The Pritchard/Pritchett Family History

The Virginia Line from
Thomas, Jamestown Immigrant
with
Related Families: Tichenell, Nestor, and Meredith

Fourth Edition

Emily Pritchard Cary

HERITAGE BOOKS
2016

HERITAGE BOOKS

AN IMPRINT OF HERITAGE BOOKS, INC.

Books, CDs, and more—Worldwide

For our listing of thousands of titles see our website
at
www.HeritageBooks.com

Published 2016 by
HERITAGE BOOKS, INC.
Publishing Division
5810 Ruatan Street
Berwyn Heights, Md. 20740

Heritage Books by the author:

*The Pritchard Family History: The Virginia Line from Thomas, Jamestown Immigrant
with Related Families of Tichenell, Nestor, and Meredith, and
Including Memoirs of Ernest Markwood Pritchard*

*The Pritchard/Pritchett Family History:
The Virginia Line from Thomas, Jamestown Immigrant
with Related Families of Tichenell, Nestor, and Meredith, Fourth Edition*

International Standard Book Numbers
Paperbound: 978-0-7884-5676-3
Clothbound: 978-0-7884-6312-9

The Pritchard/Prickett Family History

Preface

The more we learn, the less we know. Since the
publication of the third edition of *The Pritchard Family History*
in 2006, several discoveries make it clear that THOMAS
PRITCHARD, the immigrant of our line, was not, as earlier
believed, the carpenter for the London Company who arrived
on the ship *Abigaile* in 1620.

Research by Dr. Jerry O'Connell, a descendant of John
Prichard, the Revolutionary soldier and son of Thomas
Pritchard Sr. of Loudoun County, Virginia, finds that he did
indeed arrive in Jamestown in 1610, exactly as reported by
Minnie Kendall Lowther in her *History of Ritchie County, West
Virginia* published in 1911. During her journeys around the
county to gather data for her history, she recorded details from
hundreds of family bibles and official documents. Her section
on the Thomas Pritchard Jr. family states: "Mr. Pritchard was
born in 1768. His ancestors came from England and settled at
Jamestown in 1610."

The new details about the immigrant Thomas Pritchard
allow the reader to disregard the conjectures found in the past
editions and consolidate the known facts into the true
biography. This new information does not in any way gloss
over the contributions of earlier researchers who spent hours
validating the information contained in these pages. Ethel M.
Taylor labored far and above all others to gather data. For
years, she combed government archives and the court records
of every county where early Pritchards lived and died. Without
her determination and devotion to the task, many vital details
and key connections would be hidden still in dusty boxes.

Grateful thanks for priceless records are also extended

The Pritchard/Prickett Family History

to Dr. Raymond Bell, Sondra Millan Blake, Rennie Brown, Eleanor Bush, Julia Case, Jo Clark, Richard Davis, Kenneth Dennison, Joe Fasching, Pat Millan Franklin, Charlaine Gilpin, Luella M. Grantham, Pat Hickin, James Mike Holland, Betty Jones, Anne Lohr, Lee Martin, Bernard Mayhle, Mona Mattingly, Michael McGinnis, Jack Meredith, Arthur Mergy, Florence Muse, Robert Muse, Carl Nestor, Ed Oldaker, Ed Pool, Albert Prichard, Denzil Pritchard, William Pritchard, Dee Randall, Joseph Reynolds, Milton Snyder, Beverly Swanson, Dottie Thomas, Louise Throgmorton, Tina Pritchard Thompkins, Phyllis Vines, James N. Wallace, Deb Wake, and Karen White.

Because court records relied on the clerks' command of the language, the surnames of the early settlers varied in spelling. Our immigrant family arrived as Pricket or Prichet, but the surname appears in official documents as Pritchard, Prichard, Pritchet, Prichett, Pricket, Prickett, and Pritchardt. Ever since Thomas Sr. of Loudoun County, Virginia adopted Pritchard as the preferred spelling, it has remained so within my line.

The primary residences of the Pritchard family were in Virginia and the portion that became West Virginia after the Civil War. In this book, (West) Virginia is used to designate the western portion of the commonwealth until 1860 when it broke away to become a separate state. After that date, the parenthesis are removed.

All new discoveries, both additions and corrections, are eagerly welcomed.

The Pritchard/Prickett Family History

PART I – EARLY VIRGINIA PRITCHARDS

The Pritchard/Prickett Family History

THOMAS PRICKETT/PRITCHETT, THE IMMIGRANT

Dr. Jerry O'Connell has spent several decades researching the family. In the process, he consulted all the early courthouse and other records extant. From the material available, he concludes that the immigrant Thomas Pritchard (spelled Prickett and Prichett in early documents) arrived in Jamestown in the year 1610 with his brothers Miles, William, and Henry on the ship "*Starr*." At that time, they were financially able to purchase land. Miles initially came under the auspices of the London Company to make salt. He later returned to England, leaving his brothers in Virginia, but on 11 Sep 1621, the Virginia Company sent him back to the colony as a salt maker until Allhollantide, that is until 11 Nov 1622. Virginia Company records dating to January 1622 state that Maurice Berkeley had the responsibility of building a salt works and that Miles Prickett was to work under his supervision.

Miles wrote his will after returning to England. In it, he bequeathed ten pounds to the two children of his brother William Prickett, "to be equally divided as they come to age, which sum is now remaining in the hands of my brother Thomas." This suggests that he left the money with Thomas in Virginia to later present to William's children. Other bequests in the will indicate that Miles had neither wife nor children to inherit his money and land. He willed his brother John, sole executor of his estate, "two hundred acres of land lying in Elizabeth City in Virginia near Salford's Cricke." Because Miles gave Thomas money for William's sons and left Thomas

7

nothing, it may be presumed that Thomas had sufficient land and funds of his own.

The book *Virginia Immigrants and Adventurers"* by Martha W. McCartney, p. 582, lists three Prickett/Prichett residents:

Thomas Prickett/Prichet died at Warrasqueak sometime after April 1623, but before 16 Feb 1624.

William Prickett/Prichett was in possession of some land adjacent to John Bush's property in Elizabeth City on 01 Dec 1624.

Margery Prickett/Prichett was living in Elizabeth City on 15 Feb 1624. Was she the widow of Thomas?

On 16 Feb 1624, Miles was living in Elizabeth City and by 20 Sep 1624, he owned land adjacent to Robert Salford's. In early 1625, Miles shared a home with Francis Mitchell and his family. A list of patented land sent back to England in May 1625 credits Miles with 150 acres in Elizabeth City. He must have returned to England shortly afterward because his will written 30 Nov 1626 was proved on 30 Jun 1627. He is identified as a baker of the parish of Holy Cross near & without the walls of the city of Canterbury. This parish no longer exists. It was absorbed over the years into other towns and finally into Canterbury. However, much of the building is preserved. One early source says that the church records were presumed lost in the fire of London. Nevertheless, a current reliable source states that Holy Cross Parish Records are available at the Canterbury Cathedral Archives 1563-1973.

Dr. O'Connell learned that the first Virginia census taken in 1623 contains three Thomas Prichards, one living *in the maine* who arrived in 1620 on the "Abigaile" as an indentured servant to Dr. John Pott, who subsequently became deputy Governor of Virginia. This Thomas Prichard was alive and well on February 19, 1625 when he testified in a case involving tobacco owned by Dr. Pott. This Thomas did not arrive in 1610. Thus, he is not one of the Prichard brothers who immigrated in 1610 and is neither of the dead Thomas Prichards from the 1623 census.

The 1623 census lists two dead Thomas Prichards, one in Warwick County and the other in James City. The one from Warwick County left a son, also named Thomas, living in Warwick County. This son is the Captain who petitioned the House of Burgesses from Denbigh Parish in Warwick in 1656. This same Thomas appeared in Warwick court records as Lt. Colonel Thomas Prichard in 1661 and his will as Colonel Thomas Prichard is recorded in Warwick in 1689. He died in 1690 and Warwick without issue. Therefore, this Thomas is not the immigrant of 1610, but is the son of Thomas who died in Warwick before 1623.

The remaining Thomas who died before the 1623 census left a son named Thomas as wellborn (of goodly heritage) in 1618. He died in Westmoreland County in 1670. Therefore, this latter father/son combination are the progenitors of the Pritchards from the Northern Neck region of Virginia residing in Northumberland, Westmoreland, Richmond, King George, Prince William and Loudoun Counties.

The Northumberland County Orders 1652-1665, p. 58: reads: *"The deposition of Tho. Prichett, aged 37 yeares or thereabouts upon Oath sayeth that Mr. Jno Ingram & Jno Gresham is bound joyntly & severally to a bill of Acct. one piece debt cont. nineteen thousand nine hundred & sixty or seventy pounds of tobacco and further sayth not. Signed Tho Prichett, his marke, 14 Feb 1655."*

If the Thomas Pritchett/Pritchard living in Northumberland County in 1655 was 37 years of age, he most likely is the "wellborn" son of Thomas Pritchett born in 1618. We know that Thomas Prichett/Pritchard is found in Northumberland County before it segued into Old Rappahannock County and next into Westmoreland County where he died before 06 Nov 1670, the day his inventory was listed and after his widow married their neighbor, John Brooks. This adds to the proof that they are one and the same.

Thomas Pritchard is identified as living on 40 acres in Isle of Wight County, 01 May 1652, on the southeast side of a branch of Pagan Creek. He is named again in the Virginia Land Records, dated 14 Aug 1652, in which Thomas Harris is attributed with 40 acres at the head of one of the branches of Pagan Creek adjoining his own land and tracts owned by Fran Smith and Thomas Prichard. A few years later, Gloucester County Patent Book I identifies Thomas Prichard as *one of 20 people living on the S.E. side of Mattapony River, 16 Jul 1655.* This river, its name derived from the Mattaponi Indian tribe residing nearby, empties into York River about 25 miles northwest of Yorktown where the York flows into Chesapeake Bay.

Although today's Isle of Wight County is directly southwest of Newport News, separated by the James River, that name was given originally to the peninsula through which the Mattapony River flows, a spit of land between the James and York Rivers. It bears noting that this peninsula was initially part of York County, one of the eight original shires formed in 1634. A portion of York County was taken in 1651 to form Gloucester County and, in 1654, a portion of Gloucester County became New Kent County. The present day Isle of Wight County was first known as Warrascoyack, its name changed to Isle of Wight in 1637. Warrascoyack is another spelling of Warrasqueak where the immigrant Thomas Prichett

died. When placed on the map, they coincide. Because
boundary shifts and name changes were common throughout
the Virginia Colony during its early years, an individual can
have records filed in several different counties without moving
once. That happened to Pritchard land on several occasions.

One of Thomas Pritchard's early purchases was land
first granted to John Deineley (Deinley, Dainley) by Francis
Morrison, Esq., Governor and Captain General of Virginia.

*I...do give and grant until John Deinley, merchant, 550
acres of land situated on the south side of Potomack River in
the County of Westmoreland beginning at a marked Gum on
the westernmost side of the southwest branch of Pasytausy
Creeke opposite the land of Abraham Rose, extending west
northwest up a small branch 320 poles, thence south southwest
275 poles, thence east southeast parallel to the first course
until the first mentioned branch or run, finally down the said
run until the first station, the said land being due unto the said
John Deineley by and for the transportation of eleven persons
into this Colony whose names are in the records mentioned
under this patent. James City, December 04, 1661.*

Four months later, on 05 Mar 1661, John Deinley sold
the above land to Thomas Pritchard and Francis West. Less
than one year later, on 15 Jan 1662, Thomas Pritchard sold the
same 550 acres to David Anderson via his attorney John
Rynes, Francis West witness. Francis West was the son of
Francis West, an early governor of the Virginia Colony and his
third wife, Jane Davye.

Just as the counties of Warwick, Gloucester, York, and
Isle of Wight overlap, so do those on the Northern Neck, the
peninsula between the Rappahannock and Potomac Rivers.
Portions of the counties that were originally part of Old
Rappahannock County were taken to become Northumberland

The Pritchard/Prickett Family History

County in 1648, Lancaster County in 1652, Westmoreland
County in 1653, and Richmond County in 1692. In 1720, the
northernmost section of Westmoreland County was sliced off
and became King George County. While Pritchard land is
documented in all of these counties, in most cases it is the same
land.

The Northumberland County Virginia Deeds and
Orders Book for 1650-52 includes the Oath of Loyalty to the
Commonwealth signed by many residents, among them a
Thomas Prickett. Because of the county shifts mentioned
above, it is possible that he is our Thomas Pritchard.

In *The Old Families of Northumberland and their
Politics,* author John E. Manaham, a University of Virginia
history professor, remarks: *Some of the names on the list that
sound as if they might have been King's men signing against
their will are...Prickett...and others...If I were asked to
enumerate the leading families of Northumberland before the
Revolution, I should name the Gaskinses...Pritchards...
Rices...Latimores. A careful examination of the groups of
migrants to Northumberland County before 1700 show the
following: The Gloucester people following the Lees northward
- mostly Cavaliers...The significant groups direct from Isle of
Wight County were Bristol merchants and the like, presumably
slightly Roundhead...Rappahannock people descending from
North England like the Lawsons, whose characteristic name of
Epaphroditus would mark them out as Roundheads, merchants,
or broken down Royalists.*

It is interesting to observe that, for the next three
hundred years, the Pritchards often interface with families of
the above names: Lawson, Gaskin, Rice, and Lattimore.

Thomas Pritchard had land in Northumberland County,
a fact confirmed by that county's Patent Book Number 2,

which contains the following deed: *Richard Budd, 350 acres 30 Jan 1650 abutting west upon land of Mr. George Hatcher, northeast upon Dinites (sic) Creek, which divides this and a tract surveyed for Thomas Prickett; east against the mouth of the great Wickcocomico River and southeast and southwest upon aforesaid Davites (sic) Creek for transportation of seven persons.*

The formation of Northumberland County from Old Rappahannock County accounts for the fact that Thomas Pritchard ceases to be listed in the former county's records after 1652. We know that our ancestor owns land and/or has business in Old Rappahannock County by 1658 when the following transaction occurs: *On 15 Jul 1658, William Clapham and Elizabeth his wife of Lancaster County conveyed a tract of land to Capt. William Underwood of the County of Rappahannock in Virginia, lying on the North side of the River which was purchased by William Smart. Witnessed by Thomas Pritchard and Alexander Fleming.*

Was "our" Thomas Pritchard a member of the Virginia House of Burgesses in 1656 representing Gloucester County? The Grand Assembly of 1656 lists Thomas Pritchard and Thomas Ramsey as representatives for that session. The source is The General Assembly of Virginia July 30, 1619-January 11, 1978, A Bicentennial Register of Members compiled by Cynthia Miller Leonard, published by the Virginia State Library in Richmond 1978. A copy of this document is available in the Virginia Room, City of Fairfax Regional Library, Fairfax, Virginia. Because most Gloucester County records were destroyed during the Civil War and earlier, there are no extant sources to prove his presence in that county through land and other records.

At that time, Gloucester County encompassed much of

the peninsula between the York and Rappahannock Rivers. The Northern Neck found between the Rappahannock and Potomac Rivers today consists of Lancaster, Northumberland, Westmoreland, Richmond, and King George Counties. Initially, Thomas Pritchard lived in Elizabeth City County, now the city of Hampton. From there, the easiest way for him to reach Gloucester County or any place on the Northern Neck would have been by a combination of boat and horse or wagon. The land he acquired in Northumberland County soon phased into Old Rappahannock County, then into Richmond County and shortly afterward into Westmoreland County. By the next generation, King George County was formed from a portion of Richmond County, which is why his records are found in all five counties.

We do know that land he purchased is documented in Old Rappahannock County Patent No. 5, which gives land to Thomas Prichett on 21 Aug 1665 *on the north side of Dragon Swamp about three miles from Captain William Clayborne's.* Because of superfluous spelling errors in the old records, it is possible that William Clayborne and the above-mentioned William Clapham are one and the same.

The history of another parcel of Thomas Pritchard's land in Washington Parish, Westmoreland County - 300 acres - begins on 20 Oct 1666 when William Berkeley, Lt. Governor, at James City, deeds it to Phillip Wadding for transportation of six persons. This same land is sold on 28 Dec 1668 in a patent from Philip Wadding to Thomas Pritchard and Francis West. It is described as *land lying by the Great Road that goeth from the head of Popes Creek to Peperte Creek on the north side of said road (that goeth from Rappahannock County to Popes Creeke on Potomack River).* This matches the description of the land where Thomas Pritchard ultimately lived and died, so

14

we may conclude that he did not move after settling there.

Thomas Pritchard's ownership of this land and his relationship to Christopher Pritchard are both proved on 06 Jul 1695 when Christopher refers to land owned by his father, Thomas Pritchett. On that date, Christopher and his wife Jane sell to Humphrey Quesenbury of Washington Parish, Westmoreland County Virginia *9,000 pds. tobacco and casks and land assigned to Thomas Pritchett deceased, late of this County, by Phillip Wadding, except 100 acres sold to John Warde.* This document of sale confirms that Christopher Pritchard was the son of Thomas.

No other relationship between the several Pritchard families living in the Northern Neck during the late 1600s has been confirmed by primary sources. However, it is possible that Thomas Pritchard was related to the Pritchards of Lancaster County, Virginia. Located in the Northern Neck directly across the Rappahannock River from Gloucester County, Lancaster County is easily accessible from Westmoreland County by the Great Road and from all settled areas by water.

The Pritchard name appears in the following account in *The Economic History of Virginia in the 17th Century* by Bruce: *Among the principal shipwrights in Virginia in the 17th Century were John and Robert Pritchard of Lancaster County. The estate of John was appraised at 482 pounds sterling, exclusive of 101,307 pounds of tobacco.*

Are Robert and John brothers or cousins of Thomas?

In his chapter on *The Social Life of Virginia in the 17th Century*, Bruce describes the riches of Mrs. Frances Pritchard of Lancaster County, wife of Robert. *(She) possessed a printed calico gown lined with blue silk, a white striped dimity jacket, a blue silk waistcoat, a pair of scarlet sleeves with ruffles, and a Flanders lace band. These costly articles of dress were further set off by valuable jewelry. The lady's caskets contained numerous pearl necklaces, gold pendants, silver earrings, and gold hand rings.*

Another possible relative is Walter Pritchard who purchased 250 acres in Gloucester County on 06 Jun 1654. His land is described as being at the third inlet northeast of New Point Comfort.

Thomas Pritchard appears twice in Westmoreland County Records 1661-1664. Page 20: *On the 24th day of February 1663/64* (double dates indicate the calendar changes) *Thomas Pritchett was subpoenaed to this Court as a witness in behalfe of Richard Hills in a suit against David Anderson. Hills shall pay Prichett for two daies attendance on and three daies comeing to and goeing from the Court.*

He reappears on page 23: *Thomas Prichett arrested Francis Tripplet and could not make good his petition against him. Prichett shall be nonsuited.*

Because Thomas Pritchard of Westmoreland County was a second generation Virginian, his birth could have been recorded in parish or county records of Warwick, New Kent, York, Old Rappahannock, Elizabeth City, or Isle of Wight Counties. Many of the records from those counties were destroyed during the Civil War and earlier, so the proof may be gone forever. We do know that he died in Westmoreland County before 1670 and that his widow married John Brooks before 09 Nov 1670, when his inventory was listed in Westmoreland County Deeds, p. 77.

The total value of his worth was 2,000 lbs. tobacco, appraised sum. On 09 Nov 1670, it was given into the custody of *John Brooks, who intermarried with the relict* (widow) *of Thomas Pritchard.*

16

The Pritchard/Prickett Family History

A romanticist may wonder if Brooks and his neighbor's wife formed an attachment before her husband died, perhaps hastening his demise. While practical matters of that period in history point to the economic need for consolidation of single neighbors into working units, the other possibilities are fascinating. Was the lady a shrew who drove them both to the grave? Brooks' own sad end (see next chapter) heightens the suspicion that such a scenario is possible.

Both Brooks and his wife are buried in the cemetery on the Muse farm, adjacent to the George Washington Memorial Park, Westmoreland County, Virginia. The whereabouts of Thomas Pritchard's grave is not known. If tradition was followed, he most likely was buried on his own land which was inherited by his son Christopher.

The Pritchard/Prickett Family History

Sources

Biographical Dictionary of Early Virginia, 1607-1660.
Bruce. Social Life of Virginia in the 17th Century.
Coldham, Peter Wilson. English Estates of American
    Colonists; Surry, England.
Cradle of the Republic: Nutmeg Quarter, Warwick County
    Virginia.
Gloucester County Patent Book I.
Hotten, John Conden. Original Lists of Emigrants – Persons of
    Quality, Religious Exiles, Political Rebels and Others.
Journals of the House of Burgesses, Williamsburg, Virginia,
    1619-1659.
Leonard, Cynthia Miller, compiler. General Assembly of
    Virginia, Jul 30, 1619-Jan 11, 1978.
Lowther, Minnie Kendall. History of Ritchie County West
    Virginia.
Manaham, John E. Old Families of Northumberland Counties
    and their Politics.
McCartney, Martha W. Virginia Immigrants and Adventurers,
    1607-1635: A Biographical Dictionary.
Northumberland County Deeds & Orders Book 1650-1652.
Nugent, Nell Marion. Cavaliers and Pioneers Abstracts of
    Virginia Land Patents, 1623-1800, Vol. I.
Virginia Land Records in the Virginia Magazine of History and
    Biography, William & Mary Quarterly, 1982.
Rappahannock County, Virginia, Records 1656-64.
Records of the Virginia Company, July 31, 1623.
17th Century Isle of Wight: Some Isle of Wight Families.
Underwood Family of Virginia, Genealogies of Virginia
    Families V, R-Z, from Records 1656-1664.

18

Warwick County Virginia Patent Book #5.
Westmoreland County, Virginia Court Records 1661-1664.
Westmoreland County, Virginia Deeds & Wills, No. 1, 1653-1671.
Westmoreland County, Virginia Order Books, 1661-1664.

CHRISTOPHER PRITCHARD

2.

Christopher PRITCHARD I was born before 1670 in Westmoreland County, Virginia and died before 07 Jul 1730 in King George County, Virginia. He married **Jane MUSE** before 1696 in Westmoreland County, Virginia. She was born between 1660 and 1680, the daughter of **John MUSE/MEWES, Sr.**, the original settler on the Muse plantation where Popes Creek (named for the Pope family) meets the Potomac River. Although a portion of this property is now George Washington's Birthplace owned by the National Park Service, the remainder is the oldest American farm still under continual ownership by the founding Muse family.

Christopher's court records are found in deed, will, and order books of Old Rappahannock, Westmoreland, Richmond, and King George Counties, although he never moved. These scattered records can be attributed to the county name changes and overlapping borders during his lifetime of at least 60 years.

The land he owned in Washington Parish is now occupied (2015) by the farm of Corbin Muse, a descendant of John Muse and the cousin of Goodwin Muse, also a direct descendant and resident-owner of the Muse farm until his death 03 Dec 1999. In keeping with Muse family tradition that has continued from the immigrant to this day, the farm was passed on to the next male Muse in line, his nephew in this case.

Muse wives do not inherit the property from their husbands. Following the death of Goodwin Muse, his widow, Florence Jenkins Muse, was obliged to move out of the house to her own family home at Coles Point in Hague, a village at

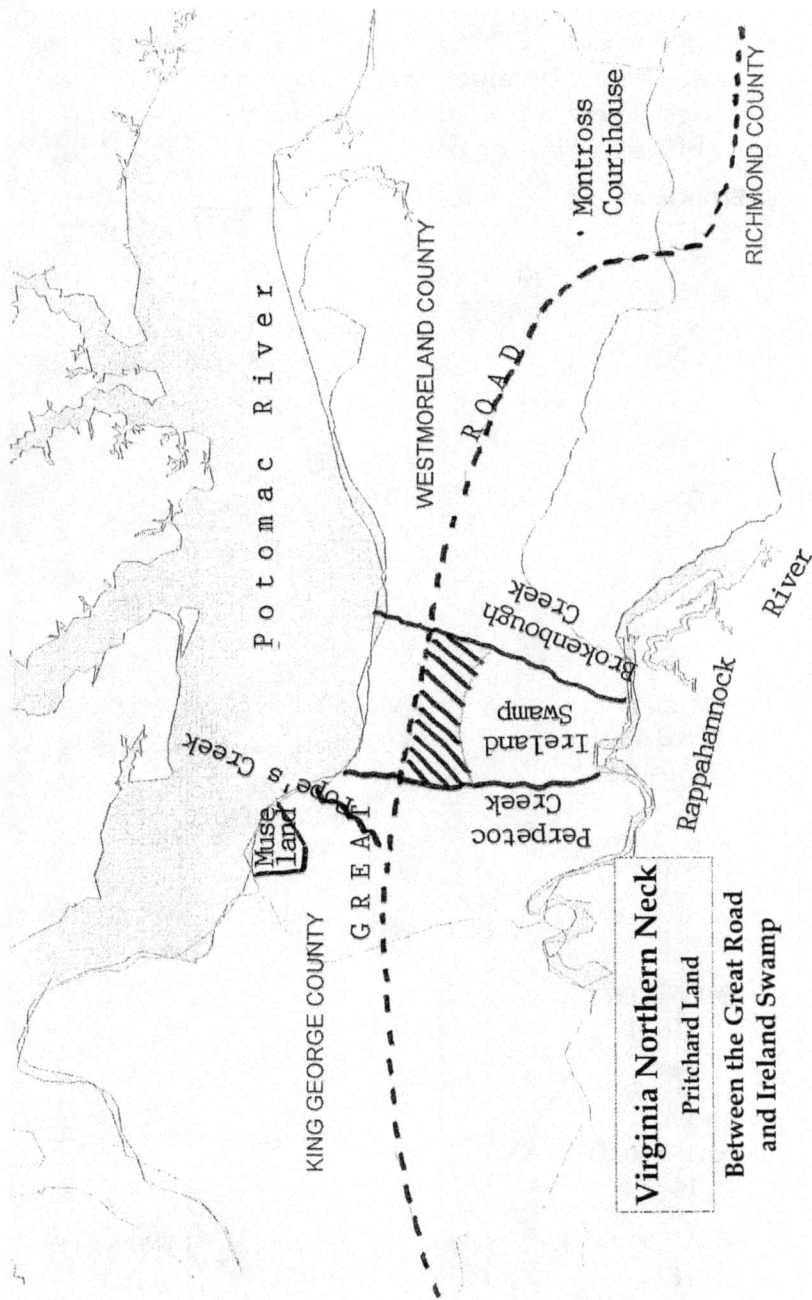

Virginia Northern Neck
Pritchard Land
Between the Great Road
and Ireland Swamp

Potomac River

Montross Courthouse

RICHMOND COUNTY

WESTMORELAND COUNTY

ROAD

Brokenbough Creek

Ireland Swamp

Rappahannock River

Perpetoc Creek

Pope's Creek

GREAT

Muse land

KING GEORGE COUNTY

20a

VIRGINIA COUNTY CHANGES - Pieces of the counties below became parts or all of new counties. There was considerable overlap and shifting of boundaries

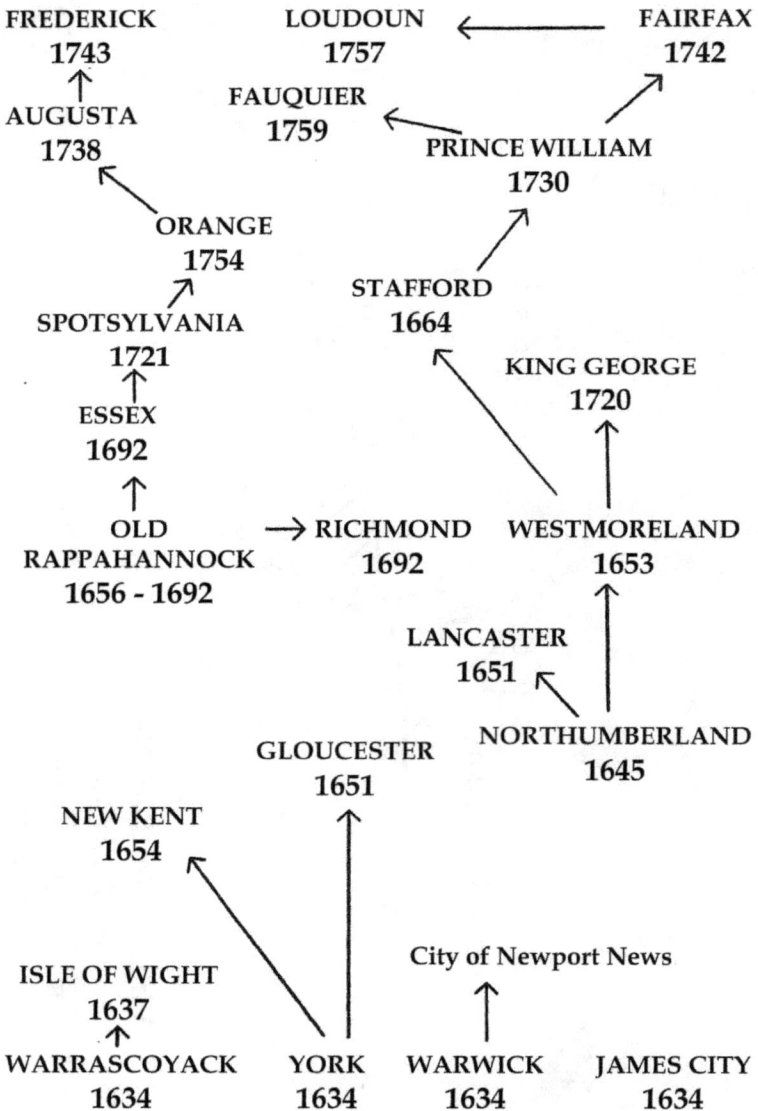

FREDERICK 1743

LOUDOUN 1757 ⟵

FAIRFAX 1742

AUGUSTA 1738

FAUQUIER 1759 ⟵

PRINCE WILLIAM 1730

ORANGE 1754

STAFFORD 1664

SPOTSYLVANIA 1721

KING GEORGE 1720

ESSEX 1692

OLD RAPPAHANNOCK 1656 - 1692

⟶ RICHMOND 1692

WESTMORELAND 1653

LANCASTER 1651

GLOUCESTER 1651

NORTHUMBERLAND 1645

NEW KENT 1654

ISLE OF WIGHT 1637

City of Newport News

WARRASCOYACK 1634

YORK 1634

WARWICK 1634

JAMES CITY 1634

20b

the southern end of Westmoreland County.

Christopher Pritchard first appears in the Westmoreland County Order Book, Pt. 1, 1690-1692 to confirm his election as Constable for *that precinct of Washington Parish where Patrick Mulberry last served.*

According to English tradition, Christopher often is the name of the second son. Therefore, it is possible that he had an older brother - or an uncle - named John, as that same Order Book contains an inventory of the estate of John Pritchett returned by Capt. Lawrence Washington, as well as notice that Capt. Washington *is entrusted with the estate of John Brookes a felo de se* (by suicide). John Brooks, who married the widow of Thomas Pritchard and mother of Christopher, was a very wealthy man for his time. On 25 May 1692, the Court orders Captain Washington to pay 1,549 pounds of tobacco to William Horton to satisfy his judgment against the Brooks estate.

Christopher Pritchard and John Quesenbury are among several persons sworn in as grand inquisitors for the County of Westmoreland Court held 31 May 1692.

On 22 Dec 1693, Christopher is named to the Westmoreland County grand jury through 25 Apr 1694.

Christopher verifies his relationship with Thomas Pritchard, as well as his connection with the Quesenbury family in the sale of land passed on to him by his father Thomas. A Westmoreland County deed dated 06 Jul 1695 states: *Know all men by these present that I, Christopher Pritchett, son and heir of Thomas Pritchett of the County of Westmoreland, do hereby alein, bargain, sell, enfieoff, and confirm all my right title and interest of the within patent unto Humphrey Quesinbury* (sic) *(except 100 acres of land more or less sold unto John Warde, lying on the North side of the Great*

21

*Road that goeth from Popes Creek to the head of Perpetoc
Creek and so East to a Locust Post and from that Post to
another Locust Post, so from these two Posts down a Point by
a line of marked trees to the branch including the above said
100 more or less)...and oblige...my wife Jane to make a due
and true acknowledgment hereof in the County Court of
Westmoreland.*

Perpetoc, or Pepetick, Creek, mentioned in several early
deeds in the area, was later renamed Brokenbrough Creek. In
Old Rappahannock County, T. H. Warner notes that it flows
into the north side of the Rappahannock River extending over
the head branches of Pope's Creek. This description, together
with the following deed, enables one to determine the
boundaries of Christopher's land on the detailed map of early
Westmoreland County which is readily available at the George
Washington Memorial gift shop.

On 31 Aug 1695, Tobias Butler of the County of
Westmoreland sold land to John Jennings of the County of
Richmond, planter. The deed identifies it as *lying in the Parish
of Washington...in the forest...beginning at a corner white oak
in a Swamp between Christopher Pritchetts and Thomas
Clators called Ireland line...along the north side of William
Jennings' plantation, crossing Ware's path...to a marked white
oak...standing almost at the head of a branch called Cattail
Swamp...till it comes to John Butler's line.*

A deed by Thomas Clayton (the above Thomas Claytor)
of Washington Parish dated 24 Feb 1696 verifies that a certain
main branch was commonly called Pritchett's Branch.

A Richmond County deed of 06 Aug 1700 from Joseph
Butler to Christopher Pritchett, carpenter, County of
Richmond, conveys land lying partly in Richmond. At that
point in history, Richmond County (the county seat now is

Warsaw) extended across a portion of Christopher's land in Westmoreland County. He did not move; the county line did.

On 06 Oct 1705, Richmond County awarded him a claim for bringing in two wolves heads with a gun, and on 03 Nov 1709, he was awarded 1,800 lbs of tobacco for 9 wolves heads. At the same court, the returns of William Carter and Christopher Pritchard, *prosessioners for one of the precincts of Sittenbourne Parish, are dismissed, the court being of the opinion they did not fall within their Cognizance.*

The Muse Family

Jane MUSE, wife of Christopher Pritchard, was the daughter of **John MUSE**, born 1633. Although tradition says that he was born in England, there is no direct evidence as to his exact place of birth. He died in Westmoreland County, Virginia in 1728. The name of his first wife, the mother of his children, is not known. His second wife was **Catherine (Lewis) MOSS-TALBOT**, a widow whose maiden name may have been **LEWIS**.

The children of John Muse and Unknown are:

i. **Thomas Muse Sr.** b. abt.1665 and died by June 1732 in Westmoreland County, Virginia. He first married **unk.** abt. 1690. He married (2) **Elizabeth (Sturman) Stewart-Murphy** by 1732 in Westmoreland County.

Children of Thomas Muse and Unknown are:

a. **John Muse**, d. by Oct. 1770; m. (1) **Mary SANFORD;** m. (2) **Elinor unk.**

b. **James Muse, Sr.** b. abt. 1700-10; d. Mar-June 1758, Cumberland Co., NC; m. **Sophia POPE** by 1732.

c. **Thomas Muse, Jr.,** b. Abt. 1712-13; d.

Oct.-Nov. 1734, Westmoreland Co., VA; m. **Sarah SANFORD** before 1730.

d. **Christopher Muse;** d. by June 1736, Westmoreland Co., VA.; unm.

e. **Elizabeth Muse,** mar. **Unk NEUMAN** by 1729.

f. **Ann Muse,** m. **unk. TAYLOR** by 1729.

g. **Daughter Muse,** m. **Unk GEORGE** by 1729.

The children of Thomas Muse Sr. and Elizabeth Stewart-Murphy are:

h. **Nicholas Muse,** b. abt. 1712-13; d. before March 1779, VA; m. (1) **Ann UNK** by 30 Nov 1832; m. (2) **Elizabeth ASBURY** 27 Nov 1749, Richmond, Co., VA.

i . **Daniel Muse,** b. after 1712; d. 1784 Richmond Co., VA; m. **Hannah DOZIER.**

ii. **John Muse,** b. 1673, d. 26 Dec 1772, Westmoreland Co., VA; m. **Ann Hopkins**.

Children of John Muse and Ann Hopkins are:

a. **Mary Muse,** b. 10 Dec 1699; d. after 1737 m.. **Robert SANFORD, Jr.** by 1725. Nine children: **Augustine, Joshua, Robert, Elizabeth, Mary, four other daughters.**

b. **William Muse,** b. 09 Jan 1701; d. aft. 1749, in VA; m. **Mary POPE**.

c. **Elizabeth Muse,** b.10 May 1704. Not named in mother's will

      d. **Edward Muse,** b. 23 Feb 1706; d. 23 Nov
        1781, Westmoreland Co., VA, m. **Ann**
        SANFORD by 1725.
      e. **Ann Muse**, b. 22 Oct, 1709; m. (1) **William**
        STUART, m. (2) **Samuel WALKER**.
      f. **Sarah Muse,** b. 01 Feb 1711; d. September
        1749; unm.
      g. **Augustine Muse**, b. 25 Aug 1715, d. by
        September 1749; unm.
      h. **Hopkins Muse,** b. 16 May 1717; d. by
        September 1749; unm.
      i. **John Muse III**, b.13 May 1719; d; by 1779;
        m. **Frances CHATTIN**, Lancaster
        County, VA.
      j. **George Muse**. This individual is
        not identified because there were six
        people named George Muse living in the
        area during mid-eighteenth century.
iii. **Mary Muse,** b. 1677; m. **Humphrey**
    QUESENBURY abt. 1695, landowner in
    Westmoreland County and youngest son of
    John QUESENBURY (1627-1717) and wife
    Ann POPE, daughter of **Thomas POPE** and
    Joanna (or Jane) DARLE, alias **GATHEY**.
Children of Mary Muse and Humphrey Quesenbury are:
      a. **Humphrey QUESENBURY, JR.**; married
        (1) **Elizabeth MOTHERSHEAD**; m.
        (2) **Elizabeth CARTER**.
      b. **Thomas QUESENBURY** married **Caroline**
        RAWLINGS.
iv. **Jane Muse**, b. abt. 1660-80; d. after April 1723; m.
    Christopher PRITCHETT by June 1696.

v. **Ann Muse**, d. after April 1723; m. **John WILLSON**.
vi. **Nicholas Muse,** b. abt. 1685; d. 1716 Westmoreland
Co., VA; m. **Mary ELLIOTT** by 1707.
According to Chambers and other researchers,
the relationship of Nicholas Muse to John
Muse, Sr. is unproven.

Children of Christopher Pritchard and Jane Muse are:
3.   i. **Thomas Pritchard,** b. abt. 1689, King George
County, VA; d. before 07 Sep 1722, King
George County, VA.
ii. **Mary Pritchard**, m. (1) **Joseph SANFORD;** m.
(2) **John REMY**.
iii. **Lydia Pritchard**, m. **Unk POWER/PORE**.
iv. **Joyce Pritchard**, m. **Henry WILLIAMS, Sr.,** who
died before 25 Sep 1717, Washington
Parish, Westmoreland County, VA; m. (2)
Francis SMITH.
v. **Sarah Pritchard**, m. **Unk GUTRAGE**.
vi. **Ann Pritchard,** m. **James DRAKE.**
vii. **Daughter Pritchard**, m. **Unk JONES**

Sources

Chambers, Dr. Roger David. A Southern Legacy:
    Descendants of John Muse of Virginia, 1994.
King George County, Virginia Deed Book 1-A, 1729-1739.
King George County, Virginia Inventory Book I, 1721-1744.
King George County, Virginia Order Book 1721-1734, Pt. 1.
Muse, Robert, letter dated 10 May 1999, states: "William
    Anderson Hagey (deceased), 2231 Bambleton Ave.,
    SW, Roanoke, VA 24025-3715, said in 1993 that
    Christopher Pritchett's daughter Mary married Joseph
    Sanford, son of Robert Sanford II (1665-1736)."
Muse (Mewes) Family of North Neck Virginia, in
    Genealogies of Virginia Families, Vol. IV, He-P.
Richmond County, Virginia Order Book No. 1, 1716-1717.
Richmond County, Virginia Order Book No 4, 1704-1708.
Richmond County, Virginia Order Book No. 5, 1708-1711.
Richmond County, Virginia Order Book No. 7, 1716-1717.
Richmond County, Virginia Order Book No. 8, 1718-1721.
Warner, T. H. Old Rappahannock County.
West, Mary Hope and Juliet Fauntleroy. The Muse Family of
    Virginia. 1939.
Westmoreland County Virginia Deeds and Wills No. 1, 1653-
    1671.
Westmoreland County Virginia Deeds and Wills No. 2, 1671-
    1699.
Westmoreland County Virginia Order Book 1690-1698.

THOMAS PRITCHARD

3.

Thomas PRITCHETT/PRITCHARD, son of No. 2, Christopher Pritchard, first appears in the records at a Richmond County Court on 03 Aug 1709. He is the recipient of a deed of lease and release for land conveyed by John Mottlin and Nathaniel Hall.

Thomas next surfaces at a Richmond County Court held 04 Oct 1716 in an action between Marmaduke Beckwith, administrator of the estate of James Phillips deceased, and Pritchett, the defendant, for 271 pounds of tobacco. The case is dismissed. At the Court continued on 04 Apr 1717, John Jennings' action of debt against Thomas Pritchett for seven hundred pounds of tobacco also was dismissed.

Thomas Pritchett may have had a brother, John, who is ordered to pay John Edwards 185 pounds of tobacco by the Westmoreland County Court on 27 Jan 1719. Nothing else is known of this John Pritchett.

Thomas Pritchett enters the Richmond County Court with Andrew Bran on 19 Oct 1720 to swear to the claim of taking up two runaway servants named Cornelius Ennis and James Welch belonging to Major John Baylor of King and Queen County. This is the final record of his brief life.

By the time Thomas dies two years later, the Pritchard property formerly situated in Richmond County is under King George County jurisdiction. At a Court for King George County on 07 Sep 1722, Thomas disappears from the records with finality. The proceedings are recorded as follows: *William Smith came into Court and made Oath that Thomas Pritchett deceased departed this life intestate so far as he knows...*

28

*William Smith, Edward Price, and Henry Woodcock personally
acknowledged their bond in Court for fifty pounds Sterling for
the said William Smith, Admin. of Thomas Pritchard's
Estate...William Carter, Christopher Pritchard, Giles Carter,
and Joseph Carpenter or any three of them are appointed...to
value and appraise all and singular the estate of Thomas
Pritchard deceased.*

Thomas Pritchard, according to court records, is known
to have had at least two sons who later become indentured to
their grandfather, Christopher. By her appearance at and
involvement in the court proceedings, **Mary DONOLY** is
likely to have been the wife of Thomas Pritchard,
Donoly/Donally being the name of her second husband.

Children of Thomas Pritchard and Mary Donoly (?) are:
4. i. **Christopher Pritchard**, between 1704 and 1711; d.
    abt. 1762, Prince William County, Virginia;
    m. **Sarah GOLLOTHAN**, abt. 1740, King
    George County, VA.
    b. **John Pritchard**, b. July 01, 1719.

During the thirteen years that mark Thomas Pritchard's
comings and goings in Richmond and King George County
Courts, his father Christopher is mentor and guardian to several
young men whose cases are recorded in court. His role as
teacher of both reading and trades verifies that he is literate,
supporting the family belief that the Virginia Pritchards have
always been able to read and write, a theory based upon each
generation's interest in and collection of books and Bibles.
Christopher Pritchard, regarded as a master carpenter and
cooper, is a man of many talents for his time. A land sale just
prior to his death identifies him as a planter.

The first formal recognition of his role in the education of young men is recorded at the Richmond County Court 04 Nov 1713 when Thomas Ffield (sic) *acknowledged to serve Christopher Pritchet till he arrive at the age of one and twenty years, he being fifteen years of age the tenth day of September last, the said Christopher Pritchet assumes to learn him to Reade and Write, the trade of a carpenter and cooper, and at the expiration of his time to pay him in like manner as is appointed by law for servants by indenture or custom.*

On 06 Jun 1717, Christopher is a member of the jury that finds George Smith guilty of selling John Tarpley's cow for his own use at the price of six hundred pounds of tobacco. His participation in local affairs continues upon his appointment by Richmond County on 01 Oct 1718 as Surveyor of the highway from Trent's plantation to Thomas Pritchet's.

At King George County Court, on 04 Mar 1725, nearly three years after the death of his son Thomas, Christopher is appointed Guardian of Christopher Pritchet, *an orphan*, son of Thomas Pritchet deceased. That same year, on 06 Nov 1725, Mary Donoly indentures her son John Pritchard to Christopher Pritchard. There is some question as to whether Mary was the second wife of Thomas; otherwise, were she his first and only wife, young Christopher would not be an orphan. Perhaps he is so designated because he is the oldest child and closer the age of indenture than his sibling.

On 01 Nov 1728, the same Court orders that John Pritchet, son of Thomas Pritchet, serve Christopher Pritchett to the age of 21 (he was born 01 Jul 1719, being nine years of age 01 Jul 1728). During the same proceedings, Henry Williams (son of Joyce Pritchard Williams and Henry Williams, Sr., deceased) is ordered to serve Christopher Pritchet to the age of 21 (he was born 12 Jan 1715, being fourteen years of age on 12

Jan 1729). The indenture of Henry Williams is approved by his mother, now Joyce Smith of Washington Parish in Westmoreland County. Her first husband, Henry Williams, Sr., died prior to 25 Sep 1717. The proceedings are witnessed by Francis Smith, Henry's stepfather, and Mary Donoly.

According to Westmoreland County Order Book for 1721-1731, p. 205, Joyce and Francis, her second husband, are ordered to appear at the Court on 27 Jun 1728 for *not repairing to their parish Church in time of Divine Service in the Month of May last past.* For this sin, they are ordered to pay five shillings or fifty pounds of tobacco. Less than one year later, on 27 Mar 1729, Joyce Smith is referred to as the relict (widow) of Francis Smith deceased. She is arrested at the suit of William Lord, gentleman for the sum of 835 pounds of tobacco which she is ordered to pay out of her deceased husband's estate.

Several months earlier, on 03 May 1728, Christopher Pritchet sells 150 acres in Hanover Parish, King George County to Martin Gollathan of Washington Parish, Westmoreland County. This may have been prophetic, as his grandson Christopher later marries Martin Gollathan's daughter, Sarah.

Christopher Pritchard I dies prior to 07 Jul 1730, when Martin Gollathan, John Jennings, and Giles Carter are appointed to appraise his estate. At the same Court, John Pritchett and Henry Williams - both bound to him by indenture - are discharged from the service of the Executor of the estate. No mention is made of his grandson Christopher, who probably has come of age by that time.

The Inventory and appraisement of Christopher's estate listed in the King George County Inventory Book I, 1721-1740 covers two pages. Some of the items included are: 13 heads of young hogs, 5 cows and calves, 2 young heifers and 4 young steers, 2 old horses, 2 old beds and old furniture, 2 feather beds and bedstead and furniture, 2 old chests and old trunk, 7 pieces of earthenware, 2 old guns, 1 brass mortar & pestle, 1 spinning wheel. The total value of the items appraised was 42 pounds, 4 shillings, 8 pence.

Little is known about Christopher's wife, Jane Muse, daughter of John, who bequeaths her one shilling in his will of 15 Apr 1723. John Muse gives the same amount to all of his living children, and the bulk of his estate to Ann Hopkins Muse, widow of his eldest son, John. Since Jane is not named as an executor of Christopher's will, it is likely that she precedes her husband in death.

Sources

Chambers, Dr. Roger David. A Southern Legacy:
Descendants of John Muse of Virginia, 1994.

King George County, Virginia Deed Book 1-A, 1729-1739.

King George County, Virginia Inventory Book I, 1721-1744.

King George County, Virginia Order Book 1721-1734, Pt. 1.

Muse, Robert, letter dated 10 May 1999, states: "William Anderson Hagey (deceased), 2231 Bambleton Ave., SW, Roanoke, VA 24025-3715, said in 1993 that Christopher Pritchett's daughter Mary married Joseph Sanford, son of Robert Sanford II (1665-1736)."

Muse (Mewes) Family of North Neck Virginia, in Genealogies of Virginia Families, Vol. IV, He-P.

Richmond County, Virginia Order Book No. 1, 1716-1717.

Richmond County, Virginia Order Book No 4, 1704-1708.

Richmond County, Virginia Order Book No. 5, 1708-1711.

Richmond County, Virginia Order Book No. 7, 1716-1717.

Richmond County, Virginia Order Book No. 8, 1718-1721.

Warner, T. H. Old Rappahannock County.

West, Mary Hope and Juliet Fauntleroy. The Muse Family of Virginia. 1939.

Westmoreland County Virginia Deeds and Wills No. 1, 1653-1671.

Westmoreland County Virginia Deeds and Wills No. 2, 1671-1699.

Westmoreland County Virginia Order Book 1690-1698.

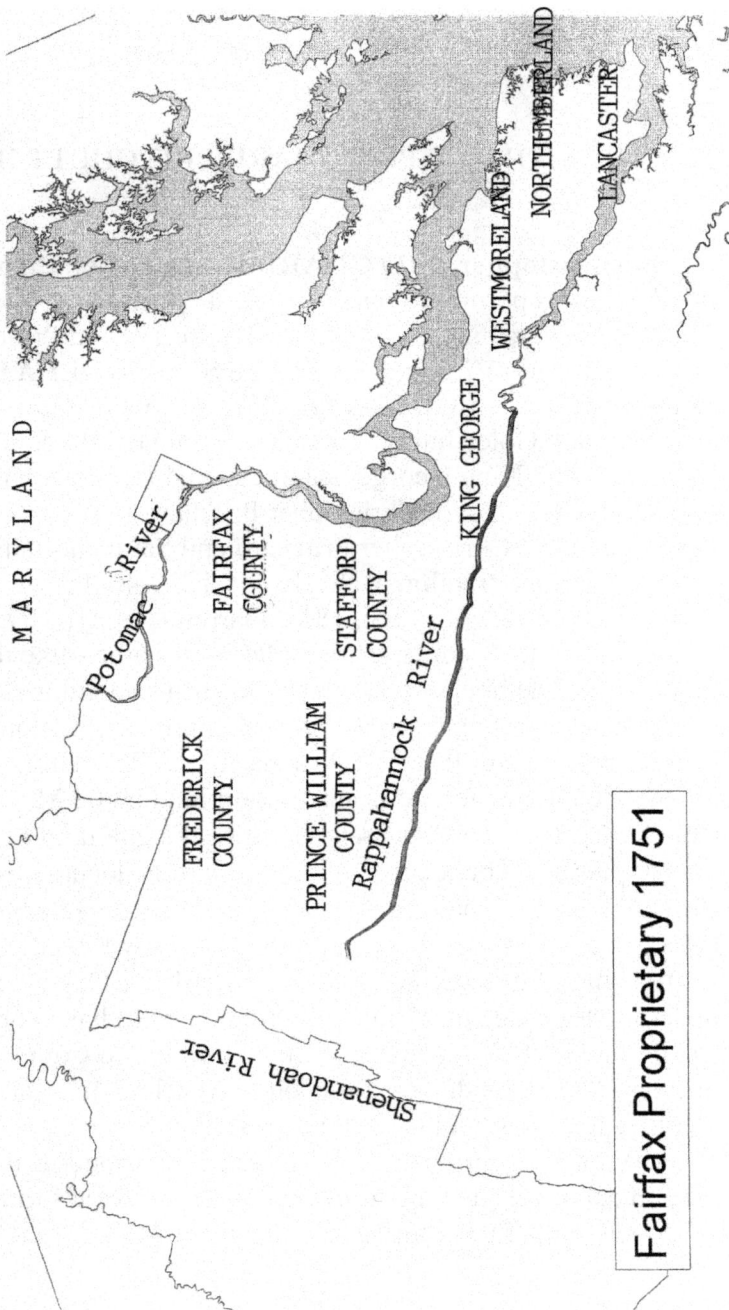

Fairfax Proprietary 1751

MARYLAND

Potomac River

FAIRFAX COUNTY

FREDERICK COUNTY

PRINCE WILLIAM COUNTY

STAFFORD COUNTY

Rappahannock River

Shenandoah River

KING GEORGE

WESTMORELAND

NORTHUMBERLAND

LANCASTER

CHRISTOPHER PRITCHARD/PRITCHETT II

4.

Christopher PRITCHARD II, son of No. 3, Thomas Pritchard, was born between 1704 and 1711 in King George County, Virginia and probably died before 1762 in Prince William County, Virginia. He married **Sarah GOLLATHAN**, daughter of **Martin GOLLATHAN** (also spelled Golathan, Golothan and Golorthum). His father, Thomas Pritchard of Richmond and King George Counties, died intestate. His grandfather was No. 2, Christopher Pritchard I.
Known child of Christopher Pritchard and Sarah Gollathan is:
5.   **Thomas Pritchard, Sr.**, b. abt. 1730-40, Prince William County, VA; d. abt. 1811, Garrett County, MD.

    In county records, Christopher's surname - like those of other family members - appears in numerous spelling variations depending upon the whims of the clerk, among them Pritchard, Prichard, Pritchett, Pritchartt, and Pritchardt.

    At a King George County Court held on 04 Mar 1725, Christopher Pritchard I is assigned to be the guardian of Christopher II. (The identification within this document of Christopher I as "uncle" of the younger Christopher appears to have been a clerk's error because the latter's will confirms his relationship as grandfather.) Christopher II must have been under the legal age of 21 in 1725, but he would have come of age by 05 Oct 1732, the date of the King George County Deed of Lease from Christopher Pritchett to Martin Gollothan identifying him as a planter. Since his grandfather died at least two years earlier (prior to 07 Jul 1730), Christopher II is indeed the subject of this document. Based on the above information, we conclude that Christopher was born 1704-1711.

The Pritchard/Prickett Family History

The land in question is 150 acres bounded by the lands of Captain Laurance Butler, Rolley Chinn, Garret O'Neal, and John Barklett. The deed confirms that *said land ...in the parish of Sittenburn was part of a grant or tract of 300 acres of land belonging to Christopher Pritchett, Grandfather to the said Christopher Pritchett...left by Christopher, the former owner, by will unto Martin Golothan and granted to the said Christopher Pritchett now in possession of the said lands.*

Christopher is married by 1732, according to the court records which state: *Then came Christopher Pritchet and Sarah his wife and acknowledged this their release unto Martin Gollathan...and Sarah wife of the said Christopher relinquished her right of dower.*

When Martin Gollothan writes his will on 20 Nov 1732, just one month later, he bequeaths to his wife Mary her wearing apparel, side saddle, and his bay horse Smoker. To his son John, he gives land, while his son Will receives ownership of his still. He also gives Christopher Prechet (sic) two ewes *and all other things lent before excepting one iron pestle and parcel of carpenters tools.* Although he mentions only two sons, he wills that his five children *be at their own liberty at sixteen, but not to have their estates till of age 20 or at the discretion of my Executors.* Christopher's role as one of three executors - the others being Mary Gollothan and Thomas Sturman - is further proof that he is at least 21 years of age. The will is witnessed by Charity Prechet (sic) *her mark.* (Who is this?)

Following the Frontier

Christopher Pritchard soon becomes caught up in the rush to settle Virginia lands to the north and west. Earlier, in 1664, a large portion of Westmoreland County - land to the west of the Rappahannock - became Stafford County. The population in that area increased so steadily that it hastened the formation of Prince William County in 1731 from portions of Stafford and King George Counties. Then in 1732, Truro Parish is carved from Hamilton Parish, which originally had coincided with the political boundaries of Prince William. This new parish includes all of Prince William County north and east of the Occoquan and Bull Run and a line running from *the head of the main branch of Bull Run by a straight cause to Ashby's Gap.*

By this time, settlers from Pennsylvania are snaking up the Valley of Virginia, following the Shenandoah River to Augusta and Frederick Counties which are formed from Orange County. Much of this western land is part of the Lord Fairfax proprietary. In 1742, Bull Run becomes the southern boundary of Fairfax County. In 1757, old Prince William County's Lower Bull Run holdings are shifted into Loudoun County. All of these changes become significant clues in tracing the Pritchard family's march, generation by generation, to the north and west.

A key document in the family history is the Lord Fairfax Grant to Christopher Pritchard dated 27 Aug 1741. Located in (then) Prince William County, it is recorded in the book of Northern Neck Grants E, 1736-1742, p. 311. Unlike most of the other grants copied on film in the Virginia State Library in Richmond, Christopher's does not include a map.

Therefore its location must be determined by tracking down the adjacent grants and sifting through them and various other records for key clues.

The deed is for 216 acres of *waste land* that adjoins the *land of Col. Carter, Connyers, Mrs. Bolan, and James Rice...beginning at two red oaks corner of Mrs. Mary Boland* (sic) *and running thence west 230 poles to a white oak in Col. Carter's Line...thence east along the said line 162 poles to a red oak in the line of James Rice deceased, then north along Rice's line 102 poles to a sycamore standing on the south side of Goose Creek near sundry cedar trees in or near the line of Connyers, thence south 110 poles to two red oak bushes in a poison field, thence south 150 poles to the beginning containing 216 acres of land together with all rights, members, and appurtenances thereunto belonging, Royal mines excepted, and a full third part of all lead, copper, tin, coal, iron mines and iron ore that shall be found thereon.*

The lands belonging to Christopher's neighbors give more clues about the location of his grant. On 10 Feb 1730, James Rice of Stafford County is granted 250 acres above Goose Creek adjacent to Jacob Lasswell, Pinehill Branch of Goose Creek. Lasswell's land, granted 07 Dec 1731, is described as 436 acres in Prince William County on a branch of Goose Creek at Secklin's branch adjacent to Thomas Owin. On 15 May 1741, Mrs. Mary Boland is granted *330 acres adjacent John Keen, Captain Elzey, Francis's Mill Branch, and Carter's Line.*

By searching the above grants and examining Virginia maps, one can conclude that Christopher Pritchard's grant on Bull Run is in the extreme western portion of Prince William County which is next claimed by Fairfax County, and finally becomes Loudoun County. Because most of the Prince William

County books were destroyed or stolen by Union troops, there are few records extant of Christopher Pritchard's life there. All that is available follows.

In the Prince William County Will Book 1734-1744, p. 271, Christopher Pritchet is a witness on 23 Mar 1740 to the inventory of Thomas Gaskins (original spelling Gascoigne, according to several sources). Gaskins' home, Laurel Wood, was located 1.5 miles west of the (then) court house on present-day State Route 630 and 1/10th of a mile south on a private road. This is north of Fredericksburg and south of the military base at Quantico. Although this site is now located in Stafford County, it was then in Prince William County. Therefore, based on his witness of the Gaskin inventory, we may surmise that Christopher has by this date moved northward from King George County and is living the neighborhood.

On 04 Oct 1743, two years after receiving the Lord Fairfax grant, Christopher again is an executor to an estate, that of Thomas Smith. His fellow witnesses are Thomas T. Davies and Susanna Smith, widow of the deceased. At that time, the Court House is located at the village of Brentsville on Davis Ford Road. Brentsville no longer exists.

When Fairfax County is formed, Christopher Pritchard's land must straddle county lines because his name appears in the Fairfax County Will Book A, #1, Part I, as a voter in the election of Burgess for the County in 1744. His signature is found under the names of both John Sturman (p. 238) and Lawrence Washington (p. 240). Presumably he was permitted two choices from the larger slate of candidates.

The last evidences of his presence in Prince William County are found on the Michaelmass Rental Rolls of 1751, 1753, and 1760.

The date and location of Christopher Pritchard's death

The Pritchard/Prickett Family History

are not known, but it may have been before 1762, as Sarah
Pritchard, his widow and mother of their son, Thomas
Pritchard Sr. of Loudoun County, is the subject of a Loudoun
County court case by John Hunsford. It is discontinued on 11
Jun 1762, but Nicholas Miner, Gentleman, and Leonard Dozer,
churchwardens for Cameron Parish in the County of Loudoun
file a complaint against her on 12 Aug 1763. The official
outcome has not been located in the extant records. Perhaps she
died before the case was concluded. One can only surmise that
these claims have to do with the widow's delinquency in
paying debts and her church tithe.

Ample court records prove that Christopher Pritchard II
was the father of Thomas Pritchard, Sr. of Loudoun County.
No other children of Christopher have been proven, although
there were several Pritchards in Northern Virginia who qualify
by their age as his descendants.

Sources

Fairfax County, Virginia Will Book A #1, Part 1.
King George County, Virginia Deed Book I, 1721-1729.
King George County, Virginia Deed Book I-A, 1729-1732.
King George County, Virginia Inventory Book I, 1721-1740.
King George County, Virginia Order Book 1721-1734.
Northern Neck Grants E, 1736-1742, by Lord Fairfax, Baron of Cameron: Land Grant for Christopher Pritchard, p. 311, Virginia State Library, Richmond, Virginia.
Prince William County, Virginia Will Book with Inventories and Accounts, 1734-1744, pp, 271-272, 438-439.
Prince William County, Virginia Will Book C, 1734-1744.
Virginia Northern Land Grants 1694-1742, Vol. I, Baltimore: Genealogical Publishing Company, 1987, Gertrude E. Gray, comp.

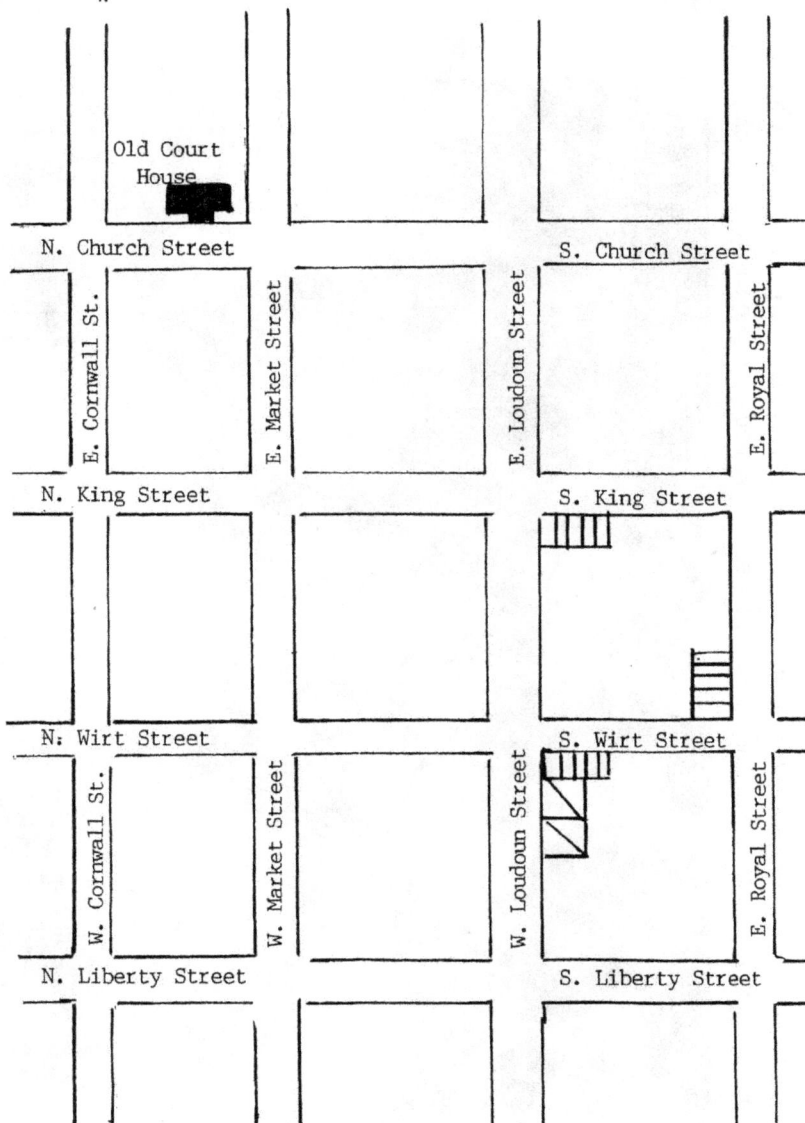

N ↔ S E W

LEESBURG, VIRGINIA

Old Court House

N. Church Street   S. Church Street

E. Cornwall St.   E. Market Street   E. Loudoun Street   E. Royal Street

N. King Street   S. King Street

N. Wirt Street   S. Wirt Street

W. Cornwall St.   W. Market Street   W. Loudoun Street   E. Royal Street

N. Liberty Street   S. Liberty Street

Houses built by Thomas Pritchard, Sr.
Additional Pritchard land

40a

Two stone houses built by Thomas Pritchard Sr. stand near the corner of E. Loudoun and S. Wirt Streets in Leesburg, Loudoun County, Virginia. Currently occupied by law firms.

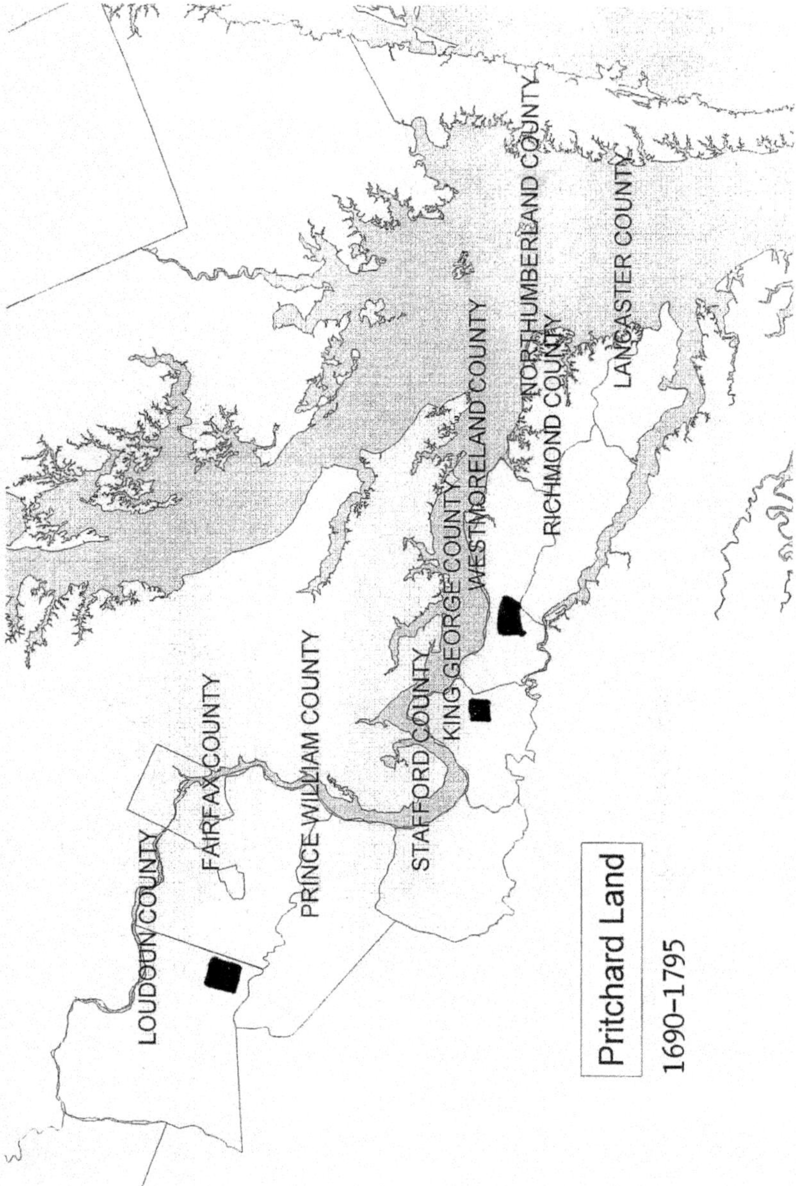
LOUDOUN COUNTY
FAIRFAX COUNTY
PRINCE WILLIAM COUNTY
STAFFORD COUNTY
KING GEORGE COUNTY
WESTMORELAND COUNTY
NORTHUMBERLAND COUNTY
RICHMOND COUNTY
LANCASTER COUNTY
Pritchard Land
1690–1795

THOMAS PRITCHARD, Sr. OF LOUDOUN COUNTY

5.

Thomas PRITCHARD, Sr., son of No. 4, Christopher Pritchard, II, was born about 1730-40 in King George, Stafford, or Prince William County, Virginia and died before 1812 in Allegany County, Maryland. He married **Rachel DAVIS** about 1759 in Loudoun County, Virginia.
Children of Thomas Pritchard and Rachel Davis are:

6.   i. **John Pritchard**, b. 29 Jul 1760, Leesburg, Loudoun County, VA; d. 28 Mar 1847, Decatur County, Indiana.

7.   ii. **Sarah Pritchard**, b. abt. 1762, Loudoun County, VA; d. Fairfax County, VA.

8.   iii. **Eleanor Pritchard**, b. abt. 1764, Loudoun County, VA; d. before 1825, Marion County, (West) VA.

9.   iv. **Thomas Pritchard, Jr.**, b. 09 Jan 1768, Loudoun County, VA; d. 24 Dec 1826, Ritchie County, (West) Virginia.

10.   v. **Elizabeth Pritchard,** b. abt. 1777; d. Marion County, (West) Virginia.

11.   vi. **William Pritchard,** b. 17 Dec 1777, Loudoun County, VA; d. April 1866, Marion County, (West) Virginia.

12.   vii. **Anne (Nancy) Pritchard,** b. abt. 1780, Loudoun County, VA; d. after 03 Oct 1850, Monongalia County, (West) Virginia.

13.   viii. **Mary Pritchard**, b. abt. 1782, Loudoun County, VA.

The Pritchard/Prickett Family History

Like his father and earlier ancestors, Thomas Pritchard, Sr. was a craftsman and pioneer at heart. The exact location of his birth is not known because of Virginia's fluctuating county borders and formation of new counties from older ones. Most importantly, the records of Prince William County where he likely was born, were destroyed by Union troops during the Civil War. Christopher II, his father, received a Prince William County land grant in 1742 from Lord Fairfax. Prince William County was formed in 1730 from Stafford and King George Counties. Fairfax County was formed in 1742 from Prince William County, Loudoun County was formed in 1757 from Fairfax County, and Fauquier County was formed in 1759 from Prince William County. These boundary shifts allowed the Pritchard family to leave traces in each county.

In 1757, Difficult Run marked the division between Loudoun and Fairfax Counties. Consequently, that stream became the boundary line of Cameron Parish, which served Leesburg and all of Loudoun County. In accordance with the Church of England law, baptisms, marriages, and deaths were recorded in the local parish regardless of a family's religious affiliation. Under ordinary circumstances, these vital statistics from the Pritchard family would have been preserved, but the Revolutionary War and public disdain for British law precipitated the decline of Cameron Parish.

A deed dated 1773 documents the sale of three acres of land near Difficult Run to Cameron Parish for the purpose of erecting a church. This church, Sugarland Chapel, was but a mile or so from Dranesville Tavern, a busy stop on Leesburg Pike, the main road between Leesburg and Alexandria, the Fairfax County seat from 1752 until 1800.

When the county line is moved several miles to the west in 1798, this fact, coupled with public outrage against the

Church of England and the monarchy, causes the parish church to lose major financial support. By 1829, both Sugarland Chapel and its graveyard have fallen into decay. Over the years, the Cameron Parish records disappeared mysteriously. Rumored earlier this century to be in the possession of someone with connections to the Virginia Theological Seminary in Alexandria, they may one day find their way to the Virginia State Library in Richmond. Since the former Cameron Parish property located partly within Fairfax County just beyond the town of Herndon is now owned privately, visitors are not welcome on the premises and its crumbling gravestones cannot be studied at present.

Goose Creek Chapel, its site designated by a state historical marker on Route 15 two miles north of Leesburg, was the first church in the county. Built by the Truro Parish Vestry in 1736 to benefit the influx of settlers, it may be where Thomas Pritchard worshipped before Cameron Parish was established. Truro Parish today encompasses Fairfax City and surrounding areas of Fairfax County.

Thomas Pritchard, Sr. first appears in Fairfax County records on 18 Oct 1752, when his petition against Ursala Jenkins, administrator of the estate of John Jenkins is heard and dismissed. Five years later, on 09 Aug 1757, he appears in Loudoun County Court to pay Catesby Cocke a debt owed him of 560 pounds of tobacco. Both Jenkins and Cocke lease their extensive land holdings to tenants. Since farming is the chief means of livelihood in the area, it is presumed that these cases revolve around land Thomas leased from them and the profits received from his crops. One of Jenkins' tracts is along Difficult Run adjacent to land owned by Charles Broadwater and extending to the Potomac River one or more miles above Great Falls. Cocke, the clerk of Stafford, Prince William, and

Fairfax Counties, is a land speculator with considerable holdings in the area above Goose Creek. Both properties are several miles east of Leesburg and would be convenient to Thomas as a tenant farmer either working or overseeing them during planting season.

Thomas Pritchard, Sr. appears to have forsaken farming by 17 May 1759, when he and his wife Rachel, now living in the town of Leesburg, are in court for the reading of the last will and testament of Rachel's aunt, Sarah Davis. Rachel, named Executrix, returns the inventory and appraisement of the estate on 11 Mar 1760.

John, their oldest son, is born 29 Jul 1760, and later serves in the Revolutionary War. It is possible that Thomas is also involved on the war front, as he is missing from the Loudoun County tax rolls during part of that period.

This possibility is raised by the existence of a Thomas Pritchard, dragoon, who appears on a list issued by the Secretary of War, 10 Aug 1790. That soldier is rewarded with 100 acres for being a member of Continental troops. He is identified on a Company payroll as a private of the 5th Troop, commanded by Captain John Hughes, in the 1st Regiment of Light Dragoons, with service of one month and a pay of eight dollars.

This may be the same Thomas Pritchard who appears on a list of Virginia soldiers receiving certificates for the balance of their full pay by an act of Assembly passed November 1781. He is paid 23 pounds, 18 shillings, 2 pence on 25 Jan 1785. A third reference is a discharge paper for *Thomas Pritchett, a gunner in the State Artillery, having served three years' time for which he stood engaged.* It is dated 02 Apr 1785, and signed by John Majarett, Major.

If he did not serve during the war, another possible

reason for Thomas Pritchard's spotty absences from Loudoun County could be land speculation in the undeveloped Ohio and Yohogania Counties of western Virginia. Located near what is now the West Virginia panhandle, Yohogania County encompassed part of the land awarded in 1789 to Washington and Greene Counties, Pennsylvania. Ohio County later became Hancock and Brooke Counties, (West) Virginia. At the 1778 court held at Augusta Town (subsequently named Washington, Pennsylvania), Oliver Miller, gentleman, returns ten shillings received from Thomas Pritchard and Philip Dougherty for swearing two profane oaths. In Ohio County, a Thomas Pritchard serves as a witness on 23 Aug 1779, in a suit of James McCullough versus John Taylor and is allowed remuneration for forty miles traveling to and from the Court for one day's attendance.

　　Other explanations for his travel away from Loudoun County may revolve around his trade. Skilled as a carpenter and a mason, Thomas Pritchard built several homes in Leesburg. He also made the railings for the Loudoun County Court House. Because the numerous court proceedings in which he is involved suggest that he was an outspoken citizen, entrepreneur, and commanding force in the area, we include herein representative accounts of his dealings.

　　His first recorded real estate deal in Leesburg is the purchase of Lot 62, one-half acre of land, from Nicholas Minor on 23 Jan 1760. Minor is a key player in the development of Leesburg, having laid out the area in lots for speculation.

　　One month later, on 26 Feb 1760, Thomas Pritchard purchases for seven pounds another half-acre lot from Minor, *Lot 10 lying in Leesburg and binding on Loudoun Street*. He proposes to build on the property a house of brick, stone, or wood with dimensions of 20 feet by 16 feet by 9 feet.

His decision to move into town from his farm is confirmed on 11 Mar 1760, when he deeds 216 acres in Cameron Parish for 32 pounds to George Vandivere of Prince Georges County, Maryland. This land deal includes most of the Lord Fairfax grant received by his father, Christopher. This is strong indication that Christopher is no longer alive and the land has been inherited by Thomas, presumably his oldest son. On 11 Apr 1774, this land is returned to Thomas Pritchard by Edward, son of the deceased George, and Ann Vandivere. Thomas and Rachel sell this same land in 1794 before leaving Loudoun County. In the deed, he is identified as a joiner (skilled carpenter).

On 12 Mar 1760, an indenture of feoffment (a grant of lands as a fee) between Nicholas Minor and Thomas Pritchard is recorded. Two days later, Thomas is among twelve men sworn in as jurors for the Loudoun County Court that continues through 15 May 1760, when Thomas, accompanied by his attorney William Ellzey, sues and wins from John Walton a debt of two pounds, six shillings and four pence.

Thomas is one of three men ordered to appear on 11 Nov 1760, to answer the complaint of Nicholas Minor, *gentleman sheriff*, for refusing to obey him when required to take John Riley.

From the time of his marriage to Rachel Davis, Thomas is frequently involved in matters regarding his in-laws. On 12 Mar 1761, he goes to court to vouch for John Davis, defendant in a suit filed by James Inger Dozer. He is there again for the same purpose on 11 Jun 1761, this suit filed by John Hardin.

On 08 Aug 1761, Thomas Pritchard and Rachel sell lot number 10, one-half acre, to Jacob Shilling. Later that year, on 12 Nov 1761, an indenture of feoffment is made between Thomas and Andrew Link. On the same day, a suit against

John Gowers is dismissed, as agreed by both parties.

He is back in Court on 09 Feb 1762, for several items, beginning with an indenture of feoffment between him and Nicholas Minor. On the same day, a petition of Sherman Chelton against him is continued until the next court.

On 09 Mar 1762, Thomas returns to court as a juror. One of the cases presented involves 50 pounds of tobacco owed Ann and George Vandivere (who earlier were in receipt of Thomas' Lord Fairfax grant acreage). The case pits John and Margaret Davis (his wife and administratrix of the estate of her deceased and former husband, Thomas Davis) against Elizabeth Davis, Margaret's daughter-in-law, who is administratrix for the estate of Thomas Davis, Elizabeth's deceased husband and Margaret's son.

On 08 Jun 1762, the aforesaid John Davis, an Ordinary keeper in Leesburg, is convicted of permitting *unlawful gaming in his house, particularly cards and dice, contrary to law.* For this misdeed, John is ordered to pay the churchwardens of Cameron Parish five pounds and costs for the care of the Poor of the Parish. On his behalf, Thomas Pritchard and George Vandivere agree to surrender themselves in the event John does not abide by the ruling. By this time, Thomas must wonder what kind of a family he has married into.

Sarah Pritchard, the widow of Christopher II and mother of Thomas, is the defendant in an attachment brought against her by Adam Patterson. It is heard first on 11 Jun 1762, and concluded on 13 Jul 1762. At the first hearing, garnishee John Hunsford delivers to the sheriff effects taken from Sarah: one gown, two aprons, one shift, one piece of an old shirt, one pair of old stays, two ribbons, and a pair of old gloves. At the second hearing, garnishee William Shrieve delivers one old paper hat, two old pairs of thread stockings, a small handkerchief, a little piece of old linen, and one yard of old ribbon. These meager items confiscated from the unfortunate lady are to be sold and the money given to the plaintiff. This siege of harassment ends on 12 Aug 1763 when Nicholas Minor, gentleman, and Leonard Dozer, Churchwardens for Cameron Parish, discontinue the suit. Perhaps Thomas has paid his mother's debts. Still, her misfortunes persist and on 12 Feb 1765, she is ordered to return to court. Nothing more is recorded. Considering the pressure she has endured, it is possible that the poor woman dies before she can be summoned again. It is interesting to speculate that Sarah's troubles with the church hierarchy may be attributed to the family's growing disenchantment with this arm of British rule. Key members of subsequent Pritchard generations have no allegiance to the Anglican traditions; they proclaim themselves strong supporters of either the Methodist or Baptist denominations.

On 15 Jul 1762, Thomas Pritchard is awarded six pounds towards the Loudoun Court House railing, the balance to be applied to a County seal. On the same day, John Davis is granted a one-year license for his Ordinary, so it appears that he is back in the town's good graces. Unfortunately this happy situation is brief. He is taken to court on 12 May 1763, by Leesburg merchants Adam and Patterson and, as usual, Thomas Pritchard agrees to cover his debts if necessary.

Thomas is seated once more as a juror on 15 Sep 1762. An order recorded on the same day that his tithable, William Mason, be added to the list of tables taken for the year indicates that Mason was either a servant or an apprentice to him.

On 10 Nov 1762, Thomas is assessed 37 pounds, 12 shillings, one and one-half pence and 6,017 pounds of tobacco for his yearly tithe. This is a large sum for that time, confirming that he is a man of means. When the Court convenes the next month on 14 Dec 1762, an indenture of feoffment is acknowledged between Thomas and James Vessell and his wife Sarah.

Thomas Pritchard is paid seventy-five pounds of tobacco by Joshua Hickman on 16 Jun 1763, for attending court three days to give evidence against Ezekiel Hickman. This windfall is diminished on 15 Sep 1763, when he is ordered to pay Christopher Perfect three pounds of current Virginia money and court costs to satisfy a debt.

On 15 Feb 1764, an indenture of foeffment is recorded between Thomas and Rachel Pritchard and John Frederick Whitmore. This arrangement is back in court on 12 Feb 1765 when Thomas Pritchard sues both John Frederick Whitmore of Frederick County Maryland and Alexander Wedner of Leesburg. The parties involved agree to dismiss the suit and the defendant is ordered to pay the costs.

Thomas returns to court on 09 Apr 1765, to sue Joseph Craig for debt, another case dismissed by mutual agreement. On the same day, the suit of Thomas Kelly against Thomas is dismissed.

Thomas must be so busy going back and forth to court that he fails to finish proper repairs to the prison. Therefore, the county assesses him on 26 Dec 1765, the cost of guarding the goal (sic) four days over Mary Duffy and May McDonald for felony. The court of 15 Oct 1766, reports that Thomas Pritchard has finished the repairs of the prison. On 11 Nov 1766, he is awarded 16 pounds and 2,560 pounds of tobacco. Two days later, he offers bail to James Abbott, the defendant in a debt case brought by John and Fleming Patterson. He is back on the jury in March, April, and May 1767 and in March, April, and May 1768. In between, however, he and John Davis are defendants in a suit by John McKenny and Susanna his wife for a debt of two pounds 18 shillings, 10 pence.

In his court dealings, Thomas Pritchard bounces back and forth between plaintiff and defendant. On 10 Aug 1768, he sues John Hough for one pound, 17 shillings, 7 pence and costs. On 14 Apr 1769, he fails to appear as defendant in a petition upon an account by Thomas Kelley. It is ruled that he owes Kelley two pounds 8 shillings, 4 pence. At the same court he is the plaintiff in a dismissed suit against Ferdinando O'Neale.

He must possess a fiery temper, for he is the subject on 15 Aug 1769, of a complaint *for behaving himself in a disorderly manner...Thereupon the said Thomas Pritchard acknowledged himself indebted to our Sovereign Lord George the third King of Great Britain...in the sum of fifty pounds...if the said Thomas Pritchard do and shall Peaceably and Orderly demean and behave himself towards all his said Majesty's Liege Subjects for one year, then this recognizance to become void.*

Is Thomas protesting British taxation? What a revelation it could be to get into the head of this brash colonist!

He is back in the real estate business by 13 Nov 1769, when an indenture of feoffment is made between Thomas and Rachel and Michael Shortz.

Thomas, a slave owner, is credited with Negroes Hazzard, Dick, and Will in the 1771 Loudoun County List of Tithables compiled by Francis Peyton of Cameron Parish.

By 29 May 1772, he is once more busy defending John Davis in suits brought by Anthony Russell and Adam and Patterson, merchants. The very next month, on 26 Jun 1772, he is ordered to pay 230 pounds of tobacco and ferriages to Aneas Campbell, a witness for him in a suit brought by Joseph Craig, who travels five miles from Maryland (across the nearby Potomac River) and attends court eight days.

After losing a case on 11 May 1774, in which Simon Triplet, gentleman, seeks damages of six pounds, 13 shillings, one-half pence and court costs from him for *nonperformance of a Certain promise*, Thomas disappears for four years from local court proceedings until June of 1778, when he is paid one pound 18 shillings, 7 pence from the estate of William Musgrove for a coffin. Alas, he loses that profit on 22 Jan 1779, when he pays 34 pounds, 3 shillings, 11 pence to the estate of William Carr Lane.

Debts begin to hound Thomas by 14 Aug 1783 when that earlier suit brought by Simon Triplett, the surviving executor of William Carr Lane, deceased, results in the judge setting payment of ten pounds seven shillings and one penny plus cost to be computed from 14 Jul 1774. Thomas is the defendant in a similar case brought by William and Hugh Neilson and heard in court on 16 Jun 1784, his debt to be computed from 19 Apr 1773.

More suits follow, and he loses again on 14 Feb 1785 in a case brought against him and Joseph Lewis by Josiah Moffett and company. *The defendants having had legal notice although solemnly called came not...It is therefore considered by the court that the plaintiffs recover against the said defendant Thomas Pritchard the sum of* 10 pounds, 14 shillings and their cost.

He is the defendant in separate cases brought 08 Aug 1785 by Samuel Canby, Joseph Smith, William Bernard Sears, and George Summers gentleman, guardian to Jetts' orphans. He loses each of these.

On 13 Feb 1787, Thomas Pritchard and John Davis are defendants in a suit brought by Benjamin Mason, and on 14

Mar 1787, he and John Linton are defendants in a suit brought by Joseph Smith for a recovery bond.

By this time, a citizen faced with such financial crises should be humbled by dwindling self-esteem, and yet the circumstances of the cases in which he figures suggest that Thomas is growing more defiant than ever.

Is it bad luck or bad temper that next propel him to go after his runaway servant man John Bryan in a suit asking 18 pounds, 13 shillings and 10 pence for twenty-two days runaway time? One can almost envision Thomas's gleeful grin as the Court orders John Bryan to *serve his Master further time according to law and the costs: tobacco rated at twenty shillings per hundred.* It is further ordered that the sheriff take John Bryan to the *Publick Whipping post and give him twenty five lashes on his bareback well laid on.*

Trouble compounds upon trouble when John Smarr, his son-in-law, sues Thomas on 09 Jun 1788, to recover eight pounds, possibly a sum Thomas has borrowed to cover his own debts. Then on 08 Sep 1788, his satisfaction at having his way is smothered when he is ordered to appear at the next Court to answer the complaint of John Bryan for not paying him his freedom due. On 11 Jun 1789, Thomas complies at last with John Bryan's petition for freedom. On the same day, however, he fails to appear as defendant in a suit brought by John Starlee, so the judge orders him to pay the plaintiff five pounds and costs.

It is easy to understand why, under pressure from these and other nagging court cases, Thomas Pritchard decides to leave Loudoun County and seek his fortune in the wilderness to the west. On 23 Mar 1794, he and Rachel forsake the prized family jewel, the Lord Fairfax grant. They sell to William Ellzey, Jr. for 40 pounds ...*all that tract of land situated in*

The Pritchard/Prickett Family History

(Loudoun County) *which was granted to Christopher Pritchard, father to the aforesaid Thomas by patent from the proprietors office dated 27 August 1741, containing 216 acres...and all houses, buildings, orchards, ways, waters, etc.* This sale is admitted to record on 10 Oct 1797.

Accustomed as he is to local court houses, it is not surprising that a suit Thomas Pritchard brings against Kimble Hicks on 15 Nov 1797, for *payment of carpenter work done by Pritchard for Hicks in 1787* continues long after the Pritchards leave Loudoun County. Eight notices from the plaintiff to the defendant and between their lawyers dated from 18 Nov 1787, until 19 Mar 1804, appear in Chancery Court records found in the Loudoun County Courthouse basement, the last bearing word that further deposition will be taken on 04 Apr 1804. No record has been located of the case's conclusion.

Before leaving Loudoun County, John Pritchard, oldest son of Thomas Sr. and Rachel, marries Annie Smarr on 12 Oct 1795. His sister Sarah marries Annie's father, John Smarr, a widower. Upon John Smarr's death, Sarah - left with two young children to raise - marries her neighbor, Cornelius Skinner. She is the only member of the immediate family who remains in Northern Virginia.

Nevertheless, other Pritchards living in Fairfax County into the 19th Century may have been related to the Thomas Pritchard family. Because most Prince William County records were lost, it is quite likely that Christopher II had more than one son, inasmuch as families at this time were very large. Possible relatives could be among the following names taken from a card file representing extensive research done by the Fairfax County Historical Society which is located in the basement of the (old) Court House adjacent to Chain Bridge Road and Little River Turnpike. These individuals lived and

53

worked near the Lord Fairfax grant.

Edward Pritchard, 22 Sep 1789, a schoolmaster, listed between James Hickie and Richard Simpson on the road from the County Line on Newgate Road to David Loofburrow's.

Philip Pritchard, 22 Sep 1789, listed between John Gibson and William Buckley on Turnpike Road from County Line to Alexandria.

Philip Pritchard, 26 Jun 1790, chain carrier on 383 acre survey for John Gibson of land near Bull Run.

Philip Pritchard, 18 Jul 1791, tithables on his plantation in Truro Parish to work on the road from the county line on the Turnpike Road leading to Alexandria and to Ox Road. Listed between John Gibson and James Donneal, Jr.

Traverse (Travis) Pritchard, 07 Mar 1795, chain carrier at Bull Run.

Lewis Pritchard, 19 Feb 1798, overseer of Old Courthouse Road from mouth of Popes Head Run to road leading to Newgate Road.

William Pritchard, 23 Sep 1801, chain carrier on 292 acres survey for heirs of Marmaduke Beckwith.

Travis Pritchartt (sic), 1807, administrator of Lewis Pritchart (sic) deceased.

Travis Pritchard, 14 Aug 1813, replaced by Benjamin Berkeley as surveyor of the road from the old county line along the Centreville Road to Francis Adams' blacksmith shop.

Travis Pritchard, 1816, trustee and attorney-in-fact for William Pritchard.

Travis Pritchard, 20 Aug 1822, administrator of Sarah Pritchard, deceased.

Travis Pritchard, 1824, administrator to estate of Rose Pritchard, deceased, widow.

Travis Pritchard, deceased 21 Mar 1825, estate

inventory recorded; widow Rose's dower in slaves and personal estate set apart.

Lewis Pritchard, 20 Jun, 1837, licensed for Ordinary until next May. With wife, deed to William Taller for all his interest in sundry lands.

21 Feb 1841. Within 30 days Rezin Williamson must open street between his and S.M. Ball's lots known as North Street and in the rear of **Pritchard's** Stable, on North side of Court House.

Leaving Loudoun County

Pioneering when America was young was usually a family affair. Like others of their generation with itchy feet, all of the immediate Pritchard family, except Sarah, already married and settled in Fairfax County, leave Northern Virginia for the wild, lush county beyond the sunset. Each is destined to carve a niche in history. As postwar pioneers seeking their fortunes, they doubtless follow the Potomac River from Loudoun County to the new frontier in Maryland. Initially, they settle at Wills Creek in Allegany County. For a brief period, they reside adjacent to the Potomac River in what is downtown Cumberland today, but they soon succumb to wanderlust and acquire land deeper in Allegany County, west of Fort Cumberland in what later becomes Garrett County. Subsequently, they obtain military lots just west of Westernport and Luke in Allegany County, now Garrett County, Maryland.

On 10 Aug 1795, a survey is made for Thomas Pritchard, Jr., who marries Nancy Tichenell in Allegany County on 06 Jan 1796. Several months later on 22 May 1796, his father purchases lots 96 and 97 containing a total of fifty acres from Michael Boyles and Frances his wife. Upon assessment, these lots are valued at 22 pounds, 2 shillings, 8 pence. With personal property that includes 16 cattle, 110 pounds 3 shillings 4 pence, Thomas Pritchard Sr. is one of eight residents of the area who are assessed with silver plate.

In 1798, John Pritchard, the oldest son, is assessed with a house and lot in the village of Selbyport and with a nearby military lot # 3294.

Ann (Nancy) Pritchard marries Davis Meredith on 08 Nov 1800, in Allegheny County. Nancy is his third wife, the other two having died.

In the Allegany County Maryland 1800 census, Thomas Pritchard, Sr. is living in the Glades. In his household are one male and one female over 45 and two males and two females between 16 and 26.

Mary L. Pritchard marries John Parker on 22 Dec 1804, in Allegany County, Maryland.

William Pritchard marries Hannah Meredith, daughter of Davis Meredith, on 18 Feb 1805, in Monongalia County, Virginia. Hannah then becomes the step-daughter of Ann (Nancy) Pritchard.

By the 1810 census, Thomas Pritchard, Jr., Richard Price, John Parker, George Furbay, and Davis Meredith - the latter four married to Thomas, Jr.'s sisters - are all living in Monongalia County, (West) Virginia.

Thomas Pritchard, Sr. is not found in the Allegany County, Maryland 1810 census, but his youngest son, William Pritchard, is living in District 1. In his household are two females over 45. Thus, Thomas Pritchard, Sr. may have died before that census is taken and his widow (Rachel) is living with William. He most definitely is dead by 1811 when William Pritchard, administrator of his estate, makes oath in Allegany County Maryland that Thomas died intestate.

The Pritchard/Prickett Family History

On 09 Jun 1813, William Pritchard makes the second account of the estate. After the widow's third is taken, money is paid to Davis Meredith, John Pritchard, George Furbay, and Thomas Pritchard, Jr. *At the request of William Pritchard of Allegany County, Maryland, acknowledgment of Thomas Pritchard and Mary* (nee Moody) *his wife, Richard Price and Eleanor his wife, George Furbay and Elizabeth his wife, Davis Meredith and Ann (Nancy) his wife, John Parker and Mary his wife, was made for a certain deed of conveyance to be executed to William Pritchard of Allegany County, Maryland.*

The proceedings are finalized on 03 Dec 1814, when William Pritchard pays Cornelius Skinner and his wife Sarah of Loudoun County, Virginia $20 for their share of land *being in the estate of Thomas Pritchard deceased lying and being in Allegany County Maryland and among the lots westward of Cumberland and distinguished by No. 96 and 97 containing 50 acres.*

This is one-ninth of Thomas Pritchard's estate. Thus, from these documents, it is concluded that the estate of Thomas Pritchard, Sr. is divided among his widow and his eight children. The final account of the estate is made by William Pritchard, administrator, on 12 Oct 1815. It is quite possible that Rachel Davis Pritchard, the widow of Thomas, Sr., died before the final settlement.

Rachel Davis Pritchard
Rachel Davis was born about 1745 in Loudoun County, Virginia and (probably) died between 1813 and 1815 in Allegany County, Maryland.

There are three Davis families in Loudoun County at the same time. One came to America from Cardigan Wales. According to the will of John Davis, who dies 09 Nov 1791, the family attended Cilfowyr (*kill-fo-weer*) Chapel in the parish of Manordeifi (*Man-or-dee-fee*), Pembrokeshire, Wales. The family relationship has been established through communication with Reverend Dafydd H. Edwards, minister of Cilfowyr until 2002 and author of the chapel's history. It was initially believed that John Davis was the uncle of Rachel Davis. According to the will of John Davis, who dies 09 Nov 1791, the family attended Cilfowyr (kill-fo-weer) Chapel in the parish of Manordeifi (Man-or-dee-fee), Pembrokeshire, Wales.

Upon his death, John Davis leaves a bequest to *the Baptist Church whereof I was a member before I emigrated to America. The said is in the principality of Wales which meets at the White House named Kilfower in the County of Pembroke and Parish of Manordeifi, the sum of one hundred pounds of Virginia currency in trust to the elders of the Baptist Church...for the proper use of the said church forever.* The family relationship has been established through communication with Reverend Dafydd H. Edwards, minister of Cilfowyr until 2002 and author of the chapel's history.

(For the complete story of this will and the possible Pritchard-Davis connection, see "Duet" by Emily Pritchard Cary, McClain Printing Company, Parsons, West Virginia, 1991; "Following Family Roots Back to Wales," by Emily P. Cary in *British Heritage*, December/January 1992/1993, pp. 16-19; and "Return to Cilfowyr" by Emily Pritchard Cary in *Y Drych*, January 1991, pp. 8 & 13.)

Although this connection seemed likely at one time, researcher James Lloyd does not believe that they are of the same family as Rachel. He has ascertained that John Davis of Cilfowyr bought property next to John Marks of Ketocton Baptist Church in 1763 and was thus far removed from the John who married Margaret and lived near the former Pritchard plantation in the "Sugarlands" near Bull Run.

He believes that Rachel's grandfather was Thomas Davis, b. 20 Sep 1699 in Neshaminack, Bucks County, Pa, the son of David Davis b. 1660. The reference is from *The History of Bucks County*, by W. W. H. Davis, p. 336. This raises the possibility that Rachel Davis's family may have been Quakers, of which there were a number in Loudoun County.

Thomas Davis Sr. dies in Loudoun County on 06 May 1758 leaving a wife Margaret. His will was proved 6 Nov 1857 in Loudoun County, Virginia.

Children of Thomas Davis Sr. and Margaret are:

    i. **Thomas Davis, Jr.**, b. about 1725, m. **Elizabeth (MINOR?).**

    ii. **John Davis** b. 1727, Loudoun County, Virginia.

    iii. **Sara Davis** b. abt. 1729 d, unm, will proved May 1759.

    iv. **Mary Davis,** b. abt. 1731, m. unk **WRIGHT**.

    v. **Elizabeth Davis** , b. abt. 1711, m. unk **THOMAS**.

    vi. **Rachel DAVIS,** b. abt. 1735.

On 06 Apr 1750, Margaret Davis declares that her son, Thomas Davis, on his death bed told her it was his desire that his clothes should not be sold. *I then asked him what he intended should be done with them and he answered to give them to his brother, John Davis, together with his saddle, or to that effect.*

Thomas Davis's account leaves money for boarding his daughter four years at 5 pounds per year, or 20 pounds. He provides for his daughter's boarding for four years. Further proof of this relationship is found in the will of Sarah Davis in which she refers to John Davis as her brother and Rachel Davis as her loving neese (sic). The will, dated 10 Mar 1759, further states: *I give and bequeath to my loving neese Sarah Plackney who is now in Carolina one case of drawers, one oval table, half my table linning* (sic)*, and half my pewter if she will either come or send for it, but if she will not, I will devise and bequeath it with the whole residue of all my worldly goods...unto my loving neese Rachel Davis, except some outstanding debts due from poor people who were drove* (sic) *by the Indians, so I remit it them and I do freely constitute and appoint the said Rachel Davis to be sole Executrix of this my last will and testament, hereby revoking annulling and making void all former or other wills by me.*

(Note: After searching many years for the surname *Plackney* in either of the Carolinas to no avail, I am inclined to conclude that Sarah was a *Hackney*. The penmanship of the original bequest is written clearly. In fact the first letter is written exactly like the P in Pritchard attached to a lower case 'l'. This certainly could be interpreted as an H. If so, then Hackney makes sense because it is a common surname in early records of Chatham County, North Carolina. Several families enumerated there have females named Sarah. In most cases, their immigrant ancestors were Quakers from England.)

Several contributors to the Davis Clearing House have submitted genealogies tying Rachel Davis to the Davis family living in Camden District, South Carolina. The location of their land is in present day Fairfield County, and the graveyard is identified as the "Davis Family Graveyard, at Monticello, South Carolina on the old Davis plantation." The following information connecting the two families has not been proven. It was submitted by Louise K. Crowder in 1959 from papers retrieved in Fairfield County Library, Winnsboro, South Carolina. This may be the third Davis family in Loudoun County.

John Davis b. 1719, Chester County, Pennsylvania, son of Rev. John Davis, m. **Cecelia Fitzhugh EDDERINGTON**. He died 15 Mar 1785, in Fairfield County, South Carolina. He lost five sons in the Revolutionary War.

Children of John Davis and Cecelia Edderington are:

    i. **Jonathan Davis** b. 1738, Loudoun County, Virginia, living 1785. (Note: Loudoun County was not formed until 1757, nearly two decades later, so he was born in either Fairfax or Prince William County, depending upon the family home site.)

    ii. **Rachel Davis**; m. **unk PRITCHARD**.

    iii. **John Davis**, b. 1748 Loudoun County, Virginia. m. **Mary WIGGINTON**.

    iv. **Elijah Davis**, b. abt. 1750, d. 1782, Revolutionary War, Tory Lt.

    v. **James Davis**, b. 1754, Loudoun County, Virginia; d. 22 Oct 1822, Fairfield County South Carolina; m. **Mary EDINGTON** (b. March 1741, d. 03 Jul 1840.), Camden District, South Carolina.

    vi. **Amos Davis**, b. 06 Aug/Sep 1757, Loudoun County, Virginia, d. 03 Mar 1840, Monticello, Fairfield County, South Carolina, m. **Mary ALBURN**.

Additional notes from other contributors to the Davis Clearing House identify **John Davis** born in Chester County, Pennsylvania as the son of **Rev. John Davis**, pastor of Second Baptist Church, Boston, Massachusetts, and grandson of **Rev. David Davis** who emigrated from Wales in 1710, pastor of Welsh Tract Church, Pennsylvania. He moved to Loudoun County, Virginia, and from there to Monticello, South

Carolina. Of his seven sons engaged in the War of the American Revolution, two survived. Three sons were successive captains of the same company. He died 15 Mar 1785, in his 66th year.

The following remarks taken from the Fairfield County Library papers describe some of his descendants:

Captain **James Davis** served our Republic as a faithful soldier in the Revolutionary War. Died 22 Oct 1822, aged 68 years.

Mrs. **Mary Davis**, relict of the late James Davis, born March 1741, died July 1840, aged 99 years.

Jonathan Davis, only son of Capt. James and Mary Davis, born 18 Aug 1786, died 05 Oct 1855, m. **Rebecca Kincaid**, daughter of **James Kincaid**.

Harriet Furman, born 23 Sep 1814, died 01 Aug 1848, eldest daughter of Jonathan and Rebecca Davis, consort of **James C. Furman**. Rebecca died at home of her son-in-law, Rev. James C. Furman of Greenville, South Carolina.

The will of John Davis of Camden District gives...*to son Jonathan Davis 1 pound sterling...to son Amos Davis, tract whereon he now lives, 150 acres and Negro Harry...to daughter Rachel Pritchard 30 pounds sterling* (is this Rachel Pritchard, wife of Thomas Pritchard, Sr.?)...*to son James Davis, plantation where I now live, 250 acres and known as Engleman's old place and & 200 acres on Sandy River known as Davis' old place & 150 acres on Rockey Creek adj. where Abraham Mayfield now lives.*

Sources

Allegany County Maryland Census, 1800 & 1810.
Allegany County Maryland Circuit Court Land Records,
    1813-1814.
Allegany County Maryland Deed Book C.
Allegany County Maryland Deed Book C.
Allegany County Maryland Deed Book E.
Allegany County Maryland Inventories, Vol. A.
Allegany County Maryland Marriage Records.
Archives of Maryland, Vol. 10505.
Atkinson, Mary David. Monongalia County, West Virginia,
    1776-1810.
Creekmore, Polly. Loudoun County Virginia 1771 Tithables
    List, in *The Virginia Genealogist*, 1973.
Crumrine, Boyd. Virginia Court Records in Southwestern
    Pennsylvania - Records of the District of West
    Augusta and Ohio and Yohogania Counties, Virginia,
    1775-1780.
DAR Lineage Book Vol. XV.
Davis Clearing House, 1916 North Signal Hills Drive,
    Kirkwood, Missouri.
Fairfax County, Virginia Order Book 1749-1754.
Fairfax County, Virginia Historical Society, Card File.
Fairfax County, Virginia Order Book 1749-1754.
Fram, Marcia Ruth. "Development may save old church,"
    Washington Star, June 12, 1979.
Historical Society of Baltimore Maryland. Old Settlers.
Hopkins, Margaret Lail, editor. Index to the Tithables of
    Loudoun County Virginia and to Slaveholders and

Slaves, 1758-1786.
List of Officers and Soldiers of the Virginia Line on
Continental Establishment.
Lloyd, James, jblloyd@kc.rr.com.
Loudoun County, Virginia 56th & 57th Regiments Militia
Records 1793-1809.
Loudoun County, Virginia Deed Book Y, 1797-1798.
Loudoun County, Virginia Order Book A, 1757-1762.
Loudoun County, Virginia Order Book B, 1763-1764.
Loudoun County, Virginia Order Book C, 1765-1767.
Loudoun County, Virginia Order Book D, 1768-July 1770.
Loudoun County, Virginia Order Book E, August 1770-April
1773.
Loudoun County, Virginia Order Book H, May 1783-May
1785.
Loudoun County, Virginia Order Book I, May 1785-
November 1786.
Loudoun County, Virginia Order Book L, September
1788-March 1790.
Loudoun County, Virginia Order Book M, March   1790-
August 1791.
Loudoun County, Virginia Order Book P, December
1792-August 1794.
Loudoun County, Virginia Order Book Q, September
1794-October 1796.
Loudoun County, Virginia Order Book R, 1796-1798.
Loudoun County, Virginia Poll Book, 1801-1821.
Loudoun County, Virginia Court Proceedings, 1763.
Loudoun County, Virginia Tithables for Cameron Parish,
1758-1799.
The Maryland and Delaware Genealogist, Vol. 10, No. 3.
Mitchell, Beth. *Beginning at a White Oak.*

Monongalia County, Virginia Deeds, Vol. 6, 1814-1816.
Mountain Democrat, Oakland, Maryland, Mary 27, 1937.
Scharf, John Thomas. History of Western Maryland, Vol. II.

Part II - THE PRITCHARD JOURNEY WESTWARD

DESCENDANTS OF JOHN PRI(T)CHARD

6.

John Pri(t)chard, oldest son of No. 5, Thomas Pritchard, Sr. and Rachel Davis, was born 19 Jul 1760 in Loudoun County, Virginia and died 28 Mar 1847 in Washington Township, Decatur County, Indiana, where he is buried in Sand Creek Cemetery. He married **Anna SMARR,** 12 Oct 1795 in Loudoun County, Virginia, the daughter of **John SMARR**, his former employer on the Smarr plantation, and **Sarah PEARL**. Their marriage was performed by John Littlejohn, an itinerant Methodist Episcopal minister. Anna was born 1774 in Cameron Parish, Loudoun County, Virginia, and died 15 Dec 1841 in Wass Township, Decatur County, Indiana.

John Pritchard served in several Virginia companies in the Revolutionary War, first enlisting in Loudoun County in Capt. Lewis' Company. His enlistment records give his occupation as farmer. In March 1781, he volunteered as private in Douglas Company, Col. Matthews' Regiment and saw a great deal of action, beginning with the battle of Guilford Court House where he was wounded in the leg. After participating in the siege of Yorktown, he was transferred to Capt. William Bearn's Company under Col. Alexander and discharged in September 1782.

By the time he returned to civilian life, the 't' in his surname was gone, perhaps because of mistakes by Army clerks, so for the rest of his life he retained the spelling used

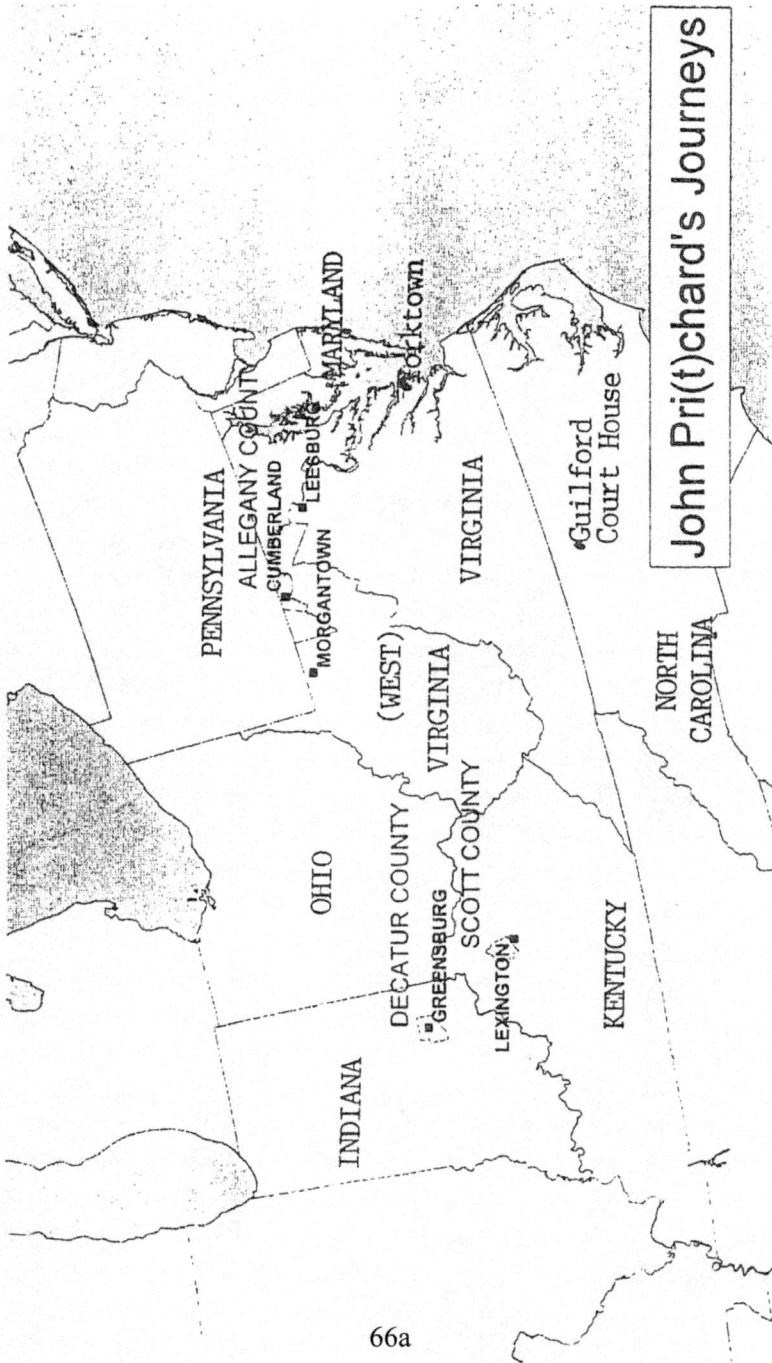

John Pri(t)chard's Journeys

OHIO

INDIANA

DECATUR COUNTY
GREENSBURG
SCOTT COUNTY
LEXINGTON

KENTUCKY

PENNSYLVANIA
ALLEGANY COUNTY
CUMBERLAND
MORGANTOWN
LEESBURG

MARYLAND
Yorktown

(WEST)
VIRGINIA

VIRGINIA

Guilford
Court House

NORTH
CAROLINA

66a

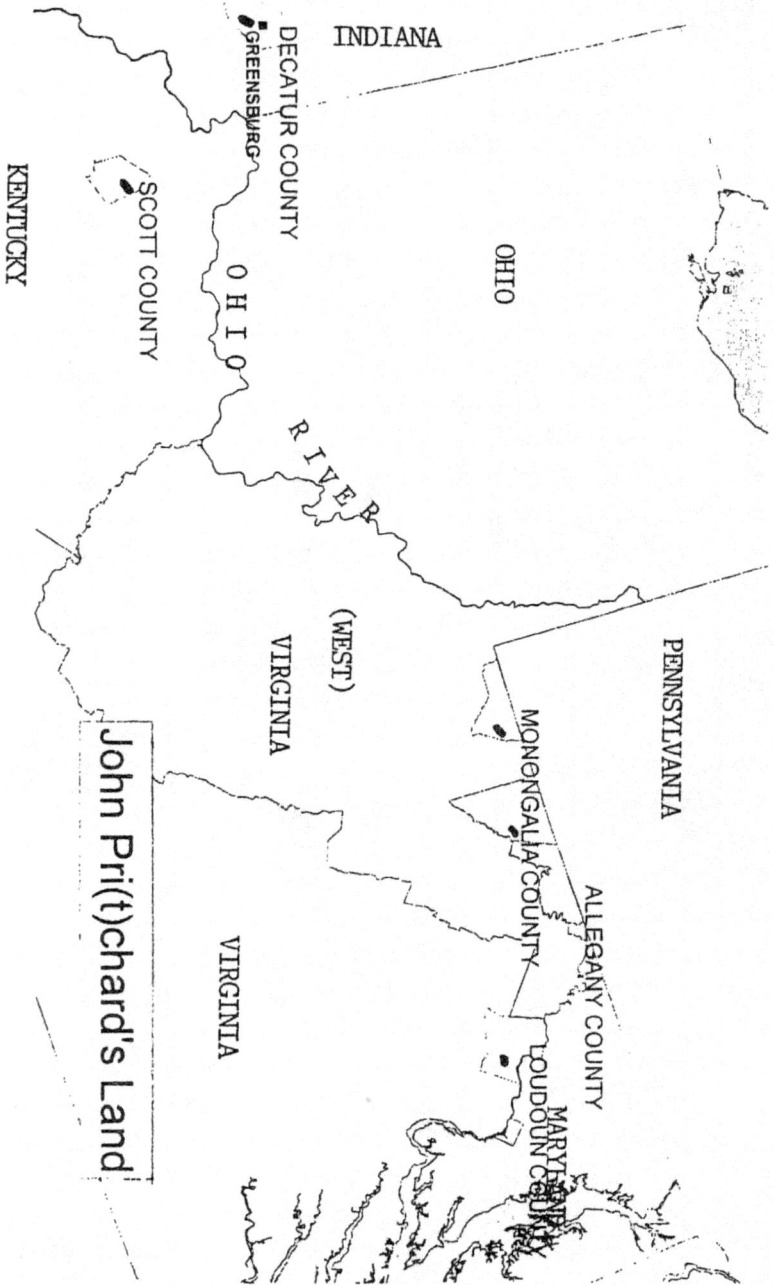

John Pri(t)chard's Land

INDIANA

DECATUR COUNTY
GREENSBURG

KENTUCKY

SCOTT COUNTY

O H I O

OHIO

R I V E R

(WEST)
VIRGINIA

VIRGINIA

PENNSYLVANIA

MONONGALIA COUNTY

ALLEGANY COUNTY

MARYLAND
LOUDOUN COUNTY

66b

throughout his Revolutionary War records. He made application for a pension in Decatur County, Indiana on 31 Oct 1833, qualifying for pension #32456 issued 14 Feb 1834.

In response to a question about the location of his home at the time he entered the service, he replied, *"I was residing at the Gum Springs in Loudoun County, Virginia and continued to reside there until the war was over. Since the Revolution I have resided in Maryland, from there I removed to near Morgantown, Virginia, from thence to Kentucky. There I resided until about six years since when I removed to Decatur County where I now reside."*

The village of Gum Springs, Loudoun County is today known as Arcola. This is adjacent to Dulles Airport, pinpointing the location of the Christopher Pritchard grant.

John Prichard first appears in court records in Hampshire County, (West) Virginia where he is a witness on 18 Apr 1789 to a sale involving a Negro woman named Cloe, one Negro servant girl named Sharlot, one Negro boy named James, livestock, and household goods.

He and Anna Smarr must have moved to Allegany County (now Garrett County), Maryland shortly after their marriage in 1795, for the Loudoun County Court orders on 09 May 1797 that John Prichard be paid eleven dollars and forty-six cents for two days attendance and (traveling) 130 miles as a witness at the petition of Joseph Moore, husband of his wife's sister Cloe.

There are several explanations as to why John Prichard dropped the 't' in his surname. Because clerks filling out many of his Revolutionary War documents used this spelling, he may have decided to adopt it for legal purposes. His younger brother, William, also eventually dropped the 't', although it was retained in some of his earlier legal papers.

The Pritchard/Prickett Family History

One intriguing factor which may have considerable bearing upon their decision is the influx into western Virginia - notably Monongalia County - of Melungeons (or Guineas) with the surname Pritchard. These people were regarded by their neighbors as "half-breeds," as they often were a mixture of Portuguese, Spanish, Turkish, Muslim, American Indian, and, more infrequently, Blacks. Since the Pritchards and other settlers in the area were proud of their English heritage, they did not wish to be mistaken for "mixed breeds." Both John and William may have chosen this means of distancing themselves from people they considered to be undesirable, because once the connection was made, it was almost impossible to undo. For example, Warner Pritchard, a Prince Georges County, Maryland native who moved to western Maryland in 1790, was listed as white in all census records prior to 1810. After his marriage on 25 Nov 1816 to Sophia Goens from the Carolinas, he was counted as a mixed breed. Not even his second marriage on 26 Jul 1835 to Ruth Dalton, a white woman, changed his listing. His descendants did not escape the prejudice until they moved to Pennsylvania.

Besides Pritchard (with a 't'), other common Melungeon surnames in western Virginia were Dalton, Goens, Kennedy, Mayle, Minard, Minor, and Norris. Along with their counterparts in North and South Carolina - many of them Lumbee/Croatan Indians - the ancestors of the West Virginia Melungeons came from several sources: (1) Iberian settlers abandoned when the English overran the Santa Elena (Beaufort, South Carolina) Colony in 1587; (2) Ottoman sailors set off on Roanoke Island, North Carolina in 1586 by Sir Francis Drake, who had freed them from their Spanish captors, then utilized them as slave labor at Cartegena in the Caribbean; (3) other Mediterranean/Middle Eastern settlers and/or

68

abandoned captives brought by the Virginia Company to Jamestown on two separate occasions in the mid-1600s. A detailed account of them is found in *The Melungeons; The Resurrection of a Proud People - An Untold Story of Ethnic Cleansing in America* by N. Brent Kennedy, with Robyn Vaughan Kennedy (Mercer University Press, Macon Georgia, September 1996.)

Like many Revolutionary War veterans, John Prichard took advantage of the military lots offered in western Maryland, but he was soon lured to Scott County, Kentucky. In 1813, he made the long trek back to Allegany County to receive his "child's share" of his father's estate. In 1833, he moved to Decatur County, Indiana, where he died. One account from a great granddaughter, Mrs. L. H. Box of Roundup, Montana, states that the former soldier and his wife were poisoned by their Negro slaves. The place, date, and circumstances are not given.

An article by Patricia Smith entitled *"Revolutionary War Veterans Buried in Decatur County, Indiana"* appears in a book published in 1976 by the Decatur County Bicentennial Committee. It contains the following observation about life in Greensburg, the county seat, John Prichard's final place of residence: *"The year Mr. Prichard died, S. Stewart was the druggist; G. W. New, a physician; John S. Scoby and Philender Hamilton were attorneys. Hamilton had an office on the east side of the square in the Stevens Bldg., and Scoby was Prosecuting Attorney. Miss Camilla Thomson taught reading, writing, art, English grammar, and geography at $2.00 per session of 12 weeks in the Presbyterian Church. Richard Talbott was sheriff and the Greensburg Repository posted a list of letters remaining in the post office and stated that, if not taken out in 3 months, they would be returned to the General*

*Post Office as dead letters. John Prichard was born as a
subject of King George. He fought for freedom for the 13
colonies, and lived to see his county becoming powerful,
expanding to embrace territories across the North American
continent."*

There are several discrepancies about the date of John
Prichard's death. On DAR records, it ranges from 21 Jun 1842
to 24 Mar 1847, the date carved on his tombstone in Sand
Creek Cemetery. The latter is most likely correct.
The children of John Prichard and Anna Smarr are:

   i. **George Washington Prichard**, m. **Elizabeth
    McCORMICK**, 30 Jul 1846, Decatur
    County, Indiana.

   ii. **John D. Prichard; m. Phoebe Ann CHANCE**,
    Dearborn County, Indiana, 12 Dec 1854.

   iii. **Rachel Prichard**, b. 11 Aug, 1798, Allegany
    County, Maryland; d. 13 Sep 1872,
    bur. Sand Creek Cemetery, Decatur County,
    Indiana; m. **John MEYERS** (12 Mar 1800-
    11 Jan 1863).

14. iv. **Nancy Prichard**, b. 19 Aug 1800, Allegany
    County, Maryland; d. 19 Jan 1883; m.
    (1) **John GRAY**; m. (2) **James WALTERS.**

   v. **Sarah (Sally) Prichard**, b. 07 Nov 1805; d. 03 Aug
    1840, bur. Sand Creek Cemetery, Decatur
    County, Indiana; m. **William FORD.**

15. vi. **Thomas Prichard**, b. about 1806; d. about 1889.

   vii.. **Elizabeth Prichard**, b. 1807; m. **unk LEE.**

16. viii. **Margaret Prichard**, b. 1811, Scott County,
    Kentucky; d. before 1851, Decatur County,
    Indiana.

17. ix. **Mary Ann Pritchard**, b. 1813 Scott County,

Kentucky; d. Marion Township, Decatur
County, Indiana.

18.	x.	**Harriet Prichard**, b. 1815 Scott County,
Kentucky.

19.	xi.	**Fanny Prichard**, b. 25 Jan 1820, Scott
County, Kentucky; d. 12 Jul 1905,
Indianapolis, Indiana.

SECOND GENERATION

14.

Nancy Pritchard, daughter of No. 6, John Prichard, was born 19 Aug, 1800 in Allegany County, Maryland and died 19 Jan 1883 in Decatur County, Indiana. She is buried in Kingston Cemetery, Fugit Township, Decatur County, Indiana. She married (1) **John GRAY**, b. 11 Dec 1759, d. 1836. She married (2) **James WALTERS**, after 1836 in Decatur County, Indiana, son of **William WALTERS** and **Elizabeth Unk**.

John Gray was a Revolutionary War Veteran who enlisted in his home state of Virginia and served under his older brother, Capt. David Gray. He fought at Yorktown, and for the service he rendered there was granted a pension and 200 acres of land in Virginia. His original headstone bears this epitaph:

> *"Remember friends as you pass by*
> *As you are now, so once was I*
> *As I am now so you must be*
> *Prepare for death and follow me."*

Child of Nancy Prichard and John Gray is:

    i. **Sarah Ann Gray, b**. 08 May 1826; d. 10 Dec 1842, bur. Sand Creek Cemetery, Washington Township, Decatur County, Indiana.

15.

Thomas Prichard, son of No. 6, John Prichard, was born about 1806, probably in Allegany County, Maryland, and died about 1889. He married **Quintilla CORBIN**, 31 Jan 1828 in Decatur County, Indiana.

Children of Thomas Prichard and Quintilla Corbin are:
20. i. **Sarah Amanda Prichard**, b. after 1828.
21. ii. **George W. Prichard**, b. 1837, Decatur County, Indiana; d. 1917.

16.

Margaret Prichard, daughter of No. 6, John Prichard, was born 1811 in Scott County, Kentucky, and died in Decatur County, Indiana. She married **Absalom D. LEE,** 05 Jun 1828 in Decatur County. He was born in Kentucky. In addition to those children listed here, he had others by a previous marriage.
Children of Margaret Prichard and Absolum D. Lee are:
  i. **James W. Lee**, b. 1837, Rush County, Indiana; d. 1920, Clinton County, Indiana; m. **Emma L. NORRIS** (b. 1861, Rush County, Indiana; d. 1880, Clinton County, Indiana.)
  ii. **Henry C. Lee**, b. 1845, Marion Township, Decatur County, Indiana.
  iii. **William H. Lee**, b. 1851, Marion Township, Decatur County, Indiana; d. 1942, Rush County, Indiana; m. **Elizabeth LEE** (b. 1861, Rush County, Indiana; d. 1890, Clinton County, Indiana).
  iv. **John Wesley Lee**, b. 07 Sep 1852, Marion Township, Indiana; d. 01 Sep 1890, Rush County, Indiana; m. **Olive Emeline AMOS** (b. 02 Jun 1850, Rush County, Indiana, d. 01 Sep 1890, Rush County, Indiana).

17.

Mary Ann Prichard, daughter of No. 6, John Prichard, was born 1813, in Scott County, Kentucky and died in Marion Township, Decatur County, Indiana. She married **Hiram CHRISTY,** 25 Dec 1834 in Decatur County, Indiana.

Hiram Christy had at least two brothers, **Henry P. CHRISTY**, who married **Mary PATTERSON** in Decatur County, Indiana on 28 Nov 1852, and **William T. CHRISTY,** who married **Elizabeth FREEMAN** in Decatur County, Indiana on 17 May 1849. He also had at least two sisters, **Martha Jane CHRISTY**, who married **Joseph B. LAYTON** in Decatur County, Indiana on 08 Jul 1852, and **Mary CHRISTY**, who married **Uriah ROBERTS** in Decatur County, Indiana on November 08, 1849.

Child of Mary Prichard and Hiram Christy is:

22.   i. **John Milton Christy**, b. 06 Sep 1839, Greensburg, Putnam County, Indiana; d. 06 Apr 1915, St. Louis, Missouri.

23.   ii. **Hiram Samuel Christy**, b. 19 Nov 1847, Greensburg, Putman County, Decatur, Indiana

The CHRISTY Family

The Christy ancestry goes back to England, according to letters written by two sons of the immigrant Samuel Christy, who married after arriving in Essex County, Virginia. His son Julius was born in Essex County about 1730.

Julius CHRISTY (c. 1730-1808) married **Agatha BARNETT** (c. 1740-1830) in Culpeper County, Virginia. They moved to Greenbrier County, Virginia before heading to the land that became Scott County, Kentucky.

Children of Julius Christy and Agatha Barnett:
  i. **Elizabeth Christy** b. abt.. 1758- d. abt. 1829 m.
     William GLASS.
 ii. **Mildred Christy** b. 1725; d. 1829; m. **Belfield
     CAVE.**
iii. **Agatha Christy** bc.1760, d.1810; m. **Francis R.
     KIRTLEY**
 iv. **Ann Christy,** b. 1762; d. 1844. m. **John LINDSEY.**
  v. **Frances Christy,** bc. 1764-1848); m. **William
     CAVE.**
 vi. **James Christy,** b. 1766, d. aft. 1847; m. **Elizabeth
     ARMSTRONG.**
 ii. **George Christy,** b. 1767, d. 1834; m. **Mary
     CAVE.**
iii. **Ambrose Christy,** b. 1768, d. 1839; m. **Mary
     BUSH.**
 ix. **John Christy,** b. 1769, d. 1848; m. **Hannah
     WHALEY.**
  x. **Sarah Christy** bc 1770; d. unk; m. **Elijah DAVIS.**
 xi. **Samuel CHRISTY** b.1783, d. 1854 m. **Mary
     "Polly" DAY** b. 1789; d. aft 1860.

Samuel Christy and Mary Polly Day were married in Scott
County, Kentucky, 11 April 1805.
Children of Samuel Christy and Mary Polly Day are:
    i. **Mariah Christy** m. **William BUSH.**
   ii. **Elizabeth Christy** m. **John HAZELRIGG.**
  iii. **Churchill G. Christy** m. **Maria COBB.**
   iv. **James Christy** m. **Catherine PARKER.**
    v. **Sarah Christy** m. **James MCCONNELL**
   vi. **Hiram Christy** m. **Mary Ann
        PRICHARD**

The Pritchard/Prickett Family History

vii **Milton Christy** m. **Lavenia VAUGHAN.**
viii. **Lucy Ann Christy** m. **William D. EUBANK.**
ix. **Samuel Christy** m. (1) **Elizabeth FREEMAN**
(2) **Margaret LOVETT.**
x. **Mary Christy** m. **Uriah ROBERTS.**
xi. **William Christy** m. **Susan ISRAEL**
xii. **Martha J. Christy** m. **Joseph LAYTON**

18.

Harriet Prichard, daughter of No. 6, John Prichard, was born 1815 in Scott County, Kentucky. She married **Thomas J. ENGLISH** 10 May 1838. He was born 1815 in Kentucky. Thomas English had at least one brother, **Joseph ENGLISH,** who married **Mary Jane LEE** in Decatur County Indiana on 27 May 1847.
Children of Harriet Prichard and Thomas English are:
i. **Joseph English,** b. 1839, Decatur County, Indiana.
ii. **Anne E. English**, b. 1842, Decatur County, Indiana.
iii. **Sarah English,** b. 1844, Decatur County, Indiana.
iv. **Martha J. English**, b. 1847, Decatur County, Indiana.
v. **Messouri A. English**, b. October 1849, Decatur County, Indiana.

19.

Fanny Prichard, daughter of No. 6, John Prichard, was born 25 Jan 1820, Scott County, Kentucky and died 12 Jul 1905 in Indianapolis, Indiana. She is buried in Hebron Adams Cemetery, Adam Township, Indiana. She married (1) **Adam**

76

HOWARD, 31 Aug 1842 in Decatur County, Indiana. He died 20 Jul 1848, age 38 years, 2 months, 20 days. She married (2) **William LOWE** 04 Jan 1850 in Indiana.
Children of Fanny Prichard and Adam Howard are:

     i. **Ann J. Howard**, b. 1842, Indiana; m. **Alexander HINDMAN**, 30 Aug 1860.

24.   ii. **Susan Howard**, b. 25 Sep 1844, Indiana; d. 11 Jul 1920.

    iii. **Charity Elizabeth Howard**, b. 09 Aug 1847, Decatur, Indiana; d. 11 Sep 1877, Kansas.

    iv. **John Steven Howard**, b. 1848, Indiana; d. 18 Jan 1903; m. **Sarah E. BARCLAY**, 13 Apr 1865.

Children of William Lowe by his first wife, step-children to Fanny Prichard are:

    v. **Elenor Lowe**, b. 1834.

    vi. **Joseph Lowe**, b. 1835.

    vii. **John Lowe**, b. 1838.

    viii. **Jonathan Lowe**, b. 1840.

    ix. **William J. Lowe**, b. 1842.

    x. **Sarah Lowe**, b. 1844.

    xi. **Phoebe A. Lowe**, b. 1845.

Children of Fanny Prichard and William Lowe are:

    xii. **Harriet J. Lowe**, b. 21 Dec 1850, Decatur County, Indiana; d. 05 Feb 1853, bur. Clarksburg Cemetery, Fugit Township, Decatur County, Indiana.

    xiii **Alice Lowe**, b. 1852; m. **John MULL**.

    xiv. **Mary M. Lowe**, b. 1855

    xv. **Gaba Lowe**, b. 1859.

    xvi. **Netta A. Lowe**, b. 1861.

    vii. **Albert Lowe**, b. 1864.

The Pritchard/Prickett Family History

THIRD GENERATION

20.

Sara Amanda Prichard, daughter of No. 15, Thomas
Prichard, was born about 1830 and died 26 Apr 1916 in Ritchie
County, West Virginia. She married **William H. EHERT**, 15
Jul, 1848, Ritchie County, (West) Virginia. She is buried in
Pine Grove Cemetery, Berea, Ritchie County, West Virginia.

We do not know how Sara reached (West) Virginia
from Indiana; however there was communication between John
Prichard and his brother Thomas, Jr, who by that time was
living in Ritchie County adjacent to Doddridge County. The
Ehert family had emigrated from Germany to Pennsylvania
after the Revolutionary War and moved to Doddridge County
about 1845, so Sara may have met William while visiting her
relatives. She most likely traveled by steamboat on the Ohio
River from Louisville to Parkersburg, (West) Virginia, then by
stagecoach to Harrisville where relatives could have met her
with horse and carriage. Her journey would have been far
easier than that undertaken in 1813 by her grandfather, John
Prichard, from Kentucky to Maryland to receive his child's
share of his father's estate.

21.

George Washington Prichard, son of No. 15, Thomas
Prichard, was born 1837 in Decatur County, Indiana and died
in 1917. He married **Phoebe KING** in 1863.
Child of George Prichard and Phoebe King is:
25.   i. **Alta G. Prichard**, b. 1865.

22.

John Milton Christy, son of No. 17, Mary Ann Prichard, was

78

born 06 Sep 1839 in Greenburg, Putnam County, Indiana and died 06 Apr 1915 in St. Louis, Missouri. He married **Martha Jane DAVIS,** 24 Oct 1867 in Indiana.

Child of John Milton Christy and Martha Jane Davis is:

26.   ii. **Thomas Newton Christy**, b. 01 Dec 1860, Crawford County, Illinois; d. 16 Apr 1943, Olney, Richland County, Illinois.

23.

Hiram Samuel Christy, son of No.17, Mary Ann Prichard, was born 19 Nov 1847, Greensburg, Decatur County Indiana. He married **Rebecca A. MORRISON,** b. 1849 Guernsey, Ohio, on 19 Aug, 1869, in Olney, Richland County, Illinois.

Child of Hiram Christy and Rebecca Morrison is:

27.   i. **Claude Bertram Christy** b. 30 Mar 1871 in Olney, Richland County, Illinois

24.

Susan Howard, daughter of No. 19, Fanny Prichard, was born 25 Sep 1844 in Indiana and died 11 Jul 1920. She is buried in South Park Cemetery, Greensburg, Decatur County, Indiana. She married **Ruben Franklin THOMAS,** 14 Apr 1869, Indiana, son of **Ruben THOMAS** and **Mary CARPER**. Ruben Franklin Thomas was a Civil War veteran 1861-1864, and prisoner, from Company I, 33rd Indiana Infantry.

Children of Susan Howard and Ruben Franklin Thomas are:

        i. **Lettie Thomas**, b. 31 Aug 1870, Decatur County, Indiana; d. 04 Jan 1871, Greensburg, Indiana.

28.   ii. **Frank Thomas**. b. 24 Oct 1871, Tipton County, Indiana; d. 05 Aug 1956, Greensburg, Indiana.

29.   iii. **Ollie Thomas**, b. 24 Jul, 1877, Tipton County, Indiana; d. 23 Apr 1937, bur. Richmond,

Indiana.

30.   iv. **Fannie May Thomas**, b. 01 Jul 1880, Decatur County, Indiana; d. 19 Feb 1924, Indianapolis, Indiana.

31.   v. **George Lucas Thomas**, b. 07 Jul 1884, Greensburg, Decatur County, Indiana; d. 31 July 1938, bur. Springfield, Clark County, Ohio.

FOURTH GENERATION

25.

Alta G. Prichard, daughter of No. 21, George W. Prichard, was born in 1865. She married **Lorenzo Albert TUSLER,** 03 Aug, 1883.
Child of Alta Prichard and Lorenzo Tusler is:
      i. **Ione Tusler**, b. Rutland, Dane County,
         Wisconsin, m. **Ernest SHELLESTAD**.

26.

Thomas Newton Christy, son of No. 22, John Milton Christy, was born 01 Dec 1860 in Crawford County, Illinois and died 16 Apr 1943 in Olney, Highland County, Illinois. He married **Naomi KOENIG**.
Child of Thomas Christy and Naomi Koenig is:
32.   i. **Beulah Christy**, b. 23 Aug 1895, Olney,
         Highland County, Illinois; d. before 1985,
         Washington, DC.

27.

Claude Bertram Christy, son of No. 23, Hiram Samuel Christy, married **Catherine Benton POPE,** b. 20 Oct 1872, on 05 Oct 1894 in Carlyle, Clinton County, Illinois,
Child of Claude Christy and Catherine Pope is:
33.   i. **June Christy.**

28.

Frank Thomas, son of No. 24, Susan Howard, was born 24 Oct 1871 in Tipton County, Indiana and died 05 Aug 1956. He is buried in South Park, Greensburg, Decatur County, Indiana. He married **Minnie Mae PREBLE** on 18 May 1904, in

Indiana.
Children of Frank Thomas and Minnie Preble are:
  i. **Alma De Louis Thomas.**
  ii. **Franklin May Thomas.**
  iii. **Ruth Thomas.**
  iv. **Lillian Thomas.**
  v. **Martha Thomas.**
  vi. **Mary Thomas.**

29.

Ollie Thomas, son of No. 24, Susan Howard, was born 24 Jul 1877 in Decatur County, Indiana and died 23 Apr 1937. He is buried in Earlham Cemetery, Richmond, Wayne County, Indiana. He married **Cora BAILEY,** 16 Oct 1895 in Greensburg, Indiana, daughter of **James BAILEY** and **Angeline COOKSEY**.

Children of Ollie Thomas and Cora Bailey are:

34. i. **Charles Howard Thomas**, b. 17 Mar 1896, Greensburg, Decatur County, Indiana; d. 16 Nov, 1951, Cincinnati, Hamilton County, Ohio.

35. ii. **Nettie Irena Thomas**, b. 09 Feb 1898, Greensburg, Decatur County, Indiana; d. 16 May 1954.

36. iii. **Myrtle May Thomas**, b. 03 Mar 1902, Greensburg, Decatur County, Indiana; d. 25 May 1977.

37. iv. **Ollie Leroy Thomas**, b. 16 May1911, Cincinnati, Hamilton County, Ohio; d. 19 Aug 1947, Boston, Wayne County, Indiana.

  v. **Mary Ellen Thomas**, b. 10 May 1914; d. after 10 1914, Cincinnati, Ohio.

38.   vi. **Thelma Corrine Thomas**, b. 13 Aug 1916,
             Cincinnati, Hamilton County, Ohio.

30.
Fannie Mae Thomas, daughter of No. 24, Susan Howard, was
born 01 Jul 1880 in Decatur County, Indiana and died 19 Feb
1924 in Indianapolis, Indiana. She married **Charles A.
BUSSEL.**
Child of Fannie Mae Thomas and Charles Bussell is:
        i. **Eddy Bussell.**

31.
George Lucas Thomas, son of No. 24, Susan Howard, was
born 07 Jun 1884 in Greensburg, Decatur County, Indiana and
died 31 Jul 1938. He is buried in Ferncliff Cemetery,
Springfield, Clark County, Ohio. He married (1) **Beulah E.
LINHELM**. He married (2) **Levena Bell SNOW,** 16 Oct
1920.
Child of George Lucas Thomas and Beulah Linhem is:
        i. **Leona Edith Thomas**, b. before 1920.
Children of George Lucas Thomas and Levena Bell Snow are:
        ii. **Florence Marie Thomas.**
        iii. **Thelma Louise Thomas.**
        iv. **Charles Albert Thomas.**
        v. **Alice Jane Thomas**

FIFTH GENERATION

32.

Beulah Christy, daughter of No. 25, Thomas Newton Christy, was born 23 Aug, 1895 in Olney, Highland County, Illinois and died before 1985 in Washington, DC. She married **William B. O'CONNELL**.
Child of Beulah Christy and William B. O'Connell is:
    i. **Jerry O'Connell**, b. 1934

33.

June Christy, daughter of No. 27, Claude Bertram Christy, married **Arthur FAKES Sr.** b. 06 Apr, 1922, Wilson County, Tennessee, on 05 May 1944 in Chicago, Cook County, Illinois.
Child of June Christy and Arthur Fakes Sr.is:
39.   i. Arthur Fakes, Jr.

34.

Charles Howard Thomas, son of No. 28, Ollie Thomas, was born 17 Mar 1896 in Greensburg, Indiana and died 16 Nov 1951 in Cincinnati, Hamilton County, Ohio. He married **Florence WERSHY,** 24 Dec 1915 in Cincinnati, Ohio.
Children of Charles Thomas and Florence Wershy are:
    i. **Alfred Charles Thomas.**
    ii. **Howard Melvin Thomas.**
    iii **Robert Leroy Thomas.**
    iv. **Harold Raymond Thomas.**

35.

Nettie Irena Thomas, daughter of No. 28, Ollie Thomas, was born 09 Feb 1898 in Greensburg, Decatur County, Indiana and died 16 May 1954. She married **William J. DURHAM,** 15 Oct 1915.

Child of Nettie Thomas and William J. Durham is:
  i. **William Herbert Durham**, b.27 Mar 1929.

36.

Myrtle May Thomas, daughter of No. 28, Ollie Thomas, was born 03 Mar, 1902 in Greensburg, Decatur County, Indiana and died 25 May 1977. She married **Epler Martin PRIVETT,** 03 Jun 1922

Children of Myrtle May Thomas and Epler Privett are:
  i. **Juanita Louise Privett**, b. Mar 1927; m.
    Unk FREEMAN.
  ii **James Thomas Privett**, b. 23 Jul 1930.
  iii. **Shirley Mae Privett**, b. 08 Oct 1931.

37.

Ollie Leeroy Thomas, son of No. 28, Ollie Thomas, was born 16 May 1911 in Cincinnati, Hamilton County, Ohio and died 19 Aug 1947 in Boston, Wayne County, Indiana. He is buried in Elkhorn Cemetery, Richmond, Indiana. He married **Ethel ADAMS**.

Child of Ollie Leeroy Thomas and Ethel Adams is:
  i. **Lowell Duane Thomas**, b. 04 Oct, 1945;
    d. 28 Feb 1946.

38.

Thelma Corrine Thomas, daughter of No. 28, Ollie Thomas, was born 13 Aug 1916 in Cincinnati, Hamilton County, Ohio. She married **Willard RIES**, 06 Oct 1936.

Children of Thelma Thomas and Willard Ries are:
  i. **Pat Lou Ries**.

ii. **Diana Lee Ries**.

39.

Arthur Fakes, Jr., son of No. 33, June Christy, married **Patricia PUISZIS,** b. 11 Aug 1947 on 19 Dec 1972 in Oak Lawn, Cook County, Illinois.

Children of Arthur Fakes, Jr. and Parricia Puiszis are:

    i. **Theresa Magdalen Fakes**, b. 31 Oct, 1979, m. **Steven Noto** on 29 Jun 2003.

    ii. **Cheryl Ann Fakes**, b. 24 Oct 1983.

DESCENDANTS OF SARAH PRITCHARD

7.

Sarah Pritchard, daughter of No. 5, Thomas Pritchard, Sr., was born about 1762 in Loudoun County, Virginia. She was married twice, first to **John SMARR** before 1789, son of **Andrew SMAW** and **Elishe Unk.** He died before 08 Jun 1795. Her second marriage was to **Cornelius SKINNER, Jr.** on 17 Aug 1799, son of **Cornelius SKINNER, Sr.** Both marriages were in Loudoun County, Virginia. Cornelius Skinner, Jr. was born 27 Feb 1767 in Woodbridge, (now) Union County, New Jersey, and died 21 Mar 1812 in Aldie, Loudoun County, Virginia. His estate, appraised in Loudoun County on 12 Apr 1814, names Sarah Skinner as his administratrix.

Sarah's first marriage to John Smarr, father of Ann who married Sarah's older brother John, produced at least two children, Fanny and Thomas. The Loudoun County marriage records report that Cornelius Skinner married Sarah Smarr, widow, of Cameron Parish, on 17 Aug 1799. Funds were paid out of John Smarr's estate to Cornelius Skinner for Fanny's maintenance and schooling in the amount of 100 pounds for 10 years. This establishes Fanny's birth at about 1789. Further confirmation of Sarah Pritchard's connection to the Smarr and Skinner families comes in a Chancery Suit noting that Cornelius Skinner intermarried with Sarah Smarr, executrix of John Smarr, deceased.

The Smarr Family

1. **Andrew Smaw**, of English ancestry, was on the list of tithables for Northampton County, Virginia in 1666. He married **Ann MORGAN**.

Children of Andrew Smaw and Ann Morgan are:

   i. **John Smaw**, m. **Joanna Unk.** In 1768, he took legal action regarding a tract of land in Northampton County, Virginia located halfway between Eastville and Cheriton.

2. ii. **Andrew Smaw**. b. Northampton County, Virginia; d. before 25 Mar 1735, Northampton County, Virginia; m. **Elishe Unk**.

Children of Andrew Smaw and Elishe are:

3. i. **John Smarr**, d. before 08 Jun 1795, Loudoun County, Virginia.

   ii. **Andrew Smarr.**

   iii. **Henry Smarr.**

   iv. **William Smarr.**

   v. **Caleb Smarr.**

3.

John Smarr, son of Andrew and Elishe Smaw, was married at least once before he married Sarah Pritchard. He married (1) **Sarah PEARL**, daughter of **William PEARL** of Fauquier County. Sarah was still living 24 May 1785 when her father made his will. He married (2) **Sarah PRITCHARD** before 1789, daughter of **Thomas PRITCHARD, Sr.** and **Rachel DAVIS**. John Smarr died between 09 Jun 1794, when he signed his will, and 08 Jun 1795, when the will was recorded at Leesburg, Loudoun County.

The will of John Smarr's father, Andrew Smaw, Jr. of Northampton County, Virginia, was probated in 1735. The name of Andrew's father, Andrew Smaw, Sr., appears on the list of tithables for Northampton County in 1666.

The spelling of the name Smaw was changed to Smarr

in Fairfax and Loudoun Counties by court clerks; all family court records are signed with their mark.

John Smarr's land deeds in Loudoun County, Virginia, together with a deed from John Hall to Joseph Lacy, pinpoint his property as east of the intersection of the Old Carolina Road and east of Middleburg, Virginia, placing it just south of the crossroads of today's Route 15 and Route 50 at Gilbert's Corner. This is within four miles of Gum Springs and the Pritchard land obtained by the Lord Fairfax Grant. The tax list of 1782-1787 credits John Smarr with 10 slaves. His son, Robert Smarr, also owned land nearby, as established by a deed from William Goff to Robert Smarr, 09 Apr 1783.

Descendants of Cornelius Skinner still live on the Skinner farm, which is located by traveling one mile south from Gilbert's Corner on Route 15, then east on Old Braddock Road two-thirds of a mile beyond the site of the Old West Ordinary House and Lacey's Tavern, which were about 800 feet from the above intersection. The Skinner farm has a common boundary with the land once owned by John Smarr. At the time of his death, John Smarr owned a plantation about 270 acres in size.

John Smarr's will names sixteen children, as well as Thomas, the seventeenth, who was born to Sarah Pritchard Smarr not long before John's death. Names of children appearing in his will who received one shilling sterling: son Perit; son Andrew; son George; daughter Elizabeth; daughter Ann; son Charles; son Samuel; son Ruben. To daughter Mary Hampton, 21 pounds ten shillings to be equally divided among her children; to daughter Jane Weadon, 21 pounds ten shillings to be equally divided among her children; to daughter Cloe More (sic), twenty pounds ten shillings; to daughter Nancy Williamson, eight pounds ten shillings to be divided among her children after her death; to son John Smarr, 20 shillings; to daughter Sarah Tilman, 20 shillings; to daughter Fanny Smarr, 32 pounds for maintenance of schooling until she marries or reaches the age of 21; the remainder of the estate to *my beloved wife Sarah Smarr and the under named children begotten of my body, vix. Robert, Mary Hampton, Cloe, Nancy, and Fanny.* Robert Smarr and Sarah Pritchard Smarr were the sole Executors on 09 Jun 1794.

The sale of John Smarr's goods lists ten Negro slaves: Minnie, Lott, Tom, Joseph, Abraham, Ben, Jonas, Rose, Will and Ellen. Sarah received three: Minnie, Lott and Tom; Robert received Joseph, Abraham, Ben, Jonas, and Rose; Jessie Williamson received the boy Will, and Josiah Weedon received Ellen. The family Bible and testaments were bought by John Pritchard, who married Ann Smarr.

Sons of John Smarr and Sarah Pearl, not necessarily in order of birth, are:

    i. **Perit Smarr**.
    ii. **Andrew Smarr** m. **Lydia MURRY**, 08 Dec 1791, Fauquier County, Virginia.
    iii. **George Smarr**.
    iv. **Charles Smarr**.
    v. **Samuel Smarr**, d. 1845, Hannibal, Missouri .
    vi. **John Smarr** m. (1) **Elizabeth REID**; m. (2) **Jane DARWIN**, South Carolina.
    vii. **Robert Smarr**, probably the oldest and joint executor of John Sr.'s will with Sarah Pritchard Smarr.
    viii. **Reuben Smarr** m. **Nancy TAYLOR**; d. 1870, Bracken County, Kentucky.

Daughters of John Smarr and Sarah Pearl are:

    ix. **Mary Smarr** m. (1) **John HAMPTON**; m. (2)

Unk JACOBS, in Fairfax County.
x. **Jane Smarr** m. **Josiah WEADON/WEEDON**.
xi. **Nancy Smarr** m. (1) **Jesse WILLIAMSON**; m. (2) **Unk BONAT**.
xii. **Sarah Smarr** m. **Edward TILMAN**.
xiii. **Ann Smarr**, b. 1774, Cameron Parish, Loudoun County, Virginia; d. 15 Dec 1841, bur. Sand Creek Cemetery, Wass Twp., Decatur County, Indiana; m. **John PRICHARD**, No. 6, 12 Oct 1795.
xiv. **Elizabeth Smarr** m. **Micajah BERKLEY**, 22 Oct 1798.
xv. **Cloe Smarr** m. **Joseph MOORE**.
Children of John Smarr and Sarah Pritchard are:
xvi. **Fanny Smarr**, b. about 1789.
40. xvii. **Thomas Smarr**, b. 18 Dec 1794, Loudoun County, Virginia; d. 28 Nov 1868, Georgetown, Kentucky

Most of the Smarrs moved away from Virginia, John Smarr, Jr. to South Carolina, Ruben Smarr to Kentucky, and Samuel Smarr to Hannibal, Missouri, although his children were born in Kentucky. Sarah Smarr and Edward Tilman lived and raised their family near Abbeville, South Carolina. Two daughters of John Smarr, Sr. of Loudoun County were married and living in Maury County, Tennessee at the time they corresponded with John Smarr, Jr. of South Carolina.

40.
Thomas Smarr, son of No. 7, Sarah Pritchard, was born 18 Dec 1794, a few months before the death of his father, John Smarr, and died 28 Nov 1868 in Georgetown, Kentucky. He

married **Eliza THOMAS**, daughter of **John THOMAS**. She was born 30 May 1811 in Bourbon County, Kentucky, and died 20 Jun 1853. Thomas Smarr played a prominent role in the development of Scott County, Kentucky, where John Prichard and Ann Smarr lived at one time. He rose to the rank of Colonel and owned an exemplary horse farm. His biography in the *Scott County History* reports that *...the old Colonel was very precise, conservative and honest...At the time of his death in his 74th year he had a large estate all of which he made.* Children of Thomas Smarr and Eliza Thomas are:

    i. **Caroline Smarr**, m. **John F. PAYNE**.
    ii. **Eleanor Smarr**, m. **Edward P. GAINES**.
    iii. **Margaret Smarr**, m. **Theodore THORNTON**.
    iv. **John T. Smarr**, m. **Fannie LOWERY**.
    v. **Susie Smarr**, m. **William H. GRAVES**
    vi. **Ann T. Smarr**, m. (1) **James THORNSBERRY**; m. (2) **James McNARY**.
    vii. **Emma Smarr**, m. **Simeon WELLS**.
    viii. **Mary Elizabeth Smarr,** died in infancy.
    ix. **William Smarr**, single, living at age 55 years.

DESCENDANTS OF ELEANOR PRITCHARD

8.

Eleanor Pritchard, daughter of No. 5, Thomas Pritchard, Sr., was born about 1764 in Loudoun County, Virginia. She has left little for history other than information about her marriage to **Richard PRICE**. Their relationship is documented in the Allegany County Maryland proceedings related to the death of her father, Thomas Pritchard, Sr.

Much more is known of her husband, Richard Price, who was born 17 Feb 1757 in Alexandria, Virginia and died 22 Jul 1834 in Marion County, (West) Virginia. He served in the Revolutionary War, No.12067. According to service records and his pension, he enlisted at Leesburg, Virginia and served one year, from January 1777, as a private under Captain Payton Harrison and Colonel Spottswood. In 1780, he spent two months under Captain Francis Russell, and in May 1781, he served under Captain Cleveland and Colonel Matthews. In 1781, he guarded prisoners from Cornwallis's captured army. During his service, he was engaged in the battles of Brandywine and Germantown and the skirmish at Bacon's Branch.

In 1794, he moved to Monongalia County, Virginia. Earlier, he married his first wife, **Nancy DALLAS**, said to be of the same line as George M. Dallas, Vice-President under James Polk. She died in 1800. It is generally accepted that Nancy Dallas was the mother of the four oldest children and Eleanor Pritchard was mother of the two youngest; the mother of numbers five through seven is disputed.

Eleanor Pritchard Price died before 13 Apr 1825 when her widower, Richard Price, married for the third time in

Monongalia County, Virginia. His wife, **Elizabeth ARNETT**, was the daughter of **Andrew ARNETT**. The surety was Joseph Shackleford. William Price, son of Richard, was the administrator of his estate. The inventory and appraisement was made in September 1834 and the final settlement recorded on 18 Oct 1839. Richard Price is buried in Lawson Cemetery, Fairview, Marion County, (West) Virginia.

Children of Richard Price and Nancy Dallas are:

41.　　i. **John Richard Price**, b. 1785; d. 06 Aug 1852, Marion County, (West) Virginia.

42.　　ii. **William W. Price**, b. 08 Feb 1788; d. 20 May 1879.

43.　　iii. **James Price**, b. 1790; d. 1848

44.　　iv. **Mary Ann Price**, b. 05 Mar 1792; d. 05 Jul 1876, Carbondale, Jackson County, Illinois.

　　　　v. **Dolly Price**, b. 22 Sep 1800; d. 15 May 1884.

　　　　vi. **Margaret "Peggy" Price**, m. **John SNIDER** 17 Jul 1804, Monongalia County, (West) Virginia.

　　　　vii. **Sarah Price**, m. **John FARMER** 18 Jan 1814, Monongalia County, (West) Virginia. Surety W. Evans; moved between 1796 and 1797 to Hardin County, Kentucky with the head of the Lincoln family, possibly Abraham Lincoln's father.

Children of Richard Price and Eleanor Pritchard are:

　　　　viii. **Nancy Price**, m. **Robert McGEE** 06 Aug 1818, Monongalia County, (West) Virginia.

　　　　xi. **Rachel Price**, m. **Daniel ARNETT** 11 Jan 1819, Monongalia County, (West) Virginia. Surety James Arnett.

SECOND GENERATION

41.

John Richard Price, son of Richard Price and Nancy Dallas, was born in 1785 and died 06 Aug 1852 in Marion County, (West) Virginia. He married **Sarah MORGAN,** daughter of **James MORGAN** and **Dorothy PRICKETT,** on 28 Feb 1825 in Monongalia County, (West) Virginia. She was born 22 Sep 1800 in Monongalia County and died in 1884 in Marion County, West Virginia.

Children of John Richard Price and Sarah Morgan are:

    i. **Lavina Price**, b. 1826, Monongalia County; m. **Andrew Meredith ARNETT** (b. 24 Jul 1823; d. 17 Jun 1888), No. 602, son of **Rachel MEREDITH,** No. 592, and **James H, ARNETT, Sr.** (see Descendants of Ann "Nancy" Pritchard).

    ii. **Melissa Price**, b. December 1828, Monongalia County.

45.   iii. **Ulysses Morgan Price**, b. December 1828, Monongalia County; d. 1923.

    iv. **Susannah Price**, b.29 Sep 1832, Monongalia County; d. 03 Nov 1872, Marion County, West Virginia; m. **John CLAYTON** before 1852.

    v. **William S. Price**, b. 1837, Monongalia County; d. 1921; m. (1) **Alcinda YOUST;** m. (2) **Caroline DAWSON**; m. (3) **Matilda MUSGROVE,** 07 Oct 1860, Marion County, West Virginia.

42.

William W. Price, son of Richard Price and Nancy Dallas, was born 08 Feb 1788, and died 20 May 1879. He married **Susanna MORGAN**, daughter of **James MORGAN** and **Dorothy PRICKETT**. She was born 08 Sep 1793 in Monongalia County, (West) Virginia, and died 15 Jan 1857. Children of William W. Price and Susanna Morgan are:

    i. **Richard Price.**

    ii. **James Price.**

    iii. **John Price.**

    iv. **Zarilda Price**; m. **Thomas ARNETT.**

    v. **Nancy Morgan Price**; m. **Boaz Burris TIBBS**, son of **Robert TIBBS** and **Castella BURRIS.**

    vi. **Sarah A. Price**, b. 1800; m. (1) **Unk McCOURTNEY**; m. (2) **John P. CLAYTON.**

    vii. **Drusilla Price**; m. **Boaz Burris COX** (b. 1821).

43.

James Price, son of Richard Price and Nancy Dallas, was born in 1790 and died in 1848. He married **Drusilla MORGAN**, daughter of **James MORGAN** and **Dorothy PRICKETT**, on 17 Sep 1818 in Monongalia County, (West) Virginia. She was born 23 May 1795 in Monongalia County, (West) Virginia, and died 19 Jul 1870 in Oregon.

Children of James Price and Drusilla Morgan are:

    i. **Mary Polly Price**, b. 11 Nov 1820, Monongalia County; m. **Martin PAYNE** 19 Apr 1838.

    ii. **Nimrod Price**, b. 09 Sep 1822; m. **America FROMAN** (b. 09 Mar 1827; d. 30 Nov 1898) on 22 Oct 1846.

iii. **Richard Price**, b. 1824; d. 1842.
iv. **Sarah Jane Price**, b. 1826; d. infant.
v. **Matilda Ann Price,** b. 11 Jan 1826; d. 06 Jul 1905;
    m. **Willoughby CHURCHILL** 11 Aug 1852.
vi. **James Dallas Price**, b.03 Mar 1830; d. 14 Sep 1908,
    Linn County, Oregon.
vii. **Margaret Amanda Price**, b. 11 Sep 1833; d. 13
    Sep 1917; m. **David RIDEOUT** 28 Feb 1852.
viii. **Oliver Price**, b. 1835; d. 16 Aug 1897, Alaska.

44.

Mary Ann Price, daughter of Richard Price and Nancy Dallas, was born 05 Mar 1792 in Monongalia County, (West) Virginia. She married. **Job PRICKETT,** son of **Josiah PRICKETT** and **Charity TAYLOR,** 10 Nov 1806, Monongalia County, (West) Virginia. The Surety was William Windsor. Job Prickett was born 18 Dec 1788 in Monongalia County, (West) Virginia, and died 18 Nov 1870 in Carbondale, Jackson County, Illinois. They moved to Illinois about 1850 and are buried in Woodlawn Cemetery, Carbondale.

Children of Mary Price and Job Prickett are:
    i. **Rebecca Prickett.**
    ii. **Josiah Prickett**, b. after 1806.
    iii. **Mahala Prickett**, b. 29 Oct 1807, Monongalia
        County, (West) Virginia; m. No.849, **Joseph**
        James PARKER.
    iv. **Isaac Prickett**, b. 1810; d. after 1880.
    v. **Isaiah Prickett**, b. 1812, Fairmont, Monongalia
        County, (West) Virginia; d. after 1880,
        probably Jackson County, Illinois; unmarried;
        1850 Census: Methodist clergyman, 39
        years old, living with Job; 1880 Census: 70

years old, carpenter, living with sister, Mary
Hill in Carbondale (insane box checked).

vi. **Nancy Dallas Prickett**, b. 1813, Monongalia
County, (West) Virginia; d. 1886, Carbondale,
Jackson County, Illinois; m. **John Pate HILL**.

vii. **Belinda Prickett**, b. 1814.

viii. **James Monroe Prickett**, b. 25 Feb 1818; d.
30 Sep 1881, Carbondale, Jackson
County, Illinois.

ix. **Oliver Perry Prickett**, b. 1820.

x. **Julia Ann Prickett**, b. March 1822, Monongalia
County, (West) Virginia; d. 17 Sep 1893,
Carbondale, Jackson County, Illinois.

xi. **William Benjamin Franklin Prickett, M.D.**, b.
1824/25, Monongalia County, (West)
Virginia; d. 16 Jul 1874, Blue Sulphur
Springs, Greenbrier County, West Virginia.

xii. **Mary D. Prickett**, b. 1831, Monongalia County,
(West) Virginia; d. 1903, Carbondale, Jackson
County, Illinois; unmarried.

xiii. **Job Prickett**, b. 1832.

THIRD GENERATION

45.

Ulysses Morgan Price, son of No.41, John Richard Price and Sarah Morgan, was born December 1828 in Monongalia County, (West) Virginia, and died 1923. He married **Rebecca ARNETT**, daughter of **William ARNETT** and **Eleanor MEREDITH**. She was born 1829 and died 1904 in Marion County, West Virginia. (See pp. 521-523 for obituary of Ulysses Morgan Price.)

Child of Ulysses Price and Rebecca Arnett is:

608.   i. **Sarah Eleanor Price**, b. 1857 (see Descendants of Ann Nancy Pritchard).

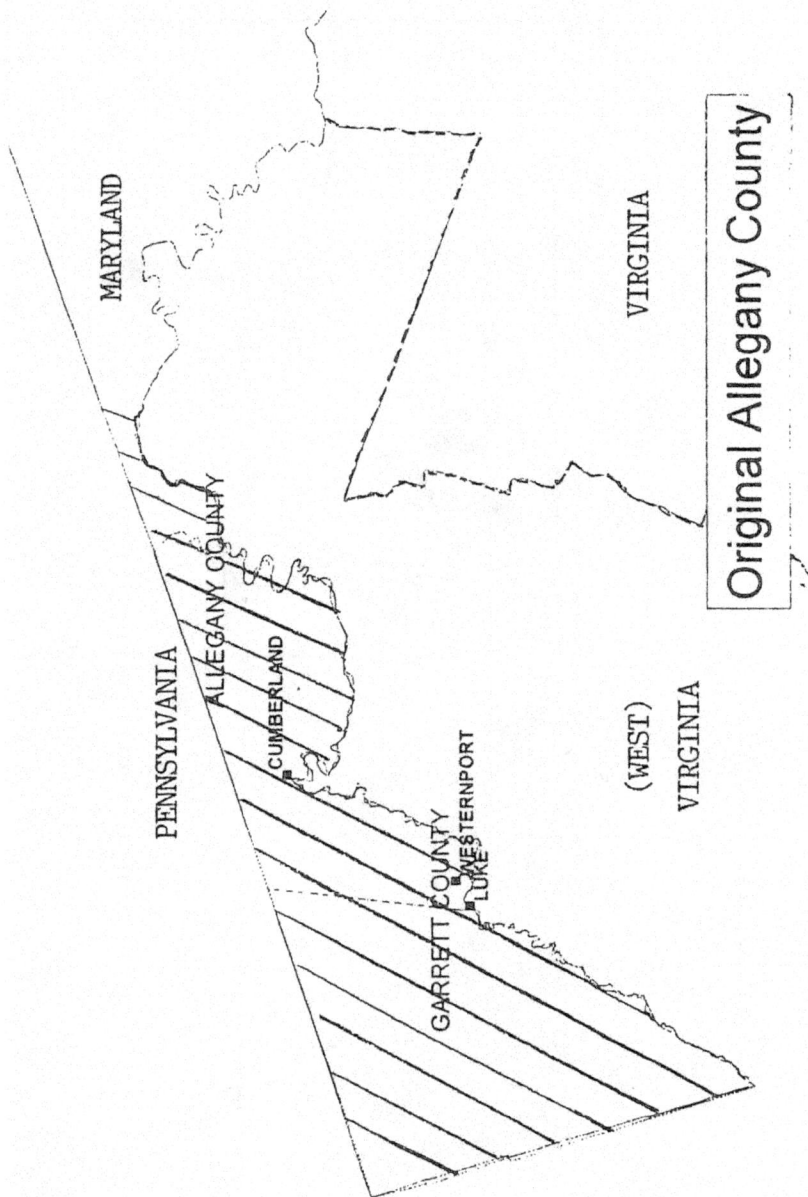

MARYLAND

PENNSYLVANIA

VIRGINIA

(WEST) VIRGINIA

ALLEGANY COUNTY

GARRETT COUNTY

CUMBERLAND

WESTERNPORT

LUKE

Original Allegany County

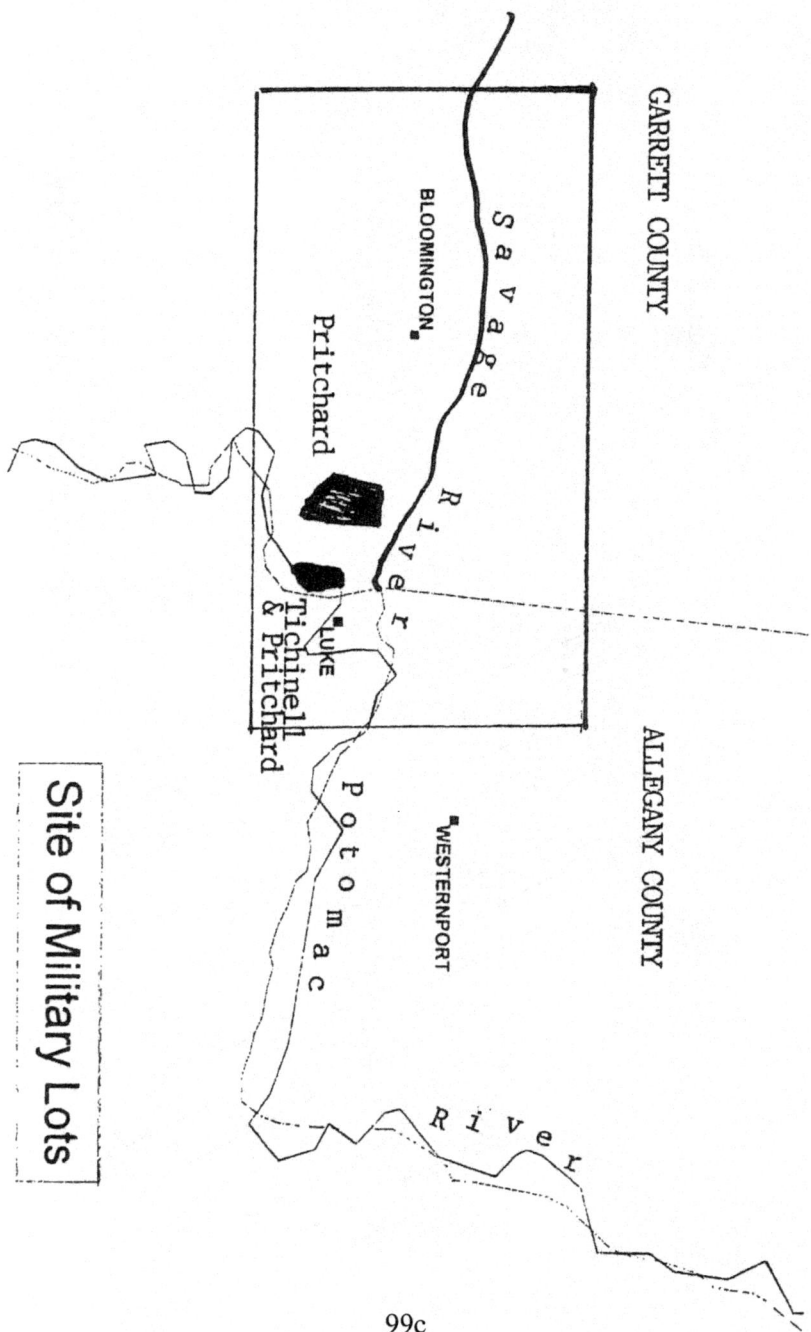

Site of Military Lots

GARRETT COUNTY

ALLEGANY COUNTY

Savage River

Potomac

River

BLOOMINGTON

Pritchard

LUKE

Tichinell & Pritchard

WESTERNPORT

99c

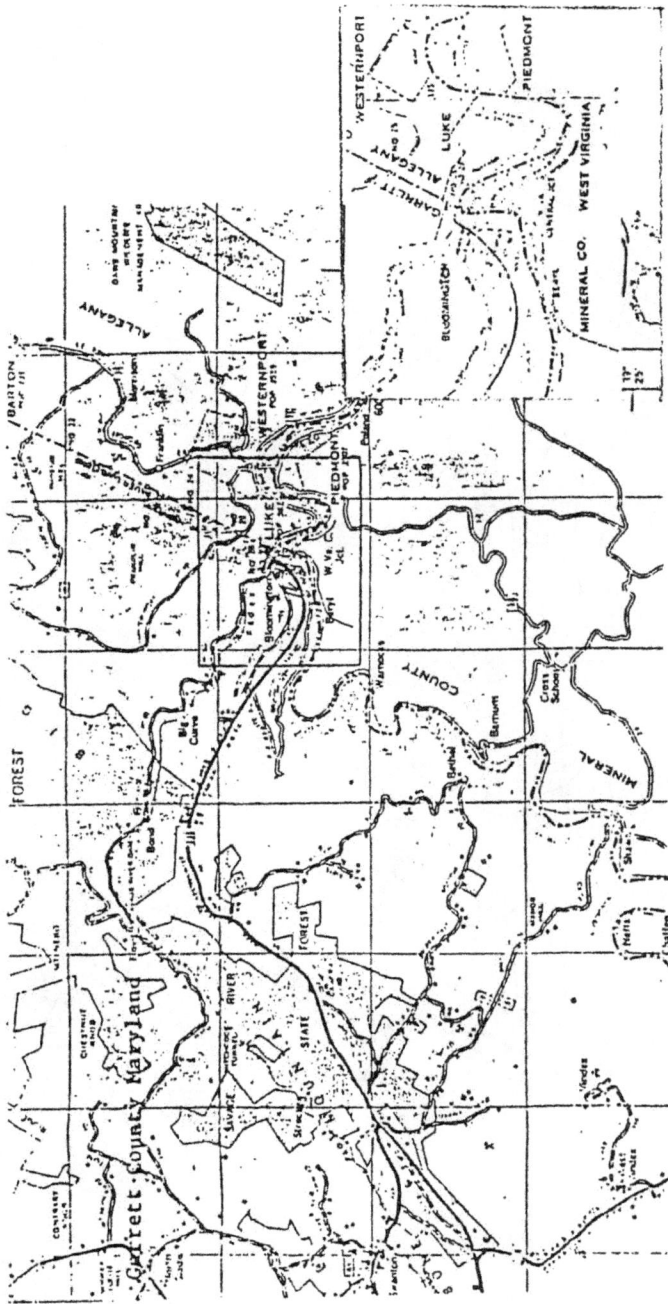

Garrett County, Maryland, location of Pritchard and Tichenell
Military Lots in the Bloomington, Luke, Westernport rectangle

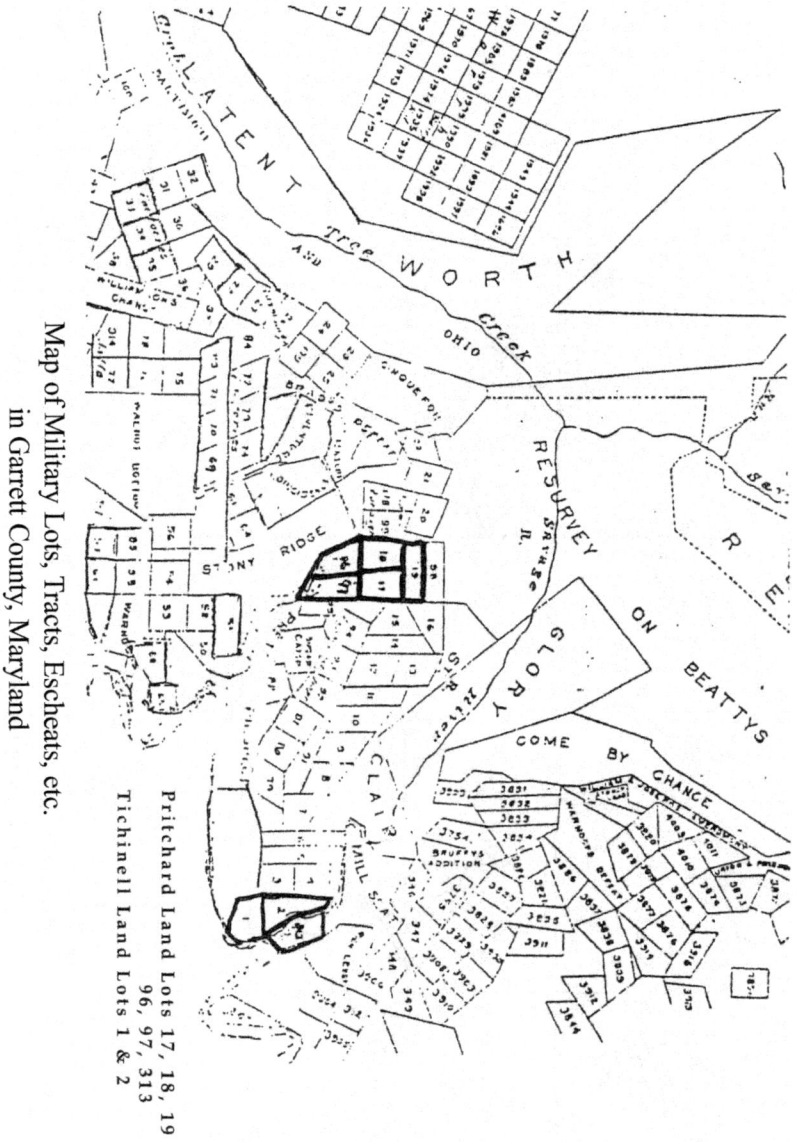

Map of Military Lots, Tracts, Escheats, etc. in Garrett County, Maryland

Pritchard Land Lots 17, 18, 19
96, 97, 313
Tichinell Land Lots 1 & 2

99e

Monongalia County Deed Book 4, p. 481, 26 May 1809
John Brant and wife Elizabeth of Allegany
County, Maryland to Thomas Pritchard
of Monongalia County, Virginia,
1,340 acres on the State Road
leading from Morgantown to Dunkards
Bottom adjoining the Monongalia Glades

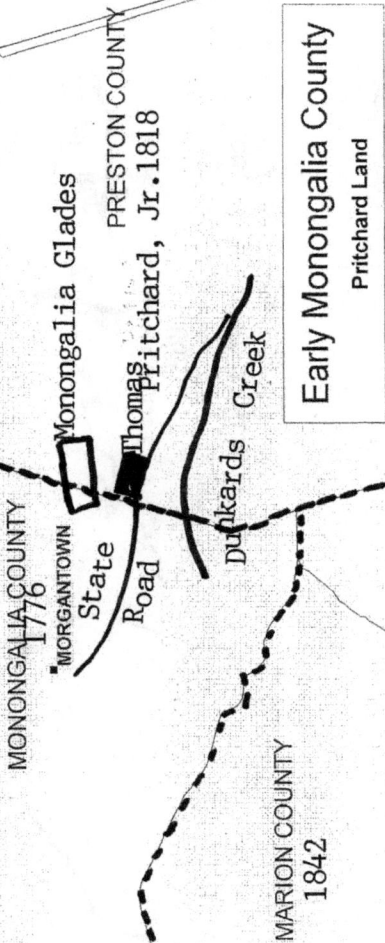

Monongalia Glades

PRESTON COUNTY

Thomas Pritchard, Jr. 1818

Dunkards Creek

MONONGALIA COUNTY
1776

MORGANTOWN

State
Road

MARION COUNTY
1842

Early Monongalia County
Pritchard Land

99f

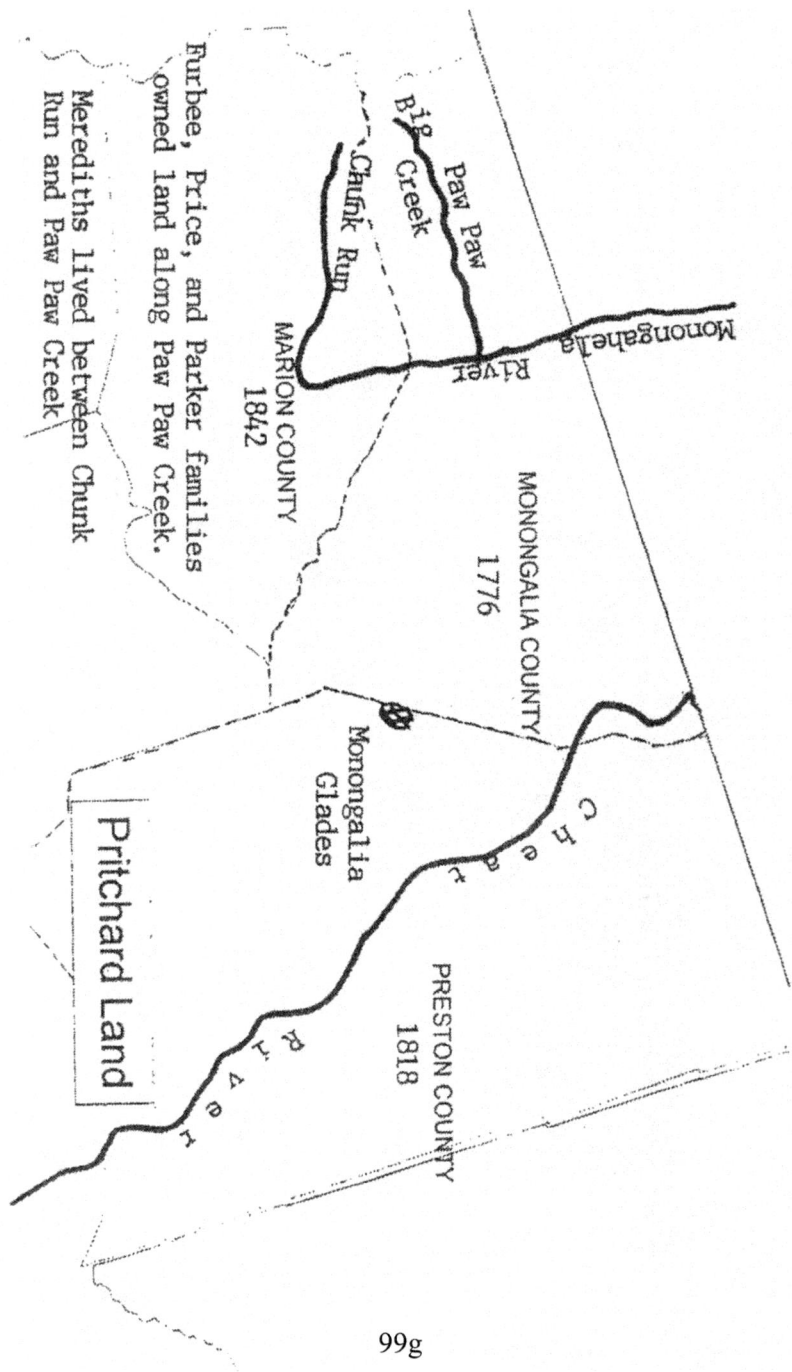

Furbee, Price, and Parker families owned land along Paw Paw Creek.

Merediths lived between Chunk Run and Paw Paw Creek

Paw Paw Creek

Big Creek

Chunk Run

MARION COUNTY 1842

Monongahela River

MONONGALIA COUNTY 1776

Monongalia Glades

Pritchard Land

Cheat River

PRESTON COUNTY 1818

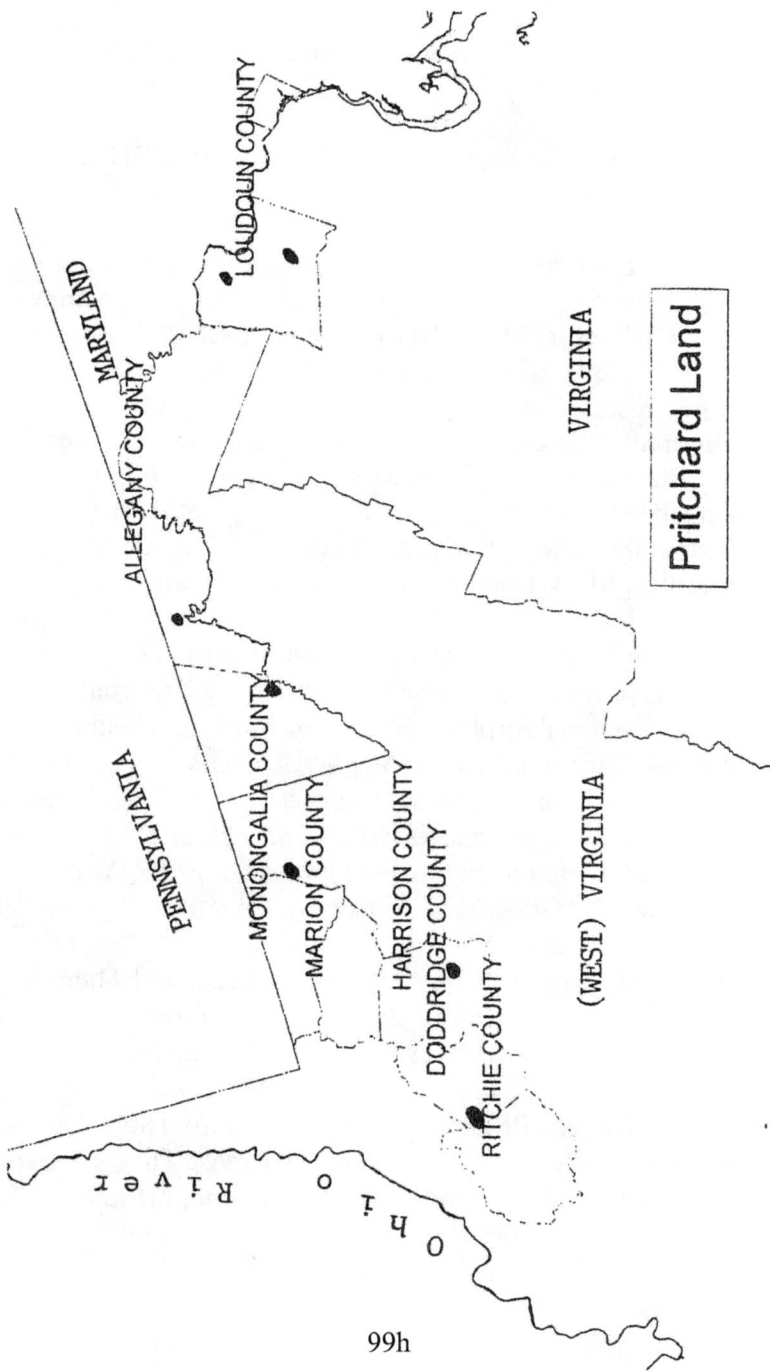

Pritchard Land

99h

DESCENDANTS OF THOMAS PRITCHARD, JR.

9.

Thomas Pritchard, Jr. son of No. 5, Thomas Pritchard, Sr., was married twice. His first wife, **Nancy TICHENAL (TICHENOR, TICHNELL),** died before 25 Oct 1812, the date of his marriage to **Mary MOODY,** in what is now Preston County, West Virginia. They had seven or eight children. (Some descendants believe that his daughter Mary was the daughter of Mary Moody. Because his daughter Elizabeth was born 20 Feb 1812, it is quite likely that Nancy died at the time of this birth, a commonplace event in pioneer families. Mary's given name is another clue.)

Two weeks after their marriage in Allegany County Maryland, Thomas became the guardian of Nancy's younger siblings, Stephen Tickenal (sic), Margaret Tickenal, and Jain (Jane) Tichenal, orphan children of Moses Tickenal, all of that county. The record states: *Stephen Tichenal being over the age of fourteen years chooses Margaret Tichenal and Thomas Prichet* (sic) *as his guardians and Margaret Titchenal and Jain Tichenal being under the age of fourteen years the court appoint the aforesaid Margaret Tichenal and Thomas Pritchet as their Guardian.*

On 09 Jan 1798, Margaret Tickenal and Thomas Pritchard, Jr. are *...allowed full amounts of the profits and interest of their wards' estate up to this date for their maintenance and support in diet, clothing, etc.*

Thomas Pritchard, Jr. is listed in the 1800 Census of Allegany County living on Georges Creek. This is the site of present day Cumberland. At the same time, his father, Thomas, Sr., is listed in Allegany County on Sandy Creek.

100

The Pritchard/Prickett Family History

On 17 Aug 1802, Thomas paid 18 shillings 9 pence for Lot 12, *westward of Fort Cumberland, Allegany County, Maryland*. The land was purchased from William McMahanon. Thomas sold part of this land on 01 Apr 1805 to John Fox for 12 shillings and Nancy relinquished her dower rights. Less than a year later, on 15 Feb 1806, he purchased lot 313 (in what is now the town of Westernport, Garrett County, Maryland) from John Boyd. On 17 Mar 1809, he sold this same lot to John Brant, who also purchased another plot of land from him on 24 Jul 1809. From this transaction forward, Thomas Pritchard, Jr. no longer appears in Allegany County records; therefore, it is concluded that he moved to Monongalia County Virginia between 17 Mar and 24 Jul 1809.

Sometime before October 1812, Thomas buried Nancy in or near The Glades, the area of Monongalia County where they were then living. This land adjacent to what is today Dunkards Bottom Road is just a few miles southwest from the present day Reedsville, West Virginia. The road originates in Monongalia County as county Route 81, becoming Route 27 in Preston County. The present day community of Gladesville named for The Glades is just a few miles southwest of the town of Reedsville. When Preston County was carved from the eastern portion of Monongalia County, the Pritchard land lay immediately east of the boundary line.

Nancy Tichenal, daughter of **Moses TICHENAL**, was born about 1767 in Morris County, New Jersey, and died about 1812 at The Glades, Preston County, (West) Virginia. She married **Thomas PRITCHARD, Jr.,** 02 Jan 1796 in Allegany County, Maryland, son of **Thomas PRITCHARD, Sr.** and **Rachel DAVIS.** Nancy Tichenal was descended from a prominent New Jersey family, most of whom retained the original spelling of Tichenor. Beginning with Nancy's father, Moses, a Revolutionary War soldier, the spelling went awry, and his descendants used a variety of forms, most ending with a single or double 'L'.

The Tichenor/Tichenal/Tichnell/Titchenell Family

1.

Martin Tichenor, the immigrant, was born before 1630, probably in England, and died after 19 Oct 1681 in Newark, New Jersey. He married **Mary CHARLES** on 16 May 1651 in New Haven Colony, daughter of **John CHARLES** and **Sarah MOSS.**

Martin Tichenor took the oath of allegiance at New Haven Colony in August of 1644. This is the first known record of him. He and Mary Charles were married by the governor. In addition to the children named in his will, New Haven records recorded Nathaniel, who was born 25 Feb 1652 and died 27 Feb 1652 and Sarah, born 1663.

The spelling of his name varies in New Haven records, but his will is signed *Tichenor*, the spelling found most often in New Jersey records. The exceptions are in a few records pertaining to his sons using one or two L's at the end of the name. Early tradition is that Martin Tichenor came from France. However, Taylor Tichenor, son of James Tichenor, whose genealogy is used in Teachenor's *Partial History of the Tichenor Family in America*, published in 1918, states that the most generally accepted tradition is that his ancestry is English, though of Dutch-Flemish derivation.

A study of the Connecticut and New Jersey colonial records cited in Harold Tichenor's *Tichenor Families in America*, published in 1988, suggests that Martin was a Puritan

and most probably came from England. It refers to notations in
Atwater's *History of New Haven* that members of the colony
settling at Milford and New Haven, like those of Massachusetts
Bay, came from Kent and Canterbury.

According to one dictionary of names, Tichenor was a
village of Hampshire England, situated on the River Itchen
near Southampton. The name of the village was originally
written *at Itchen*, since a resident was identified as being *at
Itchenor*, or one who lived by the River Itchen. Another
meaning is *dweller at the crossroads*. The name is sometimes
spelled Ticknor or Tickner, a name of Dutch origin meaning
draughtsman.

A history of Sussex, England identifies West Itchenor
as *a small parish of 546 acres lying at the mouth of Chichester
Harbor...It predates the 1066 Conquest.*

Records of many persons with similar names
christened, married, or buried in Sussex or Berkshire between
1545 and 1685 suggest that Tichenor is most likely of English
origin. The name is not found in France. Since Martin Tichenor
was a Puritan, he must have lived in England for a time, no
matter his roots.

Martin and Mary Tichenor were members of the New
Haven Church. In parish and town meetings, men and women
sat in separate divisions. For the year 1655, the seating is
recorded: *In ye seats on ye stile on both sides of the dore:
Martin Tichennor...In ye side seats all along: Goodw*
(Goodwife) *Tichennor.* On 10 Feb 1661, the seating was *below
the doore for Martine Tichnell and Sister Tichnell.* This entry
indicates that variations of the family name began early.

Martin Tichenor had a five acre lot in New Haven
which he sold on 02 Oct 1666 to join a party that founded
Newark, New Jersey. Its location was described as *at ye lower*

end of the subburbs quarter next Milford Highway.

In 1665, New Haven and Connecticut were merged into one colony. This allowed baptism of children regardless of their parents' church affiliation. When the Puritans objected to this arrangement, Robert Treat became chairman of a committee answering a call from Governor Carteret of New Jersey for homesteaders. After visiting the site in 1665, Treat and thirty families, including Martin Tichenor's, traveled there by sea. They arrived at the Passaic River in early May 1666. No sooner did they begin to unload their supplies than the Hackensack Indians confronted them to claim the land for themselves. Ultimately, the settlers purchased the land from the Indians for *fifty double-hands of powder, one hundred barrs of lead, twenty axes, twenty coats, ten guns, twenty pistolls, ten kettles, ten swoards, four blanks, four barrells of beere, ten paire of breeches, fifty knives, twenty howes, eight hundred and fifth fathem of wampem, two ancors of licquers, and three troopers coats.*

The Newark settlers built houses that were about thirty feet in length, sixteen feet in width, and one and a half stories in height. Chimneys were first made of clay and timber before stone and mortar came into use. Wood, the only fuel, served the hearthstone in the living room/kitchen. Water came from rain barrels that caught water dripping from the roof, while a nearby spring or a well dug on the premises provided water for drinking and cooking.

The first industry in town was the corn mill built in 1671. Other artisans soon arrived, among them weavers, coopers, and traveling shoemakers. The women in each household made soap and candles and dyed the cloth that they spun on spinning wheels. They made feathers of wild geese into bedding and pillows and kept beehives for honey used as both food and medicine.

Newark's first school opened in the meeting house in 1676. By 22 Oct 1719, the Puritan church was replaced by the Presbyterian form of church government. Records from the *Old Burial Ground* adjacent to the meeting house were lost in 1777 when the British captured the town.

Because of continuing Indian scares, every man between 16 and 60 was required to have his arms ready. The town drummer used his instrument to call people to church or town meetings and to scare away the Indians.

Twenty-eight Tichenors were on the Newark tax lists from 1778-1789 during the Revolution.

Children of Martin Tichenor and Mary Charles are:

   i. **Nathaniel Tichenor**, b. 25 Feb 1651/52; m. **Mary DOWNE**, 20 Jan 1663/64.

2. ii. **John Tichenor,** b. 14 Apr 1653, New Haven Colony; d. 1688, Newark, New Jersey.

3. iii. **Abigail Tichenor**, b. 01 Feb 1653/54, New Haven Colony; d. 01 Apr 1713, Newark, New Jersey.

4. iv. **Daniel Tichenor**, b. 09 Aug 1656, New Haven Colony; d. May 1728, Newark, New Jersey.

   v. **Hannah Tichenor**, b.13 Mar 1658/59, New Haven Colony; d. after 1681, Newark, New Jersey.

   vi. **Samuel Tichenor**, b. 14 Oct 1660, New Haven Colony; d. September 1688, Newark New Jersey; m. **Hannah UNK**.

   vii. **Sarah Tichenor**, b. 1663.

5. viii. **Jonathan Tichenor, b**. abt. 1663, New Haven Colony; d. aft. 1742, Newark, New Jersey.

SECOND TICHENOR GENERATION

2.

John Tichenor, son of No. 1, Martin Tichenor, was born 14 Apr 1653 in New Haven Colony, and died 1688 in Newark, New Jersey. He married **Hannah BALDWIN**, daughter of **John BALDWIN** and **Hannah OSBORNE**.
Child of John Tichenor and Hannah Baldwin is:
> i. **Martin Tichenor; m. Elizabeth CHARLES**

3.

Abigail Tichenor, daughter of Martin, was born 01 Feb 1653/54 in New Haven Colony, and died 01 Apr 1713 in Newark, New Jersey. She married **John TREAT**, son of **Robert TREAT** and **Jane TAPP**.
Child of **Abigail Tichenor** and **John Treat** is:
> i. **Sarah Treat**

4.

Daniel Tichenor, son of No. 1, **Martin TICHENOR**, was born 09 Aug 1656 in New Haven Colony, and died May 1728 in Newark, New Jersey. He married **Elizabeth BALDWIN** 1690 in Newark, New Jersey, daughter of **John BALDWIN** and **Hannah BRUEN**.

Elizabeth Baldwin is descended from a family prominent in Buckinghamshire, England. The earliest known Baldwin is **Richard BALDWIN**, m. **Ellen APUKE**.
Child of Richard Baldwin and Ellen Apuke is:
> i. **Henry Baldwin**, b. Aston-Clinton, Buckinghamshire England; d. 01 Jan 1598/99 in England; m. **Alice Unk**.

Children of Henry Baldwin and Alice are:
- i. **John Baldwin**, d. October 1637, Chesham, Buckinghanshire, England; m. **Hannah UNK**.
- ii. **Richard Baldwin**.
- iii. **Sylvester Baldwin**.
- iv. **Robert Baldwin**.
- v. **Jane Baldwin**.
- vi. **Mary Baldwin**.
- vii. **Agnes Baldwin**.

Child of John Baldwin and Hannah is:
- i. **John Baldwin Sr.**, b. Wendover, Buckinghamshire, England; d. 24 Jun 1684, Milford Connecticut; m. (1) **Mary CAMP**; m. (2) **Mary BRUEN** 1653, Milford, Connecticut.

Child of John Baldwin, Sr. and Mary Camp is:
- i. **John Baldwin Jr.**, b. 20 Mar 1647/48, Milford Connecticut; d. 1702, Newark, New Jersey; m. **Hannah BRUEN**, daughter of **Obadiah BRUEN** and **Sarah UNK**.

Child of John Baldwin, Jr. and Hannah Bruen is:
- i. **Elizabeth Baldwin**; m. No. 3, **Daniel TICHENOR** 1690, Newark, New Jersey.

Daniel Tichenor's name appears six times in the town records between 1680 and 1700. In 1684, he had *Liberty...to take up a piece of land in the Common*. He was chosen fence viewer in 1689 and pounder in 1690. The town record of 05 Mar 1693 states: *Whereas, there is much prophanation of the Lord's Day in the Time of Worship by the playing of Boys and Girls, therefore Daniel Tichenor and Thomas Lyon are chosen to look after them and to correct them for the Year ensuing.*

107

On 01 Jun 1680, Daniel was deeded 2 acres in his father's home lot. He bought 4 1/2 acres in *Little, (Tichenor's) Neck* adjacent to that lot on 03 May 1694. In 1697, he received land jointly with his brother Jonathan. On 03 Sep 1701, he had an *interest of one right* in a purchase agreement covering Indian lands west of Newark. His will of 04 Nov 1717 named his wife, Elizabeth, and children Daniel, John, Joseph, and Jane.

Children of Daniel Tichenor and Elizabeth Baldwin are:

6.　　i. **Joseph Tichenor**, b. 1680-1690, Newark, New Jersey, d. 1750, New Jersey.

　　ii. **Daniel Tichenor**, b. abt. 1704.

　　iii. **John Tichenor.**

　　iv. **Jane Tichenor.**

5.

Jonathan Tichenor, son of No. 1, Martin Tichenor, was born about 1663 in New Haven, Connecticut and died after 1742 in Newark, New Jersey.

He was named a minor in his father's will and admitted as a Planter in Newark 05 Mar 1693 or 1694. He was one of three Surveyors of Highways in 1746 or 1747.

In 1741, he testified at New Jersey Superior Court at Perth Amboy at the trial of John Penn, Thomas Penn, and Richard Penn against John Chambers regarding the boundary between Newark and Elizabeth. His horse was stolen at the trial. The Council of Proprietors 30 Mar 1742 describe him as s *...a very old man* (who) *came to give evidence...and his horse was then carried away by persons unknown. The said Tichenor was poor and paid five pounds toward the sad loss.*

Child of Jonathan Tichenor is:

　　i. **Jonathan Tichenor.**

THIRD TICHENOR GENERATION

6.

Joseph Tichenor, Sr., son of No. 3, Daniel Tichenor, was born 1680-1690 in Newark, New Jersey, and died 1750 in New Jersey. He married **Elizabeth UNK** before 1735 in New Jersey. Joseph Tichenor died in 1750. His will of 01 Mar 1750 mentions only his first five children, Moses, James, Joseph, Daniel, and Jane, all minors. Joseph, James, and Jane were over the age of 14, so they asked the court to appoint Thomas Woodruff, Jr. of Elizabeth, New Jersey as their guardian. Since Daniel and Moses were under the age of 14, they were not entitled by law to choose their guardians.

In 1731, Joseph acquired land in New Vernon, a few miles south of Morristown. A second tract of land was purchased in 1739. He also purchased land in what is known as "Turkey Pasture" from the heirs of William Penn. This is in the Great Swamp, now a wildlife preserve.

According to Harold Tichener, the records of the First Presbyterian Church of Morristown contain the words *...confest for disregarding the lot* by Joseph's name. This refers to a casting of lots to settle a dispute over establishing a church in Morristown. The people of Morristown (then called West Hanover) worshipped at the Presbyterian Church at Hanover, which was established by 1718. By 1733, the population of Morristown (so named officially in 1740) had increased. The eastern portion of the parish opposed the move, so the church resorted to casting of lots. Even though the proposed division was voted down, a Morristown church was organized and a confession for disregarding the lot was required of those who had a part in it, Joseph among them. The church records also show that he renewed his covenant 24 Apr 1743 and became a communicant in September 1749.

Children of Joseph Tichenor and Elizabeth are:

       i. **James Tichenor**, b. bef. 1736.

      ii. **Jane Tichenor**, b. bef. 1736.

7.   iii. **Joseph Tichenor, Jr.,** b. bef. 1736, Morris County, New Jersey.

8.   iv. **Daniel Tichenor**, b. 1742, Morris County, New Jersey; d. 12 Apr 1804, Nelson County, Kentucky.

9.   v. **Moses Tichenor/Tichenal**, b. bef. 19 Apr 1743, Morristown, New Jersey; d. abt. 1796, Allegany County, Maryland.

      vi. **David Tichenor**, b. bef. 01 Mar 1748/49.

     vii. **Isaac Tichenor**, b. bef. 01 Mar 1748/49.

FOURTH TICHENOR GENERATION

7.

Joseph Tichenor, Jr., son of No. 6, Joseph Tichenor, Sr., was born before 1736 in Morris County, New Jersey. He married **Unk DAY**. The Day family, well known in New Jersey, came from Milford at the time of Newark's settlement and had a plot of land (lot #21) near that of Martin Tichenor. Members of the Day family migrated to Morris County and other sections of the state, and some were connected with the Morristown Presbyterian Church when Joseph and Daniel were members. However, there is no record of a marriage between Joseph and one of the Day daughters. He may have left Morristown before this time and moved northward near Greenwood Lake in Passaic County, New Jersey.

Child of Joseph Tichenal and Miss Day is:

10.   i. **Joseph Day Tichenor,** b. 18 Jul 1762, Greenwood Lane, West Milford Twp., Passaic County, New Jersey; d. 06 Oct 1847.

8.

Daniel Tichenor, son of No. 6, Joseph Tichenor, was born 1742 in Morris County, New Jersey and died 12 Apr 1804 in Nelson County, Kentucky. He married (1) **Catherine WADE** and (2) **Anna BYRAM** on 06 May 1776 in Morris County, New Jersey, daughter of **Ebenezer BYRAM** and **Abigail ALDEN**, a descendant of **John ALDEN** and **Priscilla MULLENS** of Plymouth Colony fame.

Daniel Tichenor and Catherine Wade were Presbyterians. The births and baptisms of most of their children are recorded in the Morristown Presbyterian Church register.

He served in the Revolutionary War as a Minute Man and in Captain Isaac Halsey's Company of the Morris County Militia.

His second wife, Anna Byram, was the widow of Peter Condit, by whom she had three sons, Byram, Edward, and Lewis. Byram Condit moved to Ohio County, Kentucky in 1805 and established Condit's Ferry on Green River, now Point Pleasant. He died there about 1817/18. Edward Condit spent his life in New Jersey. He was a member of the State Legislature from 1828-1830 and was a judge of the Court of Common Pleas and member of the U.S. Congress from New Jersey for 18 or 20 years. From 1827-1861, he was a trustee of Princeton University. One of his most daring feats was a journey by horseback in 1795 to visit the Tichenors in Kentucky.

Children of Daniel Tichenal and Catherine Wade are:
- i. **Jane Tichenal.**
- ii. **Joseph Tichenal**.
- iii. **Daniel Tichenal**, b. bef. 01 May 1767.
- v. **Elizabeth Tichenal**, b. bef. 10 May 1771.
- vi. **Jacob Tichenal**, b. 08 Apr 1773.
- vii. **Timothy Tichenal**, b. 16 Jan 1775.

Children of Daniel Tichenal and Anna Byram are:
- 11. viii. **Peter Tichenal**, b. 27 Mar 1777, d. 1822.
- ix. **Jared Tichenal**, b. 18 Feb 1779.
- x. **Sarah Tichenal**, b. 1781.
- xi. **Jonas Tichenal**, b. 04 Aug 04, 1784.
- xii. **Anna Tichenal**, b. 13 Aug 1786.
- xiii. **Silas Tichenal**, b. 06 Jan 1792.
- xiv. **James Tichenal**, b. 12 Oct 1794.

9.

Moses Tichenor, later Tichenal, son of No. 6, Joseph

Tichenor, was born before 29 Apr 1743 in Morristown, New Jersey and died about 1796 in Allegany County, Maryland. He married **Margaret JACKSON** about 1762 in New Jersey.

Moses Tichenor was baptized 29 Apr 1743 at Morristown Presbyterian Church, Morristown, Morris County, New Jersey. He was willed 51 acres in Morris County by his father. On 01 Apr 1771, Moses Tichenor sold two tracts in Morristown. One tract of 24.7 acres was *adjacent to a road on the east side of Pine Brook.* The other tract of 25.5 acres was also adjacent to Pine Brook and was described as *part of the tract known by the name of Turkey Pasture.*

At the time he purchased 567 acres in two tracts on Cabbin Run in Hampshire County, (West) Virginia in September 1779, his name was spelled *Tichenal*. In the deed, he gave his residence as Morris County, New Jersey. By the time he sold that same land in 1783, he was living in Washington County, Maryland, which then included what is now Allegany and Garrett Counties. In July 1792, he sold 180 acres on the *north branch of Potowmack* in Hampshire County which he had purchased in July 1789. His residence as stated in the deed was Hampshire County. That same month, he purchased 300 acres on the Salt Rock Fork of Sandy and listed his residence as Allegany County. In 1792, he bought 52 acres in Allegany (now Garrett County) known as *Aaron's Lot*, which was located a short distance above the mouth of the Savage River. One of these tracts was probably his residence after that date. In a deed dated 1794, Moses Tichenal sold a tract of seven and one-half acres in Allegany County near the mouth of Gum Spring Run with the intention of building a sawmill and operating a coal mine on it. It was to be owned jointly by the grantee and Moses, each to have half interest. At the time of his death, he owned 268 acres.

Moses Tichenor (sic) served in the Revolutionary War in Captain Layton's Company of Morris County, New Jersey Militia in 1778, and was drafted into the Virginia Militia for a tour of duty to guard the prisoners taken at the surrender of Lord Cornwallis at Yorktown. The prisoners were confined in Frederick County, Virginia. His son, David, was enrolled as his substitute and served from November or December of 1781 until 12 Mar 1782.

Although the spelling of Moses Tichenor's name varies from the time he left New Jersey, he evidently preferred *Tichenal*. While no record of his name with that spelling has been found in New Jersey, there is one Morris County deed for his brother Daniel spelled *Tichenal*. Several spellings ending in one or two L's are in use today by Moses's descendants, none of whom, so far as is known, spell their surname Tichenor.

The administration papers that survive of Moses Tichenor's estate mention, but do not name, his widow. They do name sons-in-law John Smith and Thomas Pritchard. His grandchildren Betsey and William Smith are named with John Smith as their guardian.

His widow remarried, as evidenced by Margaret Tichenor Ryan's will recorded in Hardy County (West) Virginia 19 Oct 1818.

Children of Moses Tichenal and Margaret Jackson are:

12.   i. **David Tichenell**, b. 16 Oct 1764, Morris County, New Jersey; d. October 1853,   *
Harrison County (West) Virginia.

    *   ii. **Nancy Tichenell**, b. abt. 1767, Morris County, New Jersey; d. abt. 1812, The Glades, Preston

---

* First wife of Thomas Pritchard, Jr.

County, (West) Virginia.

13.   iii. **Joshua Tichenell**, b. abt. 1768, Morris County, New Jersey; d. Swanton, Maryland.

14.   iv. **Stephen Tichenell**, b. 10 Jun 1772, Morris County, New Jersey; d. 06 Mar 1857, Preston County, (West) Virginia.

15.   v. **Phoebe Tichenell**, b. aft. 1764, New Jersey; d. bef. 1796, Allegany County, Maryland.

    vi. **Margaret Tichenell**, b. abt. 1778, Allegany County, Maryland; d. aft. 1818. (She was living in 1818 when named in her mother's will, indicating that she was single.)

    vii. **Abigail Tichenell**, b. abt. 1778; d. aft. 1818. (She was living in 1818 when named in her mother's will.) m. **Henry DUCKWORTH**, 10 Jan 1801, Allegany County, Maryland.

    viii. **Jane Tichenell**, b. abt. 1789, Allegany County, Maryland; m. **George SEES (CEASE)**, 08 Oct 1814, Allegany County, Maryland.

The Duckworths

The Duckworth surname traces back to the Saxon chronicle compiled by monks in the 10th century. It is now in the British Museum. The name of Duckworth Fold, a town in Lancashire, was first derived from an Old English personal name Ducca, and "worth" which means a homestead (i.e. Ducca's homestead). In Baines's "History of Lancashire," the name is found as Dokeward and a number of other spellings, but by the 16th century it is found most often as Duckworth. Duckworth as a family surname is found early in both Westmoreland County, Virginia and New Jersey. The family in question may well trace back to 1664 when records in the archives of New Jersey, first series, v. 21, page 61, show a John Duckworth and 23 other people imported into the province of New Jersey under a four-year indenturement. This is registered in the "Secretary's Book of Records" dated 01 Dec 1664.

The estate of William Duckworth, yeoman, of New Hanover, Burlington County, New Jersey was appraised on 07 Mar 1727. Henry Duckworth was born there 05 Sep 1779 and died 26 May 1855 in Barbour County (West) Virginia, where he is buried at Taylor's Drain. His father was **Aaron DUCKWORTH** and his mother was **Elizabeth ABRAHAM JOHNSON.** Elizabeth was born 16 Jul 1726 in Burlington County where she and Aaron Duckworth were married on 04 Jul 1772. She died 1835 in Garrett County, Maryland. Her parents were **Abraham BRACHTHEISER JOHNSON** and **Elizabeth KULP.** Aaron Duckworth was born 28 Jan 1741 and died 1825 Garrett County, Maryland. His parents were **William DUCKWORTH** and **Mary WRIGHT/RIDGWAY.**

Child of Henry Duckworth and Abigail Tichenell:
i. **George DUCKWORTH** b. 25 Jan 1805 in George's Creek, Allegany County, Maryland. He died 27 Mar 1877 in Taylor's Drain, Barbour County, West Virginia and is buried in Taylor's Drain Cemetery. His wife, **Rachel KIGHT**, was born 04 Oct 1810 and died 18 May 1869. Her parents were **Henry Thomas KIGHT,** son of **John D. KIGHT** and **Rachel ACTON.** John D. Kight was born 16 June 1784, in Allegany County, Maryland and died 30 April 1872, in Memphis, Scotland County, Missouri. His wife, was **Anne Catherine GUNDY.** They were married 14 May 1805 at Chillicothe, Ohio. Her father, **Jacob VAN GUNDY** (13 Oct. 1765-24 Sep 1845), was an American patriot from Lancaster, Pennsylvania who is

buried in Danville, Vermilion County, Illinois.

Children of George Duckworth and Rachel Kight are:

    i. **Nancy Hizer DUCKWORTH,** b.15 Jul 1833; d. 03 May 1905.

    ii, **Thomas Jefferson DUCKWORTH**, b. abt 1834; d, 09 Nov 1874,

    iii. **Drusilla DUCKWORTH**, b. 18 Aug 1837; d. 09 Nov 1874.

    iv. **Ephraim B. DUCKWORTH,** b. 18 May 1840; d. 09 Apr 1925.

    v. **Sara DUCKWORTH**, b. abt. 1842; d. 13 Sep 1866.

    vi. **Francis DUCKWORTH**, b. Jun 1845; d. abt. 1917.

FIFTH TICHENOR GENERATION

10.

Joseph Day Tichenor, son of No. 7, Joseph Tichenor, was born 18 Jul 1762 at Greenwood Lake, West Milford Twp., Passaic County, New Jersey, and died 05 Oct 1847. He married **Jane BROWN,** 18 Jun 1785.

Children of Joseph Tichenal and Jane Brown are:

16.　　i. **James Tichenor**, b. 26 Jan 1789, West Milford, New Jersey; d. 31 Jan 1864, West Milford, New Jersey.

　　ii. **Henry Tichenor**, b. 06 Sep 1791.

17.　　iii. **Joseph Tichenor**, b. 12 Sep 1796, West Milford, New Jersey; d. 24 Jun 1883, Edwardsburg, Cass County, Michigan.

　　iv. **Bethuel D. Tichenor**, b. 13 Sep 1798, West Milford, New Jersey; d.13 Mar 1825, bur. Presbyterian Cuurch, West Milford, New Jersey; m. **Elizabeth Unk.**

　　v. **Margaret Tichenor** b.21 May 1799; d. 07 Jun 1820.

18.　　vi. **Eliza Tichenor**, b. 18 Dec 1801, West Milford, New Jersey; d. 03 Jan 1875, bur. Presbyterian Church Cemetery, West Milford, New Jersey.

　　vii. **Catherine Tichenor**.

11.

Peter Tichenor, son of No. 8, Daniel Tichenor, was born 27 Mar 1777 and died 1822. He married **Frances COTTON** 03 Sep 1797 in Nelson County, Kentucky, daughter of **John COTTON** and **Susannah SMITH.**

Children of Peter Tichenal and Frances Cotton are:

   i. **Zacheus Tichenor**, b. 27 Jun 1798.
  ii. **Byram Tichenor**, b. 1798.
 iii. **Anna Tichenor**, b. 1802.
 iv. **William Tichenor**, b. abt. 1810.
  v. **Laura Tichenor**.
 vi. **Ira Tichenor**, b. abt. 1810.
vii. **Calvin Tichenor**, b. 1813.
viii. **Silas Tichenor**, b. 26 Jun 1814.
 ix. **Emily Tichenor**, b. 1816.
  x. **Keller Tichenor,** b. bef. 1820.
 xi. **Mildred Tichenor**, b. 13 Dec 1820.
xii. **Peter Tichenor**, b. 1822.

12.

David Tichenal, son of No. 9, Moses Tichenal and Margaret Jackson, was born 16 Oct 1764 in Morris County, New Jersey, and died October 1853 in Harrison County, (West) Virginia. He married **Mary BUCKALEW** in 1790, daughter of **Andrew BUCKALEW**.

    David Tichenal served in the Virginia Militia in the Revolutionary War. His application for pension made 15 Aug 1832 reads in part: *...he was born in Morris Township in the State of New Jersey and resided* (there) *until the spring of 1780 when he removed with his father to Hampshire County, Virginia, where he resided between two and three years. From thence he removed to Allegany County in the State of Maryland where he resided upwards of twenty years. From thence he removed to the County of Harrison where he has since resided for upwards of 22 years. The applicant states that while a resident of Hampshire County, Virginia in October or November of 1780, he entered as a substitute for another person who was drafted. In this tour of duty he was detailed to*

119

guard the baggage wagons of Gen. Gates' troops.

David Tichenal served a second tour of duty in the war, also as a substitute for another person drafted in the Virginia Militia, and then...*again either in the months of November or December of 1781. His father, Moses Tichenal, was drafted for a tour of duty to guard the prisoners taken at the surrender of Lord Cornwallis at Yorktown who were confined in the County of Frederick in the state of Virginia...This applicant was enrolled as his substitute under Captain Isaac Parsons. He and the company marched to the Barracks within 4 miles of Winchester, Virginia where the said prisoners were confined. His company reached the Barracks previous to 25 Dec 1781 and remained there on duty until 12 Mar 1782, at which time he was discharged in writing. In all, he served in the Virginia Militia 12 months or more.*

David Tichenal bought 168 acres in Hampshire County Virginia in October 1807 and sold it March 1810. His residence given in both deeds was Allegany County, Maryland. He probably moved to Harrison County, Virginia soon after selling this land. The census shows him living there in 1820. In 1810, he bought 225 acres on the west side of the west fork of the Monongalia River at the mouth of Lamberts Run. He deeded this land to his son David in 1844 for *the consideration of maintaining myself and my wife, Mary, and furnishing us with the necessities of life...during our natural lives.* In addition, David Jr. received livestock, household items, three stills, blacksmith tools, guns, wagon, and books. David Sr. also bought a large acreage in Harrison County in 1825 between the Monongalia River and Romine's Mill.

David Tichenal's will, signed 17 Mar 1842, named wife Mary, sons David, Daniel, and Moses, and daughter Margaret Little, wife of Josiah Little. At the time of his death, he was living on a tract of land on Westfork River in Harrison County, Virginia opposite the mouth of Simpson's Creek. This was also the residence of his son, David, as the 1850 census lists them in the same household. He willed the tract containing 250-300 acres to sons Daniel and David after the death of their mother, provided they support *John Fox, who has resided with me for many years, should he be unable to support himself.* The residue of the estate after the death of Mary was to be divided equally between all of his children.

Children of David Tichenell and Mary Buckalew are:

19.   i. **John R. Tichenell**, b. 07 Apr 1791, Allegany County, Maryland; d. 16 Jan 1831, Fort Smith, Crawford County, Arkansas.
20.   ii. **William R. Tichenell**, b. 1793, Allegany County, Maryland; d. 19 Aug 1838, Upper Alton, Madison County, Illinois.
      iii. **Margaret Tichenell**, b. 18 Feb 1795.
21.   iv. **Moses J. Tichenell**, b. 1796, Allegany County, Maryland; d. March 1877, bur. Hepzibah Cemetery, Lamberts Run, Harrison County, West Virginia.
      v. **Andrew Jackson Tichenell**, b.12 Oct 1800.
      vi. **Daniel Tichenell**, b. 1801-1802.
      vii. **David Tichenell.**, b. 30 Jan 1805.

13.

Joshua Tichenell, son of No. 9, Moses Tichenal, was born about 1768 in Morris County, New Jersey, and died in Swanton, Allegany County, Maryland, where is buried in the Kifer Cemetery. He married **Elsie BIVINS**.

Child of Joshua Tichenell and Elsie Bivins is:

22.   i. **Moses Tichenell,** b. abt. 1805; d. 1890 in Garrett

County, Maryland.

14.

Stephen Tichenell, son of No. 9, Moses Tichenal, was born 10 Jun 1772 in Morris County, New Jersey, and died 06 Mar 1857 in Preston County, (West) Virginia. He married **Lydia MATHENY** 1802, daughter of **James MATHENY** and **Mary LaMAYNE**.

Stephen Tichenell was buried in Beach Run Hill Cemetery, Preston County, (West) Virginia. Prior to 1810, he moved from Maryland and settled on the east bank of the Cheat River at the mouth of Muddy Creek. There he built his log residence, a grist mill, and a whiskey distillery. A tract of 110 acres was surveyed for him after 1824 (exact date not readable on deed). A Preston County history states: *Beach Run Community was first settled in the late 1700s by Tichenell, Crane, May, Sypolt, and Martin families. It was first named Pleasant Hill, but later the post office name was changed to Beech Run. It is said that Stephen Titchenell used to remark jokingly, "If you want to raise preachers, raise them in a still house. That is where I raised two good ones."* Sons Daniel and Moses were ministers of the M.E. Church. Stephen's descendants have adopted the Tichenell spelling of their surname.

Children of Stephen Tichenell and Lydia Matheny are:
> i. **Mary Tichenell**, b. 12 Oct 1802.
> ii. **James Tichenell**, b. 05 Feb 1804.
> iii. **Moses Tichenell**, b. 07 Feb 1807.
> iv. **Joshua Tichenell**, b. 1811.
> v. **Margaret Tichenell**, b. 1813.
> vi. **Daniel Tichenell**, b. 14 Aug 1815.
> vii. **Rebecca Tichenell**.

   viii. **Lydia Tichenell**.
    ix. **Stephen Tichenell**, b. 06 Oct 1822.

15.

Phoebe Tichenell, daughter of No. 9, Moses Tichenal, was born after 1764 in New Jersey, and died before 1796 in Allegany County, Maryland. She married **John SMITH**. Child of Phoebe Tichenell and John Smith is:
     i. **William Smith**, b. abt. 1783.

SIXTH TICHENOR GENERATION

16.

James Tichenal, son of No. 10, Joseph Day Tichenal, was born 26 Jan 1789 in West Milford, now Passaic County, New Jersey and died 31 Jan 1864 in West Milford, New Jersey. He married **Mary FREELAND** 22 Jan 1817 in West Milford, New Jersey.
Children of James Tichenal and Mary Freeland are:
    i. **Jane Elizabeth Tichenal**, b. 16 Nov 1817.
    ii. **Margaret Tichenal**, b. 07 Jan 1820.
    iii. **John V. Tichenal**, b. 01 Jul 1822.
    iv. **Ann Mary Tichenal**, b. 24 Jul 1824.
    v. **James Joseph Tichenal**, b. 09 Nov 1826.

17.

Joseph Tichenal, son of No. 10, Joseph Day Tichenal, was born 02 Sep 1796, West Milford, now Passaic County, New Jersey and die 24 Jun 1883, in Edwardsburg, Cass County, Michigan. He married **Mary ACKERSON**.

18.

Eliza Tichenal, daughter of No. 10, Joseph Day Tichenal, was born 18 Dec 1801 in West Milford, now Passaic County, New Jersey, and died 03 Jan 1875. She is buried in the Presbyterian Church Cemetery, West Milford, New Jersey. She married **Isaac P. COOLEY**.

19.

John R. Tichenell, son of No. 12, David Tichenell, was born 07 Apr 1791 in Allegany County, Maryland, and died 16 Jan

1831 in Fort Smith, Crawford County, Arkansas. He married **Rebecca HARBERT** 03 Mar 1814 in Harrison County (West) Virginia, daughter of **Thomas HARBERT, Jr.** and **Hannah JACOBS**.

About 1819, John R. Tichenell moved his family from Harrison County (West) Virginia to Missouri. The exact location in Missouri is unknown, except that he was on the tax rolls in Gasconade Twp., Franklin County in 1819. Franklin County was very large at the time and included an area which today comprises several counties. He is said to have been a blacksmith in Missouri for four years, but by 1823 he had moved his family to the vicinity of Fort Smith, Arkansas where he settled and raised livestock. The 1830 census lists him in Crawford County, Arkansas with 12 people in his household. His house stood just below what is now the eastern approach to the Missouri Pacific Railroad bridge. The Tichenal spelling was adopted in this generation.

Children of John Tichenal and Rebecca Harbert are:

   i. **Mary Ellen Tichenal**, b. 23 Aug 1815.
   ii. **William Henry Tichenal**, b. 02 Jan 1817.
   iii. **Child Tichenal**, b. 1819.
   iv. **Child Tichenal**, b. 1820.
   v. **Child Tichenal**, b. 1822.
   vi. **Sarah Ann Tichenal**, b. 23 Dec 1823, Fort Smith Arkansas; d. 10 Feb 1900, Hackett, Arkansas; m. **Jeremiah HACKETT, Jr.** on 12 Aug 1841, James Fork, Crawford County, Arkansas.

Jeremiah Hackett, Jr. moved to Arkansas in 1836. He was a farmer and stockman. He served in the Civil War with the rank of captain in Company H, 2nd Arkansas Cavalry. He was later promoted to major. After the war, he held a number of civil offices and was elected to the Arkansas Legislature in 1866. His children were all born in Hackett, Sebastian County, Arkansas. The 1860 census lists the family in that county with real estate valued at $3,000 and personal property at $1,500.

> vii. **John R. Tichenal, Jr.**, b. 1826, Fort Smith, Arkansas; d. 08 Oct 1847, Mexico City, Mexico.
>
> viii. **David H. Tichenal**, b. 1828, Fort Smith, Arkansas; d. 04 Oct 1847, Mexico City, Mexico.

John R. Tichenal, Jr. and David H. Tichenal both served in the Mexican War in the 12th Infantry, Company C under General Pierce. John enlisted at Fort Smith on 12 May 1846. His enlistment record describes him as a farmer with hazel eyes, dark hair, fair complexion, and 5 feet, 10 inches tall. David enlisted the same time as his brother and served in the same company. His enlistment record describes him as a farmer with grey eyes, dark hair, fair complexion, and 5 feet, 6 inches tall. Both died in battle and are buried in Mexico City, Mexico.

> ix. **Susan Eliza Tichenal**, b. 23 Nov 1830, Fort Smith, Arkansas; d. 16 Jan 1865, Sebastian County, Arkansas, bur. Leard Cemetery, Cavanaugh, Arkansas; m. **George BROWNE**, 22 Mar 1852 in Arkansas.

20.

William R. Tichenell, son of No. 12, David Tichenell, was born 1793 in Allegany County, Maryland and died 29 Aug 1838 in Upper Alton, Madison County, Illinois. He married **Margaret HUNT**, daughter of **William HUNT** and **Rachel BUCKALEW**.

Children of William R. Tichenell and Margaret Hunt are:
- i. **Cassandra Tichenell**, b. 02 Apr 1819, Greensburg, Westmoreland County, Pennsylvania; d. 11 May 1855, Alton, Madison County, Illinois, bur. Short Cemetery; m. **John THOMPSON**.
- ii. **Delilah Tichenell**, b. 25 Apr 1822, Greensburg, Westmoreland County, Pennsylvania; d. 03 Oct, 1913, Madison County, Illinois, bur. Short Cemetery; m. **James Clayton TIBBETTS,** 03 Feb 1842, Madison County, Illinois.
- iii. **Julia Tichenell**, m. **Robert KENNEDY.**
- iv. **Mary Ellen Tichenell**, m. **Fielding HARRISON.**
- v. **John D. Tichenell**, b. 17 Jun 1823; d. 24 Sep 1877, Illinois, bur. Short Cemetery, Alton, Madison County, Illinois; m. **Susan M. WELCH**.
- vi. **Margaret Tichenell**, b.1826; m. **John KELL**

21.

Moses J. Tichenell, son of No. 12, David Tichenell, was born 1796 in Allegany County, Maryland and died March 1877 at Lamberts Run, Harrison County, West Virginia. He is buried in Hepzibah Cemetery. He married **Mary M. SMITH** in Harrison County, West Virginia, daughter of **John V. SMITH**.
Children of Moses Tichenell and Mary Smith are:
- i. **John B. Tichenell**, b. 05 Aug 1821.
- ii. **Sarah E. Tichenell**, b. abt. 1826.
- iii. **Thomas Edward Tichenell**, b. abt. 1828.

22.

Moses Tichenell, son of No. 13, Joshua Tichenell, was born about 1805 and died 1890 in Garrett County, Maryland. He married **Ellen ABERNATHY** 1830, daughter of **John ABERNATHY**.

Like his cousin, Moses J. Tichenell, this Moses, married to Ellen - also known as Nellie or Elen - is the namesake of his grandfather. In 1852, Moses and Ellen Tichenell sold her interest in land in Hampshire County (West) Virginia *which in any way belongs to Thomas Abernathy, deceased, who was a brother of the said Elen, wife of said Moses Tichnell at the time of his death. This land came to the said Thomas under his father John Abernathy's will.* At the beginning of the deed, their names are recorded as *Moses Tichnell and Nelly his wife.* Several times within the deed the clerk spelled her name as *Elen,* but wrote it at the end as *Ellen,* although she signed with her mark. Their residence given in the deed is Allegany County, Maryland, as in the 1850 census. That census listed Moses Tichnall (sic) aged 41 with the following in his household: Eleanore, 42; John, 19; Joshua, 16; William, 14; Mary Jane, 12; Sarah E., 10; Hester, 8; and James, 5. Eleanor's place of birth is Virginia and John's is Maryland. No other birthplaces of family members are recorded.

Children of Moses Tichenell and Ellen Abernathy are:

    i. **John M. Tichenell**, b. 23 Jun 1832, Allegany County, Maryland; d. aft. 17 Dec 1894, Garrett County, Maryland; m. **Isabella WARNICK**, 11 Feb 1858, Garrett County, Maryland.

John and Isabella lived on a farm in Maryland near Barnum, West Virginia. His will, written 17 Dec 1894, names his two children, but not his wife. However, her name is on a deed for land they sold dated just one month earlier, 17 Nov 1894. She may have died between those dates. Their daughter,

Anne Tichenell, married **George W. BRAY**. Their son,
George W. Tichenell, married **Elizabeth J. HERMAN.**

    ii.   **Joshua Tichenell**, b. 1834.

    iii. **William V. Tichenell**, b. abt. August 1836; d.
              aft. 21 Apr 1880, Garrett County, Maryland;
              m. **Sarah PAUGH**, 17 Aug 1867, Allegany
              County, Maryland.

William Tichenell had no children. A farmer, he bought
50 acres in Allegany County, Maryland (later Garrett County)
on 22 Nov 1871. This was located on or adjacent to Military
Lot 262. After his death, Sarah married (2) **John R.
KERFOOT**, a grandson of Major Armistead. A farmer, he
bought 50 acres in Allegany County, Maryland (later Garrett
County) on 22 Nov 1871. This was located on or adjacent to
Military Lot 262. When William died, Sarah sold coal and
mineral rights of the farm which she received through his will,
excepting land under and about the grave of William to the
extent of *one-half square from the center* of the grave. She also
reserved a building *located at the mouth of mines*, formerly
used as a school house, *but now occupied as a dwelling house*
for as long a time as James C. Watson and William H. Loy and
heirs need it. The name is spelled *Tichinel* on the deed. The
will of William Tichenell signed 21 Apr 1880 named only
Sarah and left everything to her.

    iv. **Mary Jane Tichenell**, b. 1838, Allegany County,
              Maryland d. June 1894, Montrose, Barbour
              County, West Virginia; m. **Rev. John
              SHARPLESS** of the M.E. South Church.

    v. **Sarah Ellen Tichenell,** b. 1840, Allegany
              County, Maryland; m. **Henry PAUGH**, a
              minister of the M. E. South Church. He died
              in Swanton, Garrett County, Maryland on the

The Pritchard/Prickett Family History

farm occupied by their son, **Stewart PAUGH**, in 1940.

vi. **Margaret Hester Tichenell**, b. 1842; m. **Benjamin TASKER.**

vii. **James W. Tichenell**, b. abt. 1845, Allegany County, Maryland; d. West Virginia; m. (1) **Mary Ann PAUGH** March 28, 1863; m. (2) **Elizabeth ARNOLD**

viii. **Elizabeth Tichenell.**

9. (Continued)

Thomas Pritchard, Jr. married for the second time on 25 Oct 1812. His new wife, **Mary MOODY**, was the daughter of **Robert MOODY, Jr.** of Greene County, Pennsylvania and **Mary Jane HUTCHINSON.** According to a biographical sketch in *The Horn Papers*, Mary's great-grandfather, **Richard MOUDY**, was an Englishman by birth and a tailor by trade. He was born about 1694 in Moulton, Suffolk, England, and died about 1744 in Paterson, Bergen County, New Jersey. **Robert MOUDY,** his father, was born about 1655 in England and died about 1705. He was the son of **Thomas MOUDY** and **A. LAWRENCE.**

Richard Moudy arrived in Philadelphia in 1712, and in 1721 established Moudy's Inn near Paterson, New Jersey. He married **Anne LOUND** about 1720 in Paterson, the daughter of **Samuel LOUND** (1672-1722) and **Prudence UNK.** Anne was born 09 Nov 1695 in Staveley, Derbyshire, England, and died about 1745 in Prince George County, Virginia.

Robert MOUDY, Sr., their son, was born 08 May 1723, in Paterson, New Jersey and died about 1794 in Greene County, Pennsylvania. He married **Lucretia GREEN** about 1753 in Bedford County, Pennsylvania. She was born about 1730 in Paterson, New Jersey and died about 1780 in Greene County, Pennsylvania.

Robert and Lucretia Moudy settled in Shippensburg, Pennsylvania in 1759. A year later, Robert joined Thomas Cresap's group of explorers and traders to the Ohio River country. For nearly two years, he made his home at the "forks" (presumably the confluence of the Ohio, Allegheny, and Monongahela Rivers), then returned to his family in 1764. By then, they were living near the Cresap home on the Potomac

River. In 1769, Robert Moudy joined a party of settlers from
Frederick County, Virginia who headed for the Monongahela
River territory. Upon locating a tract of land in Greene County,
Pennsylvania, he settled there and fathered at least four
children who grew to maturity. By 1794, his eldest son,
William MOUDY, was a merchant tailor in Greensboro.

Another son, **Robert MOODY, Jr.,** the father of **Mary
MOODY**, was born about 1754 in Bedford County,
Pennsylvania, and died 13 Dec 1838 in Greene County,
Pennsylvania. He married **Mary Jane HUTCHINSON** on 13
Apr 1785 in Cumberland County, Pennsylvania. The daughter
of **John HUTCHINSON** and **Ann CHURCH,** she was born
about 1762 in Bristol Township, Bucks County, Pennsylvania,
and died about 1806, probably in Pennsylvania. Mary Jane's
mother, **Ann CHURCH,** was the daughter of **Richard
CHURCH** and **Sarah FELL**.

Ann's mother, **Sarah FELL**, the daughter of **Joseph
FELL** and **Elizabeth DOYLE**, was born 16 Aug 1713, in
Buckingham Township, Bucks County, Pennsylvania, and died
there 11 Oct 1797. She married **Richard CHURCH** about
1745 in Bucks County. The son of **Samuel CHURCH** and
Susannah HUNGERFORD, he was born about 1710 in New
London, Connecticut, and died 11 Jun 1776 in Buckingham
Township, Bucks County, Pennsylvania.

The bondsman at the time of **Thomas Pritchard's**
marriage to **Mary Moody** was James Coburn. With his new
wife, Thomas sired eight more children. In Monongalia
County, he was a farmer, a carpenter, a justice of the peace,
and the builder of a grist mill. All of his land there ultimately
fell under the umbrella of Preston County. The deeds and other
records of family transactions in that county were lost in a fire
that destroyed the court house some years later.

The Pritchard/Prickett Family History

According to Minnie Lowther's *History of Ritchie County* published in 1911, Thomas Pritchard Jr. arrived in 1832 at the South Fork of Hughes River, below Oxford, and made the first settlement there. *A man by the name of Henry O. Middleton had given him one hundred acres of land in this wilderness so as to induce him to settle and to erect a saw and grist mill, and here some of the first lumber in the county was sawed. The old grist mill was a water-power, the wheel run in a sycamore gum, and its capacity was from eight to ten bushels a day, a marvelous improvement over the old hand mill.*

Thomas, however, did not move directly from Preston County to Ritchie County. Deeds from Harrison and Lewis Counties (West) Virginia, as well as the Census records, indicate that he owned land in both places. He purchased 130 acres of land on Gnatty Creek in Harrison County from Jonathan Radcliff on 24 Apr 1819, and several of his children were married in that county. On 19 Jun 1920, Thomas Pritchard and his wife Mary sold a 58 acre tract of land that included a mill to Jacob Romine for $2,500. This land, located on both sides of Gnatty Creek adjoining lands of Moral Bice and Sarah Radcliff and Simon Arnold, is identified today as Romine's Mill.

By 1830, Thomas is listed in the Lewis County Census, but he and his wife Mary sold land there on 01 Oct 1832 to Thomas Read. If Minnie Lowther's account is accurate, Thomas Pritchard may have gone to Ritchie County at this time to undertake construction of the mill. Its success is indicated by his eventual decision to purchase the mill site and its environs from Henry O. Middleton. Lewis County records confirm purchase of the land in 1841 by Thomas Pritchard, William Pritchard, and Thomas D. Pritchard of Lewis County.

Thomas Pritchard Jr. died 24 Dec 1846. He was buried

in White Oak Cemetery, Oxford. This is in Doddridge County, just beyond its division from Ritchie County where his son, Peter Pritchard, lived and is buried. Mary Moody Pritchard continued to live in Doddridge County. She appears in the U.S. Census for 1850, but died on 31 May 1867 and is buried beside her husband.

Children of Thomas Pritchard Jr. and Nancy Tichenell are:

46. i. **Sarah Pritchard**, b. abt. 1797, Allegany County, Maryland.
47. ii. **Peter Pritchard**, b. 01 Oct 1798, Allegany County, Maryland; d. 19 Sep 1883, Ritchie County, West Virginia.
48. iii. **Margaret Peggy Pritchard**, b. 26 Sep 1801, Allegany County, Maryland; d. 11 May 1870, Meigs County, Ohio.
49. iv. **Eleanor Pritchard**, b. November 1803, Allegany County, Maryland; d. 21 Aug 1877, Doddridge County, West Virginia.
50. v. **Anna Pritchard**, b. abt. 1805 Allegany County, Maryland, d. April 1869, Preston County, (West) Virginia
51. vi. **Katherine Pritchard**, b. 07 Jun 1807; d. 23 Mar 1879.
52. vii. **Elizabeth Pritchard**, b. 20 Feb 1812, (West) Virginia; d. 25 Mar 1876, Ritchie County, West Virginia.

Children of Thomas Pritchard Jr. and Mary Moody are:

53. iii. **Mary Pritchard**, b. (West) Virginia; d. aft. 1879, Ohio.
54. ix. **John Moody Pritchard**, b. 1814, (West) Virginia; d. 1862, Mill Pond, M.H. Davis Farm, Ritchie County.

55.   x. **Jane Pritchard**, b. 1816, Monongalia County,
        (West) Virginia; d. in Doddridge County,
        West Virginia.
56.   xi. **Thomas Dickerson Pritchard**, b. 25 Feb 1818,
        Monongalia County (West) Virginia; d. 1862,
        Gaston, Lewis County, (West) Virginia.
       xii. **William Pritchard**, b. 1820; never married;
        early schoolmaster in Ritchie County.
57.   xiii. **Samuel George Pritchard**, b. July 1823,
        Harrison County, (West) Virginia.
       xiv. **Rachel Pritchard,** b. 1824; d. in youth.
58.   xv. **Emily Pritchard**, b. 1828, Harrison County,
        (West) Virginia; died in Ritchie County, West
        Virginia.
59.   xvi. **Amos D. Pritchard**, b. abt. 1828; d. abt. 1865 in
        Civil War, Cumberland, Maryland.

SECOND GENERATION

46.

Sarah Pritchard, daughter of No. 9, Thomas Pritchard Jr. and Nancy Tichenal, was born about 1797 in Allegany County, Maryland. She married **Jacob WATSON**, son of **William WATSON** and **Elizabeth Jane PATTON**.

William Watson was born 1745 near Hagerstown, Maryland, and died May 1809 in Monongalia County, (West) Virginia. His wife, Elizabeth Jane Patton (1747-1832), was the daughter of **Robert PATTON**. William was the son of **David WATSON** and **Sarah UNK**, who were married 24 Feb 1729/30, in Prince George's County, Maryland. David died after 07 Jan 1769.

Children of William Watson and Elizabeth Patton are:

    i. **David Watson**, b. abt. 1770; d. 1855; m. **Elizabeth MENEAR** 15 Aug 1796; she died 15 Apr 1876.

*   ii. **Jacob Watson**, b. 1787, Virginia; m. (1) **Elizabeth GANDY**, 09 Jan 1812, daughter of **Samuel GANDY** and **Rachel COMBS**. Elizabeth was born 27 Mar 1787, and died 1813 in Barbour County, (West) Virginia. Jacob married (2) No. 46, **Sarah PRITCHARD**, 15 Oct 1816, in Monongalia County, (West) Virginia.

    iii. **Sarah Jane Watson**; m. **Jacob CRISS,** 16 Sep 1802, Monongalia County, (West) Virginia.

---

* Husband of Sarah Pritchard

iv. **Mary Watson**; m. **Levi GANDY**, 30 Jul 1805,
   Monongalia County, (West) Virginia.
v. **William Watson**; m. (1) **Eleanor TANSEY,**
   18 Feb 1808, Monongalia County; m.
   (2) **Margaret MUCKELROY, 14** Oct 1816,
   Monongalia County.
vi. **Nancy Watson**; m. **Thomas HOSKINSON,**
   19 Dec 1808, Monongalia County. (Her name
   appears as Jenny on the Marriage Ledger.)

Jacob Watson moved from Marion County to Barbour
County about 1812. He was first married to Elizabeth Gandy,
sister of Mrs. John Zinn of Auburn, Ritchie County, West
Virginia. One son, Otho Watson, was born of this union. After
the death of his first wife, Jacob married Sarah Pritchard. They
were the parents of George and John who, along with Otho,
were pioneer settlers on Brush Run, a small tributary of the
Middle Fork in Ritchie County. Otho Watson married Louise
Jett and made the first settlement on Brush Run in 1845. From
there, he moved to Roane County (West) Virginia where his
widow was still surviving in 1908 at the age of more than one
hundred years. The Marriage Record in the oldest Record Book
of Monongalia County shows two entries for Jacob Watson and
Sarah Pritchard: 15 Oct 1816 and 16 Oct 1815 by Rev. William
K. Smith, apparently a numerical error by the recorder. After
the second entry, it is noted that Jacob moved to Ritchie
County. It also lists his marriage to Elizabeth Gandy on 09 Jan
1812 by Joseph A. Shakleford. The family Bible spells her
name as Elisabeth.
Child of Jacob Watson and Elizabeth Gandy is:
   i. **Otho G. Watson**, b. 1813; m. **Louise JETT** (b.
      1810; d. after 1910), 1836. Otho and two of
      his sons were Union soldiers: **Jacob Watson,**

who went to Roane County, and **George Watson**, who died during the war. Their other children were **Irvin Watson; Sophia Amelia Watson** m. No. 98, **Elias PRITCHARD; Matilda Watson,** m. **Frank BOICE,** Roane County; **Unk Watson** m. **Henry COLLINS; William J. Watson; Saphira Watson**, and **Sarah Watson.**

Children of Sarah Pritchard and Jacob Watson are:

60. i. **Elizabeth Watson,** b. 1816, Harrison County, (West) Virginia.

61. ii. **Mary Watson**, b. 1817, Harrison County, (West) Virginia; d. 17 Oct 1890, Roane County, West Virginia.

62. iii. **William Watson**, b. 1818, Mercer County, (West) Virginia; d. 09 Feb 1890, Roane County, West Virginia.

iv. **Daughter Watson**, b. abt. 1820, m. **Unk CASTER.**

63. v. **George W. Watson**, b. 14 Feb 1822, Auburn, Ritchie County, (West) Virginia; d. 14 Oct 1893, Berea, Ritchie County, West Virginia.

vi. **Angeline Watson**, b. 09 Dec 1823, Auburn, Ritchie County, West Virginia; d. 10 Feb 1902; m. **Lair SIMONS** (b. March 1830; d. 1909, Auburn, Ritchie County, West Virginia) 1850.

vii. **Nancy Watson**, b. abt. 1825; m. **Unk DIVERS.**

64. viii. **Amanda Watson**, b. 1827.

ix. **Jane Watson**, b. 1828; m. **Unk ROWE.**

x. **Wilson Watson**, b. 1830; m. **Martha HESS;** buried Holbrook, Ritchie County, West Virginia.

xi. **Emily Watson**, b. 1832; never married.

65.   xii. **John Watson**, b. 1835; d. Holbrook, Ritchie
            County, West Virginia.

47.

Peter Pritchard, son of No. 9, Thomas Pritchard, Jr. and
Nancy Tichenal, was born 01 Oct 1798 in Allegany County,
Maryland, and died 19 Sep 1883 in Ritchie County, West
Virginia. He married **Elizabeth WILLIS** 15 Feb 1821 in
Harrison County, (West) Virginia, daughter of **William
WILLIS** and **Nancy Anne DOUGLASS**.

The Willis Family
1.

Richard WYLLYS was born about 1600 in Cambridgeshire,
England and died in Middlesex County, Virginia. He married
Jane NEWMARSH (or **HENMARSH**) in Middlesex County,
daughter of **William NEWMARSH** and **Katherine FLEETE**.
Child of Richard Wyllys and Jane Newmarsh is:
2.   i. **Thomas Wyllys**, b. abt. 1632; d. 1662 in
            Middlesex County, Virginia; m. **Mary**
            UNK 1654 in Lancaster County, Virginia.
Child of Thomas Wyllys and Mary is:
3   i. **John Willis Sr.**, b. 24 Nov 1658, St. Marys
            Parish, Old Rappahannock County, Virginia
            (later became Richmond County). In a deed of
            26 Apr 1701, giving the remaining 161 acres of his 261
            acre patent to his son William, John Willis, Sr.
            identifies himself as a planter. The land in
            Westmoreland County bordering Appomattox Creek
            was between the Potomack and Rappahannock Rivers
            adjacent to the land of Lt. Col. John Washington, and
            was received by him on 21 Oct 1669 (p. 283) for the

transportation of six persons. He died testate in 1715 in Richmond County, Virginia. His will and estate inventories were made in 1715 and 1716. He married **Matilda UNK**. Both John and Matilda Willis authorized Nathaniel Pope as their attorney on 01 Oct 1694.

Children of John Willis Sr. and Matilda are:

    i. **John Willis, Jr.**, b. by or before 1673, in Old Rappahannock County, Virginia. He died testate in King George County, Virginia between 06 Feb 1727-28 and 03 May 1728. He married **Mary COGHILL** (b. before 1685), daughter of **James COGHILL** and his second wife, **Mary UNK** sometime before 1698. They may have had children, but none are mentioned in their wills indicating that none survived them. Mary Coghill Willis married (2) **John JENNINGS**, who died in 1748.

4.   ii. **William Willis**, b. by 1680 in Old Rappahannock County, Virginia; d. intestate July 1716 in Hanover Parish, Richmond, County, Virginia; m. **Sarah ROSSER,** after 1701, daughter of **David ROSSER** and **Sarah SHERWOOD**, daughter of **Phillip SHERWOOD**. After the death of William Willis, Sarah married (2) **Henry WOOD**, who died abt. 1722; m. (3) **Rush HUDSON**, whose estate was assessed in 1735 by Sarah, and (4) **Edmund TURBERVILLE**. John Jr. and William Willis, their mother Sarah Willis Wood Hudson Turberville, and their extended family migrated together to the Rapidan River in

Orange County, Virginia.
Children of William Willis and Sarah Rosser are:
5.   i. **John Willis**, b. 1709/1710, King George County, Virginia; d. 1762, Orange County, Virginia; m. **Elizabeth PLUNKETT 17** January 17, 1734/35 in St. Paul's Parish, King George, Virginia, daughter of **John PLUNKETT** and **Frances FRANK**. She was born in Hanover Parish. According to *British Mercantile Claims, 1775-1893,* Elizabeth Plunkett Willis died in 1798 in Madison County, Virginia, the part created from Culpeper County in 1792. In 1737, John Willis (son of William and Sarah, and grandson of John Willis Sr.) and his wife Elizabeth Plunkett sold his Grandfather's 1669 patent to the Church Wardens of Hanover Parish, King George County, Virginia, for use as a glebe. He then moved to Orange County where he, his brother William, Joshua Hudson, and Benjamin Hawkins lived in the area of Petty's Mill Run, which was south of the Rapidan River near the present junction of highways 627 and 636.

     ii. **William Willis** named in mother's will; no further record of marriage or children.

     iii. **Sarah Willis**, m. **Benjamin HAWKINS**, had seven children.

Children of John Willis and Elizabeth Plunkett are:
     i. **Sarah Willis** m. **Walter SHROPSHIRE.**
     ii. **Margaret "Peggy" Willis** m. **Edmund TERRILL**.
6.   iii. **William Willis, Sr.**, b. 22 Feb 1742/43,

Culpeper County, Virginia; d. 21 May1833 in
Bullitsburg, Kentucky; m. **Elizabeth
GARNETT**, b. 16 April 1744, Horseshoe Farm,
Culpeper, Virginia, daughter of **Anthony
GARNETT** and **Elizabeth BOULWARE.**
  iv. **John Willis** m. **Sarah PORTER.**
   v. **Benjamin Willis** d.s.p. 1810 Orange County,
      Virginia.
  vi. **Joshua Willis** m. **Sarah THOMAS.**
 vii. **James Willis** m. (1) **Ann UNK,** m. (2) **Judith
      UNK.**
viii. **Reuben Willis** m. **Ann "Nancy" GARNETT.**
  ix. **Frances Willis** m. **William CAMP.**
   x. **Lewis Willis** m. **Edna TILMAN.**
  xi. **Moses Willis** m. (1) **Elizabeth THOMAS**; m.
      (2) **Susan WHITE.**
 xii. **Mary Willis** m. **Richard PRICE.**

6.

William Willis, Sr. and **Elizabeth Garnett** had eleven
children. Among them are William Willis the father of
Elizabeth Willis, wife of Peter Pritchard. William Willis, Sr.
and Elizabeth Garnett moved from Orange County, Virginia to
Kentucky about 1790, first to Adair County. William Willis Sr.
died May 21, 1833 in Bullitsburg, Boone County, Kentucky
and Elizabeth died in 1835, also in Boone County, Kentucky.
Children of William Willis, Sr. and Elizabeth Garnett include:
7.   i. **William Willis**, b. abt. 1769, Augusta County,
           Virginia; d. 21 Nov 1823, Harrison County,
           (West) Virginia; m. **Nancy Anne
           DOUGLASS**, daughter of **Levi DOUGLASS**
           and **Nancy Anne MERRICK.**

ii. **Isaac Willis**, m. **Anne GARNETT** and lived at "Locust Grove," the family estate and "home place," until his death in 1867. "Locust Grove" is believed to be the oldest building in Culpeper County, Virginia. It was restored in the 1970s and is now on the National Register of Historic Places.

iii. **Alexander "Sandy" Willis**.

The Douglass Family

1. **William DOUGLASS I** was born in 1642.
Child of William Douglass I is:
2.　　i. **William Douglass II**, b. 1665; d. 1747; m. **Ann UNK**.
Child of William Douglass II and Ann is:
3.　　i. **William Douglass III**, b. 1690; d. 1730; m. **Mary SCOTT**, daughter of **John SCOTT** and **Catherine UNK**, (1664-1716).
Child of William Douglass III and Mary Scott is:
4.　　i. **William Douglass IV**, b. 1720; d. 1779; m. **Mary ANDERSON**.
Child of William Douglass IV and Mary Anderson is:
5.　　i. **Levi Douglass**, b. before 1750; d. June 1789, Harrison County, (West) Virginia; m. **Nancy Anne MERRICK**, daughter of **John MERRICK** and **Ann THOMPSON**. Levi Douglass was the first white settler in Harrison County, (West) Virginia.
Child of Levi Douglass and Nancy Anne Merrick is:
6.　　i. **Nancy Anne Douglass**, b.1768 Harrison County, (West) Virginia; d. 1838, Harrison County; m.

William WILLIS 19 Nov 1794.
Child of Nancy Anne Douglass and William Willis is:
7.　　i. **Elizabeth Willis**, b .30 Dec 1798, Harrison
　　　　County (West) Virginia; d. 09 Dec 1869, Ritchie
　　　　County, West Virginia; m. No. 47, **Peter**
　　　　PRITCHARD 15 Feb 1821, Clarksburg,
　　　　Harrison County, West Virginia.

Peter Pritchard and **Elizabeth Willis** lived in Barbour County after their marriage until 1837 when they joined his father and stepmother in Ritchie County. For the next two generations, the Pritchards resided at Oxford and nearby White Oak, just across the county border in Doddridge County. Peter Pritchard was one of the earliest justices of the peace in that area and was known as "a cornerstone" of the White Oak Methodist Episcopal Church in Oxford, where he is buried.

Children of Peter Pritchard and Elizabeth Willis are:
66.　　i. **George Pritchard**, b. 10 May 1822, in Virginia;
　　　　d. 14 Oct 1902, Doddridge County, West
　　　　Virginia.
67.　　ii. **Nancy P. Pritchard**, b. 04 Aug 1823; d. 26 Nov
　　　　1903, Oxford, Ritchie County, West Virginia.
68.　　iii. **Thomas Willis Pritchard**, b. 15 Oct 1825,
　　　　Virginia; d. 30 Jun 1885, Ritchie County, West
　　　　Virginia.
69.　　iv. **Harriet Pritchard**, b. abt. 1827, Harrison County,
　　　　(West) Virginia.
70.　　v. **Anna Pritchard**, b. 26 Feb 1828, Virginia,
　　　　d. 08 Aug 1871.
71.　　vi. **William Tyler Pritchard**, b. 21 Apr 1832; d.
　　　　09 May 1911, Ritchie County, West Virginia.
72.　　vii. **John Pritchard**, b. 22 Oct 1834, Virginia; d. 05
　　　　Aug 1919, Pullman, Ritchie County, West

Virginia.
73.   viii. **Cassandra Pritchard**, b. 19 Nov 1846; d. 18
            Mar 1911, Ritchie County, West Virginia.
      xi. **Elizabeth Jane Pritchard**, b. 29 Apr 1840,
            White Oak, Ritchie County, (West) Virginia;
            d. after 1900, Fairmont, West Virginia; m. (1)
            Lewis MAXWELL (b. 1790, d. 1865), 1857.
Lewis Maxwell was the third son of **Thomas
MAXWELL** and **Janet LEWIS.** He was a member of
Congress from 1827-1833 and an early surveyor of western
Virginia. According to Minnie Kendall Lowther, p. 603, he
was a man of no small means for his time. The town of Jane
Lew in Lewis County was named by him for his mother who,
with her orphaned (fatherless) children, came to live in the
cabin of Col. William Lowther. Lewis Maxwell left no heirs,
so much of his fortune fell to his nephew, **Franklin
MAXWELL.** He was first married to **Safronia WILSON.**
After his death, his wife, Elizabeth Jane, many years his junior,
married (2) **Rev. W. H. WILEY**, a Methodist minister, on 14
Mar 1867. At their marriage, Rev. A. A. Reger officiated and
received $50 for his services, a very large amount for the time.
Elizabeth Jane had no children from either marriage.

48.
Margaret (Peggy) Pritchard, daughter of No. 9, Thomas
Pritchard, Jr. and Nancy Tichenell, was born 26 Sep 1801 in
Allegany County, Maryland and died 11 May 1870
in Meigs County, Ohio. She married **Samuel CASTER** 30 Jan
1821 in Harrison County, (West) Virginia, son of **James
CASTER** and **Drucella UNK**.
      Samuel, a farmer, is buried at Mt. Olive Cemetery,
Columbia Township, Meigs County, Ohio, as is his wife,

Margaret. They lived in Harrison and Lewis Counties, (West) Virginia and Meigs County, Ohio. Of their eleven children, Hezekiah died in infancy and Mary died in childhood. Children of Margaret Pritchard and Samuel Caster are:

      i. **Hesekiah Caster**, b. 22 May 1822; d. aft. 22 May 1822.

74.   ii. **Nancy Caster**, b. 09 Nov 1824, Harrison County, (West) Virginia

      iii. **Vincent Caster**, b. 12 Mar 1827, Harrison County, (West) Virginia; d. 26 Mar 1910, bur. Mt. Olive Cemetery, Meigs County, Ohio; m. (1) **Elizabeth CHEUVRONT**, 13 Dec 1852; m. (2) **Mary Ann YOUNG**, 25 Apr 1872, Harrison County, West Virginia.

      iv. **Salina Caster** b. 1828, m. **William MORRIS**, Harrison County, 1845

      v. **Drucella Caster**, b. 07 May 1829, Harrison County, (West) Virginia; m. **Levi WESTFALL**, 19 Nov 1847, Lewis County, (West) Virginia.

      vi. **Mary Caster**, b. 09 Oct 1831; d. child.

      vii. **Wesley Caster**, b. 16 Apr 1834, Harrison County (West) Virginia; d. 03 Mar 1923, bur. Mt. Olive Cemetery, Columbia Twp., Meigs County, Ohio; m. **Elizabeth McCLELLAN**, 27 Feb 1868, Meigs County, Ohio.

      viii. **Lewis Caster**, b. 23 Nov 1836, Harrison County, (West) Virginia; d. 11 Sep 1913, Columbia Twp., Meigs County, Ohio; m. **Lovina GREEN**, 06 Feb 1862, Meigs County, Ohio.

ix. **Emily Caster**, b. 05 Apr 1839, Harrison
County, (West) Virginia; d. 04 Aug 1930;
m. **Joshua ROMINE**, 28 Jun 1862, Meigs
County, Ohio.

75.   x. **Daniel Caster**, b. 07 Aug 1841, Harrison
County, (West) Virginia; d. 14 Aug 1914,
Oberlin, Decatur County, Kansas.

xi. **Sarah Ann Caster**, b. 14 Feb 1844,
Harrison County, (West) Virginia; d. 10 Oct
1902, Point Rock, Meigs County, Ohio;
m. **Francis Marion BOBO**, 10 Aug 1866,
Meigs County, Ohio. Note: Sarah Ann
Caster's death date has also been recorded as
17 Nov 1902.

49.

Eleanor Pritchard, daughter of No. 9, Thomas Pritchard, Jr.,
and Nancy Tichenal, was born November 1802 in Allegany
County, Maryland, and died 21 Aug 1877 in Doddridge
County, West Virginia. She married **Foster WILLIAMS** about
1821. He was born 14 Dec 1800 in New Jersey and died 28
May 1874 in Doddridge County, West Virginia. Both are
buried in the Lowther Cemetery, Holbrook, Ritchie County,
West Virginia.

Children of Eleanor Pritchard and Foster Williams are:

76.   i. **Mary Williams**, b. 25 Feb 1826, Harrison
County, (West) Virginia; d. 05 Mar 1899,
Greenwood, Doddridge County, West
Virginia.

ii. **John E. Williams**, b. 1833, Harrison County,
(West) Virginia.

iii. **Hester S. Williams,** b. 1843, Harrison County,

147

(West) Virginia.

50.

Anna Pritchard, daughter of No. 9, Thomas Pritchard, Jr. and Nancy Tichenell, was born about 1805 in Allegany County, Maryland, and died April 1869 in Preston County, West Virginia. She married **Charles C. QUEEN** 30 Aug 1828 in Harrison County, (West) Virginia, son of **Levi QUEEN** and **Catherine COBURN**. She lived at Peel Tree Creek in Harrison County. Information about her comes from the History of the Queen Family.

Children of Anna Pritchard and Charles Queen are:

77.   i. **Catherine "Katy" Rebecca Queen**, b. 24 Jun 1830, Harrison County (West) Virginia; d. 1921.

78.   ii. **Rezin P. Queen**, b. 27 Dec 1837, Harrison County, (West) Virginia; d. 16 Aug 1873, Johnstown Cemetery, Harrison County, West Virginia.

79.   iii. **Nancy Ann Queen**, b. 22 Mar 1841, Harrison County, (West) Virginia.

80.   iv. **Martha Queen**, b. 20 Jul 1843, Harrison County, (West) Virginia; d. 05 Dec 927, Clarksburg, Harrison County (West) Virginia.

81.   v. **Lemuel Queen**, b. 10 Oct 1845, Harrison County, (West) Virginia; d. Braxton County, West Virginia.

82.   vi. **Nathan Absalom P. Queen**, b. 15 Aug 1848, Peel Tree Run, Harrison County, (West) Virginia; d. 16 Oct 1911, bur. Johnstown Cemetery, Harrison County, West Virginia.

51.

Katherine Pritchard, daughter of No. 9, Thomas Pritchard, Jr. and Nancy Tichenell, was born 07 Jun 1807, and died 23 Mar 1879. She married **William B. QUEEN** 15 Oct 1827 in Harrison County, (West) Virginia, son of **Levi QUEEN** and **Catherine Coburn LOWTHER**. Katherine Pritchard was also known as Sara Catherine.

The first known Queen in West Virginia was **Charles MacQUEEN** or **MacQUAIN** born in Scotland about 1720 and died in present day Harrison County about 1755. Family tradition says that Charles was a private in the British army who performed some deed of valor that qualified him for a commission. Since no commissioned officers in the British army could be Scotttish or Irish, he shortened his name to Queen.

Charles entered a claim for 1,400 acres in what is now Harrison County, (West) Virginia and came to the colony with his wife about 1750. He died about 1755, and his wife returned to England with their son, **Charles QUEEN** (b. abt 1755, d 1806.)

In England, young Charles was apprenticed to the weaver trade and later joined the British army. After his discharge in 1770, he returned to the colonies and located in Pennsylvania where he married **Mary HEALY** in 1773. By 1785, the family had moved to the south branch of the Potomac River in Hampshire County, (West) Virginia. During the years between 1793 and 1796, they moved to Harrison County, (West) Virginia and took possession of the lands claimed by his father earlier.

Levi QUEEN, a son of Charles and Mary Healy Queen, was born about 1780. He married **Catherine Coburn LOWTHER** in Harrison County 03 Aug 1802. She was a daughter of **Jonathan COBURN** and the widow of **Joseph LOWTHER.**

The Pritchard/Prickett Family History

Children of Katherine Pritchard and William Queen are:
83. i. **Levi P. Queen**, b. 31 Jan 1829; d. 14 Feb 1854.
  ii. **Wilson Queen**, b.17 Nov 1830; d. 12 Dec 1906; m. **Susan REED**, 1876. He was a doctor.
84. iii. **Peter Queen**, b. 07 Oct 1832; d. 02 Jul 1910, Johnstown, Harrison County, West Virginia.
  iv. **Nancy Queen**, b. 15 Dec 1834; d. 24 Jan 1892, Johnstown, West Virginia; unm.
85. v. **Phineas Queen**, b. 17 Dec 1837; d. 1922, West Virginia.
  vi. **Allen Queen**, b. 15 Mar 1840; d. 09 Apr 1921, West Virginia, umn. A twin of George Queen. .
86. vii. **George Queen**, b. 15 Mar 1840; Death date unk.
87. viii. **Burrel M. Queen**, b. 07 Nov 1842; d. 1926, Johnstown, Harrison County, West Virginia.
88. ix. **Ida Matilda Queen**, b. 17 Jan 1845; d. 21 Jan 1931.
89. x. **Minerva Manassa Queen**, b. 01 May 1847; d. 27 Jan 1931, Harrison County, West Virginia.
90. xi. **James P. Queen**, b. 03 Oct 1849, Harrison County, (West) Virginia; d. 04 Jan 1926, Harrison County, West Virginia.

52.

Elizabeth Pritchard, daughter of No. 9, Thomas Pritchard Jr. and Nancy Tichenell, was born 20 Feb 1812 in Preston County, (West) Virginia and died 25 Mar 1876. She is buried in White Oak Cemetery, Pullman, Ritchie County, West Virginia. She married (1) **John C. LOWTHER,** 10 Feb 1833 in Harrison County. He was the son of **Robert LOWTHER** and **Catherine CAIN**. He was born 1804 in Harrison County, (West) Virginia. She married (2) **John HARRIS** about 1846 in Ritchie County. He was born 25 Jan, 1814 in Harrison County,

150

(West) Virginia, and died 23 Mar 1904 in Ritchie County,
West Virginia. Both are buried at White Oak, Ritchie County,
West Virginia. He may be the son of John and Nancy Harris
buried at the Harrisville Pioneer Cemetery.
Children of Elizabeth Pritchard and John Lowther are:

    i. **Evan Lowther**, b. 1834.
    ii. **Catherine Lowther**, b. 1837.
    iii. **Susan Lowther**, b. 1838.
    iv. **Columbia Lowther**, b. 1840.
    v. **Ellen B. Lowther**, b. 1843.
    vi. **India Lowther**, b. 1845.

Children of Elizabeth Pritchard and John Harris are:

    vii. **Eliza J. Harris**, b. abt. 1846; d. 1846, Ritchie County, (West) Virginia..
    viii. **George W. Harris**, b. 1847, Ritchie County, (West) Virginia; d. Harrison County, West Virginia; m. **Mary L. PRICE** (b. 1851), 06 Apr 1873, Ritchie County, West Virginia..
91.   ix. **Martha Harris**, b. 1849; d. 1908, Richwood, Nicholas County, West Virginia.
92.   x. **Millie F. Harris**, b. 1850; d. 1942, Ritchie County, West Virginia.
    xi. **Nancy Rebecca Harris**, b. 20 Apr 1853; d. 25 Jan 1876, Ritchie County, West Virginia d. 26 Jan 1876, Pullman, Ritchie County, West Virginia; m. **Wesley McCORMICK** (b. abt. 1845, Tyler County, West Virginia) 14 Nov 1872.
93.   xii.. **Alpheus F. Harris,** b. October 1858, Ritchie County, West Virginia.

53.

Mary Pritchard, daughter of No. 9, Thomas Pritchard, Jr. and (probably) Mary Moody. Minnie Lowther states that Mary was the half-sister of Peter, which strongly suggests that she was the daughter of Mary Moody rather than of Nancy Titchnell, She was born in (West) Virginia and died in Ohio. She married **William SNODGRASS** 25 Sep 1827 in Monongalia County, (West) Virginia. He served in the War of 1812. He was born 30 Jan 1783 in Monongalia County and died 20 Apr 1879. He was first married in 1807 to **Anne Nancy KING,** who died at their home in Marion County in 1834. She was the daughter of **John KING.** By his first wife, William Snodgrass had eight children. They are: **Reverend John Wesley SNODGRASS**, a minister in the Methodist Episcopal Church for 73 years, who died in Iowa at the age of 91; **Frances, Mrs. Nicholas BAKER; Martha, Mrs. Elijah MORGAN** of Marion County; **Naomi, Mrs. Davis MEREDITH** of Tyler County; **Sarah, Mrs. Solomon HAWKINS** of Ritchie County; **Isabel, Mrs. Jared HAWKINS**; **Mrs. Nancy PIERCE**; and **Comfort, Mrs. Absalom David EWING**, all of Ohio. In 1841, William and Mary Pritchard Snodgrass settled at Turtle Run in Ritchie County, West Virginia, and erected their cabin on the farm inherited by their youngest son, Thomas C. Snodgrass, and his heirs. Here William Snodgrass died in 1879 at the age of 96, and is buried in the White Oak churchyard. Mary Pritchard Snodgrass spent the later part of her life with her daughter, Margaret Pritchard Carder, in Ohio, where she is buried. Children of Mary Pritchard and William Snodgrass are:

    i. **Lamerduke Snodgrass**, b. 1830.
    ii. **John Wesley Snodgrass**, b. abt. 1833.
    iii. **William F. Snodgrass;** b. 1834; d. in Kansas.
    iv. **Frances Snodgrass**, b. 1835.

v. **Martha Snodgrass**, b. 1837.
vi. **Benjamin F. Snodgrass**, b. 1838; d. in Washington State.
vii. **Margaret A. Snodgrass**, b. 1840, Ritchie County, (West) Virginia; m. **George CARDER,** and moved to Ohio. It was at their home in Ohio that Margaret's mother, Mary Pritchard Snodgrass, died after 1879.
viii. **Thomas Corbin Snodgrass**, b. 1843; d. 1920 Ritchie County, West Virginia at the old home on Turtle Run. He married **Viola J. PRITCHARD,** daughter of No. 66, **George PRITCHARD.**
ix. **Alcinda J. Snodgrass**, b. 1845; d. child.
x. **Elizabeth Snodgrass**, b. 1848; d. infant.

54.

John Moody Pritchard, son of No. 9, Thomas Pritchard, Jr. and Mary Moody, was born 1814 in (West) Virginia and died in 1862 by drowning in the pond at his own mill on the M. H. Davis farm, Ritchie County, (West) Virginia. He married **Sarah HADDOX**, daughter of **Phillip HADDOX** and **Isabel HEWEY**. She was born in 1816 and died after 1858 in West Virginia. He is buried in an unmarked grave in the Pritchard Cemetery which the WPA located 200 feet north of County Route 22, 3.5 miles east of the Berea Post Office.
Children of John Moody Pritchard and Sarah Haddox are:
94.   i. **Phillip H. Pritchard**, b. 25 Mar 1839; d. 25 Aug 1905, Gilmer County, West Virginia, age 71.
ii. **Jason H. Pritchard**, b. 1841. Member of Company K of the 6th Regiment WV Cavalry Volunteers 1864.

95.   iii. **Jasper N. Pritchard**, b. 01 Mar 1843; d.
            March 10, 1937. His first name is sometimes
            recorded as James.
        iv. **Mary Jane Pritchard**, b. 1844; d. Colorado; m.
            Sylvester PARKER, 19 Mar 1868, Ritchie
            County, West Virginia.
         v. **Elizabeth Ann Pritchard**, b. 26 Feb 1847; d.
            Colorado; m. **William Alvin PARKER,** 17 Jun
            1868. Her name also appears as Eliza Ann.
96.   vi. **Andrew Jackson Pritchard**, b. 1849, Ritchie
            County, West Virginia.
        vii. **Henry Pritchard**, b. 22 Oct 1852, Ritchie County,
            West Virginia; d. California; m. **Josephine
            FREDERICK** b. abt. 1856, Ritchie County)
            04 May 1873, Ritchie County, West Virginia.
       viii. **Isabel Pritchard,** b. 19 Mar 1856 in Ritchie
            County; m. **Benjamin RAMSEY** (b. abt. 1852,
            Licking County, Ohio), 24 Dec 1874, Ritchie
            County, West Virginia.
        ix. **William Pritchard**, b. 1858 in Ritchie County. He
            appeared in the census on 15 Aug 1860 in
            Ritchie County; d. California.
97.   x. **Thomas Benton Pritchard**, b. 10 Aug 1858,
            Ritchie County; d. 23 Oct 1911, Salt Creek
            Township, Hocking County, Ohio.

55.

Jane Pritchard, daughter of No. 9, Thomas Pritchard, Jr. and
Mary Moody, was born 1816 in Monongalia County, (West)
Virginia, and died in Doddridge County, West Virginia. She
married **John H. GASTON** 02 Feb 1848 in Ritchie County,
(West) Virginia. He was born in 1814.

154a

George W. Harris, from a group picture of Union and Confederate Civil War Veterans in *History of Roane County, W.V.* by William H. Bishop, 1927, p. 159, photo taken in the Fall of 1921

The Pritchard/Prickett Family History

Children of Jane Pritchard and John Gaston are:
- i. **Mary E. Gaston**, b. January 1850, Doddridge County, (West) Virginia.
- ii. **Anna C. Gaston**, 21 Feb 1855, Middle Fork, Doddridge County, (West) Virginia.
- iii. **Hugh Gaston**, b. abt. 1856, Doddridge County, (West) Virginia.
- iv. **Jane E. Gaston**, b. 23 Sep 1857, Doddridge County, West) Virginia.
- v. **Rulana O. Gaston**, b. 03 Feb 1859, Camps Run, Doddridge County, (West) Virginia.

56.

Thomas Dickerson Pritchard, son of No. 9, Thomas Pritchard Jr. and Mary Moody, was born 25 Feb 1818 in Monongalia County, (West) Virginia, and died after 1896 in Gaston, (West) Virginia. He married **Mary "Polly" LOWTHER** 11 Feb 1843 in Ritchie County, (West) Virginia, daughter of **Elias LOWTHER** and **Rebecca COBURN**. Thomas D. Pritchard, a blacksmith by trade, came to the South Fork of the Hughes River with his parents. In 1848, he made his pioneer settlement at Berea, Ritchie County, where he later built his mill. His wife's father was one of Thomas Dickerson Pritchard's neighbors, Major Elias Lowther, the youngest son of Colonel William Lowther, who lived on the nearby Flanagan farm. Polly was born 20 Sep 1818 in Harrison County and died while the family lived on Slab Creek. In 1862, Thomas D. Pritchard finally went to Gaston, Lewis County, where he spent his last days. On 12 May 1883, Thomas D. Pritchard and Mary Pritchard signed a deed for 68 acres in Ritchie County. George Pritchard was a witness to the sale.

The exact date of Thomas D. Pritchard's death has not

155

been found, but he was alive in 1896 to sign a widow's pension application for Louisa Jett Watson in which he wrote that he knew her at the time of her marriage.

Children of Thomas D. Pritchard and Mary Lowther are:

	i. **Rebecca Pritchard**, b. 1844; d. 1845.
98.	ii. **Elias Robert Pritchard**, b. 29 Dec 1845, Ritchie County, (West) Virginia; d. 04 Jun 1909, Roane County, West Virginia.
	iii. **Jerusha Pritchard**, b. 1848; m. **Unk. CARPENTER**. According to oral history, she was a missionary to Spain.
99.	iv. **Thomas Tavner Pritchard**, b. 05 Apr 1849, Slab Creek, Ritchie County, (West) Virginia; d. 26 Dec 1922, Hyattville, Big Horn County, Wyoming.
	v. **Cyrus Pritchard**, b. 06 May 1851, Ritchie County, (West) Virginia; d. 10 Nov 1867, Ritchie County.
	vi. **Silas R. Pritchard**, b. 06 May 1851; d. 1865, Ritchie County, West Virginia.
	vii. **Mary J. Pritchard**, b. Abt. 1853; d. in childhood.

57.

Samuel George Pritchard, son of No. 9, Thomas Pritchard Jr. and Mary Moody, was born July 1823 in Harrison County (West) Virginia. He married **Susan DENNISON** 16 Mar 1858 in Harrison County (West) Virginia, daughter of **John DENNISON** and **Sarah SKINNER**.

Children of Samuel George Pritchard and Susan Dennison are:

i. **Rachel Pritchard**, b. 30 Jan 1858; d. child.

ii. **John Denton Pritchard**, b. 15 Sep 1860, Doddridge

County, West Virginia; d. 02 Aug 1862, Ritchie
County, West Virginia; middle name appears as
"Dennison" in birth register.

100.   iii. **Sarah Ann Pritchard**, b. 18 Dec 1862, Ritchie
County, West Virginia; d. 12 May 1940, Crystal
Springs, Randolph County, West Virginia.

101.   iv. **Mary Elizabeth Pritchard**, b. 1863, Harrison
County, West Virginia; d. 25 Feb, 1932.

     v. **Samuel Pritchard**, b. 1865, Harrison County,
West Virginia; m. **Mary A. PATTERSON**
(b. 1868, Gilmer County, West Virginia) 07
Jul 1886, Gilmer County, West Virginia.

    vi. **Salina P. Pritchard**, b. 1866, Harrison County,
West Virginia; m. **Tony ROSS**.

   vii. **Nancy Ellen Pritchard**, b. 1868, Harrison
County, West Virginia; m. **Thomas A.
McQUAIN**.

  viii. **Joseph S. Pritchard**, b. 1870.

    ix. **Margaret S. Pritchard**, b. abt, 1873, Lewis
County, West Virginia; m. **Charles Robert
SMITH, 08** Aug 1876, Ritchie County,
West Virginia.

58.

Emily Pritchard, daughter of No. 9, Thomas Pritchard and
Mary Moody, was born 1828 in Harrison County, (West)
Virginia and died in Auburn, Ritchie County, West Virginia.
She married **George W. GARRISON 25** Nov 1855 in Ritchie
County, (West) Virginia. He was born 1828 in Rockingham
County, Virginia, the son of **Lewis GARRISON** and
Elizabeth UNK.
Children of Emily Pritchard and George Garrison are:

157

    i. **Lewis Garrison**, b. 1856; became Ritchie County
       Commissioner.
   ii. **Amos Garrison**, b. 1859.
  iii. **Thomas Garrison**, b.1865.
  iv. **Martha J. Garrison**, b. 09 Nov 1866.

59.

Amos D. Pritchard, son of No. 9, Thomas Pritchard Jr. and
Mary Moody, was born about 1828 in Preston County, (West)
Virginia and died 12 Jun 1863 at the Civil War Hospital in
Cumberland, Allegany County, Maryland. He married
Clarinda MITCHEL 21 Dec 1848 in Cabin Run, Doddridge
County, (West) Virginia, daughter of **Nathaniel MITCHEL**
and **Hannah VANSANT**. Clarinda was born 09 Feb 1833 in
Harrison County, (West) Virginia and died of tuberculosis on
14 Feb 1910 in Spencer, Roane County, West Virginia.

    Amos Pritchard was a member of Company D,
Fourteenth West Virginia Regiment Volunteer Infantry. He
died of typhoid fever during the Civil War. A gravestone
bearing his name is in the military cemetery at Winchester,
Virginia. However, this may be only symbolic, as other records
say that he is buried elsewhere. He is listed in the Doddridge
County, Virginia census of 1850 with his wife Clarinda and
daughter Nancy, aged 4 months. Also in the household were
Nathaniel Mitchel, b. Ohio, age 63, Hannah b. Ohio, age 45,
and Louisa, b. Ohio, age 14. These are Clarinda's parents and
younger sister. Before moving to Ritchie County in 1832, he
lived in Preston County, (West) Virginia.
Children of Amos Pritchard and Clarinda Mitchell are:
    i. **Nancy Ann Pritchard**, abt. 1849, Doddridge
       County, (West) Virginia; m. **James STOTTS**,
       25 Oct 1871, Roane County, West Virginia.

James was born 1848.

ii. **Mary L. Pritchard**, b. 1852, Ritchie County, West Virginia; m. **Peter HARRIS**, 01 May 1872, Roane County, West Virginia. Peter was born 1851.

iii. **Emily M. Pritchard**, b. 08 May 1853; d. 16 Nov 1860, Ritchie County, West Virginia.

iv. **James Franklin Pritchard**, b. 20 May 1855, Ritchie County, West Virginia; d. 1860, Ritchie County.

v. **Henrietta "Hannah" Pritchard**, b. 03 Oct 1857, Ritchie County, (West) Virginia; d. 1860, Ritchie County.

vi. **Percis Ellen Pritchard**, b. 1860, Ritchie County, West Virginia; m. (1) **James M. TILLER**, 11 Mar 1880, Roane County, West Virginia; m. (2) **John LONG** (b. Jan 1872) in 1900.

vii. **Lucinda Jane Pritchard**, b. October 1861; m. (1) **Daniel M. MAYNE** (b. 1838) 27 Nov 1892, Roane County, West Virginia; m. (2) **Jacob LONG** (b. abt. 1850) 25 Aug 1905, Roane County, West Virginia.

Lucinda J. Pritchard, 38, and her mother, Clarinda, 67, are both listed in the 1900 Roane County census as living with her sister, Ellen Long. Lucinda states that she is single (widowed? divorced?) and Clarinda states that she has been married for 52 years, even though her husband, who died during the Civil War, has been dead for more than 35 years. Lucinda's second husband, whom she marries in 1905, may be the brother of John Long, husband of Percis Ellen, who goes by her middle name. Roane County death records list her as Pruccis Ellen Long, aged 65 years, 6 months, 28 days, making

159

her five years younger than she actually is. Although John Long is listed as head of household in 1900, it is Clarinda's house.

THIRD GENERATION

60.

Elizabeth Watson, daughter of No. 46, Sarah Pritchard, was born 1816 in Harrison County, (West) Virginia. She married **Owen WESTFALL** 23 Sep 1834 in Harrison County, (West) Virginia, son of **Zachariah WESTFALL** and **Hannah WOLF**. Owen was born 1815 in Harrison County.
Child of Elizabeth Watson and Owen Westfall is:

> i. **Harvey Westfall**, b. 1836, Lewis County, (West) Virginia.

61.

Mary Watson, daughter of No. 46, Sarah Pritchard, was born 1817 in Harrison County, (West) Virginia. She married **John JETT, Jr.,** 1836 in Harrison County, son of **John W. JETT, Sr.** and **Sarah SMITH**. He was born 1813 in Harrison County and died 23 Oct, 1889 in Roane County, West Virginia. Both are buried in Spring Creek Cemetery, Roane County.
Children of Mary Watson and John Jett are:

> i. **Otho Jett.**
> ii. **Wesley Wilson Jett**, b. 1837; d. 11 Jul 1860, Ritchie County; lived in Roane County, West Virginia.
> iii. **George Jett**, b. abt. 1838; d. child.
> iv. **William Jett**, b. 1840, Harrison County, (West) Virginia; d. 1922, Berea, Ritchie County, West Virginia; m. **Safronia/Sophronia E. LOWTHER** (b.1845; d. 1922), 11 Oct 1866, Berea, Ritchie County, West Virginia; lived at Otterslide, Ritchie County, West Virginia.

v. **Jacob Jett**, b. 1842; lived in Roane County, West Virginia.

vi. **Ellen Elizabeth Jett**, b. 1844; d. childhood.

vii. **Sylvester Jett**, b. 1846; lived at Holbrook, Ritchie County, West Virginia.

viii. **Alvin/Alden Jett**, b. 1848; lived in Charleston, Kanawha County, West Virginia

ix. **Sarah Jett**, b. abt. 1849; d. child.

x. **John Jett, Jr.**, b. abt. 1851; lived in Kanawha County, West Virginia.

xi. **Elizabeth Jett**, b. abt. 1853; d. child.

62.

William Watson, son of No. 46, Sarah Pritchard, was born 1818 in Mercer County, (West) Virginia, and died 09 Feb 1890 in Roane County, West Virginia. He married **Nancy UNK**. William Watson is listed in the 1850 Doddridge County census, age 31, as a farmer. At that time, his family included Nancy, 30; Malinda, 8; Sarah, 6; Juliet, 4; Martha and Mary, twins, age one.

Children of William Watson and Nancy are:

i. **Malinda Watson**, b. 1842.

ii. **Sarah Watson**, b. 1844.

iii. **Juliet Watson**, b. 1846.

iv. **Martha Watson**, b. 1849.

v. **Mary Watson**, b. 1849.

63.

George W. Watson, son of No. 46, Sarah Pritchard, was born 14 Feb 1822 in (West) Virginia and died 14 Oct 1863 in Berea, Ritchie County, West Virginia. He married **Susan DIVERS** in Ritchie County. Both are buried in the Auburn Cemetery.

Children of George Watson and Susan Divers are:

102.   i. **Mary C. Watson**, b. 18 Aug 1843, Auburn, Ritchie County, (West) Virginia; d. 01 Jan 01, 1914, Berea, Ritchie County, West Virginia.

103.   ii. **Martha A. Watson**, b. 1845, Barbour County, West Virginia; d. 1884 Ritchie County.

  iii. **Morgan B. Watson**, b. 1847, Military Service: Company E, 5th West Virginia Infantry, Civil War; lived in Auburn, Ritchie County, West Virginia; buried in Auburn Community Cemetery.

  iv. **Adaline Watson**, b. 1848, m. **Marshall HALL**, moved to Colorado.

  v. **Margaret "Jennie" Watson**, b. 1852, Ritchie County, (West) Virginia m. married **Francis M. SUMMERS** (b. 1850, Doddridge County, (West) Virginia), 30 Oct 1873, Ritchie County, West Virginia.

  vi. **John M. Watson**, b. 11 Aug 1854.

  vii. **Andrew J. Watson**, b. 1856.

  viii. **Alice V. Watson**, b. 1858, Ritchie County; m. **Elijah W. ADAMS** (b. 1858, Doddridge County, West Virginia), 16 Jan 1879, Ritchie County, West Virginia.

  ix. **Wilson D. Watson**, b. 1859. d. 08 Apr. 1930, Auburn, m. Nancy R. Sommerville.

  x. **Eliza Ellen Watson**, b. 12 Dec 1860, Ritchie County, West Virginia; m. **John NEWBERRY** (b, 1859, Roane County), 28 Aug 1879, Ritchie County.

  xi. **George Watson**, lived in Parkersburg, Wood County, West Virginia.

64.

Amanda Watson, daughter of No. 46, Sarah Pritchard, was born in 1827. She married **Lemuel DIVERS**. He was born in 1827.

Child of Amanda Watson and Lemuel Divers is:

    i. **Charles Divers**, b. 1848.

65.

John Watson, son of No. 46, Sarah Pritchard, was born 1835 and died in Holbrook, Ritchie County, West Virginia. He married (1) **Katherine THRASH**. She was born in Barbour County, West Virginia, and died in Holbrook, Ritchie County, West Virginia. He married (2) **Susan/Sarah MAXWELL**. John and Katherine are buried in Lowther Cemetery, Holbrook, Ritchie County.

Children of John Watson and Katherine Thrash are:

    i. **Nealy Watson.**

    ii. **Jacob M. Watson.**

    iii. **Thomas Watson.**

    iv. **David Watson.**

    v. **Scott Watson.**

    vi. **Grant Watson.**

    vii. **John "Jack" Watson.**

Children of John Watson and Susan Maxwell are:

    viii. **Laura J. Watson**, b. 1882; d. 1967; m. **Charles W. SINNETT** (b. 1873; d. 1947); both buried Auburn Community Cemetery, Ritchie County, West Virginia.

    ix. **Charles S. Watson.**

    x. **Dora Watson.**

    xi. **Sarah Watson.**

    xii. **Mary Watson.**

xiii. **Joseph Watson.**
xiv. **Morgan Watson**.

66.

George Pritchard, son of No. 47, Peter Pritchard, was born 19
May 1822 in (West) Virginia, and died14 Oct 1902. He
married **Charlotte J. ELEFRITZ** (also spelled
ELLIFRITTS), 17 Feb 1844 by Rev. George Collins in
Ritchie County, daughter of **Samuel ELEFRITZ** and **Mary
UNK**. Charlotte was born 08 Dec 1827 in Maryland, and died
1902 in Ritchie County, West Virginia. Both are buried in the
White Oak Cemetery, Ritchie County, West Virginia. George
is one of the signers of the Ritchie County Constitution of
1872.

Children of George Pritchard and Charlotte are:

104. i. **John Wesley Pritchard**, b. 02 Jan 1846, Ritchie
County (West) Virginia; d. 05 Aug 1908,
Parkersburg, Wood County, West Virginia.

105. ii. **Morgan R. Pritchard**, b.13 Dec 1847, Ritchie
County, (West) Virginia; d. 03 Apr 1915.

106. iii. **Andrew L. Pritchard**, b. 03 Mar 1850; d. 10 Mar
1878.

iv. **Viola J. Pritchard**, b. 03 Aug 1852; m. **Thomas
Corbin SNODGRASS** (1843-1920), son of No.
53, Mary Pritchard; both buried in Pullman
Cemetery, Ritchie County, West Virginia. Viola
died 1922.

v. **Mary E. Pritchard**, b. 24 Nov 1854; d. 14 Feb
1872, Ritchie County, West Virginia. Her
gravestone in White Oak Cemetery states she
was 17 years, 3 months, 20 days at time of
death.

vi. **Sara Alice Pritchard**, b. 18 Feb 1857, Ritchie County, (West) Virginia; d. 12 Jun 1877, Ritchie County, m. **Unk KIRKPATRICK**. Went by the name Alice.

107. vii. **Louis Maxwell Pritchard**, b. 11 Feb 1860, Ritchie County, (West) Virginia.

108. viii. **Helen Virginia Pritchard**, b. 16 Aug 1863, Ritchie County, West Virginia.

109. ix. **Ardena A. Pritchard**, b. 08 Sep 1867, Ritchie County, West Virginia; d. 08 Sep 1877, Ritchie County.

x. **George McNeel Pritchard**, b. 05 Oct 1873; d. 21 Dec 1890; buried Cannon Cemetery, Ritchie County, West Virginia. He went by Mack.

67.

Nancy P. Pritchard, daughter of No. 47, Peter Pritchard, was born 04 Aug 1824 in Harrison County, (West) Virginia, and died 26 Nov 1903 in Oxford, Ritchie County, West Virginia. She married **Alpheus E. HOLT/HOULT** 1841 in Harrison County, (West) Virginia. He was born 1820 in Harrison County.

Children of Nancy Pritchard and Alpheus Holt are:

i. **William E. Holt**, b. 1841.

ii. **Ella Holt**, b. 1864.

68.

Thomas Willis Pritchard, son of No. 47, Peter Pritchard, was born 15 Oct 1825 in Ritchie County, (West) Virginia and died 30 Jun 1885 in Ritchie County. He married **Amanda Virginia LAWSON** 20 Dec 1855 in Ritchie County, daughter of **William LAWSON** and **Eliza MARSHALL**. Her middle name is also recorded as Victoria. Her gravestone states that she died at 40 years, 10 months, 4 days.

The Lawson Family

The first known Lawson in Virginia is **Rowland LAWSON**, born 1617 in Northumberland, England, died 1660 in Virginia. He married **Lettice WALES**, born abt. 1626 in England. They were married abt. 1643 in Lancaster County, Virginia and left many descendants.

The first known Lawson in Maryland is **John LAWSON,** who lived at "Lynn," Popular Hill, St. Mary's County Maryland. In 1650, he was appointed as one of the Parliamentary Commissioners to govern Maryland under Oliver Cromwell, July 1654- March 1657. He was High Sheriff of St. Mary's County, 1665-1666 and Justice of the Peace, St. Mary's County in 1666. The name of his wife and children are not known. It is possible that he was the grandfather of the following John Lawson

1.

John LAWSON I is the first known ancestor of Amanda Lawson. He was born about 1698 in Baltimore County, Maryland, and died 15 Mar 1767 in Gunpowder Manor, Maryland. He married (1) **Frances DAVIS**. They lived near the border between York County, Pennsylvania and Baltimore County, Maryland. This justifies the recorded birth of his son, John Lawson II, in Pennsylvania about 1725. Although the land of John Lawson I was on the border of Pennsylvania, his estate records are in Baltimore County. Previously, he had property on Gunpowder Manor, Baltimore County, Maryland. Children of John Lawson and Frances Davis are:

167

2.   i. **John Lawson II**, b. abt. 1725, Pennsylvania.

       ii. **Mary Lawson**, b. 03 Sep 1726.

3.   iii. **Thomas Lawson**, b. abt. 1728.

       iv. **Anne Lawson**, b. 1730

       v. **Elizabeth Lawson**, b. 1733.

       vi. **Moses Lawson**, 1736.

2.

John Lawson II was born about 1725 in Pennsylvania. He married **Elizabeth UNK** 14 Nov 1748 in St. John, St. George Parish, Maryland.

Child of John Lawson II and Elizabeth is:

       i. **John Lawson III**, b. abt 1749, Maryland; d. 1797, Fayette County, Kentucky. He married **Sarah HARRATT,** Nov 1704 St. John, St. George Parish, Maryland.

Children of John Lawson III and Sarah Harratt are:

       i. **John LAWSON IV**, b. 10 Nov 1769 married **Eve HARNIST** 13 Feb 1803 Rockingham County, Virginia. She was b. 1786 in Pennsylvania and d. 23 Mar 1877. She was the daughter of **Michael HARNIST** (German).

John and Eve were among the early settlers to locate in the Beldore Hollow southeast of Elkton. John served in the War of 1812, 58 Regiment, 3rd Battalion. He was disabled and discharged near Richmond, Virginia in Oct. 1814. Both are buried in Thomas Wyant Cemetery, Beldore Area, near Elkton, Virginia.

Children of John Lawson IV and Eve Harnist are:

       i. **Moses Lawson**, b. 1804, Orange County, d. 20 Mar 1879 Rockingham County, m. **Rebecca BAUGHER**

The Pritchard/Prickett Family History

ii. **Elizabeth Lawson**, b. 21 Jul 1806, Rockingham
County, Virginia, d. 06 Feb 1890, Beldore,
Rockingham County, m. 05 Dec 1826 **David
WYANT.**

iii. **Joseph William Lawson**, b. 26 May 1809; d. 27
Feb 1894; m. **Selina SNOW** 17 Feb 1835
Orange County, Virginia.

iv. **Alfred Lawson**, b. 1810; d. 1876, Brimfield, Peoria
County, Illinois; m. **Frances Ellen WYANT,** 10
Feb 1835, Rockingham County, Virginia.

v. **Matilda Lawson**, b. 1811; m. 11 Mar 1837 **Jacob
HUPP;** lived in Shenandoah County, Virginia,
then removed to Licking County, Ohio.

vi. **Mary Lawson,** b. 1812;

vii. **Malinda Lawson**, b. Nov 1816, Rockingham
County, Virginia; m. 15 Jan 1838, Rockingham
County, **William E. MARSHALL,** b. abt.
1825, son of **Thomas MARSHALL** and
Nancy ANCELL.

viii. **Nancy Lawson,** b. 1820, Rockingham County,
Virginia; m. 11 Jan 1843 Albemarle County,
Virginia, **Nicholas A. SHIFLETT**, b. abt.
1820, son of **Absalom SHIFFLET** and **Winnie
HERRING**. Nicholas was listed in the 88th
Virginia Militia as a Private.

ix. **Theophilus Lawson**, b. 21 Oct 1821; d. 10 Jun
1890, bur. Sullivan Cemetery, Simmons Gap
Road (Rte. 628); m. 14 Apr 1844 by Rev. John
Gibson, Rockingham Co., **Margaret Caroline
HERRING**, b. Sep 1829, daughter of **Loudon
Brightberry BRUCE** and **Polly HERRING**.
Theophilus is listed in the 1860 Albermarle

169

The Pritchard/Prickett Family History

Census, Fredericksville Parish. His land in
Rockingham County came from purchase from
his father. Theophilus served in the 58th
Virginia Militia Company as a Private.

A more detailed family history of the Lawsons of Virginia is
found at http://shifletfamily.org/RFC/Lawson/index.htm. Over
the years, the Lawson families of Virginia and Maryland
intermarried.

3.

Thomas Lawson, born about 1728, married **Rebecca
WOODALL** 14 Jul 1748 in Ann Arundel County, Maryland.
Child of Thomas Lawson and Rebecca Woodall is:
4.　　i. **John Lawson, Sr.,** b. abt. 1752, Maryland; d.
　　　　aft. 1810, Harrison County, (West) Virginia.

4.

John Lawson, Sr. was born about 1752 in Maryland, and died
after 1810, probably in Beard's Run, Simpson District,
Harrison County, (West) Virginia. He married **Rebecca
SMITH** before 1779, probably in Maryland. She was born
about 1760 in Maryland or Virginia, and died between 1820
and 1840, probably in Beard's Run, Simpson District, Harrison
County, (West) Virginia.
According to Don Norman's account on the Hacker's Creek
web site, the couple came to Harrison County, (West) Virginia
in 1817. John Lawson probably moved from Maryland to the
Shenandoah Valley, where marriage records exist for some of
his children. His son John, Jr. is said to have settled in Warren
County, which borders Shenandoah County. The 1820 census
shows John, Jr. in Shenandoah County and Theophilus in

170

The Pritchard/Prickett Family History

Harrison County. The 1830 census shows John, Jr. still living in Frederick County. He died in Warren County, which was formed out of Frederick in 1836. Therefore, he probably did not move but continued living in the same place.

Children of John Lawson and Rebecca Smith are:

    i. **Nancy Lawson**, b. 1779; m. **John KELLEY.**

    ii. **Rebecca Lawson**, b. 1781; m. **James HANCOCK/HANDCOCK**, 15 Mar 1800, Shenandoah County, Virginia. They were married by William Williamson; marriage bond posted 06 Mar 1800.

    iii. **Alexander "Shauney" Lawson,** b. 1783; m. **Mary Polly CARTER** (b. abt. 1792), 23 May 1808, Fauquier County, Virginia.

5.   iv. **Theopolus Lawson**, b. 1785; m. **Rebecca HANCOCK** 1804.

    v. **William Lawson**, b. 18 Nov 1786, Shenandoah or Frederick County, Virginia; d. 18 May 1871, Beard's Run, Harrison County, (West) Virginia; m. **Rebecca GRIGSBY** (b.1792) 17 Oct 1809, Frederick County, Virginia; bur. Teter Cemetery, Coplin's Run, Harrison County, (West) Virginia.

    vi. **Mary Ann Lawson**, b. 1788.

    vii. **John Lawson, Jr.,** b. 1792, Shenandoah County, Virginia; d. Warren County, Virginia.

    viii. **Holzen Lawson,** b. 1794; m. **Hannah GRIFFITH**,11 Aug 1823, Shenandoah County, Virginia.

5.

Theopolus/Theophilis Lawson, son of John Lawson Sr., was
born 1785. He married **Rebecca HANCOCK** in 1804.
Children of Theopolus Lawson and Rebecca Hancock are:
6.   i. **William Lawson**, b. 1804, Virginia; d. before
     30 May 1850, Warren County, Virginia.
7.   ii. **Elias Lawson**, b. 1805, d. 1871, Harrison County,
     West Virginia. He married **Elizabeth TETER,**
     daughter of **George TETER** (1739-1826) and
     Mary SHARP (1773-1841) of Pendleton
     County, (West) Virginia. The surname Teter is
     derived from the German Dieter.

6.

William Lawson, son of **Theopolus Lawson** and **Rebecca
HANCOCK**, m. **Eliza MARSHALL**, daughter of **Francis
MARSHALL, Jr.** and **Phoebe HATCHER,** 01 Jun 1825 in
Shenandoah County, Virginia. The Shenandoah County
Marriage Book lists William Lawson, son of Rebecca, and
Eliza Marshall, daughter of Francis, on 20 Jun 1825.

The Marshall Family
     The earliest known ancestor of Francis Marshall in the
Colonies is **Alexander MARSHALL**, who was born 1676 in
Henrico County, Virginia. He married **Elizabeth
WORSHAM**, daughter of **John WORSHAM** and **Phoebe
UNK** about 1705. Elizabeth was born about 1679 and died 03
May 1743, in Henrico County, Virginia.
     Francis MARSHALL, Sr., son of Alexander Marshall
and Elizabeth Worsham, was born 1712 in Powhatan County,
Virginia. He married **Mary THOMPSON.**
     Francis MARSHALL, Jr., their son, was born 11 Aug

1750 and died 23 Jan 1836. He was a Captain in the Revolutionary War from the state of Virginia, according to both DAR and Tennessee State records. He is listed under SAR #56084667A-1. The listing of Tennessee Pensioners finds that Francis Marshall was 84 years of age in 1832. He served in the Virginia militia, and drew his pension in Sumner County, Tennessee, where he is buried with a DAR marker on his grave. He married (1) **Phoebe HATCHER** 1773 in Mechlenberg County, Virginia. After she died in 1809, he married (2) **Sarah JACOBS**, who survived him. Francis Marshall and Sarah Marshall are listed as charter members of Sharon Baptist Church 1827-1860, Prince Edward County, Virginia. The church records are preserved in the library of the Virginia Baptist Historical Society.

Francis Marshall, Jr. likely moved to Tennessee to be near several children who moved there earlier. His will, written in 1835, mentions *"my son David Marshall...to David Hardaway, Jess, and the heirs of Richard Marshall, certain property...my eight other children: Nancy, Phoebe, Josiah, Francis, Polly, Rebecca, Elizabeth (Eliza), and Jane. To Partheny and Malena Marshall, not yet 21, and wife Sarah Marshall."* The will was proved in 1836 and appears on p. 208 of the Sumner County, Tennessee Will abstracts 1788-1842, taken from Sumner County Will Book 2, p. 62. The Hardaway citation above refers to John Willis Hardaway Marshall, who married Elma Bertha Adkins in Pittsylvania County, Virginia. His father is listed as Francis Marshall and his mother as Phebe (sic) Hatcher. John's will proved in Sumner County, Tennessee in 1819 is evidence that he died nearly two decades earlier than his father.

Children of Francis Marshall and Phoebe Hatcher are:

    i. **John Willis Hardaway Marshall**, d. 1819,

Sumner County, Tennessee; m. **Emma Bertha ADKINS**, 1800, Pittsylvania County, Virginia.
 ii. **Francis Marshall, III,** b. abt. 1800; m. **Jane HATCHER.**
 iii. **Elizabeth "Eliza" Marshall**, b. 1801, Virginia; d. May 1874, Ritchie County, West Virginia, m. **William LAWSON,** Shenandoah County, Virginia, 20 Jun 1825.
 iv. **Nancy Marshall.**
 v. **Phoebe Marshall,** m. **Peter COUSINS.**
 vi. **Josiah Marshall**, m. **Martha BENNETT.**
 vii. **Polly Marshall**.
 viii. **Rebecca Marshall**.
 ix. **Jane Marshall,** m. **William ANTHONY**.
 x. **David Marshall**.

Children of William Lawson and Eliza Marshall are:
 xi. **John Francis Lawson**, b.08 May 1826, Warren County, Virginia; d. 11 Aug 1905, Rockingham County, Virginia; m. **Amanda LONG** (b. 26 Jul 1831; d. 09 Apr 1900), Rockingham County, Virginia).

John Francis Lawson was the first merchant in Ritchie County, (West) Virginia. The 1850 census lists John F. Lawson, 26, born in Maryland, a merchant, living with William Pritchard, 18, farmer; John Pritchard, 16, farmer, Cassandra Pritchard, 13; Jane Pritchard 10. This is the family of Peter Pritchard without George and Nancy, who probably were married by then, and Thomas Willis Pritchard, who married John's sister, Amanda Virginia Lawson in 1855. Peter Pritchard and his wife were still alive at that time, so it is not

Amanda Virginia Lawson, wife of Thomas Willis Pritchard

174b

clear why they are not listed in the census. John F. Lawson and
Amanda Long had six children before returning to their family
home in Rockingham County, where both are buried in the
Adam Long Cemetery.

ii. **Jackson Lawson**, b. 1827, Warren County,
Virginia; d. August 1854, age 27, of typhoid
fever, Warren County; m. **Demara BOOTH**,
Warren County.

iii. **Bushrod Washington Lawson**, b. 19 Apr 1829,
Warren County, Virginia; d. 1914, Fairmont,
Marion County, West Virginia; m. **Anna
PRITCHARD,** No. 70, 01 Dec 1853, Ritchie
County, (West) Virginia.

iv. **Eliza Lawson**, b. 1832, Warren County, Virginia;
d. 23 May 1854 of consumption, age 22,
Warren County; m. **James M. MATTHEWS**.

v. **Salathial Oral Lawson**, b. May 1836, Warren
County, Virginia; d. 27 Nov 1910, Travis
County, Texas; m. **Elmina MEREDITH**, No.
612.

vi. **Amanda Virginia Lawson**, b. 31 Mar 1838,
Warren County, Virginia; d. February,
1879, Ritchie County, West Virginia; m.
Thomas Willis PRITCHARD, No. 68,
20 Dec 1855.

vii. **Berthine Lawson**, b. abt. 1840; m. **Coleman
McDOUGAL**, 03 Sep 1861, Ritchie
County, West Virginia.

7.

Children of Elias Lawson and Elizabeth Teter are:

i. **Theophilus Washington Lawson**, b. 15 Jan 1838,

Harrison County, (West) Virginia; d. 14 May
1911, Harrison County, (West) Virginia; m.
Elizabeth BAILEY 12 Sep 1850, Taylor
County, (West) Virginia.

ii. **Joseph Lawson**, b.1825; d. 1884.

iii. **Hannah Lawson**, b. 1832.

iv. **Rachel Lawson,** b. 1832 (twins)

v. **Rebecca Lawson,** b. 1834.

vi. **Catherine Lawson** b. 1840

vii. **Henry Thomas Lawson**, b. 1840; d. 1916.

ix. **Melvina Elizabeth Lawson,** b. 1843; d. 1908.

Children of Theophilus Washington Lawson and Elizabeth
Bailey are:

i. **Joseph Columbus Lawson (M.D.)** b. 11 May 1852,
Harrison County, West Virginia; d. 08 Dec
1935, Auburn, Ritchie County, West Virginia;
m. **Araminita Price BUSH,** (b. 1866; d. 1924)
14 Jun, 1887 in Cumberland, Allegheny
County, Maryland.

ii. **Rachel Melvina Lawson,** b. 1854, d. 1932; m.
Jacob D. MARPLE.

iii. **Kittie Ann Lawson**, b. 1865; d. 1955.

iv. **Mary Byrd Lawson**, 1869; d. 1955; m. **Arthur
Augustus CATHER**.

v. **Silas Bailey Lawson**, b. 1874, d. 1903.

Child of Joseph Columbus Lawson and Araminita Price Bush
is:

i. **Willie Lawson**, b. 1889, Auburn, Ritchie County,
West Virginia; bc. 21 Sep 1968, Buckhannon,
Upshur County. She married **Lowery Elzy
OLDAKER,** a Methodist Minister, b. 1882;

d.1930), on 12 Oct 1911 in Auburn, Ritchie County, West Virginia.

Children of Lowery Elzy Oldaker and Willie Lawson are:

  i. **Joseph Elzy Oldaker**, b. 1812, d. 2005.

  ii, **Edward Lawson Oldaker**, b. 07 Sep 1916, Shinnston, Harrison County, West Virginia; d. 19 Apr 2011, Buckhannon, Upshur County, West Virginia; m. 12 Jul 1948, Weston, Lewis County, West Virginia. Ed Oldaker was a devoted researcher of the Lawson family. He lived and worked for many years in Mesa, Arizona, but returned to West Virginia in later years and lived to the age of 95.

  iii. **Geneva Price Oldaker**. b. 15 Oct 1918 in Shinnston, Harrison County, West Virginia; d. 2010; m. **Roy TAYLOR**

  iv. **David Lynn Oldaker**, b. 1921; d. 2004.

  v. **William B. Oldaker**, b. 1929; d. 2001.

68. (Continued)

Children of Thomas Pritchard and Amanda Lawson are:

110.   i. **Millard Fillmore Pritchard**, b. 22 Sep 1857, Ritchie County; West Virginia; d. 19 July 1927, Clarksburg, Harrison County, West Virginia. Buried Elk View Masonic Cemetery, Clarksburg, West Virginia.

111.   ii. **Sarah Eliza Pritchard**, b. 30 Mar 1859, Ritchie County, West Virginia; d. 08 Nov 1922.

112.   iii. **Giles William Pritchard**, b. 21 Jun 1861, Ritchie County, West Virginia; d. 30 Oct 1912, Fairmont, Marion County.

113.   iv. **Judson Fantley Pritchard**, b. 17 Jan 1864, Ritchie

County, West Virginia; d. 01 Apr 1946, Weston, Lewis County, West Virginia.

114.   v. **Ira Sanford Pritchard**, b. 17 Sep 1866, Ritchie County, West Virginia; d. 19 Feb 1960.

115.   vi. **Francis Ezra Pritchard**, b. 11 Sep 1870, Ritchie County, West Virginia; d. 16 Jan 1950, Ritchie County, WV.

116.   vii. **Bushrod Washington Pritchard**, b. 22 Jul 1873, Ritchie County, West Virginia; d. 17 Mar 1956, Weston, Lewis County, WV.

117.   viii. **Walter Icen Pritchard**, b. 22 Apr 1876, Ritchie County, West Virginia; d. 01 May 1953, Weston, Lewis County, WV.

69.

Harriet Pritchard, daughter of No. 47, Peter Pritchard, was born about 1827 in Harrison County (West) Virginia. She married **Henry Sleeth WALDECK** 16 Jun 1842 in Harrison County, son of **Hans WELDECK** and **Mary SLEETH**. He was born 07 Oct 1819 in Harrison County, (West) Virginia. Children of Harriet Pritchard and Henry Waldeck are:

    i. **Ebenezer Waldeck**, b. 1845.
    ii. **Virginia Waldeck**, b. 1848.
    iii. **George Waldeck**, b. 1849.

70.

Anna Pritchard, daughter of No 47, Peter Pritchard, was born 26 Feb 1828 in (West) Virginia and died 08 Aug 1871. She married **Bushrod Washington LAWSON** 01 Dec 1853 in Ritchie County, (West) Virginia, son of **William LAWSON** and **Eliza MARSHALL**. After her death, Bushrod Washington

178

Lawson married (2) **Fanny PRUNTY,** 21 Nov 1872 in Ritchie County, West Virginia, daughter of **Jacob PRUNTY,** and had five children by her. Fanny was born about 1839 in Ritchie County; Bushrod Lawson died 1914 in Fairmont, West Virginia.

Larry Heffner (lheffner@vonl.com) quotes from a poem written in 1924 by Rev. I. S. Hall honoring Bushrod W. Lawson, Thomas, John, and George Pritchard, others:
"So able in prayer, It seemed the spirit of God was there...
   Directing his mind to the throne above,
   Interceding for us through the God of love."

Children of Anna Pritchard and Bushrod Washington Lawson are:

      i. **William M. Lawson,** b. 28 May 1855; d. 20 Aug 1861.

      ii. **Elizabeth Jane Lawson,** b. 21 May 1857; d. 10 Aug 1861.

      iii. **Lydia/Lyda Lawson,** b. 09 Nov 1859, Ritchie County, (West) Virginia; m. **M. R. LOWTHER,** Ritchie County, West Virginia; d. Parkersburg, Wood County, West Virginia.

118.   iv. **Flora Odell Lawson,** b. 09 Nov 1861, Oxford, Ritchie County, West Virginia; d. 18 May 1932, Fairmont, Marion County, West Virginia.

      v. **Nancy Ellen Lawson,** b. 03 Mar 1864 in Ritchie County, West Virginia; d. 1958, Oxford, Ritchie County; m. **David CLAYTON.** Both buried Pullman Cemetery, Ritchie County, West Virginia.

      vi. **Ferris Lincoln Lawson,** b. 20 Mar 1866; d. 04 Jul 1866.

      vii. **Dora B. Lawson,** b. 08 Jul 1867; d. 07 Oct 1870.

    viii. **Alma L. Lawson,** b. 28 Jul 1869; d. 30 Sep 1878,
        bur. White Oak Cemetery.
    ix. **Paul Lawson**, b. July 1871; d. 03 Aug 1871,
        bur. White Oak Cemetery.

71.

William Tyler Pritchard, son of No. 47, Peter Pritchard, was born 21 Apr 1832 in Ritchie County, (West) Virginia, and died 09 May 1911 in Ritchie County, West Virginia. He married **Hettie Ester DAVIS**. She was born 1831 in Ohio and died 1925 in Webster County, West Virginia. She is buried in Pennsboro Masonic Cemetery, Ritchie County.
Children of William Tyler Pritchard and Hettie Davis are:
    i. **Lloyd Wallace Pritchard**, b. 1853; lived in
        Pennsboro, Ritchie County, West Virginia.
    ii. **Alice C. Pritchard**, b. 1860; m. **Unk YATES**. He
        may be the son of James Alexander and Sarah
        Jane Robinson Yates.
119.   iii. **Charles J. Pritchard**, b. abt. 1865, Doddridge
        County, West Virginia; d. Webster County,
        West Virginia, 1896.
120.   iv. **William A. Pritchard**, b. 28 Dec 1865; d. 29 Oct
        1911.
121.   v. **Olin D. Pritchard**, b. 1868; d. 1959.

72.

John Pritchard, son of No. 47, Peter Pritchard, was born 22 Oct 1834 in (West) Virginia and died 05 Aug 1919 in Ritchie County. However, his gravestone in White Oak Cemetery states that he was born 22 Oct 1832. His marriage to **Melvina COWAN** 06 Jun 1867 was performed by Rev. W. H. Wiley. Melvina was born 15 Jun 1844 and died 15 Aug 1919 in

Ritchie County, West Virginia.

John Pritchard is listed in the 1870 Census as living in Union Township, Harrisville, West Virginia. At that time, he was 36, Melvina was 30, and their daughter Cora was one. Also living with them were Peter, 71, and Nancy, 47. Evidently Elizabeth Willis Pritchard was no longer alive.

Children of John Pritchard and Melvina Cowan are:

- i. **Cora Pritchard**, b. abt. 1869; d. 1955; m. **Unk SHARPNACK**. She is buried in the Pritchard Cemetery, Ritchie County, West Virginia. Her gravestone birth date is given as 1858.

122. ii. **Laura Pritchard**, b. 10 May 1871, Ritchie County, West Virginia; d. 1935.

- iii. **Lakin Pritchard**, b. 1873, Ritchie County, West Virginia; d. 1936, Ritchie County, West Virginia; m. **Unk BELL**. His name is also spelled as Larkin. Both are buried in the Pritchard Cemetery, Ritchie County.

73.

Cassandra Pritchard, daughter of No. 47, Peter Pritchard, was born 29 Nov 1836 in Barbour County, (West) Virginia, and died 18 Mar 1911. She is buried in Bethany Cemetery, Ritchie County. She married **Harrison Ellsworth WASS** 06 Mar 1856 in Ritchie County, son of **John WASS** and **Barbara BOYER**. They were married by Rev. J. B. Hill. Harrison was born 06 Feb 1834 and died 05 Apr 1923. Cassandra was also known as Cara. Her gravestone states "Cassa" along with given name.

Harrison and Cassandra Pritchard Wass lived at the mouth of Lamb's Run on Alum Fork of Bone Creek until the close of the Civil War. Then they moved to "the old homestead above Goff's," where they lived until 1908 when they moved to Harrisonville, Ritchie County. Harrison Wass was a farmer. He served in the Union Army in Company E, 6th Reg., West Virginia Infantry.

Children of Cassandra Pritchard and Harrison Wass are:

123.   i. **William Morgan Wass**, b. 19 Jan 1857, Ritchie County (West) Virginia; d. 17 Jul 1942, Mariposa County, California

         ii. **Sophronia Jane Wass**, b. 14 Sep 1858, Ritchie County, (West) Virginia; d. 07 Jul 1860; bur. Pleasant Hill Cemetery, Ritchie County, West Virginia.

124.   iii. **Lewis Maxwell Wass**, b. 26 Sep 1860, Ritchie County, West Virginia; d. 16 Nov 1947, Mariposa County, California.

125.   iv. **Harrison Ellsworth Wass, Jr.** b. 13 Feb 1863, Ritchie County, West Virginia; d. 14 Nov 1945, Harrisville, Ritchie County, West Virginia.

126.   v. **John Anderson Wass**, b. 04 Jun 1865, Ritchie County, West Virginia; d. March 1936, Huntington, Cabell County, West Virginia.

127.   vi. **Barbara Alice Wass**, b. 01 Nov 1867, Ritchie County, West Virginia; d. 30 Nov 1962, Harrisville, Ritchie County, West Virginia.

128.   vii. **Peter Wass**, b. 19 May 1870, Ritchie County, West Virginia; d. 12 Dec 1951, Hazelgreen, Ritchie County, West Virginia.

129. viii. **Charles Grant Wass**, b.12 Sep 1872, Ritchie County, West Virginia; d. 19 Jan 1950, Harrisonville, Ritchie County, West Virginia.

130.   ix. **Roy Wass**, b. 09 Jun 1875, Ritchie County,

West Virginia; d. 04 Apr 1954, Ritchie
County, West Virginia.
131.   x. **James Rienzi Wass,** b. 27 Oct 1878, Ritchie
County, West Virginia; d. 1912, Huntington,
Cabell County, West Virginia.
xi. **Daisy Dell Wass,** b. 26 Mar 1882, Ritchie
County, West Virginia; d. 16 Jun 1904, bur.
Bethany Cemetery, Ritchie County.

74.

Nancy Caster, daughter of No. 48, Margaret Peggy Pritchard,
was born 09 Nov 1824 in Harrison County, (West) Virginia.
She married **William G. McPHERSON** 17 Mar 1846, in
Lewis County, (West) Virginia. He was born in 1805.
Children of Nancy Castor and William G. McPherson are:
i. **James McPherson,** b. 1846.
ii. **Daniel McPherson,** b. 1847.

75.

Daniel Caster, son of No. 48, Margaret Peggy Pritchard, was
born 07 Aug 1841 in Harrison County, (West) Virginia, and
died 14 Aug 1914 in Oberlin, Decatur County, Kansas. He
married (1) **Margaret TURNER** 01 Mar 1866 in Meigs
County, Ohio. He married (2) **Viola GREEN** 12 Jun 1879 in
Buffalo Park, Kansas, daughter of **Abbott Miles GREEN** and
Julia Ann CROWELL. She was born 20 Dec 1854 in Meigs
County, Ohio, and died 17 Jan 1938 in Decatur County,
Kansas.
Child of Daniel Caster and Viola Green is:
132.   i. **Bertha Fern Caster,** b. 10 Aug 1894, Decatur
County, Kansas; d. 17 Dec 1938, Rawlins
County, Kansas.

76.

Mary Williams, daughter of No. 49 Eleanor Pritchard, was born 25 Feb 1826 in Harrison County, (West) Virginia, and died 05 Mar 1899 in Greenwood, Doddridge County, West Virginia. She married **Hickman WALDO,** 20 Sep 1841 in Tyler County, (West) Virginia. He was born 28 Jan 1818 in Harrison County and died 22 Nov 1898 in Greenwood, Doddridge County, West Virginia.

      i. **Oscar Waldo**, b. 1842, Harrison County, West Virginia; d. child.

      ii. **Susan Jane Waldo,** b. 29 Feb 1844, Harrison County, West Virginia; m. **John DEBRULER,** 18 Jun 1872.

      iii. **Newton Gamaliel Waldo**, b. 11 Oct 1845, Doddridge County, (West) Virginia; m. **Rosella BOND** (b. 1852, Ritchie County), 11 Mar 1875, Ritchie County.

      iv. **Foster Williams Waldo**, b. 22 Jun 1848, Doddridge County, (West) Virginia; m. **Susan J. WISEMAN** (b. 1856, Doddridge County), 19 Oct, 1876, Ritchie County, West Virginia.

      v. **Francis Marion Waldo**, b. 04 Jun 1850, Doddridge County, (West) Virginia; m. **Gabriella DOTSON,** 14 Nov 1872, Doddridge County, West Virginia.

      vi. **Sarah Elizabeth Waldo**, b. 13 Mar 1852; m. **Wilfred D. COLLINS**, 14 Feb 1875, Doddridge County, West Virginia.

      vii. **John Edward Waldo**, b. 16 Sep 1853, Arnolds Creek, Doddridge County, (West) Virginia; m. **Charity P. BOND** (b. 1858, Ritchie County), 01 Jan 1880, Ritchie County, West Virginia.

viii. **Jasper Fenton Waldo**, b. 01 Jan 1856,
        Doddridge County, (West) Virginia; m. (1)
        Helen LAWRENCE; m. (2) **Anna**
        ELLEFRITT, 23 Dec 1880, Doddridge County,
        West Virginia.
  ix. **Sylvester Bartlett Waldo**, b. 15 Dec 1857,
        Doddridge County, (West) Virginia; m.
        Hannah GRAY, 20 Dec 1896, Doddridge
        County, West Virginia.
   x. **James Woods Waldo**, b. 17 Sep 1860,
        Doddridge County, West Virginia; m. **Avie L.**
        SHERWOOD, 07 Feb 1891, Doddridge
        County, West Virginia.
  xi. **Alice Viana Waldo**, b. 21 Jan 1863; m. **Joseph S.**
        ANKROM, 25 Dec 1891, Doddridge County,
        West Virginia.
 xii. **Thomas Grant Waldo**, b. 14 Oct 1865,
        Doddridge County, West Virginia; d. 22 Mar
        1880, Greenwood, Doddridge County; buried
        Toll Gate Baptist Cemetery, Doddridge County.
xiii. **George Hickman Waldo**, b. 26 Nov 1867,
        Doddridge County, West Virginia.

77.

Catherine Rebecca Queen, daughter of No. 50, Anna
Pritchard, was born 24 Jun 1830 in Harrison County, West
Virginia and died in 1921. She married **Joseph WHITE,** 13
Mar 1850 in Harrison County. He was born in 1829.
Children of Catherine Queen and Joseph White are:
    i. **Zachariah T. White; m. (1) Mary LORENTZ;**
       m. (2) **Betty WEST.**
   ii. **Daniel White,** b. 1853; d. 1940, Reger, Sullivan

County, Missouri; m. **Viola DOUGLASS**.

   iii. **George White; m. Olive REEDER**.

   iv. **Howard White**, b. 09 Mar 1863; m. **Cora STUART** (b. 03 Mar 1876), 12 Jul 1894.

   v. **James Queen White; m. Cora D. SIMONS**.

   vi. **Enoch White; m. Stella ADAMS**

133. vii. **Edith White**.

   viii. **Rachel Rebecca White; m. Charlie DAVISSON**.

   ix. **Abbie Ann White; m. West LOVELL**.

   x. **Elizabeth White; m. Minton LOWELL**.

78.

Rezin P. Queen, son of No. 50, Anna Pritchard, was born 27 Dec 1837 in Harrison County, (West) Virginia and died 16 Aug 1873. He is buried in Johnstown Cemetery, Harrison County. He married **Rebecca CLARK**, daughter of **Isaac CLARK** and **Martha HERZMAN**. He was killed while working at a saw mill.

Children of Rezin Queen and Rebecca Clark are:

134.   i. **Martha Ann Queen**, b. 28 Jul 1860.

135.   ii. **Marcellus Queen**, b. 14 Apr 1862.

136.   iii. **Mary Elizabeth Queen**, b. 1863; d. 1912.

137.   iv. **Sarah Catherine Queen**, b. 20 Mar 1866.

138.   v. **Lloyd C. Queen**, b. 27 Oct 1870.

79.

Nancy Ann Queen, daughter of No. 46, Anna Pritchard, was born 22 Mar 1841 in Harrison County, (West) Virginia. She married **Edwin CONLEY**.

Children of Nancy Queen and Edwin Conley are:

   i. **George Conley**.

ii. **John Conley.**
iii. **Charles Conley.**
iv. **James Conley.**
v. **Martha Conley.**
vi. **Adoline Conley.**
vii. **Salley Conley.**
139. viii. **Ella Conley.**
ix. **Fleda Conley.**

80.

Martha Queen, daughter of No. 50, Anna Pritchard, was born 20 Jul 1843 in Harrison County, (West) Virginia and died 06 Dec 1927 in Clarksburg, West Virginia. She married **William LOVE,** 15 Jun 1860 in Harrison County, son of **John LOVE** and **Mahala ROHRBOUGH**.
Children of Martha Queen and William Love are:
140. i. **Albinas Love.**
141. ii. **Earnest Love**, b. 14 Dec 1871.
142 iii. **Arnett Love.**
143. iv. **Nathan Love**, b. 01 Nov 1880.
144. v. **Ira Love.**
145. vi. **Zoie Love**, b. 05 Oct 1869.
146 vii. **Verny Love.**
viii. **Jett Love;** m. **Bell BICE**

81.

Lemuel Queen, son of No. 50, Anna Pritchard, was born 10 Oct 1845 in Harrison County, (West) Virginia, and died in Braxton County. He married **Sarah DIX,** 1865.
Children of Lemuel Queen and Sarah Dix are:
i. **Malissa Jane Queen**, b 22 Jun 1867.
ii. **Arena Queen**, b. 13 Oct, 1869.

iii. **Worton Queen**, b. 13 Dec 1872.

82.

Nathan P. Queen, son of No. 50, Anna Pritchard, was born 15 Aug 1848 in Peel Tree Run, Harrison County, (West) Virginia, and died 16 Oct 1911. He is buried in Old Johnstown Cemetery, Harrison County. He married **Sarah Jane TALBOT** in 1868. She was born in 1850 and died in 1925 at Johnstown, Harrison County, West Virginia.
Children of Nathan Queen and Sarah Talbot are:

     i. **Samuel T. Queen**, b. 25 Sep 1869, Harrison County, West Virginia; d. 15 Aug 1879, Harrison County.

147.   ii. **Floyd Dallet Queen**, b. 31 May 1875, Harrison County, West Virginia.

148.   iii. **Alvadore H. Queen**, b. 17 Aug 1880, Harrison County, West Virginia.

149.   iv. **Dowden Queen**, b. 07 Jun 1885, Harrison County, West Virginia.

150.   v. **Maude Queen**, b. 20 Jun 1887, Harrison County, West Virginia.

83.

Levi P. Queen, son of No. 51, Katherine Pritchard, was born 31 Jan 1829 in (West) Virginia and died 14 Feb 1854. He married **Anna McKINNEY**, 15 Aug 1850. She was born 03 Apr 1832, in Harrison County, (West) Virginia, and died 31 Aug 1853 in Harrison County.
Child of Levi Queen and Anna McKinney is:

     i. **William Parkey Queen**, b. 19 Mar 1852, Harrison County, West Virginia; d. 31 Jul 1853, Harrison County.

84.

Peter Queen, son of No. 51, Katherine Pritchard, was born 07 Oct 1832 in (West) Virginia and died 02 Jul 1910. He married **Martha DAVIS,** 20 Jul 1853 in Johnstown, Harrison County, (West) Virginia. She was born 29 Aug 1835 in Johnstown, Harrison County, and died 01 Jun 1909 in Johnstown. Peter was a carpenter and served in the 19th Virginia Cavalry under Col. W. L. Jackson and Capt. Coffman.

Children of Peter Queen and Martha Davis are:

      i. **Zeruah Queen**, b. 30 Nov 1856, Harrison County, (West) Virginia; d. 15 Mar 1882; m. **Morgan QUEEN** (b. 04 Oct 1849; d. 22 Jul 1919), Harrison County, West Virginia.

151.   ii. **David Lee Queen**, b.05 Dec 1866.

85.

Phineas Queen, son of No. 51, Katherine Pritchard, was born 17 Dec 1837 in (West) Virginia and died in 1922. He married **Phoebe Margaret STATEN,** 20 Jul 1856 in Johnstown, Harrison County, (West) Virginia. She was born 16 Oct 1842 in Rockbridge County, Virginia, and died August 1918.

Phineas Queen was a member of Company K, 17th Virginia Cavalry, under command of General Jenkins, until the death of the General. He then was transferred to the command of General M. Causland. Phineas went south on 14 Aug 1862 and took part in the following battles: Martinsburg, Gettysburg, Jones Cross Roads, Frederick City, and Boonsboro. It was his brigade of 6,000 men that held the 40,000 Union troops at Frederick City for four hours. His was the last regiment across the Potomac River on the retreat from Gettysburg. He also fought in the battles of Front Royal, Shepherdstown, Port

Republic, Winchester, and others. His regiment was at Lee's surrender at Appomattox Court House. He was a shoe and boot maker for over 32 years and owned a farm on Duck Creek, Harrison County.

His wife, Margaret Staten, moved to Grafton, (West) Virginia at the age of four. Her father owned what later became the B&O Railroad Yards in Grafton.

Children of Phineas Queen and Margaret Staten are:

         i. **Mary Elizabeth Queen**, b. 07 Jun 1860; d. infant.

152.   ii. **John Phineas Queen**, b. 30 Dec 1862; d. 21 May 1915, Harrison County, West Virginia.

153.   iii. **William Lloyd Queen**, b. 24 Sep 1870.

86.

George Queen, son of No. 51, Katherine Pritchard, was born 15 Mar 1840 in (West) Virginia and died 09 Apr 1921. He married **Sarah POST**, daughter of **Abram J. POST** and **Martha HENDSMAN.**

George Queen, a farmer, was a private in the Civil War. He enlisted in Company C, 31st Regiment of Virginia Volunteers on 21 May 1861. He deserted on 03 Jun 1861, but later re-enlisted. He served under General Stonewall Jackson as a member of the original Stonewall Brigade.

Children of George Queen and Sarah Post are:

154.   i. **Mary Queen**.

155.   ii. **Ella Queen**.

156.   iii. **Florence Queen**.

        iv. **Preston Queen; m. Unk KELLEY.**

157.   v. **Vida Queen.**

87.

Burrel M. Queen, son of No. 51, Katherine Pritchard, was born 07 Nov 1842 in (West) Virginia and died in 1926 at Johnstown, Harrison County, West Virginia. He married **Adelia "Delia" F. STOUT**, 23 Mar 1871, in Harrison County, West Virginia. She was the daughter of **Benjamin STOUT** and **Lydia PITCHER**. Delia was born 28 Dec 1852 in Harrison County, West Virginia, and died there on 18 Dec 1927. Burrel Queen, who owned a mill at Johnstown in Harrison County, was considered to be one of the best millers in the county. He served with his brother Phineas in the 17th Virginia Cavalry during the Civil War.

Children of Burrel Queen and Delia Stout are:

158.   i. **Augusta Maud Queen**, b. 02 Jun 1872, Harrison County, West Virginia.

159.   ii. **Percival Queen**, b. 19 Sep 1875, Harrison County, West Virginia; d. August 1906.

160.   iii. **Emmit Queen**, b. 11 Aug 1877, Harrison County, West Virginia.

        iv. **Hattie Queen**, b. 05 Mar 1880; d. 1906.

161.   v. **John Queen**, b. 14 Mar 1885; d. January 1915, Weston, West Virginia.

        vi. **Pearl Queen**, b. 23 Feb 1887.

88.

Ida Matilda Queen, daughter of No. 51, Katherine Pritchard, was born 17 Jan 1845 in Lost Creek, Harrison County, (West) Virginia, and died 21 Jan 1931. She married **Luther Martin ARNOLD**, 09 Oct 1865. He was born 04 Apr 1842 in Buckhannon Creek, Upshur County, (West) Virginia.

Children of Ida Matilda Queen and Luther Arnold are:

162.   i. **William Johnson Arnold**, b. 22 Feb 1869,

Upshur County, West Virginia.

ii. **Obie Wilson Arnold**, b. 17 Nov 1872, Upshur County, West Virginia; m. **Zona Maude TEETS** (b. 11 Aug, 1878, Upshur County, West Virginia).

iii. **Beatrice "Batie" Arnold**, b. abt. 1874, Upshur County, West Virginia; m. **Ernest POSTE.**

iv. **Nora D. Arnold**, b. abt. 1876, Upshur County, West Virginia; m. **Elmer DAWSON.**

v. **Orley Dayton Arnold**, b.16 Nov 1878, Upshur County, West Virginia; m. **Annie R. TEETS** (b. abt. 1880, Upshur County).

89.

Minerva Manassa Queen, daughter of No.51, Katherine Pritchard, was born 01 May 1847 in (West) Virginia and died 27 Jan 1931. She married **Allen J. ARNOLD,** 1871 in Harrison County, West Virginia. He was born 22 Feb 1851. Allen Arnold was the brother of Luther Arnold who married Ida Matilda, Minerva's sister.

Children of Minerva Queen and Allen Arnold are:

163.   i. **Stella Arnold**, b. 11 Aug 1878.

164   ii. **Orron Arnold**, b. 29 May 1887.

        iii. **Frank Arnold**, b. 19 Dec 1889; m. **Sophie JEFFRIES** (b. 01 Aug 1886), 02 Mar 1912.

90.

James P. Queen, son of No. 51, Katherine Pritchard, was born 03 Oct 1849 in Harrison County, (West) Virginia and died 04 Jan 1926 in Harrison County. He married (1) **Angeline BEAN**, daughter of **John BEAN** and **Martha HICKMAN**. She was born 06 Feb 1855 in Johnstown, Harrison County, and died

September 1875 in Johnstown. He married (2) **Ida DAWSON**.
She was born 19 Mar 1862, and died 05 Nov 1918.
Children of James Queen and Angela Bean are:
165.   i. **Alvertia Queen**, b. 08 Jan 1873.
166.   ii. **Angeline Queen**, b. 09 Aug 1875.
Children of James Queen and Ida Dawson are:
       iii. **Worthy Queen**, b. 26 Nov 1878.
167.   iv. **Sylvia May Queen**, b. 13 Oct 1880.
168.   v. **Levi A. Queen**, b. 25 May 1883.
       vi. **Raymond Loy Queen**, b. 20 May 1893; m. (1)
          Blanche POST, b. 12 Aug 1893; m. (2)
          Virginia ARNOLD, b. 02 Nov 1907.

91.

Martha Harris, daughter of No. 52, Elizabeth Pritchard, was
born in 1849, and died in 1908. She married **Hiram C. COX**.
He was born in 1844, and died in 1901. Both are buried at Mt.
Pisgah Cemetery, Ritchie County, West Virginia.
Children of Martha Harris and Hiram Cox are:
       i. **L. M. Cox**, b. 21 Feb 1871; d. 11 Jun 1891.
       ii. **William I. B. Cox**, b. 1873; d. 1901; buried at Mt.
          Pisgah Cemetery, Ritchie County, West
          Virginia.
       iii. **Della J. Cox,** b. 1875; d. 1902; buried at Mt.
          Pisgah Cemetery, Ritchie County, West
          Virginia.
       iv **Isa N. Cox**, b. 1879; d. 1904; buried at Mt. Pisgah
          Cemetery, Ritchie County, West Virginia.
       v. **Cosy M. Cox**, b. 1888; d. 1906; buried at Mt.
          Pisgah Cemetery, Ritchie County, West
          Virginia.

92.

Millie Frances Harris, daughter of No. 52, Elizabeth
Pritchard, was born June 1850 in Ritchie County, (West)
Virginia, and died 1942 in Pullman, Ritchie County, West
Virginia. She married **George Washington HAYHURST**, 11
Mar 1875, in Ritchie County, West Virginia. He was born June
1851 in Marion County, (West) Virginia, and died in 1926 at
Pullman, Ritchie County, West Virginia. Both Millie and
George Hayhurst are buried in the Pullman Methodist
Cemetery, in Pullman.
Children of Millie Harris and George Hayhurst are:

    i. **Leman H. Hayhurst**, b. 19 Feb 1876, Pullman,
        Ritchie County, West Virginia; d. in Ohio; m.
        Cynthia PRATT (b. 1874, Ritchie
        County, West Virginia), 21 Sep 1905, Ritchie
        County, West Virginia.

    ii. **Metta Hayhurst**, b. 1877, Ritchie County, West
        Virginia; m. **Carl WEDEKAM** (b. 1872,
        Tyler County, West Virginia), 22 Mar 1902.

    iii. **Ida L. Hayhurst**, b. January 1885, Ritchie
        County, West Virginia.

    iv. **May Hayhurst**, b. Ritchie County, West Virginia.

    v. **Juna M. Hayhurst**, b. January 1883, Pullman,
        Ritchie County, West Virginia; d. 1909,
        Pullman, Ritchie County; buried Pullman
        Methodist Cemetery, Pullman, Ritchie
        County, West Virginia.

    vi. **Zula M. Hayhurst**, b. December 1893, Ritchie
        County, West Virginia.

93.

Alpheus F. Harris, son of No. 52, Elizabeth Pritchard, was born October 1858 in Ritchie County, (West) Virginia. He married **Margaret M. MORRIS**, 25 Sep 1879, in Ritchie County, West Virginia. She was born April 1860 in Ritchie County, the daughter of **Henry S. MORRIS** and **Lydia Jane WILSON**.

Children of Alpheus Harris and Margaret Morris are:

 i. **Harley M. Harris**, b. October 1880.
 ii. **Hollis F. Harris**, b. February 1884.
 iii. **Katherine M. Harris**, b. May 1893.

94.

Phillip H. Pritchard, son of No. 54, John Moody Pritchard, was born 25 Mar 1839 and died 25 Aug 1905 in Gilmer County, West Virginia.at the age of 71. He married **Mary Jane McDONALD,** 03 Jun 1870 in Gilmer County, West Virginia. She was born 20 Jun 1851 in Ritchie County, daughter of **John McDONALD and Mary STRAIGHT,** and died in Gilmer County, West Virginia. He was a Civil War veteran.

Children of Phillip Pritchard and Mary McDonald are:

 i. **William Sanford Pritchard**, b. 03 Mar 1871, Ritchie County, West Virginia; m. **Cora BIRCHER** (b. 1876, Ritchie County), 23 Oct 1892, Gilmer County, West Virginia.
 ii. **Hulda Alice Pritchard**, b. 30 Jun 1873, South Fork, Hughes River, Ritchie County, West Virginia.
 iii. **Netta "Nettie" Bell Pritchard**, b. 05 Sep 1875, Gilmer County, West Virginia; d. bef. 1913, Vinton County, Ohio; m. **James Traverse COTTRILL** (b. 06 Jul 1868, Vinton County, Ohio; d. 09 Jan 1941), 1893, Vinton County, Ohio.
 iv. **Mary Ellen Pritchard**, b. 12 Oct 1878, Gilmer

195

County, West Virginia.
- v. **Ida Flora Lucretia Pritchard**, b.26 Jan 1881, Gilmer County, West Virginia.
- vi. **Child Pritchard**, b. 02 Oct 1889, Gilmer County, West Virginia.
- vii. **Lovey Pritchard**, b. August 1885, Horn Creek, Gilmer County, West Virginia.

95.

Jasper Newton Pritchard, son of No. 54, John Moody Pritchard, was born 01 Mar 1843 in Ritchie County, (West) Virginia, and died 09 Mar 1937 in Gulfport, Harrison County, Mississippi. A Civil War veteran, a corporal in Company K, 10th West Virginia Infantry, he is buried in the veterans' section of Green Summit Cemetery, Adelphi, Ross County Ohio. He married (1) **Mary Martha BYRD**, 23 Nov 1865, in Ritchie County, West Virginia, daughter of **John BYRD/BIRD** and **Lutecia/Letitia DILLEY.** Mary Byrd was born 1847 in Gilmer County, (West) Virginia, and died about 1878 in Ritchie County, West Virginia. He married (2) **Mardula "Maude" Merline HORNER** 16 Oct 1879 in Gilmer County. She was born in Wetzel County, Virginia and was first married to **James M. GOFF** on 10 Feb 1875 in Gilmer County. According to the following newspaper article, she died 23 Nov 1927 at the age of 67 and was buried on 24 Nov 1927 at Green Summit Cemetery in Colerain Township, Ross County, Ohio. The West Virginia marriage record lists his name as James N. Pritchard. He married (3) **Cora Belle Bethel SPEAKMAN** 08 Feb 1928 at Church of the Brethren in Circleville, Pickaway County, Ohio. They appeared in the census of 24 Apr 1930, Gulfport, Harrison County, Mississippi. Cora Belle was born on 26 Jul 1872 in Eagle Mills, Vinton

196

County, Ohio. She died 13 Aug 1936 at the age of 64 in Columbus, Franklin County, Ohio. She was buried 15 Aug 1936 at Reber Hill Cemetery, Ashville, Pickaway County, Ohio. Cora's first marriage was to **James BETHEL.** It is possible that she and James knew Orville and Wilbur Wright since the Bethels intermarried with the Wrights. Descendants of Jasper have conflicting records of his various wives and their names. The mother of John Pritchard, born 1878, is listed in West Virginia records as Miriam. This could be a recording error. According to family lore, Mardula ran off with Jasper's money and left him destitute. Jasper appears in the West Virginia census of 1890 and the Ohio census of 1910. The entire family moved to Ohio just after 1890. During the late 1920s, Jasper often traveled to Biloxi, Mississippi, with one of his grandchildren driving him back and forth. The family believes he received some sort of pension, as he seemed to have money, but did not work and family wealth was not substantial.

A Circleville, Ohio newspaper article (exact date illegible, but appears to be 1937), reads as follows:
Title*: Jasper Pritchard Passes Ninety-four Hoping to Reach His Hundredth Year;* Subtitle*: Native of West Virginia Reads Without Glasses, Shucks Corn, Walks Back and Forth to Town.*
Text: *Believed to be Circleville's oldest man, Jasper N. Pritchard celebrated his ninety-fourth birthday Sunday at the home of his grandson Russell Kneice, Circleville Twp., where he makes his home.*

Mr. Pritchard is a native of Ritchie County, West Virginia, where he farmed, made chairs and barrels, and worked as a stone mason with his father. He joined the Union army in the war of the rebellion on March 15, 1862, serving under Captain Jake Kirkendall. He was a corporal two years and a private one year. Mr. Pritchard, whose only injury in his three years' service was a bullet wound in his finger, fought at Gettysburg, Winchester, Snicker's Gap, Cedar Creek, and Richmond, and was with Grant when Lee surrendered at Appomattox Court House.

Abraham Lincoln was the first president he voted for. Mr. Pritchard has been a member of the Christian Science Church for 30 years.

Subtitle: *Married three times.* Text: *The venerable man was first married in West Virginia at the age of 26 and is survived by three sons of this marriage. His second wife, Mrs. Margaret Horner Pritchard, died in 1926. He was married the third time, his wife being Mrs. Cora Bethel Pritchard. Mr. Pritchard has 40 grandchildren and 33 great-grandchildren.*

Persons helping him enjoy his birthday anniversary were Mr. And Mrs. John Arledge, Mr. And Mrs. Alva Pritchard and son Lewis, of Gulfport, Miss., Mr. And Mrs. Roy McQuade, Mr. And Mrs. Russell Kneice and daughter and son Maxine and Leroy.

Children of Jasper Pritchard and Mary Byrd are:

169.   i. **Jason Hinson Pritchard**, b. 12 Sep 187, Smithville, Ritchie County, West Virginia; d. 01 Jul 1955, Circleville, Pickaway County, Ohio.

170.   ii. **Francis Marion Pritchard**, b. 12 Apr 1874, Ritchie County, West Virginia.

171.   iii. **Franklin Pritchard**, b. 07 Apr 1876, Smithville, West Virginia; m. (1) **Lenna McQUADE** 03 Sep 1899; Hocking County, Ohio; m. (2) **Edith BAKER** 17 Oct 1923, Franklin County Ohio; d. 05 May 1950, Columbus, Franklin County, Ohio. He was buried on 08 May 1950 at Obetz Cemetery in Obetz, Franklin County, Ohio.

The Pritchard/Prickett Family History

Children of Jasper Pritchard and Mardula Horner are:

iv. **John W. Pritchard**, b. 01 Nov 1878, Murphy
District, Ritchie County, West Virginia; d. 1954
at the age of 76 in Circleville, Pickaway County,
Ohio.

v. **Stephen U. B. Pritchard**, b. June 1880, Ritchie
County, West Virginia.

vi. **Anna Pritchard**, v. May 1881, Ritchie County,
West Virginia.

vi. **Arithienetta Pritchard**, b. 23 Jun 1884, Ritchie
County, West Virginia. She appeared in the
census on 06 Jan 1920 in Circleville, Pickaway
County, Ohio.

vii. **Ella N. Pritchard**, b. Apr 1889, Ritchie County,
West Virginia.

172.   viii. **Altie Ora Pritchard**, b. 09 Jan 1891, Hazelgreen,
Ritchie County, West Virginia; d. 26 Apr 1976,
at age 85 in Gulfport, Harrison County,
Mississippi.

ix.. **Florence Pritchard**, 07 Apr 1894 in Ohio. She died
24 Dec 1979 at the age of 85 in Circleville,
Pickaway County, Ohio

x. **Alfred Newton Pritchard**, b.12 Feb, 1897, Ross
County, Ohio; d. 01 Apr 1927 at the age of 30 in
Columbus, Franklin County, Ohio; m. **Nellie
ARMENTROUT** (b. 1889; d. 04 Mar 1958).
Alfred was a private in the Ohio 318th Aux. Tmt.
Dep. QMC during World War I. Both buried in
Forest Cemetery, Circleville, Pickaway
County, Ohio.

96.
Andrew Jackson Pritchard, son of No. 54, John Moody
Pritchard, was born in 1839. He married **Mary WILKINSON**,
daughter of **Hiram S. WILKINSON** and **Sarah UNK** on 07
Jan 1872. She was born 1850 in Ritchie County. At the time of
their marriage, his age is given in the Ritchie County Marriage
Record as 23, hers as 22. He fought in the Civil War. They
likely were also the parents of Willie B. Pritchard, born about
1870, who married Arvilla McQuaide in 1900 in Hocking
County, Ohio, at which time the records state that Willie was
age 30 and the son of Andrew Jackson and Mary Wilkinson
Pritchard. If his age recorded at that time was correct, he would
have been born two years before the marriage of his parents.
(See No. 170, Francis M. Pritchard.)
Children of Andrew Jackson Pritchard and Mary Wilkinson
are:

    i. **Susanna Pritchard**, b. 1872, Ritchie County,
      West Virginia.
    ii. **Hiram S. Pritchard**, b. 10 Feb 1877, Ritchie
      County, West Virginia.
    iii. **Martha Pritchard**, b. 30 Aug 1878, Ritchie
      County, West Virginia.
    iv. **Rosa Lee Pritchard**, b. 26 Apr 1879, Ritchie
      County, West Virginia.
    v. **Charles Pritchard**, b. 21 Oct 1883, Ritchie
      County, West Virginia.

97.
Thomas Benton Pritchard, son of No. 54, John Moody
Pritchard, was born 10 August 1858 in West Virginia and died
23 Oct 1911 in Ross County, Ohio. He married **Lucy M.
McDONALD,** 23 Nov 1876 in Gilmer County, West Virginia.

She was born 01 Apr 1856 in Ritchie County, and died 21 Jan 1940 in Ohio. Both are buried in Green Summit Cemetery, Adelphi, Ross County, Ohio. Thomas Benton Pritchard is the subject of two newspaper articles in the *Adelphi Border News* of Ross County, Ohio. The 18 Oct 1895 issue contains an item about the most recent meeting of the Cornplanter Tribe No. 173 of Adelphi at which Thomas B. Pritchard was admitted as one of four new members. The Cornplanters was a fraternal lodge which no longer exists.

The 02 Oct 1896 issue has the following item: *Thomas B. Pritchard takes the premium on raising the largest yellow yams of the season. He left one at this office the other evening that weighed 6 ¾ pounds when taken from the ground. So says Mr. Pritchard, and his word is as good as a Government bond. Another specimen of Tom's crop weighed just one pound less, and it made a mess for Dr. Barton and family. What do you think of twelve of these potatoes filling a bushel basket? What do you think of five in one hill and none weighing less than three pounds? Who knows of any other farmer or gardener that ever raised a crop of yams that could equal this?*

Children of Thomas B. Pritchard and Lucy McDonald are:

173.   i. **Larrick Pritchard**, b. 27 Mar 1879, West Virginia; d. Abt. 1970, Ohio.

174.   ii. **Leeman Lee Pritchard**, b. 01 Jul 1881; d. 24 Jan 1976, Fox Nursing Home, Laurelville, Hocking County, Ohio.

175.   iii. **Sherman Pritchard**, b. 01 Jul 1881; d. 13 Oct 1983, Chillicothe, Ross County, Ohio.

176.   iv. **Amon Lewis Pritchard,** b. 03 April 1884, Union, Ritchie County, West Virginia; d. 19 Mar 1967, Chillicothe, Ross County, Ohio.

177.   v. **Della M. Pritchard**, b. 24 Sep 1887, Salt

Creek Twp., Hocking County, Ohio.
178.   vi. **Elsie Arie Pritchard**, b. 07 Apr 1892, Salt
        Creek Twp., Hocking County, Ohio; d. Abt.
        1967.
179.   vii. **Hugh Jack Pritchard,** b. 07 Jul 1895, Salt
        Creek Twp., Hocking Co., Ohio
       viii. **Female Pritchard**, b. 17 Aug 1898, Salt
        Creek Twp., Hocking County, Ohio; d.
        17 Aug 1898 (stillborn).

98.

Elias Robert Pritchard, son of No. 56, Thomas Dickerson
Pritchard, was born 29 Dec 1845 in Ritchie County, (West)
Virginia and died 04 Jun 1909 in Roane County, West
Virginia. He married **Sophia Amelia WATSON,** 29 Mar 1868,
in Spencer, Roane County, West Virginia. She was born 22
Aug 1844 in Ritchie County, daughter of **Otho WATSON** and
Louisa JETT, and died 04 Jul 1924 in Spencer, Roane County,
West Virginia.

Elias Robert Pritchard served in the Civil War. His
gravestone is a military issue reading: E. R. Pritchard,
Company A, 6th West Virginia Cavalry. He and Sophia lived
in Smithfield District, the last area of Roane County to enforce
the range law. He died from what was called brain fever,
probably a fractured skull. He and a neighbor were in a dispute
over the property line and family tradition states that the
neighbor, Ed Post, came after him with an axe but threw it
down and picked up a tamping post and hit him over the head.
Another correspondent states that Elias hit Ed and he died.
Neither death is recorded in Roane County records, but Ed Post
is not listed in the next census.

Sophia Watson Pritchard was a widow when she died at

Elias Robert Pritchard and Sophia Amelia Watson Pritchard

8 a.m. on 04 Jul 1924 at the age of 79 from stomach or liver cancer. The attending doctor, B. A. Smith of Spencer, West Virginia, signed the medical section on her death certificate. Sophia is buried in the Watson Cemetery in Spencer. The personal and statistical particulars of her death certificate were verified on 07 Jul 1924 by Mary Pritchard of Spencer. Children of Elias Pritchard and Sophia Watson are:

180.   i. **Lewis Maxwell Pritchard**, b. 14 Mar 1869, Roane County, West Virginia; d. 1898, Roane County, West Virginia.

181.   ii. **James Robert Pritchard**, b. 18 Jul 1871, Roane County, West Virginia; d. 05 Feb 1945, Roane County, West Virginia.

182.   iii. **Darrell Duke Pritchard**, b. 20 Feb 1880, Roane County, West Virginia; d. 19 Aug 1956, Spencer, Roane County, West Virginia.

183.   iv. **Lily Alberta Boyce Pritchard,** b, 19 Dec 1881, Roane County, West Virginia, daughter of Matilda Watson Boice; adopted by Elias Pritchard and Sophia Watson, her aunt.

        v. **Alice May Pritchard**, b. 06 Sep 1884, Roane County, West Virginia; d. 25 Oct 1889, Roane County, West Virginia. The cause of her death was diphtheria, as recorded at Spencer in December 1889.

99.

Thomas Tavner Pritchard, son of No. 56, Thomas Dickerson Pritchard, was born 05 Apr 1849 in Slab Creek, Ritchie County, (West) Virginia, and died 26 Dec 1922 in Hyattville, Bighorn County, Wyoming. He married **Lucy Ann Elizabeth SUMMERS,** 04 Dec 1878, in Ritchie County. She was born 20

Mar 1852, in White Oak, Ritchie County, West Virginia, the daughter of **Elias SUMMERS** and **Maranda WILSON**. She died 30 May 1928 in Hyattsville, Bighorn County, Wyoming. Children of Thomas Tavner Pritchard and Lucy Summers are:

    i. **Martha Alice Pritchard**, b. 12 Oct 1879, Slab Creek, Ritchie County, West Virginia; d. 06 Aug 1961, Hyattsville, Bighorn County, Wyoming.

184.   ii. **Addie Miranda Pritchard**, b. 03 Sep 1881, Ritchie County, West Virginia; d. 05 Jun 1947, Boulder City, Clark County, Nevada.

    iii. **Jennie Belinda Pritchard**, b.13 Jun 1884, Ritchie County, West Virginia; d. 27 Oct 1981; m. **Ralph MERCER,** 09 Feb 1909. They had three children.

    iv. **Clara Lucinda Pritchard**, b. 10 May 1887, Harrisville, Ritchie County, West Virginia; d. 14 Feb, 1972; m. **Willard E. McGARY** August 1907. They had thirteen children.

    v. **Scipio Cortez Pritchard**, b. 06 Nov 1889, Ritchie County, West Virginia; d. 18 May 1976; m. **Ida Cook TEEPLES,** 1935. Scipio had four boys.

    vi. **Lucy Lavinia Pritchard**, b. 05 Aug 1894, Ritchie County, West Virginia; d. 26 Nov 1977; m. **John Conrad NOLL**, 24 Sep 1913. They had three children.

    vii. **James Irl Pritchard**, b. 10 Apr 1898, Ritchie County, West Virginia; d. 26 Jul 1985; m. **Thelma GARARD,** 21 Jan, 1923, Laramie, Albany County, Wyoming.

100.

Sarah Ann Pritchard, daughter of No. 57, Samuel George Pritchard, was born 18 Dec 1862 in Rockford, Ritchie County, (West) Virginia, and died 12 May 1940 in Crystal Springs, Randolph County, West Virginia. She married **Henry Mills SMITH**, son of **James Wesley SMITH** and **Sarah Nancy GARVIN**, on 21 Mar 1889 in Lewis County, West Virginia. Her age was given as 26 and his as 24 years. Henry Smith was born 18 Apr 1864 in Lewis County, West Virginia, and died 10 May 1928 in Coalton, Randolph County, West Virginia. Sarah Ann and Henry Smith are buried alongside each other in Maplewood Cemetery, Elkins, Randolph County, West Virginia.

Children of Sarah Ann Pritchard and Henry Mills Smith are:

      i. **Samuel George Smith**, b. 10 Mar 1890, d. 08 Oct 1892.

      ii. **Ellen Smith**, born 11 Jun, 1893, d. same day.

185.   iii. **Waitman Conley Smith**, b.16 Jan 1895, d. 01 Apr 1973, Kingville, Randolph County, West Virginia.

      iv. **Lena Leota Smith**, b. 25 Apr 1898, d. December 1987.

186.   v. **Claude McKinley Smith**, born 04 Oct, 1900, Walkersville, Lewis County, West Virginia; d. 17 Oct 1961, Macon, Bibb County, Georgia.

101.

Mary Elizabeth Pritchard, daughter of No. 57, Samuel George Pritchard, was born 1863 in Harrison County, West Virginia and died 25 Feb, 1932. She married **Reason DENNISON,** 04 Nov 1896.

Children of Mary Elizabeth Pritchard and Reason Dennison

are:
187.   i. **John Willis Dennison**, b. 24 Jan 1904; d. 04 Oct 1976.
188.   ii. **Dewey F. Dennison**.

FOURTH GENERATION

102.

Mary C. Watson, daughter of No. 63, George Watson, was
born 28 Aug 1843 in Auburn, Ritchie County, (West) Virginia,
and died 01 Jan 1929 in Berea, Ritchie County. She married
Arthur Green BEE before 1878 in Ritchie County, West
Virginia, son of **Ezekiel BEE** and **Mariah JOHNSON**. He
was born 18 Nov 1841 in Ritchie County, (West) Virginia, and
died 10 Sep 1922 in Berea, Ritchie County. He is buried in
Pine Grove Cemetery, Berea.

Arthur Green Bee was a member of Company G,
Fourteenth West Virginia Infantry Volunteers for the Union
during the Civil War. His father, Ezekiel Bee, was born 1800 in
Witteman, Taylor County, (West) Virginia, and died 20 Feb
1893 in Ritchie County. He married Mariah Johnson, daughter
of **Michael JOHNSON** and **Hannah HUGHES**.

The Bee Family

In her two histories of Ritchie County, West Virginia,
Minnie Kendall Lowther emphasizes that the Bee name has
had a long and prominent connection with Ritchie County,
West Virginia. *"The family were originally of Jewish
extraction of the tribe of Ephraim, but their ancestors came
from England to America in Colonial times and settled in New
Jersey. In accord with the ancient custom of their race, they
kept a record and were able to trace their lineage back to
Father Abraham, but this well-preserved record was burned in
a New Jersey house fire a century ago."* As a result, the record
of their long history was wiped out. Although Jewish in origin,
the Bee family accepted Christianity many generations ago.

207

According to tradition, four Bee brothers, Ephraim, Asa, George, and Thomas, emigrated with others from England to New Jersey some time before the Revolution. They later became actively involved in the struggle for liberty, prompted by the pursuing "British Redcoats." The Bees of Ritchie County trace their ancestry from George. His son, Asa, settled in what is now Taylor County in the late 18th century. Later, he became the first minister of the Seventh Day Baptist Church on Hughes River. Asa was a strong advocate of co-education and had no sympathy with the idea that "a woman was amply equipped for the battle of life if she could only read and spell." He taught that women's influence was the potent factor in shaping a child's mind. Three of his daughters were school teachers. Ephriam Bee was the ancestor of General Bernard Bee of the Civil War who said, "There's Jackson standing like a stone wall," hence the name Stonewall Jackson. Most of the Bees are buried in Pine Grove Cemetery, Ritchie County.

    i. **Edward J. Bee**, b. 25 May 1869, Ritchie County, West Virginia; d. 1942, Ritchie County, West Virginia; m. **Arminda CALHOUN** (b.1868; d. 1950), 18 Oct 1893, Ritchie County; both bur. Pine Grove Cemetery, Berea, Ritchie County. He was a blacksmith.

    ii. **Emma Bee**, b. 12 Apr 1872, Ritchie County.

    iii. **Gay Bee**, b. 01 Dec 1875, Ritchie County.

189. iv. **Lillian Leoti Bee**, b. 10 Jul 1878, Ritchie County, West Virginia; d. 08 Feb 1961, Houston, Texas.

    v. **James D. Bee**, b. 17 Aug 1881, Ritchie County.

    vi. **Paul D. Bee**, b. 31 May 1884, Ritchie County, West Virginia.

    vii. **Ezrith W. Bee**, b. July 1885, Ritchie County; d.

1953, Ritchie County; bur. Pine Grove
Cemetery, Berea, Ritchie County.
viii. **Martha Bee,** b.14 Aug 1887, Ritchie County;
d. infant.
ix. **Mary Bee**, b. 14 Aug 1887, Ritchie County; d.
infant.

103.

Martha A. Watson, daughter of No. 63, George W. Watson,
was born 1845 and died 1881. She married **James B.
GRIBBLE**. He was born June 1839 in Preston County, (West)
Virginia, and died 1917 in Ritchie County. James Gribble's
military service was in Company G, 14th West Virginia
Infantry, Civil War. Both are buried in Auburn Community
Cemetery, Ritchie County, West Virginia.
Children of Martha Watson and James Gribble are:
i. **M. J. Gribble**, b. 1865; d. 1919; bur.
Auburn Community Cemetery, Ritchie
County, West Virginia.
ii. **Ulysses S. Gribble**, b. 13 Feb 1867; d. 1941; bur.
Auburn Community Cemetery, Ritchie County,
West Virginia.
iii. **Dow Gribble**, b. 04 Oct 1870, Ritchie County,
West Virginia.
iv. **James M. Gribble,** b. 03 Mar 1872.
v. **Flora B. Gribble**, b. 10 Aug 1877.
vi. **Ottie S. Gribble**, b. March 1884, Ritchie County,
West Virginia; m. **C. A. MASON** (b. 1883,
Harrison County, West Virginia), 03 Dec 1905,
Ritchie County.

104.

John Wesley Pritchard, son of No. 66, George Pritchard, was born 02 Jan 1846 in White Oak, Ritchie County, (West) Virginia and died 05 Aug 1908 in Parkersburg, Wood County, West Virginia. He married **Rosalie PRICE** on 20 Oct 1870 in Ritchie County, West Virginia. She was born 26 Nov 1845 in Morgantown, Monongalia County, (West) Virginia, daughter of **Gideon PRICE** and **Rhoda UNK**, and died 03 Sep 1943 in Harrisville, Ritchie County, West Virginia. John Wesley Pritchard is buried in the Harrisville IOOF Cemetery, Ritchie County, West Virginia.

Children of John Wesley Pritchard and Rosalie Price are:

190.   i. **Gracia "Gracie" Alice Pritchard**, b. 25 May 1872, Ritchie County, West Virginia; d. 26 June 1907, Ritchie County.

191   ii. **Mary Elizabeth Pritchard**, b. 25 Dec 1874, Ritchie County, West Virginia; d. 1967, Harrisville, Ritchie County.

    iii. **Mary Pritchard**, b. 1875, Ritchie County.

    iv. **Pearl Jane Pritchard**, b. 05 Nov 1877, Ritchie County, West Virginia; m. **Ira O. WAGONER** (b. 1874, Harrison County, West Virginia), 04 Dec 1895, Ritchie County, West Virginia.

    v. **Rose Edna Pritchard**, b. 22 Aug 1879, Harrisville, Ritchie County, West Virginia; m. **John N. PRINCE** (b. 1879, Wood County, West Virginia), 22 Jun 1902.

    vi. **Laura W. Pritchard**, b. June 1886, Ritchie County, West Virginia.

    vii. **Charlotte "Lottie" Pritchard**, b. 24 Jun 1889, Oxford, Ritchie County, West Virginia; d.

08 May 1900, Harrisville, Ritchie County;
bur. IOOF Cemetery, Harrisville, Ritchie
County, West Virginia.

105.

Morgan R. Pritchard, son of No. 66, George Pritchard, was
born 13 Dec 1847 in White Oak, Ritchie County, (West)
Virginia and died 03 Apr 1915 in Oxford, Ritchie County,
West Virginia. He married **Florence E. HALL,** 18 Jan 1872 in
Ritchie County, West Virginia, the daughter of **Silas HALL**
and **Lucinda UNK**. She was born 18 Nov 1851 and died 25
Aug 1928 in Ritchie County, West Virginia. Her name is also
found as Frances E. Hall. Both are buried at White Oak
Cemetery, Ritchie County, West Virginia.
Children of Morgan Pritchard and Florence Hall are:

   i. **Son Pritchard**, b. 10 Sep 1872, Oxford,
      Ritchie County, West Virginia; d. September
      1872, Oxford, Ritchie County.
192. ii. **Coleman H. Pritchard**, b.25 Dec 1873, Oxford,
      Ritchie County, West Virginia; d. 1954,
      Harrisville, Ritchie County.
   iii. **Emma Pritchard**, b. 05 Aug 1876, Ritchie
      County, West Virginia; d. 01 Dec 1878; bur.
      White Oak Cemetery, Ritchie County, West
      Virginia.
193. iv. **Laura M. Pritchard**, b. April 1880, Ritchie
      County, West Virginia; d. 1955, Pullman,
      Ritchie County, West Virginia.
194. v. **Roscoe Clyde Pritchard**, b. 10 Sep 1882, Ritchie
      County, West Virginia.
   vi. **Luella Pritchard,** b. 11 Sep 1884, Oxford,
      Ritchie County, West Virginia; d. 09 Jul 1886;

bur. White Oak Cemetery, Ritchie County.
vii. **Wilbert C. Pritchard**, b. 02 Nov 1886, Union
District, Ritchie County, West Virginia; d.
21 Dec 1893, Pullman, Ritchie County.
viii. **Shirley E. Pritchard**, b. 04 May 1888, Oxford,
Ritchie County, West Virginia; d. 1942,
Harrisville, Ritchie County; bur. IOOF
Cemetery, Harrisville, Ritchie County.
ix. **Lola R. Pritchard**, b. 02 Dec 1891, Oxford, Ritchie
County, West Virginia; d. 30 Dec 1891; bur.
White Oak Cemetery, Pullman, Ritchie County.
x. **Florence Ruby Pritchard**, b. 28 Jul 1895,
Pullman, Ritchie County, West Virginia.

106.

Andrew L. Pritchard, son of No. 66, George Pritchard, was
born 03 Mar 1850 at White Oak, Ritchie County, West
Virginia, and died 10 Mar 1878 at Auburn, Ritchie County,
West Virginia. He married **Elizabeth "Eliza" Ellen THARP**,
07 Nov 1872, daughter of **Hezekiah THARP** and **Elizabeth
WASS**. Hezekiah Tharp is buried in Auburn Community
Cemetery, dated 09 Jan 1837-12 Apr 1899. Eliza was born 31
May 1851, and died 19 Feb 1978 in Ritchie County, West
Virginia. Both she and Andrew are buried in Auburn
Community Cemetery, Ritchie County, West Virginia.
Children of Andrew Pritchard and Elizabeth Tharp are:
i. **Grant Pritchard**, b. 06 Aug 1873, South Fork
Hughes River, Ritchie County, West Virginia.
195. ii. **Dora Alice Pritchard**, b. 02 Mar 1876, Oxford,
Ritchie County, West Virginia.

107.

Lewis Maxwell Pritchard, son of No. 66 George Pritchard, was born 11 Feb 1860 at White Oak, Ritchie County, West Virginia. He married **Sarah Frances "Fanny" PRUNTY**, 09 Apr 1882, in Ritchie County. She was born January 1861, in Ritchie County, the daughter of **Felix PRUNTY**. Both are buried in the IOOF Cemetery, Parkersburg, Wood County, West Virginia.

Children of Lewis Maxwell Pritchard and Fanny Prunty are:

    i. **Syntha Stella Pritchard**, b. 27 Apr 1883, White Oak, Ritchie County, West Virginia.

    ii. **Forest D. Pritchard**, b. May 1885, Ritchie County, West Virginia.

    iii. **Lewis C. Pritchard**, b. 10 Nov 1887, Ritchie County, West Virginia.

    iv. **Elnora Pritchard**, b. 13 Apr 1889, Ritchie County, West Virginia.

108.

Helen Virginia "Jennie" Pritchard, daughter of No. 66, George Pritchard, was born 16 Aug 1863 at White Oak, Ritchie County, West Virginia. She married **Preston G. ZINN**, 18 Feb 1886, in Ritchie County. He was born 1863 in Marion County, West Virginia.

Children of Helen Pritchard and Preston Zinn are:

    i. **Lawrence H. Zinn**, b. February 1888, Ritchie County, West Virginia.

    ii. **Lester A. Zinn**, b. January 1890, Ritchie County, West Virginia.

    iii. **Wilbur R. Zinn**, b. November 1892, Ritchie County, West Virginia.

109.

Ardena A. Pritchard, daughter of No. 66, George Pritchard, was born 08 Sep 1867 at White Oak, Ritchie County, West Virginia. She married **Frank I. KIRKPATRICK**, 03 Feb 1892 in Ritchie County, West Virginia. He was born September 1870.

Children of Ardena Pritchard and Frank Kirkpatrick are:
     i. **Leo Kirkpatrick**, b. December 1892.
    ii. **Eva G. Kirkpatrick**, b. January 1894.
   iii. **Howard G. Kirkpatrick**, b. May 1897.
   iv. **William E. Kirkpatrick**, b. June 1899.

110.

Millard Fillmore Pritchard, son of No. 68, Thomas Willis Pritchard, was born 22 Sep 1857 in Ritchie County, (West) Virginia and died 10 Jul 1927 in Clarksburg, West Virginia where he is buried in the family plot in Elk View Masonic Cemetery. He married (1) **Margaret Cerilda KELLEY** 11 Jun 1884 in Nestorville, West Virginia, daughter of **Garrett KELLEY** and **Amelia NESTOR**. He married (2) **Rosa Bell NESTOR** 12 Oct 1887 in Nestorville, West Virginia, daughter of **William G. NESTOR** and **Sarah E. LOHR**.

The Nestor Family

(For a detailed history, see *Decendants of Jacob Nestor* compiled by Carl K. Nestor, 1983.)

     Rosa Belle Nestor is descended from two lines of German immigrants, the Nestors and the Lohrs. Her earliest Nestor ancestor was **Johann Gottfried NESTLER**, who was born in Germany. He arrived in Philadelphia in 1773 on the ship "Sally." His wife died during the voyage and was buried at sea. After leaving his son Jacob with relatives in America, he returned to Germany. There are no records to indicate that he ever came back to America.

Child of Johann Gottfried Nestler is:

1.   i. **Jacob Nester**, b. Germany; d. 1844, Nestorville, Barbour County, (West) Virginia; m. (1) **Elizabeth BEDFORD** 1783 in Pennsylvania; m. (2) **Mary Magdalena DURR**,10 Oct 1785, daughter of **Andrew DURR** and **Magdalena REIGER**; m. (3) **Elizabeth Ann FANSLER** aft. 1826 in Nestorville, daughter of **Henry FANSLER.**

Jacob Nestor was a Revolutionary soldier in the Berks County, Pennsylvania Militia from 1777 to 10 Mar 1780 as a private First Class in Captain Ferdinand Ritter's Eighth Company, Third Battalion. It is believed by some descendants that Jacob was eight years old at the time he arrived in America; others believe he was twelve. The name Nester was pronounced Neshter in the early days in Berks County, Pennsylvania. This is characteristic of the Romansch dialect of German, found in southern Germany and eastern Switzerland. The name Nester today is common in the district of Heilbronn, not far from Karlsruhe, in Bockingen, and in Grankenbach (two suburbs of Heilbronn), in Kochendorf, Neckarsulm, Obereisesheim, and in the districts of Rottweil and Horb.

Jacob Nester's first wife, Elizabeth Bedford, died in 1784, a year after their marriage, leaving no children. He next married Mary Magdalena Durr, possibly near New Hanover, Pennsylvania on 10 Oct 1785, and their son George was born in 1787. The records of St. Mary Lutheran Church, Silver Run, Carroll County, Maryland (two miles south of New Hanover) show a baptism of John George Nestler 14 Oct 1787, son of Jacob and Magdalena Nestler. Records indicate that in 1791 the family moved from Pennsylvania to Piney Creek Hundred, Maryland.

In November 1797, Jacob Nester and his family were living in Georges Township, Fayette County, Pennsylvania. From there, he purchased land in Randolph County, Virginia, which later became Barbour County, (West) Virginia. There he established the town of Nestorville and is buried there, as are many of his descendants.

Mary Magdalena Durr died 09 Jul 1826. Jacob next married (3) Elizabeth Ann Fansler (b. October 1791; d. 10 Oct 1868), daughter of Henry Fansler. There were no children of this marriage.

Jacob Nester was a farmer, millwright, carpenter, shoemaker, and Lutheran minister. The original name, Nestler, was altered twice by this line. Although he appears as Jacob Nester in Revolutionary records, his son, George, adopted the spelling Nestor, which his descendants kept.

The Campbell Cemetery is a part of the original Nestorville homestead. The space was set aside by Jacob for the use of the Nestor and Hovatter families. Jacob and Mary are buried there along with all but two of their children. Children of Jacob Nester and Mary Magdalena Durr are:

2.   i. **George Nestor**, b. 30 Aug 1787, Maryland; d. 01 Aug 1866, Barbour County, West Virginia.

    ii. **Jacob Nester**, baptized 10 Jun 1786 at St. Mary Lutheran Church, Silver Run, Carroll County, Maryland.

    iii. **David Nestor**, b. 1790.

    iv. **Mary M. Polly Nestor**, baptized 19 Dec 1793, Trinity Evangelical Lutheran Church, Taneytown, Carroll County, Maryland; m.

> **John SHAVER**, 06 Aug 1813. He was a
> veteran of War of 1812. Later spelled his
> name **SHAFFER**.

v. **Catherine Elizabeth Katy Nestor**, b. 1795.

vi. **Daniel Nestor**, b. 16 Oct 1797.

vii. **John Nestor**, b. 02 Mar 1799.

viii. **Samuel Nestor**, b. 19 Apr 1805.

2.

George Nestor, son of Jacob Nestor, married **Amelia
POLAND** 05 Dec 1809 in Nestorville, Barbour County (West)
Virginia, daughter of **Martin POLAND** and **Lettice Ann
UNK.** (The surname Poland soon evolved to Poling, the
spelling used today by most descendants.)

Children of George Nestor and Amelia Poland are:

3. i. **Jacob Nestor**, b. 24 Nov 1810, Barbour County; d.
    03 Apr 1887, Barbour County, West Virginia

4. ii. **Jonas Nestor**, b. 04 May 1812, Nestorville; d.
    24 Apr 1865, Nestorville; m. **Elizabeth
    HOLSBERRY**.

iii. **Poling B. Nestor**, b. 01 Feb 1814.

iv. **Mary Nestor**, b. 1814, Nestorville; d. Nestorville;
    m. **Archibald ENGLAND**, 02 Oct 1831,
    Nestorville.

v. **Lettice Ann Nestor**, b. 20 Feb 1816, Nestorville; d.
    17 Aug 1885, Nestorville; m. **Charles
    BOYLES**, 10 Apr 1835, Nestorville.

vi. **George W. Nestor**, b. 19 Mar 1818, Nestorville; d.
    25 Jan 1893, Baileytown, West Virginia; m.
    Mary Ann HALLER. George Nestor was a
    Methodist minister.

vii. **Mary Elizabeth Nestor**, b. 23 May 1821,

Nestorville; m. **Jonas POLING**, 14 Nov 1843, Nestorville.

viii. **Sarah E. Nestor**, b. 21 Feb 1823, Nestorville; d. 08 Jun 1899, Nestorville; m. (1) **Michael Theodore HALLER**; m. (2) **J. J. RAMSEY**.

Captain Michael T. Haller, husband of Sarah E. Nestor, and Andrew Nestor, his brother-in-law, were slain at the same time. Capt. Haller was Captain of the Home Guard. Confederate soldiers in uniform, returning from the war which had ended, sent three men to Sanford Nestor's home, where the soldiers abused Nestor and his wife and robbed him as a ruse to get the Home Guard in pursuit of them and thus lead its members into a trap. The three intruders were reported to the Guard Camp and eight guards started after them, chasing them four miles to a laurel thicket, where Capt. Haller was fatally wounded. Andrew Nestor, first Sergeant of the Guards, fell to the ground and was not hit, but the Rebels caught him and led him up a ravine, a mile from the road, where they tried to force him to pray for the Confederacy. Then they shot him in the eye, mouth, and forehead. Haller fell after he was shot, but arose and then was shot several times more, his body badly mangled. His slayers took his watch and revolver and left him lying in a gore of blood. Captain Haller first was buried on top of a hill on the old Haller homestead, but 28 years later, his body was exhumed and re-interred in the Huffman Cemetery with his uniform almost intact.

x. **William Nestor**, m. 23 Jan 1824; m. **Elizabeth HARSH**.

xi. **James Nestor**, b. 23 Jul 1828, Nestorville; d. 17 Jul 1896, Nestorville; m. **Hannah SKIDMORE**. James, a blacksmith, served as Justice of the Peace around Nestorville for 24 years.

5.   xii. **Catherine Nestor, b**. 13 Mar 1831, Nestorville; d.
        04 May1895, Nestorville.
     xiii. **Andrew Nestor**, b. 12 Jul 1833, Nestorville;
        d. 24 Apr 1865, Teters Creek, Barbour
        County; m. **Margaret A. VANNOY**. He was
        killed on Teters Creek by Confederate
        soldiers; Capt. Michael Haller was killed at
        the same time.

3.

Jacob Nestor, son of George Nestor, was born 24 Nov 1810 in
Barbour County (West) Virginia and died 03 Apr 1887 in
Nestorville, Barbour County. He married **Nancy HUFFMAN**
25 Dec 1828, in Nestorville. Both are buried in the Huffman
Cemetery, Barbour County.
Children of Jacob Nestor and Nancy Huffman are:
     i. **John Nestor**, b. 1830.
     ii. **George H. Nestor**, b. 24 Feb 1832.
     iii. **Anthony Nestor**, b. 16 Feb 1834.
     iv. **Margaret Nestor,** b. 1836; m. **Gilbert HARSH**.

4.

Jonas Nestor, son of George Nestor, was born 04 May
1812 in Nestorville, and died 24 Apr 1865 in Nestorville. He
married **Elizabeth HOLSBERRY**, 19 Aug 1834 in
Nestorville, daughter of **John HOLSBERRY** and **Margaret
POLAND.** John Holsberry was born near Pittsburgh,
Pennsylvania in 1780, and died in Barbour County, West
Virginia in 1862. The father of John Holsberry (his given name
is not verified, but may also have been John) came to
Pennsylvania from Germany at the age of sixteen. All of the
people in Barbour County, West Virginia with that surname are

descended from him. He had three sons: Samuel, Conrad, and John, father of Elizabeth. Samuel married in Pennsylvania, but died without children; Conrad and John went to Ohio and bought land near Zanesville, where other settlers from New Jersey were locating about the same time. The colonists, brought down by sickness, decided to return east. They arrived in Barbour County and settled among the foothills of Laurel Hill in Glade District. Among the settlers were the Polands. Before leaving Ohio, John Holsberry became acquainted with Margaret Poland, one of the daughters, and was so enamored with her that he sold his land for almost nothing (it afterwards became very valuable) and followed the Poland family to Barbour County, where he soon was successful in winning Margaret's hand. They built their house where Kalamazoo now stands. When the War of 1812 began, John Holsberry volunteered and became a commissioned officer. He went to Norfolk, Virginia, but resigned before the close of the war because of sickness in his family. Besides Elizabeth, the children of John and Margaret Poland Holsberry were: **Rachel**, who married **Andrew STALNAKER**; **Nancy**, who married **John REGAN**; **Samuel**; **William**; **Catherine**; and **Martha**. John Holsberry died in 1862 at the age of 82. He and Margaret Poland are both buried in the M. P. White Oak Cemetery. The descendants of Conrad Holsberry drifted from Ohio down the Mississippi to Texas.

Children of Jonas Nestor and Elizabeth Holsberry are:

6.   i. **William G. Nestor**, b. 16 Aug 1835, Nestorville; d. 30 Jan 1897, Nestorville.
     ii. **Tabitha Nestor**, b. 18 Aug 1837; m. **Daniel STURMS**.
    iii. **Louisa Nestor**, b. 01 Dec 1839, Nestorville.
     iv. **Nancy Nestor**, b. 10 Feb 1843, Nestorville,

Jonas Nestor, 1812–1865, grandfather of Rosa Bell Nestor

220a

220b

    m. **Robert J. HUFFMAN**, 27 Aug 1864.
  v. **Mary Polly Nestor**, b. 23 May 1844, Nestorville;
    d. 28 Jan 1867; m. **Stingley Ebenezer**
    HUFFMAN, 19 Oct 1865, Nestorville.
  vi. **Sarah Ann Nestor**, b. 1845, Nestorville; m.
    George POLING.
  vii. **Serena Nestor**, b. 02 Jan 1848; m. **Stingley**
    Ebenezer HUFFMAN after 1867.
 viii. **Arminda Nestor**, b. 27 Mar 1850, Nestorville; d.
    1927, Nestorville; m. **George W. FRYE**.
  ix. **Melinda Nestor**, b. 14 Jul 1852, Nestorville; d.
    17 Aug 1858, Nestorville.
  x. **Peter J. Nestor**, b. 03 Dec 1853, Nestorville; d.
    16 May 1864, Nestorville.
  xi. **Henry Clay Nestor**, b. 23 May 1855,
    Nestorville; d. 21 Jul 1924, Nestorville; m.
    Laverna E. PHILLIPS, 28 May 1881.
  xii. **Barbara Margaret Nestor**, b. 04 Jun 1858,
    Nestorville; m. **Samuel SHAFFER**.

5.

Catherine Nestor, daughter of George Nestor, was born 13 Mar 1831 in Nestorville, and died 03 May 1895 in Nestorville. She married **Eli Francis Morrison HALLER** 21 Nov 1854 in Nestorville.
Children of Catherine Nestor and Eli Haller are:
  i. **Jonas Haller**, b. 10 Nov 1855, Nestorville;
    d. 04 Jan 1930, Nestorville.
  ii. **James Haller**, b. 1858; m. **Mary Ann**
    WILLIAMSON.
  iii. **George Elam Haller**, b. 1859; m. (1) **Generva**
    Palestine STALNAKER; m. (2) **Bluedell**

      POLING.
iv. **Millie Catherine Haller**, b. 02 Jan 1861,
     Nestorville; d. 07 Jan 1892, Nestorville;
     m. **William L. SHANABARGER**, 26 Mar
     1879, Nestorville.
v. **Ellsworth Haller**, b. 1863.
vi. **Mary A. Haller**, b. 1866, Nestorville; m. **Wesley
     BENNETT**, 12 May 1881.
vii. **Elizabeth Haller**, b. 25 Dec 1869, Nestorville; d.
     15 Nov 1959, Fairmont, Marion County,
     West Virginia.
viii. **Ezra Haller**.
xi. **Michael Haller**

6.

William G. Nestor, son of Jonas Nestor, was born 16 Aug
1835 in Nestorville, and died 30 Jan 1897 in Nestorville. He
married **Sarah E. LOHR 03** Dec 1857 in Nestorville, daughter
of **Jacob LOHR** and **Mary FOLTZ**.

    William G. Nestor erected a log cabin on a hill above
the town of Nestorville, seemingly a difficult place to reach,
but a wise choice because of a nearby spring which ran freely.

    The following piece, *In Remembrance of Mother, Sarah
E. Lohr Nestor*, was written by C.W. Nestor and Mary E.
Haller: *Sarah E. Nestor was born 30 Nov 1840 at New Market,
Virginia. She departed this life 02 Nov 1921, therefore being
80 years, 11 months, and 2 days old. She was united in
marriage to William G. Nestor in 1857. He preceded her to the
better world on 30 Jan 1897. There were born to this union
eight children, three boys and five girls, namely Mary E.
Haller, with whom Mother made her home, R.J. Riley and C.
W. Nestor of Nestorville, Maggie C. England of Moatsville,*

Rosa Bell Pritchard of West Union, and Icy Pearl Webster of Spencer. Alice Virginia Marsh died a number of years ago.

Sarah Lohr Nestor was the grandmother of 23 grandchildren and 24 great grandchildren. She professed faith in Christ in her 13th year and she maintained that faith. The greatest desire of her heart was to see everybody do right and to see the Church of God prosper. She loved to go to church, Sunday school, and meetings, and always went when she was able. We miss her so much at home and in church. Her great testimonies brought us all nearer to Christ.

She was a great reader of good books and the church paper, but the best book of all to her was the Holy Bible. She read it through nine times and had started through for the 10th time as far as Hosea. She was eager to get through it again, but her great suffering kept her from reading the last two months of her life.

Her last visit was to the Coves settlement at her old home where her father and mother had lived and where her sister-in-law Nancy Lohr still lives. Mother was the last of her father's family to go home. What a reunion it was for her to meet and greet her loved ones there.

She was a model mother and a true Christian. We as children and grandchildren have living evidence that she is at rest and reaping a great reward. She was a member all her life of the United Brethren Church in Christ. Her home church was Camp Valley at Nestorville and she was laid to rest in the Camp Valley Cemetery.

The Lohr Family
1..

George Lohr was the first member of Sara's line who came to America. He was born in Germany and died in Maryland. He

223

married **Maria Margaretha UNK** before 1755 in Germany or Pennsylvania. She died about 1799 in Heidelberg Township, York County, Pennsylvania. According to Anne Lohr, researcher, Georg (sic) arrived at the port of Philadelphia on 30 Sep 1754 on the ship "Edinburgh." There were several Georg Lohrs who immigrated to America about the same time, as well as a George Lohr who arrived in Philadelphia before 1752. This George settled in Berks County, Pennsylvania and appears on the tax records there in 1752. Then there was a Jerg Michael Lohr who arrived on the ship "Neptune" the same day Georg arrived. There was also a Conrad Lohr who came with Georg on the "Edinburgh." Ms. Lohr suspects that Conrad and Georg were brothers, but has not been able to prove this. Both Conrad and Georg signed the Oath of Allegiance, which she copied from microfilm at the Pennsylvania State Archives in Harrisburg. She does not know where they originated in Germany, but she noted on the Oath of Allegiance that the passengers aboard the "Edinburgh" came from either the Palatine or Wittenberg (sic).

Georg Lohr was married to Maria Margaretha (surname unknown),. It is not certain if she came with him or if they were married in America. Records of the Moravian Church of York County, Pennsylvania confirm the births of their sons, George, Jr.; Peter; and Michael, all with Johan as a first name (they went by their middle names). The girls also were born in Pennsylvania, verified by church records of Jacob Lischy, Reformed Church.

Georg died very young, shortly after the birth of their eighth child, Anna Maria, and not long after their move to Washington County, Maryland. Maria Margaretha apparently remarried, maybe even twice after the death of Georg. She returned to Pennsylvania at some point and died about 1799 in

Heidelberg Township, York County, Pennsylvania.
Children of George Lohr and Maria are:

      i. **Georg Lohr, Jr., m. UNK**. He is not listed in "Abstracts of Revolutionary War Pension Files, Vol. II," even though he served as Captain. According to one of his direct descendants, George, Jr. never filed for a pension.

2.   ii. **Peter Lohr**, b. 1757, Codorus, York County, Pennsylvania.

3.   iii. **Johan Michael Lohr**, b. 1758, York County, Pennsylvania; d. 21 Sep 1841, Augusta County, Virginia.

    iv. **Baltzer Lohr.**

    v. **Joseph Lohr.**

   vi. **Daughter Lohr.**

  vii. **Daughter Lohr.**

 viii. **Anna Maria Lohr.**

2.

Peter Lohr was born 1751 in Codorus, York County, Pennsylvania. He married **Catherine EYLER.** Peter Lohr served in the Revolutionary War, enlisting at Hagerstown, Maryland. After the war, he moved to Augusta County, Virginia where, in 1790, he purchased land. According to records at the Virginia State Library, Peter and Catherine petitioned to have part of the land become a section of Greenbrier County, (West) Virginia. It appears that Peter and a man by the surname of Osborne owned several hundred acres covering Virginia and what later became West Virginia. Peter and Catherine Eyler Lohr had at least six children: John, Nicholas, John Jacob, Christian, Barbara (who died at 14 years of age), and Mary, who married **George OSBORNE**.

From <u>Virginia Soldiers of 1776</u>, pp. 859-860: *Peter
Lohr, Private. Declaration made 25 Sep 1832 that he was born
within seven miles of Little York, Pennsylvania in 1751. He left
Pennsylvania for Maryland when very young, lived there for
some years, moved to Augusta County, Virginia 40 years ago.
He volunteered at Hagerstown, Maryland in 1776 under Capt.
John Ronalds; marched in July to New York, thence to Fort
Washington, where he remained about one month; thence to an
encampment on a stream called Tuckahoe. The British
encamped in sight of the Americans under Genl. Bell, who
retreated to White Plains, where they were overtaken about
daylight by the British, and the engagement lasted a greater
part of the day. The next morning, they marched to Croton
Bridge, thence up the North River to Fishkill, where they
crossed on the way to Philadelphia, when they were ordered to
Fort Lee. While declaring war at Fort Lee, the British attacked
Fort Washington and were successful; declarant's Regt. was
not in that fight. The fort, cannon ammunition, and a number of
Americans were captured; declarant's division retreated to
Philadelphia where they were discharged.* (Taken from
Chalkley's <u>Abstracts of Augusta</u>, Vol. II, p. 478.)
Children of Peter Lohr and Catherine Eyler are:

      i. **John Lohr**.
      ii. **Nicholas Lohr**.
     iii. **John Jacob Lohr**.
     iv. **Christian Lohr**.
      v. **Barbara Lohr**.
     vi. **Mary Lohr**, m. **George OSBORNE**.

3.

Johan Michael Lohr was born 1758 in York County,

Pennsylvania, and died 21 Sep 1841 in Augusta County Virginia. He married **Catherine Elizabeth SCHRINER**. He indicated in his Revolutionary War Pension records that he and his wife moved from Washington County, Maryland, to Berkeley County, (West) Virginia, and then to Rockingham County, Virginia, where the remaining children were born. His DAR records are under the name of Michael Lohr.

DAR Volume 61, p. 179, Mrs. Florence Lohr Trimble, ID # 60542 is original source of information.

DAR Volume 90, p. 154, Mrs. Florence I. Lohr Gardner, ID # 89785, says that Michael Lohr (1755-1835) was placed on the pension roll of Washington County, Pennsylvania for service as a private, Maryland troops. This is in error, as he lived in Washington County, Maryland. She is correct that he was born near York, Pennsylvania, and died in Rockingham County, Virginia, but the dates on this record do not match those given elsewhere.

DAR Volume 91, p. 197, Mrs. Geneva Lohr Dimond, ID # 90613 is the daughter of James Madison Lohr (1840-1904) and Mary Catherine Pringle (b. 1845), m. 1865.

DAR Volume 127, p. 314, Mrs. Lillian Reeder Lohr, ID # 126992, is wife of George D. Lohr.

DAR Volume 150, p. 78, Mrs. Mildred Lohr Rice, ID # 126993, is daughter of George D. Lohr.

In Peter and Michael's Revolutionary War declarations, they both are quoted as stating that they "remember the family moving from Pennsylvania to Maryland when they were small children."

Anne Lohr says that George, son of Michael, eventually moved to the New Market area, which is now Page County, and George's children, George Jr. and Isaac and other family members, are buried in New Market, probably at Mt. Zion

Lutheran Church. Since I have found no listing for a George, son of Michael, she must mean George, son of Georg. She says that there are a few Lohrs buried at Linville Creek Cemetery, just south of Timberville, and some near Bridgewater and Dayton. However, the majority of the Lohrs appear to have lived in the northeastern part of Rockingham County, just across the county line into Page County.

Children of Johan Lohr and Catherine Schriner are:

4. i. **Peter Lohr**, b. abt. 1782, Washington County, Maryland.

  ii. **Joseph Henry Lohr**.

  iii. **Martin Lohr**.

  iv. **Christian Lohr**.

  v. **Catherine Lohr**.

  vi. **Michael Lohr, Jr.**, b. 1787, Rockingham County, Virginia; d. 1819; m. **Mary Catherine MILLER** (b. 1794), 1810.

4.

Peter Lohr was born about 1782 in Washington County, Maryland. He married **Elizabeth SALZER**, 22 Apr 1707 In Rockingham County, Virginia. She was known as "Lizzie."

Children of Peter Lohr and Elizabeth Salzer are:

  i. **Mary Lohr**.

5. ii. **Jacob Lohr**, b. 05 May 1810, Rockingham County, Virginia; d. 28 Feb 1891, Barbour County, (West) Virginia.

  iii. **Anna Christina Lohr**, b. 23 Feb 1823; bur. Barbour County, West Virginia.

  iv. **John George Lohr**, b. 20 Mar 1825; m. **Julian MOORE**.

  v. **Peter P. Lohr**, left Barbour County for Iowa, as

did his brother, John.
vi. **John Lohr**, left Barbour County for Iowa.

5.

Jacob Lohr was born 05 May 1810 in Rockingham County, Virginia, and died 28 Feb 1891 in Barbour County, West Virginia. He married **Mary FOLTZ**, daughter of **Joshua FOLTZ**. She was born 15 Jan 1814 in Virginia, and died 06 Nov 1891 in Barbour County, West Virginia. Jacob's baptism records in Rader's Lutheran Church, Timberville, Rockingham County, Virginia lists six children for his father Peter and mother Elizabeth. Jacob was baptized on 10 Apr 1811 by the Rev. Paul Henkel. Jacob was the second child listed. The first was a female, name and DOB left blank. Anne Lohr assumes that this was Mary. This family is NOT buried at Rader's. On one visit to the old cemetery, Anne found no tombstones; perhaps they were removed over the years. She reports that the old cemetery was very unkempt and the grass not cut. Many tombstones were lying around. There is no more documentation on Peter, Elizabeth, and family in this book, another indication that they "moved on." The Barbour County, (West) Virginia census of 1860 shows Jacob as age 50, born in Virginia, and Mary as 47. Their children still at home are Joseph, 17; Henry, 14, and Mary C., 8.

Children of Jacob Lohr and Mary Foltz are:

6.   i. **Sarah E. Lohr**, b. 30 Nov 1840, New Market, Virginia; d. 01 Nov 1921, Nestorville, Barbour County, West Virginia.

    ii. **Abraham Lohr**, d. Barbour County, West Virginia. It is not clear if this Abraham Lohr, who appears in the 1870 census of Cove Township, Barbour County, West Virginia,

was the son of Jacob Lohr or of one of his
siblings.
iii. **Joseph Foltz Lohr,** b. 1843.
iv. **Henry Lohr.**
v. **Mary C. Lohr.**

6.

Sarah E. Lohr was born 30 Nov 1840 in New Market,
Virginia, and died 02 Nov 1921 in Nestorville, Barbour
County, West Virginia. She married **William G. NESTOR,** 03
Dec 1857, in Nestorville, Barbour County, West Virginia, son
of **Jonas NESTOR** and **Elizabeth HOLSBERRY.** William G.
Nestor was born 16 Aug 1835 in Nestorville, and died 30 Jan
1897 in Nestorville.
Children of William Nestor and Sarah Lohr are:
    i. **Mary Elizabeth Nestor,** b. 09 Jul 1860,
        Nestorville; d. 13 Aug 1934, Nestorville;
        m. **Jonas HALLER.**
    ii. **Robert M. Nestor,** b. 1862, Nestorville; d. 1951,
        Nestorville; m. **Rachel PHILLIPS** 06 Mar
        1880, Nestorville.
    iii. **Riley J. Nestor,** b. 21 May 1864, Nestorville; d.
        05 Apr 1956, Nestorville; m. **Virginia**
        GODWIN 03 May 1896, Nestorville.
    iv. **Charles W. Nestor,** b. 1866, Nestorville; d.1931,
        Nestorville; m. **Alda Virginia FRYE,** 26 Dec
        1896, Nestorville.
    v. **Alice Virginia Nestor,** b. 1869; m. **A. J.**
        MARSH, 15 May 1890.
7.   vi. **Rosa Bell Nestor,** b. 1872, Nestorville; d.
        09 Jan 1948, St. Marys, West Virginia;
        m. **Millard Fillmore PRITCHARD,** No.

110, 12 Oct 1887.

vii. **Margaret Cyrilda Nestor**, b. 1875, Nestorville;
m. **Baxter Michael ENGLAND** 27 Jan 1899,
Nestorville.

viii. **Icy Pearl Nestor**, m. (1) **E. W. WEBSTER**, a
Baptist minister, 04 Nov 1905; m. (2)
Dr. Unk REYNOLDS. Icy Pearl and E. W.
Webster lived in Huntington, West Virginia
and had two sons. One of them, Ellwood,
became a loan officer who used strong-arm
men to recover his investments. While in
high school, he frequently visited the
Reynolds family in St. Marys. Eugene
Reynolds remembers Ellwood as a
man-about-town with a fancy car. He boasted
that he could get Gene a date, but when Gene
arrived to pick up his date, she told him that
he would have to come back later because she
could not leave home until after her husband
went to work.

110. (Continued)

Millard Fillmore Pritchard, son of No. 68, Thomas Willis
Pritchard, was born 22 Sep, 1857 on the South Fork of the
Hughes River in Ritchie County. He died 10 Jul 1927 and is
buried in Elk View Masonic Cemetery near the Hammond
Methodist Church, Clarksburg, West Virginia, where he last
served. His first wife, **Margaret Cerilda KELLEY**, died 12
Jan 1887 shortly after childbirth. He next married **Rosa Bell
NESTOR**, the daughter of a family who were members of his
congregation in Nestorville, West Virginia. At the time of their
marriage, Millard had a two-year-old son, **Enoch**, and a baby

daughter, **Amelia Gay**. After his first wife's death, one of her relatives, Hannah Kelley Phillips, persuaded him to let her take the baby, as it was difficult for him to care for a newborn. Subsequently Hannah and her husband, Scott Phillips, went west to Oregon and he never again saw his daughter.

For most of his life, Millard was a Methodist Episcopal minister. He was converted early in life at the White Oak Methodist Church in Ritchie County. In 1883, he entered the ministry of the United Brethren Church and served in West Virginia until 1890 when he transferred to the Rock River Conference, Illinois, where he served until 1898. That year, he returned to West Virginia and entered the ministry of the Methodist Episcopal Church, remaining there until the end of his life. In West Virginia, he served at: Winifred, Parsons, Littleton, Wallace, Zane Street in Wheeling, Sistersville, St. Marys, Ash Chapel in Clarksburg, Shinnston, West Union, Pennsboro, and Hammond in Clarksburg.

A portion of a Tribute to Rev. Millard Fillmore Pritchard by Daniel Westfall, D. D. written at the time of his death, reads: *Brother Pritchard was a good preacher. His people always spoke highly of his pulpit work. He was evangelical in his type of preaching and witnessed many revivals. He was not sensational, but so sincere that he won for Christ. Preaching was his passion, and he gave himself to the work. Though seventy years of age, he knew no place for rest. During his forty-four years of ministry, he was not off more than six months' time. The funeral was conducted from the Hammond Church under the direction of District Superintendent G. D. Smith...By their presence, a large number of pastors of different denominations bore testimony to their high esteem for their fellow worker. Interment was made in the Masonic cemetery near the church.*

Reverend Millard Fillmore Pritchard, age forty, and Ernest Markwood Pritchard, age four, Winifred Junction, Kanawha County, West Virginia, 1897

Reverend Millard Fillmore Pritchard stands before one of the West Virginia churches he served and helped construct. Date and location unknown.

Rosa Nestor Pritchard and Reverend Millard Fillmore Pritchard
St. Marys, West Virginia, c. 1910

232d

Millard Fillmore Pritchard closely resembled Abraham Lincoln, had a wonderful sense of humor which he utilized in his sermons, and was greatly loved and admired by his congregations and friends wherever he went.

Rosa Belle Nestor married her minister, Rev. Millard Fillmore Pritchard, following the death of his first wife earlier in the year. She was not yet sixteen years old at the time. Their first home was in Illinois, where their three children were born, but homesickness took them back to West Virginia.

Rosa Belle was a devout Christian and her life centered around the Methodist Church. Sundays were meant for church and worship. Thursday was prayer meeting night, and the Ladies Aid met throughout the month. She designated one day a week as calling day to visit the sick or a church friend. From her meager widow's pension, she always took out a tenth, which she put in a velvet tithing bag. This was for church use only. She died suddenly on 09 Jan 1948 of a stroke while banking at the Pleasants County Bank in St. Marys, West Virginia where she lived near her daughter, Mildred Pritchard Reynolds. At 76 years of age, she lived to see three of her great-grandchildren: Patricia Gilpin, Kay Gilpin, and Randy Reynolds.

Children of Millard Pritchard and Margaret Kelley are:

196.   i. **Enoch Delmar Pritchard**, b. 11 Mar 1885, Nestorville, West Virginia; d. 24 Oct 1961, Fairmont, West Virginia.

197   ii. **Amelia Gay Pritchard**, b. 22 Dec 1886, Nestorville, West Virginia; d. 29 Sep 1959 in Washington State.

Children of Millard Pritchard and Rosa Nestor are:

198.   iii. **Helen Willa Pritchard**, b. 16 Jan 1890, Coleta, Whiteside County, Illinois; d. 13 Nov 1985,

Wallace, Harrison County, West Virginia.
199.   iv. **Ernest Markwood Pritchard**, b. 12 Sep 1893,
Coleta, Whiteside County, Illinois; d. 03 Feb
1979, Hackettstown, Warren County, New
Jersey, bur. Masonic Cemetery, Clarksburg,
Harrison County, West Virginia.
200.   v. **Mildred Edith Pritchard**, b. 16 Jan 1896,
Compton, Lee County, Illinois; d. 10 Nov 1985,
St. Marys, Pleasants County, West Virginia;
bur. Odd Fellows Cemetery, St. Marys.

111.

Sarah Eliza "Lydia" Pritchard, daughter of No. 68, Thomas
Willis Pritchard, was born 30 Mar 1859 in Ritchie County,
(West), Virginia, and died 08 Nov 1922. She married **Charles
Nimrod RATCLIFFE** about 1880. He was born about 1855 in
Ritchie County.
Children of Sarah Pritchard and Charles Ratcliffe are:
201   i. **Grace Catherine Ratcliffe**, b. 31 Mar 1881.
202.   ii. **Lloyd Foreman Radcliffe**, b. 18 Sep 1897.
(Changed surname spelling.)

112.

Giles William Pritchard, son of No. 68, Thomas Willis
Pritchard, was born 21 Jun 1861 in Ritchie County, West
Virginia, and died 30 Oct 1912 in Fairmont, Marion County,
West Virginia. He married **Catherine Hannah THOMAS**
before 1895 in Maryland. She was born 03 Jul 1869 in Ritchie
County, West Virginia and died 17 Jul 1940 in Fairmont. She
is buried in Woodlawn Cemetery, Fairmont, Marion County,
West Virginia.
Children of Giles Pritchard and Catherine Thomas are:

203   i. **Anna May Pritchard**, b. 02 May 1895, Barton,
Garrett County, Maryland; d. 19 Apr 1975,
Pittsburgh, Allegany County, Pennsylvania, bur.
Mt. Lebanon Cemetery.

204.   ii. **Daisy Ethel Pritchard**, b. 11 Sep 1897, Barton,
Garrett County, Maryland; d. 13 Aug 1984,
Pittsburgh, Allegany County Pennsylvania.

205.   iii. **Bertha Catherine Pritchard,** b. 12 Jan 1901,
Fairmont, Marion County, West Virginia; d.
05 Sep 1983.

206.   iv. **Effie Elizabeth Pritchard**, b. 22 May 1903,
Fairmont, Marion County, West Virginia.

207.   v. **Claris Edward Pritchard**, b. 18 Mar 1906,
Fairmont, West Virginia; d. 20 Dec 1971, bur.
Woodlawn Cemetery, Fairmont, Marion County,
West Virginia.

113.

Judson Fantley Pritchard, son of No. 68, Thomas Willis
Pritchard, was born 17 Jan 1864 in Ritchie County, West
Virginia, and died 01 Apr 1946 in Weston, Lewis County,
West Virginia. He married (1) **Minnie BAILEY**, b. abt 1874,
Ritchie County, West Virginia. He married (2) **Dora NORRIS**
in 1906. Judson Fantley Pritchard was a minister in the United
Brethren in Christ Church and was one of the district
superintendents in the West Virginia Conference.
Child of Judson Fantley Pritchard and Dora Norris is:

208   i. **Mark Norris Pritchard**, b.17 Aug 1908; d.
25 May 1965.

114.

Ira Sanford Pritchard, son of No. 68, Thomas Willis

Pritchard, was born 17 Sep 1866 in Ritchie County, West
Virginia and died 19 Feb, 1960. He married **Irene Brink
CLAYTON** 24 Dec 1883. She was born 18 Feb 1869 in
Ritchie County, West Virginia and died 04 Jan 1944.
Children of Ira Pritchard and Irene Clayton are:
209.   i. **Claris Clayton Pritchard**, b. September 21,
              1895; d. July 1975, Mt. Orab, Brown County,
              Ohio.
210   ii. **Dwight Ira Pritchard**, b. January 21, 1905; d.
              December 1975, Carlton, Yamhill County,
              Oregon.

115.

Francis Ezra Pritchard, son of No. 68. Thomas Willis
Pritchard, was born 11 Sep 1870 in Ritchie County, West
Virginia, and died 16 Jan 1950 in Ritchie County. He married
Maude Genevra CLAYTON 07 May 1892 in Ritchie County.
She was born 03 Jan 1876 in Ritchie County and died 18 Jan
1961. Frank Pritchard was the owner of the Pritchard
Telephone Company based in Pullman, Ritchie County.
Children of Francis Pritchard and Maude Clayton are:
211.   i. **Lora Audra Pritchard**, b. 11 Mar 1893; d.
              23 Dec 1960.
         ii. **Lela A. Pritchard**, b. 13 Apr 1894; d. 01 May
              1894.
        iii. **Bessie Amanda Pritchard**, b. 27 Aug 1897; m.
              Tony FERGUSON, 25 Dec 1920.   .
212   iv. **Eva Jane Pritchard**, b.06 May 1901, Pullman,
              Ritchie County, West Virginia; d. 06 Jun 1989
              Vienna, Wood County, West Virginia. m.
              Wheeler Shirley WILSON.
         v. **Nellie Opal Pritchard**, b. 23 Sep 1908; m.

Harley JENNINGS (b. 1887, Ritchie
County; d. 1962, Pennsboro, Ritchie County,
West Virginia) 26 Sep 1936.

116.

Bushrod Washington Pritchard, son of No 68, Thomas
Willis Pritchard, was born 22 Jul 1873 in Ritchie County, West
Virginia, and died 17 Mar 1956 in Weston, Lewis County,
West Virginia. He married **Diantha Esther SINES**. She was
born 08 Jan 1889.
Children of Bushrod Pritchard and Diantha Sines are:
213.   i. **Paul Revere Pritchard**, b.04 Sep 1908.
         ii. **Violette Amanda Pritchard**, b. 19 Dec 1909; m.
             John K. NELSON, October 1941.
         iii. **Carlos Edgar Pritchard**, b. 14 Sep 1913, d.
             December 1950.
214   iv. **Denzil Lynnwood Pritchard**, b. 10 Apr 1921.
215.   v. **Betty Lucille Pritchard**, b. 12 Feb 1924.

117.

Walter Icen Pritchard, son of No. 68, Thomas Willis
Pritchard, was born 22 Apr 1876 in Ritchie County, West
Virginia, and died 01 May 1953 in Weston, Lewis County,
West Virginia. He married **Jessie Lee JORDAN**, daughter of
Adonijah N. JORDAN (b. 04 Jan 1847, Randolph County,
West Virginia, d. 01 Nov 1930, Weippe, Clearwater County,
Idaho) and **Amanda Lee NELSON** (b. 30 Apr 1853,
Circleville, Pendleton County, West Virginia; d. 24 Mar 1926,
Weippe, Clearwater County, Idaho). Jessie Lee was born 05
Apr 1885, in Job, Randolph County, West Virginia and died 01
Mar 1969 in Seattle, King County, Washington. She and
Walter Icen Pritchard first met at a country church service.

They were married 04 Mar 1901 in Gladwin, Tucker County, West Virginia. After the birth of 12 children, she divorced him and married (2) **Preston O. PLACE** 22 Jun 1927 in Kootenai, Idaho. She married (3) **John Wesley SNYDER,** (b. 23 Feb 1874, Dry Fork, Randolph County, West Virginia; d. 27 Apr 1960, Lewiston, Nez Perce County, Idaho). Jessie and John W. Snyder were married 31 Dec 1933, Orofino, Clearwater County, Idaho. He was the father-in-law of her daughter, **Marie Alice PRITCHARD,** No. 217.

Walter Icen Pritchard had difficulty disciplining his children. Marie and Torrey left home after an altercation and Jessie soon followed Marie to Idaho. Walter traveled back and forth trying to dissuade her from divorcing him, but she did not back down. Until the divorce, he had devoted his life to the ministry in the United Brethren and Methodist Church. Because no church wanted a divorced minister, he never again was hired to preach and he died penniless.

Children of Walter Pritchard and Jessie Jordan are:

       i. **Hycle Victoria Pritchard**, b. 13 Mar 1902; d. June 1902, Ritchie County, West Virginia.

216.   ii. **Castle Cowden Pritchard**, b. 24 May 1904; d. 07 Mar 1955. After getting into trouble and outraging his father, he left home and changed his name to **Don SUTHERLAND**.

217.   iii. **Marie Alice Pritchard**, b. 12 Jan 1906, Harrisville, Ritchie County, West Virginia; d. 11 Jan 1991, Pendleton, Umatilla County, Oregon.

218   iv. **Torrey Icen Pritchard**, b. 10 Nov 1907, Jarvisville, Harrison County, West Virginia; d. 21 Mar 1979, Seattle, King County, Washington.

       v. **Amanda Talahassie Pritchard**, b. 25 Feb 1909; d.

June 1909.
219.   vi. **Sheldon Schofield "Gil" Pritchard**, b. 25 Sep 1910, Selbyville, Upshur County, West Virginia; d. 24 Feb 1990, King County, Washington.
220.   vii. **Clara Hillis Pritchard**, b. 24 Dec1912, Syracuse, Meigs County, Ohio; d. 27 Sep 1996, Pierce, Clearwater County, Idaho..
        viii. **Walter Gordon Quayle Pritchard,** b. 25 Feb 1914 in Wick, Warren County, Iowa and died 11 Dec 1998 in Yakima, Yakima County, Washington. He married **Vivian Pearl NATION,** b. 24 Jun 1908, Stanfield Junction, Umatilla County, Oregon; d. 07 Jan 1996, Yakima, Yakima County, Washington.
        ix. **Anna Jesse Pritchard**, b. 04 Jan 1916, Mt. Pleasant, Jefferson County, Ohio; d. 18 Apr 2000, Everett, Snohomish County, Washington; m. **Tolva O. GRANHOLM,** b. 28 Jul 1907; d. 12 Feb 1993, Edmonds, King County, Washington.
221.   x. **Blanche Agatha Pritchard**, b. 23 Sep 1919; Barrackville, Marion County, West Virginia d. 28 Jan 2000, Spokane, Spokane County, Washington.
222.   xi. **Fifi Lee Pritchard**, b. 31 Dec 1921 Camden-on-Gaulley, Webster County, West Virginia; d. 18 Mar 2001, Bremerton, King County, Washington.

118.
Flora Odell Lawson, daughter of No. 70, Anna Pritchard, was

born 09 Nov 1861 in Oxford, Ritchie County, West Virginia, and died 18 May 1932 in Fairmont, Marion County, West Virginia. She married **Marshall Neal PRUNTY** 30 Aug 1877. He was born 11 Sep 1852 in Oxford, Ritchie County, West Virginia, and died 14 Feb 1931 in Pullman, Ritchie County. He is the sixth of ten children of **Felix PRUNTY** and **Emily GREATHOUSE**, and great-grandson of **John PRUNTY,** the pioneer, Harrison County Legislator, and sheriff. He spent his entire life in the Oxford-White Oak-Pullman area as a farmer and stockman. During the early years of his marriage, he worked at the Pritchard Mill. Flora Lawson Prunty died at the home of her daughter, Mrs. Anna Long, in Fairmont, Marion County. Both Flora and Marshall are buried in the Pullman Cemetery. They were parents of eight children, all born at Oxford.

Children of Flora Lawson and Marshall Prunty are:

223   i. **Sylvester Orval Prunty**, b. 17 Jul 1878; d. 07 Feb, 1956, Harrisville, Ritchie County, West Virginia.

    ii. **Anna Prunty**, b. 05 Aug 1881; d. 11 Dec 1956; buried IOOF Cemetery, Harrisville, Ritchie County; m. (1) **Lee Roy WILSON,** son of **William Martin WILSON and Mary Jane NAY** (div.); m. (2) **John LONG**, railroad engineer; lived at Fairmont, Marion County; she was a practical nurse.

    iii. **Felix O. Prunty**, b. 20 Apr 1883; d. 29 Aug 1967, Newkirk, Kay County Oklahoma; m. **Ada Maude KNIGHT**, daughter of **Jerome R. KNIGHT** and **Rachel Florence JONES**; went to Oklahoma in early manhood, became very successful oil producer and cattle rancher.

iv. **Jesse Prunty**, b. 18 Jul 1885; d. 21 Mar 1967, Falls
    Church, Fairfax County, Virginia; bur.
    Bridgeport Cemetery; m. **Harvey Blaine**
    LOWTHER, son of **Wilson LOWTHER**
    and **Lucia Helen Hale GRAY,** in 1906;
    divorced in 1948.

v. **May Prunty**, b.10 Feb 1887; d.28 Dec 1925; bur.
    Pullman Cemetery; m. **Everett NAY.**

vi. **Raymond Cleo Prunty**, b. 11 Aug 1892; d.
    29 Sep 1963; bur. Lakeview Cemetery,
    Cleveland, Ohio; m. **Freda ROSS**, daughter of
    Edward ROSS and **Caroline HARDESTY**.

vii. **Carl Prunty**, b. 11 May 1896; d. same day.

viii. **Marshall Erlo Prunty**, b. 25 Mar 1900; living
    at Lexington, Kentucky in 1980; m.
    Genevieve CORDRAY, daughter of **Charles**
    Isaac CORDRAY and **Mary Alice LYNCH**;
    was an executive for Consolidation Coal
    Company, Jenkins, Kentucky.

119.

Charles J. Pritchard, son of No. 71, William Tyler Pritchard,
was born between 1870 and 1875 in Ritchie County, West
Virginia and died in Webster County, West Virginia. He
married **Ida Mae CAUTHORN**, daughter of **James**
GAWTHORNE (sic) 11 Jun 1896. The Ritchie County
marriage records give her name as Ida Cochran, 16, and his age
as 23. It states that he was born in Doddridge County, which is
possible because Pritchard lands hugged the border of the two
counties. Charles Pritchard lived in Pennsboro, Ritchie County,
West Virginia during his youth. After marrying, he lived in
Webster County, West Virginia, then moved to Nobel County,

Ohio, about 20 miles northwest of Parkersburg, West Virginia. In *Descendants of Jacob Nester*, he is identified as a resident of Nobel County, Ohio while Ida Mae's residence is Toll Gate, West Virginia. It is not known if they were separated or divorced, or if he maintained two homes.

Child of Charles Pritchard and Ida Cauthorn is:

224.   i. **Ian Hortense Pritchard**, b. 03 Jul 1902, Webster County, West Virginia; d. 28 Nov 1981, Modesto, Stanislaus County, California.

120.

William A. Pritchard, son of No. 71, William Tyler Pritchard, was born 28 Dec 1864; d. 10 Oct 1911, and was buried in the Pennsboro E.U.B. Cemetery, Ritchie County, West Virginia. He married **Minerva DAVIS,** 09 Jun 1887, in Ritchie County, West Virginia. She was born 1873 in Marion County, West Virginia. Minnie Lowther (*Ritchie County in History and Romance*, pp. 287A-288) says that William Pritchard was murdered. She notes: "The four sons (Lloyd, Charles, Olin and William) lived at Pennsboro, Ritchie County, West Virginia. William was murdered. See pages 494 and 690 Clay District Ritchie County." For more on the Davis family, see *Davis, the Settlers of Salem,* by Susie Davis Nicholson.

Child of William Pritchard and Minerva Davis is:

    i. **Bert T. Pritchard**, b. June 27, 1891, Ritchie County, West Virginia.

121.

Olin D. Pritchard, son of No. 71, William Tyler Pritchard, was born 1868 in Oxford, Ritchie County, West Virginia, and died 1959 in Oxford. He married **Roena GARRISON** 01 May

1896 in Ritchie County. She was born 1874 in Ritchie County, and died 1935 in Ritchie County. Both are buried in the Pennsboro Masonic Cemetery, Ritchie County, West Virginia. Children of Olin Pritchard and Roena Garrison are:

      i. **Clyde W. Pritchard**, b. 22 Apr 1897, Ritchie County; d. July 1983, Clarksburg, Harrison County, West Virginia.

     ii. **Dell Pritchard**, b. July 1899, Ritchie County.

122.

Laura Pritchard, daughter of No. 72, John Pritchard, was born 10 May 1871 in Ritchie County, West Virginia, and died in 1935. She married **John JOHNSON** on 08 Jan 1899 in Ritchie County. He was born February 1869 in Ritchie County. Child of Laura Pritchard and John Johnson is:

      i. **Nellie Johnson**, b. May 1900, Ritchie County; d. 1907, Ritchie County; bur. White Oak Cemetery, White Oak, Ritchie County.

123.

William Morgan Wass, son of No.73, Cassandra Pritchard, was born 19 Jan 1857 near Hall, Ritchie County, (West) Virginia and died 17 Jul 1942 in Mariposa County, California. He married **Martha Ellen "Ella" PIERPOINT** 30 Dec 1880, in Ritchie County, West Virginia, daughter of **Larkin PIERPOINT** and **Elizabeth JONES**. She was born 07 Nov 1856 in Ritchie County, and died 1940 in Mariposa County, California. Children of William Wass and Martha Pierpoint are:

      i. **Elain Wass**, b. April 1885.

     ii. **Walter Edward Wass**, b. April 1889.

    iii. **William George Wass**, b. 1892.

124.

Lewis Maxwell Wass, son of No. 73, Cassandra Pritchard, was born 26 Sep 1860 in Ritchie County, West Virginia, and died 16 Nov 1947 in Mariposa County, California. He married **Elizabeth Amarka ASHWORTH** in California, daughter of **David ASHWORTH** and **Jessina WHITE**, both born in Kentucky. The Ashworths moved to California in 1849, first to San Jose, then to Mariposa County, where they were homesteaders. They died there and are buried in Mariposa Cemetery. Elizabeth Ashworth Wass was born 15 Mar 1865 in Mariposa County, California, and died 01 Jan 1933 at Wass Ranch, Mariposa County.

Lewis Wass moved to California about 1883 to join his brother William who was already there. He bought his mother-in-law's farm and farmed until he was quite elderly, at which time he gave the farm to his son Herman. Herman's widow was still living there in 1984. Lewis, a truck gardener, sold his produce to Mariposa merchants. It is said that he was a well-known and uncommonly accurate weather forecaster, using the moon as a guide and refusing to tell anyone how he did it. He was known as Uncle Lew to the entire community.

Children of Lewis Wass and Elizabeth Ashworth are:

225.   i. **Ethel Lee Wass**, b. 25 Jan 1887, Wass Ranch, Mariposa County, California; d. 01 Apr 1969, Tulare, Fresno County, California.

226.   ii. **William "Dick" Harrison Wass**, b. 21 May 1889, Mariposa, Mariposa County, California; d. 27 Sep, 1958, Mariposa County.

227.   iii. **Lewis Maxwell Wass, Jr.**, b. 04 Jan 1893, Wass Ranch, Mariposa County, California; d. September 1982, Merced, Merced County, California.

228.   iv. **Herman H. Wass**, b. 24 Oct 1895, California; d. October 1981, Mariposa, Mariposa County, California.
229.   v. **Fred Wass**, b. 26 Nov 1898, Mariposa County, California; d. 11 Jan 1989, Mariposa County, California.
230.   vi. **Aileen May Wass**, b. 25 Nov 1906, Wass Ranch, Mariposa County, California; d. February 1994, Mariposa, County, California.

125.

Harrison Ellsworth "Ellie" Wass, Jr., son of No. 73, Cassandra Pritchard, was born 13 Feb 1863 near Hall, Ritchie County, West Virginia, and died 24 Nov 1945 in Harrisville, Ritchie County. He married **Mary "Mollie" Susan MILLER**, 27 Dec 1883 in Ritchie County. She was the daughter of **John MILLER** and **Henrietta TRIPPETT**. She was born 14 Feb 1864 in Grantsville, Calhoun County, West Virginia, and died 01 Jan 1955 in Harrisville, Ritchie County, West Virginia. Both are buried in Harrisville IOOF Cemetery, Ritchie County. Children of Harrison Wass and Mary Miller are:

231.   i. **Carrie Alice Wass**, b. 02 Feb 1885, Harrisville, Ritchie County; d. 05 Dec 1971, Harrisville, Ritchie County.
  ii. **Clyde Ellsworth Wass**, b. 09 Aug 1888, Harrisville, Ritchie County, West Virginia; d. 28 Jun 1962, Harrisville; unm; bur. IOOF Cemetery, Harrisville.
232.   iii. **Winifred Chloe Wass**, b. 25 Mar 1892, Harrisville, Ritchie County, West Virginia; d. 04 Dec 1989, Harrisville.

245

126.

John Anderson Wass, son of No. 73, Cassandra Pritchard, was born 04 Jun 1865, near Hall, Ritchie County, West Virginia, and died March 1936 in Huntington, Cabell County, West Virginia. He married **Ida Olive HAYDEN**, 04 Nov 1886, in Ritchie County. She was the daughter of **Isaac HAYDEN** and **Elizabeth THARP**. She was born March 1869 in Ritchie County, and died in 1922.

Children of John Wass and Ida Hayden are:

> i. **Maud F. Wass**, b. August 1887, Hazelgreen, Ritchie County, West Virginia.
>
> ii. **Ora Alice Wass**, b. 04 Jul 1889, Hazelgreen, Ritchie County, West Virginia; m. **Charles Cars PARKS** (b. 1882, Ritchie County), 28 Oct 1906, Ritchie County.
>
> iii. **Ada Delva Wass**, b. 19 Aug 1891, Hazelgreen, Ritchie County, West Virginia; d. 1973, Ritchie County; m. **Harry Maupin SCHEFF** (b. 16 Jul 1894, Ritchie County; d. 1973, Ritchie County.) Note: Ada's name was changed from Cassa E.; no formal documentation of name change.
>
> iv. **Goldie Pearl Wass**, b. 07 Nov 1893, Hazelgreen, Ritchie County, West Virginia; m. **Unk OLLUM.**
>
> v. **Glen Ruble Wass**, b. 07 Jul 1895, Ritchie County, West Virginia; d. 03 Feb 1902; bur. Bethany Cemetery, Hazelgreen, Ritchie County.
>
> vi. **Mamie "Minnie" Snow Wass,** b. December 1898, Ritchie County, West Virginia; m. **Unk PAYNE.**
>
> vii. **Theodore "Teddy" Roosevelt Wass**, b. 1902; d. young.

viii. **John Roy Wass**, b. 28 Jun 1903, Ritchie County,
West Virginia; d. December 1971, Huntington,
Cabell County, West Virginia.

ix. **Ruby Thelma Wass**, b. 16 Mar 1906, Ritchie
County, West Virginia; d. April 1979,
Huntington, Cabell County, West Virginia; m.
unk CHATTERTON.

x. **Hallie Paul Wass**, b. 26 Feb 1908, Ritchie County,
West Virginia; d. March 1980, Ohio.

127.

Barbara Alice Wass, daughter of No. 73, Cassandra Pritchard
Wass, was born 01 Nov 1867 in Goffs, Ritchie County, West
Virginia, and died 30 Nov 1962 in Harrisville, Ritchie County.
She married **Lathrop Columbus GOFF**, 24 Oct 1886 in
Goffs, Ritchie County. He was the son of **Marcellus GOFF**
and **Lydia SMITH**. He was born 09 Jun 1867 in Hazelgreen
(Dry Run), Ritchie County, West Virginia, and died 30 Aug
1928 in Parkersburg, Wood County, West Virginia. Both are
buried in the IOOF Cemetery, Harrisville, Ritchie County.
Children of Barbara Wass and Lathrop Goff are:

i . **Alexander Goff**, b. 19 Nov 1888, Burnt House,
Ritchie County, West Virginia; d. 21 Nov 1889.

233. ii. **Myrtle Ethel Goff**, b. 21 Oct 1890, Burnt House,
Ritchie County; d. 05 May 1964, Parkersburg,
Wood County, West Virginia.

iii. **June Leigh Goff**, b. 21 Nov 1892, Burnt House,
Ritchie County, West Virginia; d. 04 Jul 1982,
Harrisville, Ritchie County; m. **Fred GAINER**
(b. May 1890, White Pine, Calhoun County,
West Virginia; d. 1956, Cincinnati, Hamilton
County, Ohio), 07 Jun 1911, Harrisville; both

bur. IOOF Cemetery, Harrisville, Ritchie County; no children.

234   iv. **Hermione "Herma" Pearl Goff**, b. 07 May 1895, Burnt House, Ritchie County, West Virginia; d. 17 Jan 1971, Harrisville, Ritchie County.

235.   v. **Winifred Dell Goff**, b.22 Sep 1898, Burnt House, Ritchie County, West Virginia; d. 16 Mar 1989, Harrisville, Ritchie County.

236.   vi. **Fredda Marcella Goff**, b. 17 Jul 1908, Burnt House, Ritchie County, West Virginia; d. 11 Jul 1952, Parkersburg, Wood County, West Virginia.

128.

Peter Wass, son of No. 73, Cassandra Pritchard, was born 19 May 1870 in Goffs, Ritchie County, West Virginia, and died 12 Dec 1951 in Hazelgreen, Ritchie County. He married **Anna Mae MITCHELL** 18 Apr 1897 in Gilmer County, West Virginia. She was born 27 May 1873 in Berea, Ritchie County, and died 08 Jan 1961, in Hazelgreen, Ritchie County. Both are buried in Bethany Cemetery, Ritchie County.

Children of Peter Wass and Anna Mitchell are:

237.   i. **Ralph Paul Wass**, b. 06 Feb 1898, Jesse Cains Run, Ritchie County, West Virginia; d. May 1981, Ohio.

238.   ii. **Bertha Pearl Wass,** b. 05 Apr 1900, Jesse Cains Run, Ritchie County, West Virginia; d. 05 May 1991, Washington, Wood County, West Virginia.

239.   iii. **Belva May Wass**, b. 22 Feb 1901, Goffs, Ritchie County, West Virginia; d. 19 Dec 1967, Ritchie

County. West Virginia.
iv. **Daisy Hazel Wass**, b. 09 Aug 1904, Goffs, Ritchie
County, West Virginia; d. 18 Sep 1944; bur
Bethany Cemetery, Hazelgreen, Ritchie County.
240.   v. **Cecil Byrl Wass**, b. 21 Jun 1907, Goffs, Ritchie
County, West Virginia; d. May 1979,
Mariposa County, California.

129.

Charles Grant Wass, son of No. 73, Cassandra Pritchard
Wass, was born 12 Sep 1872 in Goffs, Ritchie County, West
Virginia, and died 19 Jan 1950, in Harrisville, Ritchie County.
He married (1) **Cora WASHBURN** 18 Jun 1896, in Ritchie
County, daughter of **Cyrus WASHBURN** and **Martha
SINNET**. She was born 01 Nov 1875 in Cains Run, Ritchie
County, and died 19 Jan 1904, in Hazelgreen, Ritchie County.
He married (2) **Edith CUNNINGHAM**, 30 Nov 1904 in
Ritchie County, daughter of **George CUNNINGHAM** and
Florence SNODGRASS. She was born 13 Oct 1880 in
Pennsboro, Ritchie County, and died 21 Nov 1965 in
Harrisville, Ritchie County.
Children of Charles Grant Wass and Cora Washburn are:
241.   i. **Romeo Grant Wass**, b. 09 May 1897, Ritchie
County, West Virginia; d. 04 Jan 1990,
Harrisville, Ritchie County.
242.   ii. **Hosea Harrison Wass**, b. 12 Jan 1899, Washburn,
Ritchie County, West Virginia; d. 20 Jan 1975,
Harrisville, Ritchie County.
243.   iii. **Juna Myrtle Wass**, b. 12 Sep 1900, Ritchie County,
West Virginia; d. 11 Jan 1989, Harrisville,
Ritchie County.
244.   iv. **Eva Madge Wass**, b. 20 Oct 1902, Ritchie County;

d. 05 Feb 1973, Winter Park, Orange County, Florida.

Children of Charles Wass and Edith Cunningham are:

245   v. **Harlie Graydon Wass**, b. 19 Aug 1905, Jesse Cains Run, Ritchie County, West Virginia; d. 21 Mar 1957, Harrisville, Ritchie County.

246.   vi. **Charles Fred Wass**, b. 11 Aug 1908, Ritchie County, West Virginia; d. 21 Mar 1957, Harrisville, Ritchie County.

247.   vii. **Mildred Edith Wass**, b. 17 Dec 1909, Ritchie County, West Virginia; d. 09 Feb 1973, Ritchie County, West Virginia.

130.

Roy Wass, son of No. 73, Cassandra Pritchard, was born 09 Jun 1875 in Goffs, Ritchie County, West Virginia, and died 04 Apr 1954 in Harrisville, Ritchie County. He married **Edna Maude WILSON**, 21 May 1911 in Ritchie County. The daughter of **Basil WILSON** and **Mary FOWLER**, she was born April 1880 in Ritchie County, and died 1966 in Ritchie County. Both are buried in Bethany Cemetery, Hazelgreen, Ritchie County.

Children of Roy Wass and Edna Wilson are:

   i. **Mary Wass**, b. 17 Jun 1912, Jesse Cains Run, Ritchie County, West Virginia; d .20 Jun 1912.

248.   ii. **Cassandra Wass**, b. 15 Feb 1914, Jesse Cains Run, Ritchie County, West Virginia; d. 01 Mar 1991, Boulder, Boulder County, Colorado.

   iii. **Wilson Rexroad Wass**, b. 25 Jan 1916, Jesse Cains Run, Ritchie County, West Virginia; d. May 1980, Harrisville, Ritchie County; bur. Bethany

Cemetery, Hazelgreen, Ritchie County.
249.   iv. **Daisy Delle Wass**, b. 06 Oct, 1919, Jesse Cains Run,
Ritchie County, West Virginia.
250.   v. **Josephine Jean Wass**, b. 18 Feb 1922, Jesse Cains
Run, Ritchie County, West Virginia.

131.

James Rienzi Wass, son of No. 73, Cassandra Pritchard, was
born 17 Oct 1878 in Goffs, Ritchie County, West Virginia, and
died 1912 in Huntington, Cabell County, West Virginia. He
married **Leota Maud GOFF** 1902 in Ritchie County, daughter
of **Ezra GOFF** and **Lottie SMITH**. She was born 01 Jun 1883
in Hazelgreen, Ritchie County, West Virginia, and died 24 Sep
1945 in Sarasota, Sarasota County, Florida.
Children of James Wass and Leota Goff are:
i. **Son Wass**, b. 01 Jan 1903, Ritchie County, West
Virginia; d. 03 Jan 1903; bur Bethany Cemetery,
Hazelgreen, Ritchie County.
ii. **Millie Wass**, b. abt 1905, Huntington, Cabell
County, West Virginia; d. infant.
iii. **Helen Fawn Wass**, b. 25 Jan 1907, Huntington,
Cabell County, West Virginia.
251.   iv. **Virginia Opal Wass**, b. 12 Dec 1910, Huntington,
Cabell County, West Virginia; d. February 1984,
Bradenton, Manatee County, Florida.

132.

Bertha Fern Caster, daughter of No. 75, Daniel Caster, was
born 10 Aug 1894 in Decatur County, Kansas, and died 17 Dec
1938 in Rawlins County, Kansas. She married **Tillman Joseph
TAYLOR** 27 Oct 1927 in Phillips County, Kansas. He was
born 06 Dec 1871 in Morgan County, Ohio, and died 30 Nov

1961· in Rawlins County, Kansas.
Child of Bertha Caster and Tillman Taylor is:
>   i. **Robert Joseph Taylor**, b. 16 Nov 1931, Norton
>   County, Kansas; m. **Ethel Marie JOHNSON**.

133.

Edith White, daughter of No. 77, Catherine Rebecca Queen
White, married **Benjamin WEBB**.
Child of Edith White and Benjamin Webb is:
>   i. **Cloe Webb**.

134.

Martha Ann Queen, daughter of No. 78, Rezin P. Queen, was
born 28 Jul 1860. She married **Joseph M.
WILSON/WILLIAMS**.
Children of Martha Ann Queen and Joseph Wilson/Williams
are:
>   i. **Jessie R. Wilson/Williams**, b. 30 Sep 1896.
>   ii. **Dorothy G. Wilson/Williams**, b. 18 Feb 1907.

135.

Marcellus Queen, son of No. 78, Rezin P. Queen, was born 14
Apr 1862. He married **Barbara Cora WARD.**
Children of Marcellus Queen and Barbara Ward are:
>   i. **James Queen**, b. 21 Mar 1881.
>   ii. **Britten Queen**, b. 28 Feb 1883.
>   iii. **Okey Queen**, b. October 1889.
>   iv. **Dennis Dewey Queen**, b. 28 Jan 1898.

136.

Mary Elizabeth Queen, daughter of No. 78, Rezin P. Queen,
was born 1863 and died 1912. She married **George CAIN**.

Children of Mary Queen and George Cain are:
    i. **Dennis Cain**.
    ii. **David Cain**.
    iii. **George Cain**.
    iv. **Brady Cain**.
    v. **Maud Cain**.
    vi. **Dora Cain**.
    vii. **Lloyd Cain**.

137.
Sarah Catherine Queen, daughter of No. 78, Rezin P. Queen, was born 20 Mar 1866. She married **Thomas J. MEADOWS** in 1882.
Children of Sarah Queen and Thomas Meadows are:
    i. **Thomas Lee Meadows**, b. 08 Mar 1883.
    ii. **Loney Meadows**, b. 06 Feb 1885.
    iii. **Anna Meadows**, b. 08 Mar 1887.
    iv. **Bertie Meadows**, b. 29 Dec 1889.
    v. **Emma Meadows**, b. 06 Mar 1892.
    vi. **Hazel Meadows**, b. 28 Nov 1894.
    vii. **Rose Meadows**, b. 09 Apr 1897.
    viii. **Cletus Meadows**, b. 15 Jan 1900.
    ix. **Roy Meadows**, b. 15 Dec 1903.
    x. **Ottie Meadows**, b. 30 Apr 1909.

138.
Lloyd C. Queen, son of No. 78, Rezin P. Queen, was born 17 Oct 1870. He married **Eddy LOVE** August 1893.
Children of Lloyd Queen and Eddy Love are:
    i. **Hartsell Queen**, b. 06 May 1889.
    ii. **Child Queen**, b. 22 Jun 1902.
    iii. **Ruth Queen**, b. 04 Jul 1914.

139.

Ella Conley, daughter of No. 79, Nancy Ann Queen, married **John R. COCHRAN**.

Children of Ella Conley and John Cochran are:
    i. **Gail Cochran**.
    ii. **Cline Cochran**.
    iii. **Clifford Cochran**.
    iv. **Marly Cochran**.
    v. **Harold Cochran**.
    vi. **Nellie Cochran**.
    vii. **Berd Cochran**

140.

Albinas Love, son of No. 80, Martha Queen, married **May CHAPMAN**.

Children of Albinas Love and May Chapman are:
    i. **Murdo Love**
    ii. **Leonidas Love**.
    iii. **Sarah Love**.
    iv. **Maude Love**.
    v. **Nellie Love**.

141.

Earnest Love, son of No. 80, Martha Queen, was born 14 Dec 1871. He married **Martha WARD**. She was born 12 Aug 1871 and died 09 Oct 1930.

Children of Earnest Love and Martha Ward are:
    i. **Audree Love**, b. November 1894.
    ii. **Madge Love**, b. 11 May 1901.
    iii. **Mary Love**, b. 08 Jul 1912.

142.

Arnett Love, son of No. 80, Martha Queen, married **Cora WARD**. An electrician, he was killed by electricity at the Caroline mines of the Consolidated Coal Company.
Children of Arnett Love and Cora Ward are:
  i. **Alonda Love**.
  ii. **Erma Love**.
  iii. **Chancey Love**.
  iv. **Ruth Love**.
  v. **William Love**.

143.

Nathan Love, son of No. 80, Martha Queen, was born 01 Nov, 1880. He married **Callie MASON**. She was born 11 Apr 1884.
Children of Nathan Love and Callie Mason are:
  i. **Velma Love**, b. 12 Dec 1905.
  ii. **Wesley Love**, b. 08 Jun 1915.

144.

Ira Love, son of No. 80, Martha Queen, married (1) **Bessie MALORY**. He married (2) **Elvira UNK**. He married (3) **Nancy FRANKLIN** 30 Jan 1911 in Oakland, Garrett County, Maryland. Nancy was born 09 Mar 1894 in Hamlin, Lincoln County, West Virginia, and died 08 Oct 1915 in Clarksburg, Harrison County, West Virginia. Ira married (4) **Myrtle WILSON**.
Children of Ira Love and Elvira are:
  i. **Wilma Love**.
  ii. **Mildred Love**.
Children of Ira Love and Nancy Franklin are:
  iii. **Wilma Lorena Love**, b. 09 Nov 1911,
        Clarksburg, Harrison County, West Virginia; d.

05 Jul 1991, Morgantown, Monongalia County, West Virginia; m. **Howard Hartzel JONES**, 30 Jun 1935, Elkins, Randolph County, West Virginia.

iv. **Thelma Love.**

145.

Zoie Love, daughter of No. 80, Martha Queen, was born 05 Oct 1889 in Buchannon, Upshur County, West Virginia, and died 16 Feb 1952 in Caney, Montgomery County, Kansas. She married **Arthur Deever SIMON** 22 Dec 1892. He was born 30 Oct 1871 in Phillippi, Barbour County, West Virginia, and died 08 Oct 1953 in Independence, Montgomery County, Kansas. Both are buried in Mount Hope Cemetery, Independence, Montgomery County, Kansas.

Children of Zoie Love and Arthur Deever Simon are:

      i. **Dowden Simon.**

252.   ii. **Nina Simon**, b. 01 Oct 1898, near Philippi, Barbour County, West Virginia.

      iii. **Mona Simon.**

146.

Verny Love, daughter of No. 80, Martha Queen, married **Elijah HENDERSON**.

Children of Verny Love and Elijah Henderson are:

      i. **Bassil Henderson.**

      ii. **Dyre Henderson.**

147.

Floyd Dallet Queen, son of No. 82, Nathan P. Queen, was born 31 May 1875, in Harrison County, West Virginia. He married **Josephine GRIFFITH**. She was born in Braxton

County, West Virginia.
Children of Floyd Queen and Josephine Griffith are:
>   i. **Neva Queen.**
>   ii. **Ruth Queen.**
>   iii. **Mary Jane Queen.**
>   iv. **Frances Queen.**
>   v. **Madoline Marie Queen.**

148.

Alvadore H. Queen, son of No. 82, Nathan P. Queen, was born 17 Aug 1880, in Harrison County, West Virginia. He married (1) **Frona M. HARVEY**. He married (2) **Dehl SHANABERGER**.
Children of Alvadore Queen and Frona Harvey are:
>   i. **Hazel Queen**, b. 21 Jun 1910.
>   ii. **Woodrow Queen**, b. 15 Nov 1912.
>   iii. **Kenneth Queen**, b. 01 Aug 1913.

149.

Dowden Queen, son of No. 82, Nathan P. Queen, was born 07 June 1885, in Harrison County, West Virginia. He married **Ethel SIGLEY**.
Children of Dowden Queen and Ethel Sigley are:
>   i. **Dorothy Queen**.
>   ii. **Phillip Junior Queen**.
>   iii. **Paul Queen**.
>   iv. **Mardell Queen**.

150.

Maude Queen, daughter of No. 82, Nathan P. Queen, was born 20 Jun 1887, in Harrison County, West Virginia. She married **B. J. THOMAS,** 18 Jun 1904 in Harrison County.

Children of Maude Queen and B.J. Thomas are:
  i. **Mildred Thomas**, b. 13 Apr 1905.
  ii. **Velma Thomas**, b. 25 Jan 1907.
  iii. **Blair E. Thomas**, b. 09 Apr 1918.

151.

David Lee Queen, son of No. 84, Peter Queen, was born 05 Dec 1866, in Harrison County, West Virginia. He married **Alice BAKER** 08 Aug 1889, in Harrison County. David Lee Queen was a watchmaker. After both of his sons died of influenza, he made his home with Levi A. Queen, No. 168.
Children of David Lee Queen and Alice Baker are:
  i. **Merrill Queen**, b. 17 Jun 1890.
  ii. **Cletus Queen**, b. 28 Mar 1894.

152.

John Phineas Queen, son of No. 85, Phineas Queen, was born 30 Dec 1862 and died 21 May 1915 in Harrison County, West Virginia. He married **Adaline Byrd SINCLAIR,** 28 Feb 1884, in Harrison County, West Virginia. She was born 07 May 1864, and died 11 Jun 1935.
Children of John Queen and Adaline Sinclair are:
  i. **Wesley McClelland Queen**, b. 09 Feb 1885, Harrison County, West Virginia.
  ii. **Laura Maude Queen**, b. 11 Oct 1887, Harrison County, West Virginia.
  iii. **Mary Queen**, b. 13 Apr 1890, Harrison County, West Virginia.
  iv. **Alice Belle Queen**, b. 29 Dec 1891, Harrison County, West Virginia.
  v. **Elsie Garnett Queen**, b. 20 Aug 1893, Harrison County, West Virginia.

vi. **Frank Bryan Queen**, b. 25 May 1896, Harrison County, West Virginia.

vii. **William Delbert Queen**, b. 05 Jan 1900, Harrison County, West Virginia.

viii. **Junius Basil Queen**, b. 02 Feb 1902, Harrison County, West Virginia.

153.

William Lloyd Queen, son of No. 85, Phineas Queen, was born 24 Sep 1870. He married (1) **Lula BAKER**. He married (2) **Lucy REED** 05 Sep 1901.

Child of William Lloyd Queen and Lula Baker is:

253.   i. **Glenwood Lloyd Queen**, b. 11 Jul 1896.

Children of William Lloyd Queen and Lucy Reed are:

ii. **Lena Bessie Queen**, b. 12 Oct 1902.

iii. **John D. Howard Queen**, b. 18 Feb 1904.

iv. **Lucy Blanch Queen**, b. 18 Aug 1906.

v. **Ruby Lena Queen**, b. 16 Feb 1908.

vi. **Grace Queen**, b. 12 Nov 1908.

vii. **Madge Queen**, b. aft. January 1909.

154.

Mary Queen, daughter of No. 86, George Queen, married **John McKINNEY**.

Children of Mary Queen and John McKinney are:

i. **Allison McKinney**.

ii. **Beauford McKinney**.

iii. **Hayward McKinney**.

iv. **Opaline McKinney**.

v. **Fay McKinney**.

vi. **Ferrill McKinney**.

vii. **Edna McKinney**.

viii. **Avis McKinney.**

155.

Ella Queen, daughter of No. 86, George Queen, married **Robert WILSON.**
Child of Ella Queen and Robert Wilson is:
    i. **Daughter Wilson.**

156.

Florence Queen, daughter of No. 86, George Queen, married (1) **Dudley DAVIS**. She married (2) **Forrest GILPIN.**
Children of Florence Queen and Dudley Davis are:
    i. **Hazel Davis.**
    ii. **Mary Davis.**
    iii. **Max Davis.**
    iv. **Joseph Davis.**

157.

Vida Queen, daughter of No. 86, George Queen, married **Daymond ARNOLD.**
Children of Vida Queen and Daymond Arnold are:
    i. **Lorine Arnold**, b. July 1905.
    ii. **Virginia Arnold**, b. 02 Nov 1907; m. **Raymond Loy QUEEN**, son of No. 90, **James P. QUEEN,** and **Ida DAWSON**. He was born 20 May 1893.
    iii. **Kathleen Arnold**, b. 19 Nov 1909.
    iv. **Woodrow Arnold**, b. 24 Jul 1912.
    v. **Exel Arnold.**
    vi. **Gail Arnold.**
    vii. **Marie Arnold.**

158.

Augusta Maud Queen, daughter of No. 87, Burrel Queen, was born 02 Jun 1872 in Harrison County, West Virginia. She married **Clark L. MINTER**, son of **Joe MINTER** and **Mattie STOUT**. He was born 10 Dec 1869, and died 10 March 1936. Children of Augusta Maude Queen and Clark Minter are:

    i. **Ethel Minter**.
    ii. **Harry Minter**.
    iii. **Edward Minter**, b. 13 Feb 1904.
    iv. **Freda Minter**.
    v. **Fredrick Minter**.

159.

Percival Queen, son of No. 87, Burrel Queen, was born 19 Sep 1875 in Harrison County, West Virginia. He married **Sarah LEWIS** 19 Jan 1901 in Harrison County. Children of Percival Queen and Sarah Lewis are:

    i. **Fannie Katherine Queen**, b. 16 Jun 1902.
    ii. **Denver Emmit Queen**, b. 22 Feb 1904.
    iii. **Delbert Newton Queen**, b. 18 Nov 1905; m. **Alta Mae QUEEN**. He may have gone by the name of Robert.

160.

Emmit Queen, son of No. 87, Burrel Queen, was born 11 Aug 1877. He married **Opaline McKINNEY,** 03 Apr 1930, daughter of **John McKINNEY** and No. 154, **Mary QUEEN**. Children of Emmit Queen and Opaline McKinney are:

    i. **Harold Burrel Queen**, b. 24 Apr 1931.
    ii. **Harry Felton Queen**, b. 12 Feb 1933.

161.

John Queen, son of No. 87, Burrel Queen, was born 14 Mar 1885, and died January 1915 in Weston, Lewis County, West Virginia. He married **Chlorede WARD**. He was a tailor of ladies' clothes. While working at a shop in Weston, he burned to death when a can of gasoline caught fire.

Child of John Queen and Chlorede Ward is
    i. **Martha Queen**; m. **Mike ROMER**.

162.

William "Willie" Johnson Arnold, son of No. 88, Ida Matilda Queen Arnold, was born 22 Feb 1869 in Upshur County, West Virginia. He married **Luella June HODGE**. She was born about 1872 in Upshur County.

Children of William Arnold and June Hodge are:
    i. **Orley Arnold**.
    ii. **Orbie Arnold**.
    iii. **Child Arnold**.
    vi. **Child Arnold**.

163.

Stella Arnold, daughter of No. 89, Minerva Queen, was born 11 Aug 1878. She married **Grant WHITE**.

Children of Stella Arnold and Gant White are:
    i. **Bertha White**.
    ii. **Raymond White**.
    iii. **Paul White**.
    iv. **Carl White**.
    v. **Lora White**.
    vi. **Daura White**.

164.

Orron Arnold, son of No. 89, Minerva Queen, was born 29 May 1887. He married **Bernice COBERLY** 12 Apr 1916. She was born 15 Jun 1887.
Children of Orron Arnold and Bernice Coberly are:
 i. **Clotus Arnold**, b. 16 Jan 1917.
 ii. **Dale Arnold**, b. 21 May 1920.

165.

Alvertia Queen, daughter of No.90, James P. Queen, was born 08 Jan 1873. She married **Edward SUTTON**.
Children of Alvertia Queen and Edward Sutton are:
 i. **Porter Sutton**, b. July 1896.
 ii. **Frank Sutton**, b. November 1898.
 iii. **Dick Sutton**.

166.

Angeline Queen, daughter of No. 90, James P. Queen, was born 09 Aug 1875. She married (1) **Emmet HORNBECK**. She married (2) **Richard BOYLES**.
Child of Angeline Queen and Emmet Hornbeck is:
 i. **Roscoe Hornbeck**.
Children of Angeline Queen and Richard Boyes are:
 ii. **Bertie Boyles,** b. 21 Jan 1911.
 iii. **Bessie Boyles**, b. 16 Feb 1914.
 iv. **Retha Boyles**, b. 20 Apr 1917.
 v. **Richard Boyles**, b. abt. 1918.
 vi. **Herbert Boyles**, b. 15 Mar 1920.

167.

Sylvia May Queen, daughter of No. 90, James P. Queen, was born 13 Oct 1880. She married **Judson THRASH** 02 Jul 1900.

Children of Sylvia May Queen and Judson Thrash are:
    i. **Gail Thrash**, b. 20 Aug 1902.
    ii. **Louis Thrash**, b. 26 Jan 1906.

168.

Levi A. Queen, son of No. 90, James P. Queen, was born 25 May 1883. He married **Ottie WOLF** 05 Sep 1906.
Children of Levi A. Queen and Ottie Wolf are:
    i. **Alta Mae Queen**, b. 18 Apr 1910; m. **Robert Delbert Newton QUEEN**, 24 Dec 1935.
    ii. **Haymond Allen Queen**, b. 25 Sep, 1912.
    iii. **Mamie Pauline Queen**, b. 25 Sep 1912.

169.

Jason Hinson Pritchard, son of No. 95, Jasper Pritchard and Mary Byrd, was born 12 Sep 1879, Smithville, Ritchie County, West Virginia. He appeared in the census on 15 Apr 1940 in Circleville, Pickaway County, Ohio. He died 01 Jul 1955 at the age of 84 in Circleville, Pickaway County, Ohio and was buried on 03 Jul 1955 at Green Summit Cemetery, Colerain Township, Ross County, Ohio. He married **Rachel Anna TENNIHILL,** daughter of **Samuel TENNIHILL** and **Louisa MCQUADE.** Rachel was born 03 Jul 1876, Ross County, Ohio and died 24 Oct 1938 at the age of 62 in Circleville, Pickaway County, Ohio. She was buried 27 Oct. 1938 at Green Summit Cemetery in Colerain Township, Ross County, Ohio next to her husband. The family lived on a farm near Adelphi, Ross County, Ohio until 1923, when they moved to Circleville.
Children of Jason Pritchard and Rachel Tennihill are:
    i. **Lucy Pritchard**, b. 16 Sep 1894, Salt Creek Twp., Hocking County, Ohio.
    ii. **Dessie M. Pritchard**, b. 25 Oct 1896, Salt Creek

Twp., Hocking County, Ohio.
iii. **Andrew S. Pritchard**, b. 24 Nov 1898, Salt Creek
Twp., Hocking County, Ohio.
iv. **Lee Ossie Pritchard**, b. 1903,Salt Creek Township,
Hocking County, Ohio.
v. **Ezra L. Pritchard**, b. 24 May 1904, Salt Creek
Township, Hocking County, Ohio; d. 24 Jan
1977 at the age of 72 in Circleville, Pickaway
County, Ohio.
vi. **Marvin E. Pritchard,** b. 1906 Salt Creek Township,
Hocking County, Ohio.
254. vii. **Ralph H. Pritchard**, b. 25 Apr 1912, Salt Creek
Twp., Hocking County, Ohio.
255. viii. **Edwin Lakin Pritchard**, b. 1917, Marion Twp.,
Hocking County, Ohio.
256. ix.. **Cecil Leroy Pritchard,** b. 10 Aug 1922, Salt
Creek Twp., Hocking County, Ohio.

170.

Francis M. Pritchard, son of No. 95, Jasper Pritchard and
Mary Byrd, was born 07 Apr 1876, in West Virginia. Hocking
County, Ohio
Francis M. Pritchard married **Emma Augusta STARLING** 04
Dec 1904 in Logan, Hocking County, Ohio. She was born 01
May 1885 in Hocking County, Ohio the daughter of **Ebenezer
STARLING** and **Mary PATTON,** and died 01 Jul 1936 in
Liberty Township, She was buried next to her husband in an
unmarked grave on 12 Jul 1936 at Crall Cemetery in Liberty
Township, Crawford County, Ohio at the corner of State Route
96 and Klopfenstein Road.
Children of Francis M. Pritchard and Emma Starling are:
257. i. **Ruben M. Pritchard** , b. 24 Sep 1905.

258.   ii. **Elza Owen Pritchard**, b. 08 Nov. 1906, East
           Colerain Twp., Ross County, Ohio.
       iii. **Orville Omert Pritchard,** b. 09 Apr 1908,
           Colerain Township, Ross County, Ohio. He
           appeared in the 1930 census in Logan, Hocking
           County, Ohio, and in the 1940 census of
           Whetstone Township, Crawford County,
           Ohio. He died 09 Aug 1968, Crawford County,
           Ohio.
       iv. **Homer Melvin Pritchard**, b. 16 Aug 1909 in
           Adelphi, Ross County, Ohio; d. 05 Jan, at the
           age of 52 in Bucyrus, Crawford County, Ohio.
           He was also known as Omer Milford Pritchard.
           He appeared in the census of 1930 in Sandusky
           Township, Crawford County, Ohio. He married
           Nellie May HOWARD, daughter of **James
           Peterman HOWARD** and **Victoria
           STRAWDERMAN.** Nellie was born 24 Jun
           1903 in Bucyrus, Crawford County, Ohio, and
           died 14 Feb 1988 at age 84 in Bucyrus,
           Crawford County. County, Ohio
259.   v. **Wallace Allen Pritchard**, b. 30 Jan 1911, Ohio; d.
           29 Sep. 1936, Crawford County, Ohio.
       vi. **Arthur Alvin Pritchard**, b. 27 Apr 1924, Ohio; d.
           5 Nov 1938, Bucyrus, Crawford County, Ohio;
           m. **Geraldine Vivian RICHARDSON.**05 Nov
           1938 Fremont, Sandusky County, Ohio.
       vii. **Mary Elva Pritchard**, b. 18 Aug 1916,
           Adelphi, Ross County, Ohio; m. **Harry William
           GANTZLER** 27 Nov 1938, Bucyrus, Crawford
           County, Ohio; d. 09 Apt 2001, Bucyrus,
           Crawford County, Ohio.

260.   viii. **Eunice Marie Pritchard**, b. 16 Sep 1918,
              Colerain Twp., Ross County, Ohio; d. 24 Jun
              1993, Tucson, Pima County, Arizona; m. **Lee
              Wyant MARTIN** 27 Jan 1940 Fostoria,
              Crawford County, Ohio.
          ix. **Roy Edward Pritchard**, b. 13 Sep 1920, Colerain
              Township, Ross County, Ohio; m. **Ruth Marie
              LUST** 12 May 1946, Bucyrus, Crawford
              County, Ohio
           x. **Berman Cecil Pritchard**, b. 39 Mar 1923.,
              Ohio; d. 06 Sep 1975. m. **Kathryn Ada
              NICKELL** 26 Feb 1946, Bucyrus, Crawford
              County, Ohio; d. 09 Jun 1975 Galion, Crawford
              County, Ohio.

171.

Franklin Pritchard, son of No 95, Jasper Pritchard and Mary
Martha Bird, was born 07 Apr 1875 in Smithville, Ritchie
County, West Virginia. He appeared in the census on 21 Apr
1910 in Salt Creek Township, Pickaway County, Ohio. He died
on 05 May 1950 at the age of 75 in Columbus, Franklin
County, Ohio. He was buried on 08 May 1950 at Obetz
Cemetery in Obetz, Franklin County, Ohio.
Ohio Records Vol. I, p. 58 reports that Franklin Pritchard,
farmer, age 23, married **Lenna McQuaide** (also found as
McQuade), housekeeper, age 16, on 03 Sep 1899, by James
Bethel. Lenna's consent was signed by James M. McQuaide.
Both resided in Salt Creek Twp. Neither was previously
married. Lenna's parents were **Lewis M. McQUAIDE** and
Nancy J. JINKS.
       Lenna's sister, **Arvilla S. McQUAIDE**, housekeeper
age 18, married **Willie B. PRITCHARD**, farmer, age 30, on

10 Mar 1900 by C. O. Welch, MG. The court record indicates that Willie was the son of No. 96, **Andrew Jackson PRITCHARD** and **Mary M. WILKINSON.** If his stated age is correct, he was born two years before their marriage. Willie B. Pritchard resided at Pike Run, and Arvilla resided at Apple, Hocking County. Neither was previously married. Apparently Francis M. Pritchard and Willie B. Pritchard were cousins. Children of Franklin Pritchard and Lenna McQuaide are:

    i. **John Leroy Pritchard,** b. abt. 1901, Ross County, Ohio.

    ii. **Dorothy J. Pritchard**, b. 18 May 1902, Ross County, Ohio.

    iii **Viola M. Pritchard**, b. 30 Jul 1903, Ross County, Ohio; d. 28 Jan 1991 at the age pf 87 in Circleville, Pickaway County, Ohio. She married. **Roy A. STRAWSER.**

172.

Altie Pritchard, daughter of No. 95, Jasper Pritchard and Margaret Horner, was born 09 Jan 1891 in Hazelgreen, Ritchie County, West Virginia, and died 26 Apr 1976, in Gulfport, Harrison County, Mississippi. She married **Nathan George WELCH,** who was born 24 Oct 1876 in Ohio, and died 28 Dec 1946 in Gulfport. Altie was his second wife. His parents, **George WELCH** and **Rebecca UNK** were both born in Ohio. Child of Altie Pritchard and George Welch is:

261.   i. **Mae Welch**

173.

Larrick Pritchard, son of No. 97, Thomas Benton Pritchard, was born 27 Mar 1879 in West Virginia, and died about 1970 in Ohio. He married **Gertrude PATTON** 22 Jul 1899 in

Hocking County, Ohio, daughter of **Ay PATTON** and **Mary O'HALORAND**. Both are buried in Green Summit Cemetery, Adelphi, Ross County, Ohio.

Children of Larrick Pritchard and Gertrude Patton are:

262. i. **Benton L. Pritchard**, b. 05 May 1900, Salt Creek Twp., Hocking County, Ohio; d. Abt. 1979, Ross County, Ohio.

ii. **Edith E. Pritchard**, b. 19 Jun 1902, Salt Creek Twp., Hocking County, Ohio.

iii. **Josiah Pritchard**, b. 22 May 1906, Salt Creek Twp., Hocking County, Ohio. His birth record states that his parents reside on Pike Run; their names are entered as Lark and Gertrude Patent Pritchard.

iv. **Robert H. Pritchard**, b. 11 Jun 1908, Eagle Twp., Vinton County, Ohio.

174.

Leeman Lee Pritchard, son of No. 97, Thomas Benton Pritchard, was born 01 Jul 1881 in Ritchie County, West Virginia, and died 24 Jan, 1976 in Fox Nursing Home, Laurelville, Hocking County, Ohio. He married **Nora Henrietta LADY**. A farmer, he died of congestive heart failure, and is buried in Green Summit Cemetery, Adelphi, Ross County, Ohio. Nora's name is given as Mora Lada on the birth record of their daughter, Jenivia (sic). On the birth record of daughter Della, the entry has been corrected from Mary Lady to Nora Henryetta (sic) Lady. It also states that her parents resided at Apple, probably a forgotten location name in Salt Creek Twp.

Children of Leeman Pritchard and Nora Lady are:

i. **Rebecca Pritchard**, b. 18 Jan 1904, Salt Creek

Twp., Hocking County; d. 11 Sep 1920; listed
as Becca Pritchard on Ohio Death Certificate
Index for Ross County, number 60648.

    ii. **Della Adeline Pritchard**, b. 13 May 1905, Salt
Creek Twp., Hocking County, Ohio.

    iii. **Geneva Pritchard**, b. 07 Aug 1906, Salt Creek
Twp., Hocking County Ohio.

    iv. **Denver Debs Pritchard**, b. 19 Aug 1908, Salt
Creek Twp., Hocking County, Ohio.

263.   v. **Edward Allen Pritchard**, b. abt. 1917, Logan,
Hocking County, Ohio.

    vi. **Louise Pritchard.**

175.

Sherman Pritchard, son of No. 97, Thomas Benton Pritchard,
was born 01 Jul 1881 in Ritchie County, West Virginia, and
died 13 Oct 1973 in Chillicothe, Ross County, Ohio. He
married **Bessie McDONALD**. She was born 1885 and died
1960.

Children of Sherman Pritchard and Bessie McDonald are:

264.   i. **Eugene Pritchard**, b. 1903; d. 1981.

265.   ii. **Charles Wesley Pritchard, Sr.**, b. 1905; d. 1979.

    iii. **Alice Pritchard,** b. 1906.

    iv. **Deming Alonzo Pritchard.**

266.   v. **Thomas Pritchard.**

267.   vi. **Alvin Pritchard.**

    vii. **Lela Pritchard**, b. 1917; m. **Unk GOLDMAN.**

176.

Amon Lewis Pritchard, son of No. 97, Thomas Benton
Pritchard, was born 03 Apr 1884 in West Virginia, and died 19
Mar 1967 in the Dieber Nursing Home, Chillicothe, Ross

County, Ohio. He married **Sarah Alice Hinton TENNIHILL**,
a widow, 24 Dec 1905 in Hocking County, Ohio, daughter of
Jacob HINTON (1837-15 Aug 1896) and **Leanna COX**
(1839-1922), who were married 19 Feb 1859. Sarah was born
05 May 1879, (family records indicate 1881) in Salt Creek
Twp., Hocking County, Ohio and died 28 Jan 1938 of
bronchial pneumonia, arthritis, and cancer of the right breast.
Sarah was first married to **Jacob TENNIHILL** in Hocking
County, Ohio, on 01 Oct 1896, Both Amon and Sarah Alice are
buried in Pleasant Hill Cemetery, Adelphi, Colerain Twp.,
Ross County, Ohio. Amon's birth is recorded on the Hocking
County birth register by his mother, Sarah Haddox Pritchard,
as 03 Jun 1885.

Children of Amon Pritchard and Sarah Alice Hinton are:
268. i. **Carrie Vivian Pritchard,** b. 04 May 1904; d.
         August 1990.
269. ii. **Eustace Charles Pritchard**, b. 03 Nov 1905; d.
         25 Oct 1992.
270. iii. **Alice Marie Pritchard**, b. 15 May 1907.
271. iv. **Elsie Sylvia Pritchard**, b. 21 Oct 1908.
272. v. **Eldon Berman Pritchard,** b. 03 May 1910; d.
         16 Apr 1946.
273. vi. **Marshall Edward Pritchard**, b. 12 Mar 1912.
      vii. **Thomas Virgil Pritchard**, b. 11 Jan 1916; d.
         08 Apr 1981; m. (1) **Ellen ROLAND**; m.
         (2) **Wilma PEMBER**.
      viii. **Foster Berman Pritchard**, b. 19 Sep 1918; m. (1)
         Mary SPAUN; m. (2) **Janette PRITCHARD.**
      ix. **Herald Haywood Pritchard**, b. 02 Jun 1921;
         m. **Katherine HEETER**, widow of his
         brother Eldon (see).

177.

Della M. Pritchard, daughter of No. 97, Thomas Benton Pritchard, was born 24 Sep 1887 in Salt Creek Township, Hocking County, Ohio. She married **Simon RATCLIFF**. Children of Della Pritchard and Simon Ratcliff are:

    i. **Thomas Ratcliff.**
    ii. **Cecil Ratcliff.**
    iii. **Ruth Ratcliff.**
    iv. **Verna Ratcliff.**
    v. **Virginia Ratcliff.**
    vi. **Irene Ratcliff.**
    vii. **Herald Ratcliff.**

178.

Elsie Arie Pritchard, daughter of No. 97, Thomas Benton Pritchard, was born 07 Apr 1892 in Salt Creek Township, Hocking County, Ohio, and died about 1967. She was buried in Green Summit Cemetery, Ross County, Ohio. She married (1) **Ezra REED**. She married (2) **Noke TISDALE**. She married (3) **Pearl GRAVES**. She married (4) **Alva MOORE**. Child of Elsie Pritchard and Noke Tisdale is:

    i. **Hobart Tisdale.**

Child of Elsie Pritchard and Pearl Graves is:

    ii. **Hayward Graves.**

Child of Elsie Pritchard and Alva Moore is:

    iii. **Pauline Moore.**

179.

Hugh Jack Pritchard, son of No. 97, Thomas Benton Pritchard, was born 07 Jul 1895 in Salt Creek Township, Hocking County, Ohio. He married **Iva Mae REDIFER**. Hugh was killed in Sandusky, Ohio, where he was employed by a railroad. He was mauled and killed by two men. It was later determined that Hugh was mistaken for another man. One of his assailants went free. The other died in a penitentiary fire at Columbus, Ohio.

Children of Hugh Pritchard and Iva Redifer are:

274.　i. **Darold Vernon Pritchard,** b. 23 Oct 1917.
275.　ii. **Alberta Bernadine Pritchard**, b. 25 Nov 1919.
276.　iii. **Lowell Forest Pritchard**, b. 29 Oct 1921.

180.

Lewis Maxwell Pritchard, son of No. 98, Elias Robert Pritchard, was born 14 Mar 1869 in Roane County, West Virginia, and died 1898 in Roane County, West Virginia. He married **Ida D. SMITH** 07 Oct 1891 in Roane County, West Virginia, daughter of **Whitehead SMITH**. She was born 1868, and died 1925. Dola Pritchard Pool related that her mother, Mary Kincaid Pritchard, went to work for Lewis and Ida, and may have met Darrell Duke Pritchard at their home.

Children of Louis Pritchard and Ida Smith are:

　i. **Leota D. Pritchard**, b. 18 Nov 1893.
　ii. **Earl Pritchard**, b. abt. 1895.
　iii. **Leona B. Pritchard**, b. 22 Jan 1898.

181.

James Robert Pritchard, son of No. 98, Elias Robert Pritchard, was born 18 Jul 1871 in Roane County, West Virginia, and died 05 Feb 1945 in Roane County, West Virginia. He married **Roxie WILSON** 13 Dec 1894 in Roane County, West Virginia, daughter of **William WILSON** and **Mary Polly STARCHER**. Roxie was born 02 Apr 1874 in Roane County, West Virginia, and died 30 Dec 1953 in Roane County. Photographs of them taken about 1912 include their "pet" groundhog. Both are buried in Spencer Cemetery. James Robert Pritchard's gravestone gives his birth date as 04 Jun 1872, but his family claim this is incorrect.

Children of James Pritchard and Roxie Wilson are:

277.   i. **Ira Grant Pritchard**, b. 11 Oct 1895, Roane County, West Virginia; d. 12 Jan 1984.

278.   ii. **Arty Blake Pritchard**, b. 13 May 1897, Roane County, West Virginia; d. 24 Apr 1976, Roane County, West Virginia.

      iii. **Hollie Pritchard**, b. 04 Sep 1898.

279.   iv. **Harold Dean Pritchard**, b.15 Sep 1902; d. 02 Jan 1999, Akron, Summit County, Ohio.

      v. **Orpha Alinea Pritchard**, b. 13 Jun 1904, Harrisville, Ritchie County, West Virginia; d. 21 Feb 1986, Roane County, West Virginia; m. **James Edward SCHOOLCRAFT**, 18 Feb 1935, Roane County, West Virginia.

      vi. **Effie Pritchard**, b. 1908, Roane County, West Virginia; m. **Snowdon Thorn HUFFMAN**, 14 Mar 1925, Roane County.

182.

Darrell Duke Pritchard, son of No. 98, Elias R. Pritchard, was born 20 Feb 1880. He married **Mary Elton KINCAID**, daughter of **George William KINCAID** and **Louisa Jane BURKE**, on 11 Jun 1899 in Roane County, West Virginia. Mary was born 17 Nov 1880 in Roane County, and died 25 Sep 1964 in Spencer, Roane County, West Virginia. Darrell Duke did not like his name, so he went by his initials, D. D.

    Mary Elton Kincaid was the second child born to George Kincaid and Louisa Burke. She was always called Mary, a name her grandmother, Mary Catherine Campbell

James Robert and Roxie Pritchard
with pet groundhog, ca. 1912

274a

274b

Kincaid, did not use. The Elton was from Elton Rebecca Amiss, her step-grandmother, who married her grandfather, Robert Peter Burke, after his first wife died. Elton Burke was the sister of Peter's first wife, Sarah Florence Amiss.

Mary was born and raised in the area of the county known as Looneyville. The family farm was owned until the 1960s by Mary's brother, Robert. Uncle Rob built a fine two-story home behind the home place and then removed the original house. Far behind this home, which still stands, is the original cabin site of the Kincaids. This is just below the present state route that runs through Clover.

Mary was left-handed, very neat, and highly opinionated. She was an excellent worker, homemaker, and seamstress. She knew how to pinch a penny and enjoyed making things from nothing. She had very limited schooling, and this was tainted by memories of having her left hand tied behind her back to prevent her using it to write. She had dark, penetrating eyes and a way of pursing her lips when things didn't suit her.

Albert Hammick Kincaid was the firstborn to Mary's parents. He was born 26 Jan 1879 and immediately was dubbed "Hammy." One can imagine how Mary was received in November following his death on 12 Jun 1880.

On 19 Nov 1882, a sister joined the family. She was called Hattie and listed as Mattie J. on her death record. When she passed away 22 Dec 1884, Mary was left as an only child again.

Then on 18 Oct 1885, another son, Robert Cleveland, was born. In 1887, a sister, Stella, joined the family, followed by William Homer "Widge" on 30 Aug 1889, and Pearl Hester on 20 Aug 1894.

Mary Elton Kincaid was married to Darrell Duke

Pritchard on 11 Jun 1899. Courthouse records list him as Daniel, probably a case of bad penmanship.

Mary and Darrell had eight children, two boys and six girls, including a set of twins, in the years 1900 to 1920. The last child was born 20 Jan 1920. Mary had problems during that pregnancy because of diabetes. Instead of going to a hospital where she might have had a Caesarian delivery, she remained with her family doctor, who gave Darrell the choice of saving the child or his wife. Darrell could not imagine life without his Mary, so he gave consent for the doctor to take the child. Because the baby was so large, the doctor had to deflate the head. A drill was turned into the unborn child's head so that it would collapse, and then the child was removed in pieces. It was a gruesome ordeal, but Mary's life was spared. The doctor estimated the baby's weight at twenty pounds. At the same time, he performed a hysterectomy so Mary could have no more children. From that time on, she was in excellent health.

Mary and Darrell moved to Spencer before World War I. Prior to this, they lived at Clover, where they ran a country store. In the 1940s, they moved to Ohio, outside of Sugar Grove, but later returned to Spencer where they both died, Mary on 25 Sep 1964, following an extended illness - cancer of the esophagus. She is buried beside Darrell in the Ward Cemetery next to the Gandee Chapel on land that was part of their Spring Creek farm and later owned by their daughter and son-in-lawn, Dora and Ernest Ward.

Mary Elton Kincaid Pritchard's father, George William Kincaid, called himself William and was known as "Will." One historian (Bishop, *History of Roane County,* 1927) gives his name as George Washington Kincaid, Jr. He might be right, but this was not a time when everything was always done legally, so William it was. He was born in Fayette County,

Virginia, on 05 Jan, 1850, to **George Washington KINCAID**
and his wife **Mary Catherine CAMPBELL.** The Kincaid
family moved to Roane County sometime in 1856. William
was the third child of eleven known children. He married
Louisa Jane Burke on 14 Feb 1878, in Roane County. They had
seven known children with five living to adulthood. (Provided
by Ed Pool, 1999.)
Children of Darrell Duke Pritchard and Mary Kincaid are:

      i. **Dollie Pritchard**, b. 20 Apr 1900, Roane County,
        West Virginia; d. 20 Apr 1900, Roane County.

     ii. **Lawton Pritchard**, b. 27 Sep 1901, Roane County,
        West Virginia; d. 23 Sep 1904, Roane County,
        The cause of death was an obstruction (button)

280.   iii. **Dola Pritchard**, b. 14 Aug 1903, Walnut Grove,
        Roane County, West Virginia; d. 11 Feb 1993,
        Lancaster, Fairfield County, Ohio.

281.   iv. **Dona Pritchard**, b. 10 May 1907, Roane County,
        West Virginia.

     v. **Donna Pritchard**, b. 10 May 1907; d. 24 Oct 1918
        of pneumonia following influenza, Spencer,
        Roane County, West Virginia.

282.   vi. **Dora Pritchard**, b. 04 Apr 1911.

    vii. **Lewis Pritchard**, b. 13 Dec 1912; d. 13 Dec 1912,
        Roane County, West Virginia.

   viii. **Doris Madeline Pritchard**, b. 20 Jan 1920; d. 20
        Jan 1920.

183.

Lillie Alberta Boice Pritchard, step-daughter of No. 98, Elias
Pritchard, actually was the daughter of **Frank BOICE** and
Matilda WATSON, sister of her step-mother, Sophia Watson.
Lillie was born 19 Dec 1881 in Walton District, Roane County,

West Virginia, and died 1968. She married **Isaac B.
BUTCHER** 31 Dec 1899 in Roane County, West Virginia. He
was born 1875. Known as Bertie, Lillie was raised by Sophia
and Elias Robert Pritchard as their own. After Lily's father
died, the Pritchard family changed the spelling of Boice legally
to Boyce because they did not want to be connected to the
Boice family. The reason for Matilda's death, according to the
death certificate, was consumption, but Dola Pool stated that
Matilda died following Bertie's birth. Both explanations are
probably true. The record of legal adoption action has not been
pursued, but Bertie went by the surname Pritchard. She is
buried in the IOOF Cemetery, Parkersburg, Wood County,
West Virginia.
Children of Lillie Pritchard and Isaac Butcher are:

      i. **Rex Butcher**.
     ii. **Ada Butcher**.
   iii. **May Butcher**.
   iv. **Fay Butcher**.
    v. **Euna Butcher**.

184.

Addie Miranda Pritchard, daughter of No. 99, Thomas
Tavner Pritchard, was born 03 Sep 1881 in Roane County,
West Virginia, and died 05 Jun 1947 in Boulder City, Clark
County, Nevada. She married **Robert Eaker KENNEDY,**
August 28, 1910 in Hyattville, Bighorn County, Wyoming, son
of **Frederick KENNEDY** and **Ida EAKER.**
Children of Addie Miranda Pritchard and Robert Eaker
Kennedy are:

      i. **Marguerite Amanda Kennedy**, b. 27 Mar
         1912, Lafayette, Tippecanoe County, Indiana;
         m. **William G. HUEY**, 22 Sep 1937, Denver,

Denver County, Colorado.
283.   ii. **Robert Evan Kennedy**, b. 31 Mar 1916,
              Worland, Washakie County, Wyoming.

185.

Waitman Conley Smith, son of No. 100, Sarah Ann Pritchard, was born 16 Jan 1895 in Kingsville, Lewis County, West Virginia, and died 02 Apr 1973 in Elkins, Randolph County, West Virginia. He is buried next to his wife in the Scott Family Cemetery, Norton, Randolph County, West Virginia. He married **Russie SCOTT** (b. 17 Apr 1894; d. 10 May 1952), on 02 Nov 1914, in Elkins, Randolph County, West Virginia. Waitman served with the U.S. Army Signal Corps in France during World War I. He was PFC Company C 305 Sig NB 80 Division. He had a stroke and was disabled the last years of his life. Russie died of cancer at her home on Laurel Mountain Road near Elkins, West Virginia. Her funeral services were held at 2 p.m. 13 May1952 at Kynette Methodist Church in Norton. The Rev. Ottis Linger of the Woodford Memorial Church officiated. Both Waitman and Russie are buried in the Scott Family Cemetery,
Child of Waitman Smith and and Russie Scott is:
284.   i. **Anna Lee Smith**, b. 27 Jun 1920, Coalton,
              Randolph County, West Virginia; d. 17 Feb
              1983, Macon, Bibb County, Georgia.

186.

Claude McKinley Smith, Sr., son of No. 100, Sarah Ann Pritchard, was born 04 Oct 1900 in Walkersville, Lewis County, West Virginia, and died 17 Oct 1961 in Macon, Bibb County, Georgia. He was buried October 1961 in Maplewood Cemetery, Randolph County, West Virginia. He married

Marguerite YOKUM on 06 Oct 1920. She was born 30 Nov 1899 and died 22 Mar 1966. Claude drowned in the Cheat River.
Children of Claude Smith and Marguerite Yokum are:
  i. **Claude McKinley Smith, Jr.**, b. 19 Mar 1923, Randolph County, West Virginia; retired.
  ii. **Paul E. Smith**, b. 10 Jan 1925, Randolph County, West Virginia; retired.
  iii. **Betty Jo Smith**, b. 10 Feb 1927, Randolph County, West Virginia; m. **Harold C. ROHR.**
  iv. **Winifred Jean Smith**, b. 19 Dec 1928, Randolph County, West Virginia; d. 02 Oct 1947, bur. Maplewood Cemetery, Elkins, Randolph County.
  v. **Virginia Lane Smith**, b. 20 Apr 1930, Randolph County, West Virginia; m. **George S. HOLBOROW.**

187.

John Willis Dennison, son of No.101, Mary Elizabeth Pritchard, was born 24 Jan 1904, and died 04 Oct 1976. He married **Frances L. ALLENDER.**
Children of John Dennison and Frances Allender are:
285. i. **Kenneth Wayne Dennison**, b. 14 Nov 1937, Upshur County, West Virginia.
  ii. **Norma Dennison**; m. **Roy PEYTON**, lives in Alexandria, Virginia.
  iii. **Robert Dennison**.

188.

Dewey F. Dennison, son of No. 101, Mary Elizabeth Pritchard,

married **Rhoda McCLAIN**.
Children of Dewey Dennison and Rhoda McClain are:
    i. **Rona Dennison**; m. **Richard PHILLIPS**.
    ii. **Iris May Dennison**; m. **Ray CONWAY**.

FIFTH GENERATION

189.

Lillian Leoti Bee, daughter of No. 102, Mary C. Watson, was born 10 Jul 1878 in Ritchie County, West Virginia, and died 08 Feb 1961 in Houston, Harris County, Texas. She married **Lloyd Edwin CRISS** on 07 Apr 1901. Lloyd was in the oil field business, and later had a Ford garage in Cairo. Eventually, the oil fields lured the family to Kansas.
Children of Lillian Bee and Lloyd Criss are:
> i. **Eula Criss**, lived in Shreveport, Caddo County, Louisiana.
> ii. **Paul Criss,** lived in Dallas, Dallas County, Texas.
> iii. **Louise Criss**, b. 08 Dec 1915, Ritchie County, West Virginia; m. (1) **E. H. HAWES**, 26 Dec 1937 in Texas; m. (2) **A.W. THROGMORTON**, 19 May 1953 in Kentucky.

286.   iv. **Mary Criss**.

190.

Gracia Alice Pritchard, daughter of No. 104, John Wesley Pritchard, was born 25 May 1872 in Ritchie County, West Virginia, and died 26 Jun 1907 in Ritchie County. She married **William R. HEATON**, 28 Nov 1895, in Ritchie County. He was born October 1870 in Ritchie County, and died 1959 in Ritchie County. Both are buried in the IOOF Cemetery, Harrisville, Ritchie County.
Child of Gracia Pritchard and William Heaton is:
> i. **John W. Heaton,** b. January 1900, Ritchie County, West Virginia.

191.

Mary Elizabeth Pritchard, daughter of No. 104, John Wesley Pritchard, was born 25 Dec 1974, in Harrisville, Ritchie County, West Virginia, and died 1967 in Harrisville. She married **Oliver Duffy TAYLOR,** 03 Aug 1892, in Ritchie County. He was born 1871 in Gilmer County, West Virginia, and died 1923 in Harrisville, Ritchie County. Both are buried in the IOOF Cemetery, Harrisville, Ritchie County.

Children of Mary Elizabeth Pritchard and Oliver Taylor are:

287.   i. **Gracia Alice Taylor**, b. 1894, Parkersburg, Wood County, West Virginia; d. 1972, Parkersburg.

    ii. **Wilbur Earl Taylor,** b. 09 Mar 1896, Parkersburg, Wood County, West Virginia; d. 06 May1918; bur. Harrisville, Ritchie County.

288.   iii. **Wesley Isaac Taylor**, b. 10 Oct 1898, Parkersburg, Wood County, West Virginia; d. 11 Jun 11, 1976, Parkersburg.

289   iv. **Helen Rosalie Taylor,** b, 09 Mar 1903, Harrisville, Ritchie County, West Virginia

290.   v. **Oliver Duffy Taylor, Jr.,** b. 1906, Harrisville

192.

Coleman H. Pritchard, son of No. 105, Morgan Ross Pritchard, was born 25 Dec 1873 in Oxford, Ritchie County, West Virginia, and died 1954 in Pullman, Ritchie County. He married **Eva Maude AMOS**, 01 Sep 1910, in Ritchie County. She was born 1886 in Ritchie County, and died 1970 in Harrisville, Ritchie County. Both are buried in the IOOF Cemetery, Harrisville.

Child of Coleman Pritchard and Eva Amos is:

    i. **Harlin Hall Pritchard**, b. 31 Mar 1918, Ritchie County, West Virginia.

193.

Laura M. Pritchard, daughter of No. 105, Morgan Ross Pritchard, was born April 1880 in Oxford, Ritchie County, West Virginia, and died 1955 in Pullman, Ritchie County. She married **William P. IRELAND,** 24 Aug 1899 in Ritchie County. He was born August 1876 in Ritchie County, and died 1974 in Pullman, Ritchie County. Both are buried in the Pullman Cemetery.
Child of Laura Pritchard and William Ireland is:
- i. **Claude C. "Clyde" Ireland**, b. 03 Sept 1900, Pullman, Ritchie County, West Virginia; d. 03 May 1933, Pullman; m. **Mildred DAVIS;** bur. Pullman Cemetery, Ritchie County.

194.

Roscoe Clyde Pritchard, son of No. 105, Morgan Ross Pritchard, was born 10 Sep 1882 in Ritchie County. He married **Nancy R. UNK**. She was born 1887.
Children of Roscoe Pritchard and Nancy R. are:
- i. **Nimech L. Pritchard**, b. 1912, Ritchie County, West Virginia.
- ii. **Ruby E. Pritchard**, b. July 1914, Ritchie County, West Virginia.
- iii. **Arch G. Pritchard**, b. November 1917, Ritchie County, West Virginia.
- iv. **Anna M. Pritchard**, b. December 1918, Ritchie County, West Virginia.

195.

Dora Alice Pritchard, daughter of No. 106, Andrew L. Pritchard, was born 02 Mar 1876, in Oxford, Ritchie County, West Virginia, and died 21 Feb 1970. She married **Ira D.**

COX, 30 Apr 1905 in Ritchie County, son of **Oliver COX** and
Sarah KNISELEY. He was born 30 Apr 1873, and died 10
Mar 1958. Lucille Cox Deberry provides the following
information about her parents, Ira D. Cox and Dora Alice
Pritchard, in *The History of Ritchie County, West Virginia To
1980*, p. 90: *Dora's parents, Andrew and Eliza E. Tharp
Pritchard, died young. She and her brother, Grant, were raised
by their grandparents, H. B. and Elizabeth Wass Tharp. I was
born in 1906. My younger sister, Maxie Irene, died at 18
months. My mother died when I was five, leaving my great-
grandmother, Elizabeth, again responsible for the care of a
small child. In 1929, I married a WVU senior, Max DeBerry
from Terra Alta. Our first child, Margherita, was born 10 Feb
1931. That summer, Max accepted a position in Harrisville
teaching for two years, but he wanted to become a lawyer.
After Max was appointed Assistant Prosecuting Attorney, we
moved back to Harrisville. Our second daughter, Mary Lucille
was born here. We finished building our present house at 117
West North Street in 1939...In 1944, Max was elected Circuit
Judge...My father joined us in the mid-50s, and died in 1958.*
Children of Dora Pritchard and Ira Cox are:
> i. **Elsie Lucille Cox**, b. 1906, Ritchie County, West
> Virginia; d. 1991, Harrisville, Ritchie County;
> m. **Max DeBERRY** (b. 30 Mar 1909,
> Harrisville; d. 21 Feb 1968, Harrisville),
> in 1929.
> ii. **Maxine Cox**, b. 04 Oct 1910; d. 23 Aug 1911.

196.
Enoch Delmar Pritchard, son of No. 110, Millard Fillmore
Pritchard, was born 11 Mar 1885 in Nestorville, Barbour
County, West Virginia, and died 24 Oct 1961 in Fairmont,

Marion County, West Virginia. He married (1) **Lillian McCLINTOCK**, daughter of **Willis C. McCLINTOCK** and **Alice UNK** on 23 Mar 1912 in Wetzel County, West Virginia. Lillian was born 22 Aug 1891 in Pennsylvania and died 10 Nov 1979 in Tulsa, Tulsa County, Oklahoma.

Enoch married (2) **Cora HENNEN**, daughter of **Henry HENNEN** and **Susan Catherine SIX**, in Fairmont, Marion County, West Virginia on 25 Nov 1922. She was born 18 Nov 1886 in Greene County, Pennsylvania and died 13 Jul 1970 in Wheeling, Ohio County, West Virginia. He married (3) **Dora WILSON** in Fairmont, Marion County, West Virginia in 1945. She was born 17 Oct 1896 and died in Booth, Monongalia County, West Virginia during October 1972.

Enoch was a man of many talents, business ventures, and dreams. In 1904, he ran a grocery store in Hundred, Wetzel County, West Virginia. In 1905, he taught school in Wallace, Harrison County, West Virginia. In 1906, he sold Jersey Corn Flakes in Mannington, Marion County. In the early 1920s, he worked in the oil fields of Oklahoma.

Lillian McClintock lived with her parents in Grant, Wetzel County, West Virginia, at the time of the 1910 census. Their son Willis was born there in 1912 and their daughter Kathryne was born in 1916 in Tulsa, so it is apparent that the family moved to Oklahoma after 1912 and before 1916. The 1920 U.S. census shows Enoch, Lillian, and her parents living together in Tulsa. It is likely that he and Willis McClintock were drawn to Oklahoma by a shared interest in the oil industry which was prominent in Wetzel County. Soon after 1920, Lillian divorced Enoch and married **Charles T. DAGWELL** He was born 1888 in Missouri and died 1969. The 1930 U.S. census lists the two children Enoch and Lillian had together, as Willis Dagwell and Kathryne Dagwell.

By the 1930s, Enoch had returned to West Virginia and was working in the coal mines near Fairmont. From 1952 until his death, his column, "Sam Says," ran in the Westover (West Virginia) Observer. His editors called him "The Cracker Barrel Philosopher." He died of black lung disease.
Children of Enoch Pritchard and Lillian McClintock are:
    i. **Willis Millard Pritchard**, b. 1912, d. 1970.
    ii. **Kathryne Belle Pritchard**, b.1916, Tulsa, Tulsa County Oklahoma, d. 1979.
Children of Enoch Pritchard and Cora Hennen are:
291.   iii. **Jack Pritchard**, b. 19 Sep 1925; d. 06 Sep 1991, Milwaukee, Wisconsin.
292.   iv. **Jean Marie Pritchard**, b. abt. 1930.
Child of Enoch Pritchard and Dora Wilson is:
293.   v. **Ted Delmore Pritchard**, b. 09 Apr 1941.

197.

Amelia Gay Pritchard, daughter of No. 110, Millard Fillmore Pritchard, was born 22 Dec 1886 in Nestorville, Barbour County, West Virginia, and died 29 Sep 1959. She married **John MILLER** on 02 Jan 1909.
Children of Amelia Gay Pritchard and John Miller are:
294.   i. **Mildred Louise Miller**, b. 01 Oct 1909.
295.   ii. **Artemus Kenneth Miller**, b. 13 Jun 1911.
296.   iii. **Vivian Vera Miller**, b. 12 May 1913.
297.   iv. **Ethel Gay Miller**, b. 23 Jun 1915.
298.   v. **Paul Victor Miller**, b. 22 May 1917.
299.   vi. **Garrett Stanley Miller**, b. 15 Oct 1919; d. abt. 1996.
300.   vii. **Alma Lucille Miller**, b. 12 May 1922.

198.

Helen Willa Pritchard, daughter of No. 110, Millard Fillmore Pritchard, was born 16 Jan 1890 in Coleta, Whiteside County, Illinois, and died 23 Nov 1985 in Wallace, Harrison County, West Virginia. She married **Seth ALLEN,** 05 Sep 1906 in Oakland, Garrett County, Maryland.
Children of Helen Willa Pritchard and Seth Allen are:
301.   i. **Evangeline Virginia Allen**, b. 07 May 1912, Wallace, Harrison County, West Virginia; d. 22 Oct 1985, Shinnston, Harrison County.
302.   ii. **Joe Hamilton Allen**, b. 03 Dec 1929, Wallace, Harrison County, West Virginia, d. 24 Jun 2012.

199.

Ernest Markwood Pritchard, son of No. 110, Millard Fillmore Pritchard, was born 12 Sep 1893 in Coleta, Whiteside County, Illinois, and died 03 Feb 1979 in Hackettstown, Warren County, New Jersey; He is buried in Elk View Masonic Cemetery, Clarksburg, Harrison County, West Virginia. He married **Adelaide Elizabeth STUART** 01 Jun 1927 in Clarksburg, Harrison County, West Virginia, daughter of **Albert Edward STUART** (b. 14 Mar 1867, Meadville, Crawford County, Pennsylvania; d. 28 Jan 1919 Grafton, Taylor County, West Virginia) and **Uda Dietta BELL** (b. 03 Aug 1868, Burgettstown, Washington County, Pennsylvania; d. 13 Jan 1851, Swarthmore, Delaware County, Pennsylvania).

Ernest Markwood Pritchard served in World War I at Camp Lee, Virginia, arriving there 01 Apr 1918. Following promotion to corporal, he was looking forward to a European assignment when influenza swept the camp and nearly took his life. By the time he recuperated, the Armistice had been signed,

The Pritchard family, taken at West Union, West Virginia in 1922. Left to right: Ernest Markwood Pritchard, 29; Enoch Pritchard, 37; Reverend Pritchard, 65; Rosa Bell Nestor Pritchard, 50; Mildred Edith Pritchard Reynolds, 27; Helen Pritchard Allen, 33; and Lynden Eugene Reynolds, 2.

Rosa Bell Nestor Pritchard, age 70
St. Marys, West Virginia, 1945

288b

Helen Pritchard Allen, 80; Ernest Markwood Pritchard, 76; and Mildred Pritchard Reynolds, 74; taken at the Reynolds farm near St. Marys, West Virginia in 1969, shortly after the death of Adelaide Stuart Pritchard.

288c

288d

so he returned to West Virginia Wesleyan College in Buckhannon, Upshur County, West Virginia, which he had entered prior to being drafted. There he completed a degree in education with a major in mathematics.

Upon graduating in 1921, he accepted a position teaching mathematics at Wyatt (Harrison County, West Virginia) High School for the fall, then enrolled in summer classes at Columbia University's Teachers College in New York City. After studying there for the next seven summers, he earned a Master's Degree. In the meantime, he had begun teaching at Washington Irving High School in Clarksburg, West Virginia. While rooming with the E. E. Holden family on Hall Street, Ruth Holden, then a fifth-grade student, introduced him to her teacher, Adelaide Elizabeth Stuart. Just as little Ruthie had plotted, Ernest and Adelaide quickly fell in love and were married on 01 Jun 1927. They then moved to Parkersburg, West Virginia, where Ernest was head of the math department for three years. In 1929, he accepted an offer to join AT&T in Pittsburgh, Pennsylvania and remained with that company until he retired at the age of 65.

In September 1941, just before Pearl Harbor, Ernest was transferred to Philadelphia. He, Adelaide, and their daughter Emily moved to Swarthmore, a college town on the Pennsylvania Railroad's suburban West Chester line. Teaching, however, was in his blood; by the time he retired from AT&T, he was actively teaching in local colleges. First, he became an adjunct professor of mathematics at a division of Pennsylvania State University which opened in Swarthmore shortly after the close of World War II to accommodate returning servicemen eager to take advantage of the G.I. Bill. His lesson preparations monopolized his weekends and he often stayed up long past midnight to mark exams, but he loved his work and never complained about he hours consumed by his two careers. After retiring from AT&T, he continued teaching at both Penn State and nearby Pennsylvania Military College in Chester, Pennsylvania until Adelaide's death from cancer in 1969 stole his zest for living.

Torn between their lifelong yearning to return to West Virginia and the option of staying near their grandchildren, Ernest and Adelaide Pritchard remained in the Philadelphia area until ill health dictated the final irony: their wish was granted only after their deaths. Today, both rest in the family plot in Elk View Masonic Cemetery, Clarksburg, West Virginia.

Although they never realized many of their dreams, as is the case with most of us, Ernest and Adelaide Pritchard inspired hundreds of youths to break boundaries and seek the stars through study and imagination. Those of us who were touched by them are truly fortunate.

Children of Ernest Pritchard and Adelaide Stuart are:

      i. **Ann Pritchard**, b. 20 Jan 1930; d. 20 Jan 1930.

303.   ii. **Emily Marshall Pritchard**, b. 06 Sep 1931, Pittsburgh, Allegany County, Pennsylvania.

200.

Mildred Edith Pritchard, daughter of No. 110, Millard Fillmore Pritchard, was born 16 Jan 1896 in Compton, Lee County, Illinois, and died 10 Nov 1985 St. Marys, Pleasants County, West Virginia. She is buried in the Odd Fellows Cemetery, St. Marys. She married **Lynden Eugene REYNOLDS, Sr.** 19 Jun 1919 in Clarksburg, West Virginia, son of **Franklin REYNOLDS** and **Ida RIGGS**.

Mildred Edith Pritchard was the youngest child of Rev. Millard Fillmore Pritchard and Rosa Bell Nestor. Born on the

290

same month and day as her older sister, Helen, she had an outgoing personality nourished, no doubt, by her ability to adjust to the many moves dictated by her father's profession. Throughout her life, she enjoyed mingling with others, eagerly welcomed guests into her home, and was a regular and devoted church-goer. She raised her children with the same caring and light hand that characterized her upbringing.

Her wedding announcement in a Clarksburg, West Virginia newspaper, dated 19 May 1919, reads as follows: *Reynolds-Pritchard - The marriage of Miss Mildred Edith Pritchard to Lynden Eugene Reynolds was solemnized at the home of the bride's parents in Broad Oaks at 3:30 o'clock Thursday afternoon. The ring ceremony was read by the Rev. J. B. Workman, D.D., superintendent of the Buckhannon district.*

The bridegroom is a graduate of West Virginia University. At the beginning of the war, he was commissioned first lieutenant and was stationed at Battle Creek, Michigan. He is now engaged in farming and stock breeding at Grape Island, this state.

The bride is the accomplished daughter of the Rev. and Mrs. M. F. Pritchard. The Rev. Mr. Pritchard is the pastor of the Ash Chapel Methodist Episcopal Church of this city. Mrs. Reynolds is one of the most popular young women of the communities where she is known. The bride and bridegroom left on the 5:20 train for their wedding tour. They will be at home to their friends at Grape Island after July 1.

The Reynolds farm on Grape Island, three miles north of St. Marys, West Virginia, was built before the Civil War. The family home, positioned on a rise facing the Ohio River, is constructed of white clapboard and is styled with a center hall and formal proportions, a striking sight to travelers on the river.

Lynden Reynolds was descended from early settlers in

the area. Hardesty's *History of Pleasants County* notes that when Pleasants County was formed in 1851 from Wood, Tyler, and Ritchie Counties, one of the earliest advocates of the plan *"...and perhaps its prime mover was **Daniel Reynolds**, who at that time resided and still lives upon his farm on Middle Island opposite St. Marys. This island is a tract composed of 296 acres of land, which extends for about three miles in length opposite the mouth of Middle Island Creek, its lower end lying immediately opposite the southern line of the corporate limits of the town of St. Marys. Thomas Reynolds purchased 40 acres of the lower end of this island and about the year 1806 built a cabin upon it, where he moved with his family at a time when his son, Daniel, was five years of age. After the death of his father, Daniel inherited the farm and has ever since resided upon it. In the fall of 1882, at the age of 81, he justly prides himself upon the fact that, in cutting his crop of corn, he is enabled to keep up with the athletic young men whom he employs to assist him."*

Daniel Reynolds had his coffin built 15 years before he died and occasionally got into it and jokingly remarked that he wanted to make sure it fit. He used it to dry his onions during the summer.

Thus, both Mildred and Lynden Reynolds came from hardy pioneer stock. Lynden was born 03 Apr1890 at the family homestead. His expertise in agricultural methods enabled him to contribute to the needs of local farmers and farm organizations. Lynden died in 1970 and Mildred in 1985. Both are buried in the Odd Fellows Cemetery in St. Marys. Children of Mildred Pritchard and Lynden Reynolds are:

304. i. **Lynden Eugene Reynolds, Jr.,** b. 10 Jun 1920, St. Marys, Pleasants County, West Virginia; d. 08 Aug 2002, Pataskala, Licking County,

Ohio.
305.	ii. **Millard Franklin Reynolds**, b. 08 Jul 1923, St.
Marys, Pleasants County, West Virginia; d.
31 Jan 2000 St. Marys, Pleasants County, West
Virginia.
306.	iii. **Charlaine Reynolds**, b. 08 Jul 1923, St. Marys,
Pleasants County, West Virginia; d. 17 Dec
2012, Marietta, Washington County, Ohio.
307.	iv. **Joseph Isaac Reynolds**, b. 13 May 1926, St.
Marys, Pleasants County, West Virginia.

201.
Grace Catherine Ratcliffe, daughter of No. 111, Sarah Eliza
Pritchard, was born 31 Mar 1881. She married **John Jackson
GREATHOUSE** 24 Jan 1904.
Children of Grace Catherine Pritchard and John Greathouse
are:
308	i. **Vervel Greathouse**, b. 13 May 1907.
309.	ii. **Thelma Greathouse**, b. 17 Nov 1911.
310.	iii. **Sylvia Oleta Greathouse**.
311.	iv. **Dencie Evelyne Greathouse**, b. 19 Oct 1917.

202.
Lloyd Foreman Radcliffe, son of No. 111, Sarah Eliza
Pritchard, was born 18 Sep 1897. He married **Hattie
WILFONG**.
Children of Lloyd Radcliffe and Hattie Wilfong are:
i. **Tressie Pearl Radcliffe**, b. 16 Mar 1922.
312.	ii. **Wilma Mae Radcliffe**, b. 16 Nov 1924.
313.	iii. **Ralph Leslie Radcliffe**, b. 02 Dec 1925.
iv. **Monzel Clyde Radcliffe**, b. 19 Oct 1927; d.
09 Mar 1928.

v. **Robert Lee Radcliffe**, b. 22 Jun 1931.
vi. **Lois Jean Radcliffe**, b. 02 Jul 1933.
vii. **Rosalie Alice Radcliffe**, b. 12 Nov 1935.
viii. **Clele Nadine Radcliffe**, b. 23 Jul 1937.
ix. **Betty Arlene Radcliffe**, b. 05 Apr 1939.

203.

Anna May Pritchard, daughter of No. 112, Giles William Pritchard, was born 02 May 1895 in Barton, Allegany County, Maryland, and died 19 Apr 1975 in Pittsburgh, Allegheny County, Pennsylvania. She is buried in Mt. Lebanon Cemetery. She married **Charles C. WOLFE, Sr.** 28 Oct 1916 in Pittsburgh.
Children of Anna Pritchard and Charles Wolfe are:
  i. **Catherine Virginia Wolfe**, b. 28 Jul 1917; m. **Frank LANGENBACHER**.
  ii. **Charles C. Wolfe, Jr.**, b. 13 Jul 1920; m. **Marie L. SCHMIDT**.
  iii. **James Wolfe**, b. 24 Sep 1923; d. 23 Jul 1978.
  iv. **Gloria Wolfe**, b. 04 Feb 1929; m. **John L. SCHULTE, Jr.**

204.

Daisy Ethel Pritchard, daughter of No. 112, Giles William Pritchard, was born 11 Sep 1897 in Maryland, and died 13 Aug 1984 in Pittsburgh, Allegheny County, Pennsylvania. She married **Leslie VAUGHAN** in Pittsburgh.
Child of Daisy Pritchard and Leslie Vaughan is:
  i. **Marjorie Vaughan**, b. aft. 1925.

205.

Bertha Catherine Pritchard, daughter of No. 112, Giles

William Pritchard, was born 12 Jan 1901 in Fairmont, Marion County, West Virginia, and died 05 Sep 1983. She married **Alvin E. NEININGER** 1920.
Child of Bertha Catherine Pritchard and Alvin E. Neininger is:
314.   i. **Robert E. Neininger**, b. 25 Apr 1921.

206.
Effie Elizabeth Pritchard, daughter of No. 112, Giles William Pritchard, was born 22 May 1903 in Fairmont, Marion County, West Virginia. She married **Cyrus Monroe FOSTER.**
Children of Effie Elizabeth Pritchard and Cyrus Monroe Foster are:
315.   i. **Lucille Foster**, b. 09 Jun 1924.
316.   ii. **Jean Evelyn Foster**, b. 17 Jan 1926.
         iii. **Marian Elaine Foster**, b. 15 Jun 1934; m.
              Charles NORMAN, 09 Jun 1962.

207.
Claris Edward Pritchard, son of No. 112, Giles William Pritchard, was born 18 Mar 1906 in Fairmont, Marion County, West Virginia, and died 20 Dec 1970 in Fairmont. He is buried in Woodlawn Cemetery. He married **Agatha GABLER** March 1927 in Pittsburgh, Allegheny County, Pennsylvania.
Child of Claris Edward Pritchard and Agatha Gabler is:
         i. **Claris Edward Pritchard, Jr.**

208.
Mark Norris Pritchard, son of No. 113, Judson Fantley Pritchard, was born 01 Aug 1908, and died 25 May 1965. He married (1) **Grace MOSS**. He married (2) **Ruth KENDALL**. He married (3) **Henrietta G. WENGER** 22 Jul 1939.
Children of Mark Norris Pritchard and Henrietta Wenger are:

317.   i. **Sally Pritchard**.
        ii. **Gary Pritchard**.

209.

Claris Clayton Pritchard, son of No. 114, Ira Sanford Pritchard, was born 21 Sep 1895 in West Virginia. He married **Florence Edith HOWARD** 20 Dec 1917. She was born 03 Oct 1896, and died November 1985 in Nazareth, Northampton County, Pennsylvania.
Children of Claris Clayton Pritchard and Florence Edith Howard are:

318   i. **Irene Cecelia Pritchard**, b. 08 Jan 1919.
319.   ii. **Florence Edith Pritchard**, b. 22 Dec 1920.
      iii. **Ira Sanford Pritchard II**, b. 16 Dec 1927; d. 16 Dec 1927.
320.   iv. **Claris Clayton Pritchard, Jr.**, b. 18 Dec 1927, adopted.

210.

Dwight Ira Pritchard, son of No. 114, Ira Sanford Pritchard I, was born 21 Jan 1905. He married (1) **Sylvia OSBORNE**. He married (2) **Edna Mae STAFFORD** 03 Dec1931.
Child of Dwight Ira Pritchard and Sylvia Osborne is:

321.   i. **Hope Marie Pritchard**, b. 22 Dec 1927.

Children of Dwight Ira Pritchard and Edna Mae Stafford are:

322.   ii. **Dwight Dale Pritchard**, b. 15 Sep 1933.
323   iii. **William Sanford Pritchard**, b. 09 Jul 1941.

211.

Lora Audra Pritchard, daughter of No. 115, Francis Ezra Pritchard, was born 11 Mar 1893, and died 23 Dec 1960. She married **John D. TAYLOR**. He was born 1886 and died 1939

in Pullman, Ritchie County, West Virginia.
Child of Lora Audra Pritchard and John D. Taylor is:
324.   i. **Helen Genevra Taylor**, b. 29 Feb 1932, Pullman,
            Ritchie County, West Virginia.

212.

Eva Jane Pritchard, daughter of No. 115, Francis Ezra
Pritchard, was born 06 May 1901, in Vienna, Wood County,
West Virginia. She married **Wheeler Shirley WILSON** 1922.
Children of Eva Jane Pritchard and Wheeler Shirley Wilson
are:
325.   i. **Frank Marcel Wilson**, b. 1923.
        ii. **Larry Eugene Wilson**, b. 12 Nov 1936; m.
            Donna L. JONES, 03 May 1968. Donna L.
            Jones was previously married to **William F.
            JONES**, and had by that marriage two
            children: **James F. Jones**, b. 12 Mar 1954,
            and **Karen Sue Jones**, b. 08 Jun 1962.

213.

Paul Revere Pritchard, son of No. 116, Bushrod Washington
Pritchard, was born 04 Sep 1908. He married (1) **Beulah
FITTRO** 04 Sep 1928; they divorced in 1942. He married (2)
Helen PRICE 18 Oct 1942. He married (3) **Jane MILLER**
1950; they divorced in 1952. He married (4) **Alpha May
NEWMEYER** 1956.
Child of Paul Revere Pritchard and Helen Price is:
        i. **Dianna Louise Pritchard**, b. 03 Aug 1943.
Child of Paul Revere Pritchard and Alpha Newmeyer is:
        ii. **Michael David Pritchard**, b. August 1958.

214.

Denzil Lynnwood Pritchard, son of No. 116, Bushrod
Washington Pritchard, was born April 10, 1921. He married (1)
Elizabeth CARTER 1944. She was born 25 Jul 1924 in
Windham County, Connecticut and died 04 Jan 1989, Dunkirk,
Calvert County, Maryland. She is buried in Arlington National
Cemetery. He married (2) **Marilyne H.** after 1995. Denzil
Lynnwood Pritchard was employed at the American Embassy
in Moscow for a number of years. After he retired, he and
Elizabeth ran a horse farm in Dunkirk, Maryland. He now lives
in Waynesboro, Pennsylvania.

Children of Denzil Lynnwood Pritchard and Elizabeth Carter
are:

    i. **Darrell Lynwood Pritchard**, b. 21 Jan 1947; d.
       12 Nov 2005, Gaithersburg, Montgomery
       County, Maryland.

    ii. **Karen Elizabeth Pritchard**, b. 24 Jun 1948, m.
       Unk KEENAN.

    iii. **Susan Lorraine Pritchard**, b. 06 Jan 1953; m.
       Unk MILNE.

    iv. **Meredith Lynne Pritchard**, b. 10 Dec1955;
       m..**Unk BONTA.**

215.

Betty Lucille Pritchard, daughter of No. 116, Bushrod
Washington Pritchard, was born 12 Feb 1924. She married
George Marcus ROLLS, June 1943.

Children of Betty Lucille Pritchard and George Rolls are:

    i. **Harold Samuel Rolls**, b. March 1944.

    ii. **David Paul Rolls**, b. March 1947.

    iii. **Robert Warren Rolls**, b. November 1951.

    iv. **Richard Nathan Rolls**, b. May 1956.

216.

Castle Cowden Pritchard, son of No. 117, Walter Icen
Pritchard, was born 24 May 1904 in Hendricks, Tucker
County, West Virginia and died 07 Mar 1955. He married
Louise McKEOWN. He changed his name and was known for
a number of years as Don Sutherland.
Children of Castle Cowden Pritchard and Louise McKeown
are:

      i. **Donald Pritchard**, b. 21 Apr 1931.
     ii. **Max Pritchard**, b. 15 Sep 1935.

217.

Marie Alice Pritchard, daughter of No. 117, Walter Icen
Pritchard, was born 13 Jan 1906 in Harrisville, Ritchie County,
West Virginia, and died 11 Jan 1991, in Pendleton, Umatilla
County, Oregon. She married (1) **Milton Cooper SNYDER,**
22 Jun 1925 in Orofino, Clearwater County Idaho. He was born
06 Mar 1904 in Weippe, Clearwater County, Idaho, the son of
John Wesley SNYDER and **Mary Elizabeth COOPER**. She
married (2) **Albert Ralph Ciprano STERLING,** 10 Mar 1944
at the 1st Methodist Church, Lewiston, Nez Perce County,
Idaho. Albert was born 29 Jan 1916 at Dunmore, Lackawanna
County, Pennsylvania and died 29 Sep 1988 at Milton
Freewater, Umatilla County, Oregon. A detailed history of this
family, *Maybe Milton Should Go Work in the Woods* by Milton
Lee Pritchard Snyder, was published in 2009.
Children of Marie Alice Pritchard and Milton Cooper Snyder
are:

326.   i. **Milton Lee Pritchard Snyder**, b. 15 Nov 1929.
327.   ii. **Melvin Delano Snyder**, b. 07 Jun 1933, Weippe,
             Clearwater County, Idaho; d. 15 Aug 2008 in
             Pendleton, Oregon; m. (1) **Sonya**

DAVISON, 06 Sep, 1957; m. (2) **Judy Ann LAGORE**, 09 Jun 1976, Coeur d'Alene, Koolenai County, Idaho.

218.

Torry Icen Pritchard, son of No. 117, Walter Icen Pritchard, was born 10 Nov 1907, Jarvisville, Harrison County, West Virginia. He married **Madeline Goldie BERRY** (b. 23 Feb 1917, d. 22 Sep 1996) on 01 Oct 1935.

Children of Torry Icen Pritchard and Madeline Berry are:

      i. **Jo Andre-Augustine Pritchard**, b. 04 Jan,1935.

328.   ii. **Dennis Richard Pritchard**.

     iii. **Michel Icen Pritchard**, b. 16 Jul 1939.

     iv. **Thomas Lewis Pritchard**, b. 05 Feb 1941.

     v. **Sharon Rosalie Pritchard**, b. 23 Jun 1942.

     vi. **Pamela Madaline Pritchard**, b. 19 Mar 1944.

    vii. **Sandra Kathleen Pritchard**, b. 10 Nov 1945.

   viii. **James Patrick Pritchard**, b. 05 Nov 1948.

     ix. **John Craig Pritchard**, b. 02 Jul 1950.

     x. **David Paul Pritchard**, b. 14 Oct 1952.

    xi. **Merry Lou Pritchard**, b. 20 Jul 1956.

219.

Sheldon Schofield Pritchard, son of No. 117, Walter Icen Pritchard, was born 25 Sep 1910 in Selbyville, Upshur County, West Virginia and died 24 Feb 1990, in King County, Washington. He married **Elizabeth E. BARRY** (b. 06 Jun 1911, d. 27 January 1993).

Children of Sheldon Schofield Pritchard and Elizabeth E. Barry are:

329.   i. **Betty Lee Pritchard**, b. 04 Jan, 1933.

     ii. **Sheldon Walter Pritchard**, b. 12 Dec 1936.

220.

Clara Hillis Pritchard, daughter of No. 117, Walter Icen Pritchard, was born 24 Dec 1912 in Syracuse, Meigs County, Ohio and died 27 Sep 1996 in Pierce, Clearwater County, Idaho. She married (1) **Josef SCHMID**. She married (2) **Emmett C. BONNER** (b. 15 Sep 1903, d. 29 May 1990, Idaho).

Child of Clara Hillis Pritchard and Josef Schmid is:

　　i.. **Joan Karlyn Schmid**, b. 23 Dec 1931.

Children of Clara Hillis Pritchard and Emmett Bonner are:

　　ii. **Emmett Lee Bonner**, b. 08 Aug 1934.

　　iii. **James Karl Bonner**, b. 29 May 1936.

　　iv. **Joy Bonner**, b. 21 Jan 1940.

　　v. **Timothy Parsons Bonner**, b. 02 Mar 1945.

　　vi. **Terrel Daniel Bonner**, b. 13 Jun 1946.

　　vii. **Mona Kay Bonner**, b. 28 Feb 1949.

　　viii. **Philip Martin Bonner**, b. 21 Jun 1951.

　　ix. **Willie Joe Bonner**, b. 24 Jun 1956.

221.

Blanche Agatha Pritchard, daughter of No. 117, Walter Icen Pritchard, was born 23 Sep 1919, and died 29 Jan 2000, in Spokane, Spokane County, Washington. She married **Willard W. SNYDER**.

Children of Blanche Agatha Pritchard and Willard W. Snyder are:

　　i. **Wesley Snyder**.

　　ii. **Larry Snyder**.

　　iii. **Gary Snyder**.

　　iv. **Keith Snyder**.

　　v. **Twila Gay Snyder**

222.

Fifi Lee Pritchard, daughter of No. 117 Walter Icen Pritchard, was born 31 Dec 1921. She married **Otis J. COCHRELL**. Her father named her after a French actress he admired, so infuriating his wife that she left him, calling that "the last straw."
Child of Fifi Lee Pritchard and Otis J. Cochrell is:
    i. **Ronald Cochrell**, b. 02 Dec 1947.

223.

Sylvester Orval Prunty, son of No. 118, Flora Odell Lawson, was born 17 Jul 1878, and died 07 Feb 1956 at Harrisville, Ritchie County, West Virginia, where he is buried in the IOOF Cemetery. He married (1) **Mabel KESTER**. He married (2) **Elsie D. HADDOX**, daughter of **Jonathan Hewey HADDOX** and **Safronia COLLINS**, on 31 Aug, 1913. S. O. Prunty was a prominent Harrisville attorney, retiring as Judge of the Third Judicial Circuit comprising Ritchie, Doddridge, and Pleasants Counties.
Children of S. O. Prunty and Mabel Kester are:
    i. **Orean Prunty.**
    ii. **Frances Prunty.**

224.

Ian Hortense Pritchard, daughter of No. 119, Charles J. Pritchard, was born 03 Jul 1902 in Webster County, West Virginia, and died 18 Nov 1981 in Modesto, Stanislaus County, California. She married **Frederick Leander SHAFFER** 07 Jul 1919, son of **Martin Luther SHAFFER** and **Bertie Alice HIMES**, daughter of **Joseph HIMES** and **Mary AUVIL**. Frederick Leander Shaffer was born 11 Aug 1901 in Barbour County, West Virginia and died in Modesto, California. His father, **Martin Luther SHAFFER** was the son of **Daniel N. SHAFFER** and **Sarah AUVIL** and the grandson of **William P. SHAFFER** and **Mary Magdalene NESTER**, daughter of **Daniel NESTER** and **Marion WILSON**. For more details, see section on the Nestor Family.

Children of Ian Pritchard and Frederick Leander Shaffer are:

> i. **Virginia Alice Shaffer**, b. 07 Mar 1920, Adamston, Clarksburg, Harrison County, West Virginia; bur. Greenlawn Cemetery, Liberty Addition, Clarksburg, West Virginia.
> ii. **Helen Arretia Shaffer**, b. 25 Feb 1921, Reynoldsville, Harrison County, West Virginia; m. **Harrison Clyde YEAGER**.
> iii. **Elita Maxine Shaffer**, b. 12 Oct 1922; m. (1) **Daniel Edward KOONTZ, Jr.**; m. (2) **Lloyd LEESON**, Gabbs, Nye County, Nevada.

330.
> iv. **Wilma May Shaffer**, b. 15 Jul 1926, Gladys Hollow, Harrison County, West Virginia.
> v. **Patricia Ann Shaffer**, b. 28 Oct 1952 adopted); m. **Dale FRANKLIN**, Modesto, California. *Note*: Because of the great discrepancy between Patricia Ann's age and that of her siblings, it is not clear if she was adopted by Ian and Frederick Shaffer or one of their daughters.

225.

Ethel Lee Wass, daughter of No. 124, Lewis Maxwell Wass, was born 25 Jan 1887 at Wass Ranch, Mariposa County, California, and died 02 Apr 1969 in Tulare, Fresno County, California. She married **Robert Wesley DeMOSS** 21 Oct 1907, in Mariposa, Mariposa County, California, son of **Jacob**

DeMOSS and **Sarah ELAM**. He was born 05 Dec 1878, in Mariposa County and died 06 Jul 1957 in Mariposa, Mariposa County, California.

Children of Ethel Wass and Robert DeMoss are:

331.　i. **James Wesley DeMoss**, b. 24 May 1908, Darrah, Mariposa County, California; d. 05 May 1979, Modesto, Stanislaus County, California.

332　ii. **Robert Glenn DeMoss**, b. 01 Aug 1910, Darrah, Mariposa County, California; d. 17 Feb 1995, North Fork, Fresno County, California.

　iii. **Baby DeMoss**, b. 12 Jun 1912, Darrah, Mariposa County, California; d. 12 Jun 1912.

333.　iv. **Hilda Lorraine DeMoss**, b. 13 Nov 1913, White Rock Ranch, Mariposa County, California; d. 12 Jul 1978, Plainsburg, Merced County, California.

334.　v. **Sophia Isabel DeMoss**, b. 17 May 1915, White Rock Ranch, Mariposa County, California.

335.　vi. **Lola May DeMoss**, b. 1916, White Rock Ranch, Mariposa County, California.

336.　vii. **Norma Ilene DeMoss**, b. July 1919.

　viii. **Raymond Willard DeMoss**, b. 10 Sep 1921, White Rock Ranch, Mariposa County, California; d. 18 Oct 1940, Mariposa, Mariposa County, California.

　ix. **Boy DeMoss**, b. 17 Feb 1924, White Rock Ranch, Mariposa County, California; d. 17 Feb 1924.

337.　x. **Everett Sylvester DeMoss**, b. 1926.

338.　xi. **Beverly Lee DeMoss**, b. 1928.

339.　xii. **Elzara Nadine DeMoss**, b. 1930.

226.

William "Dick" Harrison Wass, son of No. 124, Lewis
Maxwell Wass, was born 21 May 1890, in Mariposa, Mariposa
County, California, and died 27 Sep 1958 in Mariposa. He
married **Florence BAYS**. She was born 23 May 1898 in
Mariposa County, and died August 1986 in Mariposa County.
Children of William Wass and Florence Bays are:

    i. **Hazel Wass**; m. **Carl WHITE.**
    ii. **Gloria Wass.**
    iii. **Clara Wass**, b. Mariposa County, California; m.
        John ASHWORTH (b. Mariposa County,
        California).
    iv. **Clifford Wass,** b. Mariposa County, California;
        m. **Nadine UNK.**
    v. **Malcolm Wass**, b. Mariposa County, California;
        m. **Betty UNK.**
    vi. **Harry "Buck" Wass**, b. Mariposa County,
        California; m. **Marian UNK.**

227.

Lewis Maxwell Wass, Jr., son of No. 124, Lewis Maxwell
Wass, Sr., was born 04 Jan 1893, at Wass Ranch, Mariposa
County, California, and died September 1982 in Merced,
Merced County, California. He married (1) **UNK;** he married
(2) **Jennie Marie EARL**, 31 Oct 1919, in Reno, Storey
County, Nevada. She was born 13 Mar 1899, and died August
1987 in Fresno, Fresno County, California.
Children of Lewis Maxwell Wass, Jr. and Jennie Earl are:

    i. **Louis Alvin Wass**, b. 22 Nov 1920, Le Grand,
        Merced County, California; m. **Helen UNK.**
    ii. **Elizabeth Jane Wass**, b. 31 Mar 1924, Le
        Grand, Merced County, California; m. **Roy**

SCROGGINS.
340.   iii. **Lois Elvira Wass**, b. 16 Aug 1926, Merced
County, California.
iv. **William Loren Wass,** b. 06 Jul 1928, Le
Grand, Merced County, California; m. **Lois
UNK.**
v. **Lee Earl Wass**, b. 13 Feb 1933, Le Grand,
Merced County, California; m. **Flora UNK.**
vi . **Janice Louise Wass**, b. 25 May 1935, Merced
County, California; m. (1) **Alvin SANTOS**;
m. (2) **Manuel SOUZA**; m. (3) Unk
BROOKIN.
vii. **Mary Irene Wass**, b. 05 Nov 1937, Merced County,
California; m. (1) **Manuel SOUZA**; m. (2)
Adolph PETRILLO; m. (3) **Manuel SOUZA**
(remarried divorced husband).
viii. **Melva Rose Wass**, b.28 Aug, 1940; m. (1)
Jim TAYLOR; m. (2) **Unk JONES.**

228.
Herman H. Wass, son of No. 124, Lewis Maxwell Wass, Sr.,
was born 24 Oct 1895, in Mariposa, Mariposa County,
California, and died October 1981 in Mariposa, Mariposa
County, California. He married **Agnes LEAHY**. She was born
01 Jun 1904 in San Francisco, San Francisco County,
California, and died 05 Nov 1999 in Mariposa, Mariposa
County.
Children of Herman Wass and Agnew Leahy are:
341.   i. **James Russell Wass**, b.16 Jun 1923, Wass
Ranch, Mariposa County, California.
342.   ii. **Melvin Eugene Wass,** b. 25 Aug 1926, Wass
Ranch, Mariposa County, California; d.

Mariposa County.

343.   iii. **Lois June Wass**, b. 26 Jul 1930, Mariposa,
Mariposa County, California.

344.   iv. **Edna Lorraine Wass,** b. 13 Feb 1933,
Mariposa County, California.

345   v. **Alfred Leroy Wass**, b .11 Apr 1936, Mariposa
County, California.

346.   vi. **Ernest Clinton Wass**, b. 05 Mar 1938, Merced,
Merced County, California; d. 27 Aug 1963.

229.

Fred Wass, son of No. 124, Lewis Maxwell Wass, Sr., was
born 26 Nov 1898, in Mariposa County, California, and died
11 Jan 1989 in Mariposa County. He married **Beryl UNK**. She
was born 04 May 1908, and died 05 Jul 1989 in Mariposa
County.

Children of Fred Wass and Beryl unk are:

    i. **Forrest Wass.**
   ii. **Crystal Wass.**

230.

Aileen May Wass, daughter of No. 124, Lewis Maxwell Wass,
Sr., was born 25 Nov 1906 at Wass Ranch, Mariposa County,
California, and died February 1994 in Mariposa, Mariposa
County, California. She married **Carl Reuben PHILLIPS**,
February 1925 in Merced, Merced County, California. He was
born 10 Mar 1906, in Santa Barbara, Santa Barbara County,
California, and died July 1959 in Yosemite Valley, Mariposa
County, California.

Children of Aileen May Wass and Carl Phillips are:

347.   i. **Helen Eileen Phillips**, b. 11 Mar 1926, Arcata,
Humboldt County, California.

348.   ii. **Mildred Lodine Phillips**, b. 06 Jul 1928,
        Mariposa County, California.
349.   iii. **Constance Allaire Phillips**, b. 20 May 1937,
        Mariposa County, California.
        iv. **Leroy Carl Phillips**, b. 23 Oct, 1943, Merced,
        Merced County, California; d. May 1955,
        Mariposa, Mariposa County, California.

231.

Carrie Alice Wass, daughter of No. 125, Harrison Ellsworth "Ellie" Wass, was born 02 Feb 1885 in Harrisville, Ritchie County, West Virginia, and died 05 Dec 1971 in Harrisville. She married **William Shelby STOUT, Jr.**, 10 Nov 1910, in Harrisville. He was the son of **William S. STOUT, Sr.** and **Laura unk.** He was born 17 Dec 1879 in Stouts Mills, Gilmer County, West Virginia, and died 28 Dec 1938, in Harrisville. Both are buried in the IOOF Cemetery, Harrisville, Ritchie County, West Virginia.
Children of Carrie Wass and William Stout are:
        i. **Ruth Stout**, b. 29 Sep 1911.
        ii. **William Shelby Stout, III,** b. 05 Nov1913,
        Harrisville, Ritchie County, West Virginia; d.
        11 Nov 1988, Harrisville.
        iii. **Samuel Ellsworth Stout**, b. 06 Aug 1915,
        Harrisville, Ritchie County, West Virginia; d.
        02 Mar 1980, Harrisville.
        iv. **Julia Ann Stout**, b. 08 Aug 1917, Harrisville,
        Ritchie County, West Virginia; d. 1924,
        Harrisville.

232.

Winifred Chloe Wass, daughter of No. 125, Harrison

Ellsworth Wass, was born 25 Mar 1892 in Harrisville, Ritchie County, West Virginia, and died 04 Dec 1989, in Harrisville. She married **Fred Watson FOSTER**, 13 Oct 1917, in Harrisville. He was born 06 Jul 1880, in Ritchie County, and died 14 Mar 1956 in Harrisville. Both are buried in the IOOF Cemetery, Harrisville, Ritchie County, West Virginia.
Child of Winifred Wass and Fred Foster is:
350.   i. **Joseph Foster**, b. 13 May 1929, Ritchie County, West Virginia; d. 29 May 1994, Morgantown, Monongalia County, West Virginia.

233.

Ethel Myrtle Goff, daughter of No. 127, Barbara Alice Wass, was born 21 Oct 1890 in Burnt House, Ritchie County, West Virginia, and died 05 May 1964 in Parkersburg, Wood County, West Virginia. She married **Benjamin Franklin PATTON, Jr.**, 14 Jan 1913, in Harrisville, Ritchie County, West Virginia. He was the son of **Benjamin F. PATTON, Sr.** and **Evaline DePUE**. He was born 16 Dec 1878 in Harrison County, West Virginia, and died 30 Jan 1954 in Harrisville, Ritchie County, West Virginia. Ethel Myrtle (or Myrtle Ethel) Goff was originally named Cassandra L. Goff, and this was recorded in the Ritchie County birth register. Subsequently, her birth name was changed to Mirtle (sic) Ethel on 17 Oct 1890, and her birth date was changed to 21 Oct 1890. Both Ethel and Benjamin Patton are buried in the IOOF Cemetery, Harrisville.
Children of Ethel Goff and Benjamin Patton are:
         i. **Marion Carolyn Patton**, b.11 Jan 1919, Harrisville, Ritchie County, West Virginia; d. 24 Apr 1984, El Paso, El Paso County, Texas; m. **Elmer William GAUGER**, 04 Jan 1943, Charleston, Kanawha County, West Virginia. He was born

21 Aug 1919, Sheboygan, Sheboygan County,
Wisconsin. Marion Gauger is buried in El Paso,
Texas. She and Elmer Gauger had no children.

351.   ii. **Madelon Camille Patton**, b. 22 Feb 1920,
Harrisville, Ritchie County, West Virginia.

352.   iii. **Marshelline Patton**, b. 24 Jul 1923, Harrisville,
Ritchie County, West Virginia.

234.

Hermione "Herma" Pearl Goff, daughter of No. 127, Barbara
Alice Wass, was born 07 May 1895, in Burnt House, Ritchie
County, West Virginia, and died 27 Jan 1971 in Harrisville,
Ritchie County, West Virginia. She married **Thomas Jeffrey
DAVIS, Sr.**, 27 Jun 1917, son of **Thomas DAVIS** and **Aletha
LEGGETT**. He was born 19 Mar 1879 in Harrisville, Ritchie
County, West Virginia, and died 30 Jan 1962 in Harrisville.
Both are buried in the IOOF Cemetery, Harrisville.
Children of Hermione Goff and Thomas Davis are:

i. **Thomas Jeffrey Davis, Jr.**, b. 01 Sep 1918,
Harrisville, Ritchie County, West Virginia; d.
16 Feb 1981, Harrisville; m. (1) **Hilda WARD**,
1943, Montgomery, Montgomery County,
Alabama; m. (2) **Susan WHIPKEY**, 1964,
Parkersburg, Wood County, West Virginia.

ii. **George Lathrop Davis**, b. 04 May 1920,
Harrisville, Ritchie County, West Virginia; d.
06 Feb 1943, Tunisia, North Africa (World War
II).

353.   iii. **Alice Ann Davis**, b. 17 Sep 1923, Harrisville,
Ritchie County, West Virginia; d. 11 Feb 1994,
Atlanta, Fulton County, Georgia.

310

235.

Winifred Dell Goff, daughter of No. 127, Barbara Alice Wass, was born 22 Sep 1898, in Burnt House, Ritchie County, West Virginia, and died 16 Mar 1989, in Harrisville, Ritchie County, West Virginia. She married **John Edward KOEHLER, Sr.,** 09 Jun 1923 in Cincinnati, Hamilton County, Ohio. He was born 02 Nov 1900, in Reading, Hamilton County, Ohio, and died May 1972 in Cincinnati. Winifred Koehler is buried in Arlington Memorial Gardens, Cincinnati; John Koehler is buried in Hamilton Memorial Gardens, Cincinnati.

Children of Winifred Goff and John Koehler are:
354. i. **Winifred Jean Koehler**, b. 19 Sep 1925, Cincinnati, Hamilton County, Ohio.
355. ii. **John Edward Koehler, Jr.,** b. 30 Mar 1929, Reading, Hamilton County, Ohio.

236.

Fredda Marcella Goff, daughter of No. 127, Barbara Alice Wass Goff, was born 17 Jul 1908 in Ritchie County, West Virginia, and died 11 Jul 1952 in Parkersburg, Wood County, West Virginia. She married **Arthur Harry MERGY,** 12 June 1931 in Cincinnati, Hamilton County, Ohio, son of **Alfred MERGY** and **Rosalie HOLLIGER**. He was born 25 Jan 1905 in Chester, Delaware County, Pennsylvania, and died 12 Mar 1949, in Parkersburg, Wood County, West Virginia. Both Fredda and Arthur Mergy are buried in the IOOF Cemetery, Harrisville, Ritchie County, West Virginia.

Child of Fredda Marcella Goff and Arthur Mergy is:
356. i. **Arthur Eugene Mergy**, b. 03 Jul 1932, Parkersburg, Wood County, West Virginia.

237.

Ralph Paul Wass, Sr., son of No. 128, Peter Wass, was born 06 Feb 1898, in Jesse Cains Run, Ritchie County, West Virginia, and died May 1971 in Ohio. He married **Lenna Bell DAVISSON**, daughter of **Willie DAVISSON** and **Susan BRUFFEY**. Lenna was born 16 Sep 1902 in Chevauxdefrise, Ritchie County, West Virginia, and died after 1992.
Children of Ralph Wass and Lenna Davisson are:

    i. **Harold Harding Wass**, b. 17 Jan 1922.

    ii. **Ralph Paul Wass, Jr.**, b. 28 May 1924, Harrisville, Ritchie County, West Virginia.

    iii. **Elwood Edward Wass**, b. 31 Jan 1926.

357.   iv. **Betty Anadore Wass**, b. 17 Jul 1930.

    v. **Franklin Jennings Wass**, b. 09 Dec 1931.

    vi. **Elwin Davisson Wass**, b. 15 Sep 1934.

    vii. **Margaret Luron Wass**, b. 16 Oct 1937, m. **Ronald HATFIELD**.

238.

Bertha Pearl Wass, daughter of No. 128, Peter Wass, was born 05 Apr 1900, in Jesse Cains Run, Ritchie County, West Virginia, and died 05 May 1991 in Washington, Wood County, West Virginia. She married **Howard FOWLER,** 1922, in Ritchie County. He died in 1971. Bertha is buried in the IOOF Cemetery, Harrisville, Ritchie County, West Virginia.
Children of Bertha Wass and Howard Fowler are:

    i. **Howard Fowler II,** b. Ritchie County; m. **Mary Jo UNK.**

    ii. **Loretta Fowler**, b. Ritchie County; m. **Kester ELDER.**

239.

Belva May Wass, daughter of No. 128, Peter Wass, was born 2 Feb 1902, in Goffs, Ritchie County, West Virginia, and died 19 Dec 1967 in Ritchie County. She married **Ernest HATFIELD**. She is buried in the IOOF Cemetery, Harrisville, Ritchie County, West Virginia.

Children of Belva Wass and Ernest Hatfield are:

  i. **Helen Hatfield.**
  ii. **Emma Jean Hatfield.**
  iii. **Dewayne E. Hatfield,** b. 13 Feb 1938, Ritchie County, West Virginia; d. 21 Aug 1944, Ritchie County; bur. IOOF Cemetery, Harrisville, Ritchie County, West Virginia.

240.

Cecil Byrl Wass, son of No. 128, Peter Wass, was born 21 Jun 1907, in Goffs, Ritchie County, West Virginia, and died May 1979 in Mariposa County, California. He married **Elizabeth Jane BARKLEY**, daughter of **James BARKLEY** and **Catherine EWART**. She was born 01 May 1907, at Hanlin Station, Washington County, Pennsylvania, and died 01 Jul 1975, in Weirton, Hancock County, West Virginia. Elizabeth is buried at Chestnut Ridge Cemetery, Washington County, Pennsylvania.

Children of Cecil Wass and Elizabeth Barkley are:

  i. **James Edward Wass,** b. 29 Sep 1927, Goffs, Ritchie County, West Virginia.
  ii. **William C. Wass,** b. 1929.
  iii. **Richard Carl Wass,** b. 15 Sep 1931, Hollidays Cove, Hancock County, West Virginia; d. 07 Aug 1936, Eldersville, Washington County, Pennsylvania.

    iv. **Lulabelle Katherine Wass**, b. 06 Sep 1934,
        Weirton, Hancock County, West Virginia; m.
        John O. ZANEY
    v. **Joan Wass**, b. abt. 1936.
    vi. **Ruth Ann Wass**, b. 1940; m. **Richard**
        SCHULTZ.

241.

Romeo Grant Wass, son of No. 129, Charles Grant Wass, was born 09 May 1897, in Ritchie County, West Virginia, and died 04 Jan 1990, in Harrisville, Ritchie County. He married **Ida M. BICKERSTAFF** 15 Apr 1920 in Ritchie County. She was born 13 Feb 1897, in Mahone, Ritchie County, and died 19 Nov 1992 in Belmont, Pleasants County, West Virginia. Both are buried in the IOOF Cemetery, Harrisville.
Children of Romeo Wass and Ida Bickerstaff are:
358.   i. **Charles Denver Wass**, b. 08 Jul 1923,
        Smithville, Ritchie County, West Virginia.
    ii. **Donald Morgan Wass,** b. 03 Jun 1929,
        Smithville, Ritchie County, West Virginia; d.
        13 Oct 1989, Harrisville, Ritchie County;
        bur. IOOF Cemetery, Harrisville.

242.

Hosea Harrison Wass, son of No. 129, Charles Grant Wass, was born 12 Jan 1899, in Washburn, Ritchie County, West Virginia, and died 20 Jan 1975 in Harrisville, Ritchie County. He married **Gladys Willa BUSH**, 08 Nov 1924, in Coxes Mills, Gilmer County, West Virginia. She was born 1903 in Gilmer County, and died 17 Mar 1988, in Harrisville. Both are buried in the IOOF Cemetery, Harrisville.
Children of Hosea Wass and Gladys Bush are:

359. i. **Coralie Wass**, b. September 1925.
360. ii. **Herman Lawrence Wass,** b. 20 Nov 1926, Washburn, Ritchie County, West Virginia.
361. iii. **Dennis Brooks Wass**, b. 23 Sep 1928, Washburn, Ritchie County, West Virginia.
iv. **Hilda Lorianne Wass**, b. 28 Nov 1931, Washburn, Ritchie County, West Virginia; d. 1932, Ritchie County; bur. Bethany Cemetery, Hazelgreen, Ritchie County.
362. v. **Boyd Wayne Wass**, b. 03 Sep 1933, Ritchie County, West Virginia.

243.

Juna Myrtle Wass, daughter of No. 129, Charles Grant Wass, was born 12 Jan 1900, in Ritchie County, West Virginia, and died 11 Jan 1989, in Harrisville, Ritchie County. She married **Lorn Hazen SUMMERS**, 16 Aug 1919, in Ritchie County, son of **Elmore SUMMERS** and **Alice GOFF**. He was born 30 Oct 1896 in Burnt House, Ritchie County, and died 01 Dec 1976 in Harrisville, Ritchie Countyl West Virginia. Both are buried in the IOOF Cemetery, Harrisville.
Children of Juna Wass and Lorn Summers are:
i. **Gerald Summers**, b. 20 Aug 1919; d. 28 Jul 1990.
ii. **Gerald Francis Summers**, b. 05 Sep 1921, Clarksburg, Harrison County, West Virginia; m. **Mary KUKSHTEL** (b. 22 Feb 1921, Preston County), 13 Mar 1943.
iii. **Charles Edwin Summers**, b. 01 May 1924, Harrisville, Ritchie County, West Virginia; d. 13 Apr 1990, Harrisville; m. **Nancy Watson ZINN** (b. 17 Jul 1931) October 1950; bur. IOOF Cemetery, Harrisville, Ritchie County.

315

iv. **Edward Summers**, b. 06 Jul; d. June 1985.

244.

Eva Madge Wass, daughter of No. 129, Charles Grant Wass, was born 20 Oct 1902 in Goffs, Ritchie County, West Virginia, and died 05 Feb 1973 in Winter Park, Orange County, Florida. She married **Oliver Hall SMITH** 22 Apr 1923 in Ritchie County, West Virginia, son of **Arthur C. SMITH** and **Addie KELLEY**. He was born 13 Jan 1900, in Wirt County, West Virginia, and died 28 Mar 1971, in Winter Park, Orange County, Florida. Both are buried in Chapel Hills Cemetery, Weirton, Hancock County, West Virginia.

Children of Eva Madge Wass and Oliver Hall Smith are:

363   i. **Betty Lee Smith**, b. 18 Oct 1925, Steubenville, Jefferson County, Ohio.

ii. **Evelyn Louise Smith**, b. 08 Jan 1929, Steubenville, Jefferson County, Ohio; m. **Richard Gordon MORRISON**, 24 Sep 1950, Weirton, Hancock County, West Virginia.

iii. **Billy Joe Smith**, b.22 Aug 1931, Harrisville, West Virginia; m. (1) **Margie LYNCH**; m. (2) **Joann PETTY**, 15 Jan 1959.

iv. **Ruth Ann Smith**, b. 02 Aug 1936, Hollidays Cove, Hancock County, West Virginia; d. 05 Aug 1936, bur. Chapel Hills Cemetery, Weirton, Hancock County.

v. **Judith Marlene Smith**, b. 04 May1938, Weirton, West Virginia; m. (1) **David Ray RAWSON**; m. (2) **Bruce STRIPLING**; m. (3) **Virgil WENCEL**.

316b

Wass School., Jessie Cain's Run, Ritchie County, West
Virginia, 1912, or 1913. Photo provided by Mike Wilson,
Uniontown, Pennsylvania.

Front row: Left to Right
1. Hazel Simpson
2. Forest White
3. Dessie Nuzum
4. Graydon Wass
5. Fred Wass
6. Floyd Nuzum
7. Belva Wass
8. Madge Wass

Second Row: Left to Right
1. Juna Wass
2. Edith white
3. Clarence Simpson
4. Jessie Jones
5. Hosea Wass
6. Pearl Wass
7. Carter White

Back Row: Left to Right
1. Mary Hatfield
2. Dewey Wilson (Ad Wilson's son, Prudy Wilson's brother)
3. Ada Smith
4. Claude Goff, teacher
5. Romeo Wass
6. Ralph Wass

245.

Harlie Graydon Wass, son of No. 129, Charles Grant Wass, was born 19 Aug 1905, in Jesse Cains Run, Ritchie County, West Virginia, and died 21 Mar 1957 in Harrisville, Ritchie County, West Virginia. He married **Goldie Eunice RIGGS**, 30 Mar 1932, in Ritchie County, daughter of **Frank RIGGS** and **Addie UNK.** Goldie was born 25 Dec 1910, in Ritchie County, West Virginia, and died 25 Jul 1950, in Harrisville, Ritchie County. Both are buried in the IOOF Cemetery, Harrisville. Children of Harlie Wass and Goldie Riggs are:

364.   i. **Charles "Ike" Franklin Wass,** b. 06 Jan 1938, Harrisville, Ritchie County, West Virginia.

365.   ii. **John Wesley Wass**, b. 21 Aug 1947, Harrisville, Ritchie County, West Virginia

246.

Charles Fred Wass, son of No. 129, Charles Grant Wass, was born 11 Aug 1908, in Ritchie County, West Virginia, and died 27 Dec 1978, in Harrisville, Ritchie County. He married (1) **Edna PRUNTY,** 11 Nov 1931, in Ritchie County. She was born 09 Dec 1903, in Berea, Ritchie County, West Virginia, and died 19 Apr 1936, in Parkersburg, Wood County, West Virginia. He married (2) **Dorothy RUSSELSON**, 09 Mar 1941, in Ritchie County. He is buried in the IOOF Cemetery, Harrisville.

Children of Charles Wass and Edna Prunty are:

i. **Robert Eugene Wass**, b. 04 Aug 1932, Harrisville, Ritchie County, West Virginia.

ii. **Mary Joann Wass**, b. 07 Aug 1933; m. **Eugene MAPLE.**

iii. **Lois Irene Wass**, b. 11 Nov 1934; m. **Darious Winford HILL**, 10 Jun 1955.

iv. **Judith Wass; m. Unk WILSON.**
Children of Charles Wass and Dorothy Russelson are:
    v. **Sharlene Wass**, b. 08 Jul 1941, Harrisville,
        Ritchie County; m. **Richard Lee HAGER**,
        05 Nov 1960, Ritchie County, West Virginia.
    vi. **Michael Kent Wass,** b. 14 Oct 1942; m. **Linda**
        UNK.
    vii. **Judith Ann Wass**, b. 09 Apr, 1947; m. **David**
        Robert WILSON, 23 Jul 1965, Ritchie County,
        West Virginia.
    viii. **Carol Leah Wass**, b. 22 Jul 1950, Harrisville,
        Ritchie County, West Virginia; m. **Unk**
        STEVENS.

247.

Mildred Edith Wass, daughter of No. 129, Charles Grant
Wass, was born 27 Dec 1909, in Ritchie County, West
Virginia, and died 09 Feb 1973, in Ritchie County. She married
Worthy VANNOY. He was born 1909. Mildred is buried in
the IOOF Cemetery, Harrisville, Ritchie County.
Child of Mildred Wass and Worthy Vannoy is:
    i. **Charles Jimmy Vannoy.**

248.

Cassandra Wass, daughter of No. 130, Roy Wass, was born
15 Feb 1914 in Jesse Cains Run, Ritchie County, West
Virginia, and died 01 Mar 1991, in Boulder, Boulder County,
Colorado. She married **Jack RYLAND**. He died in 1972. She
is buried in Bethany Cemetery, Hazelgreen, Ritchie County,
West Virginia.
Children of Cassandra Wass and Jack Ryland are:
    i. **Linda Ryland.**

ii. **Sharon Ryland**, m. **Unk McSWIGGAN**. Their
daughter, **Tara McSwiggan**, married
Grant JACKSON and had two daughters,
Sierra Jackson and **Lily Jackson**
iii. **Kathleen Ryland.**
iv. **John Ryland.**
v. **Michael Ryland.**
vi. **Sheila Ryland.**
vii. **Bryan Ryland.**

249.

Daisy Delle Wass, daughter of No. 130, Roy Wass, was born
06 Oct 1919, in Jesse Cains Run, Ritchie County, West
Virginia. She married **Unk FLETTER.**
Children of Daisy Delle Wass and unk Fletter are:
    i. **Elizabeth Lee Fletter.**
    ii. **Barbara Fletter.**

250.

Josephine Jean Wass, daughter of No. 130, Roy Wass, was
born 18 Feb 1922, in Jesse Cains Run, Ritchie County, West
Virginia. She married **Eugene T. SULLENBERGER.** A
descendant reports that Eugene was very abusive, so she left
him and had the legal name of their child changed to Wilson,
her mother's maiden name.
Child of Josephine Wass and Eugene T. Sullenberger is:
366.   i. **Brent Wilson**

251.

Virginia Opal Wass, daughter of No. 131, James Rienzi Wass,
was born 12 Dec 1910, in Huntington, Cabell County, West
Virginia, and died February 1984 in Bradenton, Manatee

County, Florida. She married **Alton Parker BOWERS**. He
was born 25 Dec 1905, in South Carolina, and died April 1986,
in Fairview, Union County, North Carolina.
Children of Virginia Wass and Alton Bowers are:
367.   i. **Virginia Darlene Bowers**, b. 27 Feb 1933,
                Sarasota, Sarasota County, Florida.
368   ii. **Arlene Patricia Bowers,** b. 13 May 1935,
                Sarasota, Sarasota County, Florida.
369.   iii. **Barbara Ailene Bowers**, b. 06 Oct 1937,
                Sarasota, Sarasota County, Florida.
370.   iv. **Caroline Merrily Bowers**, b. 08 Aug 1942.

252.

Nina Simon, daughter of No. 145, Zoie Love Simon, was born
02 Oct 1898 near Philippi, Barbour County, West Virginia. She
married **Charles James SHUTTLEWORTH** 22 Mar 1922 in
Fairmont, Marion County, West Virginia, son of **George
Wythe SHUTTLEWORTH** and **Estella REGER**. Charles
died 26 Jan 1971 in Charleston, South Carolina and is buried in
Clarksburg, Harrison County, West Virginia.
Child of Nina Simon and Charles Shuttleworth is:
        i. **Mona Jane Shuttleworth**, b.18 Jul 1923,
                Clarksburg, Harrison County, West Virginia;
                m. **Hilary Bell MATTINGLY, Jr.**, 08 May
                1949, St. Louis, Missouri.

253.

Glenwood Lloyd Queen, son of No. 153, William Lloyd
Queen, was born 11 Jul 1896. He married **Stella A.
DOGOLYER**.
Children of Glenwood Queen and Stella A. Dogolyer are:
        i. **Billy Queen**, b. 16 Nov 1920.

    ii. **Clara Jane Queen**, b. 01 Jan 1922.
   iii. **Madge Queen**, b. 28 Aug 1928.

254.

Ralph H. Pritchard, son of No. 169, Jason Pritchard, was born 25 Apr 1912 in Salt Creek Twp., Hocking County, Ohio. He married **Dora Katherine SLARK**. She was born about 1912 in Hocking County, Ohio.
Child of Ralph Pritchard and Dora Slark is:
    i. **Ethel Lorraine Pritchard**, b. 22 Jul 1931,
       Circleville, Pickaway County, Ohio.

255.

Edwin Lakin Pritchard, son of No. 169, Jason Pritchard, was born 1917 on a farm near Adelphi, Ross County, Ohio. He married **Mildred May SNODGRASS** in 1942. She was born 1916 in Portsmouth, Scioto County, Ohio. Edwin was a watch repairman in Kingston, Ross County, Ohio. They lived in Avon Park, Okechobee County Florida in 2004, but later returned to Ohio. He died 27 Aug 2007 at the age of 90 in Circleville, Pickaway County, Ohio.
Children of Edwin Lakin Pritchard and Mildred Snodgrass are:
    i. **David Pritchard,** b. 1943; lives in central Ohio;
       Associate with Burgess and Nipel Consulting
       Engineers.
   ii. **William Pritchard,** b. 1948; left Ohio in 1971;
       lives in Addison, Dallas County, Texas.
   iii. **Thomas Jason Pritchard**, b. 26 Feb 1950;
       lives in central Ohio.

256.

Cecil Leroy Pritchard, son of No. 169, Jason Pritchard, was born 10 Aug 1922, in Salt Creek Twp., Hocking County, Ohio. He married **Mary Claretta SCHWALBAUGH,** sister of **Elsie Elizabeth SCHWALBAUGH**, who married No. 269, **Eustace Charles PRITCHARD**. Mary was born about 1924 in Hocking County, Ohio, the daughter of **Henry M. SCHWALBAUGH** and **Etta Viola LEASURE** Mary is also found as Mary Clarenda.

Children of Cecil Pritchard and Mary Schwalbaugh are:
>   i. **Robert Eugene Pritchard,** b. 14 Aug.1947, Circleville, Pickaway County, Ohio.
> ii. **Daniel Leroy Pritchard,** b. 26 May 1949, Circleville, Pickaway County, Ohio.

257.

Ruben Millard Pritchard, son of No. 170, Francis Marion Pritchard, was born 24 Sept 1905, Colerain Township, Ross County, Ohio. He married **Marie Beatrice PETERMAN,** daughter of **Bert Rufus PETERMAN** and **Laura HARRIGER**. Marie was born 17 Sep 1918 in Bucyrus, Crawford County, Ohio. She died 11 Mar 2006 at age 87 in Bucyrus, Crawford County, Ohio.

Children of Ruben Millard Pritchard and Marie Beatrice Peterman are:
>   i. **Kenneth Robert Pritchard,** b. 07 Sep 1943, Bucyrus, Crawford County, Ohio.
> ii. **Robert Eugene Pritchard**, b. 17 Dec 1945, Bucyrus, Crawford County, Ohio.
> iii. **Shirly Marlene Pritchard,** b. 24 Oct 1947, Bucyrus, Crawford County, Ohio.

258.

Elza Owen Pritchard, son of No. 170, Francis Marion

Pritchard, was born 08 Nov 1906 in Colerain Township, Ross County, Ohio. He died 02 Feb 1961 at the age of 54 in Galion, Crawford County, Ohio. He married **Elsie F. KINCAID**, daughter of **Elden C. KINCAID** and **Emma O. BAKER**. She was born 08 Mar 1913 in Marion, Marion County, Ohio. She died 15 Mar 1995 at the age of 82 in Upper Sandusky, Wyandot County, Ohio.

Children of Elza Owen Pritchard and Elsie F. Kincaid are:

    i. **Maxine Louise Pritchard,** b. 21 Nov 1933, Mount Gilead, Morrow County, Ohio.

    ii. **Rose Marie Pritchard,** b. 27 Apr 1935, Mount Gilead, Morrow County, Ohio   .

    iii. **Ruth Ellen Pritchard**, b. 11 Sep 1937, Oxford, Butler County, Ohio. She died 03 Feb 1995 at age 57 in Bucyrus, Crawford County, Ohio.

    iv. **Evelyn Lucille Pritchard,** b. 27 Nov 1945, Mount Gilead, Morrow County, Ohio. She died 30 Nov 2002 at the age of 69 in Sycamore, Wyandot County, Ohio.

    v. **Linda Kay Pritchard**, b. 30 Jul 1948, Mount Gilead, Morrow County, Ohio.

259.

Wallace Allen Pritchard, son of No. 170, Francis Marion Pritchard, was born 30 Jan 1922, Colerain Township, Ross County, Ohio. He died 29 Sep. 1956 at the age of 45 in Crawford County, Ohio. He married **Virginia Irene STEINHELFER** 19 Jul 1931, Bucyrus, Crawford County, Ohio. She was born 09 Jul 1916 in Crawford County, Ohio. She died 08 Jan 1998 at the age of 81 in Bucyrus, Crawford County, Ohio.

Child of Wallace Allen Pritchard and Virginia Irene is:

i. **Ralph Eugene Pritchard**, b. 19 Jul 1933, Bucyrus, Crawford County, Ohio.

260.

Eunice Marie Pritchard, daughter of No. 170, Francis Marion Pritchard and Emma Starling, was born 16 Sep 1918 in Colerain Twp., Ross County, Ohio and died 24 Jun 1993 in Tucson, Pima County, Arizona. She married **Lee Wyant MARTIN**, son of **William MARTIN** and **Mary BARKER** on 27 Jan 1940 in Fostoria, Crawford County, Ohio.

Children of Eunice Marie Pritchard and Lee Wyant Martin are:

i. **William Lee Martin**, b. 12 Oct 1940, Norwalk, Huron County, Ohio; d. 11 Nov 2011, Bucyrus, Ohio. He served in the U.S. Air Force from 1961-1965 and retired from Tenneco of Milan 1 after 35 years.

371.   ii. **James Leroy Martin**, b. 15 Jun 1942, Norwalk, Huron County, Ohio. He married **Lucille Ann STIMPLE,** daughter of **Dudley STIMPLE** and **Edith SMITH** on 06 Jun 1968, North Fairfield, Huron County, Ohio.

372.   iii. **Nancy Irene Martin,** 08 Jan 1951, Norwalk, Huron County, Ohio; m. (1) **Frank Makray**; m. (2) **Lazlo ZRINSZKI** 08 Apr 1988, Clark County, Nevada; lives in Tucson, Pima County, Arizona.

261.

Mae Welch, daughter of No. 172, Altie Pritchard, was the second wife of **Floyd LIZANA.** He was a butcher, sheriff's deputy, and farmer near Gulfport, Harrison County, Mississippi. Mae was a homemaker and cleaned houses. She attended the Lizana Baptist Church.

Children of Mae Welsh and Floyd Lizana are:

    i. **Melvin Lizana**, a carpenter; m. **Wanda UNK,** lives on Floyd Lizana Road, Gulfport.

    ii. **Nathan Lizana.**

    iii. **John Lizana.**

262.

Benton L. Pritchard, son of No. 173, Larrick Pritchard, was born 05 May 1900, Salt Creek Township, Hocking County. He died about 1979. He married **Mary E. TRUEX**. She was born in 1901 and died in 1993. Both are buried in Green Summit Cemetery, Adelphi, Ross County, Ohio.

Children of Benton Pritchard and Mary Truex are:

    i. **Robert Pritchard**, b. 1924; d. 1997.

    ii. **Roy Pritchard.**

    iii. **Emery Pritchard.**

    iv. **Helen Pritchard.**

    v. **Geraldina Pritchard.**

    vi. **Donna Pritchard.**

263.

Edward Allen Pritchard, son of No. 174, Leeman Lee Pritchard, was born about 1917 in Logan, Hocking County, Ohio. He married **Caroline Inez KUHLWEIN**. She was born about 1921 in Ashville, Pickaway County, Ohio. Edward was still living in Ashville in 1976 and was a milk truck driver and farmer.

Children of Edward Allen Pritchard and Caroline Kuhlwein are:

    i. **George Edward Pritchard,** b. 31 Oct 1939.

    ii. **Barbara Jane Pritchard,** b. 21 Jan 1941, Tarlton, Salt Creek Twp., Hocking County, Ohio.

iii. **Carol Lee Pritchard,** b. 16 Nov 1942, Salt Creek
Twp., Hocking County, Ohio.
iv. **Betty Louise Pritchard,** b. 01 Feb 1947,
Ashville, Pickaway County, Ohio.

264.

Eugene Pritchard, son of No. 175, Sherman Pritchard, was
born 1903 and died 1981. He married **Gaynell Marie UNK.**
She was born 1906 and died 1944.
Children of Eugene Pritchard and Gaynell Marie are:
i. **Alberta M. Pritchard**, b. 1926; d. 1966; m. **Unk
AMOS.**
ii. **Robert Pritchard.**
iii. **Phyllis Pritchard.**
iv. **Beatrice Pritchard.**

265.

Charles Wesley Pritchard, Sr., son of No. 175, Sherman
Pritchard, was born 1905 and died 1979. He married **UNK.**
Children of Charles Wesley Pritchard, Sr. and Unk are:
i. **Donna Pritchard.**
ii. **Marjorie Pritchard.**
iii. **Charles Wesley Pritchard, Jr.**
iv. **David Lee Pritchard.**

266.

Thomas Pritchard, son of No. 175, Sherman Pritchard. He
married **UNK.**
Children of Thomas Pritchard and Unk are:
i. **Benjamin Pritchard.**
ii. **Carol Ann Pritchard.**

267.

Alvin Pritchard, son of No. 175, Sherman Pritchard, married **Helen STARKEY.**

Children of Alvin Pritchard and Helen Starkey are:

  i. **Roger Pritchard.**
  ii. **Jenny Pritchard.**
  iii. **Jeannie Pritchard.**
  iv. **Jo Ann Pritchard.**

268.

Carrie Vivian Pritchard, daughter of No. 176 Amon Lewis Pritchard, was born 04 May 1904, and died 21 Aug 1990. She married **Clem SCHWALBAUGH, Sr.,** 04 Mar 1922, in Hocking County, Ohio. He was born 11 Feb 1898, and died 03 Apr 1972 in Laurelville, Hocking County, Ohio.

Children of Carrie Pritchard and Clem Schwalbaugh, Sr. are:

  i. **Berman E. Schwalbaugh,** b. 26 Apr 1924; d. 01 Oct 1960.
  ii. **Clem Schwalbaugh, Jr.,** b. 02 Dec 1929; d. 08 Nov 1997, Laurelville, Hocking County, Ohio.
  iii. **Mildred Schwalbaugh.**
  iv. **Shirley Schwalbaugh.**

269.

Eustace Charles Pritchard, son of No. 176 Amon Lewis Pritchard, was born 03 Nov 1905, in Salt Creek Twp., Hocking County, Ohio, and died 24 Oct 1992, in Berger Hospital, Circleville, Pickaway County, Ohio. He married **Elsie Elizabeth SCHWALBAUGH** on 09 Apr 1932. They were divorced prior to 1965. Elsie was the daughter of **Henry M. SCHWALBAUGH** and **Etta Viola LEASURE**, who were married 15 Oct 1910. Etta was said to be of Cherokee Indian heritage. Elsie was born 12 Sep 1914, in Salt Creek Twp., Hocking County, Ohio, and died Feb. 1987 in Anaheim, Orange County, California. Eustace Charles Pritchard owned a gas filling station. He signed his last will and testament on 05 Nov 1985, naming his oldest son, Donald Pritchard, as his executor. His obituary in the 26 Oct 1992 issue of Logan (Ohio) Daily News reads as follows: *Eustace C. Pritchard, 86, Circleville, died Saturday, October 24, in Berger Hospital, Circleville. Born 03 Nov 1905, in Hocking County, son of the late Amon and Sarah McDonald Pritchard, he was formerly married to the late Elsie Schwalbaugh Pritchard, who died in 1987. Surviving are sons, Donald Pritchard, of Kingston; Kenneth and David Pritchard, both of Florida; three daughters, Mrs. Lloyd (Helen) Williams of California; Mrs. Ralph (Betty) Coleman of Powell; and Linda Cook of Orange, California; 20 grandchildren; 23 great-grandchildren; three brothers, Hayward, Marshall, and Foster Pritchard, all of Circleville; and two sisters, Alice Nungster of Adelphi, and Elsie Downing of Laurelville. Also preceding him in death were two brothers and two sisters. Burial will be in Reber Hill Cemetery, Ashville, Ohio.*

Children of Eustace Charles Pritchard and Elsie Elizabeth Schwalbaugh are:

373.　i. **Helen Pritchard,** b. 15 Aug 1932, Williamsport, Pickaway County, Ohio.

374.　ii. **Donald Lee Pritchard,** b. 20 Oct 1934; Williamsport, Deercreek Twp., Pickaway County, Ohio; d. 16 Apr 1994.

　iii. **Betty Louise Pritchard,** b. Mar. 1936, Williamsport, Deercreek Twp., Pickaway County, Ohio; m. **Ralph COLEMAN.** Lives in Powell, Delaware County, Ohio.

375.   iv. **Kenneth Dean Pritchard**, b. 08 May 1940,
            Williamsport, Pickaway County, Ohio.
       v. **David Carl Pritchard**, b. 08 Jan 1945.
376.   vi. **Linda Sue Pritchard,** b. 08 Aug 1946,
            Williamsport, Pickaway County, Ohio.

270.

Alice Marie Pritchard, daughter of No. 176, Amon Lewis Pritchard, was born 15 May 1907. She married **Rancy NUNGSTER.**
Children of Alice Pritchard and Rancy Nungster are:
       i. **Carl Nungster.**
       ii. **Berry Nungster.**
       iii. **Bernine Nungster.**
       iv. **Anne Nungster.**
       v. **Jane Nungster.**
       vi. **Josephine Nungster.**
       vii. **Nan Nungster.**

271.

Elsie Sylvia Pritchard, daughter of No. 176 Amon Lewis Pritchard, was born 21 Oct 1908. She married **Clifford DOWNING.**
Children of Elsie Pritchard and Clifford Downing are:
       i. **Geneva Downing.**
       ii. **Margie Downing.**

272.

Eldon Berman Pritchard, son of No. 176, Amon Lewis Pritchard, was born in Pike Run, Hocking County, Ohio, on 03 May 1910, and died 16 Apr 1946, in Salt Creek Twp., Hocking County, Ohio, at the age of 35, of a ruptured stomach ulcer. He

The Pritchard/Prickett Family History

is buried in Pleasant Hill Cemetery, Adelphi, Colerain Twp., Ross County, Ohio. He married **Katherine HEETER,** daughter of **William HEETER** and **Elizabeth FORD.** She was born 14 Jun 1915, in Circleville, Pickaway County, Ohio, and died 27 Sep 1992, in Circleville. After Eldon's death, Katherine (her name is also found as Catherine and Kathryn) married Eldon's brother, **Haywood PRITCHARD.** She was a member of VFW and Eagles Auxiliaries and the Pocahontas Lodge of South Bloomfield, Pickaway County, Ohio.
Children of Eldon Pritchard and Katherine Heeter are:

    i. **Marcine Lucille Pritchard,** b. 18 Mar 1934; m. **Unk FRAZIER**; lives in Circleville, Pickaway County, Ohio.
    ii. **George Pritchard**; lives in Dighton, Bristol County, Massachusetts.

273.

Marshall Edward Pritchard, son of No. 176, Amon Lewis Pritchard, was born 12 Mar 1912 in Salt Creek Township, Hocking County, Ohio. He married (1) **Sudie PETERS**. He married (2) **Rose Ann UNK**. He married (3) **Lucille CONGROVE** 25 May 1963. Lucille is buried in Green Summit Cemetery, Ross County, Ohio.
Child of Marshall Pritchard and Lucille Congrove is:

    i. **Cindy Pritchard.**

274.

Darold Vernon Pritchard, son of No. 179, Hugh Jack Pritchard, was born 23 Oct 1917. He married **Rose Mary UNK**. She was born 1931 and died 1989.
Children of Darold Pritchard and Rose Mary are:

377.   i. **Darlene Pritchard.**

331

ii. **Debra Pritchard**
iii. **Ann Pritchard**; m. **David STILSON.**
iv. **Thomas Pritchard.**

275.

Alberta Bernadine Pritchard, daughter of No. 179, Hugh Jack Pritchard, was born 25 Nov 1919. She married (1) **Robert Jay LANE.** He died 1979. She married (2) **Kenneth N. WILSON.**
Children of Alberta Pritchard and Robert Lane are:
378.   i. **Tamara Mae Lane**, b. 1945.
379   ii. **Terry Jay Lane**, b. 1947; d. 1994.
380.   iii. **Roberta Dawn Lane**, b. 1953.
381.   iv. **Lucinda Lane**, b. 1955.

276.

Lowell Forest Pritchard, son of No. 179, Hugh Jack Pritchard, was born 19 Oct 1921. He married **Edith GAREN.**
Children of Lowell Forest Pritchard and Edith Garen are:
382.   i. **Sharon Pritchard.**
383.   ii. **Susan Pritchard.**

277.

Ira Grant Pritchard, son of No. 181, James Robert Pritchard, was born 11 Oct 1895 in Roane County, West Virginia, and died 12 Jan 1984. He married **Jessie Carrie BRADLEY** 17 Apr 1920, in Roane County, West Virginia, daughter of **Frederick O. BRADLEY** and **Bertha WELCH.** Jesse was born 29 Nov 1895, in Roane County, and died 10 Aug 1970, in Roane County. Both are buried in Clover Cemetery, Roane County. The cause of Ira's death was cardiac arrest. He served in France during World War I.

Children of Ira Grant Pritchard and Jessie Carrie Bradley are:
    i. **Freda Ann Pritchard** b. 14 Jun 1921, Roane
        County, West Virginia; m. **Glenn**
        HOLSINGER, 1947.
    ii. **Frances Jeroldine Pritchard**, b. 28 Feb 1923,
        Roane County, West Virginia; m. **Donald**
        ROTH, 1947.
384.   iii. **William Ray Pritchard**, b. 15 Feb 1924,
        Spencer, Roane County, West Virginia.

278.

Arty Blake Pritchard, son of No. 181, James Robert
Pritchard, was born 13 May 1897, in Roane County, West
Virginia, and was retired from Pennzoil Company when he
died 24 Apr 1976, in Roane County of an apparent heart attack.
He married **Anna H. BRADLEY.** He was buried at Eventide
Cemetery, Spencer, Roane County on 27 Apr 1976.
Child of Arty Pritchard and Anna Bradley is:
    i. **Ruby Bradley Pritchard;** obtained the rank of
        Colonel in the U.S. Army.

279.

Harold Dean Pritchard, son of No. 181, James Robert
Pritchard, was born 15 Sep 1902 in Spencer, Roane County,
West Virginia, and died 02 Jan 1999 in Stow, Summit County,
Ohio. He married **Bessie Mae SMITH**, daughter of **Albert
Columbus SMITH** and **Adella Frances MAY** on 15 Apr
1925 in Akron, Summit County, Ohio. Bessie died in
December 1993.

      Harold Dean Pritchard was known as "Red." His
obituary states that he died at the age of 96 still craving his
independence. He left home while in his teens and lived in

Pennsylvania until 1920 when work became scarce and he decided to join the Army. While stationed in Hawaii, Harold was accidentally shot in the left leg by another soldier. The wound did not heal properly and, at the age of 20, he lost his leg just below the knee. Harold returned to West Virginia, but, like many living near Spencer, he moved to Akron where jobs were plentiful. In February 1925, he began working for Ohio Brass in Barberton and remained there for more than 40 years. From 1925 to 1935, he was an active union member, serving as an officer and participating in some ugly strikes. In 1935, he was given a foreman's job, which he held until retiring in 1968. While working at The Brass, some of Harold's co-workers called him "Red" because of his hair color and his complexion, which would grow redder out of anger and stubbornness. For more than 70 years, starting in the 1920s and ending in 1996, Harold made certain to cast his ballot on Election Day. In his later years, he preferred Republicans, although Bessie liked to remind him that he cast four ballots for FDR. Harold and Bessie raised seven children, all of whom survive. Also surviving are 26 grandchildren, and 20 great-grandchildren. Children of Harold Dean Pritchard and Bessie Smith are:

385.   i. **John Earl Pritchard**, b. 28 Jun 1926, Akron, Summit County, Ohio.

    ii. **Helen Pritchard**, b. 10 Sep 1927, Akron, Summit County, Ohio; m. **Frank REMIS**.

386   iii. **Patricia Pritchard**, b. 30 Dec 1929, Akron, Summit County, Ohio.

387.   iv. **Lawrence Dean Pritchard**, b. 15 Sep 1931, Akron, Summit County, Ohio.

388.   v. **Charles Edward Pritchard**, b. 15 Sep 1932, Akron, Summit County, Ohio.

389.   vi. **George Lewis Pritchard**, 14 Mar 1934, Akron,

Children of Harold and Bessie Pritchard
Front: George, Helen, Patricia, Lawrence
Back: James, John, Charles, 1999

Summit County, Ohio.
390.   vii. **James Robert Pritchard**, b. 15 Aug 1938, Akron,
Summit County, Ohio.

280.

Dola Pritchard, daughter of No. 182, Darrell Duke Pritchard, was born 14 Aug 1903 in Walnut Grove, Roane County, West Virginia, and died 11 Feb 1993 in Lancaster, Fairfield County, Ohio. She married **Edward Corder POOL** 18 Dec 1921 in Spencer, Roane County, West Virginia, son of **William POOL** and **Anna ROCKHOLD**. He was born 15 Jan 1895 in Roane County, West Virginia, and died 16 Jan 1960 in Lancaster, Fairfield County, Ohio. Dola states that she was born "up the hollow" from Walnut Grove in Roane County. Her Grandma Pritchard ran the post office in her house, which Elias, her grandfather, had built. He laid up a porch and a wall around the yard out of rough stones. Mary Pritchard always gave birth to her children at her mother's house, except for Dola.
Children of Dola Pritchard and Edward Pool are:
391.   i. **Darrell Edward Poole**, b. 16 Aug 1922,
Spencer, Roane County, West Virginia; d.
22 Mar 1992, Fairfield County, Ohio.
392.   ii. **William Earl Poole**, b. 05 Aug 1924, Spencer,
Roane County, West Virginia.
393.   iii. **Walter Averill Pool**, b. 10 Jun 1926, Spencer,
Roane County, West Virginia. *Note:* Darrell
and William added an 'e' to their name, while
Walter did not.

281.

Dona Pritchard, daughter of No. 182 Darrell Duke Pritchard, was born 10 May 1907. She married (1) **Earl Austin LOWE,**

10 Mar 1925 in Roane County. A son of **Jonathan M. LOWE** and **Cordie RHODES**, he was born in Roane County 18 Mar 1904, and died 27 Jan 1934, of tuberculosis. During an interview with Ed Pool on 23 Sep 2000, Dona said that she and Earl were living on the Spring Creek farm when the house burned down one winter night. They had a little dog that stayed in the house, but that night the dog refused to come in when called. If it had not been for the little dog barking, Dona and Earl would have perished in the fire. They had only time to grab what came to hand as they left. They crossed the field barefoot to Uncle Lem Burke's home, where they were given care. Earl, whose nickname was "Hoot," was a barber and had a shop at Spencer, later at Clendenin. When he contracted tuberculosis and was hospitalized at Beckley, West Virginia, Dona took a job at the same hospital to be with him. He was buried 29 Jan 1934, in the Lowe Cemetery, Roane County. Dona married (2) **Haskell O. GRADY**, 11 Jan 1937, in Roane County. The son of **Russell GRADY** and **Ethel DALRYMPLE**, he was born 08 Apr 1911 and died 19 Nov 1978 in Roane County. He was retired from the Columbia Gas Company. Dona had no children by either husband.

282.

Dora Pritchard, daughter of No. 182, Darrell Duke Pritchard, was born 04 Apr 1911 in Roane County, West Virginia. She married **Alonzo Ernest WARD** 31 Dec 1931 in Spencer, Roane County, West Virginia, son of **Thomas WARD** and **Addie HOFF**. He was born 28 Oct 1910 in Roane County, West Virginia, and died 06 Sep 1999 in Roane County, WV at the home of his daughter, Barbara Lou Ward Owens. Ernest Ward was retired from West Virginia Department of Highways. He delivered milk from his Ward's Dairy, was a

school bus driver, an active member of the Republican Party, Gandee Chapel Church, the Lion's Club, Woodman of the World, IOOF, and a charter member of Roane County Junior Chamber of Commerce. He served on the Board of Directors of Southern States Cooperative, was a member of the Farm Bureau, and was named Farmer of the Year in the Little Kanawha Region. He was active in Soil Conservation Service, involved with Red Cross training, and was very proud that he was the first member of the Roane County 4-H Club. He was a long-time West Virginia All Star, a member of Spencer High School Harmony Boys, and enjoyed hunting, fishing, and square dancing. He was buried 09 Sep 1999 in the Ward Cemetery, Roane County, West Virginia. The Ward Cemetery is next to the Gandee Chapel Church, which is next to his longtime farm home. He bought the farm from his father-in-law, Darrell Pritchard, one of the nicest farms in Roane County. Dora's nickname was "Dote." She was a teacher.
Children of Dora Pritchard and Ernest Ward are:
394.   i. **James Ernest Ward**, b. 22 Feb 1933, Roane County, West Virginia.
395.   ii. **Barbara Lou Ward**, b. 28 Mar 1935, Roane County, West Virginia.

283.

Robert Evan Kennedy, son of No. 184, Addie Miranda Pritchard, was born 31 Mar 1916 in Worland, Wyoming. He married **Betty Lou KASER**, 03 Feb 1945 in Aurora, Kane County, Illinois, daughter of **Everett Dee KASER** and **Mabel McNEIL**.
Children of Robert Evan Kennedy and Betty Kaser are:
396.   i. **Anne Louise Kennedy**, b. 05 Jul 1946, Fond du Lac, Fond du Lac County, Wisconsin.

ii. **Carter Evan Kennedy**, b. 09 Mar 1948,
Portland, Multnomah County, Oregon.

iii. **Robert Gordon Kennedy**, b. 13 Apr 1951,
Portland, Multnomah County, Oregon.

284.

Anna Lee Smith, daughter of No. 185, Waitman Conley Smith, was born 27 Jun 1920 in Coalton, Randolph County, West Virginia, and died 27 Feb 1982 in Macon, Bibb County, Georgia. She married **Lawrence Cleveland HOLLAND, Sr.** on 07 Jun 1940 in Ludowici, Long County, Georgia. He was born 19 Aug 1917 in Graceville, Jackson County, Florida, and died 11 May 1994 in Dothan, Houston County, Alabama. Anna Lee died of cancer like her mother, grandmother, and a number of maternal aunts. She was married 41 years at the time of her death. Lawrence served with the U.S. Army in the Pacific during World War II. He was known by family and friends as L.C. Both are buried at Glen Haven Memorial Gardens on Houston Road in Dothan, Alabama.

Children of Anne Lee Smith and Lawrence Holland are:

397. i. **Nancy Ann Holland**, b. 17 Dec 1942.
398. ii. **Lawrence Cleveland Holland, Jr.**, b. 13 Aug 1944.
399. iii. **James Michael "Mike" Holland**, b. 29 Jun 1949.
400. iv. **Peggy Louise Holland**, b. 31 Aug 1950.

285.

Kenneth Wayne Dennison, son of No. 187, John Willis Dennison, was born 14 Nov 1937 in Upshur County, West Virginia. He married **Jane RAWN**. He now lives in Capshaw, Madison County, Alabama.

Children of Kenneth Dennison and Jane Rawn are:
    i. **David Dennison**, b. abt. 1965, an engineer.
    ii. **Jeff Dennison**, b. abt. 1967, computer artist.
    iii. **Daniel Dennison**, b. abt. 1971, attended George
                Mason University, Fairfax, Virginia.

SEVENTH GENERATION

286.

Mary Criss, daughter of No. 189, Lillian Bee, married **Arthur ENDSLEY**. They lived in Houston, Texas. Their sons are all engineers; their daughter is a computer scientist.
Children of Mary Criss and Arthur Endsley are:

  i. **Carter Endsley.**
  ii. **Jay Endsley.**
  iii. **Terry Endsley.**
  iv. **Cheryl Endsley.**

287.

Gracia Alice Taylor, daughter of No. 191, Mary Elizabeth Pritchard, was born 1894 in Parkersburg, Wood County, West Virginia, and died 1972 in Parkersburg. She married **Marion Reep LOW**. He was born 1895 in Butler County, Pennsylvania.
Children of Gracia Taylor and Marion Low are:

  i. **Robert Low**, b. 1917, Akron, Summit County, Ohio; m. **Phyllis Helen LaHAIE** (b. 1919; d. 1998.).
  ii. **Joseph Taylor Low**, b. 1919, Parkersburg, Wood County, West Virginia; m. **Zola Lorrayne MINER** (b.1926.)
  iii. **Mary Elizabeth Low,** b. 1921, Akron, Summit County, Ohio.
  iv. **Grace Janet Low**, b. 1926, Akron, Summit County, Ohio; d. 1977; m. **William Oliver NIGHTENGALE.**

288.

Wesley Isaac Taylor, son of No. 191, Mary Elizabeth
Pritchard, was born 10 Oct 1898, in Parkersburg, Wood
County, West Virginia, and died 11 Jun 1976, in Parkersburg.
He married **Gemma KEITH**, daughter of **Adam KEITH** and
Mary ALKIRE. She was born 18 Dec 1898, in Harrisville,
Ritchie County, West Virginia, and died 16 Jul 1982 in
Parkersburg. Both are buried in the IOOF Cemetery,
Harrisville, Ritchie County.
Children of Wesley Taylor and Gemma Keith are:

> i. **Dorothy Eileen Taylor,** b. 15 Aug 1922,
> Harrisville, Ritchie County, West Virginia; d.
> 28 Feb 1924, Harrisville; bur. IOOF
> Cemetery, Harrisville.
> ii. **Wesley Keith Taylor,** b. 1925, Harrisville,
> Ritchie County, West Virginia; d. 1927,
> Harrisville; bur. IOOF Cemetery, Harrisville.

401.　iii. **Joan Keith Taylor**, b. 1929, Parkersburg, Wood
County, West Virginia.
402　iv. **Jeannene Marie Taylor**, b. 1931, Parkersburg,
Wood County, West Virginia.
403.　v. **Doris Jacqueline Taylor**, b. 1934, Harrisville,
Ritchie County, West Virginia.

289.

Helen Rosalie Taylor, daughter of No. 191, Mary Elizabeth
Pritchard, was born 09 May 1903, in Harrisville, Ritchie
County, West Virginia. She married **Robert James WYGAL,
Sr.** He was born 1903 in Lee Creek, Wood County, West
Virginia.
Children of Helen Taylor and Robert Wygal are:

> i. **Robert James Wygal, Jr.**, b. 1926, Parkersburg,

Wood County, West Virginia.
ii. **Jack Buddington Wygal**, b. 1928, Parkersburg,
Wood County, West Virginia.
iii. **Helen Roseanne Wygal**, b. 1931, Clarksburg,
Harrison County, West Virginia.
iv. **Phillip Taylor Wygal**, b. 1942, Clarksburg,
Harrison County, West Virginia.
v. **David Ludwig Wygal**, b. 1944.

290.

Oliver Duffy Taylor, Jr., son of No. 191, Mary Elizabeth
Pritchard, was born 1906 in Harrisville, Ritchie County, West
Virginia, and died 1956 in Harrisville. He married **Eva
CURREY**. She was born 1915 in Harrisville. Oliver is buried
in the IOOF Cemetery, Harrisville.
Children of Oliver Taylor and Eva Currey are:
i. **Wendal Bryan Taylor**, b. 1935, Harrisville,
Ritchie County, West Virginia; m. **Vonda
SCHOFIELD** (b. 1937).
ii. **Carole Eileen Taylor**, b. 1937, Harrisville,
Ritchie County, West Virginia; m. **Ronald
Dean DAWSON** (b. 1934, Ritchie County).
iii. **Brenda Joyce Taylor**, b. 1941, Pennsboro,
Ritchie County, West Virginia; m. **Jerry
FLEMING**.

291.

Jack Pritchard, son of No. 196, Enoch Delmar Pritchard, was
born 19 Sep 1925 in West Virginia, and died 06 Sep 1991 in
Milwaukee, Waukesha County, Wisconsin. He married **Birgit
Elizabeth JOHNSON**. She died 15 Mar 1998 in Milwaukee.
Child of Jack Pritchard and Birgit Johnson is:

i. **Pamela Jean Pritchard, b**. 11 Jul 1949; m.
Keith BLAZICK.

292.

Jean Marie Pritchard, daughter of No. 196, Enoch Delmar
Pritchard, was born abt.1930. She married **Vincent W.
RIVIZZINO**, M.D. He died before 1995. She lives in
Middletown, Butler County, Ohio.
Children of Jean Marie Pritchard and Vincent Rivizzino are:
    i. **Sandini Rivizzino**, b. 16 Oct 1960.
    ii. **Vincent Walter Rivizzino**, b.23 Oct 1963.
    iii. **Amy Rae Rivizzino**, b. 06 Apr 1965.
    iv. **Anthony Jack Rivizzino**, b. 10 Jul 1969.

293.

Ted Delmore Pritchard, son of No. 196, Enoch Delmar
Pritchard, was born 09 Apr 1941 in West Virginia. He married
Linda RODENISH 07 Aug 1964.
Children of Ted Delmore Pritchard and Linda Rodenish are:
    i. **Ted Joseph Pritchard**, b. 23 Oct 1967.
    ii. **Kevin Keith Pritchard**, b. 04 Dec 1970.
    iii. **Shawn Michael Pritchard**, b. 12 Mar 1974.

294.

Mildred Louise Miller, daughter of No. 197, Amelia Gay
Pritchard, was born 01 Oct 1909 and died 10 Sep 1980 in
Tacoma, Pierce County, Washington. She married **J. J.
NORTON**.
Children of Mildred Louise Miller and J. J. Norton are:
404.   i. **David Dean Norton**, b. 16 Nov 1935
             Caldwell, Canyon County, Idaho.
405.   ii. **Richard Lee Norton**, b.13 Sep 1937,

Caldwell, Canyon County, Idaho.
406.   iii. **Lawrence Paul Norton**, b. 18 Mar 1940,
Caldwell, Canyon County, Idaho.

295.

Artimous K. Miller, son of No. 197, Amelia Gay Pritchard, was born 13 Jun 1911 in Napa, Napa County, California and died 13 Dec 1979 in Las Vegas, Clark County, Nevada. He is buried in Hillcrest Cemetery, Caldwell, Canyon County, Idaho. He married **Mary M. SHAFFER** (b. 13 Jul 1911) on 12 Aug 1937.
Children of Artimous Miller and Mary Shaffer are:
407.   i. **Mary Carol Miller**, b. 08 Aug 1940, Malad
City, Oneida County, Idaho.
408.   ii. **Nancy Elizabeth Miller**, b. 27 Aug 1942.
iii. **Judith Lynn Miller**, b. 16 Aug 1946; m.
Gene COLE, 1976.

296.

Vivian Vera Miller, daughter of No. 197, Amelia Gay Pritchard, was born 12 May 1913. She married **Willard W. SHAWHAN** (b. 19 May 1913, d. 02 Dec 1953, Fox Island, Kitsap County, Washington) on 29 May 1937 in Payette, Payette County, Idaho.
Children of Vivian V. Miller and Willard W. Shawhan are:
i. **Margaret G. Shawhan**, b. 12 Nov 1940, Nampa,
Canyon County, Idaho; d. 02 Mar 2014.
ii. **Gertrude M. Shawhan**, b. 14 Mar 1942, Nampa,
Canyon County, Idaho.

297.

Ethel Gay Miller, daughter of No. 197, Amelia Gay Pritchard,

344

was born 23 Jun 1915, Monroe, Benton County, Oregon, and died 01 Sep 2000, in Tacoma, Pierce County, Washington. She married **Vincent L. RATHBURN** in Colorado. Her obituary reads as follows: *Ethel Miller Rathburn died 01 Sep 2000 in Tacoma, Washington, with her family by her side. She was an active member of the First United Methodist Church in Tacoma. In her early years, she was employed as an elementary teacher. She brought over 70 foster children into her home. In later years, she was employed as a Nurses' Aide at Sharon Guest home. Ethel was very loving and giving, and always thoughtful of others. As hobbies, she enjoyed reading and crossword puzzles. Family members include her children,* ***Shirley West (Steve), Sandy Morse (Dan),*** *all of Gig Harbor;* ***Kathy Wood and Mark Holt,*** *both of Tacoma; sisters* ***Vivian Shawhan*** *of Tacoma,* ***Alma Bell*** *of Caldwell, Idaho; grandchildren* ***Paula, Tiffany, Eric,*** *and* ***Jared;*** *six great-grandchildren. She was preceded in death by her grandson* ***Christopher West.***

Children of Ethel G. Miller and Vincent L. Rathburn are:
409.   i. **Shirley I. Rathburn**, b. 23 Mar 1949, Tacoma, Pierce County, Washington.
       ii. **Sandra K. Rathburn**, b. 20 Dec 1953.

298.

Paul Victor Miller, son of No. 197, Amelia Gay Pritchard, was born 22 May 1917 in Caldwell, Canyon County, Idaho. He married **Donna Marie HESTER** (b. 18 Jul 1924) on 14 Jan 1944.

Children of Paul V. Miller and Donna Marie Hester, all born in Visalia, Tulare County, California, are:
410.   i. **Richard P. Miller**, b. 01 Dec 1944.
411.   ii. **Kathryn Miller**, b. 25 May 1947.

iii. **Steven Miller**, b. 10 Feb 1951; m. **Debra
   HAYES** (b. 03 Jun 1953) 26 Sep 1970.
412.   iv. **Cyndi A. Miller**, b. 25 June 1959.
   v. **Michael W. Miller**, b. 19 Aug 1966.

299.

Garrett Stanley Miller, son of No. 197, Amelia Gay
Pritchard, was born 15 Oct 1919 in Modesta, Stanislaus
County, California and died after 1990. He married **Dorothy
Mildred SWAFFORD** (b. 17 Jul 1920), 25 Aug 1943.
Children of Garrett Stanley Miller and Dorothy Mildred
Swafford are:
   i. **Kenneth Wayne Miller**, b. 15 Oct 1945,
      Long Beach, Orange County, California;
      electronics engineer Palo Alto, San Mateo
      County, California.
413.   ii. **Joyce Gay Miller**, b. 16 Jan 1945.

300.

Alma Lucille Miller, daughter of No. 197, Amelia Gay
Pritchard, was born 12 May 1922 in Caldwell, Canyon County,
Idaho. She married **Donald Ray BELL** (b. 16 Dec 1918 in
Norton, Norton County, Kansas) on 02 Aug 1941 in Cheyenne,
Wyoming. Donald Ray Bell died at home 20 Aug 1998. He
graduated from Gooding High School in 1936 and attended the
College of Idaho where he met his wife-to-be, Alma. They
were married while Don was serving in the U.S. Army. He
later saw duty in Europe during WWII and attended
Shrivenham College in England until he was shipped back to
the States. After the war, Don graduated from the Conn School
of Musical Instrument Repair in Elkhart, Indiana and began a
lifetime career in pursuit of music education for all who came

in contact with him. Don and Alma opened Bell's Horn Shop in Caldwell, from where he gave his wisdom on love of life to all young people in music education. He loved to make people laugh and was a master of puns. Even in retirement his love of children and education led him to continue his pursuit of knowledge. Upon his death, he left his wife, their children, one half-sister, Theda; two half-brothers, Robert and Jim, all living in Kansas, and thirteen grandchildren and great-grandchildren. Children of Alma Lucille Miller and Donald Ray Bell are:

414. i. **David D. Bell**, b. 31 Aug 1942, Olympia, Thurston County, Washington.
415. ii. **Donald S. Bell**, b. 22 Jan 1945, Portland, Multnomah County, Oregon.
416 iii. **Alma Elaine Bell**, b. 27 May1947, Boise, Ada County, Idaho.

301.

Evangeline Virginia Allen, daughter of No. 198, Helen Willa Pritchard, was born 07 May 1912 in Wallace, Harrison County, West Virginia, and died 22 Oct 1985 in Shinnston, Harrison County West Virginia. She married (1) **Paul Anson CAIN**. She married (2) **George HARDY**.
Children of Evangeline Virginia Allen and Paul Cain are:

417. i. **Helen Jane Cain**, b. 16 Jun 1929; m. **Paul WILSON**, 22 Dec 1948, Lancaster, Fairfield County, Ohio.
418. ii. **Paul Allen Cain**, b. 16 April 1933; m. **Ernestine Ann ANGELINE**, 05 Dec 1958, Shinnston, Harrison County, West Virginia.
419. iii. **David Lee Cain**, b. 28 Aug 1935, Shinnston, Harrison County West Virginia; m. **Helen FAUCHER**, Lancaster, Fairfield County, Ohio.

420.　　iv. **Joyce Ann Cain,** b. 26 Sep 1939, Gypsy, Harrison
County, West Virginia; d. 28 Nov, 1996,
Lumberport, Harrison County, West Virginia;
m. **Lawrence Albert MERRILL**, Shinnston,
Harrison County, West Virginia.

302.

Joe Hamilton Allen, son of No. 198, Helen Willa Pritchard,
was born 03 Dec 1929 in Wallace, Harrison County, West
Virginia. He married **Billie Ann DAVIS**, 21 Nov 1954,
Shinnston, Harrison County, West Virginia. He died 24 Jun
2012 in Shinnston.
Child of Joe Hamilton Allen and Billie Ann Davis is:
421.　　i. **Joe Hamilton Allen Jr**, b. 02 Dec 1968.

303.

Emily Marshall Pritchard, daughter of No. 199, Ernest
Markwood Pritchard, was born 06 Sep 1931 in Pittsburgh,
Pennsylvania. She married **Boyd Balford CARY, Jr.** (b. 29
October, Enid, Garfield County, Oklahoma; d. 18 Feb 2010,
Phoenix, Maricopa County, Arizona), son of **Boyd B. CARY,
Sr.** and **Margaret Grace McLAUGHLIN,** in Swarthmore,
Pennsylvania. Dr. Boyd Cary was a physicist in the aerospace
industry at its inception, then transferred to underwater
acoustics and invented LORAD, used by the U.S. Government
for anti-submarine warfare. Emily Pritchard is a specialist in
Gifted/Talented education and author of eight books and
hundreds of articles on music, history, ecology genealogy, and
education.
Children of Emily Marshall Pritchard and Boyd Cary are:
　　　　i. **Matthew Roger Cary**, b. 09 Sept 1954,
Philadelphia, Pennsylvania; on air personality;

lives Salt Lake City, Utah.
  ii. **Roland Mylles Cary**, b. 05 Sep 1958,
      Philadelphia, Pennsylvania; with Union
      Pacific Railroad, Omaha, Nebraska.

304.

Lynden Eugene Reynolds, Jr., son of No. 200, Mildred Edith
Pritchard, was born 10 Jun 1920 in St. Marys, Pleasants
County, West Virginia, and died 08 Aug 2002 at his home in
Pataskala, Licking County, Ohio. He married (1) **Wilma Jean
ROYE**, 04 Mar 1945. They were divorced. She died November
2003. He married (2) **Mary Evelyn WOOD**, 27 Apr 1973 in
Columbus, Ohio. Lynden "Gene" and Evelyn Reynolds lived
many years in Columbus, Franklin County, Ohio, but several
years prior to his death, they built a home in Pataskala. Evelyn
winters in Sun Lakes, Arizona near several of her daughters;
another lives near Columbus, Ohio.
Children of Lynden Reynolds and Wilma Roye are:
422.   i. **Randolph Roye Reynolds**, b. 31 Jan 1946.
423.   ii. **Lynda Renee Reynolds**, b. 15 Jan 1956.

305.

Millard Franklin Reynolds, son of No. 200, Mildred Edith
Pritchard, was born 08 Jul 1923 in St. Marys, Pleasants
County, West Virginia, and died there on 31 Jan 2000, at his
home, the family farm facing the Ohio River, which was built
before the Civil War. Millard was a U. S. Army veteran of
World War II, serving two years overseas in England, France,
and Germany, and was retired from the former Colin Anderson
Center. A longtime member of the Family Association and the
National Palatines to America, he was active in both West
Virginia and Ohio chapters of those organizations. He was a

member of St. Marys United Methodist Church, where his grandfather preached many years earlier, and the New Matamaoras Historical Society. A former football player, he was an avid West Virginia University Mountaineer sports fan and attended most of the bowl games in which they participated.

306.

Charlaine Reynolds, daughter of No. 200, Mildred Edith Pritchard, was born 08 Jul 1923 in St. Marys, Pleasants County, West Virginia. She married **Hobart GILPIN**, 15 Jul 1944 in St. Marys, West Virginia. **Millard Reynolds** is her fraternal twin. She died 17 Dec 2012, shortly after the death of Hobart on 07 Oct 2012. They were living then at Emeritus in Marietta, Washington County, Ohio.

Children of Charlaine Reynolds and Hobart Gilpin are:

424.   i. **Patricia Lynn Gilpin**, b. 18 Mar 1945, St. Marys, Pleasants County, West Virginia.
425.   ii. **Kay Walter Gilpin**, b. 18 Feb 1947, St. Marys, Pleasants County, West Virginia.
426.   iii. **Beverly Ann Gilpin**, b. 20 Feb 1950, St. Marys, Pleasants County, West Virginia.
427.   iv. **Rex Eugene Gilpin**, b. 12 Dec 1956, St. Marys, Pleasants County, West Virginia.

307.

Joseph Isaac Reynolds, son of No.200, Mildred Edith Pritchard, was born 13 May 1926 in St. Marys, Pleasants County, West Virginia. He married **Margaret McCRAY**, 20 Aug 1950, in Parkersburg, West Virginia. They lived in Willow Springs, North Carolina for many years, and recently moved to Massachusetts.

Children of Joseph Reynolds and Margaret McCray are:
428.   i. **Stephanie Ann Reynolds**, b. 12 Aug 1951,
            Parkersburg, Wood County, West Virginia.
429.   ii. **Stephen Andrew Reynolds**, b. 20 May 1954,
            Parkersburg, Wood County, West Virginia.
430.   iii. **Gregory David Reynolds**, b. 17 Sep 1959
            Parkersburg, Wood County, West Virginia
431.   iv. **Cynthia Louise Reynolds**, b. 26 Aug 1963,
            Parkersburg, Woods County, West Virginia.

308.
Vervel Greathouse, daughter of No. 201, Grace Catherine
Ratcliffe, was born 13 May 1907. She married **Roy HIBBS**.
Children of Vervel Greathouse and Roy Hibbs are:
    i. **Teresa Grace Hibbs**, b. 13 May 1929; m. **Junior
        PHILLIPS**.
    ii. **Glenna Marie Hibbs**, b. 29 Mar 1933; m.
        Charles TEETS.
    iii. **Arlene June Hibbs**, b. 13 Jun 1935.
    iv. **Velta Bell Hibbs**, b.17 Jul 1939; m. **Willard
        ERVEN**.
    v. **Richard Lee Hibbs**, b. 11 Jan 1949.

309.
Thelma Greathouse, daughter of No. 201, Grace Catherine
Ratcliffe, was born 17 Nov 1911, d. 13 Jan. 1994. She married
Glendale Rohrbough BEER 7 Apr. 1934, Buckhannon
Upshur County, West Virginia. He died 09 Aug 1970.
Children of Thelma Greathouse and Glendale Beer are:
    i. **Linda Vivian Beer**, b. 21 Dec 1940 m.
        Frank Patrick CONWAY div; m. (2)
        Gene BALL.

ii. **Jo Ann Beer**, b. 16 Oct 1944; m. (1) **Jesse BARNETT**, div; m. (2) **Ivan MITCHELL**
iii. **Allen Ray Beer**, b. 29 Sep 1947; m. (1) **Teresa CORDER;** m. (2) **Mildred McGEE**
iv. **Nancy Sharon Beer**, b. 04 Sep 1952; m. **Richard HIGGINS**.

310.
Sylvia Oleta Greathouse, daughter of No. 201, Grace Catherine Ratcliffe, married **William CASTRO**.
Children of Sylvia Oleta Greathouse and William Castro are:
    i. **William Castro, Jr.**, b. Jan 1947.
    ii. **John Castro**, b. 1949.
    iii. **David Castro**, b. 1950.

311.
Dencie Evelyne Greathouse, daughter of No. 201, Grace Catherine Ratcliffe, was born 19 Oct 1917. She married **Warren Lee TURNER**, 15 Jun 1942.
Children of Dencie Evelyne Greathouse and Warren Turner are:
    i. **Sylvia Catherine Turner**, b. Jun 1943.
    ii. **Blanch Elizabeth Turner**, b. 28 Jul 1944.
    iii. **Marilyn Lee Turner**, b. 19 Oct 1945.
    iv. **Warren John Turner**, b. 15 May 1948.
    v. **Donald Clifford Turner**, b. 11 Jun 1950.
    vi. **Mary Ann Hope Turner**, b. 22 Dec 1952.
    vii. **Rebecca Jane Turner**, b. 28 Aug 1955; d. 17 Jan 1958.

312.
Wilma Mae Radcliffe, daughter of No. 202, Lloyd Foreman

Radcliffe, was born 16 Nov 1924. She married **Carl M. STEELE**, 07 Apr 1946.
Children of Wilma Mae Radcliffe and Carl M. Steele are:
> i. **Donna Kay Steele**, b. 02 Jul 1947.
> ii. **Sherily Ann Steele**, b. 13 Mar 1950.
> iii. **Robert Carl Steele**, b. 05 Mar 1958.

313.
Ralph Leslie Radcliffe, Sr., son of No. 202, Lloyd Foreman Radcliffe, was born 02 Dec 1925. He married **Wyona CHEESEBREW** 21 Apr 1951.
Children of Ralph Radcliffe and Wyona Cheesebrew are:
> i. **Jeannie Irene Radcliffe**, b. 14 Apr 1952.
> ii. **Ralph Leslie Radcliffe, Jr.**

314.
Robert E. Neininger, son of No. 205, Bertha Catherine Pritchard, was born 25 Apr 1921. He married **Hazel Marie REESE**, 03 Jul 1941.
Children of Robert E. Neininger and Hazel Marie Reese are:
> i. **Sandra Kay Neininger**, b. 06 Mar 1946.
> ii. **Carol Ann Neininger**, b. 15 Jul 1949.
> iii. **Robert Alvin Neininger**, b. 18 Jul 1955.

315.
Lucille Foster, daughter of No. 206, Effie Elizabeth Pritchard, was born 09 Jun 1924. She married **James L. PLESHEK**.
Children of Lucille Foster and James Pleshek are:
> i. **Charles Foster Pleshek**, b. 18 Jan 1950.
> ii. **Larry Gordon Pleshek**, b. 02 Aug 1954.
> iii. **Ronald Edward Pleshek**, b. Apr 1959.
> iv. **Mark Alan Pleshek**, b. 17 Jan 1960.

316.

Jean Evelyn Foster, daughter of No. 206, Effie Elizabeth Pritchard, was born 17 Jan 1926. She married **Unk KUHN**.
Children of Jean Evelyn Foster and Unk Kuhn are:
    i. **David Jonathan Kuhn**, b. 05 Jul 1950.
    ii. **Michael Alan Kuhn**, b.11 May 1953.

317.

Sally Pritchard, daughter of No. 208, Mark Norris Pritchard, married **Darrell POWLOWSKI**.
Children of Sally Pritchard and Darrell Powlowski are:
    i. **Linda Powlowski**.
    ii. **Pamela Powlowski**.

318.

Irene Cecelia Pritchard, daughter of No. 209, Claris Clayton Pritchard, was born 08 Jan 1919. She married **Roy E. CURRY**, 30 May 1943.
Children of Irene Pritchard and Roy Curry are:
    i. **Laura Anne Curry**, b. 01 Dec 1947.
    ii. **Cecelia Irene Curry**, b. 24 Jan 1949.
    iii. **Frederick Tannahill Curry**, b. 01 Aug 1951.

319.

Florence Edith Pritchard, daughter of No. 209, Claris Clayton Pritchard, was born 22 Dec 1920. She married **John W. DITTERLINE, Jr.**, 08 Mar 1946.
Children of Florence Edith Pritchard and John W. Ditterline are:
    i. **Susan Jo Ditterline**, b. 06 Jan 1947.
    ii. **Judith Ann Ditterline**, b. 12 Apr 1948.
    iii. **Virginia Lee Ditterline**, b. 30 Nov 1955.

iv. **John Wesley Ditterline, III**, b. 30 Nov 1956.
v. **Sarah Elizabeth Ditterline**, b. 13 Jan 1959.

320.

Claris Clayton Pritchard, Jr., son of No. 209, Claris Clayton
Pritchard, was born 19 Dec 1927, adopted. He married **Lois
Elaine WEBER**, 29 May 1949.
Children of Claris Clayton Pritchard Jr. and Lois Weber are:
  i. **John Taylor Pritchard**, b. 04 Oct 1952.
  ii. **Barbara Corrine Pritchard**, b. 17 Jul 1954.
  iii. **Katherine Ann Pritchard**, b. 22 Jan 1956.
  iv. **Mark Weber Pritchard**, b. 04 Aug 1958.

321.

Hope Marie Pritchard, daughter of No. 210, Dwight Ira
Pritchard, was born 22 Dec 1927. She married **Harold
ERICKSON**.
Children of Hope Marie Pritchard and Harold Erickson are:
  i. **Steven Erickson**.
  ii. **Michael Erickson**.
  iii. **Daughter Erickson**.

322.

Dwight Dale Pritchard, son of No. 210, Dwight Ira Pritchard,
was born 15 Sep 1933. He married **Betty CAMPBELL,** 07 Jan
1956.
Children of Dwight Dale Pritchard and Betty Campbell are:
  i. **Pamela Diane Pritchard**, b. 16 Jan 1957.
  ii. **Tami Jill Pritchard**, b. 29 Feb 1960.

323.

William Sanford Pritchard, son of No. 210, Dwight Ira

Pritchard, was born 09 Jul 1941. He married **Judy C. EMERY**, 23 Feb 1957.
Child of William Sanford Pritchard and Judy C. Emery is:
    i. **Niki Dawn Pritchard**, b. 24 Jan 1958.

324.

Helen Genevra Taylor, daughter of No. 211, Lora Audra Pritchard, was born 29 Feb 1932. She married (1) **Rolly Johnson WILSON**. She married (2) **Ruffner S. ADAMS**, 08 Aug 1954.
Child of Helen Genevra Taylor and Rolly Wilson is:
    i. **Robert Douglas Wilson**.

325.

Frank Marcel Wilson, son of No. 212, Eva Jane Pritchard Wilson, was born 1923. He married **Ermalee MULLENIX**.
Children of Frank Marcel Wilson and Ermalee Mullenix are:
    i. **Randall Lee Wilson**.
    ii. **Kayla Ann Wilson**.

326.

Milton Lee Pritchard Snyder, son of No. 217, Marie Alice Pritchard, was born 15 Nov 1929. He married (1) **Ethel June BROWN**, b. 03 Jun 1930, Renton, King County, Washington), 27 Aug 1950 in Lewistown, Nez Perce County, Idaho. They were divorced. He married (2) **Dolores Jean GIBBONS** (b. 24 Aug 1946, Spokane, Spokane County, Washington) 18 Aug 1991, Tacoma, Pierce County, Washington. Milton Snyder has a Ph.D. in education. He has been superintendent of schools in Prince William County, Virginia; Oakland, California; and Federal Way School District near Seattle, Washington, and is a frequent education consultant.

Children of Milton Lee Pritchard Snyder and Ethel June Brown are:

    i. **Br**ent **Milton Snyder**, b. 05 Apr 1954, Sunnyside, Yakima County, Washington; m. (1) **Lucinda TORRES** 1979; m. (2) **Kathleen Marie SANDY** (b. 02 Sep 1960, Seattle, King County, Washington) 24 Jun 1989

    ii. **Craig Cooper Snyder**, b. 17 Feb 1956, Sunnyside, Yakima County, Washington; m. **Sarah Marie TRUCHIN** (b. 26 Feb. 1981, Long Beach, Los Angeles County, California), 09 Aug 2007. He is a high school band director.

    iii. **Mark Albert Snyder**, b. 04 Sep 1959, Sunnyside, Yakima County, Washington; m. **Kathy Lynn KIRKMAN** (b. 20 Apr 1959, Bellingham, Whatcom County, Washington) 06 Aug 1994, Bellingham Whatcom County, Washington

    iv. **Matthew Snyder**, b. 13 Oct 1960, Sunnyside, Yakima County, Washington; m. **Elizabeth JULIAN**.

327.

Melvin Delano Snyder, son of No. 217, Marie Alice Pritchard Snyder, was born 07 Jun 1933 in Greer, Clearwater County, Idaho. He married **Sonya Rae DAVIDSON**, 08 Sep 1957. She was born 31 Jan 1938 in Los Angeles, California. Melvin Snyder died 15 Aug 2008, Pendleton, Umatilla County, Oregon. He first was an engineer with General Electric, then went with Battelle Pacific Northwest Laboratories at the Department of Energy Hanford Site near Richland, Washington where he authored studies involving radioactive toxins. In 1971, he left engineering to pursue his passion for horses to

train horses at Los Alamitos Race Course in California.
Child of Melvin Delano Snyder and Sonya Rae Davidson is:
>   i. **Melvin Jeffrey Snyder**, b. 09 Nov 1959,
>   McMinnville, Yamhill County, Oregon.

328.

Dennis Richard Pritchard, son of No. 218, Torrey Icen
Pritchard, married **Unk**.
Children of Dennis Richard Pritchard and Unk are:
>   i. **Shelton Lee Pritchard**, b. 24 Aug 1958.
>   ii. **Maurice Torrey Pritchard**, b.21 Dec 1959.

329.

Betty Lee Pritchard, daughter of No. 219, Sheldon Schofield
Pritchard, was born 04 Jan 1933. She married **Unk Cramer**.
Children of Betty Lee Pritchard and Unk Cramer are:
>   i. **Kip Cramer**.
>   ii. **Scott Cramer**.
>   iii. **Michelle Elizabeth Cramer**.

330.

Wilma May Shaffer, daughter of No. 224, Ian Hortense
Pritchard, was born 15 Jul 1927 (also appears as 1925, and
1926 in other sources) in Reynoldsville, West Virginia. She
married **Dewain Leora HERROD**, son of **Ora HERROD** of
Avon, Doddridge County, West Virginia and **Vallie
THOMPSON**, in Bristol, Harrison County, West Virginia on
23 Oct 1942. The village of Bristol was bulldozed under when
the four-lane highway was constructed between Salem and
Clarksburg, but there is still a post office by that name. Dewain
was born 16 Oct 1925 in Bristol, West Virginia. In
Descendants of Jacob Nestor, Wilma's birthday is listed as 15

The Pritchard/Prickett Family History

Jul 1925, one year earlier than it appears on the Grantham-Miller Family History Research Sheet and may be a typo.
Child of Wilma May Shaffer and Dewain Herrod is:
432.   i. **Stanley Lee Herrod**, b. 23 Oct 1943,
                  Clarksburg, Harrison County, West Virginia;

331.
James Wesley DeMoss, son of No. 225, Ethel Lee Wass, was born 24 May 1908, in Darrah, Mariposa County, California, and died 05 May 1979, in Modesto, Stanislaus County, California. He married **Eve Loretta SMITH**, 06 Jun 1928, in Mariposa, Mariposa County, California. She died 07 Jun 1943, in Stockton, San Joquin County, California.
Children of James DeMoss and Ivy Wallace are:
     i. **Sherril DeMoss**, b. 1929.
     ii. **Lennis May DeMoss,** b. 1936.
     iii. **Carolyn Gay DeMoss**, b. 1941.

332.
Robert Glenn DeMoss, son of No. 225, Ethel Lee Wass, was born 01 Aug 1910, in Darrah, Mariposa County, California, and died 17 Feb 1995, in North Fork, Fresno, County, California. He married **Ivy Vernice WALLACE**, 1936, in Sacramento, Sacramento County, California. She was born 1912.
Children of Robert DeMoss and Ivy Wallace are:
     i. **Ruth Evelyn DeMoss,** b. 1942; m. **Alfred T. CORDA.**
     ii. **Ruth Ilene DeMoss**, b. 1949; m. **Michael K. STEVENS.**
333.
Hilda Lorraine DeMoss, daughter of No. 225, Ethel Lee

359

Wass, was born 13 Nov 1913, in White Rock Ranch, Mariposa County, California, and died 12 Jul 1978, in Plainsburg, Merced County, California. She married **Harry Thomas SEWARD**, 14 Jan 1933 in Mariposa County, California. He was born 04 Apr 1907, in San Francisco, San Francisco County, California, and died 10 May 1981, in Oakdale, Stanislaus County, California.

Children of Hilda DeMoss and Harry Seward are:

> i. **Robert Walter Seward**, b. 1933.
> ii. **Stanley Eugene Seward**, b. 1937.

334.

Sophia Isabel DeMoss, daughter of No. 225, Ethel Lee Wass, was born 17 May 1915, in White Rock Ranch, Mariposa County, California. She married **James Robert MURDOCK**. He was born 04 April 1907, and died May 1981 in Modesto, Stanislaus County, California.

Children of Sophis DeMoss and James Murdock are:

> i. **Shirley Ann Murdock**, b. 1942.
> ii. **Robert Douglas Murdock**, b. 1943.
> iii. **Sharon Kay Murdock**, b. 1945.

335.

Lola May DeMoss, daughter of No. 225, Ethel Lee Wass, was born 1916 in White Rock Ranch, Mariposa County, California. She married **John Eli HUGHES**. He was born 1909.

Children of Lola DeMoss and John Hughes are:

> i. **John Lester Hughes**, b. 1939.
> ii. **Gary Eugene Hughes**, b. 1941.

336.

Norma Ilene DeMoss, daughter of No. 225, Ethel Lee Wass,

was born July 1919. She married **U. V. HELBERT**. He was born 26 Dec 1918 in Quail, Collingsworth County, Texas, and died 17 Nov 1995 in Lubbock, Lubbock County, Texas.
Children of Norma DeMoss and U. V. Helbert are:
> i. **Bonnie Jean Helbert**, b. 1942.
> ii. **Dennis Wayne Helbert**, b. 1946.
> iii. **Gary Lynn Helbert**, b. 1954.

337.

Everett Sylvester DeMoss, son of No. 225, Ethel Lee Wass, was born 1926. He married (1) **Joyce M. ATHEY**. He married (2) **Lucille Bonnie BANKS**. She was born 1936.
Child of Everett DeMoss and Joyce Athey is:
> i. **Douglas Steve DeMoss**, b. 1961.

338.

Beverly Lee DeMoss, daughter of No. 225, Ethel Lee Wass, was born 1928. She married **John William GLADNEY**. He was born 1921.
Children of Beverly DeMoss and John Gladney are:
> i. **Vernon Lynn Gladney**, b. 1949.
> ii. **Michael Wayne Gladney**, b. 1954.
> iii. **Shanna Lee Gladney**, b. 1959.

339.

Elzara Nadine DeMoss, daughter of No. 225, Ethel Lee Wass, was born 1930. She married **William Edgar BEGHTEL**. He was born 25 Aug 1926, in Gilroy, Santa Clara County, California, and died 06 Oct 1981, in Tulare, Tulare County, California.
Child of Ezlara DeMoss and William Beghtel is:
433. i. **Linda Charlene Beghtel**, b. 1954.

340.

Lois Elvira Wass, daughter of No. 227, Lewis Maxwell Wass, Jr., was born 16 Aug 1926, in Merced County, California. She married **Clayton BETTENCOURT** in Merced County.
Children of Lois Wass and Clayton Bettencourt are:
    i. **Rosemary "Rosie" Bettencourt**; m. **Unk BORBA**.
    ii. **Marlene Bettencourt**.
    iii. **Harold J. Bettencourt**.

341.

James Russell Wass, Sr., son of No. 228, Herman H. Wass, was born 16 Jun 1923, in Wass Ranch, Mariposa County, California. He married **Rosa Marie ROBERTSON**. She was born 31 Aug 1925.
Children of James Wass and Rosa Robertson are:
    i. **James Russell Wass, Jr.,** b. 27 Dec 1947.
    ii. **Sherrie Mae Wass**, b. 03 Jan 1949; d. 19 Oct 1990.
    iii. **Michael Rome Wass**, b. 10 May 1954.
    iv. **Andrew Clifford Wass**, b. 12 Jun 1966.

342.

Melvin Eugene Wass, son of No. 228, Herman H. Wass, was born 25 Aug 1926, in Wass Ranch, Mariposa County, California, and died in Mariposa County. He married **Marjorie MANDLEY**. She was born 30 Aug 1942. She is the widow of No. 346, Ernest Clinton Wass.
Children of Melvin Wass and Marjorie Mandley are:
    i. **Brent Allen Wass**, b. 07 Oct 1967.
    ii. **Steven Jon Wass**, b. 10 Oct 1969.

343.

Lois June Wass, daughter of No. 228, Herman H. Wass, was born 16 Jun 1930, in Mariposa, Mariposa County, California. She married **Robert Walker SPARKS**, son of **Andrew Walter SPARKS**. He was born 10 Aug 1924, in Mariposa, Mariposa County, California.
Children of Lois Wass and Robert Sparks are:

   i. **Walter Allen Sparks**, b. 11 Jun 1950, Madera, Madera County, California.

434. ii. **Steven Wayne Sparks**, b. 25 Nov 1952, Mariposa, Mariposa County, California.

  iii. **David Michael Sparks,** b. 01 Jan 1955, Mariposa, Mariposa County, California.

344.

Edna Lorraine Wass, daughter of No. 228, Herman H. Wass, was born 13 Feb 1933, in Mariposa County, California. She married **Robert ASHBURN**. He was born 22 May 1925.
Children of Edna Wass and Robert Ashburn are:

   i. **Loraine Ann Ashburn**, b. 19 Apr 1955, Wass Ranch, Mariposa County, California.

  ii. **Mark Allen Ashburn**, b. 29 Nov 1957, Wass Ranch, Mariposa County, California.

  iii. **Amy Carol Ashburn**, b. 02 Jul 1961, Wass Ranch, Mariposa County, California.

345.

Alfred Leroy Wass, son of No. 228, Herman H. Wass, was born 11 Apr 1936, in Mariposa County, California. He married **Kathleen VEGA**.
Children of Alfred Wass and Kathleen Vega are:

   i. **Dean Allan Wass**, b. 24 April 1963, Merced,

Merced County, California.
ii. **Gary Leroy Wass**, b. 03 Oct 1967, Merced,
Merced County, California.

346.

Ernest Clinton Wass, son of No. 228, Herman H. Wass, was
born 05 Mar 1938, in Merced, Merced County, California, and
died 27 Aug 1963. He married **Marjorie MANDLEY**. She
was born 30 Aug 1942. After Ernest's his death, she married
his older brother, No. 342, Melvin Eugene Wass.
Children of Ernest Wass and Marjorie Mandley are:
i. **Erick Clinton Wass**, b. 20 Jan 1961,
Merced, Merced County, California.
ii. **Gayle Marie Wass**, b. Nov 1963, Merced,
Merced County, California.

347.

Helen Eileen Phillips, daughter of No. 230, Aileen May Wass,
was born 11 Mar 1926, in Arcata, Humboldt County,
California. She married (1) **Phillip WASS**. She married (2)
John Phillip EARL, illegitimate son of **Hugh MITCHEL** and
Jennie Marie EARL, wife of No. 227, Lewis Maxwell Wass,
Jr. John was born 17 Jan 1919. Helen married (3) **Leo Warren
DISBRO,** 11 Feb 1948, in Merced, Merced County, California.
He was born 08 Aug 1927, in Sacramento, Sacramento County,
California. She married (4) **James Bruce SUTTON**, 10 Jan
1974, in Fallon, Churchill County, Nevada. He died September
1999.
Children of Helen Phillips and Phillip Wass are:
i. **John Wass**, b. 13 Nov 1944.
Children of Helen Phillips and Leo Disbro are:
ii. **William Michael Disbro**, b. 12 Feb 1959.

iii. **Linda Marie Disbro**, b.03 Aug 1950.

348.

Mildred Lodine Phillips, daughter of No. 230, Aileen May Wass, was born July 06, 1928, in Mariposa County, California. She married **Floyd WHITE**.
Children of Mildred Phillips and Floyd White are:
  i. **David White**.
  ii. **Dennis White**.

349.

Constance Allaire Phillips, daughter of No. 230, Aileen May Wass, was born 20 May 1937, in Mariposa County, California. She married **William HULL**.
Child of Constance Phillips and William Hull is:
  i. **Janice Hull**.

350.

Joseph Foster, son of No. 232, Winifred Chloe Wass, was born 13 May 1929, in Ritchie County, West Virginia, and died 29 May 1994, in Morgantown, Monongalia County, West Virginia. He married **Dorothy WINCE**. She was born 08 Jul 1934, in Mahone, Ritchie County, West Virginia.
Child of Joseph Foster and Dorothy Wince is:
435.   i. **Thomas Alan Foster**, b. 16 Aug 1959, Parkersburg, Wood County, West Virginia.

351.

Madelon Camille Patton, daughter of No. 233, Ethel Myrtle Goff, was born 22 Feb 1920, in Harrisville, Ritchie County, West Virginia. She married **Charles Lee ZAKAIB, Sr.,** 02 May 1942, in Charleston, Kanawha County, West Virginia, son

of **Lee ZAKAIB** and **Nelle SCOTT**. He was born 29 Apr
1914, in Charleston, Kanawha County, West Virginia, and died
25 Oct 1971, in Waynesboro, Augusta County, Virginia. He is
buried at Riverview Cemetery, Waynesboro.
Children of Madeon Patton and Charles Zakaib are:

436.   i.   **Charles Lee Zakaib, Jr.**, b. March 18, 1946,
          Parkersburg, Wood County, West Virginia.
437.   ii.   **Joseph Patton Zakaib**, b. August 18, 1947, New
          York City, New York
438.   iii.   **Robert Lewis Zakaib**, b. September 21, 1953,
          Danville, Vermilion County, Illinois.

352.

Marshelline Patton, daughter of No. 233, Ethel Myrtle Goff,
was born 14 Jul 1923, in Harrisville, Ritchie County, West
Virginia. She married **Raymond Charles Arthur PURL** 28
Jun 1941, in Charleston, Kanawha County, West Virginia, son
of **Raymond PURL** and **Bessie SAFFELLE**. He was born 03
Mar 1915, in Baltimore, Baltimore County, Maryland.
Children of Marshelline Patton and Raymond Purl are:

       i. **Mara Celeste Purl**, b. 29 Aug 1950, New
         Haven, New Haven County, Connecticut; m.
         (1) **Jeffrey STROBACH**, 29 Jan 1990,
         Colorado Springs, El Paso County, Colorado;
         m. (2) **Larry B. NORFLEET** (b. 05 Jul 1947,
         Cincinnati, Hamilton County, Ohio), 29
         Jul 1994, Colorado Springs, El Paso
         County, Colorado.
439.   ii. **Linda Marion Purl,** b. 1955, Greenwich,
         Fairfield County, Connecticut.

353.

Alice Ann Davis, daughter of No. 234, Hermione Pearl Goff, was born 17 Sep 1923, in Harrisville, Ritchie County, West Virginia, and died 22 Feb 1994, in Atlanta, Fulton County, Georgia. She married **Kenneth Leroy HEWITT**, 19 Jan 1945, in Harrisville. He was born 06 Sep 1922 in Morgantown, Monongalia County, West Virginia, and died 28 Jun 1996, in Atlanta, Fulton County, Georgia. Both are buried in Arlington Cemetery, Atlanta, Fulton County, Georgia.
Children of Alice Davis and Kenneth Hewitt are:

440.   i. **William Davis Hewitt**, b. 17 Jan 1950, Atlanta, Fulton County, Georgia.
441.   ii. **Elizabeth Ann Hewitt**, b. 04 Jun 1952, Atlanta, Fulton County, Georgia.
        iii. **Susan Lee Hewitt**, b. 20 Aug 1954, Atlanta, Fulton County, Georgia.

354.

Winifred Jean Koehler, daughter of No. 235, Winifred Dell Goff, was born 19 Sep 1925, in Cincinnati, Hamilton County, Ohio. She married **Walter Boyd DUFF**, 21 Dec 1946, in Reading, Hamilton County, Ohio, son of **Hobart DUFF** and **Lela GALYEAN**. He was born 29 Mar 1926, in Lenoir City, Loudon County, Tennessee, and died 15 Mar 2000, in Cincinnati, Hamilton County, Ohio.
Children of Winifred Koehler and Walter Duff are:

442   i. **David Allen Duff**, b. 20 Jul 1948, Cincinnati, Hamilton County, Ohio.
443.   ii. **Stephen Edward Duff,** b. 25 Jul 1952, Caracas, Venezuela.
444.   iii. **Susan Kathleen Duff,** b. 04 Dec 1953, Caracas, Venezuela.

445.   iv. **Thomas Lee Duff**, b. 12 Dec 1959,
Cincinnati, Hamilton County, Ohio.

355.

John Edward Koehler, Jr., son of No. 235, Winifred Dell
Goff, was born 30 Mar 1929, in Reading, Hamilton County,
Ohio. He married (1) **Nadine Emily SMITH**, 11 Aug 1951, in
Canton, Stark County, Ohio. She was born 11 Jun 1927, in
Canton, and died 13 Apr 1982, in Flint, Genesee County,
Michigan. He married (2) **Shirley Ann BRIGGS CORBETT**,
15 Oct 1983, in Grand Rapids, Kent County, Michigan. She
was born 12 Apr 1936 in Grand Rapids, Kent County,
Michigan. She is the mother of **Robert James CORBETT**,
born 30 Jul 1961.
Children of John Koehler, Jr. and Nadine Smith are:
446.   i. **James Marven Koehler**, b. 15 Jan 1955. He
married **Susan KUHLMAN**, 04 Jun 1983.

356.

Arthur Eugene Mergy, son of No. 236, Fredda Goff, was
born 03 Jul 1932, in Parkersburg, Wood County, West
Virginia. He married **Janice Marie LONDON**, 28 Jun 1958, in
Pacific Beach, San Diego County, California, daughter of
Harry LONDON and **Mary SHOLTIS**. She was born 11 Sep
1933, in Canton, Stark County, Ohio.
Children of Arthur Mergy and Janice London are:
447.   i. **James Arthur Mergy**, b. 08 Sep 1960,
Santa Monica, Los Angeles County,
California.
448.   ii. **Judith Louise Mergy**, b. 07 Aug 1962, Santa
Monica, Los Angeles, California.

357.
Betty Annadore Wass, daughter of No. 237, Ralph Paul Wass, was born 17 Jul 1930. She married **Raymond BURWELL**, 26 Mar 1949, in Washburn, Ritchie County, West Virginia. He was born abt. 1928 in Ritchie County.
Children of Betty Was and Raymond Burwell are:
    i. **Stephen Burwell**; m. **Sharon UNK.**
449. ii. **Jill Burwell.**
    iii. **Brian Burwell**; m. **Karen UNK.**

358.
Charles Denver Wass, son of No. 241 Romeo Grant Wass, was born 08 Jul 1923, in Smithville, Ritchie County, West Virginia. He married **Hilda Aleene DAVIS**, 22 Feb 1947.
Child of Charles Denver Wass and Hilda Davis is:
    i. **Mark Donovan Wass,** b. 1957.

359.
Coralie Wass, daughter of No. 242, Hosea Harrison Wass, was born September 1925. She married **Harrel SMITH**, 21 Sep 1946. He was born 28 Jun 1918.
Children of Coralie Wass and Harrel Smith are:
    i. **Stephen Franklin Smith**, b. 13 Oct 1949; m. **Reah Maureen ADKINS**, 21 Dec 1974.
    ii. **Mark Edward Smith**, b. 06 Jul 1954.
    iii. **David Scott Smith**, b. 11 Dec 1955; m. **Lee Ann BYNUM**, 23 Jun 1979.
    iv. **Roger Lee Smith**, b. 05 May 1963; m. **Julie Lynn MILLER**, 01 Oct 1983.

360.
Herman Lawrence Wass, son of No. 242, Hosea Harrison

Wass, was born 20 Nov 1926, in Washburn, Ritchie County, West Virginia. He married **Dorainne SMITH**, daughter of **J. SMITH** and **Beulah UNK**

Children of Herman Wass and Dorainne Smith are:

    i. **Reta Jeannie Wass**, b. 10 Jan 1950; m. **Eddie GARRETT**.

    ii. **Debra Ann Wass**, b. 04 Sep1954; m. **Michael HOOVER.**

361.

Dennis Brooks Wass, son of No. 242, Hosea Harrison Wass, was born 23 Sept 1928, in Washburn, Ritchie County, West Virginia. He married **Lucy Lee HATFIELD**, October 24, 1953, in Washburn. She was born 06 Nov 1935.

Children of Dennis Wass and Lucy Hatfield are:

    i. **Robert Wesley Wass**, b. 09 Oct 1954, Parkersburg, Wood County, West Virginia.

    ii. **Kathy Ann Wass**, b. 26 Oct 1956.

362.

Boyd Wayne Wass, Sr., son of No. 242, Hosea Harrison Wass, was born 03 Sep 1933, in Ritchie County, West Virginia. He married **Patricia Gaynell HULL**, 16 Jun 1956. She was born 13 Jan 1936.

Children of Boyd Wass and Patricia Hull are:

    i. **Pamela Jeanine Wass**, b. 26 Oct 1958, Washington, Washington County, Pennsylvania.

    ii. **Leigh Ann Wass**, b. 25 Jun 1961, Washington, Washington County, Pennsylvania.

    iii. **Amy Lynn Wass,** b. 11 Jun 1967, Washington, Washington County, Pennsylvania.

iv. **Boyd Wayne Wass, Jr.,** b .28 Sep 1969,
Washington, Washington County,
Pennsylvania.

363.

Betty Lee Smith, daughter of No. 244, Eva Madge Wass, was born 18 Oct 1925 in Steubenville, Jefferson County, Ohio. She married **Donald Porter JONES**, 17 Dec 1943, in New Cumberland, Hancock County, West Virginia, son of **Alexander McCloud JONES** and **Helen Louise DUNLEVY**. They live in Globe, Arizona.

Children of Betty Lee Smith and Donald Porter Jones are:

    i. **William Terrill Jones**, b. 30 May 1945, East Liverpool, Columbiana County, Ohio; m. (1) **Virginia PERKINS**, 05 Mar 1965; m. (2) **Linda Darlene LLOYD**, 16 Sep 1972.

    ii. **Linda Dawn Jones**, b. 30 Jul 1950, Steubenville, Jefferson County, Ohio; m. **Doyl F. LIVINGOOD**, 08 Jun 1973.

    iii. **Gerald Scott Jones**, b. 28Oct 1953, Steubenville, Jefferson County, Ohio.

364.

Charles Franklin "Ike" Wass, son of No. 245, Harlie Graydon Wass, was born 06 Jan 1938, in Harrisville, Ritchie County, West Virginia. He married **Rosa Lea McDONALD**, 31 Aug 1957, in Ritchie County. She was born 05 Mar 1941, in Ritchie County.

Children of Charles Wass and Rosa McDonald are:

    i. **Royce Dean Wass**, b. 13 Apr 1959, Norfolk, Virginia.

    ii. **Lori Lynn Wass**, b. 13 Apr 1968, Parkersburg,

The Pritchard/Prickett Family History

Wood County, West Virginia.

365.

John Wesley Wass, son of no. 245, Harlie Graydon Wass, was born 21 Aug 1947 in Harrisville, Ritchie County, West Virginia. He married **Barbara HAUGHT**, 22 Mar 1969, in Ritchie County.
Children of John Wesley Wass and Barbara Haught are:
    i. **Tammy Lynn Wass**, b. 10 Oct 1970; m. **Darrell James BATTON**, 12 May 1988, Ritchie County, West Virginia.
    ii. **Melinda Wass**, b. 05 Aug 1974.
    iii. **John Michael Wass**, b. 05 Aug 1974; m. **Linda UNK.**

366.

Brent Wilson, son of No. 250, Josephine Jean Wass, was married to **Debra SPURLOCK**.
Child of Brent Wilson and Debra Spurlock is:
    i. **Michael Wilson** married **Christine BRODISCH**. They have two children, a daughter **Skyler** and a son **Thatcher**. They live in Uniontown, PA.

367.

Virginia Darlene Bowers, daughter of No. 251, Virginia Opal Wass, was born 27 Feb 1933, in Sarasota, Sarasota County, Florida. She married **James CHAMBLISS**.
Child of Virginia Bowers and James Chambliss is:
    i. **Rebecca Darlene Chambliss.**

368.

Arlene Patricia Bowers, daughter of No. 251, Virginia Opal

Wass, was born 13 May 1935, in Sarasota, Sarasota County, Florida. She married (1) **John MEARS**. She married (2) **Rolland L. KING.**
Children of Arlene Bowers and John Mears are:
    i. **John Robert Mears**, b. 13 Oct 1953,
        Sarasota, Sarasota County, Florida.
    ii. **Richard Allen Mears**, b. 03 Oct 1956,
        Sarasota, Sarasota County, Florida.
Children of Arlene Bowers and Rolland King are:
    iii. **Michael Stuart King**, b. 03 Oct 1956,
        adopted.
    iv. **Lynda Christine King**, b. 11 Feb 1961.

369.

Barbara Ailene Bowers, daughter of No. 251, Virginia Opal Wass, was born 06 Oct 1937, in Sarasota, Sarasota County, Florida. She married **Huston HUGHES**.
Children of Barbara Bowers and Huston Hughes are:
    i. **Vivian Renay Hughes,** b. 31 Oct 1957,
        Sarasota, Sarasota County, Florida.
    ii. **Donna Kathrine Hughes**, b.01 Feb 1959,
        Sarasota, Sarasota County, Florida.
    iii. **Craig Vincent Hughes**, b. 04 Apr 1961,
        Sarasota, Sarasota County, Florida.

370.

Caroline Merrily Bowers, daughter of No. 251, Virginia Opal Wass, was born 08 Aug 1942. She married **Richard FOSTER**.
Child of Caroline Bowers and Richard Foster is:
    i. **Richard Eugene Foster**, b. 27 Sep 1968,
        Sarasota, Sarasota County, Florida.

The Pritchard/Prickett Family History

371.

James Leroy Martin, son of No. 260, Eunice Marie Pritchard, was born 15 Jun 1942 in Norwalk, Huron County, Ohio. He married **Lucille Ann STIMPLE**, daughter of **Dudley STIMPLE** and **Edith SMITH**, 06 Jun 1968 in North Fairfield Huron County, Ohio.

Children of James Leroy Martin and Lucille Ann Stimple are:

    i. **Lee Dudley Martin**, b. 05 Mar 1969 in Willard, Huron County, Ohio. He served with the U.S. Army in Iraq, is an officer in the General Society of Mayflower Descendants through John Howland, Elizabeth Tilley, Joan Hurst, and Joseph Gorham. He is also a member of First Families of Ohio, Sons of the American Revolution, and Society of Civil War Families of Ohio. He graduated from Ohio State University in Columbus, Franklin County, Ohio on 10 Jun 2012, taught as a substitute teacher in Greenwich, Huron County, Ohio, and is pursuing advanced degrees in history.

    ii. **Timothy James Martin**, b. 08 Jul 1970 at Willard Memorial Hospital in Willard, Huron County, Ohio.

    iii. **Walter Allen Martin,** b. 30 Apr 1986 in Norwalk, Huron County, Ohio. He graduated *Cum Laude* from Cleveland State University, in Cleveland, Cuyahoga, Ohio, on 16 Dec 2012.

372.

Nancy Irene Martin, daughter of No. 260, Eunice Marie Pritchard, was born 08 Jan 1951 in Norwalk, Huron County, Ohio. She married (1) **Frank MAKRAY**, b. 22 Oct 1938 in

Budapest, Hungary. She married (2) **Lazslo Zrinszki** 08 Apr 1988 in Clark County, Nevada. He was born 20 Oct. 1931 in Budapest, Hungary and died on 15 Dec 2001 in Budapest, Hungary at age 70.

Children of Nancy Irene Martin and Fran Makray are:

> i. **Katherine Makray**, b. Jan 1980, Aurora, Adams County, Colorado. She married **Jeremy ELLIS**. Child of Katherine Makray and Jeremy Ellis is: **Gabriella Ellis**.

373.

Helen Pritchard, daughter of No. 269, Eustace Charles Pritchard, was born 15 Aug 1932, in Williamsport, Pickaway County, Ohio. She married (1) **Guy BOYER** before 1963. He was born about 1928, and died 11 June 1963, in Lancaster, Fairfield County, Ohio. She married (2) **Lloyd WILLIAMS** after 1964. They live in California.

Children of Helen Pritchard and Guy Boyer are:

> i. **Gary Boyer.**
> ii. **Steven Boyer.**
> iii. **Thomas Boyer.**

Child of Helen Pritchard and Lloyd Williams is:

> iv. **Brett Williams.**

374.

Donald Lee Pritchard, son of No. 269, Eustace Charles Pritchard, was born 20 Oct 1934, in Williamsport, Deercreek Twp., Pickaway County, Ohio, and died 15 Apr 1994. He married **Virginia Mae ALLEN.** She was born about 1933, in Circleville, Pickaway County, Ohio.

Children of Donald Lee Pritchard and Virginia Mae Allen are:

> i. **Valerie Pritchard.**

ii. **Carol Anne Pritchard**, b. July 02, 1959,
Circleville, Pickaway County, Ohio.
iii. **Mona Kaye Pritchard,** b. October 30, 1960,
Circleville, Pickaway County, Ohio.
iv. **Colleen Pritchard.**

375.

Kenneth Dean Pritchard, Sr., son of No. 269, Eustace
Charles Pritchard, was born 08 May 1940, in Williamsport,
Pickaway County, Ohio. He married **Marsha Jean
FELLOWS,** 15 Oct 1959, in Newington, Strafford County,
New Hampshire, daughter of **Ernest FELLOWS** and **Harriet
MOARATTY.** She was born 19 Nov 1942, in Newbury,
Merrimack County, New Hampshire. They live in Florida.
Children of Kenneth Dean Pritchard, Sr. and Harriet Moaratty,
are:
450.   i. **Kenneth Dean Pritchard, Jr.,** b. May 15, 1960.
451.   ii. **Tod Taylor Pritchard,** b. June 21, 1961.
452   iii. **Mark Douglas Pritchard, Sr.,** b. August 08,
453.   iv. **Tina Marie Pritchard,** b. April 07, 1965.

376.

Linda Sue Pritchard, daughter of No. 269, Eustace Charles
Pritchard, was born August 08, 1946, in Williamsport,
Pickaway County, Ohio. She married **Unk COOK.** They live
in Orange County, California.
Children of Linda Sue Pritchard and Unk Cook are:
i. **Aaron Cook.**
ii. **Kelly Cook,** b. August 1965.

377.

Darlene Pritchard, daughter of No. 274, Darold Vernon

Pritchard, married **UNK.**
Child of Darlene Pritchard and Unk is:
    i. **Penny Pritchard.**

378.
Tamara Mae Lane, daughter of No. 275, Alberta Bernadine Pritchard, was born 1945. She married **Thomas WEISENSTEIN.**
Children of Tamara Mae Lane and Thomas Weisenstein are:
    i. **Tab Richard Weisenstein**, b. 1965.
    ii. **Tim Jay Weisenstein**, b. 1968.

379.
Terry Jay Lane, son of No. 275, Alberta Bernadine Pritchard, was born 1947 and died 1994. He married **Cynthia SNYDER.**
Children of Terry Jay Lane and Cynthia Snyder are:
    i. **Lisa Michelle Lane**, b. 1972.
    ii. **Angela Nichol Lane**, b. 1975.

380.
Roberta Dawn Lane, daughter of No. 275, Alberta Bernadine Pritchard, was born 1953. She married **Unk WILLIAMS.**
Children of Roberta Lane and Unk Williams are:
    i. **Shawn Williams**, b. 1972.
    ii. **Robert Lee Williams**, b. 1979.

381.
Lucinda Lane, daughter of No. 275, Alberta Bernadine Pritchard, was born 1955. She married **Gene PARSLEY.**
Children of Lucinda Lane and Gene Parsley are:
    i. **Tiffany Parsley**, b. 1971.
    ii. **Samuel Jay Parsley**, b. 1973.

382.

Sharon Pritchard, daughter of No. 276, Lowell Forest Pritchard, married **Jeffrey LOUCKS**.
Children of Sharon Pritchard and Jeffrey Loucks are:
    i. **Michael Loucks.**
    ii. **Christopher Loucks.**

383.

Susan Pritchard, daughter of No. 276, Lowell Forest Pritchard, married **Unk STALEY**.
Child of Susan Pritchard and Unk Staley is:
    i. **Rose Staley.**

384.

William Ray Pritchard, son of No. 277, Ira Grant Pritchard, was born 15 Feb 1924 in Spencer, Roane County, West Virginia. He married **Mildred Doyle WILLIAMS**, 27 Dec 1946 in Spencer, Roane County, West Virginia, daughter of **Herbert WILLIAMS** and **Ila LANGFORD**. She was born 09 Dec 1925 in Spencer, Roane County, West Virginia.
Children of William Ray Pritchard and Mildred Doyle Williams are:
    i. **Jana Rae Pritchard**, b. 21 Mar 1952, South Charleston, Kanawha County, West Virginia; m. **Paul Kenneth RHAME**, 05 Jan 1974.
    ii. **Jody Kay Pritchard**, b. 27 Apr 1954, South Charleston, Kanawha County, West Virginia; m. **Richard James STOUGH**, 22 Aug 1981.
    iii. **James Reid Pritchard**, b. 20 May 1959, South Charleston, Kanawha County, West Virginia; m. **Linda Michelle FERDERER** 29 Sep1984. Divorced.

385.

John Earl Pritchard, son of No. 279, Harold Dean Pritchard, was born 28 Jun 1926 in Akron, Summit County, Ohio. He married **Joan Sarah HOUCK**, daughter of **Joseph Clarence HOUCK** and **Bernice Eleanor AICHEL** on 09 Oct 1946. She was born in Indianapolis, Marion County, Indiana, 23 Jun 1927.

Children of John Earl Pritchard and Joan Sarah Houck are:

      i. **Candace Lynn Pritchard**, b. 19 Oct 1947, Akron, Summit County, Ohio.

454.   ii. **Vicki Lee Pritchard**, b. 29 Apr 1951, Akron, Summit County, Ohio.

     iii. **John Frederick Pritchard**, b. 27 Nov 1960, Akron, Summit County, Ohio; m. **Jacqueline Ann BELL** (b. 21 Jan 1959, Barberton, Summit County, Ohio), 20 Mar 1984, Barberton, Summit County, Ohio.

386.

Patricia Pritchard, daughter of No. 279, Harold Dean Pritchard, was born 30 Dec 1929 in Akron, Summit County, Ohio. She married **Fred Junior JONES** in September 1952. He was born 14 Sep 1922 in Akron.

Children of Patricia Pritchard and Fred Junior Jones are:

      i. **Todd Michael Jones**, b. 24 Dec 1956 in Akron, Summit County, Ohio; d. 28 Aug 1994, buried in Greenlawn Cemetery, Akron.

455.   ii. **Elizabeth Marie Jones**, b. 26 Dec 1959.

387.

Lawrence Dean Pritchard, son of No. 279, Harold Dean Pritchard, was born 15 Sep 1931, in Akron, Summit County,

The Pritchard/Prickett Family History

Ohio. He married **Nancy STERLING**.
Children of Lawrence Dean Pritchard and Nancy Sterling are:
456.   i. **Adrienne Pritchard**, b. 04 Oct 1954,
        Akron, Summit County, Ohio.
457.   ii. **Renee Pritchard**, b. 18 Dec 1960, Akron,
        Summit County, Ohio.

388.

Charles Edward Pritchard, son of No. 279 Harold Dean
Pritchard, was born 15 Sep 1932 in Akron, Summit County,
Ohio. He married **Catherine PETROCEVICH** in 1954. She
was born 23 Feb 1936.
Children of Charles Edward Pritchard and Catherine
Petrocevich are:
458.   i. **Edward Pritchard**, b. 1955 Akron, Summit County,
        Ohio
459.   ii. **Patricia Pritchard**, b. 1957, Akron, Summit
        County, Ohio.
460.   iii. **Paula Pritchard**, b. 1957, Akron, Summit
        County, Ohio.
461.   iv. **Pamela Pritchard**, b. 1959, Akron, Summit
        County, Ohio.
462.   v. **Penny Pritchard**, b. 1963, Akron, Summit
        County, Ohio.
463.   vi. **Phyllis Pritchard**, b. 1966, Akron, Summit
        County, Ohio.
464.   vii. **Danya Pritchard**, b. 1971, Akron, Summit
        County, Ohio.

389.

George Lewis Pritchard, son of No. 279, Harold Dean
Pritchard, was born 14 Mar 1934 in Akron, Summit County,

Ohio. He married **Janet Sue LIAS**. She was born 04 Mar
1935 and died 12 Jun 1998 in Akron, Summit County, Ohio.
Child of George Lewis Pritchard and Janet Sue Lias is:
> i. **Lynne Pritchard**, b. 1955, Akron, Summit
> County, Ohio.

390.
James Robert Pritchard, Sr., son of No. 279, Harold Dean
Pritchard, was born 15 Aug 1948 in Akron, Summit County,
Ohio. He married **Deborah HUDSON in** September 1972.
She was born 11 Jun 1949.
Children of James Robert Pritchard and Deborah Hudson are:
> i. **Megan Pritchard**, b. 30 Oct 1977, Akron,
> Summit County, Ohio.
> ii. **James Robert Pritchard, Jr.**, b. July 1979,
> Akron, Summit County, Ohio.

391.
Darrell Edward Poole, son of No. 280, Dola Pritchard, was
born 16 Aug 1922 in Spencer, Roane, County, West Virginia,
and died 22 Mar 1992 in Fairfield County, Ohio of lung cancer.
He married **Dorothy Virginia BLUM** 06 Sep 1946, in
Norfolk, Virginia. She was born 06 Sep 1924 in Toledo, Ohio
and died 10 Apr 1991 in Indiana of lupus.
Children of Darrell Edward Pool and Dorothy Blum are:
465.   i. **Donald Darrell Poole**, b.10 Apr 1948, Norfolk,
Virginia.
466.   ii. **Linda Jean Poole**, b. 25 Aug 1951, Lancaster,
Fairfield County, Ohio.
467.   iii. **Stephen Mark Poole**, b. 01 Dec 1953,
Lancaster, Fairfield County, Ohio.
     iv. **David Timothy Poole**, b.-5 Mar 1955,

Lancaster, Fairfield County, Ohio.

392.

William Earl Poole, son of No. 280, Dola Pritchard, was born August 05, 1924 in Roane County, West Virginia. He married (1, 2, & 4) **Ruth APPEL** May 1948 in Greenup, Kentucky, daughter of **Carl APPEL** and **Mary Catherine UNK**. They divorced, but after a period of time, they remarried (2) and divorced a second time. He married (3) **Barbara BEAVER**, September 1962. Bill met Barb while helping his brother, Darrell, drill a well for Barb, who had been married first to **John KALLIMANIS**. Bill married her and they had three children. He divorced Barb after his retirement from the State of Ohio Department of Transportation (ODOT). He then remarried (4) **Ruth APPEL**, and they live (1999) in Hocking County, Ohio.

Children of William Earl Poole and Barbara Beaver are:

      i. **Annette Marie Poole**, b. 26 Jul 1963, Lancaster, Fairfield County, Ohio. She married **Unk STUDER**.

     ii. **Christine Lynn Poole**, b. 30 Jun1965, Lancaster, Fairfield County, Ohio   .

   iii. **Phillip Edward Poole**, b. 29 Aug 1967, Lancaster, Fairfield County, Ohio.

393.

Walter Averill Pool, son of No. 280, Dola Pritchard, was born 10 Jun 1926 in Spencer, Roane County, West Virginia. He married **Florence Evelyn WYNKOOP**, 24 Jul 1948, in Ashland, Boyd County, Kentucky, daughter of **Berman WYNKOOP** and **Elva CONSOLVER**. She was born 23 Mar 1931 in California Hollow, Salt Creek, Twp., Hocking County,

Florence Evelyn Wynkoop Pool, 1948; and, Walter Averill Pool, 1940

382a

382b

Ohio. The attending physician was H.S. Barton, Adelphi, Ohio.
Children of Walter Averill Pool and Florence Evelyn Wynkoop
are:
468.   i. **Walter Edward Pool**, b. 05 Jan 1952, Lancaster,
           Fairfield County, Ohio.
469.   ii. **Michael Dean Pool**, b. 21 Jun 1953, Lancaster,
           Fairfield County, Ohio.
470. iii. **William Keith Pool**, b. 17 Oct 1954, Lancaster,
           Fairfield County, Ohio.

394.

James Ernest Ward, son of No. 282, Dora Pritchard, was born
February 22, 1933 in Roane County, West Virginia. He
married **Esther Ann HEDGES,** 27 Dec 1949 in Roane
County, West Virginia, daughter of **Willie HEDGES** and **Eska
UNK**.
Children of James Ward and Esther Hedges are:
471.   i. **Ronald Gene Ward**, b   27 Dec 1950,
           Parkersburg, Wood County, West Virginia.
472.   ii. **Gary Ray Ward**, b. 30 Jan 1954.

395.

Barbara Lou Ward, daughter of No. 282, Dora Pritchard, was
born 28 Mar 1935 in Roane County, West Virginia. She
married **Donald R. OWENS** 09 Jan 1965 in the Presbyterian
Church, Anchorage, Alaska, son of **Carl OWENS** and **Pauline
WATKINS**. He was born 26 Oct 1935 in Melrose, Cherokee
County, Kansas.
Children of Barbara Ward and Donald Owens are:
473.   i. **Rebecca Fauntelle Owens**, b. 25 Nov 1966,
           Ripley, Jackson County, West Virginia.
474.   ii. **Pamela Ruth Owens**, b. 01 Oct 1969, Ripley,

Jackson County, West Virginia.
475.   iii. **Rachel Amanda Owens,** b. 25 Sep 1974,
Ripley, Jackson County, West Virginia.

396.

Anne Louise Kennedy, daughter of No. 283, Robert Evan
Kennedy, was born 05 Jul 1946, in Fond du Lac, Wisconsin.
She married **Richard CHRISINGER.**
Child of Anne Louise Kennedy and Richard Chrisinger is:
    i. **Colleen Kennedy Chrisinger,** b. 16 Jun 1969.

397.

Nancy Ann Holland, daughter of No. 284, Anna Lee Smith,
was born 17 Dec 1942 in Hinesville, Liberty County, Georgia.
She married (1) **Hollis SUBER** on 05 Sep 1960 in Macon,
Bibb County, Georgia. Hollis was born 05 Sep 1939 in Pavo,
Thomas County, Georgia. She married (2) **Raymond
LAWRENCE,** 14 Dec 1969 in Byron, Peach County, Georgia.
Raymond was born 04 Mar 1946, Olwein, Fayette County,
Iowa.
Children of Nancy Ann Holland and Hollis Suber are:
    i. **Michael Dale Suber,** b. 16 Jan 1960,
        Valdosta, Lowndes County, Georgia.
    ii. **Jackie Suber,** b. 18 Apr 1966, Moultrie,
        Colquitt County, Georgia.
    iii. **Kimberly Suber,** b. 05 Sep 1969, Moultrie,
        Colquitt County, Georgia.
Child of Nancy Ann Holland and Raymond Lawrence is:
    iv. **Scott Conley Lawrence,** b. 17 Jun 1971,
        Warner Robins, Houston County, Georgia.

398.

Lawrence Cleveland Holland, Jr., son of No. 284, Anna Lee Smith, was born 13 Aug 1944 in Elkins, Randolph County, West Virginia. He married (1) **Kathryn WALTON**; he married (2) **Dawn UNK**; he married (3) **Bobbi UNK**. Children of Lawrence Holland are:

 i. **Christy Holland.**
 ii. **Jonathan Holland.**
 iii. **Aaron Holland.**
 iv. **Anna Leigh Holland**.

399.

James Michael Holland, son of No. 284, Anna Lee Smith, was born 29 Jun 1949 in Elkins, Randolph, West Virginia. He married **Cheryl Ann GROVER** on 12 Aug 1976 in Fanwood, Union County, New Jersey. She was born 20 Apr 1957 in Boston, Suffolk County, Massachusetts. James is a veteran of the Vietnam War, serving with the U.S. Army 1st Signal Brigade, HHC 39th Signal Bn., Long Binh, S. Vietnam 1969-1970. James is known by his family and friends as "Mike." Mike is an elder at the Springs Community Reformed Church. Child of James Michael Holland and Cheryl Ann Grover is:

 i. **Rachel Marie Holland**, b. 04 Dec 1980, Macon, Bibb County, Georgia.

400.

Peggy Louise Holland, daughter of No. 284, Anna Lee Smith, was born 31 Aug 1950 in Elkins, Randolph County, West Virginia. She married **James Melvin SHED** on 09 Nov 1969 in Macon, Bibb County, Georgia. Children of Peggy Louise Holland and James Melvin Shed are:

 i. **James Stephen Shed**.

ii. **Jeremy Shed**.

EIGHTH GENERATION

401.

Joan Keith Taylor, daughter of No. 288, Wesley Isaac Taylor, was born 1929 in Parkersburg, Wood County, West Virginia. She married **Clarence Edward DYE**. He was born 1922 in Williamstown, Wood County, West Virginia.
Children of Joan Taylor and Clarence Dye are:
    i. **David Keith Dye**, b. 1955, Morgantown, Monongalia County, West Virginia.
    ii. **Darren Chris Dye**, b. 1968, Marietta, Washington County, Ohio; m. **Jodi Leigh FIZSIMMONS** (b. 1979, New Martinsville, Wetzel County, West Virginia).

402.

Jeannene Marie Taylor, daughter of No. 288, Wesley Isaac Taylor, was born 1931 in Parkersburg, Wood County, West Virginia. She married **Robert Frank SETTLE**. He was born 1931 in Belfast, Russell County, Virginia.
Children of Jeannene Taylor and Robert Settle are:
    i. **Clark Taylor Settle,** b. 1958, Parkersburg, Wood County, West Virginia; m. (1) **Gloria PIERSOL**; m. (2) **Tara Lynn BEATTY** (b. 1961).
    ii. **Douglas Bundy Settle**, b. 1960, Parkersburg, Wood County, West Virginia; m. **Daphne Dawn SIMMONS** (b. 1962).
    iii. **Jane Marie Settle**, b. 1962, Parkersburg, Wood County, West Virginia; m. (1) **David Keith BRYANT**; m. (2) **Charles Holly**

HALSTEAD, Jr.
iv. **Robert Keith Settle**, 1963, Parkersburg, Wood
County, West Virginia; m. **Barbara Lynn
SHOWALTER** (b. 1963, Weirton, Hancock
County, West Virginia).
v. **Judith Ann Settle**, b. 1967, Charleston, Kanawha
County, West Virginia; m. **Matthew William
WARNER** (b. 1966, Parkersburg, Wood
County, West Virginia).

403.

Doris Jacqueline Taylor, daughter of No. 288, Wesley Isaac
Taylor, was born 1934 in Harrisville, Ritchie County, West
Virginia. She married **Thomas Burton MONTOYA**. He was
born 1934 in Galion, Crawford County, Ohio.
Children of Doris Taylor and Thomas Montoya are:
i. **Pama Lyn Montoya**, b. 1955, Parkersburg, Wood
County, West Virginia; m. **Dean Hart
ANDERSON** (b. 1954, Salt Lake City, Salt
Lake County, Utah.)
ii. **Tara Anne Montoya**, b. 1956, Parkersburg,
Wood County, West Virginia; m. **Ferrell Ray
TOWNS** (b. 1955, Haines City, Polk County,
Florida.)
iii. **Cynthia Jeannene Montoya**, b. 1957,
Parkersburg, Wood County, West Virginia;
m. **Shaun Kelly SOWARDS** (b. 1956,
Alamosa, Alamosa County, New Mexico).
iv. **Tricia Joan Montoya**. b. 1962, Tampa,
Hillsborough County, Florida; m.
Christopher Allen COX (b. 1961, Dade City,
Pasco County, Florida).

404.

David Dean Norton, son of No. 294, Mildred Miller, was born 16 Nov 1935 in Caldwell, Canyon County, Idaho. He married **Phyllis Irene LARSON,** 31 Oct 1958. They live in Tacoma, Pierce County, Washington.

Children of David D. Norton and Phyllis Larson are:
 i. **Marla Kay Norton**, b. 27 Dec 1959.
 ii. **Kevin Lee Norton**, b. 10 Nov 1961.
 iii. **Julie Ann Norton**, b. 20 Nov 1969.

405.

Richard Lee Norton, son of No. 294, Mildred Miller, was born 13 Sep 1937 in Caldwell, Canyon County, Idaho. He married (1) **Linda Lee MITCHELL** (b.15 Aug 1940), 17 Oct 1958; divorced 1960. He married (2) **Darlene CAMPAS**, 16 Feb 1962.

Child of Richard Norton and Linda Lee Mitchell is:
 i. **Michael Scott Norton**, b, 27 Mar 1959.

406.

Lawrence Paul Norton, son of No. 294, Mildred Miller, was born 18 Mar 1940 in Caldwell, Canyon County, Idaho. He married **UNK.** He lives in Tacoma, Pierce County, Washington.

Children of Lawrence Paul Norton are:
 i. **Stephanie Norton**, b. 09 Sep 1966.
 ii. **Adrienne Norton**, b. 21 Nov 1971.

407.

Mary Carol Miller, daughter of No. 295, Artimous K. Miller, was born 08 Aug 1940 in Malad City, Oneida County, Idaho. She married **Erwin SCHWIEBERT** in 1963.

Children of Mary Carol Miller and Erwin Schwiebert are:
- i. **Kathy Schwiebert**, b. 03 Aug 1967.
- ii. **Heidi Schwiebert**, b.25 May 1969.

408.

Nancy Elizabeth Miller, daughter of No. 295, Artimous K. Miller, was born 17 Aug 1942. She married **Dan OKIMOTO** in February 1970.
Children of Nancy Elizabeth Miller and Dan Okimoto are:
- i. **Saya Okimoto**, b. 29 Aug 1971.
- ii. **Kevin Okimoto**, b. 11 Jan 1977.

409.

Shirley I. Rathburn, daughter of No. 297, Ethel Gay Miller, was born 23 Mar 1949 in Tacoma, Pierce County, Washington. She married **Steve WEST,** 1975, in Tacoma, Washington. He was born 08 Aug 1952.
Child of Shirley Rathburn and Steve West is:
- i. **Christopher West**, b. 05 Aug 1976; d. before 2000.

410.

Richard P. Miller, Sr., son of No. 298, Paul Victor Miller, was born 11 Dec 1944 in Visalia, Tulare County, California. He married **Jan WOHLFORD** on 25 Jan 1964. She was born 05 Dec 1945.
Children of Richard P. Miller and Jan Wohlford are:
- i. **Richard P. Miller, Jr.,** b. 03 Oct 1964.
- ii. **Terri Miller**, b. 07 May 1968.

411.

Kathryn Miller, daughter of No. 298, Paul Victor Miller, was

born 25 May 1947 in Visalia, Tulare County, California. She married **Dennis MONTGOMERY,** 02 Sep 1967. He was born 03 Apr 1946.
Children of Kathryn Miller and Dennis Montgomery are:
    i. **Jason Montgomery**, b. 10 Sep 1970.
    ii. **Carrie Montgomery**, b. 24 Nov 1971.

412.
Cyndi A. Miller, daughter of No. 298, Paul Victor Miller, was born 25 Jun 1959 in Visalia, Tulare County, California. She married **Larry PENA,** 17 Sep 1977. He was born 18 Feb 1955.
Children of Cyndi A. Miller and Larry Pena are:
    i. **Bethany Marie Pena**, b. 09 Mar 1981.
    ii. **Joshua C. Pena**, b. 07 Jul 1982.

413.
Joyce Gay Miller, daughter of No. 299, Garrett Stanley Miller, was born 16 Jan 1945 in Visalia, Tulare County, California. She married **Lloyd Stanley EVENSON,** October 1967, at Prince Albert, Saskatchewan, Canada. He was born 10 Jun 1944.
Children of Joyce Gay Miller and Lloyd Stanley Evenson are:
    i. **Stacy Ann Evenson**, b. 08 Aug 1971, Exeter, Tulare County, California.
    ii. **Chad Lloyd Evenson**, b. 17 Oct 1972, Visalia, Tulare County, California.
    iii. **Mandy Lynn Evenson**, b. 20 Mar 1971, Visalia, Tulare County, California.
    iv. **Leticia Gay Evenson**, b. 15 Jul 1975, Visalia, Tulare County, California.
    v. **Dustin Kyle Evenson**, b. 24 Mar 1977, Visalia, Tulare County, California.

vi. **Lylu Christian Evenson**, b. 14 Oct 1978,
Fresno, Fresno County, California.
vii. **Travis Brandon Evenson**, b. 14 Oct 1980,
Visalia, Tulare County, California.
viii. **Spencer Martin Evenson**, b. 12 Jan 1982,
Visalia, Tulare County, California.

414.

David D. Bell, son of No.300, Alma Lucille Miller, was born 31 Aug 1942 in Caldwell, Canyon County, Idaho. He lives in Redmond, King County, Washington. He married **UNK**. Child of David D. Bell and Unk is:
i. **Brett Bell**, b. 21 Oct 1966; d. 09 Feb 1970, Caldwell, Canyon County, Idaho.

415.

Donald S. Bell, son of No. 300, Alma Lucille Miller, was born 22 Jan 1945 in Portland, Multnomah County, Oregon. He married **Dorothy MILES**, 01 Jun 1971 in Caldwell, Canyon County, Idaho. She was born 15 Nov 1952.
Children of Donald S. Bell and Dorothy Miles are:
i. **Stephen D. Bell**, b. 23 Dec 1971.
ii. **Christopher Bell**, b. 02 Jan 1975.
iii. **Paul S. Bell**, b. 02 Jul 1976.
iv. **Michael A. Bell**, b. 15 Oct 1977.
v. **Alan R. Bell**, b. 03 Dec 1978.
vi. **Amelia E. Bell**, b. 19 Sep 1979.

416.

Alma Elaine Bell, daughter of No. 300, Alma Lucille Miller, was born 27 May 1947 in Boise, Ada County, Idaho. She married **Robert G. KEMPTON,** 31 Aug 1968. He was born

31 Mar 1942.
Children of Alma Elaine Bell and Robert G. Kempton are:
    i. **Malinda R. Kempton**, b. 14 Oct 1973, Boise, Ada
      County, Idaho.
    ii. **Bradley G. Kempton**, b. 11 May 1976.
    iii. **Scott G. Kempton**, b. 07 Jul 1978.

417.

Helen Jane Cain, daughter of No. 298, Evangeline Virginia
Allen, was born 16 Jun 1929 in Shinnston, Harrison County,
West Virginia. She married **Paul WILSON** 22 Dec 1948 in
Lancaster, Fairfield County, Ohio.
Children of Helen Cain and Paul Wilson are:
476.   i. **Paula Kay Wilson**, b. 04 Oct 1949.
477.   ii. **Donna Mae Wilson**, b. 07 Oct 1950.
       iii. **Karen Sue Wilson**, b. 22 Oct 1952.
478.   iv. **Brenda Lee Wilson**, b. 25 Feb 1957.

418.

Paul Allen Cain, son of No. 301, Evangeline Virginia Allen,
was born 15 Apr 1933 in Shinnston, Harrison County, West
Virginia. He married **Ernestine Ann ANGELINE** 05 Dec
1958 in Shinnston, Harrison County, West Virginia.
Children of Paul Cain and Ernestine Angeline are:
    i. **Kelly Ann Cain**, b. 07 Aug 1961; m. **Samuel
      Joseph FLEECE.**
    ii. **Kristie Jo Cain**, b. 21 Jul 1962.
    iii. **Paul Allen Cain, Jr.**, b. 20 Oct 1965.
    iv. **Steven Cain**, b. 01 June 01, 1970.

419.

David Lee Cain, son of No. 301, Evangeline Virginia Allen, was born 28 Aug 1935 in Shinnston, Harrison County, West Virginia. He married **Helen FAUCHER** in Lancaster, Fairfield County, Ohio.

Children of David Lee Cain and Helen Faucher are:

    i. **David Lee Cain, Jr.**, b. 11 Apr 1958.

    ii. **Christopher Matthew Cain**, b. 30 Nov 1969.

420.

Joyce Ann Cain, daughter of No. 301, Evangeline Virginia Allen, was born 16 Sep 1939 in Gypsy, Harrison County, West Virginia, and died 28 Nov 1996 in Lumberport, Harrison County, West Virginia. She married **Lawrence Albert MERRILL** in Shinnston, Harrison County, West Virginia.

Children of Joyce Ann Cain and Lawrence Merrill are:

479.   i. **Billie Paulette Merrill**, b. 20 Dec 1958.

    ii. **Frederick Ray Merrill**, b. 04 May 1962

    iii. **Rebecca Renee Merrill**, b. May 04, 1962.

421.

Joe Hamilton Allen, Jr., son of No. 302, Joe Hamilton Allen, Sr., was born 02 Dec 1968. He married **Kelly J. KNIGHT.** She was born 09 Nov 1972. They are divorced.

Child of Joe Hamilton Allen, Jr. and Kelly J. Knight is:

    i. **Halley Drew Allen**, b. 13 Jun 1993.

422.

Randolph Roye Reynolds, son of No. 304, Lynden Eugene Reynolds, Jr., was born 31 Jan 1946. He married **Paula DAY**. (Separated.) She lives in Crestline, San Bernadino County, California; he lives in Northern California.

Children of Randolph Reynolds and Paula Day are:
  i. **Carmen Celeste Reynolds**, b. 10 Feb 1977.
  ii. **Danielle Jo Reynolds**, b. 18 Dec 1980.

423.
Lynda Renee Reynolds, daughter of No. 304, Lynden Eugene Reynolds, Jr., was born 5 Jan 1956. She married **Peter Joseph PROCIUK**, 17 Mar 1987, in Philadelphia, Pennsylvania. They are divorced. She lives in Chester County, Pennsylvania.
Child of Lynda Renee Reynolds and Peter Joseph Prociuk is:
  i. **Asma Prociuk**, b. 17 Oct 1994.

424.
Patricia Lynn Gilpin, daughter of No. 306, Charlaine Reynolds, was born 18 Mar 1945 in St. Marys, Pleasants County. She married **Ronald Allen JEFFREY** 03 Jul 1964 in Barboursville, Cabell County. He died 07 Jul 2015.
Children of Patricia Lynn Gilpin and Ronald Allen Jeffrey are:
480.   i. **Kelly Lynn Jeffrey**, b. December 11, 1967.
  ii. **Angela Brooke Jeffrey**, b. December 05, 1971.
  iii. **Craig Allen Jeffrey**, b. February 14, 1974.

425.
Kay Walter Gilpin, son of No. 306, Charlaine Reynolds, was born February 1947 in St. Marys, Pleasants County, West Virginia. He married **Judith Lynn SWEENEY**. They live in Martinsburg, Berkeley County, West Virginia where he and his two sons are veterinarians.
481.   i. **Darin Lee Gilpin**, b. 19 Sep 1968.
482.   ii. **Brian Douglas Gilpin**, b. 20 Jun 1972.
  iii. **Julie Renee Gilpin**, b. 10 Dec 1973, m. **Bryan STAFFORD**.

426.

Beverly Ann Gilpin daughter of No. 306, Charlaine Reynolds, was born 10 Feb 1950 in St. Marys, Pleasants County, West Virginia. She married (1) **David Paul LITTMAN**, 07 Apr 1973 in Barboursville, Cabell County, West Virginia. She married (2) **Michael MORRIS**.

Children of Beverly Ann Gilpin and David Paul Littman are:

     i. **Aaron David Littman**, b. 19 Apr 1975.

    ii. **Amber Alicia Littman**, b. 13 Mar 1977.

427.

Rex Eugene Gilpin, son of No. 306, Charlaine Reynolds, was born 12 Dec 1956 in St. Marys, Pleasants County, West Virginia. He married **Kathryn Ann STEPHENSON**, 31 Dec 1977.

Children of Rex Eugene Gilpin and Katheryn Ann Stephenson are:

483.   i. **Ashlee Rexann Gilpin**, b.26 Jun 1980.

    ii. **Lydia Kathryn Gilpin**, b. December 30, 1986.

428.

Stephanie Ann Reynolds, daughter of No. 307, Joseph Isaac Reynolds, was born 12 Aug 1951. She married **Timothy MORAN**, 32 Jun 1980.

Child of Stephanie Reynolds and Timothy Moran is:

     i. **Katherine Louise Moran**, b. 23 Sep 1985.

429.

Stephen Andrew Reynolds, son of No. 307, Joseph Isaac Reynolds, was born 20 May 1954, in Parkersburg, Wood County, West Virginia. He married **Catherine KELLY**, 1984. They live in Boston, Massachusetts.

Children of Stephen Andrew Reynolds and Catherine Kelly are:

    i. **Joseph Frederick Reynolds**, b. 18 Jul 1985.

    ii. **Ryan Andrew Reynolds**, b. 16 May 1990.

430.

Gregory David Reynolds, son of No. 307, Joseph Isaac Reynolds, was born 17 Sep 1959, in Parkersburg, Wood County, West Virginia. He married **Janis L. ROSAGE**, 25 May 1985, daughter of **John Raymond ROSAGE** and **Betty Jane SPISAK**.

Children of Gregory David Reynolds and Janis Rosage are:

    i. **Julie Ann Reynolds**, 02 Nov 1989.

    ii. **Sarah Elizabeth Reynolds**, 03 Jul 1993.

431.

Cynthia Louise Reynolds, daughter of No. 307 Joseph Isaac Reynolds, was born 26 Aug 1963 in Parkersburg, Wood County, West Virginia. She married **Todd A. ROUSH**, 06 Jul 1985.

Children of Cynthia Louise Reynolds and Todd A. Roush are:

    i. **Meg-Ann Elizabeth Roush**, b. 11 Jun 1989.

    ii. **Emily Marie Roush**, b. 23 Sep 1992.

432.

Stanley Lee Herrod, son of No. 330, Wilma May Shaffer, was born 23 Oct 1943 in Clarksburg, Harrison County, West Virginia. He married **Sylviann Ellen SANDERSON**, daughter of **Lloyd Arthur Daniel SANDERSON, Sr.** and **Luella May JACKSON**, on 16 Jun 1965, in Yuma, Yuma County, Arizona. She was born 18 Nov 1944 in Winslow, Navajo County, Arizona.

Child of Stanley Lee Herrod and Sylvianna Ellen Sanderson is:
484.   i. **Jeanette Aileen Herrod**, b. 17 Jan 1968.

433.

Linda Charlene Beghtel, daughter of No. 339, Elzara DeMoss, was born 1954. She married **Michael Patrick CULALA**,
Children of Linda Beghtel and Michael Culala are:
      i. **Sean Michael Culala**, b. 1977.
      ii. **Tara Rhiannon Culala**, b. 1979.

434.

Steven Wayne Sparks, son of No. 343, Lois June Wass, was born 25 Nov 1952, in Mariposa, Mariposa County, California. He married **Nanci MILLER**. She was born 14 Jan 1952.
Child of Steven Sparks and Nanci Miller is:
      i. **Cristina Robin Sparks**, b. 28 Jan 1990,
            Sonora, Tuolumne County, California.

435.

Thomas Alan Foster, son of No. 349, Joseph Foster, was born 16 Aug 1959 in Parkersburg, Wood County, West Virginia. He married **Beverly Kay DODD**, 06 Oct, 1979, in Pullman, Ritchie County, West Virginia. She was born 16 Oct, 1957, in Parkersburg, Wood County, West Virginia.
Child of Thomas Foster and Beverly Dodd is:
      1. **Meghan Brooke Foster**, b. 22 Oct 1985,
            Clarksburg, Harrison County, West Virginia.

436.

Charles Lee Zakaib, Jr., son of No. 350, Madelon Camille Patton, was born 18 Mar 1946, in Parkersburg, Wood County,

West Virginia. He married **Pamela DUMAS**, 21 Jun 1976, in
Eden, Caswell County, North Carolina. She was born 28 May
1950, in Charlottesville, Albermarle County Virginia.
Child of Charles Zakaib and Pamela Dumas is:
> i. **Charles Lee Zakaib, III**, b. 20 Apr 1978,
> Waynesboro, Augusta County, Virginia.

437.
Joseph Patton Zakaib, son of No. 350, Madelon Camille
Patton, was born 18 Aug 1947, in New York City, New York.
He married **Beverly Lynn MONTGOMERY,** 18 Oct 1980, in
Waynesboro, Augusta County, Virginia. She was born 14 Jun
1958, in Rockbridge County, Virginia.
Children of Joseph Zakaib and Beverly Montgomery are:
> i. **Jeffrey Patton Zakaib,** b. 03 Nov 1987, Roanoke,
> Roanoke County, Virginia.
> ii. **Michael Kirkpatrick Zakaib**, b.22 Mar 1989,
> Roanoke, Roanoke County, Virginia.

438.
Robert Lewis Zakaib, Sr., son of No. 350, Madelon Camille
Patton, was born 21 Sep 1953, in Danville, Vermilion County,
Illinois. He married **Patricia Lorraine COLE**, 10 Jun 1978, in
Waynesboro, Augusta County, Virginia. She was born 11 Aug
1957.
Child of Robert Zakaib and Patricia Cole is:
> i. **Robert Lewis Zakiab, Jr.**, b. 01 Feb 1987,
> Waynesboro, Augusta County, Virginia.

439.
Linda Marion Purl, daughter of No. 351, Marshelline Patton,
was born 1955 in Greenwich, Fairfield County, Connecticut.

She married (1) **Desiderio "Desi" Alberto ARNAZ, Jr.**, son of **"Desi" AZNAZ, Sr.** and **Lucille BALL,** in Los Angeles, Los Angeles County, California. She married (2) **William BROYLES**, in Los Angeles, Los Angeles County, California. She married (3) **Lucius Alexander CARY, Sr.**, 1994, in Colorado Springs, El Paso County, Colorado. He was born 01 Feb 1963, in England, UK. She is a Broadway vocalist.
Child of Linda Purl and Lucius Cary is:
>   i. **Lucius Alexander Cary, Jr.**, b. 06 Feb 1995, Los Angeles, Los Angeles County, California.

440.
William Davis Hewitt, son of No. 352, Alice Ann Davis, was born 17 Jan 1950, in Atlanta, Fulton County, Georgia. He married (1) **Rosaline RAY**, July 1977 in Atlanta, Fulton County, Georgia. She was born in Moultrie, Colquitt County, Georgia. He married (2) **Rives Gibson DALLEY**, 08 Oct 1988, in Atlanta, Cobb County, Georgia.
Children of William Hewitt and Rives Dalley are:
>   i. **Dalley Davis Hewitt**.
>   ii. **Ann Gibson Hewitt**, b. 22 Feb 1994, Atlanta, Cobb County, Georgia.

441.
Elizabeth Ann Hewitt, daughter of No. 352, Alice Ann Davis, was born 04 Jun 1952, in Atlanta, Fulton County, Georgia. She married **Robert Jenks TAYLOR, IV**, 21 Nov 1981, in Atlanta.
Children of Elizabeth Hewitt and Robert Taylor are:
>   i. **Sarah Davis Taylor**, b. 11 Mar 1986.
>   ii. **Susan DeWitt Taylor**, b. 15 Aug 1988.

442.

David Allen Duff, son of No. 353, Winifred Jean Koehler, was born 20 Jul 1948, in Cincinnati, Hamilton County, Ohio. He married **Linda HUGHES**, 14 Feb 1981. She was born 12 Mar 1952.

Children of David Duff and Linda Hughes are:
> i. **Christopher Duff**, b. 24 Jan 1982.
> ii. **Ashley Winifred Duff**, b. 08 Jun 1983.

443.

Stephen Edward Duff, son of No. 353, Winifred Jean Koehler, was born 25 Jul 1952, in Caracas, Venezuela. He married **Angela DELANEY**, 20 Dec 1975. She was born 24 Sep 1952.

Child of Stephen Duff and Angela Delaney is:
> i. **Alexandra Duff**, b. 24 Apr 1984.

444.

Susan Kathleen Duff, daughter of No. 353, Winifred Jean Koehler, was born 03 Dec 1953, in Caracas, Venezuela. She married **Mark STERBLING**, Children of Susan Duff and Mark Sterbling are:
> i. **Christina Sterbling**, b. 26 Apr 1978.
> ii. **Lauren Michelle Unice Sterbling,** b. 22 Nov 1979.

445.

Thomas Lee Duff, son of No. 353, Winifred Jean Koehler, was born 12 Dec 1959, in Cincinnati, Hamilton County, Ohio. He married **Sheila MAYNE**, 02 Sep 1989. She was born 20 Sep 1965.

Children of Thomas Duff and Sheila Mayne are:
> i. **Travis Short Duff**, b. 16 Mar 1985.

ii. **Morgan Nicole Duff**, b. 08 Jul 1990.

446.

James Marven Koehler, son of No. 354, John Edward Koehler, was born 15 Jan 1955. He married **Susan DEAL**, 01 Oct 1987.
Children of James Koehler and Susan Deal are:
> i. **Joseph James Koehler**, b. 07 Aug 1982.
> ii. **Jonathan William Koehler**, b. 03 Jan 1989.

447.

James Arthur Mergy, son of No. 355, Arthur Mergy, was born 08 Sep 1960, in Santa Monica, Los Angeles County, California. He married **Kelly Ann FOGARTY**, daughter of **Shawn FOGARTY** and **Claudette MASTRI**. She was born 27 Sep 1963, in Bridgeport, Fairfield County, Connecticut.
Children of James Mergy and Kelly Fogarty are:
> i. **Christopher James Mergy**, b. 17 Sep 1997, Fayetteville, Cumberland County, North Carolina.
> ii. **Rebecca Madeline Mergy**, b. 13 Jun 1999, Fayetteville, Cumberland County, North Carolina.

448.

Judith Louise Mergy, daughter of No. 355, Arthur Mergy, was born 07 Aug 1962, in Santa Monica, Los Angeles County, California. She married **Barclay David NOBLE**, 29 Jun 1991, in Solana Beach, San Diego County, California. He was born 08 Apr 1962, in Los Angeles, Los Angeles County, California.
Children of Judith Mergy and Barclay Noble are:
> i. **Taylor Danielle Noble**, b. 01 Feb 1995, San

Diego, San Diego County, California.
ii. **Rachel Elizabeth Noble**, b. 05 May 1997, San
Diego, San Diego County, California.

449.

Jill Burwell, daughter of No. 356, Betty Annadore Wass,
married **Robert SMITH**.
Children of Jill Burwell and Robert Smith are:
    i. **Michael Smith**.
    ii. **Matthew Smith**.
    iii. **Bethany Smith**.

450.

Kenneth Dean Pritchard, Jr., son of No. 375, Kenneth Dean
Pritchard, Sr., was born 15 May 1960 in Circleville, Pickaway
County, Ohio. He married (1) **Margie DANNER**. He married
(2) **Wendy UNK**. He married (3) **Mary MESIAH**.
Child of Kenneth Dean Pritchard, Jr. and Margie Danner is:
485.   i. **Michael Kenneth Pritchard**, b. 07 Apr 1978.

451.

Tod Taylor Pritchard, son of No. 375, Kenneth Dean
Pritchard, Sr., was born 31 Jun 1961, in Circleville, Pickaway
County, Ohio. He married **Julie GETES** about 1981. She was
born 02 Aug 1963.
Child of Tod Pritchard and Julie Getes is:
        i. **Melanie Marie Pritchard**, b. 14 Nov 1980; adopted
            by Tod Pritchard.

452.

Mark Douglas Pritchard, son of No. 375 Kenneth Dean
Pritchard, Sr., was born 08 Aug, 1962, in Circleville, Pickaway

County, Ohio. He married (1) **Joanna HASTINGS;** m. (2) **Cindra KAYE.**
Child of Mark Pritchard and Joanna Hastings is:
  i. **Mark Douglas Pritchard, Jr.**
Children of Mark Pritchard and Cindra Kaye are:
  ii. **James Dean Pritchard.**
  iii. **Melinda Sue Pritchard.**
  iv. **Tracie Jean Pritchard**, b. 1985.

453.

Tina Marie Pritchard, daughter of No. 375, Kenneth Dean Pritchard, Sr., was born 07 Apr 1965, in Circleville, Pickaway County, Ohio. She married (1) **Edward BLAHA III,** 17 Nov 1983, Ocala, Marion County, Florida. He was born 01 Sep 1965, in Massachusetts. She married (2) **John Kenneth HART, Sr.,** 19 Feb 1985, in Ocala, Marion County, Florida. He was born 12 Jul 1960, in Ocala, Florida. She married (3) **Robert Martin TOMPKINS, 01** May 1994, Ocala, Marion County, Florida, son of **William TOMPKINS** and **Marian GESSLEIN.** He was born 27 Aug 1960, in Queens, New York. Child of Tina Pritchard and Edward Blaha is:
  i. **Michele Marie Blaha**, b. 04 Jun 1984.
Child of Tina Pritchard and John Hart is:
  ii. **John Kenneth Hart, Jr.**, b. 10 Sep 1985.

454.

Vickie Lee Pritchard, daughter of No. 385, John Earl Pritchard, was born 29 Apr 1951 in Akron, Summit County, Ohio. She married **James Nelson WALLACE**, son of **Chester James WALLACE** and **Lucille Catherine MILLER**, on 12 Jun 1976 in Akron.
Child of Vickie Lee Pritchard and James Nelson Wallace is:

486.   i. **Sarah Lucille Wallace**, b. 31 Oct 1978, Akron,
Summit County Ohio, christened 10 Dec 1978,
St. Martha's Church, Akron.

455.

Elizabeth Marie Jones, daughter of No. 386, Patricia
Pritchard and Fred Junior Jones, was born 26 Dec 1959, in
Akron, Ohio. She married **James MAGUIRE** in May 1985.
He was born 17 Nov 1961, in Akron.
Children of Elizabeth Marie Jones and James Maguire are:
    i. **Isabella Maguire**, b. 10 Aug 1996, Akron,
Summit County, Ohio.
    ii. **Aidan Todd Maguire**, b. 10 Sep 1998,
Akron, Summit County, Ohio.

456.

Adrienne Pritchard, daughter of No. 387, Lawrence Dean
Pritchard, was born 04 Oct 1954. She married (1) **Gregory
KERNS.** He was born 1953 and died about 1985. She married
(2) **Glenn SMITH.**
Child of Adrienne Pritchard and Glenn Smith is:
    i. **Clayton Smith**, b. 08 July 1992.

457.

Renee Pritchard, daughter of No. 387, Lawrence Dean
Pritchard, was born December 18, 1960, Akron, Summit
County, Ohio. She married **Matthew CARPENTER**.
Children of Renee Pritchard and Matthew Carpenter are:
    i. **Mallory Carpenter**, b. 14 Jul 1987.
    ii. **Evan Carpenter**, b.12 May 1990.

458.

Edward Pritchard, son of No. 388, Charles Edward Pritchard, was born in 1955. He married **Monica DUPLER**.
Children of Edward Pritchard and Monica Dupler are:
    i. **Joseph Bailey Pritchard**, b. 1984.
   ii. **Rae Ann Pritchard**, b. 1984.

459.

Patricia Pritchard, daughter of No. 388, Charles Edward Pritchard, was born in 1957. She married (1) **Anthony MACIAK.** She married (2) **Robert TISCHLER.** She married (3) **Dennis HOWALD**, 14 Feb 1996.
Child of Patricia Pritchard and Anthony Maciak is:
    i. **Justin Maciak**, b. 1982.
Child of Patricia Pritchard and Robert Tischler is:
   ii. **Kimberly Tischler**, b. 1994.

460.

Paula Pritchard, daughter of No. 388, Charles Edward Pritchard, was born 1958. She married (1) **Todd CRONNENWETT.** She married (2) **Lawrence THOENISSEN.** She has other marriages.
Child of Paula Pritchard and Lawrence Thoennissen is:
    i. **Patrick Thoennissen**, b. 1995.

461.

Pamela Pritchard, daughter of No. 388, Charles Edward Pritchard, was born 1959. She married (1) **Dale LISECKI** (divorced). She married (2) **Mitchell GENTRY**.
Child of Pamela Pritchard and Dale Liseski is:
    i. **April Lisecki**, b. 1979.
Children of Pamela Pritchard and Mitchell Gentry are:

   ii. **Amanda Gentry**, b. 1988.
  iii. **Anna Gentry**, b. 1991.

462.

Penny Pritchard, daughter of No. 388, Charles Edward Pritchard, was born in 1963 at Akron, Summit County, Ohio. She married **David JORDAN.**
Children of Penny Pritchard and David Jordan are:
   i. **Matthew Jordan**, b. 1988.
  ii. **Kayla Jordan**, b. 1991.

463.

Phyllis Pritchard, daughter of No. 388, Charles Edward Pritchard, was born in 1966 at Akron, Summit County, Ohio. Unmarried.
Child of Phyllis Pritchard is:
   i. **Michael Pritchard**, b. 1988.

464.

Danya Pritchard, daughter of No. 388, Charles Edward Pritchard, was born in 1971 at Akron, Summit County, Ohio. She married **Todd WILSON** in 1990.
Children of Danya Pritchard and Todd Wilson are:
   i. **Jacoby Wilson**, b. 1993.
  ii. **Emily Wilson**, b. 1996.

465.

Donald Darrell Poole, son of No. 391, Darrell Edward Poole, was born 10 Apr 1948 in Norfolk, Virginia. He married **Laura Elizabeth WARWICK,** daughter of **William C. WARWICK** and **Elizabeth ENGLISH**. They live in North Carolina.
Children of Donald Darrell Pool and Laura Warwick are:

    i. **Rebecca Elizabeth Poole**, 02 Jul 1983
   ii. **Rachel Virginia Poole**, 01 Jun 1986
  iii. **Gabriel Stanton Poole**, 27 Apr 1994
  iv. **Joshua Kincaid Poole**, 27 Apr 1994

466.

Linda Jean Poole, daughter of No. 391, Darrell Edward Poole, was born 25 August 25, 1951 in Lancaster, Fairfield County, Ohio. She married **Russell PIERCE,** 04 Jun 1975 in Fairfield County, Ohio. He was born in Mansfield, Ohio and died September 1978 in Fairfield County, Ohio in a single car crash at Grace Lutheran Church on U.S. 22 East.
Child of Linda Jean Pool and Russell Pierce is:
    i. **Omar Dylan Pierce**, b. 04 Feb 1976.

467.

Stephen Mark Poole, son of No. 391, Darrell Edward Poole, was born 01 Dec 1953 in Lancaster, Fairfield County, Ohio. He married **Barbara BRIGGS,** March 1975 in First Presbyterian Church, Lancaster, Fairfield County, Ohio, daughter of **Henry BRIGGS** and **Mary FRAZIER**.
Children of Stephen Pool and Barbara Briggs are:
    i. **Stephen Matthew Briggs Poole** b. 15 Apr 1979.
   ii. **Julia Ellen Briggs Poole**, b. 30 Dec 1981.

468.

Walter Edward Pool, son of No. 393, Walter Averill Pool, was born 05 Jan 1952 in Lancaster, Fairfield County, Ohio. He married **Martha Joyce ROWLES,** 29 May 1976, in Bremen-Bethel Presbyterian Church, Bremen, Fairfield County, Ohio, daughter of **Cyril ROWLES** and **Ruth RANSOM**. She was born 27 Jun 1953 in Lancaster, Fairfield County, Ohio.

Children of Walter Edward Pool and Martha Joyce Rowles are:
  i. **Mary Martha Pool**, b. 17 Apr 1979, Lancaster, Fairfield County, Ohio.
  ii. **Laura Belle Pool**, b. 17 Feb 1982, Lancaster, Fairfield County, Ohio.
  iii. **Amy Elizabeth Pool**, b.22 Apr 1984, Lancaster, Fairfield, County, Ohio.
  iv. **Nathan Wynkoop Pool**, b. 20 Jul 1988, Lancaster, Fairfield County, Ohio.

469.

Michael Dean Pool, son of No. 393, Walter Averill Pool, was born 21 Jun 1953 in Lancaster, Fairfield County, Ohio. He married (1) **Beth Elaine FOLZ**, 06 Nov 1981 in Municipal Court, Athens, Athens County, Ohio, daughter of **Roger FOLZ** and **Betty ARNES**. She was born 15 Oct 1954 in Cincinnati, Hamilton County, Ohio. She divorced her first husband on 16 Jan 1981. Michael married (2) **Ruth Ann YALCH,** 20 Jun 1992 in the bride's home, Bedford, Cuyahoga County, Ohio, daughter of **Steve YALCH** and **Agnes GEARO**. She was born 09 Mar 1950 in Garfield Heights, Cuyahoga County, Ohio.

Child of Michael Dean Pool and Ruth Ann Yalch is:
  i. **Darrell Michael Pool**, b. 28 Jul 1992.

470.

William Keith Pool, son of No. 393 Walter Averill Pool, was born 17 Oct 1954 in Lancaster, Fairfield County, Ohio. He married **Jane Ann BEAVERS,** 28 Jun 1980, in Amanda United Methodist Church, Amanda, Ohio, daughter of **Harold BEAVERS** and **Georgia SHARP**.

Children of William Keith Pool and Jane Ann Beavers are:

i. **Heather Adelle Pool**, b. 26 Aug 1981.
ii. **Amber Michelle Pool**, b. 03 Aug 1984.

471.

Ronald Gene Ward, son of No. 394 James Ernest Ward, was born 27 Dec 1950 in Parkersburg, Wood County, West Virginia. He married **Janice CHAMBERS**, daughter of **Frank CHAMBERS** and **Sil (Sylvia?) UNK**.
Child of Ronald Ward and Janice Chambers is:
   i. **Chad Allen Ward**, b. 17 Jul 1975; m. **Tracy WESTFALL**, 1998.

472.

Gary Ray Ward, son of No. 394, James Ernest Ward, was born 30 Jan, 1954. He married **Ginger GREY**. She was born in Indiana.
Child of Gary Ward and Ginger Grey is:
   i. **Eric Ward**, b. 1995.

473.

Rebecca Fauntelle Owens, daughter of No. 395, Barbara Lou Ward, was born 25 Nov 1966 in Ripley, Jackson County, West Virginia. She married **Philip Todd ASH,** 03 Sep 1988. in Alexander Baptist Church, Roane County, West Virginia, son of **Albert ASH** and **Camille FISHER**. He was born 19 Nov 1964 in Clarksburg, Harrison County, West Virginia.
Child of Rebecca Owens and Phillip Ash is:
   i. **Ian Matthew Ash**, b. 16 Nov 1991,
      Parkersburg, Wood County, West Virginia.

474.

Pamela Ruth Owens, daughter of No. 395, Barbara Lou
Ward, was born 01 Oct 1969 in Ripley, Jackson County, West
Virginia. She married **Theodore Matthew LEHR,** 26 Mar
1994 in Leesburg United Methodist Church, Loudoun County,
Virginia, son of **Lee LEHR** and **Dorothy BOLT**. He was born
09 Apr 1970 in Baltimore, Baltimore County, Maryland.
Child of Pamela Owens and Theodore Lehr is:

     i. **Emily Grace Lehr**, b. 22 Oct 1998,
         Martinsburg, Berkeley County, West Virginia.

475.

Rachel Amanda Owens, daughter of No. 395, Barbara Lou
Ward, was born 25 Sep 1974 in Ripley, Jackson County, West
Virginia. She married **William Edward GOOTS, Jr.** on 11
Oct 1997, at Blackwater Falls, Tucker County, West Virginia.
He was born 22 Apr 1975 in Marietta, Washington County,
Ohio.
Child of Rachel Amanda Owens and William Goots, Jr. is:

     i. **Abigail Jordan Goots**, b. 20 Oct 1999, Reedsville,
         Rockingham County, North Carolina.

NINTH GENERATION

476.

Paula Kay Wilson, daughter of No. 417, Helen Cain, was born 04 Oct 1949. She married **Robert Lee HUBER.**
Children of Paula Wilson and Robert Huber are:
    i. **Robert Lee Huber, Jr.**, b. 28 Sep 1969.
    ii. **Elizabeth Ann Huber**, b. 16 Jun 1973.

477.

Pamela Kay Wilson, daughter of No. 417, Helen Cain, was born 07 Oct 1950. She married **James Leo SMITH.**
Children of Donna Wilson and James Smith are:
    i. **James Matthew Smith**, b. 16 Jul 1971.
    ii. **Jonathan Michael Smith**, b. 18 Nov 1977.
    iii. **Jeffrey Paul Smith**, b. 17 Apr 1981.

478.

Brenda Lee Wilson, daughter of No. 417, Helen Cain, was born 25 Feb 1957. She married **Martin HINES.**
Children of Brenda Lee Wilson and Martin Hines are:
    i. **Joseph David Hines**, b. 05 Jan 1975.
    ii. **Kristoffer Garret Hines**, b. 28 Feb 1980.

479.

Billie Paulette Merrill, daughter of No. 420, Joyce Ann Cain, was born 20 Dec 1958. She married **Timothy Clark VICTOR.**
Child of Billie Merrill and Timothy Victor is:
    i. **Brandy Nicole Victor**, b. 09 Mar 1981.

480.

Kelly Lynn Jeffrey, daughter of No. 424, Patricia Lynn Gilpin, was born 11 Dec 1967. She married **Steve Eric GIBSON.**
Children of Kelly Lynn Jeffrey and Steve Gibson are:
  i. **Shaun Eric Gibson,** b. 19 May, 1989.
  ii. **Seth Jacob Gibson,** b. 04 May 1989.

481.

Darin Lee Gilpin, son of No. 425 Kay Walter Gilpin, was born 19 Sep 1968. He married **Wendy MUTO.**
Children of Darin Lee Gilpin and Wendy Muto are:
  i. **Anna Gilpin,** b. 10 Feb 1996.
  ii. **Julia Gilpin,** b. 25 Mar 1999.

482.

Brian Douglas Gilpin, son of No. 425, Kay Walter Gilpin, was born 20 Jun 1972. He married **Laura Jeane BRIGGS.**
Child of Brian Douglas Gilpin and Laura Jeane Briggs is:
  i. **Tyler Kay Gilpin,** b.14 Feb 2003.

483

Ashlee Rexann Gilpin, daughter of No. 427, Rex Eugene Gilpin, was born 26 Jun 1980. She married **Jonathan COOPER**. They live in Vienna, Wood County, West Virginia. Child of Ashlee Gilpin and Jonathan Cooper is:
  i. **Kaya Rexann Cooper**, b. 13 Nov 2003.

484.

Jeanette Aileen Herrod, .daughter of No. 432, Stanley Lee Herrod, was born 17 Jan 1968, in Clarksburg, Harrison County,

West Virginia. She married **Brian Keith SCHOONOVER**, son of **Wayne Elmer SCHOONOVER** and **Marie Fay TETER,** on 24 Jun 1995, in Sardis, Harrison County, West Virginia. Brian was born 11 Oct 1970, in Elkins, Randolph County, West Virginia. Jeanette is a school teacher. Brian majored in electrical engineering in college. He is with the FBI fingerprinting department in the Clarksburg/Fairmont area. Child of Jeanette Herrod and Brian Schoonover is:

    i. **Matthew Joel Schoonover**, b. 08 Jun 1999, Harrison County, West Virginia.

485.

Michael Kenneth Pritchard, son of No. 450, Kenneth Dean Pritchard, Jr., was born 07 Apr 1978, in Logan, Hocking County, Ohio. He married **Heather SHERLOCK**. Child of Michael Pritchard and Heather Sherlock is:

    i. **Kayla Pritchard**, b. 14 May 1998.

486.

Sarah Lucille Wallace, daughter of No. 454, Vicki Lee Pritchard, was born 31 Oct 1978 in Akron, Summit County, Ohio. She married **Jared Lee LAPHAM**, 10 Jun 2000, in St. Bernard's Church, Akron, Summit County, Ohio. He was born 26 Jan 1978, in Barberton, Summit County, Ohio. Child of Sarah Wallace and Jared Lapham is:

    i. **Adam Lee Lapham**, b. 07 Jun 2001, Akron, Summit County, Ohio.

The Pritchard/Prickett Family History

DESCENDANTS OF ELIZABETH PRITCHARD

10.

Elizabeth Pritchard, daughter of No. 5, Thomas
Pritchard, Sr., was born about 1777 in Loudoun County,
Virginia, and died after 1849 in Marion County, (West)
Virginia. She married (1) **John SMITH,** 09 Jan 1798, in
Allegany County, Maryland. He died about 1802. She then
married (2) **George FURBAY/FURBEE**. In the documents
consulted, the surname is spelled both ways interchangeably.
George was born about 1777 in Delaware, the son of **Caleb
FURBAY** and **Sarah BOWERS**. Caleb Furbay was the son of
Benjamin FURBEE who was born of English ancestry on the
Delaware/Maryland peninsula in 1693. Caleb died 16 Apr
1837. George's brothers, **Waitman Furbay,** born about 1773,
and **John Furbay,** born about 1775, went to Monongalia
County about 1790. Their younger brother, **Bowers Furbay,**
who was born about 1781, went there later.

George entered the Continental army and served in the
Battle of Brandywine and other engagements. After the close
of the Revolution, he went to the Northwest Territory and
settled on what was to become the site of Columbus, Ohio. He
remained there until the early 1800s when he went to
Monongalia County in (West) Virginia, cleared a large farm
near the Monongahela River, and formed one of the pioneer
settlements of northwestern Virginia. Considerable research
has been done by Furbay/Furbee descendants. Extensive
information is available in libraries and also at an annual
family reunion near Canton, Ohio, site of the Furbay Electric
Company.

The Pritchard/Prickett Family History

George Furbay signed his will on 03 Apr 1849 and died on 10 May 1849. At the January Court term of 1850, Elizabeth Furbay, Jeremiah Beatty, her attorney and son-in-law, and William Snodgrass appeared in person to straighten out some of the legal problems.

When examined by the court, Beatty gave the following evidence: *I wrote this will as the old man lay dying. Furbee was the second husband of Elizabeth Furbee who had children by her first husband whose name was Smith. Thomas P. Smith, Pritchard Smith, and Margaret Millan are children of Elizabeth Furbee by her first husband. At the time that I wrote the first will, Elizabeth Furbee urged the old man very hard to give her children by her first husband a part of his property. Sometime before I wrote the last paper...I was informed by Alpheus Millan, the son of Margaret Millan, that Mr. Furbee intended to see me, and he thought it likely Mr. Furbee wanted to make some alterations in his will. I then went up to see him and was told by (a neighbor) that it was not the old gentleman who wanted alterations made in the will, but it was the old lady, his wife, who desired the(m). I then went on up to Mr. Furbee to see if he wanted any alterations made and he said no.*

The George Furbee papers compiled during this hearing also contain statements by witnesses, including neighbors and relatives. William Pritchard, husband of Hannah Meredith (see Descendants of William Pritchard), was called as a witness and is quoted as testifying: *The old man Furbee's wife is my sister.* This supports the claim that William Pritchard was the son of Thomas Pritchard, Sr., rather than of William Pritchard, Revolutionary War soldier, as stated in several DAR genealogies.

Children of Elizabeth Pritchard and John Smith are:

i. **Thomas P. Smith** b. abt 1798; probably m. **Syntha LANCASTER,** daughter of **William LANCASTER** and **Elizabeth UNK**.

487.   ii. **Pritchard W. Smith,** b. 1800, Monongalia County, (West) Virginia.

488.   iii. **Margaret Smith,** b. abt. 1801, m. **Abraham MILLAN**

Children of Elizabeth Pritchard and George Furbay are :

489.   iv. **James Furbay,** b. abt. 1802, Monongalia County, (West) Virginia; d. 1885, Mannington, Marion County, West Virginia.

v. **Elizabeth Sarah Furbay**, b. about 1805, m. **Jeremiah BEATTY.**

SECOND GENERATION

487.

Pritchard W. Smith, son of No. 10, Elizabeth Pritchard and John Smith, was born in 1800 in Monongalia County, (West) Virginia. He married **Ziba/Zyba LANCASTER**, daughter of **William LANCASTER** and **Elizabeth UNK.** William Lancaster died before 18 Aug 1830, the date of his inventory. His final will settlement is dated November 1832 in Monongalia County, (West) Virginia Will Book 11. He cites his wife Elizabeth (whose will was settled December 1843); daughters Permilia Minor, Elizabeth Tennant, Melilda Climon, Syntha Smith, Zyba Smith; and sons Virgil and John. This indicates that Syntha Lancaster also married a Smith, possibly Thomas Pritchard Smith, brother of Pritchard. Thomas has not yet been found in court records, other than the mention in William Prichard's account taken prior to George Furbay's death.

Children of Pritchard W. Smith and Zyba Lancaster are:

    i. **Mary Elizabeth Smith**, b. abt. 1824; m. **Micah Andrew MORRIS** (b. 1818; d. 1867-1878), 1849, Wetzel County, (West) Virginia; son of **James MORRIS** (b. 1755, Montgomery County, Pennsylvania; d. 1834) and **Margaret UNK** (b. 1778; d. 1865), who were married 10 Oct 1794 in Greene County, Pennsylvania.

    ii. **John D. Smith**, b. 1832, Monongalia County, (West) Virginia.

    iii. **Mary Ann Smith**, b. 1835, Monongalia County, (West) Virginia.

iv. **Milton Smith**, b. 1837, Monongalia County, (West) Virginia.

v. **Rebecca Smith**, b. 1839, Monongalia County, (West) Virginia.

vi. **Cynthia Smith**, b. 1841, Monongalia County, (West) Virginia.

490. vii. **Oliver P. Smith**, b. August 1847, Marion County, (West) Virginia.

viii. **Elena Smith**, b. June 1850, Marion County, (West) Virginia.

ix. **Arthur C. Smith**, b. 1858, Marion County, (West) Virginia.

488.

Margaret Smith, daughter of No. 10, Elizabeth Pritchard and John Smith, was born about 1801 in Monongalia County, (West) Virginia. She married **Abraham MILLAN**, 15 Apr 1819, in Monongalia County, (West) Virginia. He was the son of **Abraham MILLAN** and **Nancy UNK.** He was born 12 Jan 1791 in Kent County, Maryland, and died 15 May 1857. The information about Abraham Millan comes from Dee Randall, Sondra Millan Blake, and Pat Franklin, all descendants of Elizabeth Pritchard and John Smith. There are a few discrepancies between them, such as the date of Abraham Millan's death; Sondra says he died 15 Jul 1857, while Pat says he died 15 May 1851.

Children of Margaret Smith and Abraham Millan are:

i. **Marcus Millan**, b. 05 Apr 1820; d. 1892.

ii. **Elizabeth Millan**, b. 14 Aug 1821; d. 1899.

iii. **Alpheus Millan**, b. 31 Aug 1823; d. 1866.

iv. **Sarah J. Millan**, b.14 Sep 1825; d. 1872.

v. **Nancy Millan**, b. 31 Oct 1827; d. 1847.

vi. **Caroline Millan**, b. 04 Jan 1829; d. 1846.
vii. **Thomas W. Millan**, b. 30 Aug 1831.
viii. **Benjamin Franklin Millan**, b. 17 May 1833; d. 1849.
ix. **Mary Millan**, b. 10 Mar 1835; d. 24 Jul 1885.
x. **Charlotte Millan**, b.01 Jan 1837; d. 24 Oct 1878.
xi. **George Van Buren Millan**, b. 02 Feb 1839; d. 1903.
xii. **Harriet Millan**, b. 24 Feb 1841; d. 1869.
xiii. **John Marion Millan**, b. 20 May 1843; d. 25 Jan 1918.

489.

James Furbay, son of No. 10, Elizabeth Pritchard and George Furbay, was born about 1802 in Monongalia County, (West) Virginia. He married (1) **Mary Ann BOGGESS** in 1823, daughter of **Lindsay BOGGESS** and **Ann CUNNINGHAM**, who were married 29 Mar 1827. Ann was the daughter of **John CUNNINGHAM** and **Sarah KING.** Sarah was born 11 Oct 1783 in Maryland, and died 22 Oct 1865 in Marion County, West Virginia. She was the oldest of ten children of **John KING** and **UNK.** John died in Monongalia County between 1820 and 1830 (see Descendants of John King of Monongalia County, West Virginia at: www.familytreemaker.com/users/k/i/n/James-L-King/index.html). Mary Ann Boggess was born in 1800 and died in 1838 at the age of 38, leaving eight children. James Furbay married (2) **Millie LUCAS** and died 1885 on the old family homestead. He was a farmer, merchant, stockman, and founder of Mannington, West Virginia.

Three known children of James Furbay and Mary Ann Boggess are:

           i. **George L. Furbay**, b. 08 Oct 1825, m. **Lucinda TALKINGTON**. He was a farmer.

491.   ii. **James Hilary Furbay**, b. October 18, 1827, Monongalia County, Virginia.

492.   iii. **Emily "Millie" Adeline Furbay,** b. 1829; d. 1914.

THIRD GENERATION

490.

Oliver P. Smith, son of No. 487, Pritchard W. Smith, was born August 1847 in Marion County, (West) Virginia. He married **Harriet B. WADE.**
Children of Oliver P. Smih and Harriet Wade are:
    i. **Harrison B. Smith**, b. 20 May 1889, Ritchie County, West Virginia.
    ii. **Clarence P. Smith,** b. April 1894, Ritchie County, West Virginia; m. **Iva G. SCOTT** (b. 13 Jun 1890, Ritchie County), 30 Dec 1911, Ritchie County.
    iii. **Essie Leora Smith**, b. July 1896, Ritchie County, West Virginia; m. **Charles Wesley SCOTT** (b. 04 Jan 1888, Ritchie County), 07 Dec 1911, Ritchie County.

491.

James Hilary Furbay, son of No. 489, James Furbay, was born 18 Oct 1827 and married **Sarah J. McCOY** 17 Oct 1855 in Marion County, West Virginia. He was a senator of the second senatorial district of West Virginia. The following excerpts are taken from his listing in
Biographical and Portrait Cyclopedia of Monongalia, Marion, and Taylor Counties, West Virginia:
    "He is widely known throughout the state as a man of superior business ability and unimpeachable integrity. His paternal great-grandfather, Captain Caleb Furbee, was of English parentage and birth, and settled in Delaware about the middle of the eighteenth century. When the Revolutionary War

came, Caleb espoused the cause of the colonies against his native land and entered the Continental army, where he served with honor, and distinguished himself for soldierly bearing and courage in the battle of Brandywine and other engagements. After the close of the Revolution, he went to the Northwest Territory and settled on the site of Columbus, Ohio. He remained there until the beginning of the present (19th) century, when he came to Monongalia County. He cleared up a large farm near the Monongahela River and, with others, formed one of the pioneer settlements of northwestern Virginia. Captain Furbee died on his farm when well advanced in years and covered with honors.

Caleb's son, George Furbee, was the grandfather of Senator James Hilary Furbee. George first saw the light of day in Delaware. He came west with his parents and shared their fortune in what was then considered a wilderness. He witnessed the early growth of the country and lived to see it populous and prosperous. He was a farmer and a member of the Methodist Episcopal Church, like his father before him, and died in 1862 when very comfortably situated on a fine and well-improved farm. He married Mrs. (Elizabeth Pritchard) Smith and with her reared a family of two children, James and Mrs. Sarah Beatty.

"(Their son) James Furbee was born in 1797, on the old Monongalia County homestead, and in 1849 came to what is now Mannington, where he died in 1885. After coming to Mannington, he purchased a farm of two hundred acres of land, which he cleared and devoted to stock-raising, in which he was quite successful. He also turned his attention to building up Mannington, and in 1849 opened the first store in the town. He was a Whig and Republican and a close observer of political events...Truthful, honest, and fearless he lived, and

when his last hour came, he died peacefully in the Methodist faith of his paternal ancestors. He was twice married; first to Mary L. Boggess, who died in 1838, aged 38 years, and left eight children to deplore her loss. His second marriage was with Mrs. Millie Lucas, and to this last union no children were born.

"James Hilary Furbee was reared on the farm, received his education in the select schools of his country, and then engaged in the mercantile business with his father at Mannington, which he followed for some years. A few years later, he succeeded his father in farming and stock-dealing...After the completion of the Baltimore and Ohio Railroad west of Mannington and through to Wheeling in 1852, he became ticket, freight, and express agent at Mannington, a position he held until 1866 when he engaged in the purchase, manufacture, and sale of lumber. In 1884, he and his son opened a large mercantile establishment at Mannington, which the latter has conducted successfully ever since.

"On October 17, 1855, Mr. Furbee was united in marriage with Sarah J. McCoy, a native of Tyler County and a sister to John W. McCoy of Fairmont. They have seven sons and two daughters. Senator Furbee's political career commenced in 1862 when he was appointed deputy collector of internal revenue for the first district of West Virginia, with headquarters at Wheeling. He served for five years. In 1878, the Republican party of Marion County made him its nominee for the legislature and he was elected. In 1880, the Republicans of the second Senatorial District nominated him as their candidate for the State Senate. He was elected by eight votes, but the county commissioners of Marion County threw out the returns from Benton's Ferry precinct and declared his opponent, Hon. Fountain Smith of Fairmont, to be elected. In

1886, he was the unanimous choice of his party as their candidate for State Senator and was elected by a large majority. In whatever field he labors, Senator Furbee knows no such word as <u>fail</u>, and defeat serves but to nerve him to renewed effort."

Children of James H. Furbay and Sarah McCoy are:

    i. **Mattie Furbay** m. **T. J. KOEN**, a merchant and oil speculator.

    ii. **Walter S. Furbay**, operated the Mannington Flouring Mill with his brother.

    iii. **Leslie C. Furbay** m. **Laura BEATTY**. He had a furniture and undertaking business.

    iv. **Mary J. Furbay** m. **James A. COLEMAN.**

    v. **James S. Furbay** m. **Louisa MAHAN**. He operated the Mannington Flour Mill.

493.   vi. **Howard R. Furbay**, b. 28 Feb 1866, d. 12 Dec 1919.

494.   vii. **Frank Emory Furbay**, b. 01 Oct 1867.

    viii. **Charles W. Furbay,** in the milling business.

    ix. **Guy S. Furbay**, a banker.

492.

Emily "Millie" Adeline Furbay, daughter of No. 10, Elizabeth Pritchard, was born about 1830. She married **Alpheus W. PRICHARD** (b. 31 Oct 1822), son of No. 11, **William PRICHARD**, and **Hannah MEREDITH,** on 02 Aug 1849.

Children of Emily Millie Furbay and Alpheus W. Prichard are listed under No. 499.

FOURTH GENERATION

493.
Howard R. Furbay, son of No. 491, James Hillary Furbay, married **Sallie ALTHA**. He was a member of the firm of J.H. Furbee and Sons, merchants.
Child of Howard R. Furbay and Sallie Altha is:
      i. **Russell L. Furbay**, b. 15 Jan 1898; served
         in World War I and became an attorney in
         Fairmont, West Virginia.

494.
Frank Emory Furbay, son of No. 491, James Hillary Furbay, married **Virginia H. HAGADORN,** 04 Oct 1889. He was a member of the firm of J. H. Furbee and Sons.
Children of Frank Furbay and Virginia Hagadorn are:
      i. **Robert Dater Furbay**, b. 10 Nov 1906.
     ii. **Martha Virginia Furbay**, b. 11 Mar 1912.

427

DESCENDANTS OF WILLIAM PRITCHARD

11.

William Pritchard (who later dropped the 't') was born 17 Dec 1777 in Loudoun County, Virginia and died April 1866 in Marion County, West Virginia. He married **Hannah MEREDITH,** 18 Feb 1805 in Monongalia County, (West) Virginia. The 't' was still present in his marriage application signature. Hannah was the daughter of **Davis MEREDITH** and **Amelia KNOTTS** (See Descendants of Ann "Nancy" Pritchard.)

Until recently, the ancestry of William Pritchard has been in dispute because several early DAR applicants claimed his descent from William Christopher (or Christopher William) Pritchard, a Revolutionary War soldier who was killed in battle during June 1777 in Maryland. It is possible that this soldier was a brother of Thomas Pritchard, Sr. and a son of Christopher Pritchard, recipient of the afore-noted Lord Fairfax grant in Prince William County, Virginia. The only claim that William Prichard's father was the above named soldier is found in those few DAR applications and those of several women who were later accepted into membership after citing them as evidence. It has since been proven that they were in error, as were many early DAR lineages compiled according to family "hearsay" without documentation; consequently, inaccurate information has become compounded over the years. Descendants of William Prichard have joined the DAR on these conflicting records, through no fault of theirs, but due to those early bogus applications and the confusion in names fueled by the reversal of given and middle names of the Revolutionary War casualty, and the dropped 't' in the

Pritchard surname. (For a possible explanation of the spelling change, see Descendants of John Prichard chapter.) Recent regulations prohibit future applicants from entering the DAR on William Prichard's line.

Records uncovered recently prove that William Pritchard was indeed the youngest son of Thomas Pritchard, Sr. and Rachel Davis, rather than an adopted child (heretofore presumed natural son of the soldier) raised in their household. Had he been adopted, confirmation would exist in court records, because the laws in Maryland and Virginia were very strict at that time regarding the protection of orphans. No guardianship papers have been found in Loudoun County, where records remained intact because they were hidden in Shenandoah Valley caves during the Civil War.

William Pritchard was administrator in 1813 of the estate of his father, Thomas Pritchard, Sr. in Maryland. During the process, he purchased the child's portion from each of the other heirs, his siblings. It was common in both Virginia and Maryland for the youngest son to opt for the home plantation, the older sons having already received their inheritance at the time they left home and moved westward, or married.

Further strong evidence that William was the natural son of Thomas Pritchard, Sr. and Rachel Davis Pritchard is found in the extensive George Furbay papers. The George Furbay Will, recorded in Marion County, (West) Virginia Wills Book I, pp. 114-128, contains testimony by several relatives, including William Pritchard, on behalf of Furbay's widow, Elizabeth Pritchard Furbay. On pages 124 and 125 of the Will Book, William Pritchard is quoted as saying, *I have been acquainted with George Furbee (sic) for upwards of thirty years...The old man Furbee's wife is my sister.* Therefore, it must be concluded that William Pritchard was the natural son of Thomas Pritchard.

In 1814, William Prichard moved to a portion of
Monongalia County, (West) Virginia that later became Marion
County. He died there in April 1866, and is buried along with
his son Absalom in the Asbie Rice Cemetery near Chunk's
Run. The Marion County histories list his birthplace as
Loudoun County, Virginia.

William Prichard is listed in the Allegany County,
Maryland Census of 1810 and in Monongalia County, (West)
Virginia in 1820, 1830, and 1840. Hannah does not appear in
the 1830 census, indicating that she died between 1827 and
1830, possibly when giving birth to Mary Ann. William is
living in Marion County, (West) Virginia in 1850 and 1860,
listed at ages 70 and 82, respectively. He was active in civic
affairs, as attested by his signature on many petitions.
Children of William Pritchard and Hannah Meredith are:

    i. **Amelia "Amy" Prichard**, b. 07 Mar 1806; m.
        Little CLAYTON. She must have died
        before 1828 when he married (2) No. 869,
        Rachel PARKER (see Descendants of
        Mary Pritchard).

495.   ii. **Thomas Prichard**, b. 14 Feb 1808, Allegany
        County, Maryland; d. 18 Sep 1885, Hoodsville,
        West Virginia.

496.   iii. **Margaret Ellen Prichard,** b.12 Oct 1809.

497.   iv. **Davis Prichard**, b. 09 Nov 1811, Allegany County,
        Maryland; d. 19 Jul 1891.

498.   v. **John Prichard,** b. 03 Dec 1813.

    vi. **Absalom Prichard**, b. 12 Mar 1816; m.
        Rebecca SWISHER, (b. abt. 1819,
        Monongalia County, West Virginia), 04 Mar
        1839, Monongalia County.

    vii. **William Prichard, Jr.,** b. 01 May 1818; m.
         Priscilla MINOR, 10 Apr 1845,
         Monongalia County; d. Montana.
    viii. **Rachel Pritchard,** b.14 Oct 1820; m. (1)
         Harvey COTTON; m. (2) **Squire W. C.**
         DAVIS.

499.   ix. **Alpheus W. Prichard,** b. 31 Oct 1822; d.
         28 Aug, 1884, Marion County, West Virginia.

500.   x. **Amos Newton Prichard,** b. 09 Feb 1825,
         Monongalia County, (West) Virginia; d.
         14 Sep 1909 in Mt. Lake Park, Garrett County,
         Maryland.

501.   xi. **Mary Ann Prichard,** b. 14 May 1827,
         Monongalia County, (West) Virginia.

SECOND GENERATION

495.

Thomas Prichard, son of No. 11, William Pri(t)chard, was born 11 Feb 1808 in Allegany County, Maryland, and died 18 Sep 1891 (one source says 14 Sep 1892) in Hoodsville, Marion County, West Virginia. He married **Mahala MORRIS**, daughter of **Richard MORRIS** and **Susanna STULL/STUHL**, on 11 Feb 1830. She was born 04 Dec 1809, in Delaware, and died 20 May 1898. Mahala was an older sister of Millie Morris, who married Thomas Merydith, the son of No. 12, Ann "Nancy" Pritchard, and Davis Meredith, who was the father of Thomas' mother, Hannah Meredith. Children of Thomas Prichard and Mahala Morris are:

    i. **Ezekiel D. Prichard**, b. 15 Dec 1830 Monongalia County, (West) Virginia; d. 02 Sep 1859.

    ii. **Hannah M. Prichard**, b. 09 Mar 1832, Monongalia County, (West) Virginia; m. **John HUGHES.**

    iii. **Susannah Bell Prichard**, b. 28 Oct 1833, Monongalia County, (West) Virginia; d. 06 Feb 1910, Belle Plains, Benton County, Iowa; m. **Anthony Colean BOGGESS** (b. 25 Nov 1832, Monongalia County; d. 07 Feb 1889, Page, Holt County, Nebraska), 06 Jan 1853.

    iv. **Emelia "Millie" A. Prichard**, b. 31 Oct 1835, Monongalia County, (West) Virginia; m. **William RIDGWAY.**

    v. **Richard Prichard**, b. 30 Oct 1837.

Monongalia County, (West) Virginia; Unm.
vi. **Elizabeth Prichard**, b. 09 Nov 1839,
Monongalia County, (West) Virginia; d.
12 Jan 1864.

vii. **Susan M. Prichard**, b. 21 Aug 1841, Marion
County, (West) Virginia; m. **Mart DONLEY**.

viii. **Melissa Prichard**, b. 27 Sep 1843, Marion
County, (West) Virginia; m. **Gus L.
CUNNINGHAM**.

ix. **Caroline Prichard**, b. 17 Jan 1846, Marion
County, (West) Virginia; m. **William
NEPTUNE**.

x. **Elvira M. Prichard**, b. 02 Oct 1847, Marion
County, (West) Virginia; m. **Gordon (?)
STRAIGHT**.

502. xi. **Alfred S. Prichard**, b. 21 Mar 1849, Marion
County, (West) Virginia; d. September 18,
1891.

xii. **Martha V. Prichard**, b. 30 Jun 1853, Marion
County, (West) Virginia; m. **Ed McCRAY**.

xiii. **Thomas F. Prichard**, b. 17 Sep 1855, Marion
County, (West) Virginia; d. 18 Aug 1886; unm.

496.

Margaret Ellen Prichard, daughter of No. 11, William
Prichard, was born 12 Oct 1809. She married **Thomas
FREELAND**, 22 Nov 1827, in Monongalia County, (West)
Virginia. He was born 14 Feb 1808 in Monongalia County, and
died 10 Jul 1846, in Western District, Marion County, (West)
Virginia. He was the son of **Elijah FREELAND** and **Rebecca
DICKEN.** His will filed in Marion County bequeaths one-third
of his estate to his beloved wife, Margaret; the residue to be

equally divided among his children, Jas Freeland, William Freeland, John Freeland, and daughters Amelia, Rebecca, Hannah, and Mary Ann. He appointed his "well beloved friend Davis Prichard and my wife Margaret my Executor to Execute this my last will and testament." The 1850 Census of Marion County's Western District notes that the real estate value of the Freeland dwelling is $1,260, and that Margaret, age 44, cannot write; neither can daughter Amy, age 22. Other children listed are Rebecca, 20; James, 18; Hannah, 16; Mary Ann, 13; William, 10; John, 9; and Thomas 3. Thomas was born after the death of his father.

Children of Margaret Prichard and Thomas Freeland are:

   i. **Amy Freeland**, b. 1828, Monongalia County, (West) Virginia.

503. ii. **Rebecca Freeland,** b. 1830, Monongalia County, (West) Virginia; d. 1918.

   iii. **James Freeland**, b. 1832, Monongalia County, (West) Virginia.

504. iv. **Hannah Freeland**, b. 1836, Monongalia County, (West) Virginia; d. 28 Sep 1890, Waterville, Marshall County, Kansas.

505. v. **Mary Ann Freeland**, b. 05 Apr 1837, Monongalia County, (West) Virginia; d. 05 Feb 1888, Wadestown, Marion County, West Virginia.

506. vi. **William Freeland**, b. 1849, Marion County, (West) Virginia; d. 1917.

507. vii. **John Willard Freeland**, b. 1841, Marion County, (West) Virginia.

508. viii. **Thomas Freeland, Jr.** b. 1847, Marion County, (West) Virginia; d. 1927.

497.

Davis Prichard, son of No. 11, William Prichard, was born 09 Nov 1811, in Allegany County, Maryland, and died 19 Jul 1891. He married **Emilia "Milly" DAWSON,** 26 Apr 1838, in Monongalia County, (West) Virginia. She was born 25 Feb 1812, the daughter of **George DAWSON,** and died 21 Apr 1898.

Children of Davis Prichard and Emilia Dawson are:

     i. **James Newton Prichard,** b. 1839, Monongalia County, (West) Virginia.

    ii. **Mary E. Prichard,** b. 1845, Marion County, (West) Virginia.

   iii. **Narcissa C. Prichard,** b. 1846, Marion County, (West) Virginia.

   iv. **Louise Caroline Prichard,** b. 1847.

    v. **Sarah E. Prichard,** b. 1848.

   vi. **Charles Prichard,** b. 1854.

498.

John Prichard, son of No. 11, William Prichard, was born 03 Dec 1813, in Allegany County, Maryland. He married (1) **Mary DUDLEY,** about 1840 in Monongalia County, (West) Virginia. He married (2) **Phidelia E. LAIDLEY,** 09 Feb 1847, in Marion County, (West) Virginia.

Children of John Prichard and Mary Dudley are:

509.   i. **Louise M. Prichard,** b. 02 Mar 1841, Monongalia County, (West) Virginia; d. 08 May 1926, Fort Scott, Bourbon County, Kansas.

510.   ii. **Margaret A. Prichard,** b. 21 Sep 1843, Marion County, (West) Virginia; d. 15 Nov 1915, Kansas.

iii. **Agnes F. Prichard**, b. 1846, Marion County,
(West) Virginia.
Child of John Prichard and Phidelia Laidley is:
iv. **Albert W. Prichard,** b. December 1849, Marion
County, (West) Virginia.

499.

Alpheus W. Prichard, son of No. 11, William Pritchard, was
born 31 Oct 1822 in Harrison County, (West) Virginia, and
died 28 Aug 1884 in Marion County, West Virginia. He
married No. 492, **Emily "Millie" Adeline FURBAY,** 02 Aug
1849 in Basnettville, Marion County, (West) Virginia, daughter
of **James FURBAY** and **Mary Ann BOGGESS**. She was born
about 1830. Mary Ann Boggess was the daughter of **Lindsay
BOGGESS** and **Ann CUNNINGHAM** (see Descendants of
William Pritchard). Soon after their marriage, they moved to
Forks of Buffalo, Marion County, which later became the town
of Mannington. They lived there for the rest of their lives.
Alpheus W. Prichard had his fingers in many pies: the
mercantile business, the lumber business, saw mills, and
farming. He was Mannington's first postmaster, served on the
town council, and was a member of the District Board of
Education. During his term, the District's first public (free)
school was opened. He represented Marion County in the
Virginia General Assembly in the term 1859-1860, and in the
West Virginia House of Delegates in 1870-71-72.
Children of Alpheus Prichard and Millie Furbay are:
511.   i. **Charles Albert Prichard**, b. 1850, Mannington,
Marion County, (West) Virginia; d. 1945.
512.   ii. **Arthur Lathrop Prichard**, b. 11 Mar 1857,
Mannington, Marion County, (West)
Virginia; d. 02 Sep 1938, Mannington.

iii. **Fred Alpheus Prichard**, b. 31 May1868,
   Mannington, Marion County, West Virginia;
   d. 1939, Mannington.
iv. **Mary Rose Prichard**; m. **William BURT**.
 v. **William Prichard**.
vi. **Fannie Prichard**, an artist and manager of
   Inter-Ocean Publishing Company in
   Philadelphia, Pennsylvania.

500.

Amos Newton Prichard, son of No. 11, William Prichard, was born 09 Feb 1825 in Monongalia County, (West) Virginia and died 14 Sep 1909 in Mt. Lake Park, Garrett County, Maryland. He married **Rebecca DAWSON** about 1848 in Marion County, (West) Virginia. She was born 18 Jul 1828 in Monongalia County, (West) Virginia, and died 17 Mar 1888 in Mannington, Marion County, West Virginia.

Children of Amos Newton Pritchard and Rebecca Dawson are:
   i. **William T. Prichard**, b. 1851.
513.   ii. **Absalom Wellington Prichard**, b. 07 Aug
           1852, Marion County, (West) Virginia; d.
           20 Nov 1934, Marion County.
514.   iii. **Charles Amos Prichard**, b. 06 Dec 1853, Paw
           Paw, Marion County, (West) Virginia; d.
           17 Dec 1886, Mannington, Marion
           County.
   iv. **Grace Elizabeth Prichard,** 1855.
   iv. **Belle Prichard**, b. 1857.

501.

Mary Ann Prichard, daughter of No. 11, William Prichard, was born 14 May 1827 in Monongalia County, (West)

Virginia. She married **John C. PARRISH**. He was born in 1825, and died in 1854.

Child of Mary Prichard and John Parrish is:

    i. **Amos Newton Parrish**, b. 1851.

THIRD GENERATION

502.

Alfred S. Prichard, son of No. 495, Thomas Prichard, was born 21 Mar 1849, in Marion County, (West) Virginia, and died 18 Sep 1891. He married **Sarah Ellen CUNNINGHAM,** daughter of **Ezekial CUNNINGHAM** and **Dorcas ARNETT,** on 08 Jan 1878 in Marion County. She was born 24 Sep 1854, in Marion County, and died in 1913.
Children of Alfred Prichard and Sarah Cunningham are:
    i. **John G. Prichard.**
    ii. **Dorcas M. Prichard,**
    iii. **T. F. W. Prichard.**
    iv. **Franklin A. Prichard.**
    v. **A. S. Prichard.**
    vi. **Nellie F. Prichard.**

503.

Rebecca Freeland, daughter of No. 496, Margaret Ellen Prichard, was born 1830 in Monongalia County, (West) Virginia, and died in 1918. She married **Nehemiah GLOVER.**
Children of Rebecca Freeland and Nehemiah Glover are:
    i. **John Glover.**
    ii. **Samuel Glover.**
    iii. **Ephriam Glover.**
    iv. **William Glover.**
    v. **Nehemiah Glover, Jr.**
    vi. **Isaac Glover.**
    vii. **Amos Glover.**
    viii. **Barbara Glover.**
    ix. **Margaret Glover.**

x. **Mary Glover.**
xi. **Lucy Glover.**
xii. **Leonard Glover.**

504.

Hannah Freeland, daughter of No. 496, Margaret Ellen Prichard, was born in 1834 in Job Township, Monongalia County, (West) Virginia, and died 28 Sep 1890, in Waterville, Marshall County, Kansas. She married **George KEEFOVER, Jr.,** in 1856 in West Virginia. The son of **George KEEFOVER, Sr.** and **Sarah PHILLIPS,** he was born 20 Mar 1820 in Fayette County, Pennsylvania, and died 19 Feb 1906 in Waterville, Marshall County, Kansas. Hannah Freeland was a member of the Dunkard Church in West Virginia, and joined the Baptist Church in Blue Rapids, Kansas. She traveled to Kansas on the train with her son, James, who was one year old at the time. Her obituary, in part reads, *"Hannah M. Keefover died at about age 55 years. She and her husband were amongst the earliest settlers of this part of Kansas, and a large number of relatives and friends mourn her decease...A card of thanks by her husband: To those who so cheerfully and willingly assisted in the funeral of my wife Hannah, I extend my sincere and heartfelt thanks, and especially I would not forget the ladies who so generously and affectionately rendered her all the assistance they could to make her comfortable during her long illness...We laid her among the flowers she loved so well."* Hannah was buried 01 Oct 1890 in Riverside Cemetery, Waterville, Marshall County, Kansas.

George Keefover was a farmer, school teacher, lamplighter, and flour and feed merchant. In 1884, he sold his store to his son, Thomas Keefover. His obituary reads in part: *"He died at the residence of his son, James, five miles northwest of Waterville, Kansas, 19 Feb 1906, at the age of 85 years, 10 months, and 23 days. At the age of five with his parents he moved to Morgantown, West Virginia. He worked his way through Morgantown College, fitting himself for teaching, which he followed for years after coming to Kansas. He moved with his family to Marshall County, Kansas in 1869, and located a homestead on one of our most fertile prairies near Waterville; the neighborhood, the school house, and a graveyard all bear the name of Keefover. In 1856, he was united in marriage with Miss Hannah Freeland...To this union there were five sons and a daughter. All grew to maturity and married, so that today there are eighteen grandchildren. At about twenty years of age, Mr. Keefover was converted and united with the Missionary Baptist Church, and remained a member of the same until his death. In a very early day for Kansas civilization, he gathered the children of the neighborhood and conducted a Sabbath school."*

Children of Hannah Freeland and George Keefover are:

515.   i. **Jasper H. Keefover**, b. 08 Oct 1857, Job Township, Monongalia County, West Virginia; d. 15 Jan 1944, St. Joseph, Buchanan County, Missouri.

516.   ii. **Caroline M. Keefover**, b. November 1860, Job Township, Monongalia County, West Virginia; d. 31 Oct 1900, Waterville, Marshall County, Kansas.

517.   iii. **William John Keefover**, b. 07 Dec 1864, Job Township, Monongalia County, West Virginia; d. 19 Jul 1934, Oketo, Marshall County, Kansas

518.   iv. **Thomas Willard Keefover**, b. 1867, Job Township, Monongalia County, West

Virginia; d. 1936.
519. v. **James Eddie Keefover**, b. 30 May 1869, Job Township, Monongalia County, West Virginia; d. 19 Apr 1952, Waterville, Marshall County, Kansas.
520. vi. **Frank Azim Keefover**, b. 17 Jan 1873, Walnut Township, Waterville, Marshall County, Kansas; d. 1934.

505.

Mary Ann Freeland, daughter of No. 496, Margaret Ellen Prichard, was born 05 Apr 1837, and died 05 Feb 1888, in Wadestown, Monongalia County, West Virginia. She married **John MORRIS,** 05 Apr 1857, in Wadestown, Monongalia County, West Virginia. He was born 10 Jan 1826, and died at Wadestown on 05 May 1913.
Children of Mary Ann Freeland and John Morris are:
521. i. **Charles Albert Morris**, b. 17 Jan 1858, Wadestown, Monongalia County, (West) Virginia; d. 14 Dec 1946 in Manhattan, Pottawatomie County, Kansas.
ii. **Margaret Alice Morris**, b. 1860.
iii. **Thomas J. Morris,** b. 1862; d. 1933; m. **Almira DILLE** (b. 1864; d. 1924).
iv. **Sarah Morris**, b. 1865; d. 1939; m. **Solomon M. SHRIVER** (b. abt. 1859; d. 1949).
v. **Amy Laura Morris,** b. 1868; d. 1956; m. **Ephraim Lee MARTIN** (b. 1860; d. 1949).
Vi. **Mary Josephine Morris**, b. 1870; d. 1946; m. **Marion Silas HENDERSON** (b. Abt. 1866; d. 1946).
vii. **Samuel P. Morris**, b. 1873; d. 1894.

viii. **Oella Rebecca "Bessie" Morris**, b. 1873; d.
1946; m. **Jasper Newton NAY** (b. 1869; d.
1945).

506.

William Freeland, son of No. 496, Margaret Ellen Prichard,
was born 1840 in Marion County, (West) Virginia, and died
1917. He married **Sarah A. ARNETT**. She was born in 1848.
Children of William Freeland and Sarah Arnett are:
  i. **Mary Freeland.**
  ii. **Charles Freeland**, b. 1871.
  iii. **Harry Jay Freeland**, b. 1874.
  iv. **Eleanor Freeland**, b. 1876.
  v. **Marcus D. Freeland**, b. 1878.
  vi. **Maggie B. Freeland**, b. 1879.

507.

John Willard Freeland, son of No. 496, Margaret Ellen
Prichard, was born 1841 in Marion County, (West) Virginia.
He married **Isabella McMURRAY**.
Children of John Freeland and Isabella McMurray are:
  i. **Eleanor Margaret Freeland.**
  ii. **Isabelle V. Freeland.**
  iii. **Thomas Freeland.**
  iv. **John Freeland.**
  v. **McMurray Freeland.**
  vi. **Muriel Freeland.**

508.

Thomas Freeland, Jr., son of No. 496, Margaret Ellen
Prichard, was born 1847 in Marion County, West Virginia, and
died in 1927. He married **Maria ROBEY**, who was born in

1846, and died in 1925.
Children of Thomas Freeland and Maria Robey are:
    i. **May M. Freeland**, b. 1872.
    ii. **Minerva G. Freeland**, b. 1875.
    iii. **James W. Freeland**, b. 1879.

509.

Louise M. Prichard, daughter of No. 498, John Prichard, was born 01 Mar 1841, in Monongalia County, (West) Virginia, and died 08 May 1926, in Fort Scott, Bourbon County, Kansas. She married **Jesse MILLER**, 25 Sep 1866, in Harrison County, West Virginia. He was born 08 Jun 1834, in Boothesville, Monongalia County, (West) Virginia, and died 19 Feb 1921, in Fort Scott, Bourbon County, Kansas. He is buried in Glen Dale Cemetery, Glen Dale, Marshall County, West Virginia.
Children of Louisa M. Prichard and Jesse Miller are:
    i. **John Thomas Miller**, b. 12 Jul 1867, Sardis, Harrison County, West Virginia; d. 08 Sep 1940, Fort Scott, Bourbon County, Kansas.
    ii. **Elizabeth "Lizzie" Miller**, b. 24 Sep 1869, Sardis, Harrison County, West Virginia; d. 08 Jan 1934, Gardner, Huerfano County, Colorado; m. **James SCRIMSER.**
    iii. **Margaret Vesta Miller**, b. 15 Nov 1871, Sardis, Harrison County, West Virginia; d. 22 Dec 1927, Fort Scott, Bourbon County, Kansas.
    iv. **Joseph Arthur Miller**, b. 26 Dec1873, Sardis, Harrison County, West Virginia; d. 08 May 1934, Hutchinson, Reno County, Kansas; m. **Laura Amelia HALL**, 23 Sep 1902, Devon, Bourbon County, Kansas.

    v. **Wilbur Francis Miller**, b. 10 Mar 1876, Sardis,
        Harrison County, West Virginia; d. 08 May
        1934, Halstead, Harvey County, Kansas.
    vi. **Fannie Louella Miller**, b. 10 Jun 1878, Sardis,
        Harrison County, West Virginia; d. 03 Jan 1942,
        Fort Scott, Bourbon County, Kansas.
    vii. **Harvey Festus Miller**, b. 19 Sep 1880, Fairmont,
        Marion County, West Virginia; d. 28 Mar 1965,
        Fort Scott, Bourbon County, Kansas.
    viii. **Clara Emma Miller**, b. 06 Aug 1883, Fairmont,
        Marion County, West Virginia; d. 05 Jul 1977,
        Fort Scott, Bourbon County, Kansas.

510.

Margaret A. Prichard, daughter of No. 497, John Prichard, was born 21 Sep 1843, in Marion County, (West) Virginia, and died 15 Nov 1915, in Kansas. She married **Joseph MILLER**. He was born 17 Jan 1838, in Monongalia County, (West) Virginia.
Children of Margaret A. Prichard and Joseph Miller are:
    i. **Thomas Homer Miller.**
    ii. **Clark Miller**, b. 22 Mar 1865, Harrison
        County, West Virginia.
    iii. **George Robert Miller**, b. 23 Dec 1871,
        Marion County, West Virginia.

511.

Charles Albert Pritchard, son of No. 499, Alpheus W. Pritchard, was born 1850 in Mannington, Marion County, West Virginia, and died in 1945. He never married. He enrolled in the West Virginia Agricultural College, Morgantown, in 1867 and was a student there the next year when the school became

West Virginia University. He lived nearly 95 years, outliving all the students and faculty members who were at WVU in 1868. He farmed most of his life and also was associated with his father in the operation of a general store and a lumber business. He taught school several years in Missouri and homesteaded in Kansas, but returned to West Virginia when his father died suddenly in 1884. Charles Prichard was the Mannington postmaster, served on the town council, and was a member of the West Virginia House of Delegates.

512.

Arthur Lathrop Prichard, son of No. 499, Alpheus W. Prichard, was born 11 Mar 1857 in Mannington, (West) Virginia and died 01 Sep 1938 in Mannington, Marion County. He married (1) **Mary WOODBURN** (b. 1859; d. 20 Aug 1893 in Charleston, West Virginia 12 Oct 1881. He married (2) **Katherine KIMBERLIN** (b. 23 Oct 1868; d. 08 Sep 1943) in 1895.

Children of Arthur Lathrop Prichard and Mary Woodburn are:

522. i. **Gypsy Prichard**, b. 24 Apr 1883 in Marion County, West Virginia; d. 06 Oct 1956 in Charleston, West Virginia.

ii. **Hugh Woodburn Prichard**, b. 03 Sep 1884, Marion County, West Virginia; d. 26 Mar 1918.

iii. **Lena Beryl Prichard**, b. 10 Mar 1888; d. 29 Mar 1963.

Children of Arthur Lathrop Prichard and Katherine Kimberlin are:

iv. **Helen Cotter Prichard**, b. 22 Jul 1897; d. Aug 1923 Baltimore, Maryland.

523. v. **Arthur Cornwell Prichard**, b. 07 Sep 1904, Mannington, Marion County, West

Virginia; d. 09 Dec 1990, Mannington,
Marion County, West Virginia

513.

Absalom Wellington Prichard, son of No. 500, Amos
Newton Prichard, was born 07 Aug 1852 in Marion County,
(West) Virginia and died 20 Nov 1934 in Marion County, West
Virginia. He married **Sarah Ann CONWAY,** 17 Aug 1879, in
Marion County, West Virginia. She was born November 1854
in Marion County, and died 22 Oct 1935 in Marion County.
Child of Absalom Prichard and Sarah Ann Conway is:
524.   i. **Chester Lamar Prichard**, b. 06 Nov1884,
            Mannington, Marion County, West Virginia; d.
            07 Feb 1962, Pittsburgh, Allegheny County,
            Pennsylvania.

514.

Charles Amos Prichard, son of No. 500, Amos Newton
Prichard, was born 06 Jan 1856 in Paw Paw, Marion County,
(West) Virginia, and died 17 Dec 1886 in Mannington, Marion
County, West Virginia. He married **Ida ERWIN,** 17 Feb 1881,
in Mannington, West Virginia.
Child of Charles Prichard and Ida Erwin is:
525.   i. **Charles Walter Prichard**, b. 10 May 1882,
            Mannington, West Virginia; d. 19 Dec
            1939, Mannington.

FOURTH GENERATION

515.

Jasper H. Keefover, son of No. 504, Hannah Freeland, was born 08 Oct 1857 in Job Township, Monongalia County, West Virginia, and died 15 Jan 1944, in St. Joseph, Buchanan County, Missouri at the home of his daughter Verna. He married **Amanda SIMMON**, 13 Mar 1884, in Buchanan County, Missouri. She was born 22 May 1858 in Buchanan County, Missouri, and died 06 Apr 1930, in St. Joseph, Buchanan County, Missouri. Jasper's obituary says that he moved to Kansas at the age of 12. He was a farmer, and a member of the Methodist Church in Barnes, Kansas. He died at the age of 71 years, 10 months, 24 days, and was buried in Maplewood Cemetery, Barnes, Washington County, Kansas.

Children of Jasper Keefover and Amanda Simmon are:

526.   i. **Verna L. Keefover**, b. November 1885.

527.   ii. **Raymond Jasper Keefover**, b. 25 Jul 1890, Barnes, Washington County, Kansas; d. 25 Jun 1965, VA Hospital, Topeka, Shawnee County, Kansas.

    iii. **Floyd Keefover**, b. 19 Mar 1894, Washington County, Kansas; d. 16 Aug 1895, age one year, four months, and nineteen days, Washington County, Kansas; bur. Waterville Cemetery.

528.   iv. **Iva A. Keefover**, b. 04 Jul 1896, Barnes, Washington County, Kansas; d. 04 Aug 1986, Portland. Multnomah County, Oregon.

448

516.

Caroline M. Keefover, daughter of No 504, Hannah Freeland, was born November 1860 in Job Township, Monongalia County, West Virginia, and died 31 Oct 1900 in Waterville, Marshall County, Kansas, of tuberculosis. She married **Frank J. JACQUES**, at her father's house, Walnut Township, Marshall County, Kansas, on 09 Mar 1884. He was born 1863 in Indiana, the son of **Theophilus JACQUES**, who was born 1836 in Ohio to parents who were born in Switzerland, and **Mary MISER,** whose parents were born in Ohio and North Carolina. According to family members, when Caroline's brothers went on the Oklahoma land run in 1889, James and the others stopped in Wichita and discovered that Frank had left Caroline with two small children, Rex and Harry. They took her back to Waterville where she was living with her father in the 1900 Census. The death records in the County office list her death from a tumor at 39 years. Her obituary says in part: *"...For a number of years her health has been frail but she has bravely borne hardship and struggled to keep her little family together. About two months ago, she took a severe cold and...rapidly declined...She leaves her father, five brothers, and two sons...She experienced religion in early life and in July, 1874, was baptized into the Baptist Church of Waterville...Her remains were laid to rest in the Waterville Cemetery."*

Children of Carolina Keefover and Frank Jacques are:

529.   i. **Harry E. Jacques**, b. December 1884, Nebraska; d. 1960, Shawnee Mission, Johnson County, Kansas.

         ii. **Rexford E. Jacques**, b. February 1891, Nebraska; d. 02 Dec 1956, Kansas City, Jackson County, Missouri; m. **Violet H. UNK,** taught school in

1913; became a dentist, as did his brother.

517.

William John Keefover, son of No. 504, Hannah Freeland, was born 07 Dec 1864, in Job Township, Monongalia County, West Virginia, and died 19 Jul 1934 in Oketo, Marshall County, Kansas, at the Lon Livingston Home. He married **Addie A. BINGHAM** (some records spell it Bigham), daughter of **Andrew BINGHAM** and **Eliza MATTHEWS**, on 03 Nov 1887. The service was conducted by S. T. Todd, Justice of Peace, Frankfort, Marshall County, Kansas. She was born 26 Apr 1864 in Toronto, Canada, and died 03 Jun 1926 in Oketo, Marshall County, Kansas. William John Keefover was a farmer and a Pentecostal preacher.

Children of William John Keefover and Addie Bingham are:

      i. **Archie Bingham Keefover**, b. 27 Jul 1888, Waterville, Marshall County, Kansas; d. 12 May 1952, Topeka, Shawnee County, Kansas; m. **Bertha BLACK**, 17 Feb 1914, St. Joseph, Buchanan County, Missouri; no children; bur. Maysville Cemetery, Marshall County, Kansas.

530.   ii. **Otis William Keefover**, b. 11 Jul 1889, Waterville, Marshall County, Kansas; d. 12 May 1952, Topeka, Shawnee County, Kansas.

      iii. **Claude/Clyde Keefover**, b. 22 Aug 1891, Waterville, Marshall County, Kansas; d. 28 Sep 1891; bur. Riverside Cemetery, Waterville.

531.   iv. **George Edward Keefover**, b. 15 Jul 1896, Oketo, Marshall County, Kansas; d. 08 Jul 1972, Beatrice, Gage County, Nebraska.

532.   v. **Elreno Manilla Keefover**, b. 23 Jul 1901, Oketo, Marshall County, Kansas; d. 02 Feb 1983,

The Pritchard/Prickett Family History

Manhattan, Riley County, Kansas.

518.

Thomas Willard Keefover, son of No. 504, Hannah Freeland, was born 1867 in Job Township, Monongalia County, West Virginia, and died in 1936, according to his tombstone, but the family records say 1935. He married **Maggie Melissa BINGHAM**, daughter of **Andrew BINGHAM** and **Eliza MATTHEWS**, on 06 Nov 1892, in the residence of Andrew Bingham, by Rev. E. D. Christman, Minister. Maggie was born 02 Jan 1869 in Criston, Ogle County, Illinois, and died 01 Jan 1943.

Children of Thomas Keefover and Maggie Bingham are:
  i. **Cecil Keefover**, b. ?; d. August 1978.
  ii. **Ludie Keefover**, b. 31 Aug 1902, Axtell, Marshall County, Kansas; d. 19 Jul 1969, Yakima, Yakima County, Washington; m. **Unk ROGERS**; bur. West Hills Memorial Park, Yakima, Washington.
  iii. **Liza Keefover.**
  iv. **Pauline Keefover.**

519.

James Eddie Keefover, son of No. 504, Hannah Freeland, was born 30 May 1869, in Job Township, Monongalia County, West Virginia, and died 29 Apr 1952, in Waterville, Marshall County, Kansas. He married **Elnora Sarah SCHOLFIELD,** 21 Oct 1890, in Marysville, Marshall County, Kansas, daughter of **John SCHOLFIELD** and **Sarah McCURDY**. She was born 20 Nov 1871, in Hamilton, Steuben County, Indiana, and died 21 Mar 1954, in Marysville, Marshall County, Kansas. Elnora went to Kansas with her family when she was 16 years old. She lived with her grandparents because her stepmother did not want her. Her grandfather, Samuel Scholfield, was a doctor. Elnora rode with him to help take care of the patients. She helped out as needed all of her life as a nurse to the sick. Her father got her inheritance from her mother's family and used it as her guardian. When he died, the money was left to his second family.

James separated from Elnora in 1925. He wrote (or copied) many poems, and left a clipping of his 81st birthday celebration with a poem:

> *I am burdened tonight with an old, old grief,*
> *As I gaze through the mist of the by-gone years.*
> *Memory opens the book of time,*
> *And some of the pages are stained with tears. "*

He participated in the Cherokee Strip Run to Oklahoma on 22 Apr 1889 with his brothers Will, Thomas, and Frank, his cousin Joe, and their friends Thomas Rodgers, Bill Inglesbee, George Bingham, and Bill Colgrove. Four rode in a covered wagon, the rest on horseback. They left Barnes one month ahead of time and registered at Ark City. James got a claim to land, but a brother told him there was better land ahead. He ended up with none.

Children of James Keefover and Elnora Scholfield are:

533.   i. **Walter Melvin Keefover**, b. 11 May 1892, Walnut Township, Marshall County, Kansas; d. 25 Apr 1934, Hines, Illinois.

534.   ii. **Epha Hannah Keefover**, b. 23 Mar 1894, Walnut Township, Marshall County, Kansas; d. 03 Jan 1968, Marysville, Marshall County, Kansas.

535.   iii. **Merle Arthur Hazen Keefover**, b. 12 Jun 1896, Walnut Township, Marshall County, Kansas; d.

03 Sep 1980, Marysville.

iv. **Harry Keefover**, b. 05 Dec 1898, Walnut
Township, Marshall County, Kansas; d.
06 Nov 1917, Marshall County, Kansas of blood
poisoning from scratching his arm on a
pitchfork. Last words: "Oh Papa, how beautiful
and it is miles and miles away (the beautiful,
beautiful land where Jesus is)"; bur. Riverside
Cemetery, Waterville.

536.   v. **Claude Ellis Keefover**, b. 14 Oct 1900, Walnut
Township, Marshall County, Kansas; d. 28
Feb 1992, Topeka, Shawnee County, Kansas.

537.   vi. **Thelma Sarah Keefover**, b. 05 Dec 1905, Walnut
Township, Marshall County, Kansas; d. 05 Apr
1983, Topeka, Shawnee County, Kansas.

538.   vii. **Verne Clarence Keefover**, b. 30 Jul 1908, Walnut
Township, Marshall County, Kansas.

520.

Frank Azim Keefover, son of No. 504, Hannah Freeland, was
born 17 Jan 1893 in Walnut Township, Waterville, Marshall
County, Kansas, and died in 1934. He married (1) **Daisy
DICKEY** in 1904; he married (2) **Marian UNK.**
After graduating from Waterville High School, where he gave
an oration, "Napoleon Bonaparte," he attended Cedar Rapids
Business College, followed by the Marshall County Teachers'
Institute, where he received his teaching certificate. He became
a teacher, school principal, and banker, as well as an artist and
poet. His wife published a book of his poetry. He was a
member of the Jackson Rifles and a lieutenant in the Bledsoe
Light Guards. Among his poems are two written in honor of his
mother, "The Hat My Mother Wore" and "In Kansas Out on

the Wagon Train." He was buried in the Riverside Cemetery, Marshall County, Kansas.

521.

Charles Albert Morris, son of No. 505, Mary Ann Freeland, was born 17 Jan 1858, at Wadestown, Monongalia County, West Virginia, and died 13 Dec 1946, at Manhattan, Riley County, Kansas. He married **Martha E. HAUGHT** on 17 Sep 1882. She was born at Wadestown on 07 Dec 1860, and died 01 Jul 1946 at Manhattan, Riley County, Kansas.
Child of Charles Albert Morris and Martha E. Haught is:
    i. **Velma Morris**; m. **Frank A. HAGANS.**

522.

Gypsy Prichard, daughter of No. 512, Arthur Lathrop Prichard, was born 24 Apr 1993 in Marion County, West Virginia and died 06 Oct. 1956 in Charleston, West Virginia. She married **Ralph M. "Doc" HITE** in 1908.
Children of Gypsy Prichard and Ralph M. Hite are:
    i. **Mary F. Hite Phillips.**
    ii. **Thomas Arthur Hite.**
    iii. **Ralph M. Hite**

523.

Arthur Cornwell Prichard, son of No. 512, Arthur Lathrop Prichard, was born 07 Sep 1904 in Mannington, West Virginia at the family home on Pleasant Street and died 09 Sept 1990 in Mannington in the same house where he and his wife had lived since 1963. He. He married **Mildred Emogene HUGHES,** 10 Jun 1939, in Joliet, Illinois, daughter of **Guy HUGHES** and **Mildred BUTTS.** Mildred was born 23 Jul 1906 in Springfield, Missouri. She died 09 October 2001 at home in

Manning. Both are buried in the Mannington Cemetery.
Arthur Prichard was a Presbyterian minister with pastorates in
Ohio; Pennsylvania; Wheeling, West Virginia (18 years), and
Mannington, West Virginia. For 25 years, he was chairman of
the Good Samaritan Project in Korea. This was an inter-
denominational group which opened two Christian agricultural
training schools in South Korea. He also chaired the
Westminster Foundation's Board of Directors at West Virginia
University and the Upper Buffalo Creek Watershed
Association flood control in Marion County. He returned to
Mannington in late 1960 to be the minister of the First
Presbyterian Church for a few years before retiring. After
retirement, he and his wife traveled a great deal.

Children of Arthur Prichard and Mildred Hughes are:

539.   i. **Mildred Katherine Prichard,** b. 11 Feb 1941 in Butler, Pennsylvania, and d. 25 Aug 207 in Albuquerque, New Mexico.
540.   ii. **Albert Hughes Prichard**, b. Mannington, Marion County, West Virginia.
541.   iii. **Philip Arthur Prichard**.
542.   iv. **Virginia Louise Prichard**.

524.

Chester Lamar Prichard, son of No. 513, Absalom
Wellington Prichard, was born 06 Nov 1884 in Mannington,
West Virginia and died 07 Feb 1962 in Pittsburgh, Allegany
County, Pennsylvania. He married **Edna Frances MASON** 26
Oct 1915 in Wheeling, Ohio County, West Virginia.

Children of Chester Prichard and Edna Mason are:

    i. **Susan Rebecca Prichard**, b. 27 Jan 1918, Marion County, West Virginia; m. **Frank Borton CASE**, 27 Jan 1943, Harford

County, Maryland. Frank Borton Case was a
Col. (ret.) USA.

  ii. **Sara Jane Prichard**, b. 05 Oct 1927; m.
William Corner DEAN, Ph.D., 01 Apr
1950, Erie, Erie County, Pennsylvania.

iii. **Martha Mason Prichard**, b. 23 Mar 1932; m.
Frank W. SKLEDER. She operated F.W.
Skleder Books, Pittsburgh, Allegheny County,
Pennsylvania.

525.

Charles Walter Prichard, son of No. 514, Charles Amos
Prichard, was born 10 May 1882 in Mannington, Marion
County, West Virginia and died 19 Dec 1939 in Mannington.
He married **Nellie BURCHINAL** 09 Apr 1913.
Child of Charles Prichard and Nellie Burchinal is:

543.   i. **Emily Prichard**, b. 07 Apr 1916, Mannington,
West Virginia; d. 12 Jun 1998, Elkins,
Randolph County, West Virginia.

FIFTH GENERATION

526.
Verna L. Keefover, daughter of No. 515, Jasper H. Keefover, was born November 1885. She married **Blaine P. JOHNSON**. He was born 1885 in Barnes, Washington County, Kansas, and died 12 Mar 1971, in St. Joseph, Buchanan County, Missouri. He worked at American National Bank and was a Scottish Rite 32nd degree Mason and member of Masonic Lodge No. 78. Child of Verna Keefover and Blaine Johnson is:
    i. **Willard Johnson.**

527.
Raymond Jasper Keefover, son of No. 515, Jasper H. Keefover, was born 25 Jul 1890 in Barnes, Washington County, Kansas, and died 25 Jun 1965 in the VA Hospital, Topeka, Shawnee County, Kansas. He is buried in Maplewood Cemetery, Barnes, Washington County, Kansas. He married **Olivia FELLOWS,** whose father killed himself, according to Ruth Eichelberger of Lincoln, Nebraska, a descendant. Raymond was a veteran of World War I, a member of the American Legion, and of the Odd Fellows Lodge.
Child of Raymond Keefover and Olivia Fellows is:
544.   i. **Ladd Stanley Keefover**, d. March 29, 1996, Gladstone, Clay County, Missouri.

528.
Iva A. Keefover, daughter of No. 515, Jasper H. Keefover, was born 04 Jul 1896, in Barnes, Washington County, Kansas, and died 04 Aug 1986, in Portland, Multnomah County, Oregon. She married **Guy W. WEBSTER**, 06 Feb 1921, at the

home of her sister, Mrs. P. V. Johnson. She lived in Manhattan, Kansas until 1980.

Children of Iva Keefover and Guy Webster are:

    i. **Robert O. Webster;** lives in Palo Alto, Santa Clara County, California.

    ii. **Thomas G. Webster**; a physician in Bethesda, Montgomery County, Maryland.

    iii. **Max R. Webster**; lives in Portland, Multnomah County, Oregon.

    iv. **Suzanne Webster;** lives in Portland, Multnomah County, Oregon.

529.

Harry E. Jacques, son of No. 516, Caroline M. Keefover, was born December 1884 in Nebraska, and died 1960 in Shawnee Mission, Johnson County, Kansas. He married **Ilene DAVIS**, 1921, in Kansas City, Clay County, Missouri. Harry taught at the Keefover School in 1913, later became a dentist.

Children of Harry Jacques and Ilene Davis are:

    i. **Jackie Jacques**; m. **Unk DICKERSON.**

545.   ii. **Mary Ellen Jacques**, b. 10 Mar 1922.

    iii. **Ruth Jacques.**

530.

Otis William Keefover, son of No. 517, William John Keefover, was born 11 Jul 1889 in Waterville, Marshall County, Kansas, and died 12 May 1952 in Topeka, Shawnee County, Kansas. He married **Ruth L. WARNER**, 20 Jan 1915, in Wamego, Pottawatamie County, Kansas. She was born in 1889 and died in 1952.

Children of Otis Keefover and Ruth Warner are:

    i. **Carol J. Keefover**, b.27 Apr 1917; m. **John**

The Pritchard/Prickett Family History

MURPHY.
546.   ii. **William L. Keefover**, b. 02 Jul 1920, Marietta,
           Marshall County, Kansas.
          iii. **John Wesley Keefover**, b. 12 Jun 1923.
          iv. **Luther Leroy Keefover**, b. 16 Mar 1928.
          v. **Ava Louise Keefover**, b. 12 Sep 1929; m. **Herbert**
          SEEL.

531.
George Edward Keefover, Sr., son of No. 517, William John
Keefover, was born 15 Jul 1896, in Oketo, Marshall County,
Kansas, and died 08 Jul 1972, in Beatrice, Gage County,
Nebraska. He married **Reba CHAMPAGNE**, 30 Aug 1917, in
Westmoreland, Pottawatomie County, Kansas. She was born
04 Mar 1898, in Oketo, and died 02 Nov 1988, in Wymore
Nursing Home, Gage County, Nebraska. George is buried in
the Oketo Cemetery.
Children of George Keefover and Reba Champagne are:
          i. **Donald Leslie Keefover**, b. 24 Apr 1918.
547.   ii. **Daryl William Keefover**, b. 01 Dec 1920.
548.   iii. **Stanley Dean Keefover**, b. 09 Jul 1924.
549.   iv. **George Edward Keefover, Jr.,** b. 21 Oct 1930.

532.
Elreno Manilla Keefover, daughter of No. 517, William John
Keefover, was born 23 Jul 1901, in Oketo, Marshall County,
Kansas, and died 03 Feb 1983, in Manhattan, Riley County,
Kansas. She married **Lon W. LIVINGSTON**, 03 Feb 1919, in
Marysville, Marshall County, Kansas, at the Baptist parsonage.
Lon was born in Summerfield, Kansas.
Child of Elreno Keefover and Lon Livingston is:
550.   i. **Wayne Arlo Livingston**, b. 09 Sep 1920, Barnston,

Gage County, Nebraska; d. 20 Aug 1982,
Manhattan, Riley County, Kansas.

533.

Walter Melvin Keefover, Sr., son of No. 519, James Eddie
Keefover, was born 11 May 1892, in Walnut Township,
Marshall County, Kansas, and died 25 Apr 1934, at a hospital
in Illinois, of cancer of the mouth. He married **Alice F. COX,**
30 Mar 1922, in Topeka, Shawnee County, Kansas, daughter of
Charles COX and **Kate IRWIN.** She was born 01 Sep 1904 in
Topeka, Shawnee County, Kansas, and died 24 Feb 1992 in
Colorado Springs, El Paso County, Colorado. Walter entered
the U.S. Army 15 Jun 1917 at Jefferson Barracks, Kansas, and
was sent to France. He was discharged at Camp Zachary
Taylor, Kentucky, on 14 Jun 1919. In his early years, he
worked in the Dakota wheat fields during harvesting season.
He was a member of the Masonic Lodge in Topeka, Kansas,
and Alice, his wife, was a member of the Rebekah Lodge No.
664. She was a Past Noble Grand and District Deputy President
of that Organization. She was a librarian in Marysville, Kansas
from 1949-1955. Walter was a barber. He had all of his teeth
pulled, but one, which made a lesion in his cheek and caused
the cancer.

Children of Walter Keefover and Alice Cox are:

> i. **Walter Melvin Keefover, Jr.,** b. 22 Feb 1924,
> Topeka, Shawnee County, Kansas; d. 11 May
> 1997, Peoria, Illinois; entered the U.S. Navy
> 10 Feb 1941, trained at Farragut, Idaho and the
> Naval Hospital, San Diego, California; went
> overseas 19 Jun 1944, served in Pacific theater
> during World War II: invasion of Pelelieu, Palou
> Group with First Marine Division New

Caledonia, Guadalcanal; discharged Great Lakes Naval Station, Illinois, 25 Feb 1946.

  ii. **Virginia Ann Keefover**, b. 03 Jul 1926, Topeka, Shawnee County, Kansas.

534.

Epha Hannah Keefover, daughter of No. 519, James Eddie Keefover, was born 23 Mar 1894, in Walnut Township, Marshall County, Kansas, and died in the hospital at Marysville, Marshall County, Kansas. Epha is buried in Riverside Cemetery, Waterville, Marshall County, Kansas. She married **Grover C. HEARN**, 14 Dec 1916, in Marysville. He was born 05 Jan 1888, in Little Blue Town, Washington County, Kansas, and died 17 Nov 1980, in the Marysville Nursing Home, Marshall County, Kansas. At age 12, Grover decided to stay in Kansas when his parents left to move to Oregon. He lived with his uncle and aunt, the David Campbells, farming and working on threshing crews. At age 16, he purchased a steam engine and separator for $1,500 and threshed around Waterville and western Kansas. He later purchased a sawmill and sawed lumber along Little Blue. He and Epha lived on the Stephenson place west of Waterville until it burned in January 1966, at which time they moved to Waterville.

Children of Epha Keefover and Grover Hearn are:

551. i. **Phyllis Jean Hearn,** b. 06 May 919; d. 13 Dec 1998.

  ii. **Donald Keith Hearn.**

  iii. **Robert Hearn**; m. **Mildred SWEARINGEN.**

  iv. **Floyd Hearn**, b. 16 May 1921; m. **Nellie UNK;** entered U.S. Air Force 10 Sep 1942, served in European theatre; awarded Bronze Star medal,

461

Good Conduct medal; discharged Ft.
Leavenworth, Kansas 30 Aug 1945 with rank of
Staff Sergeant.
552.   v. **Arlene Elnora Hearn**, b. 12 Sep 1925.
553.   vi. **David Hearn**, b. 24 Dec 1935.

535.

Merle Arthur Hazen Keefover, son of No. 519, James Eddie
Keefover, always thought he was born 12 June 1896 in Walnut
Township, Marshall County, Kansas, but county records say it
was 12 May 1896; they most likely are correct. He died 03 Sep
1980, in Marysville, Marshall County, Kansas, of pancreatic
cancer. He married **Gladys Ruby JACOBSON**, 16 Jun 1921,
in the home of her parents, Harbaugh Township, Waterville,
Marshall County, Kansas. She was born 07 Mar 1900 in
Harbaugh Township, and died 16 Apr 1987, in Manhattan,
Riley County, Kansas. They met at the Barnes Carnival in
August 1920, introduced by Thelma Keefover. On his 45th
anniversary, he said he hoped his children were as happy as he
was with his wife after that many years. Two hours before their
wedding, there was a downpour. The groom arrived with his
two brothers in a horse and buggy and the brothers made a
bower of wild flowers in the corner of the parlor. Judith,
Gladys's sister, was to bring a cake, but couldn't get there in
the storm, so Gladys baked a cake while waiting for her guests.
Gifts to the newlyweds were four dozen hens, 10 chicks, one
pig, one cow, dishes, pots and pans, an antique dresser, and $25
worth of groceries. Merle was a slow moving, quiet, gentle,
happy-go-lucky person who loved his family and
grandchildren. Their hobbies were gardening, fishing, going
places, and being with their family. Gladys loved music. She
played the piano for silent movies while in her early twenties,

and also played with a neighborhood orchestra. She taught
piano and violin, and said that she stayed home and memorized
music instead of going to high school. She could sit down and
play a song as soon as she heard it.

      Merle joined the U. S. Army on 05 Sep 1918 and was
stationed at Camp Funston, where he loaded bodies on wagons
during the big flu epidemic. His mother said she dreamed he
had the flu the night before receiving his letter telling her that
he was ill. He was discharged 29 Mar 1919. He was a farmer
for 42 years, and also worked at Union Pacific for two years
before being laid off in January 1946, then started at Archer-
Daniels 17 Jan 1946, and worked there until he was laid off 27
Feb 1959. He and Gladys operated a lawn care service for the
Marysville City Park, and maintained flower beds for an
elderly lady until reaching their mid-70's. Merle never had a
cold or headache, but had rheumatism in later life. One leg
shrank several inches, and he wore a built-up shoe. He used
two canes for walking.

Children of Merle Keefover and Gladys Jacobson are:

554.   i. **Wayland Rexford Keefover**, b. 28 Aug 1922,
              Walnut Township, Marshall County, Kansas.

555.   ii. **Dean Harland Keefover**, b. 29 Feb 1924,
              Waterville, Marshall County, Kansas; d.
              22 Oct 1983, Manhattan Riley County,
              Kansas.

556.   iii. **Kenneth Merle Keefover**, b. 15 Jul 1928,
              Walnut Township, Marshall County, Kansas.

557.   iv. **Darrell Leon Keefover**, b. 10 Feb 1932, Walnut
              Township, Waterville, Marshall County,
              Kansas.

558.   v. **Ramona Joyce Keefover**, b. 06 Nov, 1934,
              Randolph, Riley County, Kansas.

vi. **Romea Jacobson Keefover**, b. 06 Nov 1934, Randolph, Riley County, Kansas; d. 06 Nov 1934, Riley County, Kansas; second of set of twins; bur. Riverside Cemetery, Waterville, Marshall County, Kansas.

559.   vii. **Karen Delores Keefover**, b. 06 Dec 1936, Center Hill Township, Riley County, Kansas.

536.

Claude Ellis Keefover, son of No. 519, James Eddie Keefover, was born 14 Oct, 1900, in Walnut Township, Marshall County, Kansas, and died 28 Feb 1992, at McCrite Plaza, Topeka, Shawnee County, Kansas of a stroke. He was a barber, painter, and helped cook meals at the Moose Lodge. He married **Mary Elizabeth RICE**, 28 Aug 1922, in Marysville, Marshall County, Kansas. Mary Elizabeth was born 15 Aug 1907 and was adopted by the Rice family of Cottage Hill before she was a year old.

Children of Claude Keefover and Mary Rice are:

560.   i. **Gail Jean Keefover**, b. 21 Mar 1923, Waterville, Marshall County, Kansas; d. 23 Oct, 1995 in Georgia.
561.   ii. **Jacqueline D. Keefover**, b. 04 Mar 1925, Waterville, Marshall County, Kansas.
562   iii. **James Milo Keefover**, b. 25 Oct 1929, Waterville, Marshall County, Kansas.
563.   iv. **Joan Maxine Keefover**, b. 25 Oct 1929, Waterville, Marshall County, Kansas.
564.   v. **Deanne Charlotte Keefover**, b. 15 Sep 1932, Waterville, Marshall County, Kansas.
565.   vi. **Geraldine Keefover**, b. 06 Feb 1934, Waterville, Marshall County, Kansas.

464

566.   vii. **Rolland Rex Keefover**, b. 15 Sep 1936, Waterville,
        Marshall County, Kansas.

        viii. **Michael Clark Keefover,** b. 18 Jul 1939,
        Waterville, Marshall County, Kansas.

567   ix. **Claudette Jean Keefover**, b. 27 Sep 1943,
        Waterville, Marshall County, Kansas.

        x. **Daniel Leon Keefover**, b. 09 Sep 1945,
        Waterville, Marshall County, Kansas.

537.

Thelma Sarah Keefover, daughter of No. 519, James Eddie
Keefover, was born 05 Dec 1905, in Walnut Township,
Marshall County, Kansas and died 05 Apr 1983, in Topeka,
Shawnee County, Kansas of pancreatic cancer. She married
George E. WEHMEIER, 09 Sep 1923, in the Presbyterian
manse in Hutchinson, Rice County, Kansas. He was born 23
Jul 1899, in St. Louis, Missouri, and died 17 Apr 1961, in
Rossville, Shawnee County, Kansas of a heart attack. Thelma
was a member of the Methodist Church of Waterville, the
Rebekah Lodge, and Royal Neighbors. She was a companion
housekeeper in the Lawrence, Douglas County, Kansas area
before retiring in 1974, and still had dark brown hair, brown
eyes, and her own teeth at the end of her life. Relatives
remember her infectious laugh. George was manager of grain
elevators before his retirement in 1960. He was also a strong
man in a carnival.

Children of Thelma Keefover and George Wehmeier are:

568.   i. **Marjorie Thelma Wehmeier**, b. 04 Dec 1924,
         Waterville, Marshall County, Kansas.

569.   ii. **Donna Mae Wehmeier**, b. 18 Oct 1926,
        Waterville, Marshall County, Kansas.

570.   iii. **George Eberle Wehmeier**, b. 10 Feb 1931,

Waterville, Marshall County, Kansas.
571.   iv. **Larry Gene Wehmeier**, b. 14 Jun 1936,
            Waterville, Marshall County, Kansas; d. 21
            Sep 1995, Lawrence, Douglas County, Kansas.
572.   v. **Linda Ellen Wehmeier**, b. 10 Jan 1939,
            Waterville, Marshall County, Kansas.
       vi. **Stephen Craig Wehmeier**, b. 24 Apr 1944,
            Waterville, Marshall County, Kansas.

538.

Verne Clarence Keefover, son of No. 519, James Eddie
Keefover, was born 30 Jul 1908, in Walnut Township,
Marshall County, Kansas. He married **Alice F. COX,** 25 Oct
1934, in Lawrence, Douglas County, Kansas, daughter of
Charles COX and **Kate IRWIN** and widow of No. 533,
Walter Melvin Keefover, Sr. Alice was born 01 Sep 1904, in
Topeka, Shawnee County, Kansas, and died 24 Feb 1992, in
Colorado Springs, El Paso County, Colorado. Verne was
employed by the Union Pacific Railroad, and he also worked as
a barber. Alice was a librarian in Marysville, Waterville,
Marshall County, Kansas, where she was buried in Riverside
Cemetery.
Children of Verne Keefover and Alice Cox are:
573.   i. **Richard Lee Keefover**, b. 25 Jan 1936, Walnut
            Township, Marshall County, Kansas.
       ii. **Sherrill Keefover**, b. 22 Nov 1940, Marysville,
            Marshall County, Kansas; m. **Fred WATEK.**

539.

Mildred Katherine Prichard, daughter of No. 523, Arthur
Cornwell Prichard, was born 11 Feb 1941 in Butler,
Pennsylvania and died 25 Aug 2007 in Albuquerque, New

Mexico. She married **Theodore LAPINA**, Ph.D., from Jeannette, Pennsylvania in Mannington on 20 Dec 1960. Ted was a professor of music at the University of Wyoming in Laramie, Wyoming. They retired to Rio Rancho, New Mexico. Children of Mildred Prichard and Theodore Lapina are:

    i. **Dawn Lynn Lapina**, b. 15 Aug 1967, Alexandria, Virginia. She married **Christopher LUNDVALL** of Laramie, Wyoming in 1991. They live in Rio Rancho, New Mexico.

    ii. **Theodore Scott Lapina**, b. 14 Apr 1970, Winchester, Virginia. He married **Marie MERCADO** in 2003 and divorced in 2009. Their children are: **Massimo Lapina**, b. 24 Feb 2005, and **Tazzio Lapina**, b. 28 Oct 2007. They live in Albuquerque, New Mexico.

540.

Albert Hughes Prichard, son of No. 523, Arthur Cornwell Prichard, was born 17 Dec 1943 in Wheeling. West Virginia. He married **Cheryl Lynn FICKEY**, Ed.D., daughter of **William Lynn FICKEY** and **Mildred Angeline ROSE** of Blacksville, West Virginia, on 25 Jun 1977 in Blacksville. Cheryl Lynn was born 27 Jul 1948 in Waynesburg, Pennsylvania. They live near Morgantown, Monongalia County, West Virginia He retired from West Virginia Public Broadcasting where he served in many capacities at the TV station WNPB and was station manager at his retirement. Since then, he has been ordained a permanent deacon in the Episcopal Church.

Children of Albert Prichard and Cheryl Fickey are:

574.   i. **Zachary William Prichard**, b. 14 Nov 1979, in Morgantown, West Virginia,

ii. **Angeline Rose Prichard**, b. 17 June 1988 in Morgantown, West Virginia. She is a librarian with Salisbury University, Salisbury, Maryland.

541.

Philip Arthur Prichard, son of No. 523, Arthur Cornwell Prichard, was born 31 May 1945 in Wheeling, West Virginia. He married **Helen Suzette NAPALO** of Mannington in Mannington on 15 Jul 1972. He is a lawyer in Mannington, Marion County, West Virginia. Both children are born of Suzette and adopted by Philip.

Children of Philip Prichard and Suzette Napalo are:

575.   i. **Joseph Virgil Prichard**, b. 18 Jan 1966, Chicago, Illinois

576.   ii. **Stacie Leigh Prichard**, b. 24 Sep 1968, South Bend, Indiana.

542.

Virginia Louise Prichard, daughter of No. 523, Arthur Cornwell Prichard, married (1) **Ivan SMEJKAL** (b. 12 Jul 1948; d. 05 Mar 1986) of Mnichovice u Prahy, Czech Republic. They were divorced. She married (2) **Ted DANSBY, Jr.** 20 Oct 1989 and they currently live in Murfeesboro, Tennessee, where she teaches at Middle Tennessee State University.

Children of Virginia Prichard and Ivan Smejkal are:

577   i. **Yvonne Smejkal.**

578.   ii. **Ingrid Smejkal.**

543.

Emily Prichard, daughter of No. 525, Charles Walter Prichard, was born 07 Apr 1916, in Mannington, Marion

County, West Virginia, and died 12 June 1998, in Elkins, Randolph County, West Virginia. She married **Milford L. GIBSON**, 07 Sep 1940, in Mt. Lake Park, Garrett County, Maryland. He died 17 Aug 1994. Emily graduated from West Virginia University with a degree in journalism. She worked at Davis and Elkins College and served as a hospital and Red Cross volunteer after World War II, with more than 20 years of service in Elkins hospitals.

Children of Emily Prichard and Milford Gibson are:

        i. **Joseph Prichard Gibson**; lives in Elkins, Randolph County, West Virginia.

579.   ii. **Sarah Gibson.**

SIXTH GENERATION

544.

Ladd Stanley Keefover, son of No. 527, Raymond Jasper Keefover, died 29 Mar 1996, in Gladstone, Clay County, Missouri. He married **Janice UNK.** He was a veteran of World War II, a member of the Parkville American Legion #318, and the Newmark Baptist Church.

Children of Ladd Stanley Keefover and Janice are:

    i. **Eric Keefover;** lives in Smithville, Clay County, Missouri.

    ii. **Kim Keefover;** m. **Unk RICHARDSON**; lives in Waco, McLennan County, Texas.

    iii. **Elaine Keefover**; m. **Unk HIGH**; lives in Gladstone, Clay County, Missouri.

    iv. **Mary Keefover;** m. **Unk TRAMMELL**; lives in Gladstone, Clay County, Missouri.

    v. **Erica Keefover**; lives in Gladstone, Clay County, Missouri.

    vi. **Robert Keefover**; lives in Spring, Montgomery County, Texas.

    vii. **Cheryl Keefover**; m. **Unk JACKSON**; lives in Harveyville, Wabaunsee County, Kansas.

    viii. **Diana Keefover**; m. **Unk HINZLER**; lives in Topeka, Shawnee County, Kansas.

545.

Mary Ellen Jacques, daughter of No. 529, Harry E. Jacques, was born 10 Mar 1922. She married **Edward Frank GREER, Sr.** He was born July 1922.

Children of Mary Jacques and Edward Greer are:

    i. **Cynthia Greer**, b. 05 Mar 1948.
    ii. **Jacqueline Greer**, b. 23 Feb 1949.
    iii. **Elaine Greer**, b. 05 Feb 1951.
    iv. **Susan Anne Greer**, b. 23 Mar 1952.
    v. **Jonathan Luke Greer**, b. 1955.
    vi. **Timothy Toby Greer,** b. 05 Nov 1957.
    vii. **Edward F. Greer, Jr.,** b. 05 Dec 1959.
    viii. **Patricia Greer**, b. 24 Jan 1961.

546.

William L. Keefover, son of No. 530, Otis William Keefover, was born 01 Jul 1920, in Marietta, Marshall County, Kansas. He married **Lotta Marie HOUK**, 06 May 1948.
Children of William Keefover and Lotta Houk are:
    i. **Lynette M. Keefover;** m. **Unk COLLIER.**
    ii. **Richard D. Keefover;** m. **Cindy UNK.**

547.

Daryl William Keefover, son of No. 531, George Edward Keefover, was born 02 Dec 1920, and died June 1987. He married **Bessie BARNES.**
Children of Daryl William Keefover and Bessie Barnes are:
580.   i. **Jeanie Marie Keefover**, b. 05 Dec 1941.
581.   ii. **William John Keefover**, b. September 1947.
582.   iii. **Yvonne Elizabeth Keefover**, b. July 1950.

548.

Stanley Dean Keefover, son of No. 531, George Edward Keefover, Sr., was born 09 Jul 1924. He married **Norma Jane WATHOR.**
Children of Stanley Dean Keefover and Norma Jane Wathor are:

583.   i. **Larry Lee Keefover**, b. 16 Jan 1948.
584.   ii. **Jacqueline Rae Keefover**, b. 14 Sep 1960.

549.

George Edward Keefover, Jr., son of No. 531, George
Edward Keefover, was born 21 Oct 1930. He married **Cina
Arlene WAYMAN**.
Children of George Edward Keefover, Jr. and Cina Wayman
are:
> i. **Dianne Kay Keefover**, b. 12 Oct 1955; m.
> **James PINKERTON**.
> ii. **Scott Alan Keefover**, b. 15 Sep 1958; m.
> **Jane BILLESBACH**.
> iii. **Teresa Ann Keefover**, b. 16 Mar 1962.

550.

Wayne Arlo Livingston, son of No. 532, Elreno Manilla
Keefover, was born 09 Sep 1920 and died 20 Aug 1982 in
Manhattan, Riley County, Kansas. He married **Elsie M.
DAFFORD**, 03 Jun 1949, in Marysville, Marshall County,
Kansas.
Children of Wayne Livingston and Elsie Dafford are:
> i. **Judith Livingston**; m. **Tim ANDERSON**.
> ii. **Gregory Livingston**.
> iii. **Robert Livingston**; m. **Judy HOERMAN**.

551.

Phyllis Jean Hearn, daughter of No. 534, Epha Hanna
Keefover, was born 06 May 1919, in Blue Rapids, Marshall
County, Kansas, and died 13 Dec 1998, in Community
Memorial Hospital, Marysville, Marshall County, Kansas. She
married **Christopher A. BAKER**, 14 Feb 1947, in Waterville,

Marshall County, Kansas, son of **Lloyd BAKER** and
Elizabeth BREW. Christopher was a survivor of the Japanese
bombing of Pearl Harbor on 07 Dec 1941. He was aboard the
USS Phoenix, the last ship to leave the harbor that day. He
received the Philippine Liberation Medal with 2 stars, the
Asiatic Pacific Medal with 8 stars, and the American Defense
Medal with 1 star. He was in the U.S. Navy in both WWII and
the Korean conflict. He retired in 1981 after 30 years as a
lineman with the Kansas Power and Light.
Children of Phyllis Jean Hearn and Christopher Baker are:
    i. **Bob Baker.**
    ii. **Christine J. Baker.**

552.

Arlene Elnora Hearn, daughter of No. 534, Epha Hannah
Keefover, was born 12 Sep 1925. She married **Alyson
TRYON**, 18 Sep 1943, in Marysville, Marshall County,
Kansas. He was born 01 Nov, 1920 in Irving, Marshall County,
Kansas.
Child of Arlene Hearn and Alyson Tryon is:
    i. **Bruce Tryon**, b. 19 Nov 1951, Marysville,
        Marshall County, Kansas; m. **Eldora UNK** (b.
        18 Nov 1954), 11 May 1974.

553.

David Hearn, son of No. 534, Epha Hannah Keefover, was
born 24 Dec 1935. He married **Jo UNK.**
Children of David Hearn and Jo are:
    i. **Tonja Hearn; m. David WIENCK.**
    ii. **Travis Hearn**; m. **Mark BRINK.**

554.

Wayland Rexford Keefover, son of No. 535, Merle Arthur Keefover, was born 18 Aug 1922, in Walnut Township, Marshall County, Kansas. He married (1) **Cecile Marie HARRIS**, 11 Nov 1945, in Marysville, Marshall County, Kansas. She was born 09 Jan 1923, in Herkimer, Marshall County, Kansas, and died 23 Jul 1976, in Aurora, Arapahoe County, Colorado. He married (2) **Lela C. SPELLMAN**, 14 Mar 1978, in Evergreen, Clear Creek County, Colorado, daughter of **Edward KUHLMAN** and **Emma HILLMER**. She was born 18 Aug 1924, in Falls City, Richardson County, Nebraska, and died 23 Dec 1984, in Manhattan, Riley County, Kansas. She is buried in Hanover City Cemetery, Hanover, Washington County, Kansas. She was the operator of a Day Care center.

Wayland was a member of the Methodist Church until his first marriage, after which he belonged to Lutheran churches in Aurora, Colorado and Manhattan, Kansas, and served as elder, trustee, steward, and President of the Lutheran Laymen League.

During World War II, he was an armored gunner in the Air Corps, serving in the European theater, and went on 24 missions. He was awarded the Air Medal with three clusters, the Distinguished Flying Cross, and the Purple Heart. He was discharged September 1945 with the rank of Staff Sergeant.

In civilian life, he has been a photographer, plumber, body and fender repairman, and maintenance engineer at Moore and West Halls at Kansas State University, Manhattan, Kansas. His hobbies include playing the guitar in bands of all kinds, painting with oils and watercolor, fly fishing, hunting, carving, collecting and showing model trains and railroad memorabilia. He rides and takes pictures of old engines,

collects and sets up exhibits of old toys, teaches leather work and carving. He has served the Boy Scouts of America as adult scout, committeeman, treasurer, assistant cub master, many other positions. In Colorado, he earned the Commissioner's Arrowhead Scouter's Key, Order of the Arrow and Silver Beaver. He is docent of the Historical Society and belongs to the Miniature Railroad Club. He was president of the Metro Wildlife Association in Aurora, Colorado, a member of the American Legion Post in Manhattan, Kansas, and a member of the Grief Support Group with the Lutheran Church.
Children of Wayland Keefover and Cecile Harris are:

> i. **Tim Wayland Keefover**, b. 02 Jul 1949, Marysville, Marshall County, Kansas.
> ii. **Cindy May Keefover**, b. 26 Mar 1953, Marysville, Marshall County, Kansas; m. **Steve McWHIRT**, 26 Apr 1980.

555.

Dean Harland Keefover, son of No. 535, Merle Arthur Keefover, was born 29 Feb 1924, in Waterville, Marshall County, Kansas, and died 22 Oct 1983, in Manhattan, Riley County, Kansas of pancreatic cancer. He married **Lillian Viola GORDON**, 18 Oct 1948, in Waterville. She was born 11 Feb 1929, in Waterville. During World War II, he was in the occupation forces at Jin machi-Xamagata, Japan, and received the Asiatic Pacific Theatre Ribbon, the Victory Medal, and the Army of Occupation Medal. He worked as a mechanic at the Pontiac garage in Marysville, Kansas for 20 years, and as general maintenance technician at Haymaker and Ford Halls at Kansas State University, Manhattan, Kansas for 17 years. He was commended by the college for his conscientiousness and hard work. In his honor, the university dedicated a large trophy case and traveling trophy to Haymaker Hall to be awarded the student who exhibits the most leadership in his first year as a resident. He was buried in Riverside Cemetery, Marshall County, Kansas.

Children of Dean Keefover and Lillian Gordon are:

    i. **Velma Jean Keefover**, b. 26 Feb 1949, Marysville, Marshall County, Kansas.

    ii. **Nora Jane Keefover**, b. 23 Mar 1951, Marysville, Marshall County, Kansas; m. **Louis MINDEN.**

    iii. **Kate Elaine Keefover**, b. 18 Nov 1955, Marysville, Marshall County, Kansas.

    iv. **Rebecca Sue Keefover**, b. 16 Aug 1960, Marysville, Marshall County, Kansas.

    v. **Shelly Lea Keefover**, b. 20 Jan 1964, Marysville, Marshall County, Kansas.

556.

Kenneth Merle Keefover, son of No. 535, Merle Arthur Keefover, was born 15 Jul 1928, in Walnut Township, Marshall County, Kansas. He married **Lois Ann CLARK**, 26 Jun 1955, in the Christian Church, Marysville, Marshall County, Kansas. She was born 10 Aug 1938 in Marysville. Kenneth served in the U.S. Air Force as Engineering Specialist to the 35th Fighter Interceptor Wing at Yokota Air Base in Japan from 1949 until his discharge in 1952. Before service, he was in body and fender work. He went into TV repair in Marysville, Kansas on the GI bill, then moved in 1958 to Aurora, Arapahoe County, Colorado, where he worked for RCA/GE.

Children of Kenneth Keefover and Lois Clark are:

    i. **Gregory James Keefover**, b. 23 Dec 1956, Marysville, Marshall, Kansas.

ii. **Michael Dean Keefover**, b. 06 Oct 1961,
Aurora, Arapahoe County, Colorado; m.
Wanda Sue HERMANN (b. 27 Dec 1963,
Denver, Colorado), 11 Jun 1981, Aurora,
Colorado.

iii. **James William Keefover**, b. 01 Aug 1963,
Aurora, Arapahoe County, Colorado; m.
Debra Lynn DuPRAS (b. 26 Jun 1967,
Las Vegas, Clark County, Nevada), 26 Nov
1990 (parted by 05 May 1999).

557.

Darrell Leon Keefover, son of No. 535, Merle Arthur
Keefover, was born 10 Feb 1932, in Walnut Township,
Waterville, Marshall County, Kansas. He married **Geraldine
Joyce EAKEN**, 12 Apr 1953, in Marysville, Marshall County,
Kansas. The daughter of **Lester EAKEN** and **Viola
STANSBERRY,** she was born 17 Oct 1934, in Blue Rapids,
Marshall County, Kansas, and died 10 Mar 1999, in the
Nursing Home, Blue Rapids, Marshall County, Kansas.

While in the service, Darrell was stationed in Okinawa
and Korea. His many jobs include raising rabbits, working
harvest fields, running a filling station in Marysville, and
working for Boeing in Wichita, Kansas. He became a minister
of the Assembly of God Church at Jewell, Jewell County,
Kansas in 1950, then moved to Hoisington, Barton County,
Kansas to preach. He and his wife managed a Best Western
Motel for 15 years until 1991, when his wife became disabled
with Alzheimer's disease and he retired.

His hobbies are playing the guitar and singing. He enjoys
helping people and sends Bibles to Russia and raises money for
Christian ministries.

Children of Darrell Keefover and Geraldine Eaken are:
  i. **Delores Marie Keefover**, b. 16 Feb 1954,
      Marysville, Marshall County, Kansas; m.
      Leonard JOHNSON III, 05 Jan 1980,
      Assembly of God, Great Bend, Barton
      County, Kansas.
  ii. **Duane Darrell Keefover**, b. 08 Mar 1958,
      Wichita, Sedgwick County, Kansas; m. **Kay
      Ann WARD**, 24 Jul 1982, Wichita, Sedgwick
      County, Kansas.

558.

Ramona Joyce Keefover, daughter of No. 535, Merle Arthur
Keefover, was born 06 Nov 1934, in Randolph, Riley County,
Kansas. She married **Kenneth Gene STETTNISCH**, 16 Aug
1953, in the Methodist Church, Marysville, Marshall County,
Kansas. He is the son of **Esther Mina BIRD**. He was born 19
Apr 1932, in Barnes, Washington County, Kansas. Ramona has
worked as secretary, key punch operator, and done office work
for Stettnisch Tool and Die Company. Her hobbies are reading;
sewing; leading Bluebird, Campfire, and PTA activities for
girls; ceramics; painting; square dancing; camping; fishing;
boating; skiing; quilting; and Bible study.

Kenneth Stettnisch has worked as a farm hand, baker,
track layer for Union Pacific Railroad, machine operator, and
owner of Stettnisch Tool and Die Company. He was elected
Mayor of Barnes, Kansas April 1999. He retired with the rank
of E8 1st Sergeant from the Kansas National Guard after 21
years, during which time he served in Berlin and on riot duty at
Kansas City. His hobbies are gardening, square dancing,
building, and working at anything and everything.
Children of Ramona Keefover and Kenneth Stettnisch are:

i. **Christine Lynnette Stettnisch**, b. 23 Nov 1954, Manhattan, Riley County, Kansas; m. **Russell Lawn RUPP** (b. 02 Mar 1950, Des Moines, Polk County, Iowa), 27 Mar 1976, Overland Park, Johnson County, Kansas. Christine has had surgery for ovarian cancer, a colostomy, and was one of eight stem cell transplant patients from Kansas University Medical Center still living in 2000.

ii. **Dianna Dawn Stettnisch**, b. 31 Mar 1957, Manhattan, Riley County, Kansas; d. 27 Feb 1992, Shawnee, Johnson County, Kansas from brain and lymph node tumors; m. (1) **David Allen ESTES** (b. 21 May 1956, Kansas City, Wyandotte County, Kansas), 14 Nov 1975, Overland Park, Johnson County, Kansas; m. (2) **Michael BRYSKY** (b. 26 Nov 1952, Lawrence, Douglas County, Kansas), 19 May 1984, Overland Park, Johnson County, Kansas.

iii. **Teri Rene Stettnisch**, b. 09 Jul 1964, Kansas City Jackson County, Missouri; m. **Robert Eldon SPANGLER II** (b. 26 Oct 1962, Shawnee, Johnson County, Kansas), 09 Nov 1991, Lenexa, Johnson County, Kansas. Teri received an M.A. degree in English from Kansas University in May 1990. Robert is a system analyst with Bayer Corporation.

559.

Karen Delores Keefover, daughter of No. 535, Merle Arthur Keefover, was born 05 Dec 1936, in Center Hill Township,

Riley County, Kansas. She married **Ensley Junior SISK** on 25 Mar 1956. He was born 21 Feb 1931, in Vliets, Marshall County, Kansas. Karen has been a stenographer, enumerator, election worker, and owner of Sunflower Waterbed Stores. She enjoys bridge, decorating, collecting, and serving as a church leader.

Children of Karen Keefover and Ensley Sisk are:
- i. **Bradley Eugene Sisk**, b. 18 Aug 1959, Abilene, Dickinson County, Kansas.
- ii. **Tamara Jo Sisk**, b. 30 May 1966, Paola, Miami County, Kansas.
- iii. **Douglas Ensley Sisk**, b. 30 May 1966, Paola, Miami County, Kansas.

560.

Gail Jean Keefover, son of No. 536, Claude Ellis Keefover, was born 21 Mar 1923, Waterville, Marshall County, Kansas, and died 23 Oct 1995, in Georgia. He married **Evelyn FENIMORE**.

Children of Gail Jean Keefover and Evelyn Fenimore are:
- i. **Thomas Keefover.**
- ii. **James Keefover.**

561.

Jacqueline D. Keefover, daughter of No. 536, Claude Ellis Keefover, was born 04 Mar 1925, in Waterville, Marshall County, Kansas. She married **Joseph BERGER, Sr**. He was born 08 Mar 1921.

Children of Jacqueline Keefover and Joseph Berger are:
- 585.   i. **Eugenia Meyer Berger**, b. 04 Mar 1946.
- 586   ii. **Doyle Majors Berger**, b. 23 Dec 1952.
- 587.   iii. **Joseph Berger, Jr.**, b. 10 Aug 1957.

iv. **Randy Berger**, b. 03 Jan 1961.

562.

James Milo Keefover, son of No. 536, Claude Ellis Keefover, was born 25 Oct 1929 in Waterville, Marshall County, Kansas. He married **Unknown.**
Child of James Milo Keefover and Unknown is:
  i. **Terry Keefover.**

563.

Joan Maxine Keefover, daughter of No. 536, Claude Ellis Keefover, was born 25 Oct 1929 in Waterville, Marshall County, Kansas. She married **Forrest HAMMET.**
Children of Joan Keefover and Forrest Hammet are:
  i. **Rebecca Hammet**; m. **Unk TROXELL.**
  ii. **Richard Hammet.**
  iii. **Roxanne Hammet.**
  iv. **Robert Hammet.**

564.

Deanne Charlotte Keefover, daughter of No. 536, Claude Ellis Keefover, was born 15 Sep 1932, in Waterville, Marshall County, Kansas. She married **Robert HUMPHREY, Sr.**
Children of Deanne Keefover and Robert Humphrey are:
  i. **Robert Humphrey, Jr.**
  ii. **Kathleen Humphrey.**
  iii. **Patricia Humphrey.**
  iv. **Steven Humphrey.**
  v. **Cynthia Humphrey.**
  vi. **Sandra Humphrey.**
  vii. **Jeffrey Humphrey.**

565.

Geraldine Keefover, daughter of No. 536, Claude Ellis Keefover, was born 06 Feb 1934, in Waterville, Marshall County, Kansas. She married (1) **Unk DOVER.** She married (2) **Unk POPE.**
Child of Geraldine Keefover and Unk Dover is:
    i. **Debra Dover.**
Child of Geraldine Keefover and Unk Pope is:
    ii. **Valerie Pope.**

566.

Rolland Rex Keefover, son of No. 536, Claude Ellis Keefover, was born 15 Sep 1936, in Waterville, Marshall County, Kansas. He married **Gloria UNK.**
Children of Rolland Rex Keefover and Gloria are:
    i. **Claude Keefover.**
    ii. **Robin Keefover.**
    iii. **Gina Keefover.**

567.

Claudette Jean Keefover, daughter of No. 536, Claude Ellis Keefover, was born 27 Sep 1943, in Waterville, Marshall County, Kansas. She married **Richard SPAIN.** He was born in Manhattan, Riley County, Kansas.
Children of Claudette Keefover and Richard Spain are:
    i. **Michael Spain.**
    ii. **Ronald Spain.**
    iii. **Jackie Spain**; m. **Unk ROBINSON.**

568.

Marjorie Thelma Wehmeier, daughter of No. 537, Thelma Sarah Keefover, was born 04 Dec, 1924, in Waterville,

Marshall County, Kansas. She married **Robert R. KENNEY**, 11 Nov 1950, in Waterville.
Children of Marjorie Wehmeier and Robert Kenney are:
    i. **Terry Guy Kenney**, b. 14 Sep 1955; m.
        Trisha UNK, July 1980.
    ii. **Cynthia Ruth Kenney**, b. 01 Nov 1960.

569.

Donna Mae Wehmeier, daughter of No. 537, Thelma Sarah Keefover, was born 18 Oct 1926, in Waterville, Marshall County, Kansas. She married **Robert G. KRISCHE**, 21 Aug 1950, in Waterville.
Children of Donna Wehmeier and Robert Krische are:
    i. **Thomas Michael Krische,** b. 22 Apr 1951,
        Lawrence, Douglas County, Kansas.
    ii. **Linda Marie Krische**, b. 04 Nov 1952,
        Lawrence, Douglas County, Kansas; m.
        George Henry HEIMAN.
    iii. **Daniel Andrew Krische**, b. 17 Sep 1955,
        Lawrence, Douglas County, Kansas; m.
        Jeanne Marie BLOCK (b. 13 Apr 1956.)
    iv. **Robert Mathew Krische**, b. 25 Sep 1957,
        Lawrence, Douglas County, Kansas; m.
        Debra Jean UNK (b. 07 Sep 1957).
    v. **Nancy Annette Krische**, b. 25 Apr 1961,
        Lawrence, Douglas County, Kansas.
    vi. **Susan Diane Krische**, b. 09 Apr 1963,
        Lawrence, Douglas County, Kansas.

570.

George Eberle Wehmeier, son of No. 537, Thelma Sarah Keefover, was born 10 Feb 1931, in Waterville, Marshall

483

County, Kansas. He married **Margaret Y. HOWES**, 27 Apr 1953, in Marysville, Marshall County. Kansas.

Children of George Wehmeier and Margaret Howes are:

    i. **Craig Eberle Wehmeier**, b. 05 Jul 1955; m. **Sharon HOLDERMAN.**

    ii. **Brent Alan Wehmeier**, b. 30 Dec 1959.

571.

Larry Gene Wehmeier, son of No. 537, Thelma Sarah Keefover, was born 14 Jun 1936, in Waterville, Marshall County, Kansas, and died 21 Sep 1995, in Lawrence, Douglas County, Kansas of liver cancer. He was an alcoholic for many years, but quit about five years before becoming ill. He was a house painter. He married (1) **Beverly DAHM**, 15 Jul 1956, in Waterville, Marshall County, Kansas. Larry adopted the children of Beverly by her former h usband, whose surname is **DESBIEN.** He married (2) **Shirley UNK.**

Children of Lary Wehmeier and Beverly Dahm are:

    i. **Larry Gene Wehmeier, Jr.,** b. 10 Jul 1958, Waterville, Marshall County, Kansas.

    ii. **David Brian Wehmeier**, b. 10 Dec 1959, Waterville, Marshall County, Kansas.

    iii. **Angela Kaye Wehmeier**, b. 05 Dec 1960, Waterville, Marshall County, Kansas.

Child of Larry Wehmeier and Shirley Unk is:

    iv. **Joseph Maurice Wehmeier**, b. 09 Jan 1965.

572.

Linda Ellen Wehmeier, daughter of No. 537, Thelma Sarah Keefover, was born 10 Jan 1939, in Waterville, Marshall County, Kansas. She married **John J. McGRATH**, 19 Sep 1959, in Holton, Jackson County, Kansas.

Children of Linda Wehmeier and John McGrath are:
- i. **Gregory Dean McGrath**, b. 29 Aug 1961, Topeka, Shawnee County, Kansas.
- ii. **Steven Jay McGrath**, b. 27 Oct, 1964, Topeka, Shawnee County, Kansas.
- iii. **Jennifer Anne McGrath**, b. 07 Apr1968, Topeka, Shawnee County, Kansas; m. **Phillip A. NASITY**, 26 Jun 1993, Lenexa, Johnson County, Kansas.
- iv. **Andrea Lynn McGrath**, b. 01 Oct 1973, Topeka, Shawnee County, Kansas; m. **Jeffrey Keith ONNEN**, 20 May 1995, Prairie Village, Johnson County, Kansas.

573.

Richard Lee Keefover, son of No. 538, Verne Clarence Keefover, was born 25 Jan 1936, in Walnut Township, Marshall County, Kansas. He married **Elizabeth BARELA,** 07 Feb 1959. She was born 19 May 1941, in Manhattan, Riley County, Kansas.

Children of Richard Keefover and Elizabeth Barela are:
- 588.   i. **Ricki Renee Keefover**, b. 20 Oct 1959, Manhattan, Riley County, Kansas.
- 589.   ii. **Cynthia Lea Keefover**, b. 14 Sep 1960, Manhattan, Riley County, Kansas.
- iii. **Brian Scott Keefover**, b. 14 Jan 1966, Riverton, Fremont County, Wyoming.

SEVENTH GENERATION

574.

Zachary William Prichard, son of No. 540, Albert Hughes Prichard, was born 14 Nov 1979 in Morgantown, West Virginia. He married **Anita Arvind THEKDI** 3 Oct 2009 in Bethesda, Maryland. He is employed with American University in Washington, DC as the manager of computer labs in the School of Communications.
Child of Zachary William Prichard and Anita Arvind Thekdi is:

> i. **Meera Thekdi Prichard**, b. 28 May 2013.

575.

Joseph Virgil Prichard, son of No. 541, Philip Arthur Prichard, married **Sarah Elizabeth GERASIMEK** of Sharpsville, Pennsylvania 28 Dec 2003 in Moon Township, Pennsylvania and divorced in 2009 in Morgantown, West Virginia. Joe partnered with **Shannon JONES** of Bridgeport, West Virginia in 2009. They live outside Bridgeport, West Virginia. Joe is a musician and teacher of music.
Child of Joseph Prichard and Sarah Elizabeth Gerasimek is:

> i. **Nicholas Joseph Prichard,** b. 31 Jan 2009,
> Morgantown, West Virginia.

Child of Joseph Prichard and Shannon Jones is:

> ii. **Adeline Grace Prichard,** b. 21 Nov 2009,
> Clarksburg, West Virginia.

576.

Stacie Leigh Prichard, daughter of No. 541, Philip Arthur Prichard, married **Benjamin FRIDLEY** of Mannington, West

Virginia on 01 Jan 2007. They live in Mannington. Stacie is a speech pathologist in the Marion County Public School System.

Children of Stacie Leigh Prichard and Benjamin Fridley are:

    i. **George Arthur Fridley**, b. 08 Mar 2007, Morgantown, West Virginia.

    ii. Arden **Roy Fridley**, b. 07 Sep 2009, Morgantown, West Virginia.

577.

Yvonne Theresa Smejkal, daughter of No. 542, Virginia Louise Prichard, was born 17 Sep 1973 in Fairmont, West Virginia. She married **Michael Vaughan AYERS** 16 May 1998. They live in Brentwood, Tennessee.

Children of Yvonne Smejkal and Michael Ayers are:

    i. **Caroline Virginia Ayers**, b. 03 Mar 2000.

    ii. **Carter Vaughan Ayers**, b. 21 Apr 2003.

    iii. **Charles Philip Ayers**, b. 29 Mar 2006.

578.

Sarah Gibson, daughter of No. 543, Emily Prichard, lives in Moneta, Randolph County, West Virginia. She married **Unk PHARES.**

Children of Sarah Gibson and Unk Phares are:

    i. **Beth Phares.**

    ii. **James Phares.**

    iii. **Joseph Phares.**

    iv. **Tyler Milford Phares.**

579.

Jeanie Marie Keefover, daughter of No. 547, Daryl William Keefover, was born 05 Dec 1941. She married **David E.**

WEST.
Children of Jeanie Marie Keefover and David E. West are:
    i. **Stephen West.**
    ii. **Gregory West.**

580.
William John Keefover, son of No. 547, Daryl William Keefover, was born 21 Sep 1947. He married **UNK.**
Children of William John Keefover and Unk are:
    i. **Bobby Keefover.**
    ii. **Mathew Keefover.**

581.
Yvonne Elizabeth Keefover, daughter of No. 547, Daryl William Keefover, was born 04 Jul 1950. She married **Mark ANKROM.**
Children of Yvonne Keefover and Mark Ankrom are:
    i. **Keith Ankrom.**
    ii. **Edwin Ankrom.**

582.
Larry Lee Keefover, son of No. 548, Stanley Dean Keefover, was born 06 Jan 1948. He married **Rebecca CRANDELE.**
Child of Larry Lee Keefover and Rebecca Crandele is:
    i. **Cynthia Ann Keefover.**

583.
Jacqueline Rae Keefover, daughter of No. 548, Stanley Dean Keefover, was born 14 Sep 1960. She married **Steven Scott JONES.**
Children of Jacqueline Rae Keefover and Steven Jones are:
    i. **Alexander Jones.**

ii. **Taylor Jones.**

584.

Eugenia Meyer Berger, daughter of No. 561, Jacqueline D. Keefover, was born 04 Mar 1946. She married **Unk KURRE.** Children of Eugenia Berger and Unk Kurre are:
    i. **Kenneth Kurre**, b. 27 Jun 1968.
    ii. **Kaley Jo Kurre**, b. 01 Dec 1971.
    iii. **Shad Kurre**, b. 22 Nov 1989.

585.

Doyle Majors Berger, Sr., son of No. 561, Jacqueline D. Keefover, was born 23 Dec 1952. He married **UNK.** Children of Doyle Majors Berger and Unk are:
    i. **Doyle Berger, Jr.,** b. 27 Oct 1970.
    ii. **Greg Berger**, b. 14 May 1974.
    iii. **Melisa Berger**, b. 25 Aug 1982.

586.

Joseph Berger, Jr., son of No. 561, Jacqueline D. Keefover, was born 10 Aug 1957. He married **Laurie DeVARKIN.** Children of Joseph Berger and Laurie DeVarkin are:
    i. **Jason Berger**, b. 27 Sep 1973 (adopted).
    ii. **Aaron Berger**, b. 05 Feb 1976 (adopted).

587.

Ricki Renee Keefover, daughter of No. 573, Richard Lee Keefover, was born 20 Oct 1959, in Manhattan, Riley County, Kansas. She married **Unk REYNOLDS** and lives in San Jose, Santa Clara County, California.
Child of Ricki Renee Keefover and Unk Reynolds is:
    i. **Christina Reynolds.**

588.

Cynthia Lea Keefover, daughter of No. 573, Richard Lee Keefover, was born 14 Sep 1960, in Manhattan, Riley County, Kansas. She married **UNK** and lives in Santa Barbara, Santa Barbara County, California.

Child of Cynthia Lee Keefover and Unk is:

      i. **Cody Unk.**

DESCENDANTS OF ANN "NANCY" PRITCHARD

12.

Ann "Nancy" Pritchard was born about 1780 in Loudoun County, Virginia and died in Monongalia County (West) Virginia after 03 Oct 1850 when she was listed in the census as living with James and Rachel Arnett in the 37th district of Monongalia County. The census gives her age as 77. If this is correct, she may have been born as early as 1773. She was the third wife of Revolutionary War soldier **Davis MEREDITH**, father of Hannah Meredith, who was the wife of Ann's brother, No. 11, William Pri(t)chard. Ann and Davis were married November 8 or 9, 1800 in Allegany County, Maryland.

Thanks to Jack Meredith, Babcock Graduate School of Management at Wake Forest University, the ancestry of Davis Meredith, soldier in the Revolutionary War, is clarified. In January 2001, Jack Meredith privately published his research on the *Ancestors, Relatives, and Descendants of Job Meredith, Sr. and Lydia Meredith of 18th century Kent County, Delaware.* His analysis, based on the comprehensive dataset of the Merediths of Delaware and Maryland done by Ron Meridith (sic), gives ample proof that the information shared by numerous Meredith descendants and incorporated in several DAR applications has significant errors.

Jack Meredith credits much of the misinformation and incorrect family charts to a letter penned by Whitely W. Meredith in 1900. It narrates the fanciful story of two Meredith children abandoned in Delaware during early days of the colony. Descendants immediately took it to their hearts as gospel. However, Jack Meredith has unearthed numerous

491

earlier versions of the story, each slightly adjusted as they were narrated to subsequent generations. The story, repeated in a letter sent to Mr. L. W. Meredith of Ashland, Kentucky, was published in an Ohio newspaper. Jack Meredith retrieved a copy of the article from the files of T. O. Dillon, who received it in a letter from Rev. J. H. Meredith of Texas on 08 Apr 1942. In his letter, Rev. Meredith states that he received the article from Mrs. J. Owen Meredith of Coshocton, Ohio. In short, the information given within the letter regarding Davis Meredith's ancestry is wrong.

Furthermore, Davis Meredith is erroneously identified in some records as having been born in Radnor County, South Wales. In her *History of Ritchie County*, Minnie Kendall Lowther wrote this account: *The Merediths are of Welsh descent. Davis Meredith was born in Wales near the middle of the eighteenth century, and being a Sabbatarian, and being persecuted for his religious belief, he came to America in his young manhood shortly before the Revolution and settled in Connecticut. He took up arms in defense of his adopted county.* Except for her mention of his service in the Revolutionary War, this account is completely incorrect, though imaginative. A Davis Meredith may have emigrated from Wales to Connecticut, both Davis and Meredith being very common Welsh names, but he is not the ancestor in question. The Davis Meredith with whom we are concerned served in the Second Corps, Delaware Regiment under Colonel Henry Neill. His correct lineage is cited in the abbreviated account following.

1.

Robert Meredith, Sr., born about 1662, died in Dorchester County, Maryland in 1727. The administrator of his estate is **Job MEREDITH**. His heirs are **Hugh MEREDITH** and

Mary COOK. It is not known if Robert Meredith was born in England or Wales, or even if he was the immigrant member of this particular line. Court records show him witnessing a document in Dorchester County in 1701 concerning land at Watt's Creek. There is also a document in 1701 regarding land at Phillip's Creek and the south side of the Great Choptank, another document in 1704 regarding land at the same location, one in 1708 for land at the south side of Ingram's Creek, and one in 1712 for land at Watt's Creek once more. In *The History of Delaware, 1609-1888, Volume II,* published in 1888, author J. T. Scharf notes on page 1167 that a tract of 200 acres called "Rachel's Delight" was taken up by Robert Meredith, cordwainer (shoemaker), under warrant of 18 Sep 1735. This suggests that Rachel may have been the name of his wife, or perhaps of his mother. Jack Meredith notes that the beautiful handwriting on Robert Meredith, Sr.'s signed deed indicates his ability to read and write. The probate of his death in 1728 shows proof that he owned a large Bible, another indication that he was an educated man. Robert Meredith, Sr. and most of his descendants who follow lived at, or near, Meredith's Corner, Murderkill (also found as Mutherkill), Kent County, Delaware.

The children of Robert Meredith, Sr. are:

       i. **Job Meredith**, b. abt. 1688; d. abt. 1748.

2.   ii. **Hugh Meredith, Sr.,** b. abt. 1696, d. abt. 1753.

3.   iii. **Robert Meredith, Jr.,** b. abt. 1696; d. abt. 1753.

      iv. **Mary Meredith; m. Unk COOK.**

      v. **Joshua Meredith**, b. abt. 1716; d. abt. 1775.

2.

Hugh Meredith, Sr. (+~1696-+~1753) was married about 1721 to **Mirtle UNK.**

Children of Hugh Meredith, Sr. and Mirtle Unk are:
  i. **Nehemiah Meredith**, b. abt. 1722; married before
      1748; disappears from records after 1754.
  ii. **Hugh Meredith, Jr.**, b. abt. 1727; d. abt. 1765;
      m. abt. 1756.
  iii. **Job Meredith**, b. abt. 1727; d. abt. 1762; m.
      Patience (?) HUNN abt. 1751, daughter of
      Jonathan HUNN, administrator of his son-
      in-law's estate.
  iv. **William Meredith**, b. abt. 1732; d. abt. 1798; m.
      (1) abt. 1753; m. (2) abt. 1763.

3.

Robert Meredith, Jr. (+~1696-+~1767) was married about
1721 to **Rachel WHEELER**.
Children of Robert Meredith, Jr. and Rachel Wheeler are:
  i. **John Meredith**, b. abt. 1722; d. abt. 1767; m.
      Sophia UNK abt. 1748.
4. ii. **Job Meredith, Sr.**, b. abt. 1730; d. 1793.
  iii. **William Meredith, Sr.**, b. abt. 1730; d. abt.
      1795; m. **Phyllis GORDON** abt. 1770. Their
      son, **William Meredith, Jr.,** born abt.
      1771, married **Margaret HOPKINS.**
5. iv. **Joseph L. Meredith**, b. abt. 1734; d. abt. 1795;
      m. (1) abt. 1762, had a son, **Samuel Meredith**
      (1766-1801); m. (2) **Elizabeth GRIFFIN** or
      GRIFFITH, abt. 1768; m. (3) **Mary Woodle
      (Woods?) BOND,** abt. 1794.
  v. **Wheeler Meredith**, b. abt. 1740; d. abt. 1773; m.
      Susannah MUNCEY, abt. 1762. Their son
      Asa Meredith (1764-1812) married
      Christina (Keziah) VANPELT.

494

4.

Job Meredith, Sr. was born about 1730 and died in 1793. He married (1) **Rebecca DAVIS** about 1754. She died about 1771. He married (2) **Lydia WHITACRE/WHITAKER,** abt. 1772, daughter of **Henry WHITAKER.** Job, a farmer, served in the French and Indian War. All of his children were born in Kent County, Delaware.

Children of Job Meredith, Sr. and Rebecca Davis are:

6.   i. **Davis Meredith**, b. abt. 1757; gone from Delaware by 1785; d. 24 May 1825, Monongalia County, (West) Virginia.

      ii. **Peter Meredith**, b. abt. 1758; m. **Elizabeth BROADWAY**, 1780, gone from Delaware by 1785.

      iii. **Rachel Meredith**; m. **John KEYS.**

      iv. **Job Meredith, Jr.**, b. abt. 1762; d. 1825; m. **Elizabeth BETTS.**

      v. **Obed Meredith.**

Children of Job Meredith, Sr. and Lydia Whitacre are:

      vi. **Elizabeth Meredith**; m. **Absalom COOPER.**

      vii. **Henry Meredith**; m. **Mary Epps COBB.**

      viii. **Stephen Meredith.**

      ix. **James Meredith.**

      x. **David Meredith**; m. **Eve WELDON**

      xi. **Abner Meredith**; m. **Jane UNK.**

      xii. **Benjamin Meredith**; d. 1808; m. **Unk BELL.**

5.

Children of Joseph L. Meredith (1734-1795) and Elizabeth Griffin (married abt. 1768) are:

      i. **Martha Meredith**; m. **William ANGUISH.**

      ii. **Elizabeth Meredith**; m. **Unk FORD.**

iii. **Ann Meredith**; m. **Unk HARTSHORN.**
iv. **Joseph Meredith, Jr.**
v. **Jacob Meredith**, b. 1789; m. **Sarah UNK** abt. 1807.

6.

Davis Meredith, son of Job Meredith, Sr., was born abt. 1757 in Kent County, Delaware. He married (1) **Amelia KNOTTS** about 1782 in Delaware. He married (2) **Elizabeth UNK** after 1785 in Virginia or Pennsylvania. He married (3) **Nancy Anne PRITCHARD**, 08 Nov 1800 in Allegany County, Maryland, daughter of **Thomas PRITCHARD, Sr.** and **Rachel DAVIS**.

Among the list of founders of the Cow Marsh Baptist Church records of Kent County, Delaware are Job Meredith, Jr., Ruth Meredith, Jacob Meredith, **Davis Meredith**, Elizabeth Meredith, Luff Meredith, Levi Meredith.

Davis and his first wife, Amelia, were still living in Kent County, Delaware on 07 Apr 1786, when they joined his father Job and Job's second wife, Lydia, on a Kent County deed for land called "Maiden's Lott." Two of Davis's children were born before that date: Absalom and Hannah (about 1783 and 1785, respectively.)

Davis was enumerated in George's Township of Fayette County, Pennsylvania in the 1790 Federal Census. At that time he was +16 but -45, with one male age 16, probably Absalom, and three females, probably his wife and daughters Hannah and Rebecca. It is not known if his wife was still Amelia, or if she had died by that time and he was married to Elizabeth; the latter could be the case, as she is generally regarded as the mother of both Rebecca and New/Nue, who was born after the 1790 census. However, it is also possible that Amelia was the mother of all four children, dying prior to 1798. Rebecca consistently gave Pennsylvania as her birthplace in subsequent censuses, so she undoubtedly was born in Fayette County, Pennsylvania. Davis was still living in Fayette County on 04 Dec 1791, when he witnessed the will of Joshua Deweese. In his will, Deweese stated that he was "of Kent County, Delaware," but now living in Fayette County, Pennsylvania.

By 1796, Davis was living in Monongalia County, Virginia and serving on the fall term of the Grand Jury. He bought 400 acres on Stacks Run on 22 Sep 1796 for 150 pounds. On 13 Feb 1798, he and his wife Elizabeth sold it for 175 pounds. This is proof that his second wife was named Elizabeth; however, she was *not* Elizabeth Howell, daughter of Timothy Howell of Loudoun County, as some descendants believe. That Elizabeth married Benjamin Meredith, then moved to Belmont County, Ohio.

Elizabeth Meredith died between 1798 and 09 Nov 1800, the day Davis and Ann Pritchard were married by the Reverend William Shaw in Allegany County, Maryland, where Ann's parents and several of her siblings lived at the time. Davis and Ann lived on a 150 acre tract near Robinson's Run in Paw Paw, which he bought from Fleming and Christina Jones on 08 Jun 1801.

Several other Meredith brothers moved west. Davis picked up a deed for his brother Stephen Meredith on 08 Dec 1802 for land on Lick Run of the Dunker Bottom settlement, and one for another brother, Peter, 14 Sep 1803, probably in the area that later became Preston County. Obed Meredith, a third brother, is believed to have lived in Fayette County, Pennsylvania, just across the state line. On 20 Mar 1792, Obed joined the Seventh Day Baptist Church organized by Samuel Woodbridge at Woodbridgetown, Pennsylvania, near the present-day Uniontown, Fayette County. In his will dated 20

Aug 1799, Woodbridge left land to Hannah Meredith, as noted below.

The first-born children in pioneer families were traditionally named for a family member, often a grandparent. The belief that Absalom Meredith and Hannah Meredith were the children of Davis' first wife, Amelia, is supported by the fact that Hannah named her first daughter Amelia. The theory that Rebecca Meredith and New Meredith were children of his second wife, Elizabeth, has yet to be proved, but the naming tradition is supported by the fact that Rebecca named her first daughter after Ruth, her husband's mother, and named her second daughter Elizabeth, presumably after her own mother. Davis Meredith's remaining seven children were by Ann Pritchard, his third wife.

In 1807, Lydia Whitaker Meredith, second wife of Davis' father, died in Kent County, Delaware. The Orphans' Court proceedings list Davis Meredith as the oldest son. He had the right to accept the land upon the death of Lydia. However, Davis and his wife Ann conveyed it to his younger brother, Job Meredith, who had remained in Kent County. Delaware Deed Book K-2:252 of 11 Apr 1808 names the conveyers as: "Davis Meredith of Monongalia County, State of Virginia, and his wife Ann," thus proving that the Davis with wife Amelia in 1786, and Davis with wife Ann of Monongalia County in 1808 was one and the same, the son of Job Meredith and Rebecca Davis of Murderkill Hundred, Kent County, Delaware.

Davis Meredith died 24 May 1825 and his will was probated at the August 1825 term of Court in Morgantown, (West) Virginia. He named his wife Ann executrix and James Arnett executor in the presence of David Musgrave, Richard Morris, and John Parker.

The Pritchard/Prickett Family History

Those wishing to learn more about Jack Meredith's research and update their Meredith genealogy may contact him by email: jack.Meredith@mba.wfu.edu, or by writing to him at: Babcock Graduate School of Management, Wake Forest University, P. O. Box 7659, 3109 Worrell Professional Center, Winston-Salem, NC 27109. His telephone number is (336) 758-4467; his fax number is (336) 758-4514.

Parallel research and confirmation of Jack Meredith's data has been supplied by Meredith descendant and researcher, Phyllis Vines: jvines@charter.net.

It must be noted here that the *History of Seventh Day Baptists in West Virginia* contains several errors in its listing of the marriage of Hannah Meredith and William Pritchard: *Hannah Meredith, b. 1785 in Loudoun County, Virginia, m. 26 Feb 1803 William Pritchard, a native of Loudoun County, b. February 1777, of distinguished Welsh descent and a member of one of the old and highly respected FFV (*First Families of Virginia) *of the Valley of Virginia. William Pritchard was a devout Methodist and came to Monongalia County in 1814.*

The first error is Hannah's place of birth. She was born in Delaware. Secondly, Monongalia County, (West) Virginia marriage records prove that the marriage took place there on 18 Feb 1805. Thirdly, William Pritchard was born 17 Dec 1777. Fourthly, the Pritchards were highly regarded in Virginia, but they are not among those recognized as FFV, such as the Lee and Washington families. By the time the book was published, mistakes had crept into the oral Pritchard family history, among them accurate dates and locations of major events.

Hannah Meredith, Davis Meredith's daughter by Amelia Knotts, is listed as a member of the Woodbridge Baptist Church located in 1790 at Georges Creek, Fayette County, Pennsylvania. The following bequest from the will of

Rev. Samuel Woodbridge, minister of Woodbridge Church, Georges Creek, is dated 20 Aug 1799 and is recorded in Book I of the Fayette County Register of Wills Office, Uniontown, Pennsylvania: ...*I likewise will one-half acre of land on which the meeting house stands and an out lot, to the Seventh Day Baptist Church now meeting at Mifflin Town, etc...I likewise will to Hannah Meredith, daughter of Davis Meredith, one lot containing one quarter of an acre fronting Anon Street, Northwest side of said street, adjoining the land of James Tate.* At the time of this bequest, Davis Meredith had not yet married Ann (Nancy) Pritchard, but it is likely that his second wife had died.

Children of Davis Meredith and Amelia Knotts are:

589.　　i. **Absalom Meredith**, b. 1783, Kent County, Delaware; d. 1842, Rochester Township, Sangamon County, Illinois.

　　　ii. **Hannah Meredith**, b. 1785, Kent County, Delaware; d. before the 1830 census, Monongalia County, (West) Virginia; married No. 11, **William PRITCHARD.** (See Descendants of William Pritchard.)

Children of Davis Meredith and Elizabeth Unk are:

590.　iii. **Rebecca Meredith**, b. 1788, Fayette County, Pennsylvania.

591.　iv. **Nuw (Nue) Meredith**, b. 1792, probably Fayette County, Pennsylvania; d. abt. 1852, Ohio

Children of Davis Meredith and Ann (Nancy) Pritchard are:

592.　　v. **Rachel Meredith**, b. 29 Nov 1801, Monongalia County, (West) Virginia; d. 19 Jan 1874, Arnettsville, Marion County, West Virginia.

593.　vi. **Martha Meredith**, b. 1804, Monongalia County,

(West) Virginia; d. about May 1850 before the
1850 census.

594.   vii. **Eleanor Meredith**, b. 07 Dec 1807, Monongalia
County, (West) Virginia; d. 20 Mar 1869,
Monongalia County.

595. viii. **Thomas Meredith (Merydith)**, b. 26 Feb 1809,
Monongalia County (West) Virginia; d. 19
Apr 1890, Dexter, Cowley County, Kansas.

596.   ix. **Job John Meredith**, b. 1810, Monongalia
County (West) Virginia; d. 1881, Salem,
Harrison County, West Virginia.

597.   x. **Davis Meredith**, b. 04 Nov 1812, Monongalia
County, (West) Virginia; d. 04 Mar 1893,
Centerville, Tyler County, West Virginia.

598.   xi. **William Meredith**, b. 16 May 1815, Monongalia
County, (West) Virginia; d. 01 Sep 1896, White
Oak, Ritchie County, West Virginia.

SECOND GENERATION.

589.

Absalom Meredith, son of Davis Meredith and Amelia Knotts, was born 1783 in Kent County, Delaware, and died 1842 in Rochester Township, Sangamon County, Illinois. He married **Mary ROYAL**, 08 Oct 1807 in Monongalia County, (West) Virginia, daughter of **Thomas ROYAL** and **Hannah COOPER**. She was born 08 Jan 1787, and died in Ball Township, Sangamon County, Illinois in 1844. They first removed to Butler County, Ohio, where they had four children. Then they moved to Miami County, Ohio, where two more children were born. Finally, they moved to Sangamon County, Illinois about 27 Oct 1827, in the company of 63 persons. Children of Absalom Meredith and Mary Royal are:

599.   i. **Thomas Meredith**, b. Butler County, Ohio.
      ii. **Amy Meredith**, b. Butler County, Ohio.
      iii. **William Meredith**. Butler County, Ohio.
600.   iv. **Davis Meredith**, b. 14 June 1812, Butler County, Ohio, d. 03 Aug 1896, Sangamon County, Illinois
      v. **Joseph Meredith**, Miami County, Ohio.
      vi. **Sarah A. Meredith**, b. Miami County, Ohio.

590.

Rebecca Meredith, daughter of Davis Meredith and Elizabeth Unk was born about 1788 in Fayette County, Pennsylvania, and died 30 Jan 1875 in Marion County, West Virginia. She married **Henry NEPTUNE** 09 Oct 1806 Monongalia County, (West) Virginia. Davis Meredith was suretor and named father of Rebecca on their marriage bond. Henry was born about 1784

in Loudoun County, Virginia, and died 14 Aug 1845 in the
Paw Paw District of Marion County, (West) Virginia. Henry
and Rebecca were buried in the Neptune Family Cemetery. The
children of Rebecca and Henry Neptune are named in an
Allegany County, Maryland Equity Suit, filed 1856 in Circuit
Court by Neptune Heirs vs. Highland Coal and Iron Company.
Children of Rebecca Meredith and Henry Neptune are:

  i. **Ruth Neptune;** m. (1) **John ARNETT.** m. (2)
     Levi ARNETT.
 ii. **Davis Neptune**
iii. **John Neptune.**
 iv. **Samuel Neptune.**
  v. **Absalom Neptune.**
 vi. **Henry S. Neptune.**
vii. **Amos Alva Neptune**, b. 1826.
viii. **William H. Neptune**, b. 1829.
 ix. **Elizabeth Neptune**, b. 1833.
  x. **Alpheus Neptune**, b. 01 Aug 1848.

591.

Nuw/Nue "Nelly" Meredith, son of Davis Meredith and
Elizabeth Unk, was born about 1791-1792 in Fayette County,
Pennsylvania. He married **Dorcas SNIDER**, 04 Sep 1817, in
Monongalia County, (West) Virginia. Nuw and Dorcas soon
removed to Monroe County, Ohio, where they were
enumerated in the 1830 census, with one male born 1817-1820.
In the 1830 census, they added one male and two females born
from 1820-1830. The last record found for them in Monroe
County, Ohio is a deed (Deed Book E: 11) for the sale of land
on 31 Mar 1831 by Nuw and his wife Dorcas to Thomas
Martin. Williams's *History of Washington County, Ohio*
mentions that Nuw and Dorcas were members of the first

Methodist Church in the Paw Paw Valley of Washington
County.
Children of Nuw Meredith and Dorcas Snider are:
    i. **Mahala Meredith**; m. **Thomas J. LAW.**
    ii. **Susan Meredith**; m. **John CLINE.**
    iii. **Lydia Meredith.**
    iv. **John Meredith.**
    v. **New Meredith, Jr.**
    vi. **Nancy Meredith.**
    vii. **Rachel Meredith.**

592.

Rachel Meredith, daughter of No. 12, Ann Pritchard, named
for Ann's mother, was born 19 Oct 1801 in Monongalia
County, (West) Virginia, and died 19 Jan 1874 at Arnettsville,
Marion County, West Virginia. She married **James H.
ARNETT, Sr.,** 26 Feb 1818. Their marriage bond was dated
17 Feb 1818, and Davis Meredith was named suretor and father
of Rachel. James Arnett was born 10 Sep 1797 in Monongalia
County, son of **Andrew ARNETT** and **Elizabeth LEGGETT.**
He died 25 Feb 1880, at Arnettsville. His will dated 09 May
1877 in the Monongalia County, West Virginia Will Book is
probated 18 Mar 1880. He was the first postmaster of
Arnettsville.
Children of Rachel Meredith and James Arnett are:
601.   i. **James H. Arnett, Jr.,** b. 1820.
    ii. **William Meredith Arnett,** b. 1821.
602.   iii. **Andrew Meredith Arnett,** b. 24 Jul 1823; d.
        17 Jun 1888.
    iv. **Elizabeth Arnett,** b. 1825.
    v. **Davis Meredith Arnett,** b. 1827.
    vi. **Margaret Ann Arnett,** b. 1829; m. (1) **John**

AMOS; m. (2) **Samuel LYNCH**.
      vii. **Francis Meredith Arnett**, b. 1832.
603. viii. **Martha Ann Celia Arnett**, b. 1835.
      ix. **Jasper Meredith Arnett**, b. 1838.
      x. **Rachel Caroline Arnett**, b. 1843; m. **Elisha S. SNIDER**.

593.

Martha Meredith, daughter of No. 12, Ann Pritchard, was born about 1804 and died before the 1850 census, probably about January 1850. She married **James JONES** about 06 Feb 1824, the date of their marriage bond. Davis Meredith was named father of Martha on the bond, and David Musgrave was the suretor. James Jones was born about 1800, and died before the 1850 census. The 1850 Mortality Schedule for Marion County shows that Martha Jones died in Marion County of typhoid B, or paratyphoid fever, age 44, and James Jones died in May of typhoid B, or paratyphoid fever, age. 46. Their children were living alone in the 1850 census in Marion County, with their son, Davis Jones, as head of household. Children of Martha Meredith and James Jones are:
      i. **Davis R. Jones.**
      ii. **Harriet Jones; m. Thomas ARNETT**.
      iii. **Edgar M. Jones.**
      iv. **Amos Jones.**
      v. **Wesley Jones.**
      vi. **John N. Jones.**
      vii. **Sanford C. Jones.**

594.

Eleanor Meredith, daughter of No 12, Ann Pritchard, was born 07 Dec 1807 in Monongalia County, (West) Virginia, and died 16 Mar 1869, age 61, in Monongalia County, and was buried 20 Mar 1869. She married **William ARNETT** 13 Jan 1828 in Monongalia County, son of **John ARNETT** and **Sarah DEACON** (also found spelled Dicken and Dickens). Davis Meredith was named Eleanor's father on their marriage bond of 09 Jan 1828. William Arnett was born 06 May 1798 in Monongalia County, and died 29 Jun 1872, in Paw Paw District, Marion County, West Virginia. An account written by his son, Calvin W. Arnett, in the *Biographical and Portrait Cyclopedia of Marion County,* 1895, pp. 32-34, says that William Arnett was recognized as a prosperous farmer and an intelligent man, who always took an active part in the affairs of his community and county. The same account notes that William's grandfather, John Arnett, Sr., of Scottish ancestry, was an early settler on the Eastern shore of Virginia, where he and a brother, Andrew Arnett, lived until they moved in 1785 to the vicinity of the present village of Arnettsville, Monongalia County, where they became the owners of several hundred acres of land. John's son, John Jr., father of William, was born in Monongalia County in 1796 and died in 1872. According to the biography, he was a farmer, a great reader, and a Union man during the Civil War. William and Eleanor are buried in the Arnett cemetery, Paw Paw District.

From one grandchild of Eleanor Meredith Arnett this account comes down: *Grandmother Arnett was Eleanor Meredith, daughter of Davis Meredith, a Revolutionary soldier. She was born 07 Dec 1807 and died 16 Mar 1869. She was a real pioneer, homemaker, mother, help-mate and untiring worker. There were no idle days in her calendar except the Sabbath, which she observed with Puritan strictness. She treated our Grandpapa with the greatest consideration and respect, and the children were taught to honor him with the same respect. While visiting there many times, I have stood around with the family waiting for breakfast while Grandpapa took his "before breakfast" smoke. After he was seated at the table, the family was seated. In my imagination, I can still taste grandmother's little scalloped cakes, sweetened with maple sugar, which she always had for Sunday. She was true to every virtue that adorns private life.*

Children of Eleanor Meredith and William Arnett are:

604.   i. **Rebecca Arnett**, b. 1829, Monongalia County, (West) Virginia; d. 1904, Marion County, West Virginia.

ii. **Dorcas Arnett**; m. **Ezekiel Fielding CUNNINGHAM.**

iii. **Lavina Arnett**; m. **Joseph P. DAVIS.**

iv. **Samuel Arnett**, b. 1833, Monongalia County, (West) Virginia; d. child.

v. **John Heber Arnett**, b. 1835, Monongalia County, (West) Virginia; farmer and soldier of the 6th regiment during the Civil War.

vi. **Melissa Arnett**, b. 1837, Monongalia County, (West) Virginia; unm.

vii. **Elias Riley Arnett**, b. 1840, Monongalia County, (West) Virginia; farmer and soldier of the 6th regiment during the Civil War.

viii. **Franklin Arnett**, b. 1842, Marion County, (West) Virginia; Civil War veteran; Commissioner of the Marion County Court for six years.

ix. **Elbert Meredith Arnett**, b. 1846, Marion County, (West) Virginia; farmer; Civil War veteran in the 17th regiment, West Virginia infantry.

507

x. **Sarah Ann Arnett**, b. 1848, Marion County,
(West) Virginia; d. before 1895; m. **William FREELAND.**
605. xi. **Calvin W. Arnett.**

595.
Thomas Merydith, son of No. 12, Ann Nancy Pritchard, was
born 26 Feb 1809 in Monongalia County, (West) Virginia and
died 19 Apr 1890 in Dexter, Cowley County, Kansas. It is not
known why he changed the spelling of his surname from
Meredith to Merydith; perhaps it was for aesthetic reasons. He
married **Millie MORRIS** 14 Dec 1829, daughter of **Richard
MORRIS** and **Susanna STULL/STUHL.** Millie was born 26
Oct 1812.

The Morris Family

1.
Richard Morris, according to the Morris family history, was
one of three brothers who came to America. Two went to New
Jersey and Richard went to Delaware. As is true with most
"three brother" stories, there is no evidence proving that
Richard had two other brothers.

In 1772, Richard Morris patented 110 acres in
Botecourt County, Virginia, but in 1776, he was entitled to four
hundred acres in Monongalia County, (West) Virginia, (the
portion that is now Preston County) adjoining Samuel World,
Sr. on the waters of Sandy Creek. Fort Morris was built on his
farm in 1774, on a stream "graced by the more practical than
euphonious name of Hog Run." He received an additional 600
acres adjoining this land in the right of preemption. Thomas
Chiana, *assessee to Morris*, also received 400 acres in the *right*

of residence adjoining Richard Morris.

In 1786, Richard Morris patented 46 acres in Botecourt County, Virginia, and in 1788 he patented another 141 acres on the Jackson River. Before 1750, he married **Prudence CATT** (see Catt family history on line).

Child of Richard Morris and Prudence Catt is:

2.   i. **Zadock Morris**, b. 15 Jun 1750 in Delaware; d. 18 Dec 1842, Marion County, (West) Virginia.

2.

Zadock Morris, son of Richard Morris and Prudence Catt, married (1) **Ellen "Polly" EVANS**. He married (2) **Elizabeth DAWSON**, possibly the widow of **George DAWSON**. Zadock Morris served during the Revolution as a private in Capt. Thomas Holland's Company, Delaware Regiment, from 01 Jun 1777 to the end of the war. Zadock's pension application of 1814 indicates that he was then the father of fourteen children.

Children of Zadock Morris and Ellen Evans are:

3.   i. **Richard Morris**, b. 11 Jul 1784, Delaware; d. 1868.

      ii. **Hannah Morris**, b. 08 May 1789; d. November 1857; m. **Frederick SWISHER** (1785-1855), abt. 1812.

      iii. **Catherine Morris**; m. **John BASNETT**, 15 Sep 1804.

      iv. **Margaret Morris**; m. **George BAKER**, 08 Apr 1816.

      v. **Sarah Morris; m. Reuben G. ANDER**, 16 Jun 1817, Monongalia County, (West) Virginia.

      vi. **Fanny Morris**, m. **Thomas WHITE**, 22 Aug 1821.

    vii. **Male Morris.**

    viii. **Male Morris.**

Children of Zadock Morris and Elizabeth Dawson are:

    ix. **Male Morris.**

    x. **Male Morris.**

    xi. **Elizabeth Morris**, b. January 1809, twin. She was "insane and subject to fits."

    xii. **Ezekiel Morris**, b. January 1809, twin; m. **Sarah HAYHURST**, 1827, Monongalia County.

    xiii. **Child Morris.**

    xiv. **Zadock Morris, Jr.,** b. 01 Aug 1818; d. 22 Jan 1899; bur. Satterfield Cemetery, Marion County, West Virginia; m. **Elizabeth Unk** (1821-1892).

3.

Richard Morris, son of Zadock Morris and Ellen Evans, was born 11 Jul 1784 in Delaware, and died in 1868 in West Virginia. He married **Susanna STULL/STUHL** about 1809. She was born in 1791 and died in 1859, the daughter of **Gottfried/Godfrey STULL/STUHL** and **Barbara CARMAN.** She is buried in the Morris Cemetery in Marion County, West Virginia. Both Zadock Morris and Gottfried Stull were veterans of the Revolutionary War.

Children of Richard Morris and Susan Stull are:

    i. **Mahala Morris**, b. 04 Dec 1809; d. 19 May 1898; m. No. 495, **Thomas PRICHARD,** 1808-1885), 14 Feb 1830, son of No. 11, **William PRICHARD,** and **Hannah MEREDITH.** (See Descendants of William Pritchard.)

    ii. **Rawley Morris**, b. 06 Oct 1811; d. 22 Feb 1892; m. **Catherine BALLAH**, 16 Feb 1836.

510a

Thomas Merydith
Taken about 1876

510b

iii. **Amelia "Millie" Morris,** b. 16 Oct 1812, Fairmont, Marion County, (West) Virginia; d. 17 May 1887, Dexter, Cowley County, Kansas.

iv. **Rodney Morris**, b. 13 Mar 1814; d. 25 Sep 1905; m. **Rebecca UNK** abt. 1840.

v. **Matilda Morris**, b. 12 Feb 1816; d. 17 Aug 1904; m. **John WELLS**, 26 Dec 1836.

vi. **Malinda Morris**, b. 22 Oct 1817; d. 09 Dec 1903; bur. Merrill Cemetery, Rivesville, Marion County, West Virginia; m. **Burr MERRILL** (1806-1882), son of **Joseph MERRILL** and **Elizabeth BATTEN**, 15 Dec 1840.

vii. **Mary Jane Morris**, b. 05 Jun 1819; d. 12 Jun 1897; m. **Zeth THORN**, 14 Apr 1840.

viii. **Henry S. Morris**, b. 21 Sep 1820; m. **Lydia Jane WILSON.**

ix. **Levi Morris**, b. 21 Mar 1824; d. 1852.

x. **Ezekiel D. Morris**, b. 28 Jan 1828; m. **Catherine BRUNO/BRUNEAU**; removed to Belmont County, Ohio.

xi. **Melissa Morris,** b. 03 Nov 1830; d. 03 Oct 1896, Marion County, West Virginia; m. **John HESS.**

xii. **Richard Charles Elliott Morris**, b. 01 Apr 1836; d. 1915; m. **Evaline PITZER**, 1859.

595. (Continued)

Children of Thomas Merydith and Millie Morris are:

606.   i. **Barse Merydith**.

        ii. **George Merydith**, d. abt. 1864. Killed during Civil

---

* Wife of No. 589, Thomas Merydith

War.
607.   iii. **Rolla Merydith**, b. 22 Nov 1830; d. 1906.
608.   iv. **Caroline Matilda Merydith**, b. 02 May1832,
             Monongalia County, (West) Virginia; d.
             01 Sep 1913, Dexter, Cowley County, Kansas.
609.   v.   **Davis Merydith**, b. December 1841; d. 1890.
610.   vi. **Alvira Merydith**, b. 1846; d. 1929.
611.   vii. **William Ezekiel Merydith**, b. 1849.

596.

Job John Meredith, son of No. 12, Ann Pritchard, was born
about 1810 in Monongalia County, (West) Virginia, and died
1881 in Salem, Harrison County, West Virginia. He married
Mary Ann AMOS, 02 Nov 1837, in Monongalia County,
(West) Virginia, daughter of **Stephen AMOS** and **Elizabeth
MILLER**. Their marriage bond is dated 30 Oct 1837. Mary
Ann was born 21 Aug 1820 in Monongalia County, and died
06 Nov 1899, in Berea, Ritchie County, West Virginia.

Minnie Lowther's *History of Ritchie County* says that
Job John Meredith moved to Ritchie County as early as 1839,
the first of many settlers there from Marion County. He
initially lived at the mouth of Middle Fork and White Oak,
before settling in Berea, where his family formed a component
part of the Seventh Day Baptist Church. He was a man of
strong character and pronounced religious views. In 1881, he
moved to Salem, where he died within a few weeks. After his
death, his widow returned to her old home and is buried in the
Pine Grove Cemetery.

Children of Job John Meredith and Mary Ann Amos are:
612.   i. **Elmina Meredith**, b. February 1839, Salem,
             Harrison County, (West) Virginia; d. 18 Jul
             1912, Travis County, Texas.

512

613.   ii. **James Marshall Meredith**, b. 1842, Salem, Harrison County, (West) Virginia; d. 1912, RitchieCounty.

614.   iii. **Harriet "Hattie" Meredith,** b. 1844, Salem, Harrison County, (West) Virginia; d. 1909, Salem, Harrison County, West Virginia.

        iv. **Davis N. Meredith,** b. 1846, Salem, Harrison County, (West) Virginia; minister in the Seventh Day Baptist Church; picture of Davis N. Meredith appears in the book, *Seventh Day Baptists in West Virginia* opposite page 360; on page 212, it notes that his parents joined the new Salem Church 03 Nov, 1844, and Davis N. Meredith was taken into membership on 16 Mar 1873.

615.   v. **Alpheus A. Meredith**, b. 1848, Salem, Harrison County, (West) Virginia; d. before 1910, Ritchie County, West Virginia.

        vi. **Millie Meredith,** b. abt. 1852, Salem, Harrison County, West Virginia; d. Salem; deaf mute; unm.

        vii. **Jane Meredith**, b. abt. 1856, Salem, Harrison County, (West) Virginia; m. **Joel BEE** (b. 1845, Doddridge County,), 25 Dec 1880, Ritchie County, West Virginia.

        viii. **Nancy Lillian "Lillie" Meredith**, b. 1864, Ritchie County, West Virginia; m. **Leonard JETT.**

597.

Davis Meredith, son of No. 12, Ann Pritchard, was born 04 Nov 1812, in Monongalia County, (West) Virginia, and died 04

Mar 1893 at Centerville, Tyler County, West Virginia. He married **Naomi SNODGRASS** on 17 Nov 1833. Permission to marry was given by his mother, Ann, her signature witnessed by his brother Job Meredith and nephew Davis Pritchard. The marriage bond dated 13 Nov 1833, names **William SNODGRASS** as father of Naomi and suretor. Her mother was **Anne Nancy KING,** daughter of **John KING.** Naomi was born 25 Jul 1816 in Monongalia County, and died 17 May 1885 at Centerville, Tyler County, West Virginia. Both David and Naomi are buried in Beechwood Cemetery, Tyler County. The children were born in Ohio, before the family settled in Tyler County.

Children of Davis Meredith and Naomi Snodgrass are:

616.   i. **Nancy E. Meredith,** b. 1835; d. in Lebanon, Monroe County, Oregon.

    ii. **William Newton Meredith,** b. 1836, Liberty, Washington County, Ohio; d. 15 Sep 1869, Tyler County, West Virginia; m. **Samantha K. BEATTY,** 19 Nov 1868, Tyler County, West Virginia.

617.   iii. **John Wesley Meredith,** b. 02 Oct 1838, Liberty, Washington County, Ohio; d. 11 Jan 1937, Paden Fork, Wetzel County, West Virginia.

618.   iv. **Absalom Pritchard Meredith,** b. 1840, Washington County, Ohio; d. 1906.

    v. **Frances Lovina Meredith,** b. 1844, Liberty, Washington County, Ohio; m. **Thomas B. WATSON.**

    vi. **Thomas Pritchard Meredith,** b. 1846, Liberty, Washington County, Ohio; d. 1927; m. (1) **Elizabeth Ann HAINES;** m. (2) **Mary J. HAINES,** 19 May 1869.

619.   vii. **James Alva Meredith**, b. 28 Mar 1850, Liberty, Washington County, Ohio; d. 08 Nov 1935.
620.   viii. **Phoebe Jane "Jenny" Meredith**, b. 23 Feb 1853, Liberty, Washington County, Ohio; d. 02 Oct 1895, Alma, Tyler County, West Virginia; m. **Unk RIPLEY**.
   ix. **Lavern/Lavina Meredith**, b. 1854, Liberty, Washington County, Ohio; m. **Unk WATKINS**.
   x. **Mary Emma Meredith**, b. November 1857, Liberty, Washington County, Ohio; d. 1935, Tyler County, West Virginia; m. (1) **William GLENN**; m. (2) **Isaiah McCULLOUGH**.
   xi. **Alexander A. Meredith**, b. November 1860, Liberty, Washington County, Ohio; m. **Mary E. TAGGART**, 12 Apr 1885.
   xii. **Martha Meredith**, b. 1862, Liberty, Washington County, Ohio; d. 21 Feb 1891, Tyler County, West Virginia.

598.

William Meredith, son of No. 12, Ann Pritchard, was born 16 May 1815 in Monongalia County, (West) Virginia, and died September 01, 1896 in White Oak, Ritchie County, West Virginia. He married **Tamer/Tamar DEACON**, daughter of **John DEACON** and **Barbara HERBINGER, (**sometimes spelled **HARBINGER)**, on 12 Apr 1836. The marriage bond of 11 Apr 1836 names Tamer's mother, Barbara (widow of John), and William Baker, husband of Tamer's sister Ruth, as suretor. Tamer was born 17 Mar 1819 and died 10 Oct 1879.

   The name Deacon is spelled Decken, Dicken, Dickens and other variations early in the settlement of West Virginia, but it is firmed as Deacon by the time family members are established in Ritchie County. The Deacons were of English descent, while Barbara was born in Cumberland, Maryland of German descent. John and Barbara settled on Paw Paw Creek, eight miles from Fairmont, Marion County, where they reared a family of ten daughters and two sons. Six of their daughters married men who settled in Ritchie County. All are buried in White Oak churchyard. John Deacon contracted typhoid fever while driving his cattle across the mountains to Romney, and died at Kingwood before reaching home. Barbara cleared the family debt and raised the children. One son, Thomas, remained at the family home in Marion County, and another son, Philip, went west. **Ruth Deacon** married **William BAKER, Matilda Deacon** married **Nathan SNODGRASS, Rachel Deacon** married **Daniel MASON, Sarah Deacon** married **William PARKER**, and **Julia Deacon** married **Joseph HAWKINS. Mary Deacon** married **Daniel SATTERFIELD** and lived in Dog Comfort, Ritchie County; **Katherine Deacon** married **Aaron HAWKINS** and lived in Marion County; and **Tasy Deacon** married **Daniel MICHAEL** and lived in Marion County. **Rebecca Deacon** died in childhood. Barbara Herbinger Deacon reached the age of eighty and was blind for several years before her death. She is buried beside her husband at the old homestead in Marion County.

William Meredith and Tamer Deacon first settled in Ohio before moving to Ritchie County in 1857. Their home was near the White Oak Church, where they worshiped. Tamer died by a fall from a wagon in 1879, at the age of 60 years, 6 months, 24 days, according to her gravestone in the White Oak churchyard. After her death, William lived among his children. He died on 01 Sep 1896 at the age of 81 years, 3 months, 17 days, at the home of his youngest daughter, Mary Eleanor Lowther, Fonosville, Ritchie County.

Children of William Meredith and Tamar Deacon are:

621.   i. **Eliza Meredith**, b. 1838, Monongalia County; d. Illinois.

ii. **Rachel Meredith,** b. 1840. Monongalia County, (West) Virginia; d. before 1911, Des Moines, Polk County, Iowa; m. **Franklin C. CLAYTON** (b. 1838, Monongalia County), 03 Aug 1861, Ritchie County, West Virginia.

622.   iii. **Nancy Jane Meredith**, b. March 1844, Monongalia County, (West) Virginia.

iv. **Mary Eleanor Meredith,** b. 1847, Washington County, Ohio; d. 1934, Harrisville, Ritchie County, West Virginia; m. (1) **James N. LEGGETT** (b. 21 Mar 1847; d. 22 Jun 1872, Ritchie County), 04 Apr 1867, Ritchie County; m. (2) **William George LOWTHER** (b. 11 Feb 1839, Harrison County, (West) Virginia; d. 24 May 1921, Harrisville, Ritchie County, West Virginia), 24 Jun 1877, Ritchie County.

v. **Asbury P. Meredith**, b. 1857, Noble County, Ohio; d. 1932, Washington State; m. **Mary TAYLOR,** (b. 1859, Ritchie County, West Virginia), 09 Nov 1875, Ritchie County.

THIRD GENERATION

599.

Thomas Meredith, son of No. 589, Absalom Meredith, was born about 1809 in Butler County, Ohio. He married **Unk.**
Child of Thomas Meredith and Unk is:
> i. **Davis Meredith;** member of an Illinois Regiment,
>   d. 15 May 1864, at the battle of Resaca,
>   Georgia during the Civil War.

600.

Davis Meredith, son of No. 589, Absalom Meredith, was born 14 Jun 1812 in Butler County, Ohio, and died 03 Aug 1896 in Sangamon County, Illinois. He married **Mary NEWCOMER**, 19 Jun 1836 in Sangamon County. She was born 07 Jun 1814, in Franklin County, Ohio, and died 11 Sep 1893, in Sangamon County, Illinois.
Child of Davis Meredith and Mary Newcomer is:
623.   i. **Mary Jane Meredith**, b. 03 Dec 1842, Sangamon
>   County, Illinois; d. 10 Jan 1898, Sangamon
>   County.

601.

James H. Arnett, Jr., son of No. 592, Rachel Meredith, was born 1820 in Monongalia County, (West) Virginia. He married **Elizabeth UNK**, who was born in 1818.
Children of James Arnett and Elizabeth are:
> i. **Martha Arnett**, b. 1840.
> ii. **John C. Arnett**, b. 1842.
> iii. **Rebecca Arnett, ,** b. 1843.
> iv. **Norman Arnett**, b. 1846.

v. **William Arnett,** b. 1848.
vi. **Sanford Arnett**, b. 1850.

602.

Andrew Meredith Arnett, son of No. 592, Rachel Meredith, was born 24 Jul 1823, and died on 17 Jun 1888. He married **Lavina PRICE** on 23 Feb 1843. She was born in 1826, the daughter of No. 41, **John Richard PRICE** and **Sarah MORGAN.** Lavina was the first postmistress of Arnettsville. Before the Civil War, Andrew was a constable. In 1879, he was appointed as postmaster, and after 1881, he became a Notary Public. He is buried in the Arnettsville Cemetery in Marion County.

Child of Andrew Meredith Arnett and Lavina Price is:
624.   i. **Coleman Morgan Arnett**, b. 17 Aug 1850.

603.

Martha Ann Celia Arnett, daughter of No. 592, Rachel Meredith, was born 1835 in Arnettsville, Marion County, (West) Virginia. She married **Elias Y. SATTERFIELD**, 25 Mar 1852, and had twelve children. Elias formed a company to fight in the Civil War; one of his Lieutenants was an Arnett. Child of Martha Ann Celia Arnett and Elias Satterfield is:
     i. **Minnie Belle Satterfield.**

604.

Rebecca Arnett, daughter of No. 594, Eleanor Meredith and William Arnett, was born 1829 and died 1904 in Marion County, West Virginia. She married No. 45, **Ulysses Morgan PRICE**. He was born 14 Dec 1828 on a farm near Fairmont, then called Middleton, Virginia. His obituary in *The Fairmont Times* of 09 Jan 1923, is headed: ***Pioneer Dies at Age of 94.*** It states: *Ulysses Morgan Price died at 6 a.m. Sunday, 08 Jan 1923 at the ripe old age of 94 years and 24 days. Mr. Price resided in Fairview, Marion County for the past twenty years. He was a son of John and Sarah Price...He is a descendant of Zachariah Morgan who settled what is now known as Morgantown and was of historical fame as an Indian fighter. He was a grand-son of Richard Price, who served three enlistments in the Revolutionary War, being in our country's service throughout the entire conflict.*

He was married 03 Jan 1851 to Rebecca Arnett, and to this union nine children were born, one of which died in infancy. Of the remaining eight children, five still survive: Mrs. Ella Mockler of Mannington; Elbert of Houston, Texas; Eber G., Richard E., and Miss Malissa, all of Fairview. Samantha, Camden, and Miss Vina preceded their father to the eternal reward. There are nine grand-children and twelve great grand-children, all of whom are living. Mr. Price has been a consistent member of the Methodist Episcopal Church for seventy-four years. His remains will be placed at rest in the Arnett Cemetery.

An editorial in *The West Virginian*, 10 Jan 1923, also lauds Ulysses Morgan Price. Headed *A **Pioneer Passes**,* it begins: *With the passing of Ulysses Morgan Price, a connecting link with the pioneer past has been severed. Ninety-four years is a long, long time, and never in the world's history has such a period introduced such changes as have taken place during the lifetime of this man.*

From a boyhood spent in an untamed, uncleared wilderness, without changing his location, he passed from life in the fullness of his years within hearing of the grinding wheels of the electric cars, the hoarse voice of the automobile, and the ringing of the telephone. He stepped from the threshold of savagery to the heart of civilization during his lifetime...He has witnessed things that no other like period ever brought to man.

Children of Ulysses Morgan Price and Rebecca Arnett are:

625.   i. **Sarah Eleanor Price**, b. 1857.

    ii. **Elbert Price**; d. after 1923; lived in Houston, Texas.

    iii. **Eber G. Price**, d. after 1923; lived in Fairview, Marion County, West Virginia.

    iv. **Richard E. Price**, d. after 1923, lived in Fairview, Marion County, West Virginia.

    v. **Malissa Price**, d. after 1923, lived in Fairview, Marion County, West Virginia; unm.

    vi. **Samantha Price**, d. before 1923.

    vii. **Camden Price**, d. before 1923.

    viii. **Lavina Price**, d. before 1923.

605.

Calvin W. Arnett, son of No. 594, Eleanor Meredith, was born 14 Jun 1853 seven miles northwest of Fairmont, Marion County, (West) Virginia, and died after 1895 in Fairmont, when he was featured as a prominent citizen in the *Biographical and Portrait Cyclopedia of Monongalia, Marion, and Taylor Counties, West Virginia,* published by Rush, West & Company, Philadelphia, Pennsylvania, 1895. He married **Belle JAMISON**, daughter of **John JAMISON** of Monongalia County, on 14 Aug 1875.

    Calvin W. Arnett was reared on the farm and attended Fairmont Normal School and West Virginia University. After leaving the university, he worked with a large nursery firm, then became general manager of the Geyser Manufacturing Company for the state of West Virginia, and part of the states of Ohio and Maryland. In 1881, he moved to Fairmont and in 1891 made the first public sale of lots ever sold in the town, then purchased 25 acres of land which he cut up into lots and laid out what is known as the Arnett addition to Fairmont, resulting in formation of the Fairmont Development Company. He became an officer of the Bank of Fairmont and was elected mayor of Fairmont in 1893.

Child of Calvin W. Arnett and Belle Jamison is:

    i. **Glenn Jamison Arnett**, b. 18 Mar 1880.

606.

Barse Merydith, son of No. 595, Thomas Merydith is the father of:

626.   i. **Jimmy Merydith.**

607.

Rolla Merydith, son of No. 595, Thomas Merydith, was born 22 Nov 1830 and died 1906. He married **Jane Cornelia RIDGWAY**, daughter of **Elzy RIDGWAY** and **Jane McMUNN**.

Children of Rolla Merydith and Jane Ridgway are:

627.   i. **Martha Merydith**, b. 03 Nov 1854; d. 1931.

628.   ii. **Charles Merydith**, b. 18 Sep 1956; d. 05 Oct 1929.

629.   iii. **Edward A Merydith**. b. 01 Jan 1860; d. 06 May 1948.

    iv. **Ida Jeanette Merydith**, b. 06 Dec 1963; d. 1959.

    v. **Marietta Mayme Merydith**, b. 22 Jul 1867; d. 1961.

630.   vi. **Thomas E. Merydith**, b. 12 Oct 1869; d. 1944.

vii. **Harry E. Merydith**, b. 16 Feb 1874; d. 1963.

608.

Caroline Matilda Merydith, daughter of No. 595, Thomas Merydith, was born 02 May 1832 in Monongalia County, (West) Virginia, and died 01 Sep 1913 in Dexter, Cowley County, Kansas. She married **Charles Wesley RIDGWAY, Sr.,** 30 Mar 1852 in Monroe, Ohio, son of **Elzy RIDGWAY** and **Jane McMUNN**. Her brother Rolla married Jane, sister of her husband. Charles was born 04 Jun 1829 in Ludlow Township, Washington County, Ohio. He was disabled during the Civil War. In November 1868, he moved to Greenfield, Dade County, Missouri, then to Douglass County, Kansas in 1869, finally to Crab Creek near Dexter, Cowley County. Children of Caroline Merydith and Charles Ridgway are:

631.   i. **Amelia Jane Ridgway**, b. 27 Jun 1853, Long Eddy, Monroe County, Ohio; d. 24 Dec 1931, Dexter, Cowley County, Kansas.

         ii. **Permealia C. Ridgway**, b. 23 Jul 1855, Lebanon, Monroe County, Ohio; d. Texas. m. _?_ **HIGHTOWER**.

632.   iii. **Emma L. Ridgway**, b. 10 Feb 1858, Lebanon, Monroe County, Ohio.

         iv. **Russell Norton Ridgway**, b. 06 Feb 1860, Lebanon, Monroe County, Ohio; d. 19 Feb 1864, Mattamoras, Washington County, Ohio.

633.   v. **Charles Wesley Ridgway, Jr.,** b. 25 Aug 1862, Lebanon, Monroe County, Ohio; d. 03 Apr 1935, Dexter, Cowley County, Kansas.

         vi **Davis Archibold Ridgway**, b. 06 Sep 1864,

Mattamoras, Washington County, Ohio; d.
25 Jan 1865, Mattamoras, Washington County,
Ohio.
  vii. **Frank Sheriden Ridgway**, b. 17 Aug 1866,
        Mattamoras, Washington County, Ohio; d.
        19 Aug 1871, Cowley County, Kansas.
634. viii. **Caroline Merydith Ridgway**, b. 05 Feb 1869,
        Mattamoras, Washington County, Ohio; d.
        02 Sep 1948, Dexter, Cowley County, Kansas.
635.   ix. **Adda Lee Ridgway**, b. 07 Aug 1875, Cowley
        County, Kansas; d. February 1973. San Diego,
        California.

609.

Davis Merydith, son of No. 595, Thomas Merydith, was born
December 1841 and died 1890. He married **Sabrina SMITH**.
Children of Davis Merydith and Sabrina Smith are:
636.   i. **Nellie Merydith**.
637.   ii. **Warren Merydith**
638. iii. **Hattie Merydith**.
639.   iv. **Clarence Merydith**.
640.   v. **Ella Willmetta Merydith**, b. 13 Jan 1869; d. 06
        Sep 1919.
641.   vi. **Augusta Merydith**, b. 26 Sep 1881; d. 28 Nov
        1961.

610.

Alvira Merydith, daughter of No. 595, Thomas Merydith, was
born 1846 and died 1929. She married **Emer W. LEMASTER**
Children of Alvira Merydith and Emer W. Lemaster are:
642.   i. **Tom Lemaster**.
643.   ii. **William Septimus Lemaster, Sr.**

The Pritchard/Prickett Family History

644. iii. **Edd Lemaster**, b. 1873.
645.   iv. **Minnie M. Lemaster**, b. 26 Sep 1875; d. 16 Oct
           1961.
646.   v. **Millie J. Lemaster**, b. 27 Apr 1878; d. 1959.
647.   vi. **Anna Lee Lemaster**, b. 18 Feb 1882.
648. vii. **Bessie Edith Lemaster**, b. 18 Dec 1884.

611.

William Ezekiel Merydith, son of No. 595, Thomas Merydith,
was born 1848. He married **Mattie Mildred CALLISON**.
Children of William Merydith and Mattie Callison are:
         i. **Millie Mildred Merydith**, unm.
649.   ii. **Alpha V. Merydith**, b. 1877.
        iii. **Vinnie Ream Merydith**, b. 1879; d. young.
         iv. **Verdi Irene Merydith**, b. 1881; m. **O. E.
              KIRTLEY,** no children.
          v. **Marie Ethyl Merydith**, b. 1886; d. 1970; m.
              Earl PAINE, no children.
650.   vi. **Rose C. Merydith**, b. 12 Nov 1888; d. abt.
             1982.
651.   vii. **Morris Rolla Merydith**, b. 17 Dec 1890.
652. viii. **Frances C. Merydith**, b. 27 Dec 1892.
653.   ix. **Geneva C. Merydith**, b. 1895.
          x. **James Gertude Merydith**, b. 1897; d. young.
654.   xi. **William E. Coy Merydith**, b. 1901.

612.

Elmina Meredith, daughter of No. 596, Job John Meredith,
was born February 1839 in Salem, Harrison County, West
Virginia, and died 18 Jul 1912, in Travis County, Texas, death
certificate No. 18627. She married **Salathal Oral LAWSON**,
son of **William LAWSON** and **Eliza MARSHALL**, on 31 Oct

The Pritchard/Prickett Family History

1861 in West Virginia. He was born May 1836 in Warren
County, Virginia, and died 27 Nov 1910 in Travis County,
Texas, death certificate No. 12913. The Texas Census of 1900
listed Elmina M. as Salathial's spouse and their son, Mored B.
Children of Salathial Lawson and Elmina Meredith are:

    i. **Eva Lawson**, b. abt. 1857, Ritchie County,
(West) Virginia; m. **Unk DOAK**.

    ii. **Mandeville Lawson**, b. abt. 1861, Ritchie
County, West Virginia.

    iii. **William Lawson**, b. abt. 1862, Ritchie County,
West Virginia.

655.   iv. **Adelaide "Addie" Sylvania Lawson**. b. 15
Sep 1864, Ritchie County, West Virginia; d.
22 Jun 1944, Houston, Harris County, Texas.

    v. **Lena L. Lawson**, b. abt. 1865, Ritchie County,
West Virginia; d. bef. 1910; m. **Unk DOAK**.

    vi. **Ida S. Lawson**, b. abt. 1867, Ritchie County,
West Virginia.

    vii. **Mord B. Lawson**, b. January 1871, Ritchie
County, West Virginia.

    viii. **Mary B. Lawson**, b. abt. 1872, Ritchie County,
West Virginia.

    ix. **Roxie Lawson**, b. abt. 1878; m. **Unk FLEET**

613.

James Marshall Meredith, son of No. 596, Job John
Meredith, was born 1842 in Salem, Harrison County, (West)
Virginia, and died 1912 in Ritchie County, West Virginia. He
married **Elizabeth BEE,** 22 Dec 1864, in Ritchie County. She
was born May 1844 in Harrison County, and died 1910 in
Ritchie County. Her parents were **Ezekiel BEE** and **Mariah
JOHNSON**, daughter of **Michael JOHNSON**, an early settler

526

of Ellenboro, Ritchie County. Mariah died 09 Aug 1865. Both James and Elizabeth Meredith are buried in Pine Grove Cemetery, Berea, Ritchie County.

Children of James Meredith and Elizabeth Bee are:

    i. **John E. Meredith**, b. 01 Oct 1866, Ritchie County, West Virginia; d. 1933, Wood County, West Virginia m. **Belle W. MARSH** (b. September 1867, Ritchie County).

    ii. **Beth Meredith**, b. May 1869, Ritchie County, West Virginia.

    iii. **Seth H. Meredith**, b. 26 Jun 1869, Ritchie County, West Virginia; d. 20 Dec 1870, Ritchie County.

    iv. **Orpha Meredith**, b. March 1881, Ritchie County, West Virginia; d. 1973, Ritchie County; m. **R. Minter FOX** (b. 1879, Doddridge County, West Virginia; d. 1957 Ritchie County), 21 Aug 1909; both bur. Pine Grove Cemetery, Berea, Ritchie County.

656.   v. **Fred Meredith**, b. October 1876, Ritchie County, West Virginia; d. 1948, Berea, Ritchie County.

    vi. **Etta Meredith**, b. December 26, 1871, Ritchie County, West Virginia.

614.

Harriet "Hattie" Meredith, daughter of No. 596, Job John Meredith, was born 1844 in Salem, Harrison County, (West) Virginia, and died 1909 at Salem. She married **Preston F. RANDOLPH**. Both were teachers. She taught in the first free school in Union District, Ritchie County, at the Pleasant Hill Church in 1865. For twenty years, Preston Randolph taught in

Ritchie, Doddridge, and Harrison Counties, then turned to the mercantile business until 1902 when he founded the rural Home Voice School at Salem, a school for the correction of stuttering, a problem he himself had overcome. He lived a number of years after Harriet's death.

Children of Harriet Meredith and Preston F. Randolph are:

    i. **Ray Randolph**; d. early.

    ii. **Clyde Randolph**, professor at the State University; d. 1904, at the height of a brilliant career.

    iii. **Iva Randolph,** d. 1909; m. Professor **Joseph ROSIER** of the Fairmont Normal School. He died after 1909.

615.

Alpheus A. Meredith, son of No. 596, Job John Meredith, was born 1848 in Salem, Harrison County, West Virginia. He married **Mary L. BEE**, 01 Dec 1879. She was born 1852 in Doddridge County, (West) Virginia.

Child of Alpheus A. Meredith and Mary Bee is:

    i. **Emma Meredith**, b. December 1881, Ritchie County, West Virginia.

616

Nancy E. Meredith, daughter of No. 597, Davis Meredith, was born 1835, and died in Lebanon, Monroe County, Ohio. She married **Rollie CRAWFORD**.

Child of Nancy Meredith and Rollie Crawford is:

    i. **Sadie Crawford**, b. Lebanon, Monroe County, Ohio.

617.

John Wesley Meredith, son of No. 597, Davis Meredith, was born 02 Oct 1838, in Liberty, Washington County, Ohio, and died January 11, 1937, in Paden Fork, Wetzel County, West Virginia. He married **Elizabeth GLENN**, 19 Aug 1858, in Wetzel County. She was born 17 Aug 1839, and died in Wetzel County. Both are buried in Lazear's Chapel Cemetery, Wetzel County, West Virginia.

Children of John Meredith and Elizabeth Glenn are:

    i. **William Osborn Meredith,** b. 18 May1859; d. 11 Oct 1947.

    ii. **James Edwin Meredith,** b. 11 Jan 1861; d. 25 May 1939.

    iii. **Mary Frances Meredith,** b. 25 Sep 1862; d. in Texas.

    iv. **John Henry Meredith,** b. 17 Sep 1864; d. 10 Feb 1950; bur. Sistersville, Tyler County, West Virginia.

    v. **George Luther Meredith,** b. 13 Nov 1866; d. 15 Oct 1928.

    vi. **Naomi A. Meredith**, b. 09 Jan 1869.

    vii. **Maude Meredith**, b. 10 Apr 1870; d. 10 Apr 1870.

    viii. **Arthur A. Meredith**, b. 03 May 1873; d. 24 Apr 1954.

    ix. **Melvira Meredith**, b. 28 May 1875.

    x. **Rhoda M. Meredith**, b. 14 Sep 1878; m. **John KELLY** (b. 13 Oct 1871; d. 16 Mar 1932.)

618.

Absalom Pritchard Meredith, son of No. 597, Davis Meredith, was born 1840 in Liberty, Washington County, Ohio, and died 1906. He married (1) **Emma WHALEY**. He

529

married (2) **Catherine RILEY**, 16 Sep 1864. She was born 1839 in Sistersville, Tyler County, (West) Virginia.

Children of Absalom Meredith and Emma Whaley are:

    i. **William Mason Meredith.**
    ii. **Elmer Martin Meredith.**
    iii. **John Andrew Meredith.**
    iv. **Susanna Meredith.**
    v. **Thomas Benton Meredith.**
    vi. **Oscar Herman Meredith.**
    vii. **Child Meredith.**

Children of Absalom Meredith and Catherine Riley are:

    viii. **Jenny A. Meredith**, b. abt. 1865; m. **John B. HORNER.**
    ix. **Leo Meredith**, b. abt. 1867; d. infant.
    x. **Charles Steven Meredith**, b. 03 Jul 1868.
    xi. **Laura Laverna Meredith**, b. 03 Jul 1868; d. 24 Mar 1953.
    xii. **Gilbert B. Meredith**, b. 07 May 1872.
    xiii. **James A. Meredith**, b. 27 Jan 1875; d. April 1942; m. **Gillian JAMISON**, 17 Sep 1902.
    xiv. **Rufus Davis Meredith**, b. 27 Jan 1875; d. 03 Nov 1949.
    xv. **Emma Belle Meredith**, b. 10 Oct 1877; d. 05 Jan 1930.
    xiv. **William Henry Meredith**, b. 21 Jul 1879; d. 28 Feb 1948; m. (1) **Bertha EVANS**; m. (2) **Grace LYTTON**, 16 Jun 1938.

619.

James Alva Meredith, son of No. 597, Davis Meredith, was born 28 Mar 1850, in Liberty, Washington County, Ohio, and died 09 Nov 1935. He married **Mary Ellen DUTY**, 12 Nov

1871, in Tyler County, West Virginia. She was born in 1854 and died in 1930. Both are buried in Beachwood Cemetery, Alma, Tyler County, West Virginia.
Children of James Alva Meredith and Mary Ellen Duty are:
    i. **William Creed Meredith.**
    ii. **Nina Lee Meredith.**
    iii. **Leslie Everett Meredith.**
    iv. **John Wesley Meredith**, b. 21 Aug 1872; d. 1913.
    v. **Laura Adella Meredith**, b. 1874; d. 15 Jan 1934.
    vi. **Herbert Davis Meredith**, b. 1881.
    vii. **Charles Delbert Meredith**, b. 17 Aug 1887; d. 04 Oct 1953.
    viii. **Delcie Pearl Meredith**, b. 01 Oct 1888; d. 17 Dec 1892.
    ix. **Lloyd Biggs Meredith**, b. 1896.

620.

Phoebe Jane "Jenny" Meredith, daughter of No. 597, Davis Meredith, was born 23 Feb 1853, in Liberty, Washington County, Ohio, and died 12 Oct 1895 in Alma, Tyler County, West Virginia. She married **Thomas RIPLEY**, 12 Oct 1871. He was born 13 Aug 1843.
Children of Phoebe Meredith and Thomas Ripley are:
    i. **Mary Laverna Ripley**, b. 13 Mar 1873; d. 28 May 1950.
    ii. **Infant Ripley**, b. 16 Jan 1875; d. 24 Feb 1875.
    iii. **James Clyde Ripley**, b. 04 Jul 1881; d. 1950.
    iv. **Charles Raymond Ripley**, b. 03 Mar 1884.

621.

Eliza Meredith, daughter of No. 598, William Meredith, was born 1838 in Monongalia County, (West) Virginia, and died in

Illinois. She married **Francis G. DAY** in Ritchie County.
Child of Eliza Meredith and Francis G. Day is:
    i. **J. E. Day**, born in Ritchie County; lived in
        Auburn, Ritchie County.

622.

Nancy Jane Meredith, daughter of No. 598, William
Meredith, was born March 1844 in Monongalia County, (West)
Virginia. She married **Leander "Lee" S. CLAYTON**, 17 Dec
1874 in Ritchie County, West Virginia. He was born May 1855
in Ritchie County.
Children of Nancy Jane Meredith and Leander Clayton are:
    i. **William O. Clayton**, b. November 1879.
    ii. **Denford R. Clayton**, b. March 1882.

FOURTH GENERATION

623.

Mary Jane Meredith, daughter of No. 600, Davis Meredith, was born 03 Dec 1842 in Sangamon County, Illinois, and died 10 Jan 1898, in Sangamon County. She married **John Richard KINCAID**, 01 Jan 1863, in Illinois.

Children of Mary Jane Meredith and John Kincaid are:

657.   i. **Katherine Kincaid**, b. 30 May 1874, Sangamon County, Illinois; d. 12 May 1960, Sangamon County.

658.   ii. **Charles J. Kincaid**, b. 1878.

624.

Coleman Morgan Arnett, son of No. 602, Andrew Meredith Arnett, was born 27 Aug 1850. He married **Mariah S. PRICKETT**, 20 or 26 Dec 1872, the Rev. A. P. Sturm officiating. They lived in Arnettsville, Marion County, West Virginia at the junction of roads that became U.S. Route 19 and the Crown/Hagans Road. The house eventually burned down. Coleman was a farmer and a school teacher at Arnettsville School in 1873-74.

Children of Coleman Morgan Arnett and Mariah S. Prickett are:

  i. **Vanilla Iota "Otie" Arnett**, b. 03 Sep 1874; d. 05 Sep 1968.

  ii. **Matilda "Tillie" Lavina Arnett**, b. 25 Oct 1876.

  iii. **Desseaux Doudin (Dessa Downtain) Arnett**, b. 14 Dec 1878.

  iv. **Cora Belle Arnett**, b. 14 Feb 1882.

  v. **Effie Grace Arnett**, b. 03 Aug 1886.

    vi. **Oma Adaline Arnett**, b. 08 Mar 1889; d. 19 May
        1974.
    vii. **Dana "Dane" Coleman Arnett**, b. 01 May 1891.
659. viii. **Lillian Beatrice Arnett**, b. 08 May 1893; d. 1991,
        Arnettsville, Marion County.
    ix. **Victor Arnett**, b. 23 Dec 1898 (adopted).

625.

Sarah Eleanor Price, daughter of No. 604, Rebecca Arnett,
and No. 45, Ulysses Morgan Price, was born 1857. She married
Edward MOCKLER.
Child of Sarah Price and Edward Mockler is:
660.   i. **Robert Emmett Mockler**, b. 1879; d. 1964.

626.

Jimmy Merydith, son of No. 606, Barse Merydith, married
Unknown.
Children of Jimmy Merydith and Unknown are:
    i. **Raleigh Merydith.**
    ii. **Artie Merydith**; m. **Unk PRATT.**

627.

Martha Merydith, daughter of No. 607, Rolla Merydith, was
born 03 Nov 1854, and died 1931. She married **William
LUST.**
Children of Martha Merydith and William Lust are:
    i. **William Lust**; d. in childhood.
    ii. **Edith Lust**, d. 1968; m. **Melvin HARTINGER,**
       no children.

628.

Charles Merydith, son of No. 607, Rolla Merydith, was born

18 Sep 1856 and died 05 Oct 1929. He married **Margaret KIGANS**.

Children of Charles Merydith and Margaret Kigans are:

661. i. **Edward Merydith**, b. 1886.
662. ii. **Rolla Merydith**, b. 18 Aug 1889; d. 07 Sep 1919.
663. iii. **Ella Merydith**, b. 1895; d. 1968.

629.

Edward A. Merydith, son of No. 607, Rolla Merydith, was born 01 Jan 1860 and died 06 May 1948. He married **Rose SHANNAFELT**.

Children of Edward Merydith and Rose Shannafelt are:

664. i. **Frances C. Merydith**, b. 07 Dec 1890; d. 1925.
      ii. **Edward W. Merydith**, b. 14 May 1896.

630.

Thomas E. Merydith, son of No. 607, Rolla Merydith, was born 12 Oct 1869 and died 1944. He married **Grace BURCH**.

Children of Thomas Merydith and Grace Burch are:

      i. **Lester E. Merydith**, b. 18 Jan 1904; m. **Alice McCOY;** lived in Sun City, Maricopa County, Arizona.
665. ii. **Carroll L. Merydith**, b. 17 Sep 1905.
666. iii. **Thomas R. Merydith**, b. 02 Dec 1913.
      iv. **Donald M. Merydith**, b. 03 Apr 1914; d. 12 Jul 1933. Killed by train returning from C.C. Camp.
      v. **John W. Merydith**, b. 11 Nov 1916. Lived in Cleveland, Cuyahoga County, Ohio.
      vi. **Harry L. Merydith**, b. 28 Oct 1918. Retired from Pure Oil Company.
667. vii. **Dorothy Merydith**, b. 03 Oct 1920.

631.

Amelia Jane Ridgway, daughter of No. 608, Caroline Matilda Merydith, was born 27 Jun 1853 in Long Eddy, Monroe County, Ohio, and died 24 Dec 1931 in Dexter, Cowley County, Kansas. She married (1) **William W. BURRIS**, February 02, 1871 in Monroe County, Ohio, son of **Van BURRIS** and **Narcissa WILLIAMSON**. She married (2) **Oliver C. BRUBAKER** 11 Sep 1873 in Kansas. William Burris died 26 Aug 1872 near Erie, Neosho County, Kansas and was buried in the Erie Cemetery.

Child of Amelia Ridgway and William Burris is:

668.   i.   **Clara D. Burris**, b. 05 Feb 1872, Neosho County, Kansas; d. 11 Feb 1950, Cleveland, Pawnee County, Oklahoma.

Children of Amelia Ridgway and Oliver Brubaker are:

669.   ii.   **Fred Brubaker**, b. 25 Dec 1874, Kansas; d. 26 Apr 1946, Kansas.

670.   iii.   **Roy Preston Brubaker**, b. 26 Sep 1876, Cowley County, Kansas; d. 12 Sep1948, Kansas.

671.   iv.   **Amelia A. Brubaker**, 10 Mar 1879, Kansas; d. March 1956, Kansas.

632.

Emma L. Ridgway, daughter of No. 608, Caroline Matilda Merydith, was born 10 or 15 (Family Bible date) Feb 1858 in Lebanon, Monroe County, Ohio. She married **George A. CALLISON**.

Children of Emma Ridgway and George Callison are:

672.   i.   **George Lawrence Callison**, b. 09 Mar 1885.

673.   ii.   **James F. Callison**, b. 12 Nov 1886; d. 17 Nov 1970.

674.   iii.   **Elbert Callison**, b. 30 Oct 1890; d. 19 May 1965.

675.   iv. **Harley M. Callison**. b. 30 Nov 1892; d. 1967.

633.

Charles Wesley Ridgway, Jr., son of No. 608, Caroline
Matilda Merydith, was born 25 Aug 1862 in Lebanon, Monroe
County, Ohio, and died 03 Apr 1935 in Dexter, Cowley
County, Kansas. He married **Allie DUNLAP**. A covered
wagon is carved on his tombstone to commemorate his journey
from Ohio to Kansas in 1871.
Children of Charles Ridgway and Allie Dunlap are:
676.   i. **Ernest Wesley Ridgway**, b. 03 Aug 1892; d.
            March 1977.
677.   ii. **Ruby Caroline Ridgway**, b. 09 May 1898; d.
            30 Aug 1965.

634.

Caroline Merydith Ridgway, daughter of No. 608, Caroline
Matilda Merydith, was born 05 Feb 1869 in Mattamoras,
Washington County, Ohio, and died 01 Sep 1948 in Dexter,
Cowley County, Kansas. She married **Thomas Clayton
BROWN**, son of **William BROWN** and **Nancy
RICHARDSON**. She was known to her descendants as "Aunt
Cad."
Children of Caroline Ridgway and Thomas Brown are:
        i.   **William L. Brown**; officer in the U.S. Army; m. (1)
             Lucille BURNEY; m. (2) **Marie UNK**.
        ii. **Earl Brown**; m. **Rachel R. Unk** (1894-1924).
        iii. **Orville Brown**.
        iv. **Guy T. Brown**; b. 15 Aug 1891; d. 21 Aug 1913.
        v.   **Jack Brown**, b. 1897.

635.

Adda Lee Ridgway, daughter of No. 608, Caroline Matilda Merydith, was born 07 Aug 1875 in Cowley County, Kansas, and died February 1973 in San Diego, California. She married **Andy F. FOUDRAY**. She taught school in Enid, Oklahoma and bought a wooden chair with her first teaching paycheck. She and Andy F. Foudray lived in Tombstone, Arizona, where she was active at the Library and the Episcopal Church.
Children of Adda Ridgway and Andy Foudray are:

678.   i.   **Charles W. Foudray**, b. January 08, 1904.
679.   ii.   **Demonsthenes Foudray**, b. January 14, 1907; d. 1945.

636.

Nellie Merydith, daughter of No. 609, Davis Merydith, married (1) **Jack BROWNE**. She married (2) **Will BROWNE**.
Child of Nellie Merydith and Jack Browne is:

680.   i.   **Edith Browne**.

Child of Nellie Merydith and Will Browne is:

681.   ii.   **Mildred Browne**

637.

Warren Merydith, son of No. 609, Davis Merydith, married **Addie CHISAM.**
Children of Warren Meredith and Addie Chisam are:

     i. **Nellie Merydith.**
     ii. **Ernest Merydith; m. Pluma NEWBERRY.**

638.

Hattie Merydith, daughter of No. 609, Davis Merydith, married **Forrest ELLIOTT.**
Children of Hattie Merydith and Forrest Elliott are:

682.　i.　**Floyd Elliott**, b. June 23, 1903.
683.　ii.　**Esther Elliott**, b. April 02, 1905.
684.　iii.　**Ina Elliott**, b. April 07, 1906.
685.　iv.　**Paul Elliott, b.** July 22, 1909.
686.　v.　**Thelma Elliott**, b. February 06, 1916.

639.

Clarence Merydith, son of No. 609, Davis Merydith, married **Maybelle CHIVINGTON**.
Children of Clarence Merydith and Maybelle Chivington are:
　　i.　**Alma L. Merydith**; d. young.
687.　ii.　**Joy Jean Merydith**.
688.　iii.　**Ted Owen Merydith, Sr.**
689.　iv.　**C. Dewey Merydith**
　　v.　**Edna E. Merydith**, b. 1916; lived in Roseville, Sacramento County, California.

640.

Ella Willmetta Merydith, daughter of No. 609, Davis Merydith, was born 13 Jan 1869 and died 06 Sep 1919. She married **Lloyd SCOTT**.
Children of Ella Merydith and Lloyd Scott are:
　　i.　**James E. Scott**; d. in infancy.
690.　ii.　**Clarence Scott**.
691.　iii.　**Dewey Scott**, b. 23 Jun 1898.
　　iv.　**Lela M. Scott**, b. 19 Feb 1900; m. **Walter MAIER**.
692.　v.　**Mary Grace Scott**, b. 02 Nov 1901.
　　vi.　**Alice Scott**, b. 30 Aug 1903.

641.

Augusta Merydith, daughter of No. 609, Davis Merydith, was born 26 Sep 1881 and died 28 Nov 1961. She married **Samuel WILLIAMSON**.

Children of Augusta Merydith and Samuel Williamson are:

693.　　i.　**Lloyd Williamson**, b. 09 Aug 1905.

694.　　ii.　**William R. Williamson**, b. 17 Aug 1907; d. 10 Mar 1972.

695.　　iii.　**Ruby Mae Williamson**, b. 29 Jul 1909; d. 05 Dec 1952.

696.　　iv.　**Augusta R. Williamson**, b. 16 Jan 1920.

642.

Tom Lemaster, son of No. 610, Alvira Merydith, married **Jessie RICE**.

Children of Tom Lemaster and Jessie Rice are:

697.　　i.　**Emer W. Lemaster II**.

　　　ii.　**H. J. "Jake" Lemaster**; m. **Fern LEATHERMAN**.

643.

William Septimus Lemaster, Sr., son of No. 610, Alvira Merydith, married **Mary ALEY**.

Child of William Lemaster and Mary Aley is:

　　　i.　**William Septimus Lemaster, Jr.**

644.

Edd Lemaster, son of No. 610, Alvira Merydith, was born 1873. He married **Nellie ALEY**.

Children of Edd Lemaster and Nellie Aley are:

　　　i.　**Gail Lemaster**, b. 1907.

　　　ii.　**Elston Lemaster**, b. 1915; d. 1920.

645.

Minnie M. Lemaster, daughter of No. 610, Alvira Merydith, was born 26 Sep 1875 and died 16 Oct 1961. She married **William H. GUTHRIE, Sr.**
Children of Minnie Lemaster and William Guthrie are:
698.　　i. **Lee N. Guthrie**, b. 28 Jan 1904; d. 22 Jun 1968.
　　　ii. **Wayne Guthrie**, b. 21 Oct 1907; d. 12 Oct 1911.
699.　iii. **William H. Guthrie, Jr.,** b. 10 Jul 1911.
700.　iv. **Lois K. Guthrie**, b. 17 Jan 1915.
　　　v. **John J. Guthrie**, b. 2 Jan 1917; m. **Lucille M. RADCLIFF;** lived in Belle Plaine, Sumner County, Kansas.

646.

Millie J. Lemaster, daughter of No. 610, Alvira Merydith, was born 17 Apr 1878, and died 1959. She married **Eli H. READ**.
Children of Millie Lemaster and Eli Read are:
701.　i. **Emory William Read**, b. 21 Dec 1900; d. 1969.
702.　ii. **Thelma Read**, b. 27 Apr 1905.
　　iii. **Elva Read**, b. 05 Dec 1908.
　　iv. **Bill Read**, b. 20 Oct 1912; d. 1928.

647.

Anna Lee Lemaster, daughter of No. 610, Alvira Merydith, was born 18 Feb 1882. She married **Stewart GORDON**.
Children of Anna Lemaster and Stewart Gordon are:
　　i. **Mary Gordon**; m. **Unk BEAN**. Lived in Albuquerque, Bernalillo County, New Mexico.
703.　ii. **Mamie Gordon**, b. 18 Jun 1902.
704.　iii. **Carmen S. Gordon**, b. 05 Aug 1903.
705.　iv. **Ione Gordon**, b. 19 Jan 1905.

v. **Alice Gordon**, b. 20 Apr 1906; m. **Unk LEE**.
706. vi. **Gilbert Gordon**, b. 15 Jun 1908.

648.

Bessie Edith Lemaster, daughter of No. 610, Alvira Merydith, was born 18 Dec 1884. She married **Ray Moore McGILL**. Children of Bessie Lemaster and Ray McGill are:
707. i. **Annabel McGill**, b. 12 Dec 1905.
ii. **Clifford L. McGill**, b. 04 Sep 1907; d. 1964; m. (1) **Nora UNK**; m. (2) **Lena UNK**.
708. iii. **Dorothy Irene McGill**, b. 28 Oct 1908.
iv. **Beaulah Ray McGill**, b. 24 Feb 1918; m. **Joe GRAHAM**.
709. v. **Nellie Elizabeth McGill**, b. 14 Oct 1919.
710. vi. **Lenora Fay McGill**, b. 14 Nov 1925.

649.

Alpha V. Merydith, daughter of No. 611, William Ezekiel Merydith, was born 1877. She married **O. C. JENSON**. Child of Alpha Merydith and O. C. Jenson is:
711. i. **Wilma Jenson**.

650.

Rose C. Merydith, daughter of No. 611, William Ezekiel Merydith, was born 12 Nov 1888 and died abt. 1982. She married **Glen TURNER**. Children of Rose Merydith and Glen Turner are:
712. i. **Merydith Dean Turner**, b. 04 Dec 1915.
ii. **Jacquita M. Turner**, b. 3 Apr 1920; d, 12 Mar 2013.

651.

Morris Rolla Merydith, son of No. 611, William Ezekiel Merydith, was born 17 Dec 1890. He married **Lillie TAYLOR**. Children of Morris Merydith and Lillie Taylor are:

     i. **Billy Merydith**, b. 1920; d. in his teens.

713.   ii. **Betty Ruth Merydith**, b. 15 Feb 1927.

652.

Frances C. Merydith, daughter of No. 611, William Ezekiel Merydith, was born 17 Dec 1892. She married **John NEWSOME**.

Child of Frances C. Merydith and John Newsome:

     i. **Jean Newsome**, d. young.

653.

Geneva C. Merydith, daughter of No. 611, William Ezekiel Merydith, was born 1895. She married **Jim H. WRIGHT**. Children of Geneva Merydith and Jim H. Wright are:

714.   i. **Verdi Wright**, b. April 01, 1915.

715.   ii. **David Wright**, b. March 23, 1918.

716.   iii. **Geneva Marie Wright**, b. June 08, 1920.

654.

William E. Coy Merydith, son of No. 611, William Ezekiel Merydith, was born 1901. He married **Rachel SMITH**. Children of William E. Coy Merydith and Rachel Smith are:

717.   i. **Pearl Merydith**, b. 16 Nov 1928.

718.   ii. **Edward Merydith**, b. 10 Jan 1930.

719.   iii. **Peggie Merydith**, b. 22 Jul 1931.

720.   iv. **Joyce Merydith**, b. 16 Aug 1932.

655.

Adelaide "Addie" Sylvania Lawson, daughter of No. 612, Elmina Meredith, was born September 15, 1864 in Ritchie County, West Virginia, and died June 22, 1944 in Houston, Harris County, Texas. She married **Enoch Marsh McGINNIS** 20 Dec 1883 in Ritchie County, West Virginia, son of **David McGINNIS** and **Sarah MARSH**. He was born 08 Nov 1857 and died 12 Jan 1936.

Enoch Marsh McGinnis once owned land that became the Cinco Ranch development outside Houston, Texas. During the last years of his life, he lived with his son, **Rex Oral McGinnis**. According to the 1880 West Virginia census, he lived at home and worked as a peddler. In 1895, he moved to Katy, Harris County, Texas from Austin. In 1934, he retired from farming.

Children of Addie Lawson and Enoch McGinnis are:

721. i. **Rex Oral McGinnis**, b. 30 Jun 1885, Mole Hill, Ritchie County, West Virginia; d. 30 Jul 1960, Houston, Harris County, Texas.

722. ii. **Delsie Vertie McGinnis**, b. 30 Dec 1888, Mole Hill, Ritchie County, West Virginia; d. 17 Sep 1962, Houston, Harris County, Texas.

iii. **Kittie Vivian McGinnis**, b. 21 Oct 1891, Mole Hill, Ritchie County, West Virginia; d. 21 Mar 1970, Houston, Harris County, Texas; m. about 1920 **Charles Henry STOCKDICK** (b. 01 Jan 1879 in Missouri; d. 08 Mar 1959 in Katy, Harris County, Texas).

656.

Fred Meredith, son of No. 613, James Marshall Meredith, was born October 1876 in Ritchie County, West Virginia, and died

1948 in Ritchie County. He married **Lura BUZZARD**, 10 Apr 1909, in Ritchie County. She was born 1886 in Ritchie County, the daughter of **William BUZZARD** and **Lucinda BIRD**. Lura died 1963 in Ritchie County. She and Fred are buried in Pine Grove Cemetery, Berea, Ritchie County.

Child of Fred Meredith and Lura Buzzard is:

723.   i. **Ruby Meredith**, b. 1910, Ritchie County, West Virginia; d. 1992, Ritchie County.

FIFTH GENERATION

657.

Katherine Kincaid, daughter of No. 623, Mary Jane Meredith, was born 20 May 1874 in Sangamon County, Illinois, and died 12 May 1960 in Sangamon County. She married **Charles F. MATTHEW,** 17 Feb 1907 in Sangamon County.
Child of Katherine Kincaid and Charles F. Matthew is:
724.   i. **Mary Adelaide Matthew**, b. 21 Jun 1910.

658.

Charles J. Kincaid, son of No. 623, Mary Jane Meredith, was born in 1878. He married **Nellie DRENNAN.**
Child of Charles J. Kincaid and Nellie Drennan is:
         i. **Ruth Kincaid**, b. 28 Jul 1904.

659.

Lillian Beatrice Arnett, daughter of No. 624, Coleman Morgan Arnett, was born 08 May 1893, and died 1991 in Arnettsville, Marion County, West Virginia. She married **Simeon E. AMMONS** on 05 Nov 1910, in Rivesville, Marion County, at the First Methodist Episcopal Church, Rev. Harry C. Howard officiating. The couple moved to Jacobsburg, Belmont County, Ohio, where they were given land and a house by Simeon's father, John H. Ammons. Simeon died unexpectedly of a heart attack on 05 Nov 1913. Lillian, eight months pregnant with their second son, John Morgan, immediately fled Ohio with their first son, Billy (Charles Simeon), and returned to live with her father, Coleman Arnett. With John's inheritance from his father, Lillian purchased 22 acres and a house (the Brookover farm) between Arnettsville and Georgetown, where she married (2) **Paul A. BERRY**, son of **French BERRY**. Paul was born 17 Oct 1884, and died 25 Mar 1991. He was a coal miner and construction worker. Children of Lillian Arnett and Simeon E. Ammons are:

    i. **Charles "Billy" Simeon Ammons**, b. abt. 1912,
    ii. **John Morgan Ammons**, b. December, 1913.

660.

Robert Emmett Mockler, son of No. 625, Sarah Eleanor Price, was born 1879 and died in 1964. He married **Alberta BAUMGARTNER**, daughter of **Samuel BAUMGARTNER** and **Victoria Elizabeth SMITH**.
Child of Robert Mockler and Alberta Baumgartner is:
725.   i. **Elizabeth Eleanor Mockler**, b. 1913.

661.

Edward Merydith, son of No. 628, Charles Merydith, was born in 1886. He married **Unk.**
Child of Edward Merydith and Unk is:
726.   i. **Jack Merydith.**

662.

Rolla Merydith, son of No. 628, Charles Merydith, was born 18 Aug 1889 and died 07 Sep, 1919. He married **Jane ASTON**.
Child of Rolla Merydith and Jane Aston is:
727.   i. **Charles Wesley Merydith.**

663.

Ella Merydith, daughter of No. 628, Charles Merydith, was born 1895 and died 1968. She married **Allie WILLIAMS**.
Child of Ella Merydith and Allie Williams is:

728.   i. **Charles Williams**, b. 1908.

664.

Frances C. Merydith, daughter of No. 629, Edward A. Merydith, was born 07 Dec 1890 and died in 1925. She married **Walter HIGGINS**.
Children of Frances C. Merydith and Walter Higgins are:
729.   i. **Merydith Higgins**, b. 02 Oct 1913; d. 29 Feb 1953.
730.   ii. **Walter M. Higgins**, b. 27 Jun 1918.
       iii. **Walter W. Higgins**, b. 05 Jul 1920. U.S. Air Force; died when plane went down over Himalayan Mountains during W. W. II in 1944. His body was never found.

665.

Carroll L. Merydith, son of No. 630, Thomas E. Merydith, was born 17 Sep 1905; m. (1) **Anna PRACHHAUSER**; m. (2) **Florence UNK**; m. (3) **Adrienne UNK**. Lived in Cincinnati, Ohio.
Child of Carroll Merydith and Anna Prachhauser is:
731.   i. **Betty Ann Merydith**, b. 24 Jan 1936.
Child of Carroll Merydith and Adrienne Unk is:
       ii. **Carrol N. Merydith**, b. 20 Nov 1941; m. **Cheri UNK**; lived in Concord, Contra Costa County, California.

666.

Thomas R. Merydith, son of No. 630, Thomas E. Merydith, was born 02 Dec 1913. He married **Margaret HEYWORTH.** They lived in Cleveland, Cuyahoga County, Ohio.
Children of Thomas Merydith and Margaret Heyworth are:

   i. **Carole Merydith**, b. 24 Oct 1941; lived in Westlake, Cuyahoga County, Ohio.

   ii. **Alice Merydith**, b. 28 Nov 1942; m. **Richard WASOSKY**; lived in Sagamore Hills, Cuyahoga County, Ohio.

732. iii. **Christine Merydith**, b. 18 Aug 1948.

   iv. **Tracy Merydith**, b. 09 Aug 1956; lived in Strongsville, Cuyahoga County, Ohio.

   v. **Alexis Merydith**, b. 23 Apr 1959; lived in Middleburg Heights, Cuyahoga County, Ohio.

667.

Dorothy Merydith, daughter of No. 630, Thomas E. Merydith, was born 03 Oct 1920. She married **Archie DAYMONT**. They lived in Auburn, Cayuga County, New York.

Children of Dorothy Merydith and Archie Damont are:

733. i. **Thomas Daymont**, b. 05 Jul 1945.

   ii. **Richard Daymont**, b. 25 May 1947.

   iii. **Judy Daymont**, b. 25 Sep 1953.

   iv. **Cindy Daymont**, b. 21 Feb 1962.

668.

Clara D. Burris, daughter of No. 631, Amelia Jane Ridgway, was born 05 Feb 1872 in Neosho County, Kansas, twelve miles north of Erie, near Canville Creek, and died 11 Feb 1950 in Cleveland, Pawnee County, Oklahoma. She married (1) **John Preston BROWN** 16 Feb 1892 in Kansas, son of **William BROWN** and **Nancy RICHARDSON**. They were married by Rev. Turnelson. She married (2) **Austin Bennett BERRY**.

Children of Clara Burris and John Brown are:

   i. **John Homer Brown**, b. 03 Oct 1894, Loyal, Kingfisher County, Oklahoma; d. September

1968, Kansas City, Jackson County, Missouri;
m. **Ruth HOGAN** 13 Jan 1923.
734.   ii. **Forest Leroy Brown**, b. 21 Mar 1897, Loyal,
Kingfisher County, Oklahoma; d. 30 June
1986, Boise, Ada County, Idaho.

669.

Fred Brubaker, son of No. 631, Amelia Jane Ridgway, was
born 25 Dec 1874 in Kansas and died 26 Apr 1946 in Kansas.
He married **Marguarette LEFLER**.
Children of Fred Brubaker and Marguarette Lefler are:
735.   i. **Erma A. Brubaker**, b. 28 Nov1909, Kansas.
737.   ii. **Orin C. Brubaker**, b. 17 Jan 1911, Kansas.
737.   iii. **Eula M. Brubaker**, b. 07 Aug 1920, Kansas.
738.   iv. **Vesta G. Brubaker**, b. 22 May 1924, Kansas.
          v. **Ivan F. Brubaker**, b. 08 Jul 1930, Kansas; m.
             Winnie HANKINS.

670.

Roy Preston Brubaker, son of No. 631, Amelia Jane
Ridgway, was born 26 Sep 1876 in Cowley County, Kansas
and died 12 Sep 1948 in Kansas. He married **Gertrude
Josephine JOY,** 27 Apr 1904 in Kansas. Gertrude died 24 Mar
1919. She died four days after her daughter Millie, both during
the flu epidemic.
Children of Roy Brubaker and Gertrude Joy are:
          i. **Millie Ruth Brubaker**, b. 20 Aug 1907; d. 20 Mar
             1919.
          ii. **Olin Leroy Brubaker**, b. 14 Aug 1909; d. 28 Aug
              1970; m. (1) **Dorothy GALE,** 28 Sep 1946; m.
              (2) **Elizabeth WRIGHT,** 11 Dec 1956.
          iii. **Naomi Faith Brubaker**, b. 06 Aug 1911; d. 25

Feb 1995, Albuquerque, Bernalillo County, New Mexico; m. **Deane KIPP**, 25 Apr 1954.

739.　iv.　**Howard Joy Brubaker**, b. 27 Feb 1914; d. 22 Dec 1997, Calexico, Imperial County, California.

740.　v.　**Lucille Lillian Brubaker**, b. 12 Dec 1918; d. 31 Aug 1994, Halstead, Harvey County, Kansas.

671.

Amelia A. Brubaker, daughter of No. 631, Amelia Jane Ridgway, was born 10 Mar 1879 in Kansas and died March 1956 in Kansas. She married **Edgar A. RONEY**.
Children of Amelia Brubaker and Edgar Roney are:

　　i.　**Alma A. Roney**, b. 05 Oct 1912; m. **Joe E. MORTON**.

　　ii.　**Raymond Roney**, b. 25 Dec 1917.

672.

George Lawrence Callison, son of No. 632, Emma L. Ridgway, was born 09 Mar 1885. He married (1) **Amy BELKNAP**. She died five months later in a house fire. He married (2) **Imogene SHERMAN,** who married (2) **Unk ZILER**. George Callison died of influenza during W.W.I.
Children of George Callison and Imogene Sherman are:

741.　i.　**Doyle L. Callison Ziler**, b. 1913.

742.　ii.　**Jarrett W. Callison**, b. 1915.

743.　iii.　**William Donavan Callison Ziler**, b. 1916.

673.

James F. Callison, son of No. 632, Emma L. Ridgway, was born 12 Nov 1886 and died 17 Nov 1970. He married (1) **Pearl L. HANDY**. He married (2) **Jessie BOOTH**.
Children of James Callison and Pearl Handy are:

      i. **Robert Callison**, b, 1913; d. 1939.
744.   ii. **James E. Callison**, b. 1915.
Children of James Callison and Jessie Booth are:
745.   iii. **James Callison**.
746.   iv. **Marilyn Callison**.
     v. **Verda E. Callison**; m. **Gary JONES** (dec.)

674.

Elbert Callison, son of No. 632, Emma L. Ridgway, was born 30 Oct 1890 and died 19 May 1965. He married (1) **Helen Ruth LIMPP.** She died 22 Sep 1950. Helen Limpp was first married to **Dillon TAYLOR.**
Child of Helen Limpp and Dillon Taylor is:
747.   i. **Jacqueline Taylor**
Child of Elbert Callison and Helen Limpp is:
748.   ii. **Dianna Lee Callison**, b. 11 Dec 1943.
Elbert Callison married (2) **Lucy Martin Tucker** 15 Aug 1952.

675.

Harley M. Callison, son of No. 632, Emma L. Ridgway, was born 30 Nov 1892 and died 1967. He married **Caroline JARVIS.**
Children of Harley Callison and Caroline Jarvis are:
749.   i. **Martha Louise Callison**, b. 28 Feb 1921.
750.   ii. **Mary Helen Callison**, b. 08 Feb 1923.

676.

Ernest Wesley Ridgway, son of No. 633, Charles Wesley Ridgway, Jr., was born 03 Aug 1892 and died March 1977. He married (1) **Letha DAY**. He married (2) **Gladys Koonce MEIRES** after 1956. He lived in Dexter, Cowley County,

552

Kansas.
Children of Ernest Ridgway and Letha Day are:
751.   i.   **Charles Wesley Ridgway**, b. 19 Nov 1916.
752.   ii. **Catherine E. Ridgway**, b. 10 Jun 1918.
753.   iii. **Violet V. Ridgway**, b. 22 Nov 1921.
754.   iv. **Ernest E. Ridgway**, b. 21 Oct 1926; d. 16 Dec
             1964.

677.

Ruby Caroline Ridgway, daughter of No. 633, Charles
Wesley Ridgway, Jr., was born 09 May 1898 and died 30 Aug
1965. She married **Homer C. POWERS**.
Child of Ruby Ridgway and Homer Powers is:
755.   i.   **Richard D. Powers**, b. 01 Oct 1924.

678.

Charles W. Foudray, son of No. 635, Adda Lee Ridgway,
was born 08 Jan 1904. He married **Norma TRENT**.
Child of Charles W. Foudray and Norma Trent is:
756.   i.   **Samuel H. Foudray**, b. 14 Sep 1935.

679.

Demonsthenes Foudray, son of No. 635, Adda Lee Ridgway,
was born 14 Jan 1907 and died 1945. He married **Luella S.
Schwab ALVIA**. He lived in San Diego, California.
Child of Demonsthenes Foudray and Luella Alvia is:
757.   i.   **Patricia Schwab Foudray**, b. 13 Mar 1940.

680.

Edith Browne, daughter of No. 636, Nellie Merydith, and Jack
Browne married **Carl KEMNER**.
Children of Edith Browne and Carl Kemner are:

    i. **Ruth Kemner**.
   ii. **Carl C. Kemner**.
  iii. **Jack W. Kemner**.

681.

Mildred Browne, daughter of No. 636, Nellie Merydith, and Will Browne, married **Alfred J. GABRIELSON**. She lived in Ontario, Orange County, California.
Child of Mildred Browne and Alfred Gabrielson is:
758.   i. **Doris Gabrielson**.

682.

Floyd Elliott, son of No. 638, Hattie Merydith, was born 23 Jun 1903. He married **Gladys RANDALL**. He lived in Gresham, Multnomah County, Oregon.
Children of Floyd Elliott and Gladys Randall are:
759.   i. **Mayron Elliott**.
760.   ii. **Elouise M. Elliott**.

683.

Esther Elliott, daughter of No. 638, Hattie Merydith, was born 02 Apr 1905. She married **Dan A. JOHNSON**. She lived in Ponca City, Kay County, Oklahoma.
Children of Esther Elliott and Dan Johnson are:
761.   i. **Miles H. Johnson**, b. 05 Feb 1932.
762.   ii. **Maralyn E. Johnson**, b. 05 Aug 1936.

684.

Ina Elliott, daughter of No. 638, Hattie Merydith, was born 07 Apr 1906. She married **Russell BRYAN**. She lived in Ponca City, Kay County, Oklahoma.
Children of Ina Elliott and Russell Bryan are:

763.   i. **Phyllis C. Bryan**, b. 29 Jun 1928.
764.   ii. **Lawrence E. Bryan**, b. 27 Oct 1930
765. iii. **Melva I. Bryan**, b. 16 Mar 1934.

685.

Paul Elliott, son of No. 638, Hattie Merydith, was born 22 Jul 1909. He married **Edna JOHNSON**. He lived in Santa Rosa, Sonoma County, California.
Children of Paul Elliott and Edna Johnson are:
766.   i. **Joy V. Elliott**.
767.   ii. **Melba Elliott**.
      iii. **Delbert D. Elliott**. b. 02 Jun 1936.

686.

Thelma Elliott, daughter of No. 638, Hattie Merydith, was born 06 Feb 1916. She married (1) **Melvin WRIGHT**. She married (2) **Roy McCLAFLIN**. She married (3) **Norman HULL**.
Children of Thelma Elliott and Melvin Wright are:
768.   i. **Janice K. Wright**.
      ii. **Owen T. Wright**; m. **Pamilia FRIDDLE**.

687.

Joy Jean Merydith, daughter of No. 639, Clarence Merydith, married (1) **Munro MITCHELL**. After his death, she married (2) **Barney NICHOLS**. She lived in Orinda, Alameda County, California.
Children of Joy Merydith and Munro Mitchell are:
769.   i. **Bruce Mitchell**.
770.   ii. **Delbert Mitchell**.
771. iii. **Lloyd Mitchell**.

688.

Ted Owen Merydith, Sr., son of No. 639, Clarence Merydith, married **Jane SHEPPARD**. He lived in Springfield, Lane County, Oregon.
Children of Ted Owen Merydith and Jane Sheppard are:
      i. **Ted Owen Merydith, Jr.**
772.   ii. **Steve Merydith**
      iii. **Ruth Merydith**; m. **Randy PRICE**.

689.

C. Dewey Merydith, son of No. 639, Clarence Merydith, married **Jane SERLES**. He lived in Portland, Multnomah County, Oregon.
Children of C. Merydith and Jane Serles are:
      i. **Janis K. Merydith**.
      ii. **Rodney Merydith**.
      iii. **Anne Merydith**.

690.

Clarence Scott, son of No. 640, Ella Willmetta Merydith, was born 27 Feb 1896. He married **Elizabeth REED**.
Child of Clarence Scott and Elizabeth Reed is:
      i. **Melba R. Scott**, b. 28 Mar 1917.

691.

Dewey Scott, son of No. 640, Ella Willmetta Merydith, was born 23 Jun 1898. He married **Esther JUDGE**. Lived in Stillwater, Payne County, Oklahoma.
Child of Dewey Scott and Esther Judge is:
      i. **Shirley Scott**.

692.

Mary Grace Scott, daughter of No. 640, Ella Wilmette Merydith, was born 02 Nov 1901. She married **John BRIDAL**. Children of Mary Scott and John Bridal are:

773.   i. **Loy Donna Bridal**, b. 16 Jun 1936.
774.   ii. **Arthur S. Bridal**, b. 09 Mar 1937.

693.

Lloyd Williamson, son of No. 641, Augusta Merydith, was born 09 Aug 1905. He married **Freda Lee BOHLEN**. He lived in Choctaw, Oklahoma County, Oklahoma.
Children of Lloyd Williamson and Freda Lee Bohlen are:

     i. **Lloyd K. Williamson**; d. young.
775.   ii. **Larry B. Williamson**, b. 21 Jun 1943.
    iii. **Dean A. Williamson**, b. 23 Jul 1956; lived in Jones, Oklahoma County, Oklahoma.

694.

William R. Williamson, son of No. 641, Augusta Merydith, was born 17 Aug 1907 and died 10 Mar 1972. He married **Vearl M. HARRIS**
Children of William R. Williamson and Vearl M. Harris are:

776.   i. **Russell L. Williamson**, b. 30 May 1929.
777.   ii. **Rose Marie Williamson**, b.15 Jun 1942.

695.

Ruby Mae Williamson, daughter of No. 641, Augusta Merydith, was born 19 Jul 1909 and died 05 Dec 1952. She married **James V. WILSON, Sr.**
Children of Ruby Mae Williamson and James V. Wilson are:

     i. **James V. Wilson, Jr.**, b. 04 Dec 1937; lived in Bakersfield, Kern County, California. (Div.)

778.   ii. **Noel R. Wilson**, b. 14 Apr 1941.
        iii. **Linda J. Wilson**, b. 12 Mar 1944; m. **Michael L. NICHOLLS**; lived in Logan, Rich County, Utah.
        iv. **Thomas J. Wilson**, b. 06 Feb 1946; m. **Gail HAGEL**; lived in Carson, Orange County, California.
779.   v. **Wilma R. Wilson**, b. 25 Nov 1948.

696.

Augusta R. Williamson, daughter of No. 641, Augusta Merydith, was born 16 Jan 1920. She married **Lee Martin DOOLEY**. She lived in Ripley, Payne County, Oklahoma.
Children of Augusta Williamson and Lee Dooley are:
780.   i. **Marilyn J. Dooley**, b. 10 Jul 1937.
781.   ii. **Sammy M. Dooley**, b. 03 Apr 1945.
        iii. **Dorothy R., Dooley**, b. 17 Apr 1951; m. **Keith TIET** (b. 1950).

697.

Emer W. Lemaster II, son of No. 642, Tom Lemaster, married **Beula CRUM**.
Children of Elmer W. Lemaster and Beula Crum are:
782.   i. **Barbara K. Lemaster**, 02 Nov 1935.
783.   ii. **Thomas A. Lemaster, Sr.**, 15 Sep 1938.
784.   iii. **Edwin W. Lemaster**, 27 Apr 1940.

698.

Lee N. Guthrie, son of No. 645, Minnie M. Lemaster, was born 28 Jan 1904 and died 22 Jun 1968. He married **Hazel M. GILLILAND**.
Children of Lee N. Guthrie and Hazel Gilliland are:

785.   i. **Lee Guthrie**, b. 15 Mar 1930.
786.   ii. **Lynn G. Guthrie**, b. 03 Feb 1933.
       iii. **Lehrie Guthrie**, b. 14 Aug 1939; d. 16 Jun 1963.

699.

William H. Guthrie, Jr., son of No. 645, Minnie M. Lemaster, was born 10 Jul 1911. He married **Ruth W. WESTACOTT**.
Child of William Guthrie and Ruth Westacott is:
787.   i. **Richard P. Guthrie**, b. 05 Nov 1940.

700.

Lois K. Guthrie, daughter of No. 645, Minnie M. Lemaster, was born 17 Jan 1915. She married **Phileman GIROD**. They lived in Towanda, Butler County, Kansas.
Children of Lois K. Guthrie and Phileman Girod are:
788.   i. **Phillip G. Girod**, b. 14 Mar 1939
       ii. **Barbara J. Girod**, b. 22 Nov 1940.
       iii. **Charles I. Girod**, b. 03 Dec 1946; d. 25 Sep 1965.
789.   iv. **Linda A. Girod**, b. 11 Jan 1949.

701.

Emory William "Wick" Read, son of No. 646, Millie J. Lemaster, was born 21 Dec 1900 and died 1969. He married **UNK**
Child of Emory Read and Unk is:
       i. **Emory William Read**.

702.

Thelma Read, daughter of No. 646, Millie J. Lemaster, was born 27 Apr 1905. She married **Clay PHILLIPS**.
Children of Thelma Read and Clay Phillips are:
       i. **Carol J. Phillips**.

ii. **Tom Phillips**.

703.

Mamie Gordon, daughter of No. 647, Anna Lee Lemaster, was born 18 Jun 1902. She married **Charles D. WILSON**. They lived in Canon City, Fremont County, Colorado.
Children of Mamie Gordon and Charles D. Wilson are:
790.   i. **William Gordon Wilson**, b. 03 Jan 1925.
791.   ii. **Donna L. Wilson**, b. 20 Feb 1928.
792.   iii. **Morris Duane Wilson**, b. 20 Feb 1928.

704.

Carmen S. Gordon, son of No. 647 Anna Lee Lemaster, was born 05 Aug 1903. He married **Lelia POTS**. They lived in Englewood, Arapahoe County, Colorado.
Children of Carmen Gordon and Leila Pots are:
    i. **Thomas Gordon**, b. 16 Mar 1942; d. 23 Mar1942.
793.   ii. **Sue Gordon**, b. 01 Apr 1944.
794.   iii. **Kay Gordon**, b. 28 Oct 1947.

705.

Ione Gordon, daughter of No. 647, Anna Lee Lemaster, was born 19 Jan 1905. She married **Earl PETTET**.
Child of Ione Gordon and Earl Pettit is:
795.   i. **Carma Pettet**.

706.

Gilbert Gordon, son of No. 647, Anna Lee Lemaster, was born 15 Jun 1908. He married **Pauline HOYT**. They lived in Dexter, Cowley County, Kansas.
Children of Gilbert Gordon and Pauline Hoyt are:
796.   i. **Jean Gordon**, b. 31 Aug 1929.
797.   ii. **Joe Gordon**, b. 25 Oct 1934.

798.   iii. **Rhea Gordon**, b. 20 Nov 1940.

707.

Annabel McGill, daughter of No. 648, Bessie Edith Lemaster, was born 12 Dec 1905. She married **Ernest WADE**. They lived in Wichita, Sedgwick County, Kansas.
Children of Annabel McGill and Ernest Wade are:
799.   i. **Marjorie Iona Wade**, b. 16 Apr 1925.
          ii. **Eugene E. Wade**, b. 05 Jun 1927.
800.   iii. **Raymond E. Wade**, b. 25 Aug 1929.

708.

Dorothy Irene McGill, daughter of No. 648, Bessie Edith Lemaster, was born 28 Oct 1908. She married **Herbert E. ROBERTSON**. They lived in Wichita, Sedgwick County, Kansas.
Child of Dorothy McGill and Herbert Robertson is:
801.   i. **John F. Robertson**, b. 11 Jul 1941.

709.

Nellie Elizabeth McGill, daughter of No. 648, Bessie Edith Lemaster, was born 14 Oct 1919. She married **Jack WHYDE, Sr.** They lived in Arkansas City, Cowley County, Kansas.
Children of Nellie McGill and Jack Whyde are:
802.   i. **Jack Whyde, Jr.,** b. 18 Jan 1938.
803.   ii. **Dorothy Louise Whyde**, b. 19 Nov 1939.
804.   iii. **Tom Whyde**, b. 21 Sep 1942.
805   iv. **Robert Whyde**, b. 01 Nov 1950.
          v. **David Whyde**, b. 03 Oct 1958.

710.

Lenora Fay McGill, daughter of No. 648, Bessie Edith

Lemaster, was born 14 Nov 1925. She married (1) **William L. BRIDGES**. She married (2) **Warren SPEARS**. She lived in Sherman, Grayson County, Texas.

Children of Lenora McGill and William Bridges are:
- i. **William Bridges**, b. 18 Apr 1944; d. 1944.
- 806. ii. **Michael L. Bridges**, b. 20 Sep 1945.
- 807. iii. **Patrick Bridges**, b. 17 Jun 1947.
- 808 iv. **William D. Bridges**, b. 13 Nov 1948.
- 809. v. **Lee James Bridges**, b. 29 Oct 1951.
- vi. **Steven Bridges**, b. 27 Sep 1952; m. **Donna L. BRITT**; lived in Sherman, Grayson County, Texas.
- vii. **Hank W. Bridges**, b. 11 Nov 1954.
- viii. **Jesse J. Bridges**, b. 09 Apr 1956.
- ix. **Elizabeth A. Bridges**, b. 28 Jun 1957.

Children of Lenora McGill and Warren Spears are:
- x. **David W. Spears**, b. 12 Jan 1963.
- xi. **Kathryn K. Spears**, b. 08 Dec 1971.

711.

Wilma Jenson, daughter of No. 649, Alpha V. Merydith, married **Frederick SULLIVAN, Sr**. She lived in Austin, Lee County, Texas.

Children of Wilma Jenson and Frederick Sullivan are:
- 810. i. **Sherwood M. Sullivan**.
- ii. **Frederick Sullivan, Jr.**, b. 1918; d. 1921.
- 811. iii. **Godfrey R. Sullivan**, b. 1920.
- 812 iv. **Gerald I. Sullivan**, b. 1922.
- 813. v. **Fred M. Sullivan**, b. 1930

712.

Merydith Dean Turner, Sr., son of No. 650, Rose C.

Merydith, was born 04 Dec 1915. He married **Doris MONTGOMERY**.
Children of Merydith Dean Turner and Doris Montgomery are:
814.   i. **Merydith Dean Turner, Jr.**
       ii. **Judy M. Turner.**
      iii. **Marcia Turner**; m. **David KIER.**
      iv. **Valerie Turner.**

713.

Betty Ruth Merydith, daughter of No. 651, Morris Rolla Merydith, was born 15 Feb 1927. She married **Don BEARD**. She lived in Lipscomb, Lipscomb County, Texas.
Child of Betty Merydith and Don Beard is:
      i. **Monica Beard**, b. 12 Apr 1955.

714.

Verdi Wright, daughter of No. 653, Geneva C. Merydith Wright, was born 01 Apr 1915. She married **Virgil TERREL**. She lived in Lake Tenkiller, Cherokee County, Oklahoma.
Child of Verdi Wright and Virgil Terrel is:
      i. **Gary Terrel**, b. 09 Sep 1939; m. (1) **Gayle PRITCHARD**; m. (2) **Judy FRANK**; lives in Amarillo, Potter County, Texas.

715.

David Wright, son of No. 653, Geneva C. Merydith, was born 23 Mar 1918. He married **Faye TERREL**. He lived in Tahlequah, Cherokee County, Oklahoma.
Children of David Wright and Faye Terrel are:
815.   i. **Jim H. Wright**, b. 27 Nov 1942.
      ii. **Paula Wright**, b. 06 Oct 1944; m. (1) **William GILTNER**; m. (2) **Robert HALEY**.

iii. **Scott Wright**, b. 27 Sep 1952.

716.

Geneva Marie Wright, daughter of No. 653, Geneva C. Merydith Wright, was born 08 Jun 1920. She married **Marvin BROWN**. They lived in Lake Tenkiller, Cherokee County, Oklahoma.

Child of Geneva Wright and Marvin Brown is:

816.   i. **Ethyl Marlene Brown**, b. 29 Mar 1940.

717.

Pearl Merydith, daughter of No. 654, William E. Coy Merydith, was born 16 Nov 1928. She married **Leroy THOMPSON**. They lived in Amarillo, Potter County, Texas.

Child of Pearl Merydith and Leroy Thompson is:

    i. **Matthew A. Thompson**, b. 27 Dec 1958.

718.

Edward Merydith, son of No. 654, William E. Coy Merydith, was born 10 Jan 1930. He married **Barbara PERRY**. They live in Booker, Lipscomb County, Texas.

Children of Edward Merydith and Barbara Perry are:

817.   i. **Debrah Merydith**, b. 29 Jan 1954.

    ii. **Becky Merydith**, b. 15 Sep 1956; m. **Lefty MINFELL**; lives in Woodward, Woodward County, Oklahoma.

719.

Peggie Merydith, daughter of No. 654, William E. Coy Merydith, was born 22 Jul 1931. She married **C. T. DUKE**. They live in Darrowzett, Lipscomb County, Texas.

Children of Peggie Merydith and C. T. Duke are:

818.   i. **Sheril Duke**, b. 04 Oct 1951.
       ii. **John Duke**, b. 06 Sep 1953.
      iii. **Kevin Duke**, b. 21 Nov 1958.

720.

Joyce Merydith, daughter of No. 654, William E. Coy
Merydith, was born 16 Aug 1932. She married **Jim HODGES**.
They live in Richmond, Hanover County, Virginia.
Child of Joyce Merydith and Jim Hodges is:
       i. **Jan Hodges**, b. 01 Jul 1961.

721.

Rex Oral McGinnis, son of No. 665, Addie Sylvania Lawson,
was born 30 Jun 1885 in Mole Hill, Ritchie County, West
Virginia and died 30 Jul 1960 in Houston, Harris County,
Texas. He married **Ruth O'BRYAN** 21 Dec 1917 in Houston,
Texas, daughter of **Oliver O'BRYAN** and **Ruth NOURSE**.
Ruth was born in Abbeville, Vermilion Parish, Louisiana in
1895 and died at Van Nuys, Los Angeles County, California in
1970.
Children of Rex McGinnis and Ruth O'Bryan are:
819.   i. **Charles David McGinnis**.
       ii. **Maureen McGinnis**.

722.

Delsie Vertie McGinnis, daughter of No. 665, Addie Sylvania
Lawson, was born 30 Dec 1888 in Mole Hill, Ritchie County,
West Virginia and died 17 Sep 1962 in Houston, Harris
County, Texas. She married (1) **Robert Emmett LOVEJOY**
about 1910, son of **Reise LOVEJOY** and **Lucinda
HORNSBY**. He was born 1879 and died 1963. They were
divorced in 1935, and she married (2) **George Sparks**

HERRON about 1950 in Houston, Texas. Delsie was George's second wife. George Sparks Herron, a World War I veteran, was inducted into the U.S. Army in San Antonio, Texas on 17 Aug 1917, serial No. 2215183, and was discharged from the Army in Fort Worth, Texas on 20 Jun 1919. The children of C. David McGinnis and Eloise McGinnis called him Grandpa George. He was buried at Forest Park Cemetery, Lawndale, Houston, Texas.

Children of Delsie McGinnis and Robert Lovejoy are:

820.   i. **Rex Emmett Lovejoy**, b. 22 Oct 1911; d. 07 Jul 1992, California.
821.   ii. **Lesta Delsie Lovejoy**.
822. iii. **Donna Ruth Lovejoy**, b. 06 Oct 1923, Houston, Harris County, Texas; d. 31 Mar 1986, Houston, Texas.

723.

Ruby Meredith, daughter of No. 656, Fred Meredith, was born 1910 in Ritchie County, West Virginia, and died 20 Jun 1992, in Ritchie County. She married **Otha BRITTON**. He was born 1906 and died 1963 in Ritchie County. Both are buried in Pine Grove Cemetery, Berea, Ritchie County.

Child of Ruby Meredith and Otha Britton is:

823.   i. **Sandra Sue Britton**, b. February 1941, Parkersburg, Wood County, West Virginia.

SIXTH GENERATION

724.

Mary Adelaide Matthew, daughter of No. 657, Katherine Kincaid, was born 21 Jun 1910 in Sangamon County, Illinois. She married **William J. HUNT,** 08 Feb 1937.
Child of Mary Adelaide Matthew and William J. Hunt is:
      i. **Susan Hunt**, b. 08 Mar 1941; m. **J. Nicholas HAMILTON**, 19 Sep 1959, Springfield, Sangamon County, Illinois.

725.

Elizabeth Eleanor Mockler, daughter of No. 660, Robert Emmett Mockler, was born 1913. She married **A. Kyle BUSH,** M.D., son of **Ivan BUSH** and **Meta HAYES**. They lived on Bush Avenue in Philippi, Barbour County, West Virginia.
Children of Elizabeth Eleanor Mockler and A. Kyle Bush are:
824.   i. **Robert Kyle Bush**, M.D., b. 1944.
825.   ii. **Eleanor Caroline Bush**, b. 1947.

726.

Jack Merydith, son of No. 661, Edward Merydith, married **Wilma UNK.**
Child of Jack Merydith and Wilma Unk is:
      i. **Brent W. Merydith.**

727.

Charles Wesley Merydith, **Sr.**, son of No. 662, Rolla Merydith, married **Emma LAMBERT.** They lived in Melrose Park, Cook County, Illinois.
Children of Charles W. Merydith and Emma Lambert are:

i. **Constance J. Merydith.**
ii. **Jane Ann Merydith,** b. 15 Nov 1945; m.
   John S. ALEO (Div.).
826. iii. **Jean Elizabeth Merydith**, b.19 Mar 1949.
iv. **Charles Wesley Merydith, Jr.,** b. 22 Dec 1952.

728.

Charles Williams, son of No. 663, Ella Merydith, was born 1908. He married **Unknown.**
Child of Charles Williams and Unknown is:
    i. **Charles L. Williams**, b. 1936; m. **Karen NELSON.**

729.

Merydith Higgins, son of No. 664, Frances C. Merydith, was born 02 Oct 1913, and died 09 Feb 1953. He married **Annie Theo LINDSEY**. She lives in DeLeon Springs, Volusia County, Florida.
Child of Merydith Higgins and Annie Lindsey is:
    i. **Alice Cornelia Higgins**, b. 1952; m. (1)**UNK_ SMITH,** (Div.); m. (2) **UNK,** (Div.).

730.

Walter M. Higgins, son of No. 664, Frances C. Merydith, was born 27 Jun 1918; he married **Dorothy CRUICKSHANK**.
Children of Walter Higgins and Dorothy Cruickshank are:
827. i. **Walter M. Higgins, III,** b. 1944.
828. ii. **Susan Merydith Higgins**, b. 1945.
829. iii. **Allison B. Higgins**, b. 1950.
iv. **Jane Frances Higgins**, b. 1956.

731.

Betty Ann Merydith, daughter of No. 665, Carroll L.
Merydith, was born 24 Jan 1936. She married **Joseph
HAWLIK.**
Children of Betty Ann Merydith and Joseph Hawlik are:
    i. **Jami Hawlik**, b. 1959.
    ii. **Joseph Hawlik, Jr.**, b. 1961.
    iii. **Scott Hawlik**, b. 1965.
    iv. **David Hawlik**, b. 1966.

732.

Christine Merydith, daughter of No. 666, Thomas R.
Merydith, was born 18 Aug 1948. She married **David BLAIR**.
They live in Sheffield Lake, Cuyahoga County, Ohio.
Child of Christine Merydith and David Blair is:
    i. **Nathan Thomas Blair**, b. 1975.

733.

Thomas Daymont, son of No. 667, Dorothy Merydith, was
born 05 Jul 1945. He married **Ellen GERSON**.
Child of Thomas Daymont and Ellen Gerson is:
    i. **Joshua Matthew Daymont**, b. 1975.

734.

Forest Leroy Brown, son of No. 668, Clara D. Burris, was
born 21 Mar 1897 in Loyal, Kingfisher County, Oklahoma and
died 30 Jun 1986 in Boise, Ada County, Idaho. He married
Katherine Marie COMER, 27 Nov 1921 in Cedar Vale,
Chautauqua County, Kansas, daughter of **Thomas COMER**
and **Emma BAKER.**
Children of Forrest Brown and Katherine Comer are:
830.   i. **Beverly Ann Brown**, b. 28 Sep 1931, Oklahoma

City, Oklahoma County, Oklahoma.

831.   ii. **Carrol Comer Brown**, b. 13 Feb 1937, Florence, Marion County, Kansas.

735.

Erma A. Brubaker, daughter of No. 669, Fred Brubaker, was born 28 Nov 1909 in Kansas. She married **John R. MILLER**, June 1927, in Kansas. They lived in Protection, Comanche County, Kansas.

Children of Erma Brubaker and John Miller are:

832.   i. **Jack R. Miller**, b. 01 May 1928.

833.   ii. **Phyllis M. Miller**, b. 25 May 1930.

834.   iii. **Jerry A. Miller**, b. 14 Mar 1935.

        iv. **Sandra L. Miller**, b. 14 Jan 1945; m. **Steven H. HURT**; lives in San Jose, San Mateo County, California.

736.

Orin C. Brubaker, son of No. 669, Fred Brubaker, was born 17 Jan 1911 in Kansas. He married **Ethel L. GRAHAM**.

Children of Orin Brubaker and Ethel Graham are:

        i. **Shirley A. Brubaker**, b. 02 Oct 1935; m. **Howard W. POORY**.

        ii. **Donald D. Brubaker**, b. 20 Dec 1939; m. **Sharon L UNK**.

835.   iii. **Nancy L. Brubaker**, b. 04 Sep 1944.

        iv. **Mary J. Brubaker**, b. 25 Jul 1950; m. **Hubert WOOLDRIDGE**.

737.

Eula M. Brubaker, daughter of No. 669, Fred Brubaker, was born 07 Aug 1920 in Kansas. She married **Ancil A. WOOD**.

Children of Eula Brubaker and Ancil Wood are:
836.   i. **Carol M. Wood**, b. 22 Jul 1943.
837.   ii. **Melva K. Wood**, b. 20 Aug 1945.
838.   iii. **Anthony W. Wood**, b. 02 Sep 1948.
      iv. **James R. Wood**, b. 21 Mar 1950; m. **Connie SWEANEY.**

738.

Vesta G. Brubaker, daughter of No. 669, Fred Brubaker, was born 22 May 1924 in Kansas. She married **R. C. MARSHALL**.
Children of Vesta Brubaker and R. C. Marshall are:
      i. **Ronnie D. Marshall**, b. 13 Nov 1951.
      ii. **Phillip W. Marshall**, b. 01 Nov 1952.
      iii. **Susan D. Marshall**, b. 25 Feb 1961.

739.

Howard Joy Brubaker, son of No. 670, Roy Preston Brubaker, was born 27 Feb 1914 and died 22 Dec 1997 in Calexico, Imperial County, California. He married **Mary Louise EWALD,** February 1946.
Children of Howard Brubaker and Mary Ewald are:
      i. **Barbara Ann Brubaker**, b. 14 Jul 1948; m. a UMC minister; lives in Des Moines, Ankeny County, Iowa.
839.   ii. **William Lee Brubaker**, b. 13 Dec 1951.

740.

Lucille Lillian Brubaker, daughter of No. 670, Roy Preston Brubaker, was born 12 Dec 1918 and died 31 Aug 1994 in Halstead, Kansas from a malignant brain tumor. She married (1) **Eldon HOOVER,** 17 Feb 1945. She married (2) **Richard**

HUEBERT, 01 Aug, 1957.
Child of Lucille Brubaker and Richard Huebert is:
> i. **Gene Richard Huebert**, b. 08 Aug 1959.

741.

Doyle L. Callison Ziler, son of No. 672, George Lawrence
Callison, was born 1913. He married (1) **Mary
CARPENTER**. He married (2) **Lois HOLLINGWORTH**. He
was a County Judge in Sierra Blanca, Hudspeth County, Texas.
He went by his step-father's surname, **ZILER**.
Child of Doyle Callison Ziler and Lois Hollingworth is:
> i. **Mary Linda Ziler**.

742.

Jarrett W. Callison, son of No. 672, George Lawrence
Callison, was born 1915. He married **Mildred C. BOYER**. He
lived in El Paso, El Paso County, Texas.
Child of Jarrett Callison and Mildred Boyer is:
> i. **Patricia M. Callison**; m. **Patrick ATTEL**.

743.

William Donavan Callison Ziler, son of No. 672, George
Lawrence Callison, was born 1916. He married **Anna
RIGNEY**. He went by his step-father's surname, **ZILER**.
Children of William Ziler Callison and Anna Rigney are:
> i. **Diane Ziler**, b. 1946; m. **James McCONNELL**.
> ii. **Jean Ziler**, b. 1950; m. **Thomas W. MORGAN**.
> iii. **Sally Ziler**, b. 1954.

744.

James E. Callison, son of No. 673, James F. Callison, was
born 1915. He married (1) **Mildred LONG**. He married (2)

Mary L. HOY. He lived in Portland, Multnomah County, Oregon.

Child of James E. Callison and Mildred Long is:

840.   i. **Jimmy G. Callison**, b. 19 Oct 1935.

Children of James E. Callison and Mary L. Hoy are:

841.   ii. **Sidney Mac Callison**, b. 12 May 1942.

       iii. **Melissa F. Callison**, b. 15 Jul 1958.

745.

James Callison, son of No. 673, James F. Callison, married **Willadean SHOFFIELD**. He lived in Albany, Dougherty County, Georgia.

Children of James Callison and Willadean Shoffield are:

      i. **Wanda Sue Callison**.

      ii. **James Albert Callison**.

746.

Marilyn Callison, daughter of No. 673 James F. Callison, married (1) **Melvin DAVIS**. She married (2) **Leo MEADOWS**. She lived in Winfield, Cowley County, Kansas.

Children of Marilyn Callison and Melvin Davis are:

      i. **Renee Davis**.

      ii. **Malianda Davis**.

747.

Jacqueline Taylor, daughter of Helen Limpp Calliston and Dillon Berry Taylor, was born 25 May 1927. She married **Robert Ellis SHACKELFORD** (b. 19 Nov. 1928; d. 18 Apr 1946) on 18 Apr 1946. She died 12 Mar 2013 and is buried in Natrona, Kansas.

Children of Jacqueline Taylor and Robert Shackelford are:

      i. **James Dillon Shackelford**, b. 12 Jan 1949.

ii. **Nancy Kay Shackelford**, b. 14 Aug. 1952.

748.

Dianna Lee Callison, Ph.D., daughter of No. 674, Elbert Callison and Helen Limpp, was born 11 Dec 1943. She married (1) **Russell MAY**, 30 Jun 1961 (div. 1969). She married (2) **John PARMLEY** (d. December 01, 1998), 29 Jul 1989. She married (3) **Dr. Woodrow Hodges** and lives in Kenosha, Wisconsin. She is a retired Dean of Academic Services, Central Community College in Nebraska.
Children of Dianna Callison and Russell May are:

       i. **Randy Lee May**, b. 21 Apr 1965; d. 05 Jan 1991.
842.   ii. **Kelly Sue May**, b. 30 Sep 1967.
843.   iii. **Misti Michelle May**, b. 16 Apr 1969.

749.

Martha Louise Callison, daughter of No. 675, Harley M. Callison, was born 08 Mar 1921. She married **Charles C. JONES**. He died 29 Oct 2007. They lived in Norman, Cleveland County, Oklahoma.
Children of Martha Louise Callison and Charles C. Jones are:

       i. **Charles Clinton Jones**, b. 22 Dec 1945.
       ii. **Michael A. Jones**, b. 21 Aug 1948.
       iii. **Caroline M. Jones**, b. 23 Jun 1960.
       iv. **David C. Jones**, b. September 1965. Died.

750.

Mary Helen ("Sally") Callison, daughter of No. 675, Harley M. Callison, was born 08 Feb 1923. She married **Robert W. POOL**. He died 1969.
Children of Mary Helen Callison and Robert W. Pool are:

       i. **Robert D. Pool**, b. 08 Jan, 1946; m. **Unk**

GAYE. He died 06 Sep 2010.
  ii. **Dennis C. Pool**, b. 23 Feb 1950.

751.

Charles Wesley Ridgway, son of No. 676, Ernest Wesley
Ridgway, was born 18 Nov 1916. He married **Mary B.
WILSON**.
Children of Charles Wesley Ridgway and Mary B. Wilson are:
844.   i. **Charlene Ridgway**.
845. ii. **Ernestine M. Ridgway**, b. 03 Feb 1945.
846. iii. **Sherrel J. Ridgway**, b. 07 Aug 1948.
    iv. **Leon W. Ridgway**, b. 16 Dec 1950; m.
     Caroline CONROES.
    v. **Charles L. Ridgway**, b. 22 Jun 1952; m. **Debra
     GILPIN**.

752.

Catherine E. Ridgway, daughter of No. 676, Ernest Wesley
Ridgway, was born 10 Jun 1918. She married **Floyd L.
REEVES**.
Children of Catherine E. Ridgway and Floyd L. Reeves are:
847.   i. **Everett W. Reeves**, b. 06 Jun 1939.
848. ii. **Larry D. Reeves**, b. 26 Jan 1941.
849. iii. **Norman K. Reeves**, b. 25 Jul 1945.

753.

Violet V. Ridgway, daughter of No. 676, Ernest Wesley
Ridgway, was born 22 Nov 1921. She married (1) **Owen
STOVER**. She married (2) **Robert M. IRETON**.
Child of Violet Ridgway and Owen Stover is:
850.   i. **Phillips L. Stover**, b. 28 Mar 1943.
Children of Violet Ridgway and Robert M. Ireton are:

    ii. **Robert Dean Ireton**, b. 27 Jul 1949.

   iii. **Harry W. Ireton**, b. 15 Aug 1950.

   iv. **John Steven Ireton**, b. 09 Jan 1953.

    v. **Brenda K. Ireton**, b. 16 Sep 1960.

   vi. **Michael G. Ireton**, b. 12 May 962.

754.

Ernest E. Ridgway, son of No. 676, Ernest Wesley Ridgway, was born 21 Oct 1926 and died 16 Dec 1964. He married (1) **Eula BENNETT**. He married (2) **Anna M. KINGSBURG**. He married (3) **Wanda TETRICK**.

Child of Ernest E. Ridgway and Eula Bennett is:

851.   i. **Rita R. Ridgway**, b. 30 Apr 1947.

Children of Ernest E. Ridgway and Anna Kingsburg are:

   ii. **Cathy A. Ridgway**, b.18 Apr 1952; m. **Chris STEWART**; lives in Manhattan, Pottawatomie County, Kansas.

   iii. **Ronda J. Ridgway**, b. 24 Nov 1958; lives in Sonoma, Napa County, California.

755.

Richard D. Powers, son of No. 677, Ruby Caroline Ridgway, was born 01 Oct 1924. He married **Barbara VEST**. They live in Manhattan, Pottawatomie County, Kansas.

Children of Richard Powers and Barbara Vest are:

    i. **Stephen B. Powers**, b. 26 Aug 1953.

   ii. **Laura J. Powers**, b. 08 Nov 1955.

   iii. **John M. Powers**, b. 22 Dec 1960.

756.

Samuel H. Foudray, son of No. 678, Charles W. Foudray, was born 14 Sep 1935. He married **Martha N. Pizoati**

SEGGSON. He lived in Paramount, Orange County, California.
Child of Samuel H. Foudray and Martha N. Pizoati Seggson is:
852.   i. **Robin W. Pizoati**.

757.
Patricia Schwab Foudray, daughter of No. 679, Demonsthenes Foudray, was born 13 Mar 1940. She married **Allen SCHUH**.
Children of Patricia Foudray and Allen Schuh are:
      i. **Peter A. Schuh**.
      ii. **Erika A. Schuh**, b. 27 Oct 1969.

758.
Doris Gabrielson, daughter of No. 681, Mildred Browne, married **John B. BOTHELL**. She lived in Chino, San Bernadino County, California.
Children of Doris Gabrielson and John Bothell are:
      i. **John D. Bothell**.
      ii. **Jane Bothell**.

759.
Mayron Elliott, son of No. 682, Floyd Elliott, married **Bobbie J. SHMIDL**.
Children of Mayron Elliott and Bobbie Schmidl are:
      i. **Michael Elliott**.
      ii. **Patti Elliott**.

760.
Elouise M. Elliott, daughter of No. 682, Floyd Elliott, married **Nate WILSON**.
Children of Elouise Elliott and Nate Wilson are:

    i. **Larry Wilson.**
    ii. **Jeanne Wilson.**

761.

Miles H. Johnson, son of No. 683, Esther Elliott, married **Marsia UNK**
Children of Miles Johnson and Marsia Unk are:
    i. **Michael Johnson.**
    ii. **Lina Johnson.**
    iii. **Timothy Johnson.**

762.

Maralyn E. Johnson, daughter of No. 683, Esther Elliott, married **Douglas ROLAND**.
Children of Maralyn Johnson and Douglas Roland are:
    i. **Douglas Roland, Jr.**
    ii. **Darrel Roland.**
    iii. **Curtis Roland.**

763.

Phyllis C. Bryan, daughter of No. 684, Ina Elliott, was born 29 Jun1928. She married **Billie W. ROBERTS**.
Children of Phyllis Bryan and Billie Roberts are:
    i. **Charles R. Roberts**, b. 1955.
    ii. **Perry S. Roberts**, b. 1958.

764.

Lawrence E. Bryan, son of No. 684, Ina Elliott, was born 27 Oct 1930. He married **Mary E. THOMPSON**, who was born in 1930.
Children of Lawrence Bryan and Mary Thompson are:
    i. **Mary C. Bryan**, b, 1951.

    ii. **Cheryl L. Bryan**, b. 1953.
   iii. **Jane E. Bryan**, b. 1958.

765.

Melva I. Bryan, daughter of No. 684, Ina Elliott, was born 16 Mar 1934. She married **Lawrence MABRY.**
Children of Melva Bryan and Lawrence Mabry are:
    i. **Elaine Mabry**, b. 1953.
   ii. **Lynette Mabry**, b. 1955.
  iii. **John Mabry**, b. 1957.

766.

Joy V. Elliott, daughter of No. 685, Paul Elliott, married **Larry THOMPSON.**
Children of Joy Elliott and Larry Thompson are:
    i. **Susan Thompson.**
   ii. **Brent Thompson.**

767.

Melba Elliott, daughter of No. 685, Paul Elliott, married **Ward UPSON.**
Children of Melba Elliott and Ward Upson are:
    i. **Cynthia Upson.**
   ii. **Kathy Upson.**
  iii. **Diane Upson.**

768.

Janice K. Wright, daughter of No. 686, Thelma Elliott, married **George PAYTON**.
Children of Janice Wright and George Payton are:
    i. **George Payton, Jr.**
   ii. **Gerry Payton.**

iii. **Glenn Payton.**

769.
Bruce Mitchell, son of No. 687, Joy Jean Merydith, married **UNK.**
Children of Bruce Mitchell and Unk are:
    i. **Laurie Mitchell.**
    ii. **Bill Mitchell.**
    iii. **Nancy Mitchell.**

770.
Delbert Mitchell, son of No. 687, Joy Jean Merydith, married **UNK.**
Children of Delbert Mitchell and Unk are:
    i. **John Mitchell.**
    ii. **James Mitchell.**

771.
Lloyd Mitchell, son of No. 680, Joy Jean Merydith, married **UNK.**
Children of Lloyd Mitchell and Unk are:
    i. **Kim Mitchell.**
    ii. **Scott Mitchell.**

772.
Steve Merydith, son of No. 688, Ted Owen Merydith Sr. married **Gail SANDS.**
Child of Steve Merydith and Gail Sands is:
    i. **Scott S. Merydith.**

773.
Loy Donna Bridal, daughter of No. 692, Mary Grace Scott,

was born 16 Jun 1936. She married **Dr. Ralph R. MARKLAND.** They lived in Oklahoma City, Oklahoma County, Oklahoma.

Children of Loy Donna Bridal and Ralph Markland are:

    i. **Ralph J. Markland,** b. 1963.

    ii. **Mary L. Markland,** b. 1964.

    iii. **Donna E. Markland,** b. 1968.

774.

Arthur S. Bridal, son of No. 692, Mary Grace Scott, was born 09 Mar 1937. He married **Betty L. SHARP.** She was born in 1941. They lived in Cashion, Kingfisher County, Oklahoma.

Children of Arthur Bridal and Betty Sharp are:

    i. **Anita J. Bridal,** b. 1963.

    ii. **Sharon L. Bridal,** b. 1967.

775.

Larry B. Williamson, son of No. 693, Lloyd Williamson, was born June 21, 1943. He married **Janice M. HANSON.** They lived in Midwest City, Oklahoma County, Oklahoma.

Children of Larry B. Williamson and Janice Hanson are:

    i. **Jane R. Williamson,** b. 1968.

    ii. **Kristen J. Williamson,** b. 1972.

776.

Russell L. Williamson, son of No. 694, William R. Williamson, was born 30 May 1929. He married **Joan RICKSTREW,** who was born in 1935. They lived in Dover, Kent County, Delaware.

Child of Russell Williamson and Joan Rickstrew is:

    i. **Michael Williamson,** b. 1956.

777.

Rose Marie Williamson, daughter of No. 694, William R. Williamson, was born 15 Jun 1942. She married **Larry HULL.** They lived in Macomb, Pottawatomie County, Oklahoma. Children of Rose Marie Williamson and Larry Hull are:

    i. **Larry D. Hull,** b. 1970.
    ii. **Kimberly D. Hull.**

778.

Noel R. Wilson, son of No. 695, Ruby Mae Williamson, was born 14 Apr 1941. He married **Janice PUTNAM**, who was born in 1943. They lived in Bakersfield, Kern County, California.
Children of Noel Wilson and Janice Putnam are:

    i. **Steven N. Wilson,** b. 1968.
    ii. **Samuel D. Wilson**, b. 1972.

779.

Wilma R. Wilson, daughter of No. 695, Ruby Mae Williamson, was born 25 Nov 1948. She married **John E. GRAHAM.**
Child of Wilma Wilson and John Graham is:

    i. **John David Graham**, b. 1972.

780.

Marilyn J. Dooley, daughter of No. 696, Augusta Williamson, was born 10 Jul 1937. She married **Donald R. BEENE**, who was born in 1935. They lived in Cushing, Payne County, Oklahoma.
Children of Marilyn Dooley and Donald Beene are:

    i. **David R. Beene**, b. 1956.
    ii. **Lea Ann Beene**, b. 1959.

781.

Sammy M. Dooley, son of No. 696, Augusta Williamson, was born 03 Apr 1945. He married **Barbara J. SPIVA.** They lived in Ripley, Payne County, Oklahoma.
Children of Sammy Dooley and Barbara Spiva are:
    i. **Lori Jo Dooley**, b. 1966.
    ii. **Michele L. Dooley**, b. 1970.

782.

Barbara K. Lemaster, daughter of No. 697, Emer W. Lemaster, II, was born 02 Nov 1935. She married **Larry J. OBERLE.** They lived in Minden, Kearney County, Nebraska.
Children of Barbara Lemaster and Larry Oberle are:
    i. **Scott J. Oberle**, b. 1958.
    ii. **Jesse K. Oberle**, b. 1959.
    iii. **Clark C. Oberle, b. 1967.**

783.

Thomas A. Lemaster, son of No. 697, Emer W. Lemaster, II, was born 15 Sep 1938. He married **Gilene C. SIMMONS**. They lived in Abilene, Taylor County, Texas.
Children of Thomas Lemaster and Gilene Simmons are:
    i. **Marcie L. Lemaster**, b. 1958.
    ii. **Thomas A. Lemaster, Jr.**, b. 1959.
    iii. **Stephen C. Lemaster**, b. 28 Jan 1963; d. June 1963.
    iv. **Brett C. Lemaster**, b. 1964.

784.

Edwin W. Lemaster, son of No. 697, Emer W. Lemaster, II, was born 27 Apr 1940. He married **Carol A. NORMAN**. They lived in Edinburg, Hidalgo County, Texas.

Children of Edwin Lemaster and Carol Norman are:
  i. **Matthew J. Lemaster**, b. 1968.
  ii. **Ann Marie Lemaster**, b. 1971.

785.

Lee Guthrie, son of No. 698, Lee N. Guthrie, was born 15 Mar 1930. He married **Patricia UNK.**
Children of Lee Guthrie and Patricia Unk are:
  i. **Iric J. Guthrie,** b. 1957.
  ii. **Janales K. Guthrie**, b. 1959.
  iii. **Michael M. Guthrie**, b. 1965.

786.

Lynn G. Guthrie, son of No. 698, Lee N. Guthrie, was born 03 Feb 1933. He married **Mavis A. SEYMORE.** She was born in 1934.
Children of Lynn Guthrie and Mavis Seymore are:
  i. **Denise D. Guthrie**, b. 1955.
  ii. **Steven L. Guthrie**, b. 1961.
  iii. **Michael L. Guthrie**, b. 1966.

787.

Richard P. Guthrie, son of No. 699, William H. Guthrie, Jr., was born 05 Nov 1940. He married **Dian C. MURRAY.**
Children of Richard P. Guthrie and Dian C. Murray are:
  i. **Christopher D. Guthrie**, b. 1967.
  ii. **Jay Matthew Guthrie**, b. 1970.
  iii. **Patrick R. Guthrie**, b. 1975.

788.

Phillip G. Girod, son of No. 700, Lois K. Guthrie, was born 14 Mar 1939. He married **Sharon K. MAXWELL.**

The Pritchard/Prickett Family History

Children of Phillip Girod and Sharon Maxwell are:
    i. **Andrea Girod**, b. 1968.
    ii. **Suzanne K. Girod**, b. 1975.

789.

Linda A. Girod, daughter of No. 700, Lois K. Guthrie, was born 11 Jan 1949. She married **Steven P. PIERCE**, who also was born in 1949.
Children of Linda Girod and Steven Pierce are:
    i. **Shane S. Pierce**, b. 1971.
    ii. **Flint G. Pierce**, b. 1973.

790.

William Gordon Wilson, son of No. 703, Mamie Gordon, was born 03 Jan 1925. He married **Wynona Mae UNK.** They live in Canon City, Fremont County, Colorado.
Children of William Gordon Wilson and Wynona Mae Unk are:
    i. **Gary Stewart Wilson.**
    ii. **Kyanna Sue Wilson**; m. **Loren REISWIG.**
    iii. **Kendra Kay Wilson.**
    iv. **Kayla Ann Wilson.**
    v. **Kimley Dee Wilson.**

791.

Donna L. Wilson, daughter of No. 703, Mamie Gordon, was born 20 Feb 1928 (twin). She married **Alvin H. HAZELL.** They are divorced.
Children of Donna Wilson and Alvin Hazell are:
853.   i. **Sheridan Hazell.**
854.   ii. **David H. Hazell.**

792.

Morris Duane Wilson, son of No. 703, Mamie Gordon, was born 20 Feb 1928 (twin). He married **Barbara BULLARD**. They are divorced.

Child of Morris Duane Wilson and Barbara Bullard is:
    i. **Lisa Gay Wilson.**

793.

Sue Gordon, daughter of No. 704, Carmen Gordon, was born 01 Apr 1944. She married (1) **Gade R. CONGROVE**. She married (2) **Steven MURO**. She lived in Englewood, Arapahoe County, Colorado.

Children of Sue Gordon and Gade Congrove are:
    i. **Gene R. Congrove**, b. 1965.
    ii. **Gordon S. Congrove**, b. 1967.

794.

Kay Gordon, daughter of No. 704, Carmen Gordon, was born 28 Oct 1947. She married **Cecil GUTIERROZ**. Children of Kay Gordon and Cecil Gutierroz are:
    i. **Margaret Helen Gutierroz,** b. 1967; dec.
    ii. **Ginnia Marie Gutierroz**, b. 1972.

795.

Carma Pettet, daughter of No. 705, Ione Gordon, married **Bob MAURING**. They lived in Winfield, Cowley County, Kansas.

Children of Carma Pettet and Bob Mauring are:
    i. **Erie Lee Mauring.**
    ii. **Robert Earl Mauring.**
    iii. **Carla Ann Mauring.**

796.

Jean Gordon, daughter of No. 706, Gilbert Gordon, was born 31 Aug 1929. She married **Bill FLOWER**.
Children of Jean Gordon and Bill Flower are:
- i. **Scotty Meeker Flower**, b. 1949.
- ii. **Mike Flower**, b. 1950, Dodge City, Ford County, Kansas.
- iii. **Kris Flower**, b. 1953.
- iv. **Paul Flower**, b. 1958, Winfield, Cowley County, Kansas.

797.

Joe Gordon, son of No. 706, Gilbert Gordon, was born 25 Oct 1934. He married **Florence FLOYD**. They lived in Winfield, Kansas, where he did custom kitchen work in Winfield and Wichita, Kansas.
Children of Joe Gordon and Florence Floyd are:
- i. **Steve Gordon.**
- ii. **Susan Gordon.**
- iii. **Stewart Gordon.**

798.

Rhea Gordon, daughter of No. 706, Gilbert Gordon, was born 20 Nov 1940. She married **Ron SLOAN**, a Christian Church minister in Wichita, Sedgwick County, Kansas.
Children of Rhea Gordon and Ron Sloan are:
- i. **Kimberly Sloan**, b. 1966.
- ii. **Jennifer Sloan**, b. 1975.

799.

Marjorie Iona Wade, daughter of No. 707, Annabel McGill, was born 16 Apr 1925. She married **Floyd D. SANBURN**.

Children of Marjorie Wade and Floyd Sanburn are:
855.   i. **Sandra J. Sanburn,** b. 1949.
       ii. **David L. Sanburn,** b. 1950.
      iii. **Steven E. Sanburn,** b. 1952.
856.   iv. **Tresca A. Sanburn,** b. 1953.
        v. **Michiel G. Sanburn,** b. 1954.
       vi. **Floyd D. Sanburn, Jr.,** b. 1959.
      vii. **Marie K. Sanburn,** b. 1961.
     viii. **John G. Sanburn,** b. 1962.

800.

Raymond E. Wade, son of No. 707, Annabel McGill, was born 25 Aug 1929. He married **LaVonne GRAHAM**.
Child of Raymond Wade and LaVonne Graham is:
        i. **Jerome Wade,** b. 1967.

801.

John F. Robertson, son of No. 708, Dorothy Irene McGill, was born 11 Jul 1941. He married **Linda LOUK**.
Children of John Robertson and Linda Louk are:
        i. **Curt E. Robertson,** b. 1959.
       ii. **Daren Lee Robertson,** b. 1960.

802.

Jack Whyde, Jr., son of No. 709, Nellie McGill, was born 18 Jan 1938. He married (1) **Unk;** he married (2) **Unk.**
Children of Jack Whyde and Unk are:
        i. **Steven J. Whyde,** b. 1958.
       ii. **Larry Whyde,** b. 1960.
      iii. **Janet Whyde,** b. 1963.

803.

Dorothy Louise Whyde, daughter of No. 709, Nellie McGill, was born 19 Nov 1939. She married **Ray CHAPMAN.**
Child of Dorothy Louise Whyde and Ray Chapman is:
    i. **Deborah Chapman**, b. 1958.

804.

Tom Whyde, son of No. 709, Nellie McGill, was born 21 Sep 1942. He married **Cynthia UNK.**
Children of Tom Whyde and Cynthia Unk are:
    i. **Nannette Whyde,** b. 1966.
    ii. **Chris Whyde**, b. 1968.

805.

Robert Whyde, son of No. 709, Nellie McGill, was born 01 Nov 1950. He married **UNK.**
Child of Robert Whyde and Unk is:
    i. **Steven L. Whyde**, b. 1969.

806.

Michael L. Bridges, son of No. 710, Lenora McGill, was born 20 Sep 1945. He married **Janet JOHNSON.**
Children of Michael Bridges and Janet Johnson are:
    i. **Michael L. Bridges, Jr.,** b. 1963.
    ii. **Timmy W. Bridges**, b. 1966.
    iii. **Malissa V. Bridges**, b. 1968.
    iv. **Eric Roy Bridges,** b. 1970.

807.

Patrick Bridges, son of No. 710, Lenora McGill, was born 17 Jun 1947. He married **Carolyn CALLOWAY.**
Child of Patrick Bridges and Carolyn Callaway is:

The Pritchard/Prickett Family History

i. **Chad Erin Bridges**, b. 1968.

808.
William D. Bridges, son of No. 710, Lenora McGill, was born 13 Nov 1948. He married **Janet M. NEWMAN**.
Children of William D. Bridges and Janet Newman are:
i. **Rebecca Ann Bridges**, b. 1972.
ii. **Lenora Fay Bridges**, b. 1974.

809.
Lee James Bridges, son of No. 10, Lenora McGill, was born 19 Oct 1951. He married **Victoria CHILDRESS**.
Children of Lee James Bridges and Victoria Childress are:
i. **Scott Christopher Bridges**, b. 1972.
ii. **Brian James Bridges**, b. 1973.

810.
Sherwood M. Sullivan, son of No. 711, Wilma Jenson, married (1) **Inga Bruaunde NEERGAARD**. He married (2) **Mollie MILLER**. He lived in Los Gatos, San Mateo County, California.
Children of Sherwood Sullivan and Inga Neergaard are:
i. **Michael Sullivan**; lived in Palo Alto, San Mateo County, California.
ii. **Jenny Marie Sullivan.**
iii.**Christina Sullivan**

811.
Godfrey R. Sullivan, son of No. 711, Wilma Jenson, was born in 1920. He married **Viola WALLACE** and lived in Waco, McLennan County, Texas.
Children of Godfrey R. Sullivan and Viola Wallace are:

     i. **Augusta V. Sullivan**, b. 1944.

    ii. **Karl James Sullivan**.

  iii. **Meredith Sullivan**, b. 1952; m. **Rev. Unk
       LINDSAY.**

  iv. **Godfrey R. Sullivan, Jr.**

812.

Gerald I. Sullivan, son of No. 711, Wilma Jenson, was born in 1922. He married **Geraldine UNK.** They lived in Newport Beach, Orange County, California.

Child of Gerald L. Sullivan and Geraldine Unk is:

     i. **Karen Sullivan**, b. 1953; m. **Tom
       HENDERSON**; lives in Atlanta, Fulton
       County, Georgia.

813.

Fred M. Sullivan, son of No. 711, Wilma Jenson, was born in 1930. He married (1) **Grace UNK.** He married (2) **Charlotte HESS.** He married (3) **UNK.**

Children of Fred Sullivan and Grace Unk are:

     i. **Shirley Grace Sullivan**.

    ii. **Fred Sullivan**.

Children of Fred Sullivan and Charlotte Hess are:

  iii. **Diane Sullivan**.

  iv. **Juliette Sullivan**.

    v. **Lewis Sullivan**.

  vi. **Christopher Sullivan**.

Children of Fred Sullivan and **Unk** are:

  vii. **Robert Sullivan**.

 viii. **John Sullivan**.

  ix. **Jenny Sullivan**.

    x. **Janet Sullivan**.

814.

Merydith Dean Turner, Jr., son of No. 712, Merydith Dean Turner, Sr., married **Harriet LEONARD.**
Child of Merydith Dean Turner, Jr. and Harriet Leonard is:
    i. **Daniel Benton Turner.**

815.

Jim H. Wright, son of No. 715, David Wright, was born November 17, 1942. He married **Jeannie CARTER.**
Child of Jim H. Wright and Jeannie Carter is:
    i. **Mark Wright**, b. 1967.

816.

Ethyl Marlene Brown, daughter of No. 716, Geneva Marie Wright, was born 29 Mar 1940. She married **Amon HIZER,** and lived in Nevada, Vernon County, Missouri.
Children of Ethyl Brown and Amon Hizer are:
    i. **Lori Marie Hizer**, b. 1970.
    ii. **Holly Dot Hizer**, b. 1973.

817.

Debrah Merydith, daughter of No. 718, Edward Merydith, was born 29 Jan 1954. She married **Danny HERRINGTON**. They lived in Spearman, Hansford County, Texas.
Child of Debrah Merydith and Danny Herrington is:
    i. **David Edward Herrington**, b. 1974.

818.

Sheril Duke, daughter of No. 719, Peggie Merydith, was born 04 Oct 1951. She Married **Garland NICHOLS.** They live in Petrolia, Wichita County, Texas.
Child of Sheril Duke and Garland Nichols is:

      i. **Coby Ben Nichols**, b. 1975.

819.

Charles David McGinnis, son of No. 721, Rex Oral McGinnis, married **Eloise Ann GARRETT**, daughter of **James GARRETT** and **Gloria ASHORN**
Children of Charles McGinnis and Eloise Garrett are:
      i. **Michael David McGinnis**.
857.   ii. **Mark James McGinnis**.
858.   iii. **Marilyn Ruth McGinnis**.

820.

Rex Emmett Lovejoy, son of 722, Delsie Vertie McGinnis Lovejoy, was born 22 Oct 1911 in Houston, Harris County, Texas, and died 07 Jul 1992 in California. In 1966, his address was 5815 Compass Drive, Los Angeles, 45, CA. He married **Myrtle Flora ROWLETT**, 28 Apr 1935 in Houston, Texas, She was born in 1910 and died in 1994, the daughter of **George ROWLETT** and **Mattie RICHEY**.
Children of Rex Lovejoy and Myrtle Rowlett are:
859.   i. **Paul Gordon Lovejoy**.
      ii. **Sylvia Joyce Lovejoy**.
    iii. **Benjamin Elliott Lovejoy**.

821.

Lesta Delsie Lovejoy, daughter of No. 722, Delsie Vertie McGinnis Lovejoy, married **J. Alan KING.** He was born in 1910 and died in 1977. They lived at 6645 Lindy Lane, Houston, Texas. Lesta continued to live there after his death.
Children of Lesta Delsie Lovejoy and J. Alan King are:
860.   i. **Kay King**.
      ii. **Carroll Alan King**, b. 10 Oct 1944 in

Houston, Texas, d. 17 Sep 1952 of
leukemia in Houston Texas. He was a
stepchild.
iii. **Ray King.**
iv. **Wade King**.

822.

Donna Ruth Lovejoy, daughter of No. 722, Delsie Vertie
McGinnis Lovejoy, was born 06 Oct 1923 in Houston, Harris
County, Texas, and died 31 Mar 1986 in Houston, Texas. She
married **Arnold A. HENDERSON**.
Children of Donna Ruth Lovejoy and Arnold A. Henderson
are:
861.   i. **Lisa Henderson.**
862.   ii. **Dana Henderson.**
        iii. **Tanya Henderson**.

823.

Sandra Sue Britton, daughter of No. 723, Ruby Meredith, was
born February 1941 in Parkersburg, Wood County, West
Virginia. She married **Darrel SMITH**.
Children of Sandra Britton and Darrel Smith are:
        i. **Kathy Lynn Smith.**
       ii. **Kelly Sue Smith.**

The Pritchard/Prickett Family History

SEVENTH GENERATION

824.
Robert Kyle Bush, M.D., son of No. 725, Eleanor Mockler, was born in 1944 and married **Betty Jean WHITE**, daughter of **Charles WHITE** and **Virginia HANNA**.
Children of Robert Bush and Betty Jean White are:
    i. **Elizabeth Bush**.
    ii. **Sarah Bush**.
    iii. **Catherine Bush**.

825.
Eleanor Caroline Bush, daughter of No. 725, Eleanor Mockler, was born in 1947 and married m. **Patrick Ross ESPOSITO**.
Children of Eleanor Caroline Bush and Patrick Ross Esposito are:
    i. **Patrick Ross Esposito, Jr**.
    ii. **Cara Marie Esposito**.

826.
Jean Elizabeth Merydith, daughter of No. 727, Charles Wesley Merydith, was born 19 Mar 1949. She married **Eugene BELLINE**. They were divorced.
Child of Jean Merydith and Eugene Belline is:
    i. **Jacqueline J. Belline**.

827.
Walter M. Higgins, III, son of No. 730, Walter M. Higgins, was born in 1944. He married **Candise S. CONSOLVO**. They lived in Gaithersburg, Montgomery County, Maryland.

595

Children of Walter M. Higgins, III, and Candise S. Consolvo are:

    i. **Amy Elizabeth Higgins**, b. 1971.

    ii. **Walter John Higgins**, b. 1974.

828.

Susan Merydith Higgins, daughter of No. 730, Walter M. Higgins, was born in 1945. She married **Melvin J. O'BILLOVICH**. They lived in Eugene, Lane County, Oregon.

Children of Susan Higgins and Melvin O'Billovich are:

    i. **Anthony Robert O'Billovich**, b. 1970.

    ii. **Jonni Jane O'Billovich**, b. 1975.

829.

Allison B. Higgins, daughter of No. 730, Walter M. Higgins, was born in 1950. She married **David H. BRYANT.** They are divorced.

Child of Allison Higgins and David Bryant is:

    i. **Michael Paul Bryant**, b. 1973.

830.

Beverly Ann Brown, daughter of No. 734, Forrest Leroy Brown, was born 28 Sep 1931 in Oklahoma City, Oklahoma. She married **Donald Reuben SWANSON,** 27 Dec 1953, in Caldwell, Canyon County, Idaho, son of **Reuben SWANSON** and **Lela ALLINGTON**.

Children of Beverly Ann Brown and Donald Swanson are:

863.   i. **Michael Lee Swanson**, b. 08 Nov 1954, Caldwell, Canyon County, Idaho.

864.   ii. **Donald Kirt Swanson**, b. 08 Nov 1956, Caldwell, Canyon County, Idaho.

The Pritchard/Prickett Family History

831.

Carol Comer Brown, son of No. 734, Forrest Leroy Brown, was born 13 Feb 1937 in Florence, Marion County, Kansas. He married **Hazel (Billie) Viola WHITBY,** 24 Nov 1962, in Carey, Blaine County, Idaho.
Children of Carol Comer Brown and Hazel Viola Whitby are:
865.   i. **Pamela Marie Brown**, b. 08 Feb 1966, Yakima, Yakima County, Washington.
    ii. **Karen Kae Brown**, b. 23 Oct 1968, Renton, King County, Washington; m. **Walter Anderson TURNER**, 13 Feb 1993, San Diego, San Diego County, California.

832.

Jack R. Miller, son of No. 735, Erma B. Brubaker, was born 01 May 1928. He married **Dorothy M. PAINES**. He lives in Sunnyvale, San Mateo County, California.
Children of Jack Miller and Dorothy Paines are:
    i. **Mark R. Miller**, b. 25 May 1956.
    ii. **Joan D. Miller**, b. 11 Jul 1957.
    iii. **Ann M. Miller**, b. 02 Dec 1958.
    iv. **Judith D. Miller**, b. 22 Feb 1963.
    v. **Michael J. Miller**, b. 11 Oct 1965.

833.

Phyllis M. Miller, daughter of No. 735, Erma Brubaker, was born 25 May 1930. She married **Roger P. JOHNSON**. They lived in San Jose, San Mateo County, California.
Children of Phyllis Miller and Roger Johnson are:
    i. **Timothy W. Johnson**, b. 02 May 1959.
    ii. **David F. Johnson**, b. 30 Oct 1962.

597

834.

Jerry A. Miller, son of No. 735, Erma Brubaker, was born 14 Mar 1935. He married **Patsy OSWALT**.
Children of Jerry Miller and Patsy Oswalt are:
  i. **Derrick S. Miller**, b. 28 Aug 1953.
  ii. **Courtney J. Miller**, b. 06 May 1967.

835.

Nancy L. Brubaker, daughter of No. 736, Orin C. Brubaker, was born 04 Sep 1944. She married **Terry L. FIREBAUGH**.
Children of Nancy Brubaker and Terry Firebaugh are:
  i. **Roger E. Firebaugh**, b. 27 Feb 1970.
  ii. **Ginger L. Firebaugh**, b. 14 Jun 1971.

836.

Carol M. Wood, daughter of No. 737, Eula M. Brubaker, was born 22 Jul 1943. She married **Donald D. WALDSCHMIDT**.
Children of Carol M. Wood and Donald Waldschmidt are:
  i. **Jill A. Waldschmidt**, b. 06 Jan 1964
  ii. **Jana S. Waldschmidt**, b. 16 Nov 1965.
  iii. **Jay A. Waldschmidt**, b. 19 May 1967.

837.

Melva K. Wood, daughter of No. 737, Eula M. Brubaker, was born 20 Aug 1945. She married **Raymond CASE**.
Children of Melva K. Wood and Raymond Case are:
  i. **Craig A. Case**, b. June 02, 1968.
  ii. **Kelly R. Case**, b. June 05, 1973.

838.

Anthony W. Wood, son of No. 737, Eula M. Brubaker, was born 02 Sep 1948. He married **Thelma L. BING**.

Children of Anthony W. Wood and Thelma L. Bing are:
- i. **Michael L. Wood**, b. 26 Aug 1970.
- ii. **Chad A. Wood**, b. 28 Jun 1973.

839.

William Lee Brubaker, son of No. 739, Howard Joy Brubaker, was born 13 Dec 1951. He married **Mary UNK**. He lived in Bakersfield, Kern County, California.
Children of William Lee Brubaker and Mary Unk are:
- i. **Child Brubaker**, b. 1985.
- ii. **Child Brubaker**, b. 1987.
- iii. **Child Brubaker**, b. 1989.
- iv. **Child Brubaker**. b. 1991.

840.

Jimmy G. Callison, son of No. 744, James E. Callison, was born 29 Oct 1935. He married **Marcia BLACK**.
Children of Jimmy G. Callison and Marcia Black are:
- i. **Barbara Callison**, b. 1958.
- ii. **Andrew Callison**, b. 1961.
- iii. **William Callison**. b. 1969.

841.

Sidney Mac Callison, son of No. 744, James E. Callison, was born 12 May 1942. He married **Rhoda KNOX**.
Children of Sidney Mac Callison and Rhoda Knox are:
- i. **Timothy M. Callison**, b. 01 Oct 1962.
- ii. **Bradley J. Callison**, b. 19 Apr 1966.
- iii. **Jennifer J. Callison**, b. 15 Jul 1972.

842.

Kelly Sue May, daughter of No. 748, Dianna Lee Callison, was born 30 Sep 1967. She married Dr. **Paul STERN**, 07 Aug 1999.
Children of Kelly Sue May and Paul Stern are:
    i. **Rowley Garrett Stern**, b. 16 May 2000.
    ii. **Callison "Callie" May Stern**, b. 28 Jan 2002.
    iii. **Bryson Thomas Stern**, b. 08 Dec 2003.

843.

Misti Michelle May, Ph.D., daughter of No. 748, Dianna Lee Callison, was born 26 Apr 1969. She married **Scott GOLTL**, 15 Apr 2000. They are divorced 2012. She is a DVM and the owner of Southview Veterinary Clinic in McPherson, Kansas.
Children of Misti Michelle May and Scott Goltl are:
    i. **Caroline Sue Goltl**, b. 28 Jul 1997.
    ii. **Andrew Paul Goltl**, b. 10 Nov 2000.

844.

Charlene Ridgway, daughter of No. 751, Charles Wesley Ridgway, married **Unk MURPHY**.
Children of Charlene Ridgway and Unk Murphy are:
    i. **Shannon Murphy**.
    ii. **Shelley Murphy**.

845.

Ernestine M. Ridgway, daughter of No. 751, Charles Wesley Ridgway, was born 03 Feb 1945. She married **Neal BEARD**.
Children of Ernestine M. Ridgway and Neal Beard are:
    i. **Tammy Beard**, b. 24 Jun 1963.
    ii. **Renee Beard**, b. 13 Jul 1967.
    iii. **David Beard**, b. 23 Jan 1969.

846.

Sherrel J. Ridgway, daughter of No. 751, Charles Wesley Ridgway, was born 07 Aug 1948. She married (1) **Samuel BYINGTON**. She married (2) **Michael MURPHY**.
Child of Sherrel J. Ridgway and Samuel Byington is:
    i. **Sammy Byington**, b. 16 Dec 1966.
Children of Sherrel Ridgway and Michael Murphy are:
    ii. **Michael Murphy, Jr.,** b. 24 Feb 1970.
    iii. **Jeffrey Murphy**, b. 22 Jun 1971.

847.

Everett W. Reeves, son of No. 752, Catherine E. Ridgway, was born 06 Jun 1939. He married **Douria BANISTER**. He lived in Houston, Harris County, Texas.
Children of Everett W. Reeves and Douria Banister are:
    i. **Sherry Reeves**, b. 10 Jul 1961.
    ii. **Weslena Reeves**, b. 19 Sep 1962.
    iii. **Floyd J. Reeves**, b. 07 Jan 1964.

848.

Larry D. Reeves, son of No. 752, Catherine E. Ridgway, was born 26 Jan 1941. He married **Janice GORDON**. He lived in Dexter, Cowley County, Kansas.
Children of Larry D. Reeves and Janice Gordon are:
    i. **Pammie Reeves**, b. 11 Dec 1962.
    ii.**Tammie Reeves**, b. 11 Dec 1962.
    iii.**Teresa Reeves**, b. 07 Jul 1964.
    iv. **Lisa Reeves**, b. 20 Dec 1966.

849.

Norman K. Reeves, son of No. 752, Catherine E. Ridgway, was born 25 Jul 1945. He married **Diana L. BURKHEART**.

Children of Norman K. Reeves and Diana L. Burkheart are:
    i. **Jim Alan Reeves**, b. 18 Dec 1972.
    ii. **Lynn Ann Reeves**, b. 28 Jul 1975.

850.
Phillips L. Stover, son of No. 753, Violet V. Ridgway, was born 28 Mar 1943. He married **Jessie McBRIDE**.
Children of Phillips L. Stover and Jessie McBride are:
    i. **Jerry Stover**, b. 15 Oct 1965.
    ii. **Larry Stover**, b. 11 Aug 1967.
    iii. **Perry Stover**, b. 28 Oct 1971.

851.
Rita R. Ridgway, daughter of No. 754, Ernest E. Ridgway, was born 30 Apr 1947. She married **Rex MEDCALF**. She lived in Wichita, Sedgwick County, Kansas.
Children of Rita Ridgway and Rex Medcalf are:
    i. **Craig Medcalf**.
    ii. **Jason Medcalf**.

852.
Robin W. Pizoati, son of No. 756, Samuel H. Foudray, married **Elaine RICKE**.
Child of Robin Pizoati and Elaine Ricke is:
    i. **Linda Pizoati**.

853.
Sheridan Hazell, daughter of No. 791, Donna L. Wilson, married **Don L. CRAWFORD**.
Children of Sheridan Hazell and Don Crawford are:
    i. **Michael C. Crawford**.
    ii. **Shawni D. Crawford**.

854.
David H. Hazell, son of No. 791, Donna L. Wilson, married **Tonda BELLAGARDT.**
Child of David Hazell and Tonda Bellagardt is:
    i. **Daniel D. Hazell.**

855.
Sandra J. Sanburn, daughter of No. 799, Marjorie Iona Wade, was born in 1949. She married **Juan ARNALDI**.
Children of Sandra Sanburn and Juan Arnaldi are:
    i. **Jennifer R. Arnaldi**, b. 1972.
    ii. **Sara Jeanne Arnaldi**, b. 1974.

856.
Tresca A. Sanburn, daughter of No. 799, Marjorie Iona Wade, was born in 1953. She married **Charles PERKINES.**
Child of Tresca Sanburn and Charles Perkins is:
    i. **Rebecca A. Perkines.**

857.
Mark James McGinnis, son of No. 819, Charles David McGinnis, married **Darna Elaine SHORT**.
Children of Mark McGinnis and Darna Short are:
    i. **Charles David McGinnis II.**
    ii. **Trevor Matthew McGinnis.**
    iii. **Shawn Ryan McGinnis.**

858.
Marilyn Ruth McGinnis, daughter of No. 819, Charles David McGinnis, married **Raymond Ellis LOREE**.
Children of Marilyn McGinnis and Raymond Loree are:
    i. **Krista Shaye Loree.**

ii. **Alyse Nicole Loree.**
iii. **Blake Sterling Loree.**
iv. **Ariana Evangeline Loree.**
v. **Hanah Rachelle Loree.**

859.

Paul Gordon Lovejoy, son of No. 820, Rex Emmett Lovejoy, married **Irene LABORIUM.**
Children of Paul Gordon Lovejoy and Irene Laborium are:
    i. **Randal Elliott Lovejoy.**
    ii. **Jennifer Leigh Lovejoy.**
    iii. **Timothy Lance Lovejoy.**

860.

Kay King, daughter of No. 821, Lesta Delsie Lovejoy, married **Harold Mark WELCH, Jr.**
Child of Kay King and Harold Welch, Jr. is:
    i. **Harold Mark Welch III.**

861.

Lisa Henderson, daughter of No. 821, Donna Ruth Lovejoy, married **Robert WHITE.**
Children of Lisa Henderson and Robert White are:
    i. **Ruth White.**
    ii. **Josh White.**

862.

Dana Henderson, daughter of No. 821, Donna Ruth Lovejoy, married **Louie KREUGER.**
Children of Dana Henderson and Louie Kreuger are:
    i. **Mike Kreuger.**
    ii. **Max Kreuger.**

iii. **Fred Kreuger**.
iv. **Tiger Kreuger**.
 v. **Wayne Kreuger**.
vi. **Victor Kreuger**.

EIGHTH GENERATION

863.
Michael Lee Swanson, son of No. 830, Beverly Ann Brown, was born 08 Nov 1954 in Caldwell, Canyon County, Idaho. He married **Teresa Rae OLTMAN,** 08 Oct 1977 in Boise, Idaho, daughter of **Ray OLTMAN** and **Frances Ruth UNK**.
Children of Michael Lee Swanson and Teresa Oltman are:
    i. **Ryan Michael Swanson**, b. 15 Feb 1985,
        Sacramento, Sacramento County, California.
   ii. **Kimberly Rae Swanson**, b. 10 May 1991,
        Sacramento, Sacramento County, California.

864.   .
Donald Kirt Swanson, son of No. 830, Beverly Ann Brown, was born 08 Nov 1956 in Caldwell, Canyon County, Idaho. He married **Penny Jean SEMAN,** 04 Aug 1984 in Tacoma, Pierce County, Washington, daughter of **Clarence SEMAN** and **Martha SYLSTAD**.
Children of Donald Kirt Swanson and Penny Seman are:
    i. **Ashley Marie Swanson**, b. 19 Jun 1988,
        Portland, Multnomah County, Oregon.
   ii. **Kayla Ann Swanson**, b. 27 Nov 1990,
        Portland, Multnomah County, Oregon.
  iii. **Shelby Jean Swanson**, b. 25 Apr 1996,
        Bellevue, King County, Washington.

865.
Pamela Marie Brown, daughter of No. 831, Carrol Comer Brown, was born 08 Feb 1966 in Yakima, Yakima County, Washington. She married **Stephen Todd LAWRENCE,** 12

Jun 1993 in Bakersfield, Kern County, California, son of
Richard LAWRENCE and **Susan DEWEY**.
Children of Pamela Brown and Stephen Lawrence are:
- i. **Connor Forrest Lawrence**, b. 27 May 1996, Boise, Ada County, Idaho.
- ii. **Madison Grace Lawrence,** b. 10 May 2000, Boise, Ada County, Idaho.

DESCENDANTS OF MARY PRITCHARD

13.

Mary Pritchard, the youngest daughter of No. 5, Thomas Pritchard, Sr. and Rachel Davis, was born in Leesburg, Loudoun County, Virginia about 1782. A marriage bond between Mary Pritchard and (1) **Charles ROBERTS** is dated 04 Mar 1799. When the rest of the family moved away, she may have remained behind with her sister Sarah, perhaps to plan for her approaching marriage because Robert Smarr, the son of Sarah's first husband, gives oath on the bond as to Mary's age. She would have been 17 at that time, if her birth date is accurate. A record of the actual marriage has not been located. Therefore, there are two possibilities. The first is that Charles Roberts died soon after the marriage; the second is that the marriage never took place. The latter possibility may be the case inasmuch as Allegany County, Maryland marriage records list Mary Pritchard, using her maiden name, as the bride of (2 ?) **John PARKER** on 22 Dec 1804 in Westernport, Allegany County, Maryland. This date appears in several sources, including the *Cyclopedia* cited below (pp. 110-112) and the diary of Reverend Shaw.

According to the *Biographical and Portrait Cyclopedia of Monongalia, Marion, and Taylor Counties, West Virginia*, John Parker was born about 1770 in Westernport, Maryland and died about 1840 in Monongalia County, (West) Virginia. His will was probated in the December term of 1840. He settled about 1795 in the portion of Monongalia County, Virginia which became the Paw Paw District of Marion County, West Virginia. He was a blacksmith by trade, but he also farmed and was a pioneer of Methodism, being a local minister of the Methodist Episcopal Church. He was first married to **Elizabeth NEPTUNE**, by whom he had two children, William and Joseph James. They are identified in an equity suit brought by the heirs of John and Ruth Neptune in 1856 in Allegany County, Maryland. He married second **Mary PRITCHARD**, by whom he had four children.

Children of John Parker and Elizabeth Neptune are:

866.　　i. **William Parker**, b. abt. 1801, Allegany County, Maryland; d. 1838, Monongalia County, (West) Virginia or Indiana.

867.　　ii. **Joseph James Parker,** b. September 23, 1803, Allegany County, Maryland; d. 06 Nov 1873, Agency, Wapello County, Iowa.

Children of Mary Pritchard and John Parker are:

868.　　iii. **John D. Parker**, b. 1807, Marion County, West Virginia; d. 1879, Marion County, West Virginia.

869.　　iv. **Rachel Parker**, b. 24 Jul 1808, Monongalia County, (West) Virginia; d. 27 Mar 1861, Marion County, West Virginia.

870.　　v. **Eliza Parker,** b. 27 Dec 1810, Monongalia County, (West) Virginia; d. 30 Jul 1892, Marion County, West Virginia.

871.　　vi. **Eli Parker**, b. abt. 1815, Monongalia County, (West) Virginia; d. after 17 Sep 1834.

SECOND GENERATION

866.

William Parker, son of John Parker and Elizabeth Neptune, was born about 1801 in Allegany County, Maryland, and died about 1838 in Monongalia County, (West) Virginia or Indiana. Lowther's History of Ritchie County, West Virginia says that the family moved to Indiana in 1830. After his death there in 1832 (another source says that he died in 1838), the family then returned to West Virginia. Sarah, his wife, was head of the household in both the Monongalia County Census of 1840 and the Marion County Census of 1850. On December 27, 1822, William Parker married **Sarah DEACON** daughter of **John DEACON** (also found as **DICKEN** and **DECKON**) and **Barbara HERBINGER** (also found as **HARBINGER**), who was born in Cumberland, Maryland. Tamar Deacon, sister of Sarah, married No. 598, William Meredith. (See Descendants of Ann Pritchard for additional details about the Deacon family.) Sarah Deacon was born about 1805 in Monongalia County, (West) Virginia, and died after 01 Jun 1860 in Marion County or Ritchie County. She is not found in the Marion County Census after 1860.

Children of William Parker and Sarah Deacon are:
872.　　i. **John Parker II,** b. abt. 1823, Monongalia County, (West) Virginia; d. December 1895, Pullman, Ritchie County, West Virginia.
　　ii. **Thomas H. Parker**, b. 1825; d. 10 Jun 1885; m. **Caroline BOONE** 13 Oct 1850.
　　iii. **Rachel Parker**, b. 28 Sep 1827; d. 16 Jan 1896; m. (1) **George Washington TOOTHMAN** 02 May 1846, Marion County, (West) Virginia; m. (2)

Calder H. **PARRISH** 06 Sep 1868.
iv. **Philip W. Parker**, b. 1831; d. 28 Jun 1894,
Marion County, (West) Virginia; m. **Julia
BOGGESS** 20 Apr 1851.
873.   v. **George Washington Parker**, b. abt. 1832; d.
1885, Chevauxdefrise, Ritchie County, West
Virginia.
vi. **Luvina Parker**.

867.

Joseph James Parker, son of John Parker and Elizabeth
Neptune, was born 1804 in Maryland and died in 1860 in
Monongalia County, West Virginia. He married **Mahala
PRICKETT** on 25 Sep 1824, daughter of **Job PRICKETT**
and No. 40, **Mary Ann PRICE**, who was the daughter of
Richard PRICE, husband of No. 8, Eleanor Pritchard, and
Nancy DALLAS, his first wife. Mahala was born 29 Oct 1807,
in Monongalia County, (West) Virginia.
Children of Joseph James Parker and Mahala Prickett are:
i. **Elizabeth Ann Parker**, b. 1827, Monongalia
County.
ii. **Mary Harriet Parker**, b. 11 Mar 1828,
Monongalia County; d. 23 Aug 1855,
Marion County, (West) Virginia.
iii. **William Parker**, b. 1831.
iv. **Josiah Parker**, b. 1832.
v. **James M. Parker**, b. 1834.
vi. **Sabrina Parker**, b. 1836.
vii. **Newton Parker**, b. 1841.
viii. **Sophronia Parker**, b. 1841.
ix. **Margaret Cornelia Parker**, b. 1842.
x. **Oliver W. Parker**, b. 24 Feb 1844.

xi. **Pinkney M. Parker**, b. 1846.
xii. **Buckney M. Parker**, b. 1847.
xiii. **Joseph Luther Parker,** b. 15 Apr 1848.

868.

John D. Parker, son of No. 13, Mary Pritchard, and John Parker, was born in 1807 on the old family homestead in Monongalia County, Virginia, and died there in 1879. By that time, it had become part of Marion County, West Virginia. He married (1) **Rebecca CLAYTON**, daughter of **Elisha CLAYTON,** who was also the Suretor of the marriage. Rebecca was born 28 Feb 1813 in Monongalia County, (West) Virginia, and died 01 Oct 1856. Both she and John are buried in the William Parker cemetery, Paw Paw District, Marion County, West Virginia. John D. Parker was a Methodist minister, as well as a farmer. He and Rebecca had seven children, two sons and five daughters, but only one is verified and listed here. When Rebecca died at the age of 43, he married (2) **Amelia "Millie" HARTLEY** on 20 Aug 1857 in Marion County. Amelia was born about 1811 in Virginia, and died July 01, 1894 in Marion County, West Virginia.
Child of John D. Parker and Rebecca Clayton is:
874.   i. **Eli L. Parker**, b. 15 Jul 1840.

869.

Rachel Parker, daughter of No. 13, Mary Pritchard, was born 24 Jul 1808 in Monongalia County, (West) Virginia. She died 27 Mar 1851 in Marion County, West Virginia. Rachel married **Little CLAYTON,** 02 Oct 1828 in Monongalia County, (West Virginia). John Parker was Suretor. Little Clayton was born 06 Sep 1806 in Monongalia County, (West) Virginia, and died 13 Mar 1895 in Marion County, West Virginia. He married (1)

Amelia "Amy" PRICHARD, oldest daughter of **William PRICHARD**, No. 11. Little Clayton and Rachel are buried in the William Parker Cemetery, Paw Paw District, Marion County.

870.

Eliza Parker, daughter of No. 13, Mary Pritchard, was born 17 Dec 1810 in Monongalia County, (West) Virginia and died 30 Jul 1892 in Marion County, West Virginia. The date comes from her gravestone in the Arnettsville Cemetery, Grant District, Marion County, West Virginia. She married **Thomas Alfred ATHA,** 17 Oct 1871 in Marion County, West Virginia. He was born about 1831 and died 1873 in Marion County, West Virginia. At that time, Eliza was 61 years of age and Thomas was 40. The disparity in their ages and the swiftness of his death following their marriage further compounds the curious citation in the 1880 Marion County Census naming Eliza as the mother of Ann Eliza Parker Arnett.

871.

Eli Parker, son of No. 13, Mary Pritchard, was born about 1815 in Monongalia County, (West) Virginia and died after 17 Sep 1834 when he was named in his father's will. He married **Rosey COWEN** on 24 Oct 1833 in Monongalia County, (West) Virginia.

THIRD GENERATION

872.

John Parker II, son of No. 866, William Parker, was born about 1823 in Monongalia County, (West) Virginia, and died December 1895 at Pullman, Ritchie County, West Virginia. He married **Nancy SNODGRASS** 22 Apr 1847 in Ritchie County, officiated by T. W. Snodgrass. She was the daughter of **Isaac SNODGRASS** and **Hannah UNK**. In her *History of Ritchie County, West Virginia,* Minnie Lowther reports that John Parker went to Indiana with his parents as a child, but returned to West Virginia and moved to Ritchie County in 1838 when he was only seventeen years old. He and Nancy built a home on the waters of White Oak, where he erected a saw mill near the present site of the White Oak Church. Lowther describes him as the first miller of the area, "that honest, rugged type of miller of those early days." He operated his mill for several years before removing to a farm on Slab Creek. From there he moved to Pullman, where he is buried in the Pullman Churchyard.

Children of John Parker and Nancy Snodgrass are:

      i. **Sylvester Parker;** m. **Mary Jane PRITCHARD**, daughter of No. 54, John Moody Pritchard, remained at Pullman.

     ii. **James Parker**, remained at Pullman.

   iii. **William Alvin Parker**; m. **Elizabeth Ann PRITCHARD**, daughter of No. 54, John Moody Pritchard, moved to Colorado.

   iv. **Rose Parker**; m. **Unk FOSTER**; moved to Colorado.

    v. **Eli Parker**, moved to Washington State.

vi. **Luvina Parker**, m. **Unk WILSON;** moved to
    Washington State.
vii. **Elsie Parker**, m. **Unk HOWE;** moved to Upshur
    County, West Virginia;
viii. **Usebius Parker**, moved to Parkersburg, Wood
    County, West Virginia.
ix. **Frank Parker**, moved to Clarksburg, Harrison
    County, West Virginia.

873.

George Washington Parker, son of No. 866, William Parker,
was born about 1832 and died in 1885 at Chevauxdefrise,
Ritchie County, West Virginia. He married **Mary BOONE** on
22 Apr 1852 in Marion County. They settled in White Oak,
Ritchie County in 1854, remaining there eight years before
moving to Chevauxdefrise in 1862. Mary Boone Parker lived
until 1909. Both are buried in the Kendal Burial Ground,
Ritchie County.
Children of George Washington Parker and Mary Boone are:
    i. **Ella Parker**; m. **Conrad MATHENY**,
       Harrisville, Ritchie County, West Virginia.
   ii. **Josiah Parker,** lived in Washburn, Ritchie
       County.
  iii. **Leroy Parker**, lived in Pennsboro, Ritchie
       County.
   iv. **Laura Parker**, m. **Unk GOODWIN**, lived in
       Cairo, Ritchie County.
    v. **Lena Parker**, m.**Unk COX**, lived in Cairo,
       Ritchie County.
   vi. **Festus Parker**, moved to Washington State.
  vii. **Sarah Parker**, m. **Unk FOSTER**, moved to
       Colorado.

The Pritchard/Prickett Family History

viii. **Iva Parker**, m. **Unk LOWTHER**, lived in Yellow
Creek, Ritchie County.

874.

Eli L. Parker, one son of No 868, John D. and Rebecca
Clayton Parker, was born 15 Jul 1840 and married **Elizabeth
MURRAY** 24 Jan 1863. He taught school until enlisting in the
federal army in company "F," 12th regiment, West Virginia
volunteer infantry, Captain Pitcher's company, and served as a
private in the Civil War until 04 Mar 1864, when he was
discharged to accept the office of second lieutenant of
company "E," third West Virginia mounted infantry. On 14
Dec 1864, he was promoted to first lieutenant and transferred
to company "D" of the same regiment. He was promoted to
captain 30 Mar 1865 and served until being honorably
discharged 22 May 1866 after reinforcing Colonel Fleming
who was surrounded by Indians at Cottonwood, Colorado. A
Methodist minister, he was a member of the West Virginia
House of Delegates 1884-1885.

Children of Eli L. Parker and Elizabeth Murray are:

i. **John W. Parker**, owner of a planing mill at
Rivesville, Marion County, with his brother.
ii. **Lincoln E. Parker**.
iii. **Nora Parker**, m. **George E. SATTERFIELD**, a
farmer, Marion County.
iv. **F.W. Parker**, a traveling salesman representing
Franklin Davis Nursery.
v. **Grace Parker**.
vi. **Charles B. Parker**.
vii. **Sallie Parker**

616

SOURCES

Allegany County Maryland Deed Books.

Allegany County Maryland Marriage Records.

Barnes, Robert, comp. Maryland Marriages 1801-1820.

Bell, Raymond Martin. List of Inhabitants, 1800 or before, of Washington County, Pennsylvania.

Biographical and Portrait Cyclopedia of Monongalia, Marion, and Taylor Counties, West Virginia.

Brown, Chloe Della Foltz. John Bathes Foltz and Margaret Horminghuser Foltz of Shenandoah County, Virginia and Fairfield County, Ohio, with Early History and Records of Father George Peter Foltz and Grandfather Joseph Foltz of Shenandoah County, Virginia, 1751-1797.

Brown, Jacob. Brown's Miscellaneous Writings.

Caster, Bertha, Records of.

Caster Cemetery Records, Meigs County, Ohio.

Caster Family Sketches.

Conrad, Henry C. History of the State of Delaware.

Crumrine, Boyd. Virginia Court Records in Southwestern Pennsylvania - Records of the District of West Augusta and Ohio and Yohogania Counties, Virginia.

Cunningham, John N. History Autobiography and Genealogical History: Ancient Meredith Line.

Dearborn County, Indiana Office of the Clerk of Circuit Court Marriage Book 9.

Decatur County Indiana Bicentennial Committee, Revolutionary War Veterans Buried in Decatur County, Indiana, by Patricia Smith, 1986.

Decatur County Indiana Cemeteries.

Decatur County Indiana Deed Books A, B, C, & D.

Delaware Archives I.

Dille, Thomas Ray, comp. Marriage Bonds filed in Monongalia County Virginia, now West Virginia 1796-1850. Published in Daughters of the American Revolution Magazine, Vols. 62, 63, 64, and 66.

Doddridge County (West) Virginia Death Records, West Virginia State Archives, Charleston, WV.

Fansler, Homer Floyd. History of Tucker County West Virginia.

Fathergill and Noble. Virginia Tax Payer List 1782-1787.

Fauquier County Virginia Will Book 2.

Fayette County, Pennsylvania, Will Book 7.

Frazier, Griffin Guy. James Frazier: Chapter IV - The Merediths.

Gaddis, Emma Frances Loar. The Loar Genealogy with Cognate Branches, 1774-1947.

Gaines, B.O. The History of Scott County Kentucky, 3 vols. Georgetown, Kentucky.

Granthan, A.R. and L.M., Grantham-Miller Family History Research, Congress, Arizona.

Harrison County (West) Virginia Census 1820.

Harrison County (West) Virginia Deed Books.

Harrison County (West) Virginia Highway Map.

Harrison County (West) Virginia Court Order Book and Minutes 1814-1820.

Harrison County (West) Virginia Tithable List 1784-1824.

Holmes, Maurice, comp. Early Land Holders of Decatur County Indiana.

Jewell. Loudoun County Marriage Records 1751-1880.

Kennedy, N. Brent. The Melungeons: The Resurrection of a Proud People - An Untold Story of Ethnic Cleansing in America," Mercer University Press, Macon, GA, September 1996.

Kent County, Delaware Deed Book Y.

King, Estelle Stewart. Abstracts of Wills, Inventories and Administration Accounts of Loudoun County Virginia 1757-1800.

Leckey, Howard L. The Ten Mile County and its Pioneer Families - Greene and Washington Counties, Pennsylvania.

Lewis County (West) Virginia Census 1930.

Lewis County (West) Virginia Deed Books.

Loudoun County Virginia Deed Book N.

Loudoun County Virginia Minute Book 1780-1783,

Loudoun County Virginia Old Chancery Suits M 1330-File.

Loudoun County Virginia Order Book R 1796-1798.

Loudoun County Virginia Will Book E.

Lowther, Minnie Kendall. History of Ritchie County (West) Virginia.

Lowther, Minnie Kendall. Ritchie County in History and Romance.

Marion County (West) Virginia Genealogical Club. Marion County Paw Paw District Map.

Marion County (West) Virginia Genealogical Club. Map of boundaries of Monongalia and Preston Counties, 1818.

Marion County (West) Virginia Genealogical Club. Map of Monongalia County 1821.

Marion County (West) Virginia Genealogical Club. Map of Monongalia County Union Magisterial District, 1886.

Marion County (West) Virginia Wills, Vols.1-3, 1842-1903.

Maryland and Delaware Genealogist, Vol. 10, No. 3.

Maryland Historical Society, Baltimore, Maryland. Old

Settlers.

Meigs County Ohio Death Records, Book 2.

Meigs County Ohio Marriage Books 2, 3, 4.

Merydith Family Bible.

Monongalia County (West) Virginia Appraisement Book 4.

Monongalia County (West) Virginia Census 1810.

Monongalia County (West) Virginia Estate Settlements, Book 4.

Monongalia County (West) Virginia Land and Personal Property Tax Lists 1783-1821.

Monongalia County (West) Virginia Order Book Vol. 3, 1806-1810.

Morris, Earle H. Marriage Records Harrison County, (West) Virginia 1784-1850.

Mountain Democrat, Oakland, Maryland, May 17, 1937.

Nestor, Carl K. Descendants of Jacob Nester 1761-1844.

New Jersey Historical Society Collections, Vol. VI, Supplement.

Ohio: Cross Roads of the Nation - Records and Pioneer Families in Ohio, Vol. 5, No. 2.

Power, John Carroll. History of the Early Settlers of Sangamon County, Illinois, Centennial Record, 1876.

Prichard, Arthur C. An Appalachian Legacy: Mannington Life and Spirit.

Queen Family History.

Randolph, Corliss. Seventh Day Baptists in West Virginia, 1905.

Revolutionary War Veterans Buried in Decatur County Indiana.

Rubincam, Milton, ed. Genealogies of Pennsylvania Families From the Pennsylvania Magazine of History and Biography.

Rush, Peggy Frances. The Willis Family of the Northern
    Neck in Virginia, 1669-1737.
Scharf, John Thomas. History of Western Maryland, Vol. II.
Scott County Kentucky Census 1800 & 1810.
Shannon, William G. and Sara Belle Shannon. The Smarr
    Family.
Slevin, Ruth, comp. Decatur County Indiana Marriage
    Records 1822-1852, Book A through G.
Spangler, D.V. History of the Welsh Tract Baptist Church,
    Pencader Hundred, New Castle County, Delaware.
State of Maryland Land Grant to Thomas Pritchard Jr.,
    Maryland Hall of Records.
Teachenor, Richard Bennington. A Partial History of the
    Tichenor Family in America, Descendants of Martin
    Tichenor.
Tichenor, Harold A. Tichenor Families in America, 1988.
Wardell, Patrick G. Virginians & West Virginians,1607-
    1870, Vol. 3.
Wardell, Patrick G. Virginia/West Virginia Genealogical
    Data from Revolutionary War Pension and Bounty
    Land Warrant Records, Vol. 3.
Warren County Virginia Book A.
Wertz, Mary Alice. Marriages of Loudoun County, Virginia,
    1757-1853.
West Virginians in the Revolution.
Wiley, S.T. History of Preston County West Virginia.
Zinn, Melba Pender. Monongalia County (West) Virginia
    Records of the District Superior and County Courts,
    Vol. 2, 1800-1803.
Zinn, Melba Pender. Monongalia County (West) Virginia
    Records of the District Superior and County Courts, 11-
    1812 and 1814-1820.

The Pritchard/Prickett Family History

INDEX

ABERNATHY, Ellen, 128; John, 128.

ACKERSON, Mary, 124.

ACTON, Rachel, 116.

ADAMS, Elijah W.; Ethel, 85; Ruffner S., 356; Stella, 186.

ADKINS, Emma Bertha, 174; Rhea Maureen, 369.

AICHEL, Bernice Eleanor, 379.

ALBURN, Mary, 61

ALDEN, Abigail, 111; John, 111

ALEO, John S., 568.

ALEY, Mary, 540; Nellie, 540.

ALKIRE, Mary, 341.

ALLEN, Evangeline Virginia, 288, 347-348; Halley Drew, 394; Joe Hamilton, 288, 348; Joe Hamilton Jr., 348, 394; Seth, 288; Virginia Mae, 375-376.

ALLENDER, Frances L., 280.

ALLINGTON, Lela, 596.

ALTHA, Sallie, 427.

ALVIA, Luella S. Schwab, 553.

AMMONS, Charles "Billy" Simeon, 547; John Morgan, 547; Simeon E., 546-547.

AMOS, Unk, 327; Eva Maude, 283; John, 504-505; Mary Ann, 512-513; Stephen, 512

ANCELL, Nancy, 169.

ANDER, Ruben G., 509.

ANDERSON, Dean Hart, 388; Mary, 143; Tim, 472.

ANGELINE, Ernestine Ann, 347; 393.

ANGUISH, William, 495.

ANKROM, Edwin, 488; Joseph S., 185; Keith, 488; Mark, 488.

ANTHONY, William, 174.

ASH, Albert, 410; Ian Matthew, 410; Philip Todd, 410.
ASHBURN, Amy Carol, 363; Loraine Ann, 363; Mark Allen, 363; Robert, 363.
ASHORN, Gloria, 593.
ASHWORTH, David, 244; Elizabeth Amarka, 244-245; John, 305.
ASTON, Jane, 547.
ATHA, Thomas Alfred, 63.
ATHEY, Joyce M., 361.
ATTEL, Patrick, 572.
AUVIL, Mary, 302; Sarah, 303.
AYERS, Caroline Virginia, 487; Carter Vaughan, 487; Charles Philip, 487; Michael Vaughan, 487.
BAILEY, Cora, 82; Elizabeth, 176; James, 82; Minnie, 235.
BAKER, Alice, 258; Bob, 473; Christine J., 473; Christopher A., 472-473; Edith, 198; Emma, 570; Emma O., 324; George, 509; Lloyd, 473; Lula, 259; Nicholas Morgan, 153; William 516.
BALDWIN, Agnes, 107; Elizabeth, 106, 107; Hannah, 106; Henry, 106; Jane, 108; John, 106, 107; John Jr. 107; John Sr., 107; Mary, 107; Richard, 106, 107; Robert, 108; Sylvester, 107.
BALL, Gene, 351; Lucille, 400.
BALLAH, Catherine, 510.
BANKS, Lucille Bonnie, 361.
BANISTER, Douria, 601.
BARCLAY, Sarah E., 77.
BARELA, Elizabeth, 485.
BARKER, Mary, 325.
BARKLEY, Elizabeth Jane, 313-314; James, 313.
BARNES, Bessie, 471.
BARNETT, Agatha, 74.

BRYANT, David H., 596; David Keith, 387; Michael Paul, 596.

BRYSKY, Michael, 479.

BUCKALEW, Andrew, 119; Mary, 120; Rachel, 126

BULLARD, Barbara. 586.

BURCH, Grace, 535.

BURCHINAL, Nellie, 456.

BURKE, Louisa Jane, 274

BURKHEART, Diana L., 601-602.

BURNEY, Lucille, 537.

BURRIS, Castella, 96; Clara D., 537, 549-550; Van, 536; William W., 536.

BURT, William, 437.

BURWELL, Brian, 369; Jill, 369, 403; Raymond, 369; Stephen, 369.

BUSH, A Kyle, 567; Araminita Price, 176; Catherine, 595; Eleanor Caroline, 567, 595; Elizabeth, 595; Gladys Willa, 314; Ivan, 567; Mary, 75; Robert Kyle, 565, 595; Sarah, 595; William, 75.

BUSSELL, Charles A., 83; Eddy, 83.

BUTCHER, Ada, 278; Euna, 278; Fay, 278; Isaac B., 278; May, 278; Rex, 278.

BUTTS, Mildred, 454.

BUZZARD, Lura, 544-545; William, 545.

BYINGTON, Sammy, 601; Samuel, 601.

BYNUM, Lee Ann, 369.

BYRAM, Anna, 111-112; Ebenezer, 111.

CAIN, Brenda Lee, 393; Brady, 253; Catherine, 150; Christopher Matthew, 394; David, 253; David Lee Jr., 394; David Lee Sr., 347; Dennis, 253; Dora, 253; George, 252-253; Helen Jane, 347, 393, 412; Joyce Ann, 348, 394; Kelly Ann, 393; Kristie Jo, 393; Lloyd, 253; Maud, 253; Pa. 412; Paul

Allen Jr., 393; Paul Allen Sr., 347, 393; Paul Anson, 347-348; Steven, 393.

CALHOUN, Arminda, 208.

CALLISON, Andrew, 599; Barbara, 599; Bradley J., 599; Dianna Lee, 552, 574; Elbert. 536, 552; George A., 536-537; George Lawrence, 536, 551; Harley M., 537, 552; Helen Limpp, 574; James, 552, 573; James Albert, 573; James E., 552, 572-573; James F., 536, 551-552; Jarrett W., 551, 572; Jennifer J., 599; Jimmy G., 573, 599; Marilyn, 552, 573 Martha Louise, 552, 574; Mary Helen, 552, 574; Mattie Mildred, 525; Melissa F., 573; Patricia M., 572; Robert, 562; Sidney Mae, 573, 599; Timothy M., 599; Verda E., 552; Wanda Sue, 573; William, 599.

CALLOWAY, Carolyn, 589-590.

CAMP, Mary, 107; William, 142.

CAMPAS, Darlene, 389.

CAMPBELL, Betty, 355; Mary Catherine, 277.

CARDER, George, 154.

CARMAN, Barbara, 510

CARPENTER, Unk. 156; Evan, 405; Mallory, 405; Mary, 572; Matthew, 405.

CARPER, Mary, 79.

CARTER, Elizabeth, 25, 298; Mary Polly, 172.

CARY, Boyd Balford Jr., 348-349; Boyd Balford Sr., 348; Lucius Alexander Jr., 400; Lucius Alexander Sr., 400; Matthew Roger, 349; Roland Mylles, 349.

CASE, Craig A., 598; Frank Borton, 455-456; Kelly R., 598; Raymond, 598.

CASTER, Unk, 138; Bertha Fern, 183, 251-252; Daniel, 147, 183; Drucella, 146; Emily, 147; Hesekiah, 146; James, 146; Lewis, 146; Mary, 146; Nancy, 146, 183; Salina, 146; Samuel, 145-147; Sarah Ann, 147; Vincent, 146; Wesley, 146.

236-237; Rebecca, 612; William O., 532.

CLIMON, Melilda, 419.

CLINE, John, 505.

COBB, Maria, 75; Mary Epps, 495.

COBERLY, Bernice, 263.

COBURN, Catherine, 149-149; Jonathan, 149; Rebecca, 155.

COCHRAN, Berd, 254; Clifford, 254; Cline, 254; Gail, 254; Harold, 254; John R., 254; Marly, 254; Nellie, 254.

COCHRELL, Otis J., 302; Ronald, 302.

COGHILL, James, 140; Mary, 140.

COLE, Gene, 344; Patricia Lorraine, 399.

COLEMAN, James A., 426; Ralph, 329.

COLLIER, Unk P. 96, 471.

COLLINS, Henry, 138; Safronia, 302; Wilfred D., 184.

COMBS, Rachel, 136.

COMER, Katherine Marie, 569-570; Thomas, 569.

CONDIT, Bryam, 113; Edward, 113; Lewis, 113; Peter, 113.

CONGROVE, Gade R., 586; Gene R., 586; Gordon S., 586; Lucille, 331.

CONLEY, Adoline. 187; Charles, 187; Edwin, 186-187; Ella, 187, 254 Fleda, 187; George, 186; James, 187; John, 187; Martha, 187; Salley, 187.

CONROES, Caroline, 575.

CONSOLVER, Elva, 382.

CONSOLVO, Candise S., 595-596.

CONWAY, Frank, 352; Ray, 281; Rebecca Jo Ann, 352; Sarah Ann, 447.

COOK, Unk, 376, 493; Aaron, 376; Kelly, 376; Mary, 493..

COOKSEY, Angeline, 82.

COOLEY, Isaac P., 124.2; Jonathan, 413; Kaya Rexann, 413; Mary Elizabeth, 299.

CORBETT, Robert James, 368; Shirley Ann Briggs, 368.

Katherine, 516; Mary, 516; Matilda, 516; Rachel, 516; Ruth,
516; Sarah, 506, 516; 610; Tamar, 515-517; Tasy, 516.
DEAL, SUSAN, 402.
DEAN, William Corner, 456.
DeBERRY, Max, 285.
DEBRULER, John, 184.
DELANEY, Angela, 401.
DeMOSS, Baby, 304; Beverly Lee, 304, 361; Boy, 304, 361;
Carolyn Gay, 359; Douglas Steve, 361; Elzara Nadine, 304;
Everett Sylvester, 304, 361; Hilda Lorraine, 304, 359-360;
Jacob, 303-304; James Wesley, 304, 359; Lennis May, 359;
Lola May, 304, 360; Norma Ilene, 304, 360- 361; Raymond
Willard, 304; Robert Glenn, 304. 359; Robert Wesley, 303-
304; Ruth Evelyn, 359; Ruth Ilene, 359; Sherril, 359; Sophia
Isabel, 304, 360.
DENNISON, Daniel, 339; David, 339; Dewey F., 206, 280-
281; Iris May, 281; Jeff, 339; John, 156; John Willis, 206, 280;
Kenneth Wayne, 280, 338-339; Norma. 280; Reason, 205-206;
Robert, 280; Rona, 281; Susan, 156-157.
DEPUE, Evaline, 309.
DESBIEN, Unk, 484.
DeVARKIN, Laurie, 489.
DEWEY, Susan, 607.
DICKEN, Rebecca, 433.
DICKERSON, Unk, 458.
DICKEY, Daisy, 453.
DILLE, Almira, 442.
DILLEY, Letitia/Lutecia, 196.
DISBRO, Leo Warren, 364-365; Linda Marie, 365; William
Michael, 364
DITTERLINE, John W., Jr., 354; John Wesley III, 355; Judith
Ann, 354; Sarah Elizabeth, 355; Susan Jo, 354; Virginia Lee,

254.
DIVERS, Unk, 138; Charles, 164; Lemuel, 164; Susan, 162-163.
DIX, Sarah, 187-188.
DOAK, Unk, 526.
DODD, Beverly Kay, 398.
DOGOLYER, Stella A., 321-322.
DONLEY, Mart, 433.
DONOLY, Mary, 29-31.
DOOLEY, Dorothy R., 558; Lee Martin, 558; Lori J., 583;
Marilyn J., 558, 582; Michele L., 583; Sammy M., 558, 583
DOTSON, Gabriella, 184.
DOUGLASS, Levi, 142, 143; Nancy Anne, 139, 142, 143-144;
Viola, 186; William I, 143; William II, 143; William III, 143;
William IV, 143.
DOVER, Unk, 482; Debra, 482.
DOWNE, Mary, 105.
DOWNING, Clifford, 330; Geneva, 330; Margie, 330.
DOYLE, Elizabeth, 132.
DOZIER, Hannah, 24.
DOZER, Leonard, 39.
DRAKE, James, 26.
DRENNAN, Nellie, 546.
DUCKWORTH, Aaron, 116 Drusilla, 117. Ephraim B., 117;
Francis, 117; George, 116-117; Henry, 116; John, 116-117;
Nancy Hizer, 117; Sara; 117; Thomas Jefferson, 117, William,
116.
DUDLEY, Mary, 435-436.
DUFF, Alexandra, 401; Ashley Winifred, 301; Christopher,
401; David Allen, 367, 401; Hobart, 367; Morgan Nicole, 402;
Stephen Edward, 367, 401; Susan Kathleen, 367, 401; Thomas
Lee, 368, 401; Travis Short, 401; Walter Boyd, 367-368

76; Messouri A., 76; Sarah, 76; Thomas J., 76.
ERICKSON, Daughter, Harold, 355; Michael, 355; Steven, 355.
ERVEN, Willard, 351.
ERWIN, Ida, 447.
ESPOSITO, Cara Marie, 595; Patrick Ross Jr., 595; Patrick Ross Sr., 595.
ESTES, David Allen, 479.
EUBANK, William D., 76.
EVANS, Bertha, 530; Ellen "Polly", 510.
EVENSON, Chad Lloyd, 391; Dustin Kyle, 391; Leticia Gay, 391; Lloyd Stanley, 391-392; Lylu Christian, 392; Mandy Lynn, 391; Spencer Martin, 392; Stacy Ann, 391; Travis Brandon, 392.
EWALD, Mary Louise, 571.
EWART, Catherine, 313.
EWING, Absalom David, 153.
EYLER, Catherine, 225-226.
FAKES, Arthur Jr, 84, 86; Arthur Sr., 84; Cheryl Ann, 86; Theresa Magdalen, 86.
FANSLER, Elizabeth Ann, 215; Henry, 215.
FARMER, John, 94.
FAUCHER, Helen, 347, 394.
FELL, Joseph, 132; Sarah, 132.
FELLOWS, Ernest, 376; Marsha Jean, 376; Olivia, 457.
FENIMORE, Evelyn, 480.
FERDERER, Linda Michelle, 378.
FERGUSON, Tony, 236
FICKEY, Cheryl Lynn, 467; William Lynn, 467.
FIREBAUGH, Ginger L., 598; Roger E., 598; Terry L., 598.
FISHER, Camille, 410.
FITTRO, Beulah, 297.

GARVIN, Sarah Nancy, 205.
GASTON, Anna C., 155; Hugh, 155; Jane E., 155; John H., 154-155; Mary E., 155; Rulana, 155.
GATHEY, Joanna 25.
GAUGER, Elmer William, 309-310.
GAWTHORNE, James, 241.
GAYE, Unk, 574-575.
GEARO, Agnes, 409.
GENTRY, Amanda, 407; Anna, 407; Mitchell, 406-407.
GEORGE, Unk, 23.
GERASIMEK, Sarah Elizabeth, 486.
GERSON, Ellen, 569.
GESSLEIN, Marian, 404.
GETES, Julie, 403.
GIBBONS, Dolores Jean, 356.
GIBSON, Joseph Prichard, 469; Milford I., 469; Sarah, 469, 487; Seth Jacob, 413; Shaun Eric, 413; Steve Eric, 413.
GILLILAND, Hazel M., 558-559.
GILPIN, Anna, 413; Ashlee Rexann, 396, 413; Beverly Ann, 350, 396; Brian Douglas, 395, 413; Darin Lee, 395, 413; Debra, 575; Forrest, 260; Hobart, 350; Julia, 413; Julie Renee, 395; Kay Walter, 350, 395; Lydia Kathryn, 396; Patricia Lynn, 350, 395; Rex Eugene, 350, 396; Tyler Kay, 413.
GILTNER, William, 563.
GIROD, Andrea, 585; Barbara J., 559; Charles I., 559; Linda A., 559, 585; Philemon, 559; Philip G., 559, 584-585; Suzanne K., 585.
GLADNEY, John William, 361; Michael Wayne, 361; Shanna Lee, 361; Vernon Lynn, 361.
GLASS, William, 75.
GLENN, Elizabeth, 529.
GLOVER, Amos, 439; Barbara, 439; Ephriam, 439; Isaac, 439;

John, 439; Leonard, 440; Lucy, 440; Margaret, 440, Mary, 440;
Nehemiah Jr., 439; Nehemiah Sr., 439-440; Samuel, 439;
William, 439.
GODWIN, Virginia, 230.
GOFF, Alexander, 247; Alice, 315; Ethel Myrtle, 248, 309-
310; Ezra, 251; Fredda Marcella, 248, 311; Hermione
"Herma" Pearl, 248, 310; James M., 196; June Leigh, 247-248;
Lathrop Columbus, 247-248; Leota Maude, 251; Marcellus,
248; Myrtle Ethel, 247; Winifred Dell, 249, 312, 367, 368.
GOLDMAN, Unk 270.
GOLLATHAN/GOLLOTHAN, Martin, 31, 34; Sarah, 29, 34-
39.
GOLTL, Andrew, 600; Caroline Sue, 600; Scott, 600.
GOODWIN, Unk, 615.
GOOTS, Abigail Jordan, 411; William Edward, Jr., 411.
GORDON, Alice, 542; Carmen S,, 541, 560; Gilbert, 542, 500-
561; Ione, 541. 560; Janice, 601; Jean, 560, 587; Joe, 560, 587;
Kay, 561. 586; Lillian Viola, 475-476; Mamie, 541, 560; Mary,
541; Phyllis, 494; Rhea, 561, 587; Sue, 561, 586; Steve, 587;
Stewart, 541-542, 587; Susan, 587; Thomas, 561.
GRADY, Haskell O., 336; Russell, 336.
GRAHAM, Ethel L., 570; Joe, 542; John David, 582 John E.,
582; LaVonne, 588.
GRAVES, Hayward, 272; Pearl, 272; William, H., 92.
GRAY, Hannah, 185; John, 70, 72; Lucia Helen Hale, 241.
GREATHOUSE, Dencie Evelyne, 293, 352; Emily, 240; John
Jackson, 293; Sylvia Oleta, 293, 352; Thelma, 293, 351-352;
Vervel, 293, 351.
GREEN, Abbott Miles, 183; Lucretia, 131; Lovina, 146; Viola,
183.
GREER, Cynthia, 471; Edward Frank Jr., 471; Edward Frank
Sr., 470-471; Elaine, 471; Jacqueline, 471; Jonathan Luke, 471;

Michael Theodore 218-219; Millie Catherine, 222.

HALSTEAD, Charles Holly Jr, 387-388.

HAMILTON, J. Nicholas, 567.

HAMMET, Forest, 481; Rebecca, 481; Richard, 481; Robert, 481; Roxanne, 481.

HAMMET, Forrest, 481; Rebecca, 481; Richard, 481; Robert, 481, Roxanne, 481.

HAMPTON, John, 90.

HANCOCK/HANDCOCK, James, 171; Rebecca, 171, 172.

HANDY, Pearl L., 551-552.

HANKINS, Winnie, 550.

HANNA, Virginia, 595.

HANSON, Janice M., 581.

HARBERT, Rebecca, 125; Thomas, Jr, 125.

HARBINGER/HERBINGER, Barbara, 515-517, 610.

HARDESTY, Caroline, 241.

HARDY, George, 347.

HARNIST, Eve, 168; Michael, 168.

HARRATT, Sarah, 168.

HARRIGER, Laura, 323.

HARRIS, Alpheus F., 151, 194-195; Cecile Marie, 474-475; Eliza J., 151; George W. 151; Harley M., 195; Hollis F., 195; John, 150-151; Katherine M., 195; Martha, 151, 193; Millie Frances., 151 194; Nancy Rebecca, 151; Peter, 159; Vearl M., 557.

HARRISON, Fielding, 127.

HARSH, Elizabeth, 218; Gilbert, 219.

HART, John Kenneth Jr., 404; John Kenneth Sr., 404.

HARTINGER, Melvin, 534.

HARTLEY, Amelia "Millie, 612.

HARTSHORN, Unk, 497.

HARVEY, Frona, M., 257.

HASTINGS, Joanna, 404.

HATCHER, Jane, 174; Phoebe, 172-174.

HATFIELD, Dewayne E., 313; Emma Jean, 313; Ernest, 313; Helen, 313; Lucy Lee, 370; Ronald, 312.

HAUGHT, Barbara, 372; Martha E., 454.

HAWES, E. H., 282.

HAWKINS, Aaron, 516; Benjamin, 141; Jared, 153; Joseph, 516; Solomon, 153.

HAWLIK, David, 569; Jami, 569; Joseph Jr, 569; Joseph Sr,, 569; Scott, 569.

HAYDEN, Ida Olive, 246-247; Isaac, 246

HAYES, Debra, 346; Meta, 567.

HAYHURST, George Washington, 194; Ida L., 194; Juna M., 194; Leman H., 194; May, 194; Metta, 195; Sarah, 510; Zula M., 194.

HAZELL, Alvin H., 585; Daniel D, 603; David H., 585, 603; Sheridan, 585, 602.

HAZELRIGG, John, 75.

HEALY, Mary, 149.

HEARN, Arlene Elnora, 462, 473; David, 462, 473; Donald Keith, 461; Floyd, 461-462; Grover C., 461-462; Phyllis Jean, 461, 472-473; Robert, 461; Tonja, 473; Travis, 473.

HEATON, John w., 282; William R., 282.

HEDGES, Eska, 383; Esther Ann, 383; Willie, 383.

HEETER, Katherine, 271, 331; William, 331.

HEIMAN, George Henry, 483.

HELBERT, Bonnie Jean, 361; Dennis Wayne, 361; Gary Lynn, 361; U. V., 361.

HENDERSON, Arnold A., 594; Bassil, 256; Dana, 594, 604-605; Dyre, 256; Elijah, 256; Lisa, 594, 604; Marion Silas, 442; Tanya, 594; Tom, 591.

HENDSMAN, Martha, 190.

HINTON, Jacob, 271.

HINZLER, Unk, 470.

HITE, Mary F., 454; Ralph M., 454; Ralph M. "Doc", 454; Thomas Arthur, 454.

HIZER, Aon, 592; Holly Dot, 592; Lori Marie, 592.

HODGE, Luella June, 262.

HODGES, Jan, 565; Jim, 565; Woodrow, 574.

HOERMAN, Judy, 472.

HOFF, Addie, 336.

HOGAN, Ruth, 550.

HOLBOROW, George S., 280.

HOLDERMAN, Sharon, 484.

HOLLAND, Aaron, 386; Anna Leigh, 385; Christy, 385; James Michael, 338, 385; Jonathan, 385; Lawrence Cleveland Jr., 338, 385; Lawrence Cleveland Sr., 338; Nancy Ann, 338, 384; Peggy Louise 338, 385-386; Rachel Marie, 385.

HOLLIGER, Rosalie, 311.

HOLLINGWORTH, Lois, 572

HOLSBERRY, Catherine, 221; Elizabeth, 217, 219-221, 230; John, 219; Martha, 221; Nancy, 221; Rachel, 221; Samuel, 221; William, 221.

HOLSINGER, Glenn, 333.

HOLT/HOULT, Alpheus E., 166; Ella 166; William E., 166.

HOOVER, Eldon, 571; Michael, 370.

HOPKINS, Margaret, 494.

HORNBECK,Emmet, 263; Roscoe, 263.

HORNER, John B., 530; Mardula "Maude" Merline, 196-199.

HORNSBY, Lucinda, 565.

HOSKINSON, Thomas, 137.

HOUCK, Joan Sarah, 379; Joseph Clarence, 379,

HOUK, Lotta Marie, 471.

HOWALD, Dennis, 406; James Peterman, 266; Nellie May,

266.
HOWARD, Adam, 77; Charity Elizabeth, 77; Florence Edith, 296; John Steven, 77; Susan, 79-80.
HOWE, Unk, 615.
HOWES, Margaret Y., 484.
HOY, Mary L., 572-573.
HOYT, Pauline, 560-561.
HUBER, Elizabeth Ann, 412; Robert Lee Jr., 412; Robert Lee Sr., 412.
HUDSON, Deborah, 381; Rush, 140.
HUEBERT, Gene Richard, 572; Richard, 571-572; Rush, 141.
HUEY, William G., 278-279.
HUFFMAN, Nancy, 219; Robert J., 221; Snowdon Thorn, 274; Stingley Ebenezer, 221
HUGHES, Craig Vincent, 373; Donna Kathrine, 373; Gary Eugene, 361; Guy, 454; Hannah, 207; Huston, 373; John, 432; John Eli, 361; John Lester, 361; Linda, 401; Mildred Emogene, 454-455; Vivian Renay, 373.
HULL, Janice, 365; Kimberly, 582; Larry, 582; Larry D., 582; Norman, 555; Patricia Gaynell, 370; William, 365.
HUMPHREY, Cynthia, 481; Jeffrey, 481; Kathleen, 481; Patricia, 481; Robert Jr., 481; Robert Sr., 481; Sandra, 481; Steven, 481.
HUNGERFORD, Susannah, 132.
HUNN, Jonathan, 494; Patience, 494.
HUNT, Margaret, 126-127; Susan, 567; William, 126; William J., 567.
HUPP, Jacob, 169.
HURT, Steven H., 570.
HUTCHISON, Mary Jane, 131-132; John, 132.
IRELAND, Claude C. "Clyde," 284; William P., 284.
IRETON, Brenda K., 576; Harry W., 576; John Steven, 576;

Donald Porter, 371; Donna L., 297; Edgar M., 505; Elizabeth, 243; Elizabeth Marie, 379, 405; Fred Junior, 379; Gary, 552; Gerald Scott, 371; Harriet, 505; Howard Hartzel, 255; James, 505; James F., 297; John N., 505; Karen Sue, 297; Leonard III, 478; Linda Dawn, 371; Michael A., 574 Rachel Florence, 240; Sanford C., 505; Shannon, 486; Steven Scott, 488; Taylor, 488; Timothy W., 598; Todd Michael, 379; Wesley, 505; William F., 297; William Terrill, 371.
JORDAN, Adonijah N., 237; David, 407; Jessie Lee, 237-239; Kayla, 407; Matthew, 407.
JOY, Gertrude Josephine, 550-551.
JUDGE, Esther, 556.
JULIAN, Elizabeth, 357.
KALLIMANIS, John, 382.
KASER, Betty Lou, 337-338; Everett Dee, 337.
KAYE, Cindra, 404.
KEEFOVER, Alexander, 488; Archie Bingham, 450; Ava Louise, 459; Bobby, 488; Brian Scott, 485; Caroline M., 441, 449-450, 458; Carol J., 458; Cecil, 451; Cheryl, 470; Christine Lynette, 479; Cindy May, 475; Claude, 482; Claude/Clyde, 450; Claude Ellis, 453, 464-465; Claudette Jean, 465, 482; Cynthia Ann, 488; Cynthia Lea, 485, 490; Daniel Leon, 465; Darrell Leon, 463, 477-478; Daryl William, 459, 471; Dean Harland, 463, 475-476; Deanne Charlotte, 464, 481; Delores Marie, 478; Diana, 470; Dianna Dawn, 479; Dianne Kay, 472; Donald Leslie, 459; Duane Darrell, 478; Elaine, 470; Elreno Manilla, 450-451, 459-460; Epha Hannah, 452, 461-462; Eric, 470; Erica, 470; Floyd, 448; Frank Azim, 442, 453-454; Gail Jean, 464, 480; George Jr., 440-442; George Sr., 440; George Edward Jr., 459, 471, 472; George Edward Sr., 450, 459; Geraldine, 464, 482; Gregory James, 476; Gina, 482; Gloria, 482; Harry, 453; Iva A., 448, 457-458; Jacqueline D., 464,

LANGFORD, Ila, 378.
LAPHAM, Adam Lee, 414; Jared Lee, 414.
LAPINA, Dawn Lynn, 467; Massimo, 467; Tazzio, 467;
Theodore, 466-467; Theodore Scott, 467.
LARSON, Phyllis Irene, 389.
LAW, Thomas J., 504.
LAWRENCE, A., 131; Connor Forrest, 607; Helen, 185;
Madison Grace, 607; Raymond, 384; Richard, 607; Scott
Conley, 384; Stephen Todd, 606-607.
LAWSON, Adelaide "Addie" Sylvania, 526, 544; Alexander
"Shauney", 171; Alfred, 169 Alma L., 180; Amanda Virginia,
166-167, 175, 177-178; Anne, 168; Berthine, 175; Bushrod
Washington, 175, 178-180; Catherine, 176; Dora B., 179-180;
Elias, 173, 175-176; Eliza, 175; Elizabeth, 169; Elizabeth
Jane, 179; Eva, 526; Ferris Lincoln, 179; Flora Odell, 179,
238-241; Hannah, 176 Henry Thomas, 176; Holzen, 171; Ida
S., 526; Jackson, 175; John, 167, John I, 167-168; John II, 168-
170; John III, 168; John IV, 168-170; John Jr., 171; John Sr.,
170-171; John Francis, 174-175; Joseph, 176; Joseph
Columbus, 176; Joseph William, 169 Lena L., 526;
Lydia/Lyda, 179; Kittie Ann, 176; Malinda, 169; Mandeville,
526; Mary, 168. 169; Mary Ann, 171; Mary B., 525; Mary
Byrd, 176; Matilda, 169; Melvina Elizabeth, 176; Mord B.,
526; Moses, 168; Nancy, 169, 171; Nancy Ellen, 179; Paul,
180; Rachel, 176; Rachel Melvina, 176; Rebecca, 171, 176 ;
Rowland, 167; Roxie, 526; Salathial Oral, 175, 525-526; Silas
Bailey, 176; Theophilus/Theopolus 169-170, 171, 172;
Theophilus Washington, 171, 175-176; Thomas, 168. 170;
William, 166, 171, 172, 525.526; William M., 179; Willie
(female), 176-177.
LAYTON, Joseph, 76; Joseph B. 74.
LEAHY, Agnes, 306-307.

McPHERSON, Daniel, 183; James, 183; William G., 183.

McQUADE/McQUAID, Arvilla S., 267; Lenna, 198, 267; Lewis M., 267; Louisa, 264.

McQUAIN, Thomas A., 157.

McSWIGGAN, Unk, 320; Tara, 321.

McWHIRT, Steve, 475.

MEADOWS, Anna, 253; Bertie, 253; Cletus, 253; Emma, 253; Hazel, 253; Leo, 573; Loney, 253; Ottie, 253 Rose, 253; Roy, 253 Thomas Lee, 253; Thomas J., 253.

MEARS, John, 373; John Robert, 373; Richard Allen, 373.

MEDCALF, Craig, 602; Jason, 602; Rex, 602.

MEIRES, Gladys Koonce, 552.

MENEAR, Elizabeth, 136

MERCADO, Marie, 467.

MERCER, Ralph, 204.

MEREDITH, Absalom, 500, 5502, 19; Absalom Pritchard, 514, 529-530; Abner, 495; Alexander A., 515; Alpheus A., 513, 528 Amy, 502; Ann, 497; Arthur A., 529; Asa, 496; Asbury P., 517; Benjamin, 495; Beth, 527; Charles Delbert, 531; Charles Steven, 530; David, 495; Davis, 56, 153, 431, 491-501, 502, 504, 513-515, 518, 529, 530, 531, 532, 534; Davis N., 513; Delcie Pearl, 531; Eleanor, 99, 5012, 505-508, 520, 521, 522; Eliza, 517, 531-532; Elizabeth, 495, 497, 498; Elmer Martin, 530; Elmina, 175, 512, 525-526; Emma, 528; Emma Belle, 530; Etta. 527; Frances Lovina, 514; Fred, 527, 544-545; Hannah, 56, 426, 428-431, 500, 510; Harriet "Hattie", 513, 527-528; Henry, 495; Herbert Davis, 531; Hugh, 492; Hugh Jr., 494; Hugh Sr., 493, 495; Jack, 492; Jacob, 496; James, 4956; James A., 530; James Alva, 515, 530-531; James Edwin, 529; James Marshall, 513, 526-527; Jane, 513; Jennie A., 530; Job, 493, 494, 495; Job Jr., 495; Job Sr., 494. 495; Job John, 501, 512-513, 526, 527. 528, 529; John, 494, 504; John

Andrew, 530; John E., 527; John Henry, 529; John Wesley, 514, 529, 531; Joseph, 502; Joseph Jr., 496; Joseph L., 494, 495-496, 497; Joshua, 493; Laura Adella, 531; Laura Laverna, 530; Lavern/Lavina, 515; Leo, 530; Leslie Everett, 531; Lloyd Biggs, 531; Lydia, 504; Mahala, 504; Martha, 495, 500-501. 502, 505, 515; Mary, 493; Mary Eleanor, 517; Mary Emma, 515; Mary Frances, 529 Mary Jane, 518, 533; Maude, 529; Melvira, 529; Millie, 513; Nancy, 504; Nancy E., 514, 528; Nancy Jane, 517, 531; Nancy Lillian "Lillie", 513; Naomi A., 529; Nehemiah, 494; New/Nuw/Nue Jr,, 500, 504; New/Nuw/.Nue Sr. "Nelly", 501, 503-504; Nina Lee, 531; Obed, 495; Orpha, 527; Oscar Herman, 530; Peter, 495; Phoebe Jane "Jenny", 515, 531; Rachel, 495. 500, 502, 504, 504-505, 517, 520; Rebecca, 500, 502-503; Rhoda M., 529; Robert Jr., 493, 495-496; Robert Sr., 492-493; Ruby, 545, 566; Rufus Davis, 530; Sara A., 502; Seth H., 527; Stephen, 495; Susan, 504; Susanna, 530; Thomas, 502, 518; Thomas Benton 530; Thomas Pritchard, 514;Wheeler, 494; William, 494, 501, 502, 515-517, 532; William Jr., 49; William Sr., 494; William Creed, 531; William Henry, 530; William Mason, 530; William Newton, 514; William Osborn, 529

MERGY, Alfred, 311; Alpha V., 526; Arthur Eugene, 311, 368; Arthur Harry, 311; Christopher James, 402; Frances C., 526; Geneva C., 526; James Arthur, 368, 402; Judith Louise, 368, 402-403; Rebecca Madeline, 402.

MERRICK, John, 143; Nancy Anne, 142, 143.

MERRILL, Billie Paulette, 394, 412; Burr, 511; Frederick Ray, 394; Joseph, 511; Lawrence Albert, 348, 394; Rebecca Renee, 394.

MERYDITH, Adrienne, 549; Alexis, 549; Alice, 549; Alma L., 539; Alpha V., 525, 542; Alvira, 512, 524-525; Anne. 556; Artie, 534; Augusta, 524, 539-540; Barse, 511, 522, 535;

MULLENS, Priscilla, 111.

MULLENIX, Ermalee, 356.

MUNCEY, Susannah, 494.

MURDOCK, James Robert, 360; Robert, 360; Sharon Kay, 360, Shirley Ann, 360.

MURO, Steven, 587.

MURPHY, Unk, 600; Jeffrey, 601; John, 458-459; Michael Jr., 601; Michael Sr., 601; Shannon, 600; Shelley, 600.

MURRAY, Dian C., 584; Elizabeth, 616.

MURRY, Lydia, 90.

MUSE, Ann, 24, 25; Augustine, 25; Christopher, 24; Daniel, 24; Edward, 24; George, 25; Hopkins, 25; Elizabeth, 24; Jane, 20, 23-26; James Sr., 23; John Sr., 20-26; Mary, 24-25; Nicholas, 24; Thomas Jr, 23; Thomas Sr., 23-24; William, 24.

MUSGROVE, Matilda, 95.

MUTO, Wendy, 413.

NAPALO, Helen Suzette, 468.

NASITY, Phillip A., 485.

NAY, Jasper Newton, 443; Mary Jane, 240.

NEERGAARD, Inga Bruaunde, 590.

NEININGER, Alvin E., 295; Carol Ann, 353; Robert Alvin, 353; Robert E., 295, 353; Sandra Kay, 353.

NELSON, Amanda Lee, 237; John K., 237; Karen, 568.

NEPTUNE, Absalom, 503; Alpheus, 503; Amos Alva, 503; Davis, 503; Elizabeth, 503, 609; Henry S., 503; John, 503; Ruth, 503; Henry, 502-503; Samuel, 503; William, 433; William H., 503.

NESTLER, Johann Gottfried, 214-216.

NESTER/NESTOR, Alice Virginia, 230 Andrew, 219 Anthony, 220; Arminda, 221; Barbara Margaret, 221; Carl K., 215; Catherine, 219, 221-222; Catherine Elizabeth Katy, 217; Charles W., 230; Daniel, 217, 303; David, 216; George, 216,

217-219; George H., 220; George W., 217; Henry Clay, 221;
Icy Pearl, 231; Jacob, 215-217, 219; James, 218; John, 217.
220; Jonas, 217; 219-220, 230; Lettice Ann, 217; Louisa, 220;
Margaret, 220; Margaret Cyrilda, 231; Mary, 217; Mary
Elizabeth, 217-218, 230; Mary Magdalene, 303; Mary M.
Polly, 221; Melinda, 221; Nancy, 220-221; Peter, J., 221;
Poling B., 217; Riley J., 230; Robert M., 230; Rosa Bell, 214,
231, 231-234; Samuel, 217; Sarah Ann, 221; Sarah E., 118;
Serena, 221; Tabitha, 220; William, 218; William G., 214; 220;
222-223; 230-231.
NEUMAN, Unk, 24.
NEWBERERY, John, 163; Pluma, 538.
NEWCOMER, Mary, 518.
NEWMAN, Janet M., 590.
NEWMARSH, Jane, 139; William, 139.
NEWMEYER, Alpha May, 297.
NEWSOME, John, 543.
NICHOLLS, Michael L., 558.
NICHOLS, Barney, 555; Coby Ben, 593; Garland, 592-593.
NIGHTENGALE, William Oliver, 340.
NICKELL, Kathryn Ada, 267.
NOBLE, Barclay David, 402-403; Rachel Elizabeth, 403;
Taylor Danielle, 402-403.
NOLL, John Conrad, 204.
NORFLEET, Larry B., 367.
NORMAN, Carol A., 583-584; Charles, 295.
NORRIS, Dora, 235; Emma, 73.
NORTON, Adrienne, 389; David Dean, 343, 389; J. J., 343-
344; Julie Ann, 389; Kevin Lee, 389; Lawrence Paul, 344, 389;
Marla Kay, 389; Michael Scott, 389; Richard Lee, 343-344,
389; Stephanie, 389.
NOURSE, Ruth, 565.

NUNGSTER, Anne, 330; Bernine, 330; Berry, 330; Carl, 330; Jane, 330; Josephine, 330; Nan, 330; Rancy, 330
OBERLE, Clark C., 583; Jesse K., 583; Larry J., 583; Scott J., 583.
O'BILLOVICH, Anthony Robert, 596; Jonni Jane, 596; Melvin J., 596.
O'BRYAN, Oliver, 565; Ruth, 565.
O'CONNELL, Jerry, 84; William B. O'Connell, 84.
O'HALORAND, Mary, 269.
OKIMOTO, Dan, 390; Kevin, 390; Saya, 390.
OLDAKER, David Lynn, 178; Edward Lawson, 177; Joseph Elzy, 177; Lowery Elzy, 176-177; Geneva Price, 177; William B., 177.
OLLUM, Unk, 246.
OLTMAN, Frances. Ruth, 606; Ray, 606; Teresa Rae, 606.
ONNEN, Jeffrey Keith, 485.
OSBORNE, George. 226; Hannah, 107; Sylvia, 296.
OSWALT, Patsy, 598.
OWENS, Carl, 383; Donald R., 3383-384; Pamela Ruth, 383-384, 411; Rachel Amanda, 384, 411; Rebecca Fauntelle, 383..
PAINE, Earl, 525;
PAINES, Dorothy M., 597.
PARKER, Buckney M., 612; Catherine, 75; Charles B., 616 Eli, 609, 613, 614; Eli L., 612, 616; Eliza, 609, 613; Elizabeth Ann. 611; Ella, 615 Elsie, 615; Festus, 615; Frank, 615; F.W. 616; George Washington, 611, 615-616; Grace, 6176 Iva, 615; James M., 611, 614; John, 56. 608-609, John Parker II, 610, 614-615; John D., 609, 612, 617; John W., 616; Joseph James, 97; 609, 611-612; Joseph Luther, 612; Josiah, 611, 615; Laura, 615; Lena, 615; Leroy, 615; Lincoln E., 616; Luvina, 611, 615; Margaret Cornelia, 611; Mary Harriet, 611; Newton, 611; Nora, 616; Oliver W., 611; Philip W., 611; Pinkney M., 612;

PHARES, Unk, 487; Beth, 487; James, 487; Joseph, 487; Tyler
Milford, 487.
PHILLIPS, Carl Reuben, 307-308; Carol J., 559; Clay, 559-
560; Constance Allaire, 308, 365; Helen Eileen, 307, 364-365;
Junior, 351; Laverna E., 221; Leroy Carl, 308; Mildred Lodine,
308 365; Rachel, 230; Richard, 281; Sarah, 440; Scott, 233;
Tom, 560.
PIERCE, Flint G., 585; Omar Dylan, 408; Russell, 408; Shane
S., 585; Steven P., 585.
PIERPOINT, Larkin, 243; Martha Ellen "Ella", 243-244.
PIERSOL, Gloria, 387.
PINKERTON, James, 472.
PITCHER, Lydia, 192.
PITZER, Evaline, 511
PIZOATI, Linda, 602; Robin W., 577, 602.
PLACE, Preston O., 238.
PLESHEK, Charles Foster, 353; James L., 353; Larry Gordon,
353; Mark Alan, 353; Ronald Edward, 353.
PLUNKETT, Elizabeth, 141-142; John, 142.
POLAND, Amelia, 217-219; Margaret, 219; Martin, 217.
POLING, Bluedell, 221-222; George, 221; Jonas, 218.
POOL, Amber Michelle, 410; Amy Elizabeth, 409; Darrell
Michael, 409; Dennis C., 575; Edward Corder, 335; Heather
Adelle, 410; Laura Belle, 409; Mary Martha, 409; Michael
Dean, 383, 409; Nathan Wynkoop, 409; Robert D., 574-575;
Robert W., 574-575; Walter Averill, 226, 335, 382-383; Walter
Edward, 383, 408-409; William, 335; William Keith, 383, 409-
410.
POOLE, Annette Marie, 382; Christine Lynn, 382; Darrell
Edward, 335, 381-382, 407, 408; David Timothy, 381-382;
Donald Darrell, 381-382, 407-408; Gabriel Stanton, 408;
Joshua Kincaid, 408; Julia Ellen Briggs, 408; Linda Jean, 381-

7-8; Thomas Sr,, 34; William, 7-8; William Benjamin Franklin, 99.;
PRINCE, John N., 210.
PRITCHARD, PRITCHETT, Addie Miranda, 204, 278-279, 338; Adrienne, 380, 405; Alberta Bernadine, 273, 332, 377, 378; Alberta M., 327; Alfred Newton, 199; Alice, 270; Alice C., 180; Alice Marie, 271, 330 Alice May, 203; Altie Ora, 199, 268; Alvin, 270, 328; Amanda Tallahassee, 238 ; Amelia Gay, 232, 233, 287. 343. 344. 345, 346; Amon Lewis, 201, 270-271, 329, 331, 332; Amos D., 135, 158-160; Andrew Jackson, 154, 200, 268; Andrew L, 165, 212, 285, 285; Andrew S., 265; Ann, 26, 290, 332; Anna, 134, 144, 148, 175, 178-180, 199; Anna Jesse, 239; Anna M., 284; Anna May, 235, 294; Anne "Nancy", 41, 491-501, 505, 506, 507, 509; Arch G., 284; Ardena A., 166, 214; Arithienetta, 199; Arthur Alvin, 266; Arty Blake, 274, 333; Barbara Corrine, 355; Barbara Jane, 326; Beatrice, 327; Benjamin, 327; Benton L., 269, 326; Berman Cecil, 267; Bert T., 242; Bertha Catherine, 235, 294-295; Bessie Amanda, 236; Betty Lee, 300, 358; Betty Louise, 329; Betty Lucille, 237, 298; Betty Louise, 329; Blanche Agatha, 239, 301; Bushrod Washington, 178, 237, 297-298; Candace Lynn, 379; Carlos Edgar, 237; Carol Ann, 327; Carol Anne, 376; Carol Lee, 327; Carrie Vivian, 271, 328; Cassandra, 145, 182-184, 244, 245, 246, 247, 248, 249, 250, 251, 252; Castle Cowden, 238, 299; Cecil Leroy; 265, 323-324;Charles, 200; Charles Edward, 334, 380; Charles J., 180, 241-242; Charles Wesley Jr., 327; Charles Wesley Sr., 270, 327; Charlotte "Lottie", 210-211; Christopher I, 15, 20-26; 29-32; Christopher II, 34-39; Cindy, 331; Clara Hillis, 239, 301; Clara Lucinda, 204 Claris Clayton Jr., 296. 355; Claris Clayton Sr., 236, 296, 354, 355; Claris Edward, 235, 295; Clyde W., 243; Coleman H., 211, 283-284; Colleen, 376; Cora, 181; Cyrus, 156; Daisy Ethel, 235, 294; Daniel

Start

Millard, 265; 323; Ruby Bradley,. 333; Ruby E., 284; Ruth
Ellen, 324; Salina, 157; Sally, 296, 354; Samuel, 157; Samuel
George, 135 156-157, 206, 207; Sandra Kathleen, 300; Sarah,
26, 47, 53, 87-92, 135, 136-139, 162; Sarah Alice, 166; Sarah
Ann, 157, 205; Sarah Eliza, 177; Sarah Eliza "Lydia," 234;
Scipio Cortez, 204; Sharon, 332, 378; Sharon Rosalie, 300
Shawn Michael, 343; Sheldon Schofield "Gil," 239, 301-302,
358; Sheldon Walter; 300; Shelton Lee, 358; Sherman, 201,
270, 328-329; Shirley E., 212; Shirly Marlene, 323; Silas R.,
156; Stephen U.B., 199; Susan, 332, 378; Susan Lorraine, 298;
Susanna, 200 Syntha Stella, 213; Tami Jill, 355; Ted Delmore,
287, 343; Ted Joseph, 343; Thomas, 7-17; 28-32, 270, 32, 332;
Thomas Benton, 154, 201-202, 269, 271-273; Thomas
Dickerson, 135, 155-156, 206; Thomas Jason, 322; Thomas Jr,
41, 55, 100-102, 131-135; Thomas Sr, 41-62, 102. 496;
Thomas Lewis, 300; Thomas Tavner, 156 203-204, 278;
Thomas Virgil, 271; Thomas Willis, 144, 167-168, 175, 177-
178; Tina Marie, 376, 404; Tod Taylor, 376, 403; Torrey Icen,
238, 301. 358; Tracie Jean, 404; Travis, 54; Valerie, 375;
Vickie Lee, 379, 404-405, 414; Viola J., 153 165; Viola M.,
268; Violette Amanda, 237; Wallace Allen, 266; 324-325;
Walter Gordon Quayle, 239; Walter Icen, 178, 237-239, 299,
300, 301, 302, 303; Wilbert C., 212; William, 41, 135, 154 (See
also Prichard); William A, 180, 242, 322; William Christopher,
397; William Ray, 333, 378; William Sanford, 195, 296, 355-
356; William Tyler, 144, 180, 242, 243; Willie B., 201; 269;
Willis Millard, 287.
PRIVETT, Epler Martin, 85; James Thomas, 85; Juanita
Louise, 85; Shirley Mae, 85.
PROCIUK, Asma, 395; Peter Joseph, 395.
PRUNTY, Anna, 240; Carl, 241; Edna, 318-319; Fanny, 179;
Felix, 213, 240; Felix O., 240; Frances, 302; Jacob, 179; Jesse,

560; Emory William Sr., 541, 559; Thelma, 541, 559-560.

REDIFER, Iva Mae, 272-273.

REED, Elizabeth, 556; Ezra, 272; Lucy, 259; Susan, 150.

REEDER, Olive, 186.

REESE, Hazel Marke, 353.

REEVES, Everett W., 575, 601; Floyd J., 601; Floyd L., 575;
Jim Alan, 602; Larry D., 575, 601; Lisa, 601; Lynn Ann, 602;
Norman K., 575, 601-602; Pammie, 601; Sherry, 601; Tammie,
601; Teresa, 601; Weslena, 601.

REGAN, John, 220.

REGER, Estella, 3221

REID, Elizabeth, 91.

REIGER, Magdalena, 215.

REISWIG, Loren, 585.

REMIS, Frank, 334.

REMY, John, 26.

REYNOLDS, Unk, 489; Carmen Celeste, 395; Charlaine, 293,
350; Christina, 489; Cynthia Louise, 351, 397; Daniel, 292;
Danielle Jo, 395; Dr., 231; Franklin Montgomery, 290;
Gregory David, 351, 397; Joseph Frederick, 397; Joseph Isaac,
293, 350-351; Julie Ann, 397; Lynda Renee, 349, 395; Lynden
Eugene Jr., 292-293, 349; Lynden Eugene, Sr., 290-293;
Millard Franklin, 293, 349-350; Randolph Roye, 349, 394-395;
Ryan Andrew, 397; Sarah Elizabeth, 397; Stephanie Ann, 351,
396; Stephen Andrew, 351, 396-397.

RHAME, Paul Kenneth, 378.

RHODES, Cordie, 336.

RICE, Jessie, 540; Mary Elizabeth, 464-465.

RICHARDSON, Unk, 470; Geraldine Vivian, 266; Nancy,
537, 549.

RICHEY, Mattie, 593.

RICKE, Elaine, 602.

RICKSTREW, Joan, 581.

RIDEOUT, David, 98.

RIDGWAY, Adda Lee, 524, 538; Amelia Jane, 523, 536; Caroline Merydith, 524, 538; Catherine E., 553, 575, 602; Cathy A., 576; Charlene, 575, 600; Charles L., 575; Charles Wesley Jr. 523. 537, 553, 575; Charles Wesley Sr., 523- 524; Davis Archibold, 523-524; Elzy, 522, 523; Emma L., 523, 536-537; Ernest E., 553, 576; Ernest Wesley, 537,552- 553; Ernestine M., 575, 600; Frank Sheriden, 524; Jane Cornelia, 523-524; Leon W., 575 Mary Wright, 116; Permealia C., 523; Rita R., 576, 602; Ronda J., 576; Ruby Caroline, 537, 554; Russell Norton, 523; Sherrel J., 575, 601; Violet V., 553, 575-576; William, 432.

RIES, Diana Lee, 86; Pat Lou, 85; Willard, 85-86.

RIGGS, Frank, 318; Goldie Eunice, 318; Ida Anderson, 290.

RIGNEY, Anna, 572.

RILEY, Catherine, 530.

RIPLEY, Unk, 515; Charles Raymond, 531; Infant, 532; James Clyde, 531; Mary Laverna, 531; Thomas, 531.

RIVIZZINO, Amy Rae 343; Anthony Jack, 343; Sandini, 343; Vincent W. 343; Vincent Walter, 343.

ROBERTS, Billie W., 578; Charles, 608; Charles R., 578; Perry S., 578; Uriah, 74, 76.

ROBERTSON, Curt E., 588; Daren Lee, 588; Herbert E., 561; John F., 561, 588; Rosa Marie, 362.

ROBEY, Maria, 443- 444.

ROBINSON, Unk, 482.

ROCKHOLD, Anna, 335.

RODENISH, Linda, 343.

ROGERS, Unk, 451.

ROHR, Harold C., 280.

ROHRBOUGH, Mahala, 187,

SMEJKAL, Ingrid, 468; Ivan, 468; Yvonne, 468, 487.
SMITH, Unk, 568; Albert Columbus, 333; Anna Lee. 279, 338;
Arthur C., 316, 420; Bessie Mae, 333-335; Bethany, 403; Betty
Jo, 280; Betty Lee, 316, 371; Beulah, 370; Billy Jo, 316;
Charles Robert, 157 Clarence P., 423; Claude McKinley Sr,
205, 279; Claude McKinley Jr., 280; Clayton, 405; Cynthia,
420; David Scott, 339; Darrel, 594; Dorainne, 370; Edith, 325,
374; Elena, 420; Ellen, 205; Essie Leora, 423; Eve Loretta,
359; Evelyn Louise, 316; Francis, 26, 31; Glenn, 405; Harrel,
369-370; Harrison B., 423; Henry Mills, 205; Ida D., 273; J.
370; James Leo, 412; James Matthew, 412; James Wesley,
205; Jeffrey Paul, 412; John, 123, 416-418; John D., 419; John
V. 127; Jonathan Michael, 412; Joyce, 31; Judith Marlene, 316;
Kathy Lynn, 594; Kelly Sue, 594; Lena Leota, 205; Lottie,
251; Lydia, 247; Margaret, 418, 420-421; Mark Edward, 369;
Mary Ann, 419; Mary Elizabeth, 419; Mary M., 127;
Matthew, 403; Michael, 403; Milton, 420; Nadine Emily, 368;
Oliver Hall, 316; Oliver P., 420, 423; Paul E., 280; Pritchard
W., 418, 419-420; Rachel, 543; Rebecca, 170, 420; Robert,
403; Roger Lee, 369; Ruth Ann, 316; Sabrina, 524; Samuel
George, 205; Sara. 161; Stephen Franklin, 369; Susannah, 118;
Thomas P., 418; Victoria Elizabeth, 548; Virginia Lane, 280;
Waitman Conley, 205, 279; Whitehead, 273; William, 122;
Winifred Jean, 280.
SNIDER, Dorcas, 503-504; Elisha, 505; John, 94.
SNODGRASS, Alcinda J., 153; Benjamin F., 153; Comfort,
153; Elizabeth, 153; Florence, 249; Frances, 153, 154; Hannah,
615; Isaac, 614; Isabel, 153; John Wesley, 15; Lamerduke,
152; Margaret A., 153; Martha, 153, 154; Mildred May, 322;
Nancy, 614; Naomi, 153, 513-515; Nathan, 516; Sarah, 153;
Thomas Corbin, 153, 165; William, 152-153, 514; William F.,
152.

STURMS, Daniel, 220.

SUBER, Hollis, 384; Jackie, 384; Kimberly, 384; Michael Dale, 385.

SULLENBERGER, Eugene R., 320

SULLIVAN. Augusta V. 591; Christina, 590; Christopher, 591; Diane, 591; Fred, 562, 592; Frederick Jr., 562; Frederick Sr., 562; Fred M., 563, 591; Gerald I., 562, 592; Godfrey R., Jr., 591; Godfrey R. Sr., 562, 590-591; Janet, 591; Jenny, 591; Jenny Marie, 590; John, 591; Juliette, 591; Lewis, 591; Karen, 5921 Karl James, 591; Meredith, 591; Michael, 590; Robert, 591; Sherwood M., 562, 590; Shirley Grace, 591.

SUMMERS, Charles Edwin, 315; Edward, 316; Elias, 204; Elmore, 315; Francis M., 163; Gerald, 315; Gerald Francis, 315; Loran Hazen, 315-316; Lucy Ann Elizabeth, 203-204.

SUTHERLAND, Don, 238.

SUTTON, Dick, 263; Edward. 263; Frank 264; James Bruce, 364; Porter, 263.

SWAFFORD, Dorothy Mildred, 346.

SWANSON, Ashley Marie, 606; Donald Kirt, 596, 606 Donald Reuben, 596; Kayla Ann, 606; Kimberly Rae, 606; Michael Lee, 596 606; Reuben, 596; Ryan Michael, 606; Shelby Jean, 606.

SWEANEY, Connie, 571.

SWEARINGEN, Mildred, 461.

SWEENEY, Judith Lynn, 395.

SWISHER, Frederick, 509; Rebecca, 430.

SYLSTAD, Martha, 606.

TAGGART, Mary E., 515.

TALBOT, Sarah Jane, 188.

TALKINGTON, Lucinda, 422.

TANSEY, Eleanor, 137.

TAPP, Jane, 106.

Ellen, 82; Mildred, 258; Myrtle May. 82, 85; Nettie Irena, 82, 84-85; Ollie, 79, 82-83; Ollie Leroy, 82, 85; Robert Leroy, 84; Ruben, 79; Ruben Franklin, 79-80; Ruth, 82; Thelma Corrine, 83, 85-86; Thelma Louise, 83, Velma, 258.

THOMPSON, Ann, 143; Brent, 579; John, 127; Larry, 579; Leroy, 564; Mary, 172; Mary E., 578-579; Matthew A., 564; Susan, 579; Vallie, 358.

THORN, Zeth, 511.

THORNSBERRY, James, 92.

THORNTON, Theodore, 92.

THRASH, Gail, 264; Judson, 263-264; Katherine, 164; Louis, 264.

THROGMORTON, A. W., 282.

TIBBS, Boaz Burris, 96 Robert, 96.

TIBBETTS, James Clayton, 127.

TICHENAL, Ann Mary, 124; Anna, 112; Daniel, 112 David, 120-122 (see also Tichenell); David H., 126; Eliza, 124 Elizabeth, 112; Jacob, 112; James, 112, 124; James Joseph, 124; Jane, 113; Jane Elizabeth, 124; Jared, 112; John R., 124-126; John R. Jr., 126; John V., 124; Jonas, 112; Joseph, 113, 124; Margaret, 124; Mary Ellen, 125; Moses, 101-102; Peter, 112 (see also Tichenor); Sarah, 112; Sarah Ann, 125; Silas, 112; Susan Eliza, 126; Timothy, 112; William Henry, 125.

TICHENELL, Abigail, 115; Andrew Jackson, 121; Anne, 129; Cassandra, 127; Daniel, 121, 122; David, 114, 121; Delilah, 127; Elizabeth, 130; George W., 129-130; James, 122; James W., 130; Jane, 115; John B., 127; John D., 127; John M. 128-129; John R., 121, 125-127; Joshua, 115, 116, 121, 122, 124, 129; Julia, 127; Lydia, 123; Margaret, 115, 121, 122, 127; Margaret Hester, 130 Mary, 122 Mary Ellen, 127; Mary Jane, 129; Moses, 121, 122, 127-130; Moses J., 121, 127-130; Nancy, 55; 100-102, 114, Phoebe, 115 123; Rebecca, 122;

Sarah E., 127; Sarah Ellen, 129-130; Stephen, 115, 122-123; Thomas Edward, 127; William R., 121, 126-127; William V., 129-130.

TICHENOR, Abigail, 105 107, 116; Anna, 119; Bethuel D., 118; Byram, 119; Calvin, 1219 Catherine, 118; Daniel, 105, 106, 107, 108, 110, 111-112; David, 110, 119-121; Eliza, 118; Emily, 119; Hannah, 105; Henry, 119; Ira, 119; Isaac, 110; James, 110, Jane, 108, 111, 118; Jonathan, 105, 108; John, 105, 106, 107, 108, 109; Joseph, 108, 109, 117; Joseph Jr, 110, 111; Joseph Sr., 109-110; Joseph Day, 111, 116, 118; Keller, 119; Laura, 119; Margaret, 118; Martin, 102-105; Mildred, 119; Moses, 110, 112-115; Nathaniel, 105; Peter, 118-119; Samuel, 105; Sarah, 105; Silas, 119 Stephen, 116; William 119; Zacheus, 119.

TICKENAL, Jain (Jane), 101 Margaret, 101; Moses, 101; Stephen, 101.

TIET, Keith, 558.

TILLER, James M., 159.

TILMAN, Edna, 142; Edward, 91.

TISCHLER, Kimberly, 406; Robert, 406.

TISDALE, Hobart, 272; Noke, 272

TOMPKINS, Robert Martin, 404; William, 404.

TOOTHMAN, George Washington, 610.

TORRES, Lucinda, 357.

TOWNS, Ferrell Ray, 388.

TRAMMELL, Unk, 470.

TREAT, John, 106; Sarah, 106.

TRENT, Norma, 553.

TRIPPETT, Henrietta, 245.

TROXELL, Unk, 481.

TRUCHIN, Sarah Marie, 357.

TRUEX, Mary E., 326.

Franklin Jennings, 312; Fred, 245, 307; Gary Leroy, 364; Gayle Marie, 364; Glen Ruble, 246; Gloria, 305; Goldie Pearl, 246; Hallie Paul, 247; Harlie Graydon, 250, 318; Harold Harding, 312; Harrison Ellsworth Jr., 182, 245, 309, 310; Harrison Ellsworth Sr., 181-183; Harry "Buck", 305; Hazel, 305; Helen Fawn, 251; Herman H. 245, 306-307; Herman Lawrence, 315, 369-370; Hilda Lorraine, 315; Hosea Harrison, 249, 314-315; James Edward, 313; James Rienzi, 183, 251; James Russell Jr., 362; James Russell Sr,, 306, 362; Janice Louise, 306; Joan, 314; John, 181, 364 John Anderson, 182, 246-247; John Michael, 372; John Roy, 247; John Wesley, 318, 372; Josephine Jean, 251, 321, 372; Judith, 319; Judith Ann, 319; Juna Myrtle, 249, 315-316; Kathy Ann, 370; Lee Earl, 306; Leigh Ann, 370; Lewis Maxwell, 182, 244-245, 304, 306, 307, 308, 362; Lewis Maxwell Jr., 244, 305-306; Lois Elvira, 306, 362; Lois Irene, 318; Lois June, 307, 363; Lori Lynn, 371-372; Louis Alvin, 305; Lulabelle Katherine, 314; Malcolm, 305; Mamie "Minnie" Snow, 24246; Margaret Luron, 312; Mark Donovan, 369; Mary, 250; Mary Irene, 306; Mary Joann, 318; Maud F., 246; Melinda, 372; Melva Rose, 306; Melvin Eugene, 306, 362; Michael Kent, 319; Michael Rome, 362; Mildred Edith, 250 319; Millie, 251, 320; Ora Alice, 246; Pamela Jeanine, 370; Peter, 182, 248-249, 313, 314; Phillip, 364; Ralph Paul Jr., 312; Ralph Paul Sr., 248, 312; Reta Jennie, 370; Richard Carl, 313; Robert Eugene, 318; Robert H., 270; Robert Wesley, 370; Romeo Grant, 249, 314; Roy, 182-183, 250-251; Royce Dean, 371; Ruby Thelma, 247; Ruth Ann, 314; Sharlene, 319; Sherrie Mae, 362; Sophronia Jane, 182; Steven Jon, 362; Tammy Lynn, 372; Theodore "Teddy" Roosevelt, 246; Virginia Opal, 251, 320-321; Walter Ed4ard, 243; William C., 313; William "Dick" Harrison, 243, 305; William George, 243; William Morgan, 182, 243;

Craig, 466.
WEISENSTEIN, Tab Richard, 377; Thomas, 377; Tim Jay, 377.
WELCH, Bertha, 332; George, 268; Harold, Jr., 605; Harold Mark III, 605; Mae, 269, 325-326; Nathan George, 268; Susan M., 127.
WELDON, Eve, 496.
WELLS, John, 512; Simeon, 92.
WENCEL, Virgil, 316
WENGER, Henrietta G., 295-296.
WERSHY, Florence, 84.
WEST, Betty, 185; Christopher, 390; David E., 487-488; Gregory, 488; Stephen, 488; Steve, 390.
WESTACOTT, Ruth W., 559
WESTFALL, Harvey, 161; Levi, 146, Owen, 161; Tracy, 410; Zachariah, 161.
WHALEY, Emma, 529-530; Hannah, 75.
WHEELER, Rachel, 494.
WHIPKEY, Susan, 310
WHITACRE/WHITAKER, Henry, 495; Lydia, 495,
WHITBY, Hazel "Billie" Viola, 597.
WHITE, Abbie Ann, 186; Bertha, 262; Betty Jean, 595; Carl, 262, 305; Charles, 595; Daniel, 185-186; Daura. 262; David, 365; Dennis, 365; Edith, 186, 252; Elizabeth, 186; Enoch, 186; Floyd, 365; George, 186; Grant, 262; Howard, 186; James Queen, 186; Jessina, 244; Joseph, 185-186; Josh, 604; Lora, 262; Paul, 262; Rachel Rebecca, 186; Raymond, 262; Robert, 604; Ruth, 604; Susan, 142; Thomas, 509; Zachariah T., 185.
WHYDE, Chris, 589; Cynthia, 589; David, 561; Dorothy Louise, 561, 589; Jack Jr., 561, 588; Jack Sr., 561; Janet, 588; Larry, 588; Nannette, 589; Robert, 561, 589; Steven J., 588; Steven L., 589; Tom, 561, 589.

WIENCK, David, 473.
WIGGINTON, Mary, 61.
WILEY, Rev. W. H., 145.
WILFONG, Hattie, 293-294.
WILKINSON, Hiram S., 200; Mary, 201; 268.
WILLIAMS, Unk, 377; Allie, 547-548; Brett, 375; Charles, 548, 568; Charles L., 568; Foster, 147-148; Henry Jr. 30-31; Henry Sr., 26; Herbert, 378; Hester S., 147-148; John E., 147; Lloyd, 375; Mary, 147, 184-185; Mildred Doyle, 378; Robert Lee, 377; Shawn, 377.
WILLIAMSON, Augusta R., 540, 558; Dean A., 557; Jane R., 581; Jesse, 92; Kristen J., 581; Larry B., 557, 581; Lloyd, 540, 557; Lloyd K., 557; Mary Ann, 221; Michael, 581; Narcissa, 536; Rose Marie, 557, 581; Ruby Mae, 540, 557-558; Russell L., 557, 581; Samuel, 539-540; William R., 540, 582.
WILLIS/WYLLIS, Alexander "Sandy", 143; Benjamin, 142; Elizabeth, 140-146; Frances, 142; Isaac, 143; James, 142; John, 139; John Jr., 140-142; John Sr., 139-140; Joshua, 142; Lewis, 142; Margaret "Peggy", 112; Mary, 142; Moses, 142; Reuben, 142 Richard, 139; Sarah, 141; Thomas 139; William, 140, 141-144; William Sr., 141-144.
WILLSON, John, 25.
WILSON, Unk. 319, 615; Basil, 250 Brenda Lee, 393, 412; Brent, 320, 372; Charles D., 560; Donna Mae, 393; Donna L., 560, 585; Dora, 286-287; Edna Maude, 250; Emily, 407; Frank Marcel, 297, 356; Gary Stewart, 585; Jacoby, 407; James V. Jr., 557; James V. Sr., 557-558; Jeanne, 578; Karen Sue, 393; Kayla Ann, 356, 585; Kendra Kay, 585; Kenneth N., 333; Kimley Dee, 585; Kyanna Sue, 585; Larry, 578; Larry Eugene, 297; Lee Roy, 240; Linda J., 558; Lisa Gay, 586; Lydia Jane, 195, 511; Maranda, 204; Marion, 303; Mary B., 575; Michael, 372; Morris Duane, 560, 586; Myrtle, 255; Nate, 577-578;

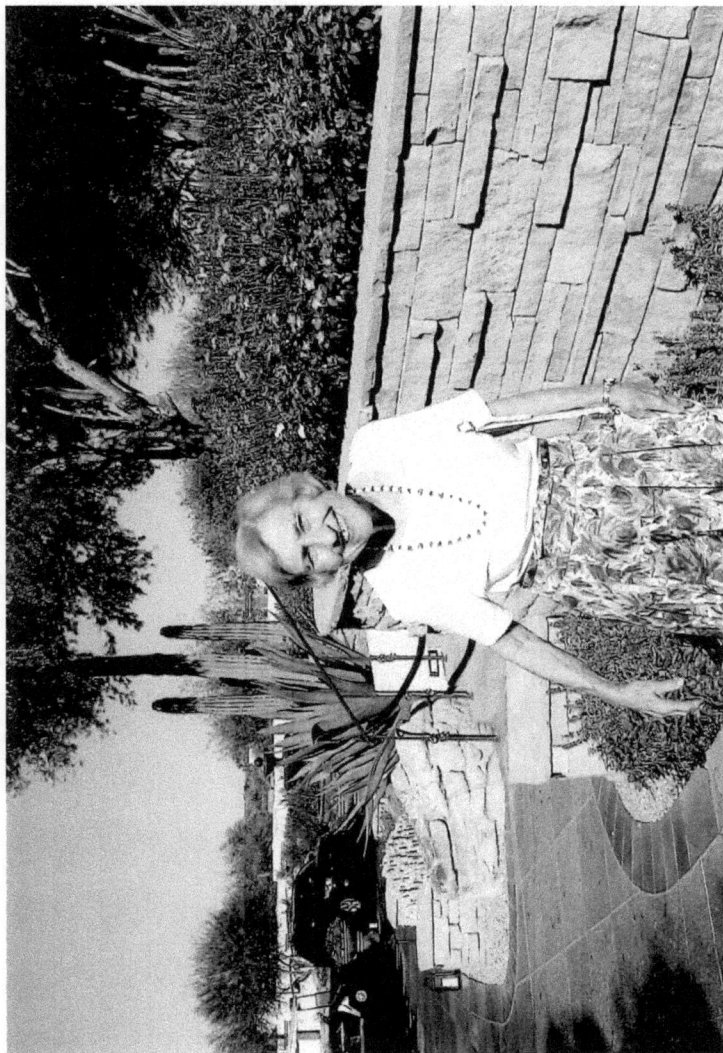

Emily Pritchard Cary, Scottsdale, Arizona, 2015

700a